DATE			

BRITTLE POWER

BRITTLE POWER

Energy Strategy for National Security

Amory B. Lovins
L. Hunter Lovins

BRICK HOUSE PUBLISHING COMPANY
Andover, Massachusetts

Published by Brick House Publishing Co., Inc.
34 Essex Street
Andover, Massachusetts

Production Credits:
Editor: *Jack Howell*
Edited by *Nancy Irwin*
Designed and Produced by *Mike Fender*

Typeset in new Baskerville and Caslon 540 by
dnh Typesetting, Cambridge, Massachusetts

Printed by Book Press; Brattleboro, Vermont

Library of Congress Cataloging in Publication Data

Lovins, Amory B., 1947–
  Brittle power.

  Bibliography: p.
  Includes index.
  1. Energy policy—United States. 2. United
States—National security. I. Lovins, L.
Hunter. II. Title.
HD9502.U52L67   1982   333.79'0973   82-4159
ISBN   0-931790-28-X   AACR2

Printed in the United States of America

Contents

v

PART THREE: NATIONAL ENERGY SECURITY

Foreword

The professional fraternity of those who deal regularly with questions of national security has its own language, its own rituals, its own stylized forms of well-worn argument. Most strategic analysts, for example, obligingly sort themselves out into two herds—those who advocate only an "assured destruction" mission for our strategic forces and those who support also a "counterforce" capability. They then find some specific piece of new hardware about which they can conveniently disagree, and they do, interminably—ringing all the changes on a ritualized dispute while the public looks on with a mixture of boredom, fear, and confusion.

Look out, fraternity, here come Hunter and Amory Lovins.

The authors of this fascinating, disturbing, and—in its own way—hopeful book disrupt this well-worn debate in a number of healthy ways. They insist on taking seriously one of our society's most troubling vulnerabilities—the extremely fragile nature of the way it acquires, transmits, and uses energy.

Because they take seriously a problem which has grown, under our noses, while we have almost all refused to think about it, they will doubtless hear some try to argue that the threats they describe could not realistically become manifest. But the vulnerabilities are so numerous—to the weather, to accidents arising from complexity ("one damned thing leads to another"), to a handful of terrorists, to the detonation of even a single smuggled nuclear weapon—that denying the plausibility of such threats is unlikely to prove persuasive. The authors' recommended solutions for a more resilient energy system—greater end-use efficiency and redundant, decentralized, simple, and renewable energy sources—thus appear in a very different light than that in which such recommendations have often appeared before. In the hands of the authors, these are not solutions that derive from a desire to take to the hills with a bag of Krugerrands to abandon a decaying society, nor are they steps that resist the use of modern technology or demand special subsidies. The Lovinses seek rather to persuade us not to resist what the free market and millions of citizens and local governments are already doing in their own self-interest.

Efforts to stereotype the authors' approach in terms of the traditional natural security debate will prove to be a difficult exercise. In their critique of the false sense of certainty about the predictability of failure and the other dangers that accompany excessive centralization of authority and excessive reliance on highly quantified analysis, the authors have much in common with the military officers, Members of Congress, and others who have led the criticism of the reigning theology of systems analysis in the Pentagon. The Lovinses face honestly the devastation that could be caused by the use of nuclear weapons and what our society could do to reduce the damage to itself if such a horror should ever occur. In this their thinking has certain common threads with those who take civil defense seriously. (Consequently we fully expect that some member of the pure strain of the assured destruction school of strategic analysis, ever vigilant in defense of doctrine, will angrily argue that they risk making nuclear war more likely by trying to mitigate any damage that might occur from it.). Those who identify national security with the current way we do our energy business will wax wroth. Those who believe that everything necessary has been accomplished if we can just avoid reliance on Persian Gulf oil will find cold comfort. The managers of the government's huge energy programs will grind their teeth.

In the meantime, the people, local governments, and a growing share of the business community go on quietly insulating their houses, installing their woodburning stoves, building passive solar buildings, using the wind and rebuilding small dams to generate electricity, and lowering the cost of photovoltaics. If we get out of their way, they will soon make America progressively less and less a fragile power.

As Carl Sandburg once said of us, "this old anvil laughs at many broken hammers."

–ADMIRAL THOMAS H. MOORER (USN RET)

–R. JAMES WOOLSEY

Admiral Thomas H. Moorer, former Chairman of the Joint Chiefs of Staff and former Chief of Naval Operations, is Senior Associate at the Georgetown Center for Strategic and International Studies.

R. James Woolsey, former Under Secretary of the Navy and former General Counsel to the Senate Armed Services Committee, practices law in Washington, D.C.

Acknowledgments

The official study which gave rise to this book was suggested and commissioned by Mr. Bardyl Tirana, then Director of the Defense Civil Preparedness Agency, and carried out under the auspices of that Agency's successor, the Federal Emergency Management Agency, through the vehicle of the President's Council on Environmental Quality. Mr. Tirana's and our belief that the subject deserved such an examination in depth grew out of a seminar which he and Dr. Frank Kapper kindly arranged for Mr. Lovins to give for Armed Forces energy directors and others in the Office of the Joint Chiefs of Staff, and another seminar set up by Dr. Robert Hayes at the National Defense University. Throughout the contract we received valuable help and guidance from our Project Managers, Mr. George Divine of FEMA and Dr. John Davidson of CEQ, and administrative aid from our colleagues Jeffrey Knight, Esq. of Friends of the Earth (the contracting organization) and Mr. Jim Harding of the International Project for Soft Energy Paths, a project of Friends of the Earth Foundation.

For the content of this book we are alone responsible, but we owe an intellectual debt to many vicarious contributors. We thank especially: Dr. Jan Beyea (formerly at Princeton University and now with the National Audubon Society); Captain Howard Bucknell III (USN Ret.) and his colleagues at the Energy and Security Project at The Mershon Center of The Ohio State University; Dr. William Clark of the Institute for Energy Analysis at Oak Ridge, for incisive comments and papers on biological resilience; Mr. Wilson Clark, whose independent but parallel work helped to bring energy vulnerability to public attention; Dr. Paul Craig of the University of California; Mr. F.R. Farmer and his colleagues in the nuclear industry who generously shared their insights into the principles of resilient design; Dr. Karl Gawell and Mr. Bruce Green of the Solar Energy Research Institute; Ms. Tina Hobson of the U.S. Department of Energy; Professor C.S. Holling of the University of British Columbia (now director of the International Institute for Applied Systems Analysis), to whom we owe the whole concept of resilience; Col. William Holmberg (USMC Ret.) of the U.S. Department of Energy; Dr. Paul Hoover (also at The Mershon Center); Dr. Edward Kahn of Lawrence Berkeley Laboratory; Mr. Fran Koster, formerly director of solar programs at the Tennessee Valley

Authority; Dr. Florentin Krause (International Project for Soft Energy Paths); Dr. Enver Masud of the Department of Energy and Dr. Bud Miles of Systems Control, Inc., who kindly shared with us their latest research results on dispersed electrical systems; The RAND Corporation (a seminar venue); Professor Bent Sørensen of Roskilde University in Denmark, one of our earliest teachers about renewable energy; Dr. Peter Steen and his colleagues at the Swedish Defense Research Establishment, pioneers in parallel research; Dr. David Sternlight (who first introduced us and has helped ever since) and The Atlantic Richfield Company; and Commissioner Gene Varinini of the California Energy Commission.

Among the most useful review comments on the FEMA draft were those by Dr. Melvin Conant, Mr. Peter Gleick, Mr. H. Richard Holt, Professor Barry Hyman, Dr. David Morris, Mr. John R. Newell, Ray Watts, Esq., and Dr. Zdanek Zofka. If any errors have evaded them and several dozen other reviewers, and still lurk somewhere in this text, they are of course our sole responsibility, and we shall be most grateful to anyone who points them out.

In the difficult task of translating our FEMA report into plainer English and clearer logic, we have incurred many new debts: foremost to Dr. Jim Gray of Tandem Computer Corporation for his help in restructuring Chapter Thirteen, and Mr. E.R. Baugh PE (of the Ralph M. Parsons Co. and Small Scale Technology, Inc.) for re-educating us about grid interconnections.

Mr. Alec Jenkins worked hard to distill into a few dozen pages his wealth of experience in mobilizing communities to improve their energy resilience. We have greatly benefited from his insights and, with his kind permission, have sought to share them here, mainly in Chapter Seventeen. We hope his skill and patience will be rewarded by the rapid spread of his excellent ideas. He and we are grateful for the patience of Monica, Alex, and Jenny Jenkins during his writing.

In preparing his material, Mr. Jenkins was aided by two research consultants: on production lead times for wind and hydro systems, Roy Pitts, who is a solar advisor at the California Energy Commission and studying architecture at the Sacramento City College; and on community activity, Carolyn Jane Danahy, who will finish her studies in environmental and policy planning at the University of California at Davis in 1982.

The two maps on page 171 were prepared by Dr. Edward Hillsman, Dr. William Eberle, and Mr. Paul Johnson, and were made available to us by Dr. Robert Honea, all of the Oak Ridge National Laboratory. We thank them all.

Our research was greatly facilitated by Mr. Tom Lutgen and his helpful colleagues at the Research Library of *The Los Angeles Times,* and by two devoted research assistants who indefatigably tracked down obscure references: Mr. Gabriel Gorenstein near the beginning and Mr. Kenneth A. Anderson near the end. Mr. Anderson's editorial insights were also most helpful. Our voluminous paperwork was faithfully handled by the staff of the International Project for Soft Energy Paths: notably Ms. Cissy Wallace, Mr. John Fore, Ms. Katy Slichter, and Ms. Elyse Axell. The writing was made possible by two miraculous machines: one to which Mr. Patrick Heffernan and Dr. Ruthann Corwin hospitably gave us visiting rights after we had lent it to them, and another which, through the kindness of the Los Angeles Office of Lanier Business Products (especially Mr. Chad Farling), we were later able to rent. Our editor (Nancy Irwin), production manager (Mike Fender), and publisher (Jack Howell) also performed their customary wonders in guiding us smoothly through the complex process of converting fuzzy thoughts into crisp typography. And for the typography itself we are enduringly grateful for the dedicated professionalism of the staff of DNH Typesetting—especially Ruth Goodman, David Roh, Mary Meltaus, and Don Leamy.

Finally, we are indebted beyond words to Mr. Chris Cappy for his frequent help, and to Mrs. Farley Hunter Sheldon for her tolerance, professional guidance, and personal support, during the throes of our writing.

Amory B. Lovins
L. Hunter Lovins

Hanover, New Hampshire
17 April 1982

Part 1 Brittle Power

Chapter One
National Energy Insecurity

The United States has for decades been undermining the foundations of its own strength. It has gradually built up an energy system prone to sudden, massive failures with catastrophic consequences.

The energy that runs America is brittle—easily shattered by accident or malice. That fragility frustrates the efforts of our Armed Forces to defend a nation that literally can be turned off by a handful of people. It poses, indeed, a grave and growing threat to national security, life, and liberty.

This danger comes not from hostile ideology but from misapplied technology. It is not a threat imposed on us by enemies abroad. It is a threat we have heedlessly—and needlessly—imposed on ourselves.

Many Americans' most basic functions depend, for example, on a continuous supply of electricity. Without it, subways and elevators stall, factories and offices grind to a halt, electric locks jam, intercoms and televisions stand mute, and we huddle without light, heat, or ventilation. A brief faltering of our energy pulse can reveal—sometimes as fatally as to astronauts in a spacecraft—the hidden brittleness of our interdependent, urbanized society. Yet that continuous electrical supply now depends on many large and precise machines, rotating in exact synchrony across half a continent, and strung together by an easily severed network of aerial arteries whose failure is instantly disruptive. The size, complexity, pattern, and control structure of these electrical machines make them *inherently* vulnerable to large-scale failures: a vulnerability which government policies are systematically increasing. The same is true of the technologies which deliver oil, gas, and coal to run our vehicles, buildings, and industries. Our reliance on these delicately poised energy systems has unwittingly put at risk our whole way of life.

The United States has reached the point where
• a few people could probably black out most of the country;

1

• a small group could shut off three-fourths of the natural gas to the eastern U.S. in one evening without leaving Louisiana;

• a terrorist squad could seriously disrupt much of the oil supply to the nation or even to the world;

• one saboteur could incinerate a city by attacking certain natural gas systems;

• a few people (perhaps just one person) could release enough radioactivity to make much of the U.S. uninhabitable; and

• a single hydrogen bomb could probably do *all* these things simultaneously.

These vulnerabilities are increasingly being exploited. This book documents—based on a far from exhaustive search—significant recent assaults on energy facilities, other than during an actual war, in forty countries and, within the United States, in at least twenty-four states. Scarcely a week passes in which no new attack is reported. Their rate is quickening. Oil tankers and terminals, oil wells and platforms, refineries, pipelines, storage facilities, coal and uranium mines, hydroelectric dams, power plants, transmission lines, substations, switching centers, control systems, nuclear facilities—all have proven to be tempting targets. Disruption of energy is becoming a terrorists' fad.

How did we become so vulnerable?

America's energy vulnerability is an unintended side effect of *the nature and organization of highly centralized technologies.* Complex energy devices were built and linked together one by one without considering how vulnerable a system this process was creating. Through such incremental adhocracy, our nation has drifted haphazardly from one kind of energy vulnerability to another.

In the mid-nineteenth century the United States shifted from wood to coal in search of more secure and abundant supplies. In the years following the 1919 coal strike, dependence shifted again to oil and gas;[1] today they provide three-quarters of our energy. When World War II U-boats sank coastal oil tankers, and labor problems snarled railway coal shipments, the nation's response was to build oil and gas pipelines, ignoring in turn *their* serious vulnerabilities.[2]

The 1973–74 Arab oil embargo made it painfully obvious that oil shipped from an unstable area halfway around the world can be cut off at will, priced almost at will, and used as a tool of international blackmail. Analysts and politicians suddenly woke up to energy vulnerability. But the crisis management mentality focused their attention so exclusively on foreign oil that they overlooked the many other forms of energy vulnerability that had (luckily) not yet been so dramatically exploited. As a result, policymakers rushed to relieve oil dependence without considering the new vulnerabilities which their favored substitutes for foreign oil might create.

Again in 1979, when a one percent reduction in world oil availability during the Iranian revolution triggered gasoline lines and a one hundred twenty percent price increase in the United States,[3] this narrow conception of energy vulnerability diverted attention from a more comprehensive understanding of how to guarantee secure supplies of *all* kinds of energy in the face of *all* possible disruptions—foreign or domestic, civil or military, accidental or deliberate, foreseen or unforeseen. The result: hasty proposals for synthetic fuel plants, power stations, and Arctic gas projects that would in their own way be even less secure than the foreign oil they were meant to replace.

In short, the oil crises of the 1970s, far from raising our leaders' consciousness about the fragility of *all* these centralized energy sources, diverted their attention away from all but *one* type of vulnerability. For this reason, most investments proposed to replace foreign oil would actually make our energy supplies *more* vulnerable, in other and even less tractable ways.

Ironically, the oil cutoffs and price hikes also renewed the development of alternative energy technologies. The end of cheap oil combined with rapid technological progress to produce new opportunities for simultaneously reducing oil dependence *and* other energy vulnerabilities. It became possible to build a resilient energy system out of ingredients that were actually the cheapest and fastest-growing options available—ones that would spread even faster in a truly competitive marketplace. Thus an energy policy consistent with free market principles, individual choice, and local autonomy would also be the easiest way to provide lasting energy security for a free society—if the foundations of that security were clearly understood.

Unfortunately, these more resilient energy options had a very low official priority. Thus a double oversight arose. The problem was defined narrowly—how to reduce dependence on imported oil—because no one had organized the thousands of warning signs sprinkled through the daily news reports into a coherent, recognizable pattern showing the full range of potential vulnerabilities. As a result, the answer was defined narrowly to be the rapid deployment of any familiar technology which could substitute for foreign oil. Thus, despite a multitude of studies, conferences, books, and television specials on energy, almost nobody looked beyond the conventional definition of the problem to seek a solution truly consistent with national security.

That was a central task of an analysis which the Defense Civil Preparedness Agency (the civil defense arm of the Pentagon) commissioned in

1979. Released on 13 November 1981 by the Federal Emergency Management Agency (DCPA's successor), that research[4] is the basis for this book. Extensively reorganized, rewritten, and supplemented to make it useful to a wider audience, it seeks

- to analyze the full range of potential disturbances to energy systems, their causes, their often unexpected effects, and their interactions with each other;
- to show why traditional engineering measures meant to make energy systems more *reliable* in the face of expected technical failures may make them less *resilient* against unexpected disruptions;
- to identify specific design principles that can make major failures in our energy system structurally impossible;
- to discuss how these principles can be embodied in efficient, diverse, dispersed, and sustainable energy technologies, and patterns of organizing those technologies, which are already available and practical;
- to show that such measures yield great inherent resilience—making failures both less likely and less dangerous—without added cost, and indeed at *less* cost than more vulnerable energy options; and
- to describe how governments, corporations, communities, and individuals can actually implement a resilient energy policy for the United States while at the same time meeting their own economic and security needs.

Purpose and scope

This broader concern with the security of energy supplies does not mean that dependence on foreign oil is not a serious problem. When the Secretary of Defense, referring to oil dependence, stated that "there is no more serious threat to the long-term security of the United States than that which stems from the growing deficiency of secure and assured energy resources,"[5] he was right in a wider sense, as this book will show—but also exactly as he meant it.

The global oil problem *is* real, difficult, and urgent. Buying foreign oil cost America nearly ninety billion dollars in 1980 alone—equivalent, as Deputy Secretary of Energy Sawhill put it, to the total net assets of General Motors, Ford, General Electric, and IBM, or to nearly forty percent of total U.S. exports. Further, the proprietors of much of the oil are neither friendly nor reliable; and the far-flung supply lines can readily be cut by the Soviet Union, Colonel Qadafi, or the Palestine Liberation Organization. Oil is in any case a finite resource that will become scarce. These obvious dangers have led our government to take various precautions against interruptions of oil imports. Even those precautions are not enough: virtually all assessments of American oil dependence find that a major interruption of world oil trade would gravely damage national and global security.[6] Yet even *eliminating* oil imports—as this book shows how to do within this decade—would barely begin to reduce America's *total* inventory of critical energy chokepoints.

Energy is more than oil, and energy security is far more than ability to keep the oil coming. Thus the emphasis here is on energy security problems *other* than foreign oil—not through a lack of concern about it, but through an even deeper concern that it is only a small part of an immense problem. It is bad enough that foreign oil supplies are vulnerable. It is far worse that all the rest of our major energy sources—domestic oil, the non-oil half of our energy today, and most of the officially proposed replacements for oil tomorrow—are at least as vulnerable as foreign oil itself. And it is worst of all that these dangers to our domestic energy system are so little recognized.

Three nuances of this analysis might be misunderstood if not made explicit. First, many of the vulnerabilities identified in the energy system probably have counterparts elsewhere: for example, in the supply of food,[7] water, and industrial products.[8] This is an unfortunate but unavoidable consequence of the structure of our society. As Congress's Joint Committee on Defense Production remarked:

> An increasingly complex, technology-dependent, industrial economy in the United States has made citizens more than ever vulnerable to the effects of disasters and emergencies over which they have little or no control and to which they cannot successfully respond as individuals.[9]

We recognize that energy vulnerability may be a parable for the wider fragilities of our society. However, we do not argue, on that ground or on any other, for the transformation (let alone the dismantlement) of the industrialized corporate economy. The merits of alternative patterns of social and economic evolution, though worth analyzing, remain beyond the scope of this work. It is the purpose of this analysis to explore only those *incremental, technological* choices which would increase *energy* security (and minimize direct economic costs) while maintaining and enhancing precisely the industrial patterns of production, organization, and control which prevail in the United States today. Thus the analysis explicitly assumes unchanged values and lifestyles. It is possible that other patterns might be preferable for various reasons, including greater resilience both in energy supply and otherwise. However, such questions of personal preference are not a part of this analysis and will remain outside our brief.

Second, any analysis of vulnerabilities must be so framed as not to provide a manual for the malicious. Great care has therefore been taken— including independent review by more than fifty experts from the military, civilian government, industrial, and academic communities—to omit those concepts, technological details, and references which could be useful to an adversary with enough skill and insight to mount an effective assault in the first place. That is, the material presented here should be grossly insufficient to help persons who do not have such skill, but superfluous to those who do. This book is a warning, but not a cookbook. Citations are omitted where necessary to protect a specific point of vulnerability from being identified (or to honor a source's wish that a statement not be attributed). No proprietary or classified information has been used or received. The official predecessor of this book[10]—virtually identical in technical substance—underwent formal government classification review before being released for unlimited public distribution.

Some residual risk will nonetheless remain—perhaps the price of free and informed discussion in a democracy. We believe the only thing more dangerous than discussing these distressing matters is *not* discussing them; for if only terrorists are aware of what they can do—and energy-related attacks around the world demonstrate weekly that they are—then the real dangers embodied in present energy policy will persist and sooner or later will be exploited. Reported attacks on centralized energy facilities are steadily (and, of late, rapidly) becoming more frequent, more sophisticated, and more violent. Not to recognize and combat this trend is to surrender to it—benefitting nobody but the enemies of a free society.

Third, energy security is more than a military problem. Military power, to be sure, rests more than ever on secure supplies of energy. The Allied loss of five hundred fifty-two oil tankers in World War II would have spelled defeat had not American industry, fueled mainly by domestic coal, been able to build nine hundred and eight more.[11] Europe would have run out of oil during the Suez crisis if American oil fields had not been able to provide enough extra "surge" capacity to make good our allies' deficit.

But the flexibility of the 1950s had disappeared by the time the Vietnam war hastened our nation's shift to being a net importer of oil. Vietnam was our first largely oil-fueled war, directly using somewhat over one million barrels of oil per day—about nine percent of national oil use, or nearly twice the fraction lost in the 1973–74 Arab oil embargo.[12] Any future wars may have to be fought largely with oil shipped from foreign countries in foreign tankers by foreign crews.[13] Fighting a replica of World War II today with ninety percent of our oil imports cut off (corresponding to a virtual closure of sea lanes by submarine warfare) would require roughly half the nation's oil.[14] This would imply at best drastic civilian rationing and at worst a serious advantage against an enemy that happened to enjoy relatively secure access to oil.[15] To make matters worse, modern weapons tend to use highly refined fuels—it takes almost two barrels of crude oil to make one barrel of military jet fuel.[16] And they also use fuels voraciously—the fuel consumption of a modern main battle tank, for example, is measured in gallons per mile, not miles per gallon. Despite such vast fuel requirements, today's military stockpiles are miniscule (in 1978, about one month's peacetime use).[17] Securing the fuels that enable our military establishment to fulfill its national security mission is thus a matter of direct and intense concern to the Pentagon.[18]

Furthermore, secure and equitable access to adequate energy is vital also to preserve national and global economic and political stability[19]—without which turmoil, revolutionary doctrines, and political extremism can flourish. Fair access to energy is also essential to ensure that competing domestic interests within a diverse society are resolved peacefully—lest civil disorders, domestic terrorism, or an erosion of mutual respect and governmental legitimacy put at risk the democratic process that is itself a cherished national interest. In an era when simply having to wait in line to buy gasoline has led some Americans to shoot each other, while others must choose daily between heating and eating, this hazard to our most deeply held political values cannot be taken lightly.[20] A nation without shared and durable principles, social cohesion, economic integrity, and a sustainable system of production is weakened in the world:[21] it may find itself unable to preserve, or forced to choose between, its most vital national interests.

Directly and indirectly, therefore, energy security is a pillar of national strength. The commitment of tens of billions of dollars for a Rapid Deployment Force for the Mideast oilfields bespeaks military planners' anxiety. Yet few of those planners see vital energy security objectives as being achievable primarily by military means.[22] The Defense Department's 1978 Annual Report calls instead for a primarily domestic, *civilian* solution to the energy problem: expansion of domestic fuel reserves, diversification, substitution, conservation, and stockpiling.[23] Thus the Pentagon has pragmatically recognized that stronger armies cannot achieve energy security. What the Pentagon has not yet recognized is that civilian energy planners, focusing exclusively on foreign oil, tend to propose substitutes which armies will be even *less* able to defend. This book describes instead an approach to energy security that will both enhance military preparedness and make it less necessary.

All authors must set boundaries to their subject. The important topics *not* considered here include, among others,

• U.S. military and defense policy and the threats it addresses;[24]

• most of the social, political, and psychological dimensions of preparedness;[25]

• the vulnerabilities of most systems other than energy supply;

- the merits of U.S. energy policy on grounds other than security;
- how the government could be better organized to improve energy security; and
- how the thesis applies in detail to other countries (though many close analogies will be evident from the scores of international examples cited).

Organization

To our knowledge, this book and the official report from which it is derived[26] are the first thorough analysis of energy vulnerability in its widest sense.[27] It has been edited with the needs of many different audiences in mind, especially those without a technical background or training in economics. To simplify new and sometimes difficult concepts, concrete examples have been used in place of elaborate theories and mathematical formulations. Illustrative anecdotes from many fields—biology, aeronautics, computer science, nuclear engineering, telecommunications, and more—seek to borrow from a wider experience without encumbering the reader with excess technical baggage. Concepts from diverse disciplines are therefore translated into ordinary language, at the occasional cost of some specialized details.

The text is organized into three sections. The first, following this introductory chapter, surveys

- the general types of disturbances to which energy systems are prone (Chapter Two);
- the often unpredictable ways in which failures can evolve (Chapter Three);
- the generic properties which make today's energy system vulnerable (Chapter Four);
- a case study (the 13–14 July 1977 blackout of New York City) of how these properties can cause a major failure and hamper recovery (Chapter Five);
- the aftermath and consequences of major energy failures (Chapter Six); and
- the risk of disruption by sabotage or acts of war (Chapter Seven).

Part Two illustrates and elaborates these concepts by tracing how these vulnerabilities apply to four specific cases—liquefied energy gases (Chapter Eight), oil and gas (Chapter Nine), centralized power stations and associated electric grids (Chapter Ten), and nuclear power (Chapter Eleven). Chapter Twelve finds that bipartisan government policy is seeking to expand these particularly vulnerable systems.

After examining the grave vulnerabilities of the present energy system, the book describes inherently resilient alternatives. Part Three

- explores the elements of a design science for making any system resilient (Chapter Thirteen);
- applies the resulting principles to the energy system (Chapter Fourteen);
- examines in greater detail how increased energy productivity can prevent, delay, and limit failures (Chapter Fifteen);
- surveys the opportunities offered by inherently resilient supply technologies (Chapter Sixteen); and
- discusses the role of federal, state, and local governments, of private industry, and of grassroots programs in rapidly achieving energy resilience (Chapter Seventeen).

This last chapter, and some examples in the two preceding ones and in the last part of Chapter Six, are based on longer drafts by our valued colleague Alec Jenkins. They reflect his vast experience in pioneering community-based energy preparedness programs throughout the United States.

Finally, three Appendices at the end of the text incorporate technical material—on net economies of scale and on the technical and economic status of appropriate renewable sources. This material is useful to technical readers but not essential to the development of the main argument.

Recognizing that much of this material will be fresh and novel to scholars of preparedness and of energy policy, we have retained extensive notes, cited by superscript numbers and listed by chapter starting on page 391. Those notes in turn refer to nearly twelve hundred consolidated references, listed alphabetically by author starting on page 429. And because examples concerning a particular country, technology, or concept may be scattered through several chapters, an index of places and subjects begins on page 469.

This analysis is not definitive. It answers some questions and raises others. By breaking new ground, it has pushed us, and probably our readers, well beyond our accustomed disciplines and patterns of thought. It is presented here not just for arcane private debate among energy and military experts, but for wide political discussion. The fundamental concepts of energy security, long ignored by the responsible professionals, should not be limited to experts, for they concern basic choices about the structure and even the survival of our society. Our aim, then, is to provoke informed reflection and discussion—professional, political, and above all public—on a grave and overlooked threat to national and individual security, a threat that is properly the concern of every citizen. We solicit your views, your participation, and your personal initiative in building a more resilient energy system as one key component of a more enduring society.

Chapter Two
What Can Go Wrong?

This book analyzes those threats to national security which are expressed through the energy system. It deals especially with "the degree to which an energy supply and distribution system is unable to meet end-use demand as a result of an unanticipated event which disables components of the system. The kinds of events referred to are sudden shocks, rare, and of large magnitude."[1] Later chapters will develop this theme in detail, including threats which cannot be foreseen. First, however, this chapter briefly surveys the main kinds of foreseeable threats that can affect various energy systems.

Threats which can be identified in advance include

- natural events;
- aggressive physical acts (war, terrorism, and sabotage, all considered more fully in Chapter Seven);
- failures of complex technical and economic systems; and
- accidental failure or deliberate disruption of the devices that control these systems.

Some of these disruptions have mainly a tangible physical or economic effect; others, mainly psychological. Collectively, they offer a formidable array of hazards to modern society. We now consider these four types of disruptions in turn.

Natural events

Perhaps the most familiar threats to all aspects of daily life, including energy supply, are those commonly called "natural disasters"—though they may in fact be caused or aggravated by human activity. (For example, flooding can be caused by dam failure or by building on a flood plain. Unstable climatic conditions may be related to such stresses as carbon dioxide and particulate emissions, clearing of forests, and creation of urban "heatislands.") For some natural disasters that are sudden and castastrophic, like earthquakes, volcanic eruptions, and tidal waves, the areas at risk are broadly known but the times are not. General precautions are commonly taken, such as reinforcing buildings and improving communications equipment for disaster relief services. But these steps offer only partial protection from both direct damage[2] and its wider consequences.[3]

Severe weather, the most common kind of natural disaster, occurs frequently in a country as large as the United States. In 1973–75, an average of about three dozen major episodes per year caused damage totalling about a half-billion dollars per year.[4] Each region has a characteristic range: "hurricanes are especially likely . . . in Florida, droughts in Texas, tornadoes in Oklahoma, and blizzards in Wisconsin."[5] Other events include windstorms, ice storms, hailstorms, landslides, lightning, dust storms, and floods, both singly and in various combinations. Simple rain can be a disaster—when upwards of a foot comes at one time, as it did on 3–5 January 1982 in a Northern California deluge. In storms which killed three hundred fifty-four people in 1960, ice deposits over eight inches in diameter built up on wires.[6] Tornado winds can exceed five hundred miles per hour.[7] Conditions as extreme as any in the world can occur in seemingly innocuous places: in New Hampshire's White Mountains, the officially recorded maximum windspeed is two hundred thirty-one miles per hour, and a temperature drop of sixty Fahrenheit degrees in forty minutes has been unofficially observed in July.

Few parts of the United States are essentially free from extremes of weather, though the frequency of extremes varies widely. In many areas, "normal" bad weather is also disruptive, with routine snowfalls, spring thaws, ice break-ups, and so forth snarling transportation and communication for days or weeks each year.[8] This is also common in other countries: in the Soviet Union, for example, "seven out of ten . . . roads become impassable" during the spring thaw, and again during autumn rains[9]—the same autumn rains that left the 1941–42 German offensives bogged down in mud.

Since fuel and power are transported outdoors over long distances, "a large portion of the fuel movement . . . in the United States is vulnerable to disruption from inclement weather, and all forms of fuel shipment are subject to disruption by natural disaster."[10] The winter of 1976–77, for example, was twenty-two percent colder than normal,[11] and particularly cold in the Midwest. "The Ohio River froze bank to bank [,] blocking barge traffic [carrying] . . . both fuel oil and coal. Coal [wetted at the mine face to suppress dust] froze solidly in rail cars, sometimes requiring blasting to remove it. Winter snows impeded truck movements of heating oils, gasoline, and [liquefied petroleum gas]."[12]

How disruptive bad weather is depends on the mix and the flexibility of fuel use in the area. The Ohio River freeze-up hit a region that both depends heavily on coal (which was why the one-hundred-nine-day 1978 miners' strike had such an impact on the Midwest)[13] and moves much of that coal by barge. "Water carriers are, by and large, . . . most subject to weather . . . —freezing, flooding, and drought [which makes navigable channels shallower and narrower] can all have very disruptive impacts."[14]

Slight differences in the nature of the disruption can greatly change its consequences. The winter of 1977–78, though nearly as cold as that of 1976–77, caused virtually none of its dislocations in fuel delivery,[15] both because the local details of how the weather affected fuel shipments were different and because people were better prepared the second time.

Abnormal weather affects not only the supply of energy but also the need for energy. This interaction may make matters much worse. During 1975–77, for example, California got sixty percent less rainfall than the 1931–77 average.[16] This reduced the region's hydroelectric output by about forty percent. That deficit made hydro-dependent Pacific Gas & Electric Company burn an extra fifty million barrels of oil, and was largely responsible for raising PG&E's operating expenses by thirty percent.

Meanwhile, however, water allotments for agriculture—which normally uses eighty-five percent of California's water—were reduced by over sixty percent. Efforts to pump up more groundwater to make up this loss used about one billion kilowatt-hours of additional electricity. The interaction between energy and water problems could have been even worse if proposed coal slurry pipelines had been operating: they would have had such a low water priority that their operation would probably have been cut back severely. The result: two supposedly independent energy systems— hydroelectricity and coal-electric—would have failed at the same time.

As drought persisted in the Western states, the Eastern two-thirds of the country simultaneously suffered record cold. This raised heating costs by an estimated four to eight billion dollars and increased oil imports by approximately one hundred fifty million barrels. Thus drought in the West and cold in the East caused oil imports to increase by a total of about two hundred million barrels worth six billion dollars—not an insignificant contributor to a weak dollar and a tight world oil market.

Meanwhile, also caught short, the unprepared natural gas industry burned twelve percent of its stored gas in November 1976 (compared to zero the previous winter). Some systems were withdrawing gas from wells when they normally injected it. One major pipeline company sold its reserves prematurely. Some areas where gas was stored were so cold that the pumps were not powerful enough to retrieve the stored gas.[19] Gas supplies ran short, putting over a million people out of work in twenty states and costing up to one hundred million dollars in unemployment benefits.

Over forty-five percent of the gas shortfall was in Ohio, already hard hit by disrupted deliveries of coal and fuel oil.

Perhaps the most disturbing feature of this disruptive weather is that the same characteristic pattern which causes Western drought and Eastern cold typically causes simultaneous cold weather in Europe and Japan.[18] If this happened when world oil supplies were tight, it could greatly increase pressures on the global oil market. Oil shortfalls in the 1970s were only a few percent of total supply. A simultaneous cold spell throughout the north temperate zone could roughly double this gap.

The possibility of bad weather, then, heightens vulnerability to routine shortages or disruptions of energy supply. Likewise, a deliberate disruption can be timed to coincide with bad weather. Thus in Britain, the onset of winter is commonly associated with militancy among fuel and power workers, who remember how effectively the miners' strike toppled the Heath Government in 1974. Sabotage of electric grids could likewise be timed to coincide with peak loads, or with the unavailability of major plants, or both.

Weather fluctuations can affect wide areas for periods of weeks, months, or even years, as in the Sahelian drought. In the U.S. in 1980–81, extreme cold in the Midwest and Northeast, and extreme heat in the South (nationally, the summer of 1980 was thirteen percent hotter than normal), caused as much dislocation as a major hurricane, but spread over a far longer period. There is ample precedent for such fluctuations. In the summer of 1816, for example, frosts were reported in every month in New England and New York, with similarly severe weather in Western Europe. And such "freak weather" will probably become more common, not less. Most climatologists agree that global weather patterns in the past decade or so have fluctuated from the average much more than they did earlier in this century, and will probably continue to do so.[19]

In fact, at several times in the past seventy thousand years—perhaps as often as once every thousand to ten thousand years—there may have been abrupt drops of average temperature by about nine Fahrenheit degrees. (That is nearly three times the margin by which the U.S. winter was colder in 1976–77, when the Ohio River froze, than the previous winter.)[20] Indeed, many scientists suspect that global climate may well be "almost-intransitive"[21]—subject to abrupt changes from one mode of behavior to another, brought about by very small, seemingly random causes but, once changed, reluctant to change back again. The size and nature of events that can trigger such climatic lurches are not yet known.

Climatic fluctuations on time-scales longer than year-to-year are particularly insidious. The Colorado River Compact of 1927, for example, allocated water based on average flows for the previous decade, but subsequent average flows have been smaller by as much as a million acre-feet per year. The abnormality of the Compact's base years has been a fruitful source of litigation ever since.[22] Such gradual changes in rainfall patterns could disrupt not only hydropower but also conventional power stations (which require abundant supplies of cooling water). They could also, of course, require major changes in agriculture, with large effects on energy use and food supply.[23]

When climate—or any other environmental influence—changes, different organisms adapt at different rates and to different degrees. This fact can be at least as important for energy use as the change itself.[24] Even localized, seemingly trivial environmental change can cause awkward biological adaptations. For example, the young of the Asiatic clam *Corbicula fluminea*, too small to be stopped by screens, adapt enthusiastically and prolifically to the warm, protected, and food-laden water flow in the artificial environment of the fresh-water-cooled steam condensers in power stations. Some stations, pumping little but clams, must shut down twice daily to shovel them out.[25]

Deliberate actions

A second category of threats to a stable energy supply is those caused by human action. Such actions may arise either outside the United States (wars, embargoes, interruptions of commerce) or domestically (sabotage, terrorism, riots, strikes, lockouts, oligopolistic withholdings of supply, judicial injunctions, permit suspensions, declarations of air pollution emergency). Some of these disruptions spring from a desire to harm the system. Others are pursued with commendable motives, not in order to shut off energy supplies; but the result can be equally disruptive.

Malicious intervention has one crucial difference—so obvious that it is often overlooked. If natural disasters happen to strike a point of weakness, that is an unfortunate coincidence; but malicious actions deliberately seek out and *exploit* vulnerabilities so as to maximize damage and limit possible responses. Thus identifiable vulnerabilities can *invite* attack tailored to take advantage of them. If that attack in turn is foreseen, one can try to forestall it by reducing the vulnerabilities that it might exploit. Such reductions will in turn create their own, perhaps different, vulnerabilities—which may be lesser or greater than the original ones—thereby inviting new forms of attack, and so on. This iterative, coevolutionary process reduces total vulnerability to attack only if it carefully anticipates the new vulnerabilities created by responses to earlier ones. Otherwise, like France, a country seeking to reduce Mideast oil dependence may become equally dependent on a central electric grid which (as later chapters will show) can be turned off even more easily than oil.

Vulnerabilities can be unexpected by both attacker and victim. The Iranian revolution's dramatic effect on world oil prices was probably as big a surprise to Iran as to oil importers. Vulnerabilities can be exploited accidentally: Iran's bombing of Iraqi oil facilities was meant to hurt Iraq, not Italy, France, Brazil, and India. Surface vulnerabilities may be less important than deeper ones: a military attack meant to maximize immediate damage may do less long-term harm than an attack meant to hamper recovery.[26] Modern, highly accurate nuclear warheads, for example, make possible recovery-hampering attacks on such points of vulnerability as oil refineries in the United States[27] and certain Soviet installations crucial to agriculture.[28] Outwardly similar vulnerabilities can be exploited by different means because they arise from different causes. For example, both the U.S. and the U.S.S.R. have highly vulnerable transportation sectors, but in different ways. The Soviets lack a highly articulated network of rail, canal, and especially road routes, and each is already too overtaxed to take up much slack from the rest. The U.S., on the other hand, has such a network (especially of roads) and vehicles to run on them, but lacks a secure supply of fuel for those vehicles.[29]

Mistakes

Many modern technical systems are liable to sudden, large-scale failure because they rely on elaborate design and construction techniques: the complexity and technical adventurousness of these techniques are conducive to serious mistakes. These technical failures are sometimes called "industrial accidents," but "accidents" are always caused by something—ignorance, carelessness, overconfidence, or a combination. Common sites of major failures include buildings, bridges, water or sewage plants, dams, locks, tunnels, aircraft, trains, or containments for toxic or hazardous substances. Most of these sites are important to the energy system, along with other, more specialized, pieces of plumbing and equipment. Major failures may be manifested or accompanied by fires, explosions, physical collapses, leaks, spills, and so forth. These failures often occur in sequences (derailments causing spills causing fires causing further releases) which greatly amplify the effects. (Such a chain reaction caused a 1946 explosion, largely from ammonium nitrate fertilizer on shipboard, whose force—equivalent to four to six thousand tons of TNT—leveled much of Texas City.[30]) Many technical failures could be prevented or mitigated by the design precautions developed for energy systems in Part Three.

Though technical failures are not the main focus of this study, they offer cautionary tales. A National Aeronautics and Space Administration missile worth hundreds of millions of dollars had to be blown up shortly after launch because one misplaced minus sign in a computer program put it on the wrong trajectory. Analogously, had there been a nuclear war during a substantial period in the 1960s, all U.S. missile warheads would reportedly have missed their targets by a wide margin, owing to a systematic error in reentry calculations. A radar image of the rising moon once caused a U.S. nuclear attack alert; once this was fixed, a flock of geese caused a new alert.[31] In a recent fifteen-month period the U.S. had one hundred fifty-one false attack alerts, four of them serious.[32]

The great care applied to such matters is clearly not always enough: a fire incinerated three Apollo astronauts in 1967, and a Space Shuttle nitrogen purge error suffocated a worker in 1981. Both events occurred during extremely high-technology launch-pad operations where the utmost precautions were presumably being taken. Some technical systems are simply so complex that they exceed the limits of attainable reliability and foresight—a problem to which the next chapter returns.

Command, control, and communications disruptions

Any system is by definition most vulnerable to disruption through its control mechanisms—those meant to affect its operation most by applying the least perturbation. The management structures and procedures for using these control systems, and the communications systems used to provide their input and transmit their output, share in this enhanced vulnerability. As systems grow more complex, the volume and speed of information flow needed to control them grow until only computers can cope with these demands. Computers' undiscriminating willingness to do what they are told, however nonsensical, increases control vulnerability further. And finally, through computers, the ability to affect much by little becomes concentrated in one place, perhaps accessible electronically from many other places.

For example, a Swedish Government assessment of "The Vulnerable Society" notes that the central computer of the National Social Insurance Board, in the northern town of Sundsvall, sends over fifty million payments or financial messages per year (at a peak rate of half a million per day) to Sweden's eight million people. Computer failure

> would affect large numbers of [people] . . . , chiefly those . . . with the least social and economic protection. [Non-military] threats to the computer . . . might include terrorism for political purposes, fire or water damage [or disruption by magnetic or electric fields or by reprogramming]. Even a lengthy power cut might have serious repercussions. Other critical situations might arise, for instance, from an industrial dispute involving personnel working with the computer.[33]

Because of this dependence on a single fragile computer, small groups of systems analysts and programmers, even disgruntled individuals, can now constitute a national threat—which is why Swedish computer experts are being compartmentalized to "redistribute dependence among [more] people."[34]

The Sundsvall computer's product is information, including instructions to transact financial affairs. The product of energy systems, however, is delivered electricity or fuel, so the designers have tended to concentrate on ensuring the supply of that product, rather than on ensuring proper control of the *information which controls its delivery*. Most assessments of energy vulnerability, likewise, deal with crude disruptions—oil embargoes, pipeline or transmission line sabotage—when in fact the greatest vulnerability may well lie in misuse of control systems. This subject is explored further, with specific examples, in later chapters.

The first practical demonstration that the worst vulnerabilities may arise within control systems is today coming not from energy systems but from telephones. Highly intelligent and dedicated "phone phreaks" (or, as they prefer to be called, "communications hobbyists") are causing serious loss of revenues for both public and private telecommunications companies in the U.S. An estimated twenty percent of the traffic on ARPANET, a defense-related electronic network, is unauthorized. Some supposedly secure military communications links have been accidentally penetrated by experimenting students. Phone phreaks' ingenuity generally keeps them several steps ahead of security precautions. Using microcomputers, they can break codes and discover passwords by automatic dialing. They can read, change, or delete supposedly secure data and programs in computers a continent away.[35] Using pseudonyms, they collaborate via computer teleconferencing networks and newsletters. Some are specifically devoted to technical measures for fooling control systems into giving something for nothing (such as free phone calls, telex, water, electricity, gas, gasoline, photocopying, computer time, and cable TV).[36] Contacts via such computer networks are anonymous and essentially untraceable. Phone-linked computers can also be used to implement automatic sequences of events, including destructive events, at great distances.[37]

Some newsletters of "anti-system technology" even focus entirely on ways to "crash" telephone and time-sharing computer systems—something that occasionally results from random intervention, but is much easier to accomplish with understanding and purpose. It appears that one person, without compromising identity or location, can crash most or all of a corporate or commercial telephone network and keep it down more or less indefinitely, perhaps causing significant damage to electromechanical components in the process. Most—with sufficient effort, perhaps all—communications and computer systems whose entry is controlled by electronic passwords rather than by physical barriers are vulnerable to penetration, misuse, and disruption. The systems which control electric grids, oil and gas pipelines, and other complex energy facilities are no exception.

Physical barriers, of course, are not an absolute bar to physical penetration by stealth or force. The physical vulnerability of some control systems, like the control room of a nuclear reactor, may suggest a need for a duplicate control room, located away from the reactor, to be used if the first one is taken over. (Such a proposal has already been rejected by the Nuclear Regulatory Commission, though some alternative control equipment for basic shutdown functions is provided.) But such duplication also increases vulnerability to capture, or simply to interception and misuse of the communications channels, as in computer and telephone networks today. False control signals can then be combated by encoding, but this increases operational delays and errors: recall the thirty-seven minutes it took for a technician to find the "all clear" tape after accidentally broadcasting a tape announcing a Soviet nuclear attack.[38] In this game of threat and countermeasure, problems simply cascade. The design principle seems to be "One damned thing leads to another." To the extent that deliberate intervention in a control system can be combated, it is seldom by adding yet more layers of complexity, but rather by a quite different strategy—of resilient design (Chapter Thirteen).

The vulnerability of controls is especially marked in computerized financial systems. An adversary could probably crash the U.S. (and international) banking system simply, anonymously, and untraceably by using electronic funds transfer to make hundreds of billions of dollars vanish instantaneously.[39] The needed techniques are not unduly difficult. In 1980, four thirteen-year-olds brought chaos to some Ottawa commercial computers while playing with a microcomputer at their New York private school.[40] Fraud, sabotage, and coercion using electronic banking has already reached alarming (if largely unpublicized) proportions. If a computerized embezzlement is detected (many cannot be), that fact itself is frequently an effective lever for blackmail, lest the victimized organization lose public confidence or have to pay higher insurance premiums. It is doubtless encouraging to potential computerized thieves that of the few caught so far, most have been rewarded with lucrative jobs as security consultants. As will become clear in later chapters, if financial computers are this vulnerable despite the immense effort devoted to protecting their data, the farflung and far less well protected computers which control modern energy systems may be even more vulnerable, with results at least as serious.

Chapter Three

How Systems Fail

The previous chapter's brief list of the main events that can disrupt the energy system seriously understates the problem. Failures in complex systems are seldom simple. Simple threats can and often do act in bizarre ways on the complex interdependencies that bind those systems together. *"The assessment of vulnerability, therefore, cannot rest on a mechanical collection of assessments of the vulnerability of separate parts."*[1]

"Mechanical collection," however, is what most vulnerability studies do. At best, they assess energy vulnerability (for example) for stringing together the individual vulnerabilities of fuel sources, processing plants, storage and transmission and distribution facilities, and so forth. But considering the energy system as a mere collection of components, without considering how they must be bound together to work as a whole, ignores the crux of the problem: interactions, combinations, feedback loops, higher-order consequences, and links across the system boundary. The complexity of these links may defy complete analysis, but is easily illustrated by anecdotes.

Complexity

The sheer complexity of many technical systems can defeat efforts to predict how they can fail. A modern nuclear power plant, for example, typically contains

some fifty miles of piping, held together by twenty-five thousand welds; nine hundred miles of electrical cables; eleven thousand five hundred tons of structural steel; and a hundred thousand cubic yards of concrete. Countless electric motors, conduits, batteries, relays, switches, switchboards, condensers, transformers, and fuses are needed. Plumbing requirements in the various cooling systems call for innumerable valves, seals, drains, vents, gauges, fittings, pipe hangers, hydraulic snubbers, nuts, and bolts. Structural supports, radiation shields, ductwork, fire walls, equipment hatches, cable penetrations, emergency diesels, and bulkheads must be installed. Instruments must be provided to monitor temperatures, pressures, chain-reaction power levels, radiation levels, flow rates, cooling-water chemistry, equipment vibration, and the performance of all key plant components.[2]

Not surprisingly,

The sequence of human and mechanical events leading to the two most serious power reactor failures in the U.S. [at Browns Ferry, where a technician testing for air leaks with a candle caused a fire that burned sixteen hundred electrical cables, and at Three Mile Island] were excluded from . . . analysis in the most comprehensive study of reactor safety ever undertaken. Clearly it is possible to construct systems sufficiently complex that all probable states of the system are not foreseeable[3].

Recent reactor failures "must give pause to one's acceptance of any claim of high reliability for a particular system, based solely on probabilistic analysis [which tries to foresee all the ways in which it can fail]." 0004]

Many failures from one source

Perhaps the largest single cause of unpredicted failures in complex systems is that multiple components, supposedly independent and redundant, can all fail at the same time for unforeseen reasons. These can be "common-mode" failures—multiple failures of identical, redundant components in the same *manner*—or "common-cause" failures—multiple failures, caused by a single initiating *event*, of components that are different from each other but are supposed to do the same task.[5] For example, identical valves can all fail at the same time if they are all exposed to conditions for which they were not designed, or if they were designed or built wrongly: a common-mode failure. Different energy systems that are supposed to back each other up independently—for example, programs for mining coal, making oil from shale, and generating electricity from coal and uranium—could all fail to be built because Wall Street will not pay for them or because Westerners do not want them: a common-cause failure.

Common-mode and common-cause failures *cannot* be identified simply by cataloguing individual failure modes and their probabilities. In a spectacular example, the afterheat removal system in the Oak Ridge Research Reactor failed for several hours during operation in 1969, even though it had three identical channels backing each other up. In each channel, there were three separate operator errors, two equipment installation errors, and three design errors (including one that did not affect the outcome because the circuit in which it occurred was inoperable for other reasons). The system would have worked if any *one* of these twenty-one failures (seven identical errors or equipment failures in each of three channels) had not occurred. The post-mortem stated:

> This is almost unbelievable, especially in view of the importance that is attached to the single-failure criterion wherein no·single failure shall prevent proper [operation]. . . .
> . . . It must be concluded that present tools and methods are ineffective in uncovering the source of common mode failure. . . . [R]eliability analysis would have uncovered nothing. The single-failure analysis would also have been ineffective.[6]

Damage to the core was prevented only because a less reliable back-up system, which the failed ones had replaced, happened still to be available and functioning.

Common-mode and common-cause failures tend to be more important in actual nuclear reactor accidents than random failures of chains of components in sequence. The varieties of common-mode nuclear safety failures are legion. In one memorable case, a technician adjusting the trip points in several supposedly independent safety channels happened to calibrate them all to an inoperable range, simply by setting his voltmeter selector switch on the wrong decade position. In another case, a key circuit failed because a test procedure simultaneously destroyed a diode and confirmed that it was in good order.

A popular sampler anthologized from official reports of such incidents in U.S. commercial nuclear power reactors notes common-mode failures caused by such diverse circumstances as:

- failure of a power supply which was required to run supposedly independent circuits;
- disabling of four independent power sources when a transformer failed in such a way as to hurl a wire across a major electrical conductor;
- incorrect installation or manufacture of supposedly redundant equipment, so that all units failed in the same way;
- improper soldering, which kept electricity from flowing properly in separate and supposedly independent circuitry;
- floats which leaked, filled up, and sank, all in the same manner, so they all provided the same wrong indication of a liquid level;
- wiring errors copied consistently onto wiring diagrams;
- supposedly independent equipment all being water-damaged from being stored together outdoors;
- redundant machines all disabled by the same contaminated lubricating oil;
- independent pumps whose inlet strainers all became clogged by the same kind of debris;

- redundant pipes which all froze because the thermostat on one protective heater had been miswired; and
- common-mode failure so peculiar that its origin was never discovered.[7]

Another instance concerned control rods, which are drive into a reactor core to blot up excess neutrons and damp down the nuclear reaction, or drive out of the core to let the reaction speed up. Unfortunately, the control rods moved out when commanded to move either in or out, because their two-phase, three-wire drive motor, after one wire became disconnected, could start up on the remaining phase, a possibility which its designers had not expected. It turned out, however, that the windings of the drive motor were interacting with the windings of another motor, belonging to a cooling blower, that had been wired in parallel with them. In yet another case, relays designed to be fail-safe—opening if their power failed—stuck shut because of sticky paint. Similar relays had proven highly reliable for thirty years, but investigation disclosed that new staff at the manufacturer's new plant had put the paint on thicker.[8]

Unpredictable interactions

How could a twenty-nine-cent switch, burned out by improper testing, cause grotesque failures to cascade throughout the Apollo Thirteen spacecraft, so crippling it that the three astronauts barely coaxed it back to Earth?[9] That spacecraft was designed with the utmost care by highly qualified people who tried as hard as they could to make it reliable. They knew exactly what was in the blueprints, and the blueprints showed the way the spacecraft had been built. Unfortunately, "when one of the . . . oxygen tanks blew up[,] it developed that there were 'relationships among the gears' which the designers knew nothing about."[10] Likewise, in 1980, as simple an initiating event as dropping a wrench socket down an Arkansas missile silo led to the explosive ejection of a megaton-range Titan warhead into a nearby field.

The complexity of even the most advanced technical systems, however, is dwarfed by that of biological and social systems, as a simple example illustrates. The World Health Organization attacked malaria-carrying mosquitos among the inland Dayak people of Borneo with verve and abundant DDT. The people became much healthier, but the roofs of their longhouses started falling down. The DDT had killed a parasitic wasp which had previously controlled thatch-eating caterpillars. Worse, the cats started to die: they had built up lethal doses of DDT by eating lizards which had eaten poisoned mosquitos. Without the cats, the woodland rats flourished. Faced with sylvatic plague, the WHO had to parachute live cats into Borneo. This example "shows the variety of interactive pathways that link parts of an ecological system, pathways . . . [so] intricate . . . that manipulating one fragment causes a reverberation throughout."[11]

A further example extends the concept. Farmers in the Cañete Valley (on the coast about a hundred miles south and east of Lima, Peru) shifted in the 1920s from sugar cane to cotton. This developed a mildly annoying but economically tolerable infestation by seven native insect pests. In 1949, persistent, highly toxic, broad-spectrum pesticides, such as DDT and toxaphene, became cheaply available for distribution by aircraft throughout the confined valley. The pesticides offered an opportunity to decrease crop damage dramatically and hence increase yields and profits. That initial result was followed within a few years, however, by the emergence of six new cotton pests that had not previously been a problem; then, six years later, by the return of the original seven pests, now equipped with pesticide resistance. Despite heavier and more frequent spraying and the use of organophosphorus insecticides, "the cotton yield plummeted to well below yields experienced before the synthetic pesticide period. The average yield in 1956 was the lowest in more than a decade, and the costs of control were the highest." The near-bankrupt farmers were forced into a sophisticated program of integrated pest management based on reformed farming practices, minimal use of biocides, and fostering of beneficial insects. As any ecologist might predict, once biological balance was restored, pest levels dwindled and yields increased to the highest levels in the valley's history. This is, however, a story of luck. The farmers might well have caused irreversible damage: their effort to achieve a narrowly defined objective (eliminating seven insect pests) in the cheapest and simplest way had generated "a series of unexpected and disastrous consequences explicitly because of the narrow definition of the objective and the intervention."[12]

The Borneo and Cañete examples illustrate four key properties of ecological or other complex systems:

> By encompassing many components with complex feedback interactions between them, they exhibit a *systems* property. By responding not just to present events but to past ones as well, they show an *historical* quality. By responding to events at more than one point in space, they show a *spatial* interlocking property, and through the appearance of lags, thresholds, and limits they present distinctive *non-linear* structural properties. . . . [E]cosystems are characterized not only by their parts but also by the interactions among those parts. It is because of the complexity of the interactions that it is so dangerous to take a fragmented view, to look at an isolated piece of the system. By concentrating on one fragment and trying to optimize the performance of that fragment, we find that the rest of the system responds in unexpected ways.[13]

These biological insights have even been applied to urban renewal, rent

control, and freeway construction, where they have predicted and explained phenomena that had long baffled analysts of urban socioecono-
mics. For example, this approach shows why building freeways decreases
anticipated travel times, changes land-use patterns, generates more traffic,
increases anticipated travel times, and hence creates an apparent need for
still more freeways.[14] Similarly, in societies as diverse as the United States
and Sri Lanka, dams and levees to protect flood plains tend to encourage
building in those high-risk areas, vastly increasing the damage when an
extraordinary flood sooner or later overwhelms the defenses—precisely
the opposite of what was planned.[15]

These unexpected, paradoxical properties of natural and social systems—properties derived from their very complexity—are precisely those
that are critical to the conceptual basis of effective energy preparedness.
For example, viewing security as solely an outgrowth of military strength
would be as misleadingly narrow a view as supposing that cotton can be
grown profitably in the Cañete Valley only by using more and more pesticides—and that using them will in fact have the desired effect.

But it is impossible to do only one thing: every sword has at least two
edges. Thus a purely military conception of national security dangerously
neglects (for example) the energy vulnerabilities described in this book—
and does nothing to guard against the economic, ecological, and social instabilities which can destroy the very country one is seeking to defend.
Similarly, if we suppose that the answer to the Arab oil embargo is simply
to expand the domestic supply of all forms of energy, we may merely substitute one class of vulnerabilities for another. Defining a problem too narrowly can "solve" it by making it into someone else's problem—shoving it
into an adjacent pigeonhole that is someone else's responsibility. Thus one
can "solve" the energy problem, for a time, by making it into a problem of
insecurity, inflation, climate, nuclear proliferation, inequity, etc. Whether
in energy, military, or biological terms, focusing on only one aspect of security at a time ignores the interactions among all aspects. Subtle, higher-
order interactions can be a greater threat to stability than direct, first-or-
der consequences. Where cause-effect relationships are too complex to
understand intuitively, attempted solutions can make a problem worse: *the
cause of problems is often prior solutions.*

Indeed, when problems get complicated enough, wrestling with them
may create *more* problems than are solved. Two IBM scientists found, for
example, that the more they tried to "debug" a massive computer program, the more "bugs" their manipulations introduced. Their efforts to
fix it became ever more complicated and time-consuming, yet produced
ever weirder side effects in supposedly independent parts of the program.[16]

Some systems analysts, such as the mathematician Roberto Vacca, believe that poorly understood interactions may prove collectively so unmanageable as to lead to the breakdown of industrial society.[17] The Swedish vulnerability study, citing this view, found "similar apprehensions among technicians, biologists and sociologists."[18] But one need not extend the idea that far to see how the ripples of a single event can spread far beyond its intended area of influence—especially in the energy system, which influences and is influenced by virtually every aspect of our society. Perhaps the following extended qualitative illustration can convey the flavor of these unexpected interactions, feedback loops, and potential instabilities in modern techno-economic systems and how they bear on energy preparedness.[19] The following example is of course highly selective, but is not a wholly tongue-in-cheek description of recent trends.

Tracing higher-order consequences: an illustration

The United States pursued for many years a policy of promoting the use of more energy while holding its price down through regulation and subsidy. Because the energy looked cheap, its users did not know how much was enough, and so they grossly underinvested in energy productivity. The resulting emergence of the United States as a massive net importer in the world oil market harmed many U.S. allies. It harmed the economies of some oil-exporting countries which were being asked to lift oil at a rate detrimental to their reservoirs or economies or both. It devastated the Third World, which was unable to compete for the oil. The value of the dollar fell. Dollar-denominated oil prices rose.

The U.S. then needed even more foreign exchange to pay for the oil. It earned this in three main ways: by depleting domestic stocks of commodities (which was inflationary, left the forests looking moth-eaten, and left holes in the ground where orebodies used to be); by exporting weapons (which was inflationary, destabilizing, and of controversial morality); and by exporting wheat and soybeans (which inverted Midwestern real-estate markets and probably raised domestic food prices). Exported American wheat enabled the Soviets to divert capital from agriculture to military activities. This in turn increased pressure on the U.S. to raise its own (inflationary) defense budget—which it had to do anyhow to defend the sea lanes to bring in the oil and to defend the Israelis from the arms sold to the oil-exporting Arabs. (From this point of view, the best form of Middle Eastern arms control might be American roof insulation.)

With crop exports crucial to the balance of payments, pressure mounted for even more capital-, energy-, and water-intensive agribusiness. Fencerow-to-fencerow planting and cultivation of steep and marginal land raised the rates of topsoil loss above those of the Dust Bowl era—a dump-truck-load of topsoil passed New Orleans in the Mississippi River each *second,* and more soil was compacted, burned out, or sterilized. Heavy chemical inputs and a severely narrowed genetic base impaired free natural life-support systems. Still more oil was needed for fertilizers, pesticides, herbicides, irrigation, and desalination. All of these increased the stress on remaining natural systems and threatened uncontrollable epidemics of crop pests with an evolved resistance to chemical pesticides. More energy was needed to pump the vanishing groundwater from greater depths and to purify drinking water contaiminated with nitrate runoff. More coal strip mines and power plants, using still more water and land, were needed to supply the energy. The capital intensity of modern agribusiness, coupled with fluctuations in markets and weather, became unsustainable in the 1980 recession, when land values (on whose inflation farmers had borrowed heavily to pay their carrying charges) stopped inflating, instantly creating thousands of mini-Chryslers out of Midwestern farms.

The spiral sped faster as artificial financial incentives demanded quicker returns. The Ogallala Aquifer under the High Plains was drawn down three to ten feet per year and recharged less than half an inch per year. It was already half gone when the lifting rate, during the four dry months of the year, surpassed the full annual flow of the Colorado River past Lee's Ferry. Two-fifths of America's feedlot cattle came to be grown on grains made of Ogallala groundwater. Growing enough of the grain to put enough weight on a feedlot steer to put an extra one pound of meat on the table came to consume about a hundred pounds of lost, eroded topsoil and over eight thousand pounds of mined, unrecharged groundwater.[20] To replace imported oil, some people started to make the corn into ethanol fuel, but because of the unsustainable farming practices, each bushel of corn consumed about two bushels of topsoil.

Meanwhile, excessive substitution of apparently cheap inanimate energy for people exacerbated structural unemployment: the people who got jobs fixing the automatic machines looked more productive, but the people displaced by the machines had no jobs. A tax system left over from an era of plentiful capital and scarce labor, and therefore designed to subsidize capital investment and tax employment, also increased unemployment. This worsened poverty and inequity, which increased alienation and crime. High oil prices and the collapse of the automobile industry hastened the decay of the urban Northeast. Priorities in crime control and health care were stalled in part by the heavy capital demands of building and subsidizing the energy sector. At the same time, the energy sector itself—by its extraordinary capital intensity and its noxious emissions—contributed to the unemployment and illness at which those social investments were aimed. Energy prices and oil balance-of-payments deficits helped to drive inflation. Inflation and unemployment fed civil unrest. The growing vulnerability of the energy system to strikes, sabotage, and protest required greater guarding, surveillance, and erosion of civil liberties, which would in time encourage a drift towards a garrison state.

This, coupled with consolidation of oil and uranium cartels and a widespread failure to address the energy security needs of developing countries hit hardest by oil prices, encouraged international distrust and domestic dissent, feeding further suspicion and repression. On the horizon loomed energy-related climatic shifts that could jeopardize agriculture, especially in the Midwestern breadbasket, and so endanger a hungry globe. The competitive export of arms, reactors, and inflation from rich countries to poor countries made the world more inequitable, tense, and anarchic. Plans proceeded to create, within a few decades, an annual flow of tens of thousands of bombs' worth of plutonium as an item of commerce within the same international community that had never been able to stop the heroin traffic. Nuclear bomb capabilities crept towards the Persian Gulf from several directions.

All of this is rather a lot, of course, to blame on underpriced energy. But the point of this tracing spree, exploring some possible consequences of a supposedly simple action, is that the elements of national security must be considered as an *interdependent whole*. Their bizarrely intricate connections keep on working whether we perceive them or not.

Surprises

The United States does not yet have—and may not have for a very long time if ever—all the information needed to foresee all important consequences of our actions. This does not mean that we dare not do anything. It does mean that we need to view any reductionist catalogue of national security concerns with a certain wariness and humility. However thoughtful the catalogue, it cannot capture the most important sources of risk— the higher-order interactions within a complex system and the surprises from outside it. Taken together, four factors—unavoidable ignorance of how some things work, unpredictable changes in the environment in which things work, the influence of unexpected events not taken into account, and changes in technology and society—make it *impossible in principle* to foresee all risks.[21]

As an example of how many surprises may be lurking beyond the range of our attention, consider one narrow area of concern: the stability of regional and global climate. These are some of the unexpected energy-climate interactions whose existence was first widely revealed during the 1970s:

• "Forcing" the nitrogen cycle by using synthetic nitrogen fertilizer increases the incidental production of nitrous oxide by denitrifying bacteria in the soil (especially if acid rain makes the soil more sour). Some of the nitrous oxide diffuses up to the stratosphere. There its photochemical products attack the ozone layer, especially at altitudes above about fifty miles. This in turn changes the heating and circulation of the upper atmosphere. Some analysts believe that near-term rates of artificial nitrogen fixation might be climatically significant.[22]

• Radioactive krypton gas routinely released by nuclear reactors and reprocessing plants can apparently alter atmospheric ionization and hence the distribution of electric charge in the atmosphere (the "fairweather potential gradient"). This change has unknown but potentially large effects on nimbus rainfall (such as monsoons and thunderstorms) and other processes important to global agriculture and heat transport. This charge-altering effect may become important at krypton concentrations hundreds or thousands of times less than those of radiological health concern, possibly including present or near-term levels.[23]

• An oil spill in the Beaufort Sea, where drilling is now underway, could arguably spread under the fragile Arctic sea ice, and work its way to the surface through seasonal melting on top and freezing on the bottom. In about ten years this could make the top of the ice gray, increase its solar absorptivity, and so lead to a probably irreversible melting of the sea ice, with dramatic effects on hemispheric weather patterns.[24]. Present levels of soot in Arctic air may also be worrisome, since even faintly gray snow absorbs heat much better than pristine white snow.[25]

• Fluctuations in the behavior of charged particles in the upper atmosphere over Antarctica have been correlated with power surges in the North American electrical grid—apparently coupled, and very greatly amplified, through some sort of resonance effect. The climatic relevance of this linkage, if any, is unknown.[26]

These examples could as well have been taken from many other areas of earth science (or from biology or even political and social science) as from climatology. Their point is not that there is lot we don't yet know about climatology; it is rather that the future is a cornucopia of surprises. One scientist, hearing of the unexpected discovery that certain propellent gases in aerosol cans could deplete the ozone layer, exclaimed, "What the hell else has slipped by?" A great deal, concludes William Clark of the Oak Ridge Institute for Energy Analysis, "has slipped by, and always will."[27] That is as true of energy as of any other field.

Most energy policy analysts spend their professional lives coping with the consequences of a singular event in 1973. That event, the Arab oil embargo, surprised them: "The acute dependence of the western economies on a continuous oil supply was (rightly or wrongly) not viewed as hazardous, because supply was treated as a fixed function of geology rather than a variable function of politics."[28] Yet the same analysts who were so caught by surprise in 1973 cheerfully go on today to assume a surprise-free future. It is not going to be like that at all.

In 1974, a list was drawn up of the twenty most likely surprises in energy policy over the next decade or two.[29] Near the top of the list were "a major reactor accident" and "a revolution in Iran." Number twenty on the list, of which no examples could be given, was "surprises we haven't thought of yet." There will be many of those, not only because there is so much still unknown about how the world works, but because *rare events do happen.*

A principle enunciated by George Orwell and E.B. White, and known to discomfited experimental scientists as the Totalitarian Law of Physics, states that "whatever is not forbidden [by the laws of physics] is compulsory"—it will happen sooner or later. There are many possible events which may be individually very rare: their probabilities may be vanishingly small. But these surprises are also almost infinitely numerous, so *collectively* they will catch up with us, and one or another of them is likely to occur fairly frequently. We live in a world full of nasty surprises, and had better prepare for it.

National security, therefore, requires not only that we calculate the probability of foreseeable kinds of failure. Our designs must also include the broader philosophy of resilience in the face of the incalculable: lunatics, guerrillas, Middle East wars, freak winters, social turmoil, and those unpredicted high-technology failures which all experts insist are impossible—until, like the 1965 Northeast blackout, they happen. True preparedness requires not merely an explicit readiness for foreseeable threats—the subject of the next nine chapters—but also an implicit readiness for unforeseeable and imponderable threats. The theme of unforeseeable threats to complex, interactive systems, and the design principles for resilience that flow from the inevitability of such threats, will return for full development starting in Chapter Thirteen. This theme is the key to designing an energy system that can survive the surprise-*full* future.

Chapter Four

What Makes the Energy System Vulnerable?

Most commercial fuels and power in the United States today are delivered through a long, intricate chain of events and equipment. From mines in Appalachian hollows or Wyoming badlands, trains haul coal hundreds of miles to power plants. Arab and Alaskan oil is pumped perhaps a thousand miles through pipelines over desert or wilderness. Tankers haul the oil out of the Arctic or halfway around the globe, and deliver it to refineries and tank farms occupying hundreds of acres. The concentrated, high-quality refined products and natural gas move another thousand miles or so via elaborate networks of pipelines, barges, ships, trains, and trucks. Electricity moves hundreds of miles through sophisticated transmission lines. All these processes depend on massive, highly capital-intensive, long-lead-time facilities which are are extremely complex, both technically and socially, and which operate continuously under precise controls.

In this structure lie the seeds of brittleness:

- The energy system's components are complex, so they are prone to fail, and when they do, it is often hard to diagnose and fix them.
- The components are organized in complex patterns, so they may interact with each other in complicated ways which are not always well understood.
- The components are subject to unexpected, unpredictable disturbances from outside.
- These disturbances may cause sudden system-wide failures on a massive scale.
- The proper functioning of the whole system is profoundly important to people's well-being, to social cohesiveness, and to national survival.

Because the energy system is familiar and usually dependable, one is

30

tempted to suppose that it will always be able to resist disruption in the future, even if it is tested in ways—such as concerted terrorist attacks—to which it has not yet been exposed. But in fact, as will be shown both in principle and from practical examples, the very properties of the modern energy system that make it such a visible and impressive technical achievement also make it peculiarly vulnerable to the threats described in the previous two chapters.

The energy system cannot cope with threats for which it was not designed: it grew up in a quieter, more stable era of history than we are able to look forward to. Lately it has also been evolving, through a combination of many subtle trends, in a way that makes it vulnerable as a system to threats against which each of its components was supposed to have been secure.

The structure of today's energy system makes it prone to major disruptions because of the following attributes:[1]

• dangerous materials;
• limited public acceptance;
• centralization of supplies;
• long haul distances;
• limited substitutability;
• continuity and synchronism in grids;
• inflexibility of energy delivery systems;
• interactions between supposedly separate energy systems;
• high capital intensity;
• long lead times;
• specialized labor and control requirements; and
• potential for misuse of energy distribution systems.

These attributes are now considered in turn.

Dangerous materials

Many of the forms in which energy is commonly delivered are hazardous in their own right. Though accidental electrocution is uncommon, defective electric wiring is among the leading causes of fires (poorly installed and maintained wood stoves are gaining fast). But the main danger arises from the high energy density of fuels—the energy carriers which, by being burned, directly supply eight-seven percent of all energy delivered in the United States.

The high energy content of a given volume of fuel is in large measure the property which makes it valuable. It is what makes the fuel a fuel. But our familiarity with everyday fuels may lead us to underestimate their formidable ability to cause harm. (Hence the need for safety signs in some filling stations reminding us, "Gasoline is designed to explode.") A gallon of average gasoline, for example, contains as much energy as a strong horse produces in forty-nine hours' work. A standard gasoline pump (pumping at about thirteen gallons per minute) delivers fuel energy at the remarkable rate of twenty-nine million watts. Thus a twenty-pump station, when all its pumps are working, is delivering energy about as fast as a six-hundred-megawatt power station, which is quite a large one.[2]

Most fuels are, by intent, highly flammable or explosive. The amounts of fuel present even in the most dispersed stages of distribution, such as tank trucks, are sizable hazards. A nine-thousand-gallon tank truck of number two fuel oil contains the energy equivalent of a small nuclear explosion—three-tenths of a kiloton. Even though the two would not behave the same (the oil fire would release its energy not as prompt radiation or blast but as radiant heat), the heat from a tank-truck fire would suffice to melt nearby cars. In refinery accidents, burning oil flows have covered as much as forty-two acres—an essentially unextinguishable conflagration—and vapor explosions have devastated as much as twenty-nine acres.[3] A 1976 oil tanker explosion in Los Angeles Harbor broke windows twenty-one miles away.[4] The hazard is not limited to petroleum-derived fuels: at least one worker was killed in the 6 March 1981 explosion of a large ethanol tank in São Paulo, Brazil.[5]

Gaseous fuels, being harder to contain, increase the hazard:

> With vast quantities of a highly explosive substance [natural gas] being carried at very high pressures in a steel pipeline with a wall thickness ranging from a tenth of an inch to half an inch, often near or through populated areas, the potential for catastrophe is considerable.[6]

> A gas pipeline can be bombed over a considerable length by a single charge. It will blow up by itself if a break allows air into the line. An air-gas mixture, under [the] right conditions, can explode and detonate over miles of terrain, through cities and industrial centers . . . . The writer observed an eight-inch spiral weld line that unwound and came out of its ditch for a distance of eight miles. A larger line would result in a worse situation. Detonation can occur even in a two-inch line.[7]

Compared to, say, piped water, this is an impressive potential for mischief, demanding meticulous care. Such energy density increases the likelihood of serious consequences from an initial disruption, whether from natural disaster, deliberate attack, or technical failure. The ready availability of such materials as natural gas, propane, and gasoline also expands the destructive capability of terrorists, permitting them to make bombs whose detonation inside even the most heavily reinforced major structures can demolish them.

Stored energy can also be gravitational, as in the potential of water behind a dam to sweep away whatever is below it if the dam bursts. This potential has often been exploited in wartime. Occasionally it is demonstrated in peacetime, accidentally or (as in the recent collapse of a sludge dam in the Kentucky coalfields) deliberately.[8]

Still another manifestation of high energy density is the radioactivity of nuclear materials. Pure fissionable materials (such as uranium-235 or plutonium-239) contain more than a million times as much energy per pound as pure hydrocarbon fuels. They are mildly radioactive; many of their fission and activation products are intensely so. Despite extensive precautions, the possibility of accidental or deliberate releases remains. Since the threat cannot be sensed without special equipment and can have long-term consequences with high emotional impact, even the possibility of a minor release can have major social effects:

> More than any other type of peacetime disaster, . . . nuclear emergencies could cause mass panic . . . . [T]he prime danger comes . . . from the [wide] dispersal of radioactive material . . . , impossible to detect without special instruments, [and which] could cause fearsome and unpredictable consequences: cancer, sterility, and gross birth defects . . . for many years after . . . release.[9]

Since there is no way to tell whether most such injuries were caused by radiation or by something else, the perpetrators of a release can be blamed for far more harm than they did. Conversely, people cannot be sure the release was *not* the cause of their affliction, and actual victims may be unable to prove causality as a basis for just compensation. These perplexing issues, now being raised in class actions by persons exposed to the Three Mile Island releases and to fallout from military nuclear weapons tests in the 1950s, have aroused considerable public attention and anxiety. Some other substances used in energy devices, such as polychlorinated biphenyls (PCBs) in old transformers, and even the electromagnetic emissions of very-high-voltage power lines, raise broadly similar concerns.

Limited public acceptance

Such anxiety is only one of many reasons why many people, from a wide variety of backgrounds and beliefs, many not want to have to bear the social costs of major energy facilities. The sources of opposition can include a desire to preserve a particular way of life (an important issue in rural Western areas threatened with boom-town development); concern about a wide range of environmental impacts (water use, loss of habitat or endangered species, biomedical effects of power lines on people and farm animals, potential danger from liquefied natural gas (LNG) or nuclear plants, oil pollution, nuclear proliferation, noise, coal dust, heat releases, esthetic damage); desire to defend certain social structures or values (free enterprise, small business, local self-reliance); or even perceived vulnerability itself.

It does not matter here how far these diverse concerns are justified or how widely they are shared. The important thing is that they represent views sincerely and strongly held by citizens of a democracy who believe they are entitled to give their views political and practical effect. Many historical examples suggest, too, that attempts to bypass or suppress such concerns bear high political costs and often turn out in hindsight to be a refusal to listen to warnings of serious errors in policy.[10]

For present purposes, however, it is sufficient to note that major energy facilities of any kind—like highways, water projects, chemical factories, or toxic waste dumps—can come to represent to many people a highly visible focus for grievances about the project itself or broader issues. By threatening direct and undesired impacts or by symbolizing perceived inequities, such a facility can be, from the standpoint of civil disturbances, an attractive nuisance. Nuclear facilities, particularly in Europe, are clearly among the most prominent lightning-rods for such social tensions:[11] hence the official interest in assessing how likely it is that opposition to such plants might motivate some people to attack them.[12]

Centralization of supplies

Primary fuel sources—oil and gas fields, coal mines, uranium mines— have to be where the fuel is in the ground. Dams have to be where the water is. Refineries and power plants have to be so sited that it is not too costly to supply their fuel and deliver their products. The usual result of these logistical and economic requirements is to site major energy sources and conversion plants relatively far from their final users. Earlier in American history, heavy industry tended to go where the energy was, and cities followed the factories. Thus the mill towns of New England went to the waterpower, and later an industrial heartland grew in the Midwest near the coalfields.

But in this century, people become more mobile, new technologies were developed for cheaply moving fuels thousands of miles to market, and convenient near-urban sites for new plants were exhausted. For those reasons, the distance between major energy facilities and their customers has steadily risen. This increasing geographic separation has had two obvious effects. It has concentrated the facilities themselves into a small area (for example, near Western coalfields), making them more vulnerable to all sorts of disruptions. And it has made the connecting links longer and hence more tenuous, exposing them to mishaps over a longer distance.

But a more subtle social result of the separation may be equally important: the automatic allocation of the delivered energy and of its side effects or social costs to *different groups of people* at opposite ends of the transmission lines, pipelines, and rail lines. This divorce of benefits from costs is considered admirable at one end but, often, unjust at the other. Politically weak rural people usually do not want to live in "zones of national sacrifice" for the benefit of "slurbians" a thousand miles away. At the same time that this refusal is being asserted, the planners and builders of most modern energy projects are forced—by the projects' very scale and complexity—to organize their work through institutions that may be, or at least appear to be, remote and unresponsive to local needs.

These trends have together led in the United States to more than sixty "energy wars"—violent or near-violent conflicts over siting—now in progress. They reflect an intensity and breadth of social unrest that any student of energy vulnerabilities must take seriously. Archetypal, perhaps, is the long-running rebellion by politically conservative farmers in northern Minnesota who nightly dismantle high-voltage power lines that have been built diagonally across their land under a political process which they consider unjust and illegitimate.[13] An anthropologist who has named, analyzed, and often succesfully predicted the course of this and other "energy wars" persuasively argues that they often reflect an underlying conflict between a network and a hierarchy.[14] (The network generally wins.)

Additional social feedback loops can further heighten the risk that social unrest will spill over into deliberate disruption of energy systems. For example, social conflict and tension may increase if massive energy projects seem to be increasing inequities or economic insecurities to the projects' neighbors or customers or both. If people do not want the plants near them, that rejection—together with the general difficulty of siting and guarding large numbers of plants—may heighten pressures for further centralization in remote, paramilitarized enclaves like "nuclear parks."[15] Such concentrations of unwelcome energy plants have been seriously proposed to be built on the energy scale of the Mideast oil fields—the same degree of centralization whose vulnerability was the rationale for building nuclear plants in the first place.

Long haul distances

A large, recently built power station delivers its electricity an average distance of about two hundred twenty miles—as far as from Washington, D.C. to New York City. If its customers were evenly spread out (rather than clustered in an urban area as they usually are), they would occupy an area of more than ten thousand square miles—so huge is the station relative to the needs of the average customers. Some electricity travels much farther: British Columbia hydroelectricity goes as far as Southern California and Arizona, and some Churchill Falls (eastern Canadian) hydroelectricity probably gets nearly to Florida.

The average barrel of oil lifted in the United States is transported a total of about six to eight hundred miles before final use.[16] The average unit of natural gas probably moves even farther. In 1974, sixty-six percent of U.S.-mined coal was hauled an average of three hundred miles by rail, and twenty-one percent—much of it in the Ohio River Valley—travelled an average of four hundred eighty miles by barge.[17] Remote Western strip mining and exploitation of Arctic and offshore petroleum resources will greatly increase the average haul lengths. "The average distance we have moved our energy sources has continuously increased . . . , and all signs point to an even greater extension of these vital supply lines."[18] Longest of all—halfway around the world—are the supply lines for Mideast oil.

These long haul lengths increase vulnerability to all types of hazards. Different fuel delivery systems, of course, have different vulnerabilities. "The [California] pipeline network contains fewer parallel links than the highway net, and has less excess capacity for carrying fuel. Therefore, it is more vulnerable to disruption by earthquake. However, it is less vulnerable to a Teamsters' Union strike."[19] A few heavily used arteries of fuel transport make several different forms of energy (oil, coal, coal-fired electricity) simultaneously vulnerable to localized events: for example, in the case of the Ohio River, to freezing, bridge collapses, or river fires like the gasoline barge fire which recently closed a fifteen-mile stretch of the river for two days.[20]

Limited substitutability

Until such recent developments as the commercialization of fluidized-bed boilers,[21] few of which are yet in use, it was costly and uncommon for boilers to be designed to burn more than one or at most two kinds of fuel. It is especially hard to handle both solid and fluid fuels, because they require different kinds of equipment to store and feed them, and the duplication of investment would normally be unattractive. Indeed, the whole infrastructure for processing, moving, and using fuels, whether directly or via electricity, has been built on the assumption that several competing fuels will always be readily available in essentially unlimited quantities. The engineer's task was simply to decide which of those fuels would be cheapest in the near term and and to procure a device for burning just that fuel. The lifetime of these devices typically ranges from one to several decades. Accordingly, a complex pattern of past investments now locks each region and each industry into a relatively inflexible pattern of fuel and power use, limiting its adaptability to interruptions in the supply of any particular form of energy.

This problem is perhaps most familiar to electric utilities, whose hundred-plus billion dollars' worth of power stations represent the largest fixed industrial asset in the whole economy. Past fuel interruptions (the 1973–74 oil embargo, the 1978 coal strike, the 1975–77 Western drought, occasional natural gas curtailments, generic nuclear shutdowns) have highlighted regional concentrations on one or another fuel. Utility plans for 1989 reflect continuing fuel specialization of different kinds in virtually every region: over seventy-five percent coal dependence in the East Central states; over fifty percent oil in the Florida and Southern California/Nevada regions; over twenty-five percent oil in the New York, New England, North California/Nevada, and Arizona/New Mexico pools; over fifty percent gas in South Central; twenty-five to fifty percent nuclear in New England and in the Pennsylvania/New Jersey/Maryland and Chicago areas; and over sixty percent hydro in the Pacific Northwest.[22]

This might at first sight look like healthy diversity; but it also guarantees that a major interruption in the supply of *any* of these sources will put at risk the electrical supplies of at least one substantial region. Utilities in one region have some capacity to interchange power with those in a different region whose fuel vulnerabilities are different: in recent years, coal power has been "wheeled" to oil-short areas and, during the 1977–78 coal strike, vice versa.[23] But this interchange capacity is limited in scope; it does not apply to the whole country, since the eastern and western grids connect via only one small line in Nebraska, and the Texas grid is connected to neither. Moreover, interchange introduces new vulnerabilities (explored more fully in Chapter Ten).

Throughout the energy system, the ability to substitute is limited not only between different fuels but also between different types of the *same* fuel. There are different kinds of coal, for example, whose content of ash varies by up to a hundredfold; of sulfur, by at least tenfold; and of heat, by at least twofold. Conventional furnaces can burn coal only within a specified, often rather narrow, range of chemical and physical properties. On a home scale, most woodstoves are designed to burn hardwood *or* softwood efficiently, cleanly, and safely—but not to be able to burn either indiscriminately (without special design features). Oil is refined into an immense variety of products ranging for tar to watch oil. Just among the many grades of fuel oils and of motor vehicle fuels, there is often only a limited range of interchangeability for a given use. Even crude oil comes in many varieties, differing in specific gravity (heaviness), viscosity, chemical composition, and trace impurities such as sulfur and heavy metals.

Refineries normally need to blend crude oils of different composition— a logistical problem of considerable complexity at the best of times:

In some areas of the country large refinery complexes depend on a specific crude oil supply [whose] . . . interruption . . . could shut down [the] . . . plant. If this refinery were the sole supplier of particular feedstock[s] to a petrochemical plant which was one of a very few making specific products, such as toluene, tetraethyl lead, butadiene, specific solvents, or other chemicals, the loss could be . . . of strategic importance.[24]

Refineries designed for low-specific-gravity crudes cannot suddenly switch to high-gravity crudes without developing "bottlenecks" which limit their capacity. Refineries meant for sweet (low-sulfur) crudes are not built of the special alloys required to withstand the severely corrosive sour (high-sulfur) crudes. Waxy crudes requires special handling: some do not flow until heated to the temperature of a warm room.

There are similar restrictions on the purity, dryness, and heat content of natural gas suitable for various kinds of processing, transmission, and use. Even in storage of liquid fuels, "clean" tanks, barges, tankers, and so forth are not interchangeable with "dirty" ones contaminated by crude oil or heavy fuel oils; cleaning vessels is costly and time-consuming.

In many complex ways, therefore, prolonged disruption of normal fuel supplies can severely constrain the ability of the fuel-processing and fuel-using industries to cope. In many cases the modifications needed for oil refineries, for example, to switch to a different kind of crude take many months and cost many millions of dollars; it is not just a matter of turning valves.[25]

Continuity and synchronism in grids

Fossil fuels are in general straightforward and relatively cheap to store in bulk. With reasonable care to protect piles of coal from spontaneous combustion and tanks of crude oil from collecting moisture, stocks are fairly durable. Nuclear fuels are still cheaper and more durable to store: for a ten-year supply of low-enriched uranium fuel, warehousing charges are infinitesimal, and carrying charges add less than one percent to the delivered price of electricity. With more trouble and cost, natural gas can be stored in substantial amounts either as a gas (in tanks or underground) or as a very cold liquid (Chapter Eight). This is not to say that storage of fuels is free from risk: on the contrary, oil and gas stocks are prone to fire and nuclear stocks to potential theft. The point is rather that at least technically and economically, all fuels can be readily stored in bulk.

But for electricity, such storage is uniquely awkward and expensive. Thus the central supply of electricity requires a *continuous, direct connection* from source to user. Interruptions of central electric supply, having no buffer storage, are instantaneously disruptive. The grid exposes large flows of energy to interruption by single acts at single points, and there is only limited freedom to reroute the flow around the damage.

Furthermore, centralized supply grids cannot discriminate well between users. Electricity for a water heater, which may be unaffected by a few hours' interruption, must bear the high cost of the extreme reliability required for subways and hospital operating theaters. And the grid is all-or-nothing: it *must* be so reliable *because* its failure is so catastrophic, blacking out a wide area simultaneously. If your heating oil delivery fails to arrive, you can put on a sweater or go next door. If the electric grid fails, there is no unaffected next door: everyone who relies on the electric grid is in the same boat at the same time.

Another reason why electrical grids require continuous, meticulous management[26] is that they carry electrons in a particular, precisely defined time pattern of variation that is *synchronous throughout the grid*. Departures from synchronism can seriously damage equipment and can even cause the whole grid to break down. The exacting requirement for synchronism raises serious problems of grid stability which are examined further in Chapters Five and Ten.

Natural gas pipeline grids have a requirement of their own that is somewhat analogous to synchronism in electric grids. While electric grids can transmit power at levels varying all the way down to zero, gas pipelines cannot, because if pressure falls below a certain level, the pumps can no longer move the gas. In practice, this means that gas grids must keep input in step with output. If coal barges or oil tankers cannot deliver fast enough to keep up with demand, there is simply a corresponding shortage at the delivery end. But if a gas grid cannot supply gas fast enough to keep up with demand, it can cease working altogether. In January 1977, calling on stored gas and adding grid interconnections was not enough to keep up the grid pressure, so major industrial customers had to be cut off, causing dislocations in Ohio and New York (as noted earlier).

The alternative would have been even worse, because the collapse of gas pressure could not have been confined to the transmission pipelines. Without a continuous supply of high-pressure gas, the retail gas distribution system too would have been drained below its own critical pressure. If distribution pressure collapses, pilot lights go out in innumerable buildings, including vacant ones. A veritable army of trained people then has to go immediately into each building, turn off the gas to prevent explosions, and later return to restore service and relight all the pilots. This occasionally happens on a local level, but has hardly ever happened on a large scale. It is such a monumental headache that gas companies strive to avoid it at all costs.[27] Indeed, the gas industry generally considers it an abstract problem—much as the electric power industry considered a regional blackout until it happened in 1965. Yet, ominously, an extortionist threatened a few years ago to cause a brief interruption in Philadelphia's gas supply—long enough to extinguish the pilot lights, but short enough to cause instant and widespread "urban redevelopment" shortly thereafter.

Inflexibility of energy delivery systems

A monumental study of the U.S. energy transportation system identified six aspects of system flexibility:

- adaptability to changes in volume carried (throughput);
- adaptability to different operating fuels;
- sensitivity to weather;
- ability to change delivery routes;
- ability to build facilities quickly; and
- ability to ship several different fuels jointly.[28]

Another attribute not mentioned by the study, but also important, is

- ability to reverse direction.

Several of these qualities deserve brief amplification.

Volume   Normal fluctuations in demand, let alone the ability to substitute for other interrupted supplies, make it desirable to be able to change the amount of energy transmitted, quickly and within wide limits. All present means of coal transportation have this property insofar as they need no fixed or minimum throughput. (This may not be true of proposed slurry pipelines.) Railroad and barge traffic cannot greatly expand without overloading key track sectors, locks, and so on, but at least within those limits the volume is free to fluctuate. For oil, trucks provide the greatest ability to expand, provided there are enough trucks and open roads; railways and waterways are intermediate in flexibility, since they have fixed trunk routes but can move equipment along them to where it is most needed (and, in the case of railways, can add spur lines). Oil pipelines are the least flexible, having fixed routes and—barring major modifications—fixed maximum capacities. Most pipelines, however, can reduce their throughput over a substantial range with little penalty save in profits.

The ability to concentrate modular fuel-carrying vehicles where they are most needed paid off in 1940–42. At that time, the Atlantic Seaboard was ninety-five percent dependent on coastal tankers that were vulnerable to German submarines (and oil shipments to England were wholly dependent on these same tankers). Twenty thousand idle railway tank cars were reconditioned and put into oil-hauling service "almost overnight."[29] Barrel-loaded boxcars and tanks built for synthetic rubber were pressed into service. The oil unit trains "were highballed from one railroad to another" on "fifty railroads and fifty-six routes," achieving a peak shipment rate of nine hundred thirty thousand barrels per day. Commandeered barges also moved an average one million three hundred thousand barrels per day on the Mississippi. It was a heroic response to a desperate problem.

Surprisingly, the same need might arise even today. There is still no crude oil pipeline serving the East Coast refineries (New Jersey, Pennsylvania, Delaware), so an interruption of Atlantic or Gulf tanker traffic would shut them down. The Colonial Pipeline System, with a capacity of about two million one hundred thousand barrels per day, provides the only substantial capacity for importing refined products to the East Coast, but none for crude. The immense increase in oil demands over the past forty years has made America far more dependent on such major pipelines than we were on coastal shipping in World War II. Should the Colonial Pipeline not operate, replacing its product flow would require the equivalent of more than two hundred World War II T–2 tankers (each of sixteen thousand deadweight tons) on a continuous thirteen-day round-trip shuttle between Galveston and New York. This is approximately the whole U.S. coastal tanker capacity, and enough to cause a monumental traffic jam in the ports.[30] And this would substitute for the delivery of refined products by just one major pipeline: it would not even provide a drop of crude oil for the isolated East Coast refineries.

Facilities construction Liberty Ships showed the importance of being able to build up an extra stock of equipment to meet unexpected needs. This is equally true in responding to major energy emergencies. In general, it is faster to build trucks than other fuel-transporting devices, and once built, they can be deployed where needed. The roads they use are multi-purpose, rather than being specialized to move energy, as gas pipelines and power lines are. On the other hand, trucks are usually the most costly and energy-intensive way of moving fuels. Railway and waterway facilities, though cheaper, take much longer to build and are usually too costly for any but large users.

Speed and joint shipment Electricity moves instantaneously; natural gas is the next fastest; then, usually, oil, which can travel thousands of miles by pipeline in a week or two; and (in most cases) the slowest is coal. In coal shipment, the cheapest method (barge) is also the slowest, least flexible, and most vulnerable to weather. The most flexible in routing (truck) is also the costliest; railways offer various compromises between flexibility and economy. All can keep different kinds of loads separated.

So, surprisingly, can pipelines. For example, the Colonial system, the largest and probably the most complex in the world, accepts minimum batches of seventy-five thousand barrels, occupying a twelve-mile length of pipe (an amount which takes an hour and a half to pass a fixed point).[31] Each batch is separated from adjacent batches of different composition by inflating between them a water-filled rubber "batching sphere" that fits the inside pipe diameter. Constant monitoring of the specific gravity of transmitted product enables operators to divert the "interface"—the small mixing zone formed by leakage around the batching sphere—into holding vessels for reseparation or blending into products of saleable purity. The order of batching is carefully defined to minimize contact between incompatible products, and a full product sequence requires ten days. For products more viscous than the lighter heating oils, pipeline shipment is impractical.

Reversibility Oil and gas transmission pipelines now in operation are generally unidirectional.[32] They can be reversed, and have been, by modifying valves and compressors.[33] Oil tank trains are even more easily reversible, requiring only appropriate loading/unloading equipment.[34] Electrical grids are usually reversible without modification, subject to requirements of safety, metering, and stability (Chapter Ten).

In contrast, the 1978 coal strike showed that coal generally flowed only one way. The federal government had extensive authority to protect coal distribution, to require emergency electric interties, and to mandate allocations and sales of coal, but not physically to move coal.[35] Regardless of what the law allowed, most of the coal was sitting in power plant depots where foresighted utility managers had stockpiled it. And most of the depots had equipment only for *un*loading coal onto piles, not for *re*loading it for shipment to someplace else.[36] Such inflexibility in redistributing scarce fuel supplies can greatly hamper the response to an energy emergency.

In summary, then, the systems which transport fuels and power around the United States are not infinitely flexible. The transportation patterns have some slack, but not enough to accommodate all foreseeable disruptions. Major changes in how much of which fuel travels where may require many years to accomplish. The loss of particular fuel transport arteries could indeed cause energy shortages in the midst of surplus, simply because there may not be enough alternative pathways to get the energy to the people who need it.

Interactions between energy systems

Most of today's systems for supplying energy, and many for using it, require additional, auxiliary supplies of another kind of energy in order to operate. Interruptions of one kind of energy supply can therefore cause interruptions in others. Most home furnaces, for example, burn oil or gas but need electricity to ignite them, pump their fuel, and distribute their heat. The pumps at gasoline filling stations generally run on grid electricity. Most municipal water plants (and sewage treatment plants that do not burn their own methane byproduct)[37] require grid electricity to operate;[38] the water in turn is needed, among other things, to fight fires, run power plants, and cool refinery columns. Most oil refineries depend so heavily on grid electricity[39] that a blackout may cause them "extremely serious" damage.[40] About half of U.S. domestic oil extraction depends on electrical supplies,[41] for example to drive the motors that pump the wells. In turn, all the heavy machinery used throughout the energy industry depends on a continuous supply of lubricants from the oil industry.

Failure of power for dewatering coal mines can flood them so badly as to force their abandonment. Except for the tiny fraction of U.S. coal carried in slurry pipelines, virtually all coal transportation depends on diesel fuel,[42] so a cutoff of imported oil "may threaten our supply lines for coal as well."[43] Likewise, many power stations depend on diesel generators for safe shutdown and to run critical control and protective circuits if the stations and their grid supplies fail.

Some fuels are coproducts of others (natural gas liquids from natural gas processing, for example). Some fuels, like heating oil or propane, can become scarce if a shortage of, say, natural gas forces buyers to substitute.[44]

In short, any disturbance in the intricately interlinked web of fuel and power supplies can spread out in complex ripple effects at all levels, from primary supply to end use, complicating substitutions and making the initial shortage much worse.

Another worrisome interdependence of supposedly independent energy systems can arise from their being built close to each other or to equipment that provides other critical services. Broken water mains can short out electric cables. Fire and explosion can propagate between nearby pipelines or through a tank farm: people were recently evacuated from five square miles of Franklin Township, New Jersey, when a fire at a natural gas pipeline compressor station threatened to engulf two nearby propane tanks.[44] Earthquakes can cause gas mains to break and explode or burn over a wide area simultaneously, destroying energy facilities that survive the initial shock.[45] On a smaller scale, exploding gas mains can simultaneously disable electric and telephone cables located in the same tunnels under city streets. During the British conversion to North Sea gas, some public telephone booths started exploding: the higher gas pressure was too much for old joints, and the leaking gas entered adjacent telephone cable conduits and seeped up into the booths, ready for someone to walk in with a lighted cigarette.

High capital intensity

Modern energy systems tend to be among the most capital-intensive investments in the entire economy. A central power station is the most capital-intensive device in all industry. It requires several times as many dollars' investment to produce an annual dollar of output as a mechanized factory does. Such capital intensity reflects the degree to which the project commits scarce resources, and thus indirectly measures the difficulty of building (or rebuilding) it with limited resources.

In general, synthetic fuel and frontier (Arctic and offshore) oil and gas systems require about ten times as much capital (per unit of capacity for delivering additional energy to final users) as did the traditional direct-fuel systems—such as Appalachian coal, Texas oil, and Louisiana gas—on which the American economy was built. Central electric systems, in turn, are about ten times more capital-intensive still[46]—about a hundred times as capital-intensive as most of the fuel supplies we depend upon. The resulting capital charges generally exceed operating costs and profits. Carrying charges for a plant costing, say, two billion dollars (such as one producing fifty thousand barrels of synthetic fuel per day) can easily exceed half a million dollars per day, or six dollars per second—payable whether the plant runs or not.

This has important operational, social, and financial consequences. First, the designers will be unable to afford much redundancy—major back-up features that cost a lot but are seldom used. Second, there will be a strong temptation to skimp on downtime for routine maintenance—a temptation commonly indulged in reactor operations. A similar reluctance to shut down oil refineries for maintenance if they can be kept running without it means that minor leaks which in prior years would have been quickly fixed are now often allowed to continue for a year or more. The prevalence of known but unfixed leaks and other faults greatly increases both the likelihood of fire and the workers' exposure to toxins and suspected carcinogens. These economically motivated risks are a chief cause of refinery strikes by the Oil, Chemical and Atomic Workers' Union.

The economic need for capital-intensive plants to run nearly continuously places a high premium on the correctness of engineering expectations that they will prove reliable. Technical mistakes, bad weather, external interference, or other factors can produce massive economic penalties as well as disrupting energy supplies. For example, the financial fallout from the Three Mile Island accident—in reduced bond ratings, higher cost of money, lower investor confidence, and the like—may cripple General Public Utilities even more than the direct costs of the clean-up or of buying replacement power. High capital intensity also commonly reflects a degree of complexity that hampers diagnosis and repair of faults and limits available stocks of costly spare parts (Chapter Six). The corresponding managerial complexity places additional stress on another scarce resource, especially scarce in emergencies—the attention of gifted managers.

Another result of high capital intensity is limited ability to adapt to fluctuating demands. Higher demand may require new capacity which the supplier cannot afford, while lower demand reduces the revenues needed to keep paying off the high capital charges. In this light, the Natural Gas Policy Act of 1978, passed in the wake of the 1976–77 winter gas shortages and giving absolute priority to residential and small commercial users, may have a perverse effect.[47] These users, who under the law may not be interrupted, have the most temperature-sensitive demand—their needs go up the most in cold weather. Industrial customers, who must be interrupted first, have the least temperature-sensitive demand. In a cold-weather gas shortage, a utility with many uninterruptible customers might reap windfall profits from unexpected extra sales. At the same time, a utility selling mainly to interruptible industrial customers might go into the red by losing the sales it was counting on to pay its capital charges, which continue regardless. To maximize profits, utilities may therefore seek to raise their proportion of uninterruptible, temperature-sensitive customers to keep from going broke. But this would increase total national vulnerability to a cold-weather gas shortage.

Long lead times

The many (typically about ten) years required to build a major energy facility contribute to its capital cost and investment risk. Long lead time requires foreknowledge of demand, technological and political conditions, and costs further into the future, when forecasts are bound to be more uncertain. This uncertainty imposes a severe financial penalty on bad guesses, especially building more plants than turn out to be needed—a diseconomy of scale considered further in Appendix One.

Frequently, long lead times require that major developmental facilities be built, or at least their designs frozen, right on the heels of finishing earlier plants—before enough operating experience has been gained to show where the design needs to be improved. This tendency to run ahead of sound engineering experience tends to encourage costly mistakes which may seriously affect long-term energy supplies. Congress's decision, in the panic following the Iranian revolution, to subsidize dozens of huge synthetic fuel plants—each dozens of times the size of any that had been built before and many using wholly unproven processes—may well turn out to be a mistake of this kind.

Long lead times also create risk *even if forecasting is perfect*. When people consider in 1982 a billion-dollar commitment to a plant that cannot be finished until 1992 and must then operate into, say, the 2020s, they want to know with confidence the conditions of finance, regulation, and demand throughout this period. But they want this certainty in a society whose values and institutions are in rapid flux—a society that changes its politicians every few years. If democracies are to retain their flexibility and adaptiveness, they must remain free to change their minds. This is not a problem of accurate forecasting but of maintaining political degrees of freedom essential to the American concept of government. It means that the certainty desired by the promoters of costly, long-lead-time technologies simply cannot be given. This tension—perhaps a fundamental incompatibility between the characteristics of many modern industrial investments and those of a pluralistic political system in a changing world—is bound to express itself somehow. It is an inherent source of vulnerability in those facilities or in the adaptability of our institutions or both. Certainly it points up a solid advantage of short-lead-time energy alternatives.

Specialized labor and control requirements

Modern society is becoming disturbingly dependent on skills possessed by small numbers of highly organized people. Air traffic controllers, for example, are virtually irreplaceable, at least on short notice. Their 1982 strike and dismissal has caused widespread disruption, casting a financial shadow over the airline industry for years into the future. The sympathy strike by just a few dozen Canadian controllers at Gander, Newfoundland snarled North Atlantic air traffic for two days.[48] A twenty-four-hour strike by fifteen hundred British controllers and allied staff (presumably five hundred per shift) did what Hitler was unable to do—close British airspace.[49]

Likewise, modern systems for the continuous bulk delivery of energy are exceedingly complex and require meticulous automatic and manual control—control which can be understood, run, and maintained only by a few highly trained specialists. There are a few exceptions: railway loading operations are almost unique in having so far largely resisted automation, retaining human judgment instead of computerization.[49] But gas and oil pipelines and electric grids are already almost completely computerized. This is indeed essential because of their complexity. And with the computers come new vulnerabilities, arising from both the equipment and the people who operate it.

An oil pipeline, for example, needs several dispatchers, but they could not unaided keep track of the status of pumps, valves, flow rates, batch locations, schedules, metering, costs, and so forth.[50] This requires a sophisticated network of computer-controlled instruments and communication devices. In one major pipeline system,

> One small room, in a large southern city, houses the complete . . . control system [for] . . . several states. . . . Forced entry to the computerized center [and low-technology sabotage] . . . could suddenly put the entire system back on hand operation. Each control valve, of many hundreds, would have to be visited, but . . . only a few men are available to run the system. There are no repair crews except contract crews in most cases.[51]

The Plantation and Colonial pipelines, supplying most of the Eastern Seaboard's refined products, parallel each other and interconnect at many vulnerable points; moreover, the control systems for both are in the *same building.* "A repeat of the University of Wisconsin action [a major bombing of a computer center in 1970] by saboteurs could do serious damage to these operations."[52] (Colonial has since installed a back-up control center, but most of the control vulnerability remains.) Even the failure of electric power can be a serious embarrassment—as when, on 18 July 1981, many oil-industry control centers were blacked out for forty miles around New Orleans, a major pipeline and oil-gathering center.[53]

Perhaps most dependent on control automation are electric grids, where transient events such as lightning bolts or routine circuit interruptions often require action within hundredths of a second to prevent damage. Effecting control decisions throughout the far-flung grids of wires and pipelines requires complete dependence, therefore, on computer decisions not first checked by human judgment, and on electronic telecommunications links. The disturbing consequences of this dependence are explored in later chapters.

The specialized nature of the control systrems, and of the operations needed to maintain both them and the devices they control, concentrates immense power in few hands. The economic and social cost of energy disruption, let alone the direct financial damage incurred by carrying charges on idle equipment, places "power to the people" in the hands of very small numbers of people who are well aware of that power. Its exercise has already changed the course of history: Iranian oilfield workers in 1978 precipitated the fall of the Shah by all but shutting down their country's oil and gas exports,[54] while their counterparts in the power industry blacked out most of Teheran.[55]

Such power can also be used to achieve narrower ends. Shortly after a coal strike had brought down the Heath Government in 1974, an official of the British power workers' union remarked, "The miners brought the country to its knees in eight weeks; we could do it in eight minutes." His colleagues have since repeatedly threatened national blackouts as a prelude to negotiations for various desired concessions, including (in one recent instance) basic wages of up to fifty thousand dollars per year.[56] Ironically, the Conservative Government's well-known desire to reduce vulnerability to future coal miners' strikes by substituting nuclear power would increase vulnerability to disruption by workers in power plants and power dispatching centers, who are even more specialized and nearly as militant.

Power workers blacked out increasing areas of Israel during a strike in 1981.[57] Electrical supplies have become a bargaining chip in Australia[58] and elsewhere, as have water supplies, sewage treatment, and other utilities essential to public health and safety. In a few instances, too, threats have been a prelude to violence. Striking power workers sabotaged a plant in Argentina in 1976.[59] In a Puerto Rican power workers' strike in 1973, National Guardsmen were unable to prevent sabotage of remote transmission lines, leaving forty-five cities partly or wholly blacked out, and seriously affecting water and telephone service.[60] In the next strike, in 1977–78, a vital transmission line was bombed,[61] and explosions at three substations blacked out thirty thousand San Juan households.[62] By the time the strike was over, more than two hundred acts of sabotage had been reported, doing four million dollars' damage.[63] Sabotage and bombing persisted after another power strike in 1981.[64] Later chapters cite other examples of damage to power, oil, and gas equipment in mainland U.S. strikes.

Of course, such incidents are far from the norm: the overwhelming majority of workers in the world's energy industries refrain from abusing their physical control over their complex equipment. But however responsibly a union or management controlling key energy facilities may behave, the very possibility of disruption tends to foster suspicion and intolerance—just the argument raised in 1982 against rehiring fired air traffic controllers.

Potential for misuse of energy distribution systems

Virtually all analyses have considered the vulnerability of energy systems only to *interruptions* of supply. Many systems can, however, be interfered with in other ways at least as damaging—large-scale versions of putting sugar in a gasoline tank. A few examples make the point:

• It would probably not be difficult to introduce a foreign substance into crude oil being stored or pipelined to many refineries. Such substances might include radiotoxins which will neither affect nor be affected by processing but would be widely dispersed by subsequent burning of the refined products. Like a suspicion of botulin toxin in canned foods, they could make substantial amounts of petroleum products unfit for use (or, for that matter, for destruction by conventional means), and could be an effective means of extortion.[65] Alternatively, certain substances could be introduced which are potent poisons of refinery cracking catalysts. There are technical reasons why it would be difficult to make this form of sabotage effective, but it could be important in specialized circumstances, and could at least have considerable nuisance value.

• The national grid of natural gas pipelines—over a million miles for transmission and distribution—offers an inviting route for dispersing unpleasant materials. In early 1981, the Environmental Protection Agency (EPA) found that natural gas systems in Southern California, Chicago, and Long Island had become accidentally contaminated with liquid polychlorinated biphenyls (PCBs). Manufacture of this extremely persistent and toxic liquid was banned in the U.S. in 1976, but it is still widely used in older transformers, capacitors, and similar equipment.[66] Not only retail distribution systems but also some segments of interstate pipelines and their gate stations were contaminated. EPA thinks the PCBs may have entered the gas lines as a pump or compressor lubricant many years ago, perhaps via leaky seals. The PCBs detected in retail customers' meters are not so far believed to mean that burning the gas had actually released significant amounts of PCBs indoors. Nonetheless, there are cheap, very disagreeable substances which could be deliberately introduced in bulk into the national gas grid from any of thousands of loosely supervised access points. Such substances could be widely distributed and released before likely detection. Some could contaminate the inside of the pipelines—the third largest fixed asset in all American industry—so as to make them very difficult to clean up. To determine whether a major public hazard could be caused in this way would require further analysis at an indiscreet level of specificity; but it appears there is, at a minimum, a potential for causing public anxiety and disruption.

• Another category of potential threats might involve the fuel distribution system or local storage tanks. Some organisms promote the gelling of liquid oil: fungi and bacteria, for example, turned oil stored in South African goldmines into a gel that was very hard to re-extract.[67] Although the bacteria developed to eat oil slicks at sea are more effective in the laboratory than in field conditions, certain bacteria and fungi are a well-known cause of deterioration in jet fuel and other refined products stored in tanks containing a little air. (So far as is publicly known, such organisms cannot thrive in an airless environment.)[68] In the 1960s, the Central Intelligence Agency commissioned a study by the University of Houston concerning microorganisms which could be added to oil (presumably refined products in particular) to hasten its decomposition.[69] While the results of that research are not published, it is known that some refined products can be stored for only a few months to years unless stabilized by special additives.[70] Presumably *de*stabilizing additives, whether microbiological or otherwise, also exist. It is hard to say whether such additives could become a credible threat to oil storage and processing facilities. But strikingly effective instances of biological sabotage are already known, ranging from releasing moths in a cinema to sowing the spores of certain mushrooms which, on sprouting, hydraulically fracture any concrete that has meanwhile been poured over them. The adaptability of organisms and the ingenuity of some amateur biologists suggest that biological threats cannot be discounted. Already, such accidental infestations as Mediterranean fruitfly, gypsy moth, *Corbicula* in power plants (Chapter Two), kudzu vines on much Southern land, and water hyacinths on waterways suggest a considerable potential for mischief.

• Finally, an analogous problem may exist with electricity, because as much harm can be caused by increasing as by interrupting its supply. Some manipulations of electrical control systems may be able to increase grid voltages to levels which damage not only generating and transmission equipment but also widely dispersed distribution and end-use equipment. This has already happened by accident, as in restoration after the July 1977 New York blackout described in the next chapter. Alternatively, persistent low voltage or operation of only one of several phases on multiphase lines can cause epidemics of burned-out motors and other equipment over a wide area: an oilfield operation lost one hundred fifty-three motors in one evening in this way.[71] Repairing such widespread damage to end-use devices can be extremely slow and costly. As noted above, too, analogous interference with gas distribution pressures can endanger large numbers of customers simultaneously, even on the scale of an entire city.

The elaborate technical system which fuels and powers America, then, is built in such a way that it is inherently prone to large-scale failures which can be difficult to predict, prevent, contain, control, and repair. So far, this country has experienced relatively few prolonged and widespread failures of energy supply. We pride ourselves on having the most reliable energy system on earth. But our relative success so far does not prove that the engineers have succeeded in designing the system so it cannot suffer such failures. Rather, it may mean that our nation has been very lucky, especially in the small number of people who have so far had the skill and the desire to exploit the opportunity to cause massive dislocation. That the latter view is more plausible than the former will become clearer as the following eight chapters apply the general observations above to specific instances, starting with a case study of one of the most celebrated energy failures of recent years—the overnight failure of the New York City electrical grid on 13–14 July 1977.

Chapter Five
Case Study: The 1977 New York Blackout

The failure of the main electric power grid in New York in July 1977 was not the first or the largest to occur there. On 9 November 1965, a cascading power failure originating in a malfunctioning relay in Canada interrupted the electrical supply of most of the Northeastern United States. Some thirty million people were blacked out for anywhere from one to thirteen and one-half hours. A load totalling nearly forty-four thousand megawatts—twenty-three percent of the total 1965 U.S. peak demand—was lost.[1] Only customers with isolated or emergency systems had power: all telephone exchanges, most hospitals, a housing project and two shopping centers in the middle of New York City, and some scattered office buildings and factories.[2] Everyone else was plunged into darkness. The utilities were shocked; the public was outraged. There were hearings, investigations, reports, and—supposedly—changes to ensure it could never happen again.

On 13 July 1977, three days after the Chairman of Consolidated Edison Company of New York had said he could "guarantee" that a recurrence was remote,[3] nearly nine million people were blacked out for five to twenty-five hours through "a combination of natural events [lightning], equipment malfunctions, questionable system design features, and operating errors," coupled with serious lack of preparation to use available facilities to prevent complete failure.[4]

A complex, cascading failure

Geography and operational circumstances laid the groundwork for the July 1977 blackout. Most cities import part of their power rather than generating enough for their own needs within their own boundaries. New York City, however, relies particularly heavily on imports of bulk power.

51

Because it is much cheaper to take high-voltage power lines over land than under water, most of the imports arrive through a narrow corridor from the north, where power is available at relatively low cost and can be delivered overland without expensive underwater cables. This clustering of lines increases vulnerability to storms and sabotage.

There are some interconnections in other directions, but in July 1977, one key link was inoperable. Its phase-regulating transformer, after causing several earlier local power failures, had failed beyond repair ten months earlier (it eventually took over a year to replace).[5] Three generating plants on the Con Ed system were also down for repair. The Indian Point Two nuclear plant (eight hundred seventy-three megawatts of electrical capacity) had a failed pump seal. Two fossil plants were also out of action: Bowling Point Number Two (six hundred one megawatts), with a boiler problem, and Astoria Number Six (seven hundred seventy-five megawatts), with a turbine failure. Within the Con Ed area, therefore, only three thousand nine hundred megawatts was being generated to serve a load of six thousand one hundred megawatts. The rest was being imported through six interties. It is the successive failure of these transmission systems, and their interaction with local generators, that led to the system failure. There was plenty of generating capacity available in the "pool" of adjacent utilities with which Con Ed was interconnected, but events developed in such a way that by the late evening of 13 July 1977, there was no way to deliver that power to the city.

Perhaps the best description of the failure sequence is by Philip Boffey in *Science* magazine:

> The trouble began . . . when lightning struck a[n imperfectly grounded transmission-line] tower in northern Westchester County and short-circuited two . . . [high-voltage] lines. . . . [P]rotective relays . . . triggered circuit breakers to open at both ends of the affected lines, thus isolating the problem from the rest of the system. This is exactly what the circuit breakers are supposed to do. However, they are also supposed to reclose automatically once the fault dissipates, and this they failed to do. One transmission line failed because of a loose locking nut [which released air pressure from a circuit breaker][6] . . . ; the other because a reclosing circuit had been disconnected and not yet replaced . . . .
>
> Two other facilities also tripped out of service. . . . A nuclear reactor [Indian Point Three] shut down automatically when the circuit breaker that opened to contain the lightning fault also [by a design fault] deprived the reactor of any outlet for its power. . . . [Another high-voltage line]—a major tie across the Hudson—tripped out because a protective timing device was designed improperly. . . . Thus, in one stroke of misfortune, Con Ed lost three major transmission lines and its most heavily loaded generator. Even so, Con Ed regained its equilibrium by importing more power on the remaining tie lines and by increasing its own generation somewhat [but did not restore a safety margin] . . . .
> Then lightning struck again . . . and short-circuited two more [high-voltage] . . . lines. Again there was a malfunction. One line closed automatically

[but] . . . the other remained open because a relay had been set primarily to protect a nuclear reactor (which, ironically, was out of service) rather than to facilitate reclosing of the line. . . . The loss of the line . . . caused a temporary power surge that tripped out another [high-voltage] . . . line. This should not have happened but did, because of a bent contact on a relay.

Con Ed's control room succumbed to confusion and panic. . . . [The] system operator [assumed] . . . a particular transmission line was still in service [and] . . . failed to read a teletype [saying it was down]. . . . Moreover, because of Con Ed's antiquated control room layout, he was unable to see a more dramatic indicator in another room—a flashing screen with a high-pitched alarm. The personnel there knew the line was out but failed to tell him. . . . [H]e ignored [seven] . . . suggestions from the power pool that he shed load. Then, as the situation deteriorated, he . . . dumped his . . . responsibility on his boss, the chief system operator, who sat at home in the dark reading diagrams by a kerosene lantern and issuing orders over the phone. . . . The chief ordered voltage reductions—but these were too little and too late. Eventually he also ordered that a block of customers be disconnected. Whereupon the confused operator [rendered the load-shedding control panel inoperable by apparently turning] . . . a master switch the wrong way.

The performance of Con Ed's generators was equally erratic. Con Ed's system operator delayed eight minutes . . . before requesting a fast load pickup from generators that were supposedly able to respond in ten minutes. He [then] got only half the power he expected—and only thirty percent of what Con Ed had incorrectly told the power pool it could provide. Some equipment malfunctioned; other units were undergoing routine inspection but had not been removed from the fast-start capability list; some were not even manned. [All the night-shift operators had been sent home, and the remote-start capability had been removed some years earlier.[7] At most fifty-five percent of Con Ed's total in-city generating capacity was actually operable.[8]] Similarly, when Con Ed sounded the maximum generation alarm some ten minutes after the second lightning strike, it again failed to get the anticipated response from its thirty-minute reserve generators.

As the system cascaded toward collapse, heavy overloads caused the failure or deliberate disconnection of all remaining ties to neighboring utilities. Con Ed['s] . . . last hope was an automatic load shedding system that had been installed after the 1965 blackout. [It] worked beautifully to disconnect customers. . . . But it also unexpectedly caused a rapid rise in system voltage that caused a major generator to shut down. . . . The remaining generators could not restore equilibrium. Eventually, protective relays shut them down to prevent damage . . . [and] the city was blacked out.[9]

Nearly twelve weeks later, on 26 September 1977, another thunderstorm tripped four transmission lines with six lightning bolts. Automatic reclosing equipment again failed to perform, shutting down forty percent of Con Ed's generation. Only a more alert operator response in shedding Westchester County loads prevented a second, more serious blackout from spreading again across the city. On that occasion, the equipment failures included an out-of-service instrumentation channel at Indian Point Three, a wiring error in a relay, deactivation of a reclosing circuit by the unexplained placing of a switch in the wrong position, and a defective relay.[10] Like earlier equipment faults, these resulted from "serious failures in inspection and testing."[11] Though local trip systems prevented in July 1977 most of the serious damage that the 1965 blackout had caused to fifteen hundred megawatts—several billion dollars' worth—of generating equipment,[12] many of the underfrequency relays meant to shed load automatically in 1977 did not initially operate.

Human error and oversight

Serious, multiple operator errors, reminiscent of those identified in the Three Mile Island accident by the Kemeny and Rogovin reports, also dominated the July 1977 blackout. Many training and procedural problems[13] had already been identified in the 1965 blackout,[14] but they had not been fixed. Lack of unambiguous linguistic conventions like those used in air traffic control contibuted to the confusion:[15] different operators concealed their meaning from each other and, on occasion, from themselves. The system operator was apparently hard of hearing anyway[16], perhaps contributing to his poor performance in communicating over the telephone from a noisy and doubtless chaotic control room.

The July 1977 blackout was of a type that none of the official design criteria or operating instructions had foreseen. The State's investigator concluded:

> The inability to achieve stable isolated operation [i.e., without interties to adjacent areas] stems from a general failure to think through the problems that transmission losses can create. For example, virtually no planning consideration has been given to the generation reserves needed in the event of transmission losses. Installed generation reserve capacity is determined solely with reference to potential *generation* shortages. Similarly, the Pool's minimum operating reserve criterion . . . is designed to meet generation shortages, not transmission losses [, and] . . . assumes sufficient transmission exists to deliver the members' . . . reserve capacity to the system suffering the shortage. Where disturbances on the bulk transmission system severely limit the ability to transfer power, the Pool's existing reserve requirements are inadequate.[17]

This had already been clearly noted in the 1965 Federal Power Commission report to President Johnson—"Cascading power failures are usually the result of insufficient capability within . . . transmission links"—but neither Con Ed nor Pool criteria followed the logic. The reason Con Ed had not realized that load shedding would produce overvoltage and trip the Big Allis generator at Ravenswood was simply that they had never analyzed the behavior of an isolated Con Ed system.[18] (Most utilities still have not done so. For example, when transmission failures led to the isolation of St. Louis from the Midwestern grid on 13 February 1978, the utility was equally startled.[19] By luck, the city had at the time a surplus of capacity rather than a deficit, so the frequency rose rather than falling, and electric service did not collapse.)

Unexpected complications

The July 1977 New York power failure produced unexpected secondary consequences which seriously hampered recovery. There was inadequate light and power for troubleshooting or manually operating major substations.[20] Auxiliary equipment at power stations—lubricating and cooling pumps, boiler feedwater pumps, and so forth—failed gradually with declining voltage, compromising and in some cases modestly damaging major equipment.[21] (Declining frequency probably also damaged turbine blades through vibration.)[22] Assessment of the status of equipment, and coordination of early restoration efforts, was also hampered by the complete failure of Con Ed's UHF and VHF radio networks. The main repeater had two power sources; one had failed before the blackout and the other failed to start. The back-up power supply to the back-up repeater station also failed to operate. This triple failure also exposed shortcomings in radiotelephones and direct telephone lines. The back-up radio repeater was not repowered until another emergency power source could be hooked up two and a half hours later.[23]

Most dismaying was the unexpectedly rapid loss of pressure in oil needed to insulate and cool the main high-voltage underground power cables. After the 1965 blackout, standby generators had been provided to operate generator lubricating pumps and other key protective equipment in power stations. The Federal Power Commission had then recommended installing standby power for pumping oil to the underground cables too—as Commonwealth Edison Co. had done, for less than half a million dollars, in the underground Chicago cable system. Apparently Con Ed was unaware of this recommendation. That cost them at least five hours in recovery time in 1977.[24] They thought the cables would hold oil pressure for four to six hours,[25] but pressure actually decayed much faster. This caused many short-circuits and some equipment damage, causing further delays which lost more oil pressure. Finally it was necessary to bring in portable generators to run the oil pumps, restore all oil pressure throughout the length of the cables, and monitor pressure at all terminations and connections before the cables could be safely re-energized.[26]

This experience illustrates the warning that in restoring a failed power grid to operation,

> there are urgent time constraints due not only to the need for restoring service to critical loads but also due to the fact that the condition of some unenergized system components will degrade with time, making restoration even more diffi-

cult. For instance, pressurized circuit breakers with electric heaters may fail due to [liquefaction of the special insulating gases inside them] . . . or loss of air pressure; this will occur more rapidly in cold weather, and they may not become operable again until hours after the restoration of auxiliary service. Also, the capacity of stand-by batteries for operation of critical facilities will be limited. Another time constraint . . . is the time required to carry out the many hundreds of switching operations necessary to excise failed equipment and lost loads and to secure whatever portions of the system . . . remain operable.[27]

Electric grid restoration is

a complicated, demanding process. Even if all system elements are ready for service, there are three basic problems to be solved: First, the system . . . must be synchronized with neighboring systems through interconnections; second, substantial time must be allowed for the large steam-turbine generators to be brought up to full output; and third, as generator output becomes available, it must be matched by gradually increasing the connected customer load [which is often beyond the utility's direct control save by switching large areas], so that an approximate balance of generation and load is maintained. Solution of these problems usually involves "sectionalizing" the system.[28]

Picking up lost loads in the wrong order, or in excessively large blocks, may further damage equipment. Worst of all, some power stations have no "black-start" capability—that is, they cannot restart in isolation, but only if supplied with outside power for auxiliaries or synchronization or both. Some stations which are supposed to have this capability occasionally turn out not to.

Clearly, the improvisations that restoration of a crashed grid may require are so complex that only people of exceptional ability can be expected to do them smoothly without considerable practice. Yet opportunities for such practice are almost nil, and simulation exercises for more than routine local outages are very rare. Utilities are reluctant to join neighboring utilities in preparedness drills (or in installation of costly reliability interties), because they would have to pay the cost of a benefit shared by others. In general, too, utilities have much experience of coping with localized failures, but little if any experience of improvising in the face of large-scale failures that limit help from adjacent areas—the position Con Ed was in with its grid completely isolated.

The restoration procedures of the Northeast Power Coordinating Council at the time of the 1977 New York blackout read simply:

1. Restore frequency to sixty [cycles per second].
2. Establish communication with system operators of adjacent systems.
3. Synchronize with adjacent systems.
4. Coordinate restoration of any load previously shed.[29]

It is hard to escape the impression that if adjacent areas are also down, or if damage to equipment has been widespread, most utilities' ability to cope would be quickly overwhelmed. Con Ed's was certainly stretched to the limit.

Just as reactors do not read nuclear safety analyses, and therefore do not know that they are supposed to suffer only one simple failure at a time, so the New York grid did not fail according to simple textbook patterns. The textbooks never contemplated such a massive failure. The blackout showed how a complex sequence of unforeseen and interactive technical and human failures is not only possible but likely. It also illustrated how recovery measures meant to cope with simple failures do not work when many things have gone wrong and more dominoes are falling every minute.

Mitigation

The 1977 blackout also revealed, however, some good news—some respects in which such failures can be controlled and contained if not prevented. For one thing, even a little advance warning is invaluable in containing the damage if the warning is used effectively. In the blackout,

> most of the nearly two hundred subway trains then on the tracks managed to crawl to the nearest stations, thanks to a warning from a quick-witted dispatcher; still, seven trains carrying [fewer than] a thousand passengers were stuck between stations for [several] hours—and the entire system folded thereafter for the duration.[30]

Deterioration of power supplies and drivers' reports of dark or flashing signals enabled dispatchers to order trains into stations via a two-way radio system spanning the two hundred thirty miles of tunnels. This "decisive action" avoided major strandings; all passengers were evacuated within three and a half hours with no reported injuries.[31] (In contrast, hundreds of rush-hour commuters were stuck between stations without warning when a saboteur switched off power to the central Stockholm subway.)[32] On 9 September 1981, when Lower Manhattan was suddenly blacked out, subways were able to use the last bit of their fading power supply to crawl into stations, but three hundred people were stranded in various skyscraper elevators, and officials were reluctant to rescue some of them "because of fears that the elevators might go out of control in a sudden resumption of power."[33]

An intriguing and little-known feature of the New York blackout is that part of a grid which operates at twenty-five cycles per second (mostly for railways), and most of a direct-current grid, were able to continue normal operation within the city while the main public grid, operating at sixty cycles per second, crashed. This was possible because the two "oddball" minigrids—relics of the earliest days of the U.S. utility industry—did not depend on the sixty-cycle-per-second grid for synchronization and were easily isolated from it. Unfortunately, they served such relatively small areas that they were not able to provide a bootstrap for recovery operations.

Local standby generators generally worked well, maintaining operations at bridges and tunnels (most of which were normally powered from the New Jersey side anyway), hospitals, fire and police stations, and airports. (Flights were suspended overnight, however, and thirty-two aircraft diverted, because obstruction lights on New York skyscrapers were out.) Surface transit worked, though some fuel had to be imported from New Jersey for buses. Subway officials controlled flooding by dispatching emergency pumps and compressors.[34] Though most hospital emergency generators worked, four hospitals needed police emergency generators, and thirteen other establishments, mainly medical, needed emergency generators repaired. Con Ed dispatched eighteen of its fifty portable generators throughout the city to run lifesaving equipment. Had the hospitals used their own generating plants routinely, as is common in Europe, rather than only in emergencies, they would have achieved higher reliability and obtained their heating and hot water as a virtually free by-product (Appendix One).

The 1977 New York blackout nicely illustrates that the reasons modern energy systems fail, and the reasons they are hard to restore, are considerably more complex than appears from newspaper headlines. It is very much more involved than simply blowing and replacing a household fuse. But even this example does not fully capture some of the difficulties likely to arise in repairing major failures, especially if they damage major items of equipment or extend over a wide area. These problems of restoration, and the costs which the failure can exact from our society, are the subject of the next chapter.

Chapter Six
Picking Up the Pieces

Modern energy technologies rank among the greatest achievements of engineering. They embody great skill and a considerable investment of scarce resources. Often, to achieve the greatest technical efficiency, they are custom-designed for unique local circumstances, so that there is no other plant quite like them. For these reasons, it is difficult to stock major spare parts for them.

Spare Parts

Recovery from major failures is often limited by the availability of spare parts. It used to be customary for electric utilities to keep on hand extra sets of large generator coils, large bearings, and so forth. But with higher unit costs (owing to larger unit sizes) and greater manufacturing specialization, and with the added burden of ad valorem inventory taxes and recent high interest rates, spares have greatly dwindled.[1] Only the smaller, cheaper, more frequently needed items are now commonly stocked.[2] Thus replacement of any sizeable item that fails is likely to require a protracted special order. Only after the 1977 blackout did Con Ed decide to procure a spare for a phase-regulating transformer whose unavailability had contributed greatly to the blackout and which had previously caused four lesser outages. The spare took over a year to manufacture.

Spare parts may be lost in a major accident if they are stored in vulnerable locations.[3] For example, when Typhoon Karen struck Guam in November 1962 with sustained winds of one hundred seventy miles per hour and gusts up to two hundred seven miles per hour, repair to badly disrupted electrical distribution systems was "materially lengthened" by the total loss of vital spare parts which had been stored in light sheet-metal buildings.[4] The proprietors of the Trans-Alaska Pipeline are running a similar risk: they propose to store spare pumps at the pumping stations themselves. This would save having to ship them to the site of a failure (a difficult task, especially in winter). But it would also increase the likelihood that mishap or sabotage would destroy both original and spare at the same time.

Spare parts may be effectively lost, too, by becoming inaccessible. A five-mile stretch of canal along the Gulf Coast, for example, contains an astonishing concentration of oil-well service companies whose capacity, vital to the entire offshore and near-shore oil industry, could be bottled up by something as simple as a failed lock or drawbridge.

Few energy companies have retained the on-site manufacturing capabilities they had when they did much of their own machine-shop work. Many utilities do have portable substations of modest size, and some have spare-part sharing arrangements with adjacent utilities. Still, most major items have to be imported from relatively remote manufacturers, who may have shortages or production problems of their own. The complexity of modern energy equipment is tending to increase resupply problems and lead times. Professor Maynard Stephens, for example, in one of a series of pioneering studies of the fragility of the oil and gas industry, surveyed in 1969 the ready availability of three-phase explosion-proof electric motors—a key component of most oil and gas facilities. He found the total stock of the four main U.S. manufacturers to be only twenty-two motors of one hundred fifty horsepower and up, with smaller sizes faring little better. Most larger sizes required special ordering with delivery delays of months. Just replacing the explosion-proof motors required for a single small crude-oil distillation plant "could use up the nation's entire supply of [such] motors."[5] Some key components, such as transformers, seem scarcer yet. Even such mundane items as the hoses and couplings needed to unload oil tankers often require special ordering.[6] And there are of course limits to the insurance that spare parts inventories can provide: "One pipeline company keeps two of each important piece . . . of critical equipment on hand, but if three items of the same [type] were damaged, as much as nineteen months' months delay could be created."[7]

Repair times, facilities, and skills

In the best of circumstances, and based on data from 1967 when many components were smaller and simpler than today's, estimated repair times for seriously damaged major components of power systems or other major energy facilities are daunting.[8] Typically hundreds, and in some cases thousands, of person-days are required to repair substantial damage: an estimated twenty-three thousand person-days, for example, for a seriously damaged boiler. Most major repairs require not only small tools and welders but also heavy cranes and hoists. Transporting heavy items like generator rotors and transformers is an exacting task when transport systems are working normally. In the event of widespread disruption, it could prove impossible. Such items as large transformers, for which spares are often too costly to keep, must nowadays be returned to the manufacturer for many of the repairs that might be needed. Cannibalizing existing equipment is seldom feasible, because "Interchangeability of major equipment is generally not possible due to severe matching problems. Thus, repair or replacement of such components will pose a major post-[nuclear-]attack problem."[9]

Another estimate[10] suggests that a minimum of several weeks would be needed to restore a modestly damaged power station to operation under ideal conditions, including absolute availability of expertise, labor, money, and parts, no radiation or other interfering conditions, and no conflicting priorities. The history of even minor repairs in high-radiation-field areas of nuclear plants suggests that it would not take much radiological or chemical contamination to complicate repairs enormously and even to exhaust available pools of skilled workers: some welds have required hundreds of welders over a period of months, each exposed to the quarterly limit in just a few minutes' work.

For some types of repairs to damaged energy systems, national manufacturing capacity is already strained to keep up with routine demand, let alone the exigencies of large-scale emergency repairs. Large tubular steel is an obvious example. Pipe over about twelve inches in diameter is normally special-ordered, as are the large motors and other special components associated with it.[11] If Mideast oil systems suffered major pipe damage, digging up existing U.S pipelines, cutting them into sections, flying them to the stricken area, and rewelding them might be faster than manufacturing new pipe.

In such an emergency, needs for equipment and trained personnel, too, would dwarf any standby capacity—as was arguably the case when, during the Three Mile Island accident, industry experts from around the world converged on Middletown. Automation has so reduced the number of field employees in the oil and gas industry "that the system could not suddently revert to hand operation." Since most company repair crews have been disbanded in favor of specialized contractor crews, "Should a number of areas be damaged at once, they could not be repaired in any suitable time to serve an emergency."[12] Recovery from limited damage is hard enough; damage to, say, several refineries in the same area would be "a catastrophe"; damage to many throughout the country would be virtually unrepairable because of the shortage of skills and parts.[13]

If major energy facilities are so damaged that they must be substantially rebuilt or replaced, construction lead times (neglecting any regulatory approval periods) would probably not be much shorter than in routine practice—around five or six years for a sizeable coal-steam power plant, about eight for a nuclear plant. (Subsequent chapters will contrast this nearly irreducible lead time—required by the sheer scale and complexity of the technologies—with lead times measured in weeks or months for many alternative energy sources.)

Elaborate plants also require exotic materials and fabrication techniques. These are available only if the highly interdependent industrial economy is intact and flourishing, and if certain strategic minerals can be obtained from abroad. A single nuclear power plant, for example, includes in its replaceable core components one hundred nine metric tons of chromium, two and two-thirds tons of gadolinium, at least fifty-five tons of nickel, twenty-four tons of tin, and over eleven hundred tons of hafnium-free zirconium (which is made by only one main U.S. supplier).[14] Once used in a reactor, these materials are often so irradiated that they cannot be recycled. Other major energy facilities also depend substantially on imported strategic minerals for which there are strongly competing uses, particularly for military equipment.[15] High technologies, for energy as for other purposes, also depend on an industrial infrastructure which is itself easily disrupted. And once it is disrupted, it is very difficult to reestablish.[16]

Propagating failures

For these reasons, if a major energy source fails, its interconnections with other sources may provide help (back-up and restarting)—or they may merely propagate the failure. This applies not only to different parts of, say, an interconnected electric grid, but also to all energy sources in their complex interconnectedness, and even to the whole interwoven fabric of our high-technology industrial society. If an interdependent energy system collapses, the need of device A to have energy from B and vice versa before either can operate may enmesh recovery efforts in rapidly spreading chaos.

The wider interdependencies of the stricken energy system on materials and equipment drawn from an energy-intensive industrial system may prove even more unsustainable. Seen in microcosm by a utility engineer trying to bootstrap one damaged power plant up the critical path to recovery, inability to get spare parts from a local warehouse is a local, specific obstacle. But from a macro point of view,[17] thousands of similar localized breaks in a previously seamless web of industrial relationships could collectively signal its unraveling on a large scale.[18] Only if materials, skills, and equipment are *locally available* to cope with disruptions can one be confident of keeping that web coherent and coordinated. Crucial to that availability is information that enables people and organizations on the spot to harness their latent ingenuity. This theme will recur as later chapters explore technologies that are very accessible to large numbers of potential improvisers.

The dependence of modern industrial societies on continuous, highly reliable supplies of high-grade energy—not only for day-to-day comfort but to maintain the complex web of production that keeps the whole society going—is a relatively recent phenomenon. The Netherlands today uses about as much oil as all Western Europe did in 1950. We are accustomed to suppose that civilization would be impossible with, say, only half as much energy as we use today; yet the industrialized countries used only half as much as recently as 1960, when they were at least half as civilized as now.

Unfortunately, once that dependence, like a physiological addiction, has been built up, abrupt withdrawal—perhaps due to a major failure of energy supply—is disproportionately painful. A world which *suddenly*, without time to increase its energy efficiency or to take the other precautions described later in this book, had only half as much energy as it was used to, would not be like the world of 1960. It might be more like the world of 1860 or even 1360, because such a sudden loss could so devastate the accustomed structure of industry. In such a world, the most powerful and sophisticated nations on earth might suddenly find themselves grappling with the problems of daily survival that have for so long been confined chiefly to the poorest nations.

The cost of failure

What if we don't pick up the pieces fast enough? And even if we do, is there some way to estimate the cost of major energy failures, so that we can determine how hard it is worth trying to prevent them? Such an estimate might be easier to make if there were a history of such failures. But the extreme degree of energy dependence and fragility of energy supply which are so worrisome today have no precedent in human history. The only failures we have experienced have been relatively small and, for the most part, localized. As the next six chapters show, episodes like the New York blackout are trivial in comparison with the failures of supply which could readily occur in an energy system as precarious as the one that runs the United States today.

For the relatively minor failures of energy supply which have already occurred, however, there are abundant data to show how often they happened and how long they lasted. For example, during the past decade about sixty significant failures of bulk electrical supply have been reported per year in the United States, averaging about two hundred fifty megawatts each. An interruption five times that size, corresponding to roughly one hundred thousand customers, has occurred about once a year. The 1977 New York blackout, because complete restoration took twenty-five hours, heads the list based on a "severity index" (the product of megawatts times customers times hours), with an index of three hundred eighty-eight billion. Other power failures less well known, such as the 16 May 1977 Florida blackout with an index of nineteen billion (thirty-two thousand megawatts, one million three hundred thousand customers, four and a half hours), have been far from negligible. Several other interruptions were nearly as severe, including one in March 1976 that left parts of Wisconsin blacked out for as long as nine days.[19]

But while there are plentiful statistics on the size, frequency, duration, and location of supply failures, estimating their cost to society is difficult and controversial. This is not surprising. There is no theoretical basis for quantifying the value of *delivering* a unit of energy.[20] Quantifying the value of a unit *not* delivered raises even thornier problems. For example, not all kilowatt-hours or barrels of oil are created equal. The lack of one may cost a life while the lack of another may represent no loss at all. The direct costs may be high in, say, agriculture if the failure prevents a harvest, causes the mass suffocation of hogs or poultry dependent on ventilation, or causes dairy cows to dry up or die because they cannot be milked.[21] Yet on another farm, or even on the same farm at another time of year, the damage may be negligible. Vital seed banks whose long-term value to American agriculture may be measured in GNP-years are regularly endangered by power failures,[22] but because this potential value is prospective and not yet realized, it is barely even counted.

Utility experts have tried in many studies to figure out how much an outage (power failure) costs. For simplicity, they commonly assume that failure to serve a ten-kilowatt demand is ten times as important as failure to serve a one-kilowatt demand, but this may well be untrue in both economic and human terms. Duration, degree of warning, and foreknowledge of likely duration are also important. Despite extensive research into outage costs,[23] the results are highly subjective, fail to capture many important features of heterogeneous demands, and differ amongst themselves by nearly a hundredfold.

One partial measure, however, is how much people are willing to pay (within their means, which may be limited) to gain emergency energy supplies. Among the four thousand factories closed in the natural gas shortage of 1976–77 were about seventy percent of South Carolina's textile mills—a sector that provides forty-four percent of that state's manufacturing payrolls. (Six of the closed plants never reopened, and nine moved elsewhere.) One company, Spring Mills Corporation, willingly paid almost five times the usual price for trucked-in propane.[24] In four other states, a survey showed that one hundred affected businesses were willing to pay an average of twenty-six times the average 1978 price to get emergency gas—the equivalent of two hundred sixty dollars per barrel. (In contrast, businesses on interruptible gas were used to substituting and were scarcely willing to pay any premium.)[25] A similar survey after the Key West, Florida power curtailment in summer 1978 showed that firms were willing to pay a fortyfold premium to get enough electricity to stay in operation.[26]

Such estimates only measure private costs to a manufacturer—not even the downstream costs to other firms which lose *their* suppliers. But the social costs are much wider. Does one draw the boundary at lost income, life, health, comfort, crops, industrial production, gross national product?[27] At the looting of a blacked-out city?[28] How can one assess downstream economic consequences? In the 1978 coal strike, Congressman Brown of Ohio suggested to the Secretary of Labor that "there is imminent danger of having lights go out across the state of Ohio," only to be told, "That is not a national emergency." But Congressman Brown then went on to state that "the entire [U.S.] economy will grind to a halt very quickly without Ohio's glass, rubber, steel, and thousands of other component[s]. . . ."[29] If he were right, where would one draw the line in calculating the costs of the coal strike?

The July 1977 New York blackout again offers a useful window into the social complexity of energy supply failures. Direct costs were estimated to be made up thirty-nine percent of riot damage, twenty-four percent of national economic costs, and the rest of various social and economic costs. The total was some three hundred ten million dollars, or seven percent of a national average GNP-day.[30] Con Ed's Chairman thought that figure too low.[31] He was probably right: most later analyses suggest that a more realistic estimate might be of the order of a billion dollars, or about a hundred dollars per person throughout the blacked-out area.

This is largely because the social brittleness that made intolerable "an outage of any period of time in certain areas of our city"[32] appeared in uncontrollable riots. Nobody knows, however, why there was extensive rioting in the 1977 blackout and not in others. In the 1965 Northeast blackout, the New York crime rate actually declined,[33] and the Chairman of the Federal Energy Regulatory Commission has stated that "In the more than two hundred major bulk power interruptions which have occurred throughout the country over the past seven years, the 1977 New York blackout was the only one recording a significant degree of social losses."[34]

On one level, the damage was tidied up: the city administration "sees actual benefits in that the [1977] blackout led to forming stronger merchants' associations and anti-crime programs."[35] And of the more than three thousand people arrested for looting, over a thousand were convicted and sentenced. But class action suits charging gross negligence—one totalling ten billion dollars[36]—continue to haunt Con Ed. A Small Claims

Court judge in New York City ruled that the utility "must reimburse . . . complainants [mostly for food spoilage] unless the [utility] company can prove it was not guilty of negligence."[37] The suits, including one by the City to recover fifty million dollars' expenses and the same again in punitive damages from Con Ed, proceeded to trial, with "severe implications" for the utility industry if the plaintiffs succeeded, in effect, in "making the utilities insurers of public safety."[38] On 19 November 1981, the New York State Court of Appeals unanimously ruled against Con Ed in a leading food spoilage suit by a grocery store, finding the utility "grossly negligent" and clearing the way for the other complainants.[39] The lawyers will doubtless be busy for years to come.

The direct financial consequences of failure can be catastrophic for particular companies or for whole industries. Three Mile Island may be the end of the Babcock & Wilcox nuclear enterprise; it may well push General Public Utilities over the brink of insolvency; it has reduced the NRC's credibility; and it has focused investors' attention on the possibility of catastrophic loss in an industry that was already having trouble attracting funds.[40] Con Ed, or any other company blamed (rightly or wrongly) for a major energy failure, may yet pay such a price. A single event may seal the fate of an industry that is already financially precarious and has little safety margin left for maneuver. Most of the electric utility industry in the United States is presently in this condition and likely to stay that way. Neither individual companies nor the industry as a whole can afford multibillion-dollar mistakes.

It may well turn out that the most lasting and severe effects of the New York blackout will not be financial losses, crime, or other things expressible in statistics. Rather, the greatest effect may be the unquantifiable loss of confidence in the city's social future[41] and in the institutions that are supposed to protect its citizens from such complete breakdown of social order—much as the most lasting effect of the Iranian hostage-taking may turn out to be loss of public confidence in our government's ability to foresee and forestall hostile foreign actions. Such a psychological shock is deep and lasting, and can change what people do far more than mere economic signals can. For example, in Britain, for several years after the 1974 coal strike, more electrical generating capacity was installed privately—in the form of expensive standby generators in homes and factories—than publicly, simply because many people placed a very high premium on not being turned off. This degree of private investment bespeaks an anxiety that surely represents a substantial social cost.

For all these reasons, it is difficult to quantify the cost of failure. Some types of failures, however, are clearly so unacceptably vast that it would be worth paying a very high price for effective insurance against them. Part Three of this book will show that the extra cost of that insurance can actually be *negative*. That is, an energy system in which catastrophic failures are impossible can cost less to build and operate than one in which such failures are plausible and even frequent. The general vulnerabilities surveyed above give an enormous incentive for achieving such a resilient energy system, even if it *did* cost extra. To illustrate this fact, the next six chapters will show how these general types of vulnerability can translate into specific major failures which have already occurred or which have so far been avoided only by great good luck.

Chapter Seven
War and Terrorism

Accidental failures in energy systems randomly hit points of weakness and resources needed for recovery. Deliberate attacks, however, seek out these vulnerabilities and exploit them to maximize damage. The trend towards ever more centralized energy technologies creates opportunities for devastating attacks of a kind and on a scale never before possible. This has long been foreseen by military planners. The first American post-Hiroshima strategic review recommended dispersion of industrial facilities as a civil defense measure,[1] and the same principle is considered desirable in the Soviet Union.[2] Neither country has seriously practiced it.

Centralized facilities as military targets

Even when energy systems were considerably simpler than modern electrical grids, they proved attractive targets in wartime. The Energy and Defense Project found several such cases instructive.[3] Hitler's Germany used electricity for three-fourths of industrial motive power, as well as for all electrochemical processes (arc furnaces, electrolysis, production of synthetic nitrogen and oil and rubber). Four-fifths of the electricity came from central steam plants. These were highly concentrated: in 1933, one and four-tenths percent of the thermal plants provided over half the total output, and five percent of the plants provided four-fifths of the output. The Allies, however, mistakenly assumed that despite this inviting concentration of generating capacity, German grid interconnections provided enough flexibility of routing that power stations did not deserve a high priority as bombing targets. Thus power stations escaped substantial targeting until the vast bombing raids of 1944.

Rarely has there been a costlier error in military planning. The Nazis were delighted: they felt, and responsible officials including Goering and Speer said afterwards, that systematic targeting of power plants would have curtailed the war, perhaps by two years. They could not understand why the Allies had passed up such an effective targeting strategy.[4] U.S. analysts later realized that early Allied bombing of major power plants and substations "would have had a catastrophic effect on Germany's war production."[5]

The Allies were also late to exploit similar opportunities to interdict the Nazis' liquid fuel supplies. On 1 August 1943, a single raid destroyed three hundred fifty thousand barrels of oil and half the refining capacity at Ploesti (Romania), then a key German source. But still earlier bombing of other German oil facilities, especially those making aviation fuel, would have greatly curtailed World War II.[6] By early 1944, about a fifth of the German oil supply—about seventy thousand barrels per day—was being made from coal in twenty-six synthetic fuel plants, most of which had been built in the Ruhr area during the 1930s. When those plants were belatedly targeted for precision bombing, the synfuel output plummeted by more than ninety percent in just a few months[7]—starkly confirming German analysts' fears. (Meanwhile, the Luftwaffe had delayed attacks on Russian power plants in the hope of capturing and using them. By the time the Nazis had been driven back, making this a forlorn hope, the plants were no longer within their bombing range.)[8]

Protection by dispersion

In striking converse to this centralized vulnerability, Japanese electrical production in World War II was relatively decentralized.[9] Seventy-eight percent came from small, highly dispersed hydroelectric plants that were not individually attractive targets. The largest single dam supplied less than three percent of Japan's electricity. The more centralized thermal plants, though they provided only twenty-two percent of the total electricity, were so comparatively vulnerable to urban bombing raids that they sustained ninety-nine and seven-tenths percent of the damage. The contrast between these centralized plants and the dispersed hydro plants (seventy-eight percent of the output but only three-tenths of one percent of the damage) impressively demonstrates the military advantages of not putting all one's energy eggs in a few baskets.

Similarly, North Vietnamese energy facilities were not a primary target during the Vietnam war because, like the Japanese hydro plants in World War II, they were too small and dispersed to be worth attacking.[10] But in the Korean War, the centralized hydroelectric dams on the Yalu River, serving North Korea and China, did become a target. The U.S. also bombed a concentrated energy target—a Cambodian oil refinery—during the 1975 *Mayaguez* incident.[11]

At least since then, if not for longer, the People's Republic of China has reportedly taken military vulnerability to heart in dispersing energy facilities. For example, a third of China's rural electricity, a quarter of its hydro generation, and thirty-six percent of its total hydro capacity in 1981 came from more than ninety thousand small hydro sets, often generating only kilowatts or tens of kilowatts each[12]—enough to run an American house or neighborhood. Furthermore, seven million small anaerobic digesters (a fifteenfold increase during 1975–78) provide fertilizer, and about a third of the units provide reliable supplies of biogas. This local fuel is used for cooking and lighting, and in some cases for operating diesel generators in the general range of five to forty kilowatts of electric output.[13] To date, the dispersed biogas plants serve only four percent of the Chinese population, but they are not yet widely used in the parts of the country that are climatically most favorable.[14] Chinese planners are well aware of the military benefits of even this modest dispersion.

A similar philosophy of dispersion is apparently applied, so far as practicable, in Israel. Oil and power facilities are carefully divided into relatively small, dispersed pieces. It was not lost on Israeli planners that their jets destroyed virtually the whole of Syria's oil installations (and two main power stations) in a half-hour early in the Six Days' War because they were so highly concentrated geographically. Thus, when Arab sabotage of Israeli power lines blacked out Negev settlements, Elath was not affected because that city had built its own generators as a precaution.[15] But mere dispersion of generating capacity is not always enough to ensure resilience—as Israel found out in 1979 when a transmission failure cascaded, New York-style, and blacked out virtually the whole country at once.[16] (Later chapters will diagnose the missing ingredients for making a power grid "crashproof.")

Energy in jeopardy

Rhodesia made the same mistake as Syria—centralized oil depots—and paid for it when Black nationalist guerrillas blew one up in December 1978 (Chapter Nine). Likewise, June 1980 opened with a strong, simultaneous attack on three key South African plants:[17] the two SASOL synfuel plants already built (which are planned, with one more now under construction, to provide nearly half the country's liquid fuels by 1984), and the Natref refinery, the smallest of four in the country. The attack seriously damaged SASOL One. The failure of some explosive charges to go off (although seven bombs did)[18] narrowly saved SASOL Two, six times as large and just starting operation, from destruction. Millions of gallons at the refinery and its tank farms burned in a fire that was visible fifty miles away. The plants, along with the key pipelines carrying crude oil from Durban to the industrial heartland of the Witwatersrand, and other highly centralized energy and industrial facilities in South Africa, remain under threat.[19] And South Africa is not averse to making or supporting such attacks on its neighbors: it is believed to be implicated in the destruction of oil facilities in the Angolan port of Lobito in 1980,[20] in the unsuccessful 1981 mining of a key Angolan oil pipeline,[21] and in the 1981 burning of Angola's oil refinery.[22]

Similar attacks have become more common in guerrilla wars since Egyptian saboteurs burned British oilfields in Libya in 1956.[23] At this writing, guerrillas are said to be closing in on dams and power plants in such countries as Chile and Angola. Ecuadorean troops foiled a 1976 attack on a major oil pipeline,[24] but recent reports suggest a continued threat there and in the Guatemalan oilfields. In 1969, Israeli commandos cut power lines from the Aswan High Dam to Cairo.[25] Guerrillas claimed to have blacked out the Soviet-controlled airport at Jalalabad, Afghanistan, by sabotaging a power station.[26] The bombing of three pylons carrying a power line from Jinja to Kampala sharply curtailed power and water supplies to the Ugandan capital in 1979.[27] Iran announced in July 1981 that it had blacked out large areas of Iraq by bombing a hydroelectric station in Kurdistan.[28] Guerrillas sabotaged "power relay facilities in Kaohsiung," Taiwan, in January 1976.[29]

On 14 June 1978, Red Brigades terrorists caused six hundred thousand dollars' damage and blacked out part of Rome for several hours with a series of bombs in a power station.[30] Accident or sabotage in a San Juan power plant blacked out Puerto Rico on 10 April 1980, shortly after the plant's chief engineer was kidnapped.[31] Much of San Juan was blacked out again when two power stations were bombed seven months later.[32] San Salvador was blacked out on 6 February 1981 by the bombing of a power plant—the fourth attack on power installations in four days.[33] A few months later, guerrillas were reportedly a few miles from a dam providing half of El Salvador's electricity.[34] A third of the country was blacked out in early November 1981,[35] and over Christmas, seven bombings of transmission lines blacked out three more Salvadorean cities.[36] In just four months in 1981, Salvadorean guerrillas made one hundred fifty attacks on the electric grid, blacking out some cities in the transmission-dependent eastern third of the country for as long as seven weeks; and in January 1982 they blew up another million-dollar San Salvador power plant.[37]

Later chapters document significant recent sabotage to energy facilities in many of the sixteen above-mentioned countries and in twenty-four more: Argentina, Bolivia, Brazil, Cyprus, the Federal Republic of Germany, France, India, Iran, Ireland, Japan, Kuwait, Lebanon, Mozambique, The Netherlands, Nicaragua, Portugal, Qatar, Saudi Arabia, Singapore, Spain, Sweden, Turkey, the United Kingdom, and the mainland United States. The attacks cited in these forty countries are only a sampling of items from the public press. It is likely that many such incidents

are not reported· in many countries they would be considered state se-
crets·: A fuller search, too, would doubtless turn up more instances.

Concern over the military vulnerability of centralized energy facilities is
not unique to beleaguered countries (like Israel) or those like China which
have a decentralist and civil-defense-oriented tradition. For example, the
French military establishment reportedly wishes to reduce national vulnerability by decentralizing the energy system.[38] This desire was doubtless
heightened by the "impossible" cascading failure of virtually the entire
French electric grid on 19 December 1978, with lost production officially
estimated at nearly one billion dollars.[39] The security benefits of the
greatest possible energy decentralization, especially through the use of renewable sources, form a key component of at least one of the several lines
of official French energy policy.[40] Even in the Soviet Union—where central electrification has been a sacred tenet of the Communist Party since
Lenin declared Communism to consist of "collectives plus electrification"—there is

> reportedly a standing argument between the Soviet military and the Politbu-
> ro. . . . The military argues that decentralized energy systems are of primary
> importance for civil defense and therefore essential to Soviet national security.
> The Politburo insists on centralization of primary energy systems in order to
> ensure party control, and is apparently prepared to risk a significant degree of
> national security to do so.[41]

Electronic vulnerability

The new technical dimensions of modern warfare and of modern energy systems have recently combined to produce new types of vulnerability
which are not related just to the size or centralization of individual plants,
but also to how they are controlled and interconnected. For example, just
as oil and gas pipelines must be remotely monitored and controlled at
hundreds of points by sophisticated computers and electronic communications, so no part of the synchronous electric grid can function without
continuous communications from centralized, computerized control
points. Utility and regional power pool dispatchers must be in constant
contact with each other and with devices and staff in the field. This control and communication system now faces a novel threat from nuclear
warfare—a threat that makes the physical vulnerability of particular plants
to nuclear attack pale by comparison.[42]

The new vulnerability is caused by "electromagnetic pulse" (EMP)—a
brief but very powerful electromagnetic field produced by nuclear explosions at high (or, with limited range, at low) altitude. The pulse reaches its
full intensity in about ten billionths of a second—a hundred times as fast
as lightning—and hence cannot be stopped by ordinary lightning arres-
tors, but only by special cabinets and other equipment designed for this

purpose. Its peak strength may be fifty thousand volts per meter, or six million watts per square meter—six thousand times the peak density of sunlight. And a single one-megaton hydrogen bomb exploded at an altitude of sixty to three hundred miles can produce this electromagnetic blink over a radius of five hundred to fourteen hundred miles.[43] A single blast high over the central United States could blanket almost the entire lower forty-eight states with an intense pulse—at least twenty-five thousand volts per meter.[44]

Any metal object—power lines, telephone lines, wires, instrument cabinets—would pick up the pulse like an antenna, focusing its energy into any delicate electronic circuitry in the area. The result: *instantaneous, simultaneous failure* of all unhardened electrical and electronic systems, including electric grid and pipeline controls, telephones, and other telecommunications except fiber optics. Many of the failures would require major repairs. Most power grid controls would be damaged functionally (burned-out transistors) or operationally (erased computer memory):[45] integrated circuits are about ten million times as prone to EMP burnout as vacuum tubes.[46] Power lines act as long antennas, collecting the pulse over great distances. The induced surges—as high as thirty thousand megawatts[47]—could damage insulators and transformer windings, and would probably burn out many end-use devices that happened to be operating from line voltage at the time.[48]

With the prospect of grid controls knocked out, transmission and distribution systems themselves damaged, and power plants probably damaged too, it is no wonder that the Defense Civil Preparedness Agency concluded that, because of EMP, "no reliance should be placed on the presumed availability of electric power during and immediately following a nuclear attack."[49] Design trends in the power industry are tending to increase the likelihood of EMP damage,[50] and "the extreme difficulty and expense of protecting the grids has discouraged utilities from taking virtually any action."[51]

EMP may have another, even more dramatic effect. Especially in newer nuclear plants which use solid-state electronic devices extensively,[52] the safety and control systems on operating nuclear power reactors may be disabled.[53] This could cause a simultaneous epidemic of uncontrollable core meltdowns in dozens of plants across the country.[54] Although this possibility is very hard to analyze, it cannot be excluded on the basis of present knowledge.[55] A fuller report to the Nuclear Regulatory Commission is due in 1983.[56] (This problem has apparently not been analyzed at all in Europe, or in Canada, whose reactors would be equally blanketed by a North American EMP.)

The Joint Chiefs of Staff want to spend seven billion dollars over the next few years to make military command, control, and communications systems more resistant to such disruptions as EMP.[57] No such program is envisaged, however, for protecting the civilian electric power grid or its controls, nor for protecting other vital parts of the energy system. If concerns about nuclear power plants' vulnerability to EMP proved justified, such a blast would not leave much of a country to defend. It might even turn out that Strategic Air Command bomber crews, racing for their planes to carry out their doomsday missions, might be unable to reach their EMP-hardened aircraft because the pulse would have burned out the electric ignitions in their cars.[58]

The terrorist threat

EMP is at one extreme of the spectrum of military threats to the energy system: an instantaneous flash of invisible radiation that could shut off virtually all energy supplies across the entire United States at once. At the other extreme, but still a formidable threat, is localized terrorist attack. The next four chapters survey some of the main energy targets that saboteurs might find most attractive, in order to determine how much damage they could do. But achievable damage also depends on the resources which a terrorist group could bring to bear against major energy facilities. These resources deserve a brief survey as background for the specific examples to follow in Part Two.

Most of the literature dealing with terrorist threats to energy facilities deals with nuclear facilities,[59] which tend to be the most carefully guarded and the most resistant to attack. But most studies that are commonly quoted to reassure the public that such plants are very resistant to sabotage expressly *exclude* the possibility of "military action and damage by foreign agents or subversive organizations."[60] In practical effect, therefore, such studies consider only lone disgruntled employees and the like. But international terrorist groups have far greater resources, and some can even call on the resources of wealthy governments. Governments in turn may find such a connection useful for their own ends:

> Finding modern conventional war inefficient, uneconomical, and ineffective, some nations may be drawn to exploit the demonstrated possibilities and greater potential of terrorism, and employ terrorist groups or tactics in surrogate warfare against other nations. This requires an investment far smaller than the cost of a conventional war; it debilitates the enemy; and it is deniable.[61]

Even the short list of attacks cited above (later chapters list many more) suggests that this pattern has already begun to emerge: guerrilla attacks on centralized energy facilities are arguably the cheapest and most effective way to attack another country. Significantly, attacks on key energy facilities are among the prime tactics used by Soviet-trained guerrillas throughout the world today. Similar tactics are of course available to any other attackers, whether working on their own or as surrogates for others. Who are some of these possible attackers, and what are their strengths and resources?

There are believed to be about fifty terrorist organizations in the world, with an estimated total of about three thousand active members, and perhaps an equal number of peripheral supporters. A hard core of about two hundred members constitutes the "primary transnational threat."[62] Because several groups sometimes participate jointly in an action, it is hard to estimate how many terrorists might join in a single attack on a particular energy facility.

In the U.S., where the nuclear regulatory philosophy encourages formulation of specific threat levels which licensees are to guard against, there is a long-running debate over this number. It has risen steadily during the past ten years. At first it was thought to be "several," meaning three, of whom one could be an insider, and there was a consensus that security systems even at nuclear plants—the best-guarded of all types of major energy facilities—were not adequate for this threat.[63] Upgraded security measures were then again outrun by a heightened threat estimate of a "small group" (six), aided by up to two insiders. More recently, after several official studies, a consensus has emerged that "fifteen highly trained men, no more than three of [whom] . . . work within the facility . . . , [the insiders to include] anyone up to the higher levels of management," is a reasonable threat level.[64]

But this debate is reminiscent of the disputations of medieval theologians, since the history of criminal and terrorist enterprises clearly shows that attackers bring with them "as many as they need . . . to do the job, and no more. The fact that most came with a handful of persons, three to six, thus does not represent an upper limit on their capacity" but only their estimate of what would be "necessary to accomplish their mission."[65] More stringent security precautions might deter some attackers, but would simply elicit a stronger assault from really determined attackers who thought the price was worthwhile.

Indeed, what most protects energy facilities is not that they have fences and guards, but rather that relatively few people have an intense desire to attack them. As the physicist and physician Dean Abrahamson has pointed out, vastly more aircraft have crashed on purpose (e.g., through being shot down) than by accident. Given "the inherent frailty of a technology that puts hundreds of people in a cylinder of aluminum moving at six hundred miles per hour some seven miles up in the air," it is not airport security systems or other defenses that mainly serve to limit the crashes of civilian airliners, but rather the relative lack of incentive to cause crashes. Since the incentive to shoot down military aircraft is much higher, people often do so.

Unfortunately, the incentive to attack major energy facilities is very large if one is seeking a means of causing economic hardship, or death and destruction, or both. As soon as people come onto the world stage who have such incentives, the sense of security encouraged by past freedom from attacks becomes groundless. Human intention, which brings technological systems into being, can also disrupt them. Generally a much lower technology is needed to make disorder than order. What matters most is intention and incentive.

Another warning against underestimating what a few committed attackers can do comes from a review of past commando raids. Most of the raids

> were carried out against protected targets at least as well armed as the commandos, conditions that would hardly seem to bode well for the raiders. Yet, with the advantages of greater flexibility and tactical surprise, the raids succeeded three-fourths of the time and against some targets whose defenses could have prevailed against much larger forces: if one excludes those failures that were not due to enemy action, the commandos were successful almost ninety percent of the time. This rate of success speaks highly for the professional skill and ingenuity of the raiders, and particularly for their use of surprise. (It also bodes ill for the use of mathematical engagement models [or security plans] in which force ratios determine the outcome.)[66]

The success of such raids depends on accurate intelligence and precise planning—especially in such operations as the destruction of eleven bridges in one night during Israel's fight for independence from Britain, or raids in which British and Israeli commandos seized and carried off German and Egyptian radar bases, respectively.[67] Similar attributes determined the success of task-force crimes. "In the forty-five cases reviewed, criminals were able to assemble teams of as many as twenty people (yet remain undiscovered), breach thick walls and vaults and neutralize modern alarm systems, and devote up to two years of planning for a single 'caper'."[68] Considerable technical sophistication has also been displayed.[69] "In 1970, an electronics expert connected with organized crime was detected in what appeared to be an elaborate method of monitoring the activities of the Chicago police. He was cruising near the Chicago Police Department's lake front headquarters in a converted mine-sweeper laden with radio-intercept equipment."[70]

It is commonly asserted that no group as big as, say, a dozen people could be assembled and trained for a nuclear plant attack without coming to the authorities' attention; but larger groups in past criminal efforts have escaped both notice beforehand and capture afterwards. Indeed, thirteen mercenaries training with automatic weapons for jungle warfare were arrested for trespassing *after* five days of secret maneuvers on the borders of the Crystal River nuclear power plant in Florida.[71]. They were observed more or less by accident, and nobody knew who they were—whether they were "a drug-offloading operation, a subversive group trying to get the power plant or a CIA operation," according to the sheriff. His aide added: "If they were the real McCoy, we wouldn't have been any match for 'em. . . . This damn sure oughta wake up the nuclear power industry. . . . A good assault team could have taken that plant."[72] The month after the thirteen mercenaries were released on their own recognizance, two of them were rearrested with guns and explosives in Miami, where it was believed they were about to plant a bomb.[73]

Insiders and security lapses

Such a straightforward light-infantry group is a less formidable threat, however, than just one or two insiders with knowledge of and access to the plant's vital areas. Aid from insiders has characterized many of the biggest and smoothest thefts and hijackings.[74] (Impersonation of insiders has also worked every time it was tried.)[75] "In the . . . theft [of nearly six million dollars] from Lufthansa at the JFK Airport, a ten-year Lufthansa employee was promised three hundred thousand dollars (more than any other participant) . . . [simply to leave] his post for more than an hour and a half."[76] A Bank of New Mexico burglary on the high-security Sandia nuclear base in 1955 appears to have had inside help on the base.[77] Other examples cited in Chapter Eleven indicate that even nuclear facilities requiring the most stringent clearance and vetting of employees may harbor potential criminals. The former security director of the Atomic Energy Commission was himself sentenced to three years' probation in 1973 after borrowing two hundred thirty-nine thousand dollars from fellow AEC employees, spending much of it at the racetrack, and failing to repay over one hundred seventy thousand dollars.[78]

A particularly worrisome sort of insider help is security guards. The guard forces at nuclear power plants are claimed to be better selected, trained, and equipped than guards at any other energy facilities. Nonetheless, as of 1977, guard forces at many reactors not only were of low quality, but had a turnover rate of a third to a half per year, with departing guards taking with them an intimate knowledge of up-to-date security arrangements.[79] A local newspaper reporter got a job as a security guard at Three Mile Island, then prepared a series of articles which the utility unsuccessfully sought an injunction to suppress[80] on the grounds that—as the utility's lawyers put it—revealing "the specific details of the security system . . . presents a significant, serious, grave security threat. . . . there is a threat to the health of the public, and national security is involved if someone gets in there to hold the plant hostage for whatever reason."[81]

A U.S. Marshals Service review of reactor guard forces in 1975 found they had weak allegiance, high turnover rate, poor background checks and supervision, inferior equipment, weak legal authority, poor rapport with local police, poor mobility, no uniform physical fitness standards, low public confidence, and little training.[82] Many of these weaknesses persist today.[83] Eleven guards at the Trojan nuclear plant were even charged in 1980 with bulk sales of various illegal drugs. At many plants during 1980–81, guards were reported to be drunk on the job.[84] The pre-employment background of guards has been a particularly sore point since a convicted and paroled armed robber got a job as a security guard under an alias at the former Kerr McGee plutonium fuel fabrication plant in Oklahoma. He was found out and fired in 1974, then six months later arrested in connection with an attempted bank robbery in which a woman was shot.[85]

Even with honest guards, breaches of security are fairly common. A woman working at Browns Ferry forgot she had a pistol in her purse and carried it through a guardpost undetected in February 1980.[86] General Accounting Office auditors in 1977 "were able to pick the locks and open several doors to vital areas of [a nuclear power] plant by using a screwdriver or a piece of wire . . . found on the ground near the door."[87] Other breaches of security too numerous to mention have elicited Nuclear Regulatory Commission fines of utilities on almost a monthly basis. A Phoenix, Arizona security consultant to nuclear utilities has stated that at the peak of a nuclear plant's security, he has yet to observe one that he can't break into undetected.[88] For the convenience of intruders who do not want to rely only on the laxity or corruptibility of security guards, the Nuclear Regulatory Commission thoughtfully publishes many detailed plans and analyses of nuclear plants' security systems, including a computer program for determining terrorists' most promising modes of entry and attack, and a technical survey of the best ways to break through thirty-two kinds of fences and barriers used at nuclear plants.[89]

Nuclear plants are arguably the fattest target for terrorists, and the only major class of energy facilities whose security is supposedly enforced by stringent government regulation. The discouraging picture of security at nuclear plants, then, hardly gives one confidence that other, and in many respects more vulnerable, energy facilities can withstand a significant terrorist attack.

Terrorist resources

Such a conclusion becomes quite unavoidable when one considers the balance of physical forces between terrorists and defenders of major energy plants. Except at the eleven federal facilities handling nuclear bomb materials, where recently installed protective devices include armored cars with light machine guns, U.S. nuclear plants are defended by small numbers of guards with conventional light arms. Non-nuclear energy facilities generally have less than that—typically a few pistol-toting people who, in

John McPhee's phrase, look as if they could run the hundred yards in four minutes. Such guard forces are clearly no match for the sort of firepower that even a handful of terrorists could deploy against an energy facility. These potential weapons include the following main categories:

• Firearms: past terrorist and criminal attacks have used all available civilian and military firearms up to and including heavy machine guns, twenty-millimeter cannons, antitank guns, and recoilless rifles. Modern counterinsurgency arms now available to terrorists include "tiny—some less than fifteen inches long—silent submachine guns."[90] Automatic weapons are readily available.[91] "Enough weapons and ammunition to outfit ten combat battalions numbering eight thousand men were stolen from U.S. military installations around the world between 1971 and 1974."[92]

• Mortars—especially well suited for attacks on spent fuel pools, switchyards, and other facilities unprotected from above. A single North Vietnamese mortar team caused about five billion dollars' damage in a few minutes to the U.S. airbase at Pleiku. Technical progress continues:

> A Belgian arms manufacturing firm has … developed a disposable, lightweight, silent mortar which can be used against personnel and also fires a projectile with a spherical warhead designed to produce a "shattering effect" suitable for the "destruction of utilities, communications, and light structures." The full field unit, which weighs only twenty-two pounds, includes the firing tube plus seven rounds. All seven rounds can be put in the air before the first round hits.[93]

• Bazookas and similar unguided rockets. "In August 1974, ninety antitank weapons were stolen by a Yugoslav national who was an employee of the U.S. Army in Germany."[94] These were recaptured, but many more were stolen and later turned up in the hands of criminals and terrorists. Their shaped-charge warheads are specifically designed to penetrate thick armor. World War II-vintage bazookas have a range of twelve hundred feet. The Korean War version, of somewhat shorter range, is in service with National Guard and Reserve units. The 1970s version, the U.S. Light Antitank Weapon (LAW), is a five-pound, hundred-dollar rocket effective at a thousand feet against stationary targets. It is shoulder-fired from a disposable tube and can penetrate nearly three inches of armor plate.[95] One was unsuccessfully fired at a West Coast police station in 1974; many have been stolen.[96] The similar Soviet RPG-7 ("Katyusha") is commonly used by Palestinian terrorists and was used in a Paris airport attack in January 1975. Both, and counterparts such as the French "Strim" F-1, are portable, suitcase-sized, and easy to conceal or disguise. "[T]here has not been a recent Soviet-influenced conflict in which the recipients of Russia's support were not carrying RPG-7s."[97] Still deadlier versions are now under development, with ranges far greater than a thousand feet.

• Light, precision-guided rockets designed for shoulder-firing against aircraft (like the Soviet SA-7 or "Strela" and the U.S. "Redeye," both of which have terminal infrared guidance and a range of several miles). Redeye weighs under thirty pounds and is about four feet long; its successor, "Stinger," is no bigger but is faster, longer-range, and more accurate.[98] The British "Blowpipe" is radio-guided by its aimer. The supersonic, tripod-mounted Swedish RB-70 has laser guidance, "weighs under one hundred eighty pounds, breaks down into three smaller packages, and can be operated by one man with minimal training." These latter two missiles can shoot down aircraft approaching head-on. Palestinian terrorists have Strela rockets and were arrested with some near the Rome Airport in September 1973 and at the edge of the Nairobi airport in January 1976.[99] A Strela may have been used to shoot down two Rhodesian passenger planes in the past three years. It is the rocket whose reported possession by an alleged Libyan assassination squad caused such anxiety in the White House in December 1981. A Strela rocket could be used for standoff attacks on stationary energy facilities, or to shoot down incoming airborne security forces.

• Analogous precision-guided munitions (PGMs) designed for antitank use. The U.S. "Dragon" and "TOW" rockets and the Soviet "Sagger" are wire-guided, use laser target acquisition, have ranges of a mile or two, weigh generally under thirty pounds, and can be carried and operated by one person. The French/German "Milan," somewhat smaller and with semiautomatic guidance, is even more portable and is being deployed by the tens of thousands.[100] The Dragon, TOW, and Sagger shaped-charge warheads "can pierce several feet of homogeneous armor plate,"[101] or five times their own diameter.[102] They are more commonly available than their anti-aircraft counterparts. It would not be surprising if at least hundreds of them were in terrorists' hands today. They are ideal for standoff attacks against even semihardened energy facilities, as well as for attacking any vehicles in which security forces would be likely to arrive.

• Specialized rockets and grenades. The German-designed antitank "Armbrust 300," designed for urban warfare, "has no backblast, making it possible to fire the weapon from inside a room—something no rocket launcher can do now. The Germans expect to produce the 'Armbrust' in large quantities."[103] A new projectile that can be fired from the U.S. M-79 grenade launcher (many of which have reportedly been stolen) "is capable of penetrating two inches of armor plate and igniting any fuel behind it."[104] A more conventional rocket-propelled grenade was used in the 15 September 1981 Heidelberg attempt to assassinate General Kroesen, U.S. Army Commander in Europe. Another has been used to blow up an oil depot in Azerbaijan.[105]

• Poison gas. In April 1975, terrorists stole three quarts of mustard gas from German Army bunkers; several cities, including Stuttgart and Bonn, were threatened with a gas attack.[106] The "Alphabet Bomber" threatened in 1974 to "destroy the entire personnel of Capitol Hill" with two tons of sarin nerve gas, and had in fact assembled all but one of the ingredients needed to make it.[107] A letter bomb containing a vial of nerve gas has reportedly been intercepted in the United States.[108] Viennese police in 1975 arrested German entrepreneurs for conspiring to sell tabun nerve gas in the Middle East.[109] They had already made a quart of it—a mere whiff of which would cause unconsciousness in five seconds and death within five minutes—and packed it into bottles, capsules, and spray cans.[110] Methods of making such substances have been published, and some highly toxic nerve gas analogues are commercially available in bulk as organophosphorus insecticides. An inhaled lethal dose of sarin nerve gas to a normally respiring adult is about a thirty-thousandth of an ounce. VX nerve gas, whose method of preparation has also been printed, is ten times this toxic by inhalation and three hundred times as toxic by contact.[111] It can be made by a "moderately competent organic chemist, with limited laboratory facilities" and willingness to take risks.[112] Nonlethal incapacitating gases like Mace® are also widely available. A U.S. Army black-hat team reportedly demonstrated in 1969 and 1970 that a gas attack on the Capitol and White House air-conditioning systems could readily have killed everyone inside, including the President, the Congress, and most of their staffs.[113] The security precautions taken at these buildings are presumably more stringent than at most energy facilities.

• Explosives, including breaching, shaped, platter, airblast, and fuel-air detonation charges. These are readily available at a wide range of sophistication, ranging from plastic explosives and specialized cutting and penetration jets to the crude seventeen-hundred-pound truckload of fertilizer/fuel-oil explosive which destroyed the Army Mathematics Research Center at the University of Wisconsin in 1970.[114] (Such a charge at ten yards' range produces overpressures of the order of one hundred fifty pounds per square inch—six times the level which severely damages reinforced concrete.) Many tons of commercial explosives are stolen every year,[115] and probably over a million Americans are trained in their use. Many types of high explosives can be homemade.[116] Military explosives come in many varieties, some of which are invisible (liquids which soak into the soil) or can be so well disguised as to be recognizable only by experts. Military explosives and fuses are often available to terrorists. Soviet-made limpet mines have been routinely used to sabotage power facilities in southern Africa.[117] Nuclear explosives may also become available, and offer special capabilities which are considered separately in Chapter Eleven.

• Aircraft. The same group that caused one death and six million dollars' damage with the homemade truck bomb at the University of Wisconsin had also tried to sabotage a power station supplying a munitions plant, and had made an unsuccessful aerial attack in a stolen airplane against the same munitions plant.[118] Fixed-wing aircraft have been used in several bombing attempts, particularly in Northern Ireland. Helicopters have been used in jailbreaks in the U.S.,[119] Mexico, and Eire, and by Pfc. Robert K. Preston in his 17 February 1974 landing on the White House lawn. Palestinian terrorists have recently used even a hot-air balloon to enter Lebanon, and of course Nazi commandos often used gliders with great success. Commercial and, on occasion, even military aircraft are hijacked throughout the world, and could be used for access, weapon delivery, or kamikaze attack. The remote control devices used by hobbyists could probably be adapted to make sizable fixed-wing aircraft into pilotless drones, or similarly to operate boats or other vehicles by remote control.

• Ships, small submersible vessels, and frogmen are undoubtedly available to terrorists. Ships carrying torpedoes, depth charges, and guided rockets may be available. Portable missiles can be fired even from a rowboat; one was fired from a speedboat in 1972 by Palestinian commandos against an Israel-bound Liberian oil tanker in the Red Sea straits between Ethiopia and Yemen.[120]

• Tanks and similar vehicles are sufficiently available at National Guard and Army bases, where a wide variety of other sizable weapons have been stolen in the past, that it is not unrealistic to contemplate their hijacking. Some incidents of this kind have already occurred. Just heavy construction equipment, which is commonly available to civilians and is frequently stolen from construction sites, lends itself to adaptation, and could readily be armored to withstand the light-infantry arms issued to guards. In Louisiana in 1967, a large construction crane was driven into three large transmission line towers to destroy them.[121] In July 1977, an earthmover struck a valve on the Trans-Alaska Pipeline, spewing hot oil over five acres of tundra.[122]

• Other relevant equipment available to terrorists includes sophisticated communication and interception equipment, electronic countermeasures systems for jamming or spoofing communication or guidance signals, radar, night vision devices, industrial lasers for metal-cutting or other uses (a small handheld laser temporarily blinded the pilot and crew of a Los Angeles Police Department helicopter in October 1981), gas and plasma cutting torches capable of penetrating any material, robots, and computers. Within a few years, "research" rockets capable of sending hundreds of pounds for thousands of miles will become commercially available, and so will accurate inertial guidance systems.

• Military munitions, available to governments worldwide via the generous export policies of the major military powers, add a new dimension to the previous list, because such munitions are often even more effective for the specialized tasks for which they are designed.[123] For example, some aerial bombs can reportedly penetrate ten yards or more of concrete,[124] and certain artillery rounds can pierce five feet of concrete after travelling twenty miles. Newly developed munitions can apparently penetrate heavily hardened targets and then explode inside them. In the coming years, the gradual evolution and spread of military hardware can be expected to offer terrorists more channels for obtaining this specialized equipment, just as they have done in the past.

The point of this catalogue of terrorist resources is not to claim that all the means listed have been used to attack energy facilities (though in fact many have). Rather, it is to give fuller meaning to the description, in the next four chapters, of the specific characteristics which make four major types of energy system highly vulnerable to attack—including especially their potential not just to stop working but to do great harm to their neighbors.

A growing danger

There are, unfortunately, many people eager to exploit any potential to do great harm by a dramatic act. In the past decade, "there have been on the average two terrorist incidents per day somewhere in the world."[125] Increasingly, as the previous and following examples show, those attacks have focused been on centralized energy systems. As a U.S. Department of Energy compilation shows, between 1970 and mid-1980 there were at least one hundred seventy-four incidents of sabotage or terrorism against energy facilities in the United States and at least one hundred ninety-two abroad, as shown in Table One.[126]

Thus, by this official count, attacks on energy facilities are *already* occurring at a rate averaging one every three weeks in the United States and one every ten days throughout the world. That rate, as the citations in the following chapters show, is rapidly accelerating. To understand the dangers of this emerging pattern, we must understand not only what has already happened, but what could happen in the future—if we do not begin to make the energy system far more resilient.

Table One   Attacks Against Energy Facilities: 1970–1980

Target	Domestic	Foreign
Powerline	55	48
Power station or substation	43	21
Pipeline	27	54
Oil or gas storage facility	15	15
Nuclear energy support facility	15	32
Oil refinery	6	12
Oil well	5	1
Hydroelectric facility	4	2
Mine [coal or uranium]	2	2
Coal train	1	–
"Nuclear weapon association"	1	–
Oil tanker	–	3
Oil train	–	1
Nuclear waste freighter	–	1
TOTAL	174	192

SOURCE: U.S. Department of Energy

Part 2 Disasters Waiting to Happen

Chapter Eight
Liquefied Natural Gas

Natural gas can be sent by pipeline over long distances. For a price, it can be piped from North Sea platforms to the British mainland, from Algeria to Italy, or from Siberia to Western Europe. But pipelines are not a feasible way to send gas across major oceans—for example, from the Mideast or Indonesia to the United States. A high-technology way to transport natural gas overseas has, however, been developed in the past few decades, using the techniques of cryogenics—the science of extremely low temperatures.

In this method, a sort of giant refrigerator, costing more than a billion dollars, chills a vast amount of gas until it condenses into a colorless, odorless liquid at a temperature of two hundred sixty degrees Fahrenheit below zero. This liquefied natural gas (LNG) has a volume six hundred twenty times smaller than the original gas. The intensely cold LNG is then transported at approximately atmospheric pressure in special, heavily insulated cryogenic tankers—the costliest non-military seagoing vessels in the world—to a marine terminal, where it is stored in insulated tanks. When needed, it can then be piped to an adjacent gasification plant—nearly as complex and costly as the liquefaction plant—where it is boiled back into gas and distributed to customers by pipeline just like wellhead gas.

Approximately sixty smaller plants in North America also liquefy and store domestic natural gas as a convenient way of increasing their storage capacity for winter peak demands which could otherwise exceed the capacity of trunk pipelines supplying the area. This type of local storage to augment peak supplies is called "peak-shaving." Such plants can be sited anywhere gas is available in bulk; they need have nothing to do with marine LNG tankers.

LNG is less than half as dense as water, so a cubic meter of LNG (the usual unit of measure) weighs just over half a ton.[1] LNG contains about thirty percent less energy per cubic meter than oil, but is potentially far more hazardous.[2] Burning oil cannot spread very far on land or water, but a cubic meter of spilled LNG rapidly boils into about six hundred twenty cubic meters of pure natural gas, which in turn mixes with surrounding air. Mixtures of between about five and fourteen percent natural gas in air are flammable. Thus a single cubic meter of spilled LNG can make up to twelve thousand four hundred cubic meters of flammable gas-air mixture. A single modern LNG tanker typically holds one hundred twenty-five thousand cubic meters of LNG, equivalent to twenty-seven hundred million cubic feet of natural gas. That gas can form between about twenty and fifty billion cubic feet of flammable gas-air mixture— several hundred times the volume of the Great Pyramid of Cheops.

About nine percent of such a tankerload of LNG will probably, if spilled onto water, boil to gas in about five minutes.[3] (It does not matter how cold the water is; it will be at least two hundred twenty-eight Fahrenheit degrees hotter than the LNG, which it will therefore cause to boil violently.) The resulting gas, however, will be so cold that it will still be denser than air. It will therefore flow in a cloud or plume along the surface until it reaches an ignition source. Such a pume might extend at least three miles downwind from a large tanker spill within ten to twenty minutes.[4] It might ultimately reach much farther—perhaps six to twelve miles.[5] If not ignited, the gas is asphyxiating. If ignited, it will burn to completion with a turbulent diffusion flame reminiscent of the 1937 *Hindenberg* disaster but about a hundred times as big. Such a fireball would burn everything within it, and by its radiant heat would cause third-degree burns and start fires a mile or two away.[6] An LNG fireball can blow through a city, creating "a very large number of ignitions and explosions across a wide area. No present or foreseeable equipment can put out a very large [LNG]... fire."[7] The energy content of a single standard LNG tanker (one hundred twenty-five thousand cubic meters) is equivalent to seven-tenths of a megaton of TNT, or about fifty-five Hiroshima bombs.

A further hazard of LNG is that its extreme cold causes most metals to become brittle and contract violently. If LNG spills onto ordinary metals (that is, those not specially alloyed for such low temperatures), such as the deck plating of a ship, it often causes instant brittle fractures. Thus failure of the special cryogenic-alloy membranes which contain the LNG in tanks or tankers could bring it into contact with ordinary steel—the hull of a ship or the outer tank of a marine vessel—and cause it to unzip like a banana, [8] a risk most analyses ignore.[9] LNG can also seep into earth or into insulation—the cause of the Staten Island terminal fire that killed forty workers in 1973. Imperfectly insulated underground LNG tanks, like those at Canvey Island in the Thames Estuary below London, can even create an expanding zone of permafrost, requiring the installation of heaters to maintain soil dimensions and loadbearing properties that are essential to the integrity of the tank.

The potential hazards of LNG are illustrated by the only major LNG spill so far experienced in the U.S.—in Cleveland in 1944.[10] A tank holding four thousand two hundred cubic meters of LNG, part of America's first peak-shaving LNG plant, collapsed. Not all the spillage was contained by dikes and drains. Escaping vapors quickly ignited, causing a second tank, half as large, to spill its contents. "The subsequent explosion shot flames more than half a mile into the air. The temperature in some areas reached three thousand degrees Fahrenheit." Secondary fires were started by a rain of LNG-soaked insulation and drops of burning LNG.[11] By the time the eight-alarm fire was extinguished (impeded by high-voltage lines blocking some streets), one hundred thirty people were dead, two hundred twenty-five injured, and over seven million dollars' worth of property destroyed (in 1944 dollars). An area about a half-mile on a side was directly affected, within which thirty acres were gutted, including seventy-nine houses, two factories, and two hundred seventeen cars. A further thirty-five houses and thirteen factories were partly destroyed. [12] The *National Fire Protection Association Newsletter* of November 1944 noted that had the wind been blowing towards the congested part of the area, "an even more devastating conflagration . . . could have destroyed a very large part of the East Side."

It is noteworthy that the plant's proprietors had taken precautions only against moderate rates of LNG spillage. They did not think a large, rapid spillage was possible. "The same assumption is made today in designing dikes" around LNG facilities.[13] The Cleveland plant, like many today, was sited in a built-up area for convenience; the proximity of other industrial plants, houses, storm sewers, and so forth was not considered. Less than six thousand three hundred cubic meters of LNG spilled, mostly on company property, whereas a modern LNG site may have several tanks, each holding up to ninety-five thousand cubic meters. And the cascading series of failures in two inner and two outer tanks was probably caused by a single minor initiating event.[14]

The future of LNG in the United States is highly uncertain, largely for economic reasons. LNG shipment requires highly capital-intensive facilities at both ends and in between. Their coordination is a logistical feat that exposes companies to major financial risks: "if any of [the system's components is not ready on time] . . . , the entire integrated system collapses."[15] Like the nuclear fuel cycle, LNG projects require exquisite timing but often do not exhibit it—as when Malaysia was "caught with finished [LNG] carriers before their fields and facilities were ready to begin production."[16] This uninsurable financial exposure by prospective LNG buyers provides a bargaining chip to sellers, who can simply raise the price and dare the buyers to write off their tankers, terminals, and regasification plants.

This actually happened in 1980–81. Algeria—the major LNG exporter, and the sole source of LNG exports to the U.S. during 1979–80—abruptly demanded that its LNG be priced at the energy equivalent of OPEC oil, more than a trebbling of earlier prices. The U.S. government, which had just negotiated a much lower gas price with Canada and Mexico, rejected the Algerian demand. On 1 April 1980, Algeria cut off LNG deliveries to the El Paso Natural Gas Company, idling its costly tankers and its terminals at Cove Point, Maryland and Elba Island, Georgia. A third of the Algerian shipments continued to arrive—via the older (1968–71) Distrigas operation in Everett, Massachusetts, which uses an oil-linked pricing structure and Algerian-owned ships. But by late 1981, the Cove Point and Elba Island facilities were still sitting as hostages to price agreement with Algeria. (So was a nearly completed terminal at Lake Charles, Louisiana.) Algeria has somewhat moderated its initial demands, but it and other LNG exporters still intend to move rapidly to oil parity. Partly for this reason, the proposed Point Conception (California) LNG terminal seems unlikely to be built. Argentina, which has never before exported LNG, now proposes to build a liquefaction plant to ship over eight hundred million dollars' worth of LNG per year to the idle Cove Point and Elba Island plants, but market conditions seem most unfavorable for this project. Acknowledging the bleak economic outlook, El Paso in February 1981 "wrote off most of the equity ($365.4 million) in its six tankers which hauled Algerian LNG to the East Coast" [17]—a sizable loss even for such a large company. Of course the tankers might be revived under some new price agreement; but the investors would then have no guarantee that history would not simply repeat itself. Their massive investment would continue to hold them hostage to demands for higher prices.

The economic difficulties of LNG arise not only in the international marketplace but also in the domestic one. New, and probably existing, LNG imports cannot compete with domestic gas (let alone with efficiency improvements and some renewable options). Recent drilling has vastly expanded the reserves of relatively cheap domestic natural gas. Recent geological evidence suggests that enormous reserves can be tapped at prices well below that of imported LNG. LNG has so far been saleable only by "rolling in" its high price with very cheap (regulated) domestic gas, so that customers see only an average of the two. Gas deregulation will probably increase domestic supply and reduce domestic demand so much further as to squeeze LNG out of the market entirely.

Despite these uncertainties, some LNG is now being imported into the U.S., and facilities are available for more. Even though the present imports are only about a thousandth of all U.S. natural gas supplies, they represent a disturbing vulnerability: not so much in interrupted energy supply as in the damage which the LNG facilities—tankers, terminals, storage tanks, and trucks—could do to their neighbors.

LNG tankers

Fourteen LNG terminals are operable worldwide. Some are sited in major urban areas, including Boston Harbor and Tokyo Harbor. (Another, built in Staten Island, New York, has remained mothballed since its fatal 1973 fire, though in February 1980 it was proposed that it be completed and used as a peak-shaving LNG storage facility.) In 1980 the world fleet contained about eighty specially insulated, double-hulled tankers of several designs.[18] Their average LNG capacity was somewhat over fifty thousand cubic meters; the largest held one hundred sixty-five thousand cubic meters—"enough to cover a football field to a depth of one hundred thirty feet."[19] A modern standard LNG tanker of about one hundred twenty-five thousand cubic meters is about a thousand feet long, one hundred fifty feet abeam, and cruises at twenty knots. It is fueled partly by the gas (normally between an eighth and a quarter of one percent per day) that constantly boils off as warmth seeps in through the thermal insulation. LNG tankers carry unique safety equipment and are subject to special rules, usually involving escorts and traffic restrictions, when moving in harbor.

Once moored, a tanker discharges its LNG cargo in ten to fifteen hours. The rate of LNG flow ranges up to one hundred ninety cubic meters per minute—equivalent to about seventy-five thousand megawatts, or the rate at which about seventy giant power stations send out energy. The pipes used in this operation are exposed on the jetty, and lead to at least two tankers' worth of storage tanks, contained (with limitations noted below) by dikes. A typical LNG storage tank, of which most terminals have several, is one hundred forty feet high by one hundred ninety feet in diameter. It holds ninety-five thousand cubic meters of LNG with a heat content equivalent to a quarter of an hour's total energy consumption for the entire United States, or to the energy released by more than forty Hiroshima bombs.

LNG tankers have a fairly good safety record, but projections that it will continue are unpersuasive.[20] Even the limited reports available show some spills.[21] One LNG carrier has gone aground, and three failed certification owing to cracked insulation[22]—a loss of three hundred million dollars for Lloyds of London. Double-hulled LNG tankers—unlike single-hulled, pressurized tankers used for liquefied petroleum gas—are relatively resistant to damage by collision or light attack. They could, however, be pierced by certain weapons available to international terrorists, including limpet mines. Onboard sabotage would be relatively straightforward. Manipulation of onboard valves could in some circumstnaces rupture the LNG tanks from overpressure.[23] Alternatively, all LNG tanker designs allow internal access below the tanks, and if a tank were deliberately ruptured, ducts open at both ends and running the full length of the cargo area would help to distribute liquid.[24] Any such substantial spillage of LNG onto the steel hull would probably shatter it. The General Accounting Office warned that "Only an expert would recognize some types of explosive material as explosives. One LNG ship crew member, trained in the use of explosives, could cause simultaneous tank and hull damage . . . [which] might initiate an extremely hazardous series of events." (Ships carrying liquefied propane and butane, described below, are even more easily sabotaged.)[25]

LNG terminals and storage tanks

The enormous amounts of LNG and, if it leaks, of flammable vapors make LNG terminals and storage areas highly vulnerable. The world's largest LNG gasification plant, built at Arzew, Algeria at a cost of over four billion dollars, narrowly escaped destruction one night a few years ago when a gas cloud from a leaking tank drifted through it and dispersed without igniting. The Tokyo Harbor terminal has luckily escaped damage in several marine fires and explosions, including at least one major one from a liquid gas tanker. The Canvey Island LNG terminal downriver from central London recently had its third narrow escape from disaster when a two-hundred-thousand-ton oil tanker collided with a Shell oil jetty that protrudes into the river upstream of it at Coryton.[26] On that occasion, the gush of oil was stopped before it caused a major fire that could have spread downriver to the LNG plant. Years earlier, this very nearly happened when the Italian freighter *Monte Ulia* sheared off that same oil jetty, causing a melange of burning oil and trash barges to drift downriver. A change of wind, fortuitous currents, and desperate firefighters stopped the fire just short of the LNG terminal.[27] One known and one suspected incident of arson aboard a Texaco tanker have also recently also endangered the Canvey Island LNG terminal.[28] At a similarly exposed position in Boston Harbor lies the Everett Distrigas LNG terminal. It is near Logan Airport, and its ship channel lies under the flight path for at least one runway. In 1973, a Delta DC-9 on an instrument landing crashed into the seawall short of that runway. Had a gas tanker been in the channel at the time, the errant plane could have missed it by as little as a few feet.[29]

LNG terminals are vulnerable to natural disasters or sabotage. So are the far more numerous peak-shaving LNG plants. (In 1978 the U.S. had forty-five such plants, each storing more than twenty-three thousand cubic meters—three and a half times the total spill in the 1944 Cleveland disaster.) An audit of five LNG and LPG sites by the General Accounting Office, the independent watchdog agency of the U.S. government, found that at three of the sites, tanks had very small earthquake safety margins; "two of these three sites, including three large tanks, are located next to each other in Boston Harbor."[30]

In Japan, LNG tanks are normally built underground, where they are better protected from mishap and spills are more likely to be contained. In the United States, LNG tanks are normally built aboveground and surrounded by dikes. But General Accounting Office calculations and experiments suggest that most dikes meant to contain minor leaks will in fact fail to contain at least half of any sudden, major spill. Some thin dikes could fail altogether.[31] Abrupt, massive releases are indeed possible, as in Cleveland in 1944, because "if the inner tank alone fails for any reason, it is almost certain that the outer tank will rupture from the pressure and thermal shock."[32] It also appears that relatively small cracks or holes in a large, fully loaded LNG tank could cause it to fail catastrophically by instant propagation of the crack.[33]

This proneness to brittle fracture implies that relatively small disruptions by sabotage, earthquake, objects flung at the tank by high winds, etc. could well cause immediate, massive failure of an above-grade LNG tank. Certainly enough weaponry is available to pierce such a tank with ease. The General Accounting Office confirms that the equipment stolen from National Guard armories includes

small arms, automatic weapons, recoilless rifles, anti-tank weapons, mortars, rocket launchers, and demolition charges. A large number of commercially available publications provide detailed instructions on the home manufacture of explosives, incendiaries, bombs, shaped charges, and various other destructive devices. All the required material can be bought at hardware stores, drug stores, and agricultural supply outlets. . . . It is not unusual for international terrorist groups to be armed with the latest military versions of fully automatic firearms, anti-aircraft or anti-tank rockets, and sophisticated explosive devices.[34]

The General Accounting Office also found, however, that such sophistication would not be necessary to cause a major LNG release. Live firing tests "confirmed that the double-wall structure of [LNG] . . . tanks affords limited protection even against non-military small arms projectiles, and that devices used by terrorists could cause a catastrophic failure of the inner wall."[35] Some tanks allow access to the insulation space through ground-level manholes, or are built in the air on pilings, thus greatly increasing the effectiveness of explosive charges.

In 1978, none of the sixteen LNG facilities visited by the government auditors had an alarm system. Many had poor communications and back-up power sources. Guarding was minimal—often one unarmed watchman. Procedures were so lax that "Access to all of the facilities we visited would be easy, even for untrained personnel."[36]

LNG shipments by truck

More than seventy-five insulated, double-walled trucks deliver LNG from terminals to over one hundred satellite distribution tanks in thirty-one states,[37] chiefly in urban areas.[38] Some LNG may also be imported by truck from Montréal to New England.[39] More than ninety truckloads of LNG can leave Boston's Everett Distrigas terminal in a single day.[40] Though puncture-resistant, the trucks have points of weakness and a very high center of gravity, encouraging rollover accidents.[41] Each truck carries forty cubic meters of LNG, with a heat content equivalent to a quarter of a kiloton of TNT, or about a fiftieth of a Hiroshima yield.

Before LNG trucks are loaded, they are not inspected for bombs, nor are the drivers required to identify themselves properly.[42] Security is only marginally better than for potato trucks.[43] LNG trucks are easily sabotaged. The double walls "are relatively thin, . . . and can be penetrated by a fairly small improvised shaped charge. Properly placed, such a charge would cause LNG to discharge into the insulation space, causing the outer jacket to fracture and disintegrate."[44] Further, a truck could be hijacked from its fixed route for extortion or for malicious use of its cargo. It is "particularly dangerous, because [it allows] . . . the easy capture, delivery, and release of a large amount of explosive material any place the terrorist chooses."[45]

At least twelve LNG truck accidents had occurred in the United States by 1978. Two caused spills.[46] One driver blacked out after driving far more than the permitted number of hours and falsifying his logbook.[47] Luckily, both spills were in rural areas and neither ignited. Most LNG trucks leaving the Everett facility travel on the elevated Southeast Expressway, a hazardous road within a few blocks of the crowded Government Center area. In the first four months of 1977 alone, there were four serious accidents on the Southeast Expressway involving tractor-trailer trucks, one of which fell off onto the streets below.[48] An LNG truck would almost certainly break open in such an accident.[49] The entrances to the Sumner and Callahan Tunnels are about a hundred yards downhill from the Southeast Expressway.[50] The area is also laced with basements, sewers, and subway tunnels into which the invisible, odorless vapor would quickly spill.

"The forty cubic meters of LNG in one truck, vaporized and mixed with air into flammable proportions, are enough to fill more than one hundred and ten miles of six-foot sewer line, or sixteen miles of a sixteen-foot-diameter subway system."[51] That is enough, if the gas actually went that far and did not leak out partway, to fill up virtually the entire Boston subway system. An LNG spill into a sanitary sewer would vaporize with enough pressure to blow back methane through domestic traps into basements.[52] Even if buildings are not involved, sewer explosions can damage large areas. Early on 13 February 1981, for example, an hour before rush-hour traffic, miles of streets in Louisville, Kentucky were instantly torn up by an explosion of hexane vapor, which had apparently leaked into the sewer system from a factory a mile from the point of ignition.[53] Such explosions can do great damage with only a few cubic meters of flammable liquids,[54] and have been used for sabotage.[55]

Analogous hazards of liquefied petroleum gas (LPG)

Liquefied petroleum gas ("LP Gas")—the kind so commonly seen in metal bottles in rural areas and trailer parks—consists almost entirely of either propane or butane. These are by-products separated from natural gas at the wellhead or, on occasion, derived from other parts of the petroleum system. Unlike LNG, LPG is not regasified and piped to customers, but rather delivered directly as a liquid. This is possible because propane and butane liquefy at normal temperatures under modest pressure, or alternatively with moderate cooling at atmospheric pressure.[56] Because LPG is delivered to retail customers as a liquid, it requires many small shipments. Yet because those shipments make up about three percent of all U.S. energy supplies, vehicles carrying LPG are ubiquitous. It is a far older and better-known fuel than LNG, yet is less well studied and regulated—even though in some respects it may be even more hazardous than LNG.

About eighty-five percent of the LPG in bulk storage is kept under pressure in underground salt domes or caverns;[57] the rest is stored aboveground in tanks, often small ones. As these tanks are generally pressurized rather than chilled, they do not require insulation as LNG tanks do. Instead, they have only a single wall and hence are easily penetrated or destroyed. In 1978 the U.S. had twenty aboveground LPG storage facilities with capacities greater than twenty-three thousand cubic meters.

Most LPG is transported through some seventy thousand miles of high-pressure pipelines. The rest travels in sixteen thousand pressurized railcars (as opposed to LNG, which does not move by rail) and in twenty-five thousand pressurized tank trucks, whose squat cylindrical outlines are a daily sight on our highways. A large LPG truck, like its LNG counterpart, holds about forty cubic meters. But unlike an LNG truck, it is under pressure and is single-walled. It is therefore more vulnerable to breakage through accident or sabotage. LPG trucks are also more likely to explode in fires, both because they are uninsulated and because their cargo creates very high pressures by boiling when exposed to heat.

Many LPG truck accidents have occurred worldwide[58]—often through faulty repairs, delivery procedures, or valve operations.[59] A truck laden with thirty-four cubic meters of LPG, for example, overturned in 1973 on a mountain road above Lynchburg, Virginia, creating a fireball more than four hundred feet in diameter.[60] Four people were burned to death at the site, and three more at a distance by the radiant heat. In a far more destructive accident near Eagle Pass, Texas in 1975, a thirty-eight-cubic-meter LPG tank broke loose from its trailer. Two explosions blew the front of the tank about sixteen hundred feet and the rear (in three pieces) some eight hundred feet. Sixteen people were killed and thirty-five injured.[61] In Berlin, New York, in 1962, a twenty-eight-cubic-meter LPG semi-trailer jack-knifed, hit a tree, and split. The tank was propelled eighty feet back up the road, spewing gas as it went. After some minutes, the gas, having spread over about five acres, ignited and burned in a few seconds, engulfing ten buildings and causing ten deaths and seventeen injuries.[62] And in West St. Paul, Minnesota, a midnight LPG delivery fire in 1974 killed four people and demolished large sections of three apartment buildings.[63]

LPG railcars, each containing about one hundred fifteen cubic meters (equivalent to about an eighteenth of a Hiroshima yield),

> are involved in many of the ten thousand railroad accidents that occur in this country each year. There are often more than ten consecutive LPG cars on a train. Each car can form a ten-second fireball about [four hundred feet] . . . in radius.[64]

This can cause third- and second-degree burns out to nearly three thousand feet and to one mile respectively.[65] The range can be even larger. In 1973, a slightly oversized railcar of LPG developed a small leak while being unloaded. The ensuing small fire burst the tank after nineteen minutes, causing a fireball nearly a thousand feet in diameter. Thirteen people were killed. Many of the ninety-five people injured were standing along a highway a thousand feet from the track.[66]

The General Accounting Office's safety study of both LPG and LNG notes a further danger of LPG tankers and railcars:

> If vapors from one LPG car ignite, the fire may rupture an unpunctured car in a "Boiling Liquid Expanding Vapor Explosion," or BLEVE [where sudden depressurization rapidly boils and expels the LPG as an aerosol-vapor-air mixture]. Each fire and explosion contributes to the heating and weakening of neighboring cars and makes additional explosions more likely. A BLEVE can rocket a forty-five-thousand-pound steel section of a tank for a quarter of a mile. This is what happened in a derailment near Oneonta, New York, in 1974. LPG vapor from a crushed LPG car quickly ignited and formed a fireball. Fire fighters attempting to cool down several other LPG cars were caught in a subsequent explosion; fifty-four were injured. . . . In a 1974 railyard accident near

Decatur, Illinois, an LPG railcar was punctured; the resulting cloud did not ignite immediately, but spread and then exploded over an area one-half by three-quarters of a mile. [The blast was felt forty-five miles away;[67] such unconfined vapor-air explosions are similar to those caused by military fuel-air bombs, some of which use propane.] There were seven deaths, three hundred forty-nine injuries, and twenty-four million dollars in damage [including blast damage out to two and a half miles]. Litter and debris . . . covered twenty blocks of the city. . . . LPG railcars travel through densely populated areas of cities, even cities which prohibited LPG storage.[68]

LPG trains could easily be derailed at any desired point: "youth gangs frequently place obstacles on tracks which delay freight trains in New York City just to harass the trainmen,"[69] and similarly in Los Angeles.[70] Sabotage causing serious damage to trains has occurred across the U.S.,[71] including trains carrying LPG (which fortunately did not leak)[72] and chlorine (whose leakage in a Florida derailment killed eight people and injured nearly a hundred).[73]

LPG railcars are only a tenth as numerous as tankers carrying other hazardous cargoes, and are thus likely to occur in the same trains with chlorine, oil, industrial chemicals, and so forth. Such cargoes and LPG can endanger each other. Railcars spend a good deal of time sitting in switchyards where they are subject to tampering and fires. Ammunition trains have blown up in switchyards. A few years ago, a chemical tank car being shunted in Washington State exploded with the force of several World War II blockbusters. A forty-hour fire in a railcar of toxic ethylene oxide recently shut the Port of Newark and curtailed flights at Newark International Airport for fear of an explosion that could hurl shrapnel for a mile.[74] Far less would be enough to breach an LPG railcar. Its steel wall is only five-eighths of an inch thick, and "can be easily cut with pocket size explosive devices [or by] many other weapons commonly used by terrorists. . . ."[75] A small leak can be dangerous because LPG vapor is heavier than air even when it warms up (unlike LNG vapor, which is heavier than air only so long as it remains chilled). LPG vapor can therefore flow for long distances along the ground or in sewers or tunnels. When a mixture of between about two and nine percent LPG vapor in air reaches a small spark, it will ignite or explode.

LPG terminals, as well as shipments by road and rail, penetrate the most vulnerable parts of our industrial system. The General Accounting Office has published an aerial photograph of a major LPG receiving terminal near Los Angeles Harbor.[76] Its propane storage tanks, a stone's throw from the Palos Verdes earthquake fault, are surrounded on one side by a large U.S. Navy fuel depot and by a tank farm, and on the other side by a dense residential area that runs for miles. All are within the range of an LPG conflagration. Marine LPG tankers add to the hazard and can endanger the terminal itself. In 1974, the LPG tanker *Yuyo Maru* collided and burned in Tokyo Bay with the loss of thirty-three crew. In 1968, the small Swedish LPG tanker *Claude*, having collided with a freighter in Southampton water, was abandoned by her crew and shortly thereafter by her pilot (who supposed the crew must know what was good for them). *Claude* drifted under reverse power, went aground, was towed to a refinery, and started to have a chartered vessel pump off her cargo. But when one hose sprang a leak, *Claude* was again precipitately abandoned by that vessel, rupturing all the hoses and pipelines.[77] It was only luck and the courage of a few remaining crewmen that got the valves shut before the gas cloud ignited, for it could well have destroyed the refinery too.

In 1977, a fifty-thousand-cubic-meter refrigerated propane tank in Qatar, designed by Shell International on a pattern similar to that of tanks in the Los Angeles terminal, suddenly collapsed, sending liquid propane over the dike. The resulting explosion destroyed the LPG facility surrounding the tank. In France, eleven people died and seventy were injured when vapor from a leaking butane tank was ignited by a truck passing more than five hundred feet away, leading to the explosion of eight butane and propane tanks.[78] In a little-noted incident on 30 January 1981, an FB-111 aircraft crashed a quarter-mile from the edge of the tank farm in the second largest LPG/LNG facility in New England (in Newington, New Hampshire). The plant is about two miles from the center of Portsmouth (population about twenty-seven thousand), two and a half miles from a nuclear submarine base, and three-quarters of a mile from Pease Air Force Base with its huge fuel depot. For comparison, the direct fireball radiation alone from the burning of thousands of cubic meters of LPG can start fires and cause third-degree burns at ranges of a mile or more.[79]

The risk from liquefied energy gases (LEG)

In practical effect, the most densely industrialized and populated areas in America have potential bombs in their midst, capable of causing disastrous explosions and firestorms without warning. As the General Accounting Office summarized, describing both LNG and LPG by the generic term "liquefied energy gases" (LEG):

Successful sabotage of an LEG facility in an urban area could cause a catastrophe. We found that security precautions and physical barriers at LEG facilities are generally not adequate to deter even an untrained saboteur. None of the LEG storage areas we examined are impervious to sabotage, and most are highly vulnerable.[80]

Moreover,

In many facilities, by manipulating the equipment, it is possible to spill a large amount of [LEG] . . . outside the diked area through the draw-off lines. LEG storage facilities in cities are often adjacent to sites that store very large quantities of other hazardous substances, including other volatile liquids. Thus, a single cause might simultaneously destroy many tanks, or a spill at one facility might cause further failures at adjacent facilities.[81]

These might include ports, refineries, tank farms, or power stations. For example, although the Cove Point, Maryland LNG terminal is not near a city, it is five miles upwind—well within plume range—of the Calvert Cliffs nuclear power plant, which probably could not withstand being enveloped in a fireball.

The General Accounting Office report concluded:

> Nuclear power plants are built to higher standards than any other type of energy installation, much higher than those for LEG installations. Nevertheless, they are never located in densely populated areas. We believe that new large LEG facilities also should not be located in densely populated areas.[82]

LNG shipments and facilities likewise perforate America's industrial heartland. Even the most sensitive "chokepoints" are put at risk. In February 1977, for example, LNG was being trucked along the Staten Island Expressway and across the Verrazano Narrows and Goethals Bridges.[83] Seven Mile Bridge, the only land access to the lower Florida Keys, was heavily damaged by a recent propane-truck explosion,[84] which could as well have occurred on any urban bridge in America. It is apparently common for LNG shipments to pass near major oil, gas, and nuclear facilities, few if any of which could withstand envelopment in a burning gas cloud. While many local authorities would like to restrict such shipments before a catastrophe, the regulation of such interstate commerce is federally preempted; and so far, despite the devastating criticisms by the General Accounting Office, the dozen or so responsible federal agencies have done little of substance to improve safety.

Perhaps additional LNG imports, brought by eighty-plus large tankers into a half-dozen U.S. terminals, will never happen as enthusiasts once hoped, if only for the economic reasons alluded to earlier. But unless tackled directly, the clear and present dangers from present LNG and—on a far greater scale—LPG operations will persist. Later chapters will show that all the energy now supplied by LNG and LPG can be replaced by much cheaper sources which do not compromise national security.

Chapter Nine
Oil and Gas

Oil, gas, and natural gas liquids, which together supply nearly three-quarters of America's total primary energy, are transported, processed, stored, delivered, and marketed by an extraordinarily complex technical system. A veteran observer of that system noted in a classic study that

> The system is delicately balanced and extremely vulnerable and can be readily interrupted or damaged by natural disasters, by sabotage, or by enemy attack. An attack concentrated on the system, or even on certain segments or fragments of it, could bring industrial activity and transportation to a standstill.[1]

A followup study of the natural gas system alone identified an ominous trend:

> . . . as the industry becomes more efficient, handling larger volumes of gas and products, as flow lines extend farther seaward linking more deep water platforms, [the] . . . frailty of the system is increasing. There are critical locations and junction points that concentrate facilities and large gas volumes into centers which are easy targets. . . . Unfortunately, there appears to be a trend away from flexibility of the system. . . . The Icarian nature of expansion of the industry increases vulnerability daily.[2]

For these reasons, "international terrorism, 'hit' squads and saboteurs are matters of immediate and deepening concern to the petroleum industry," involving "a whole spectrum of targets—refineries, pipelines, tankers, drilling rigs, offshore production platforms, storage tanks and people."[3]

The links between the oil and gas industry and other equally vulnerable systems are intricate, pervasive, and increasing.

> Our present economy is so finely tuned, because of the need to effect as much efficiency as possible, that an interdependence has been developed between transportation, manufacturing, electric power generation and the petroleum and natural gas industry, [so] that one can hardly exist without the other. Each

100

depends on and each serves the other. A widespread failure of one industry is certain to seriously affect another. The natural gas industry cannot function without pipe, electric motors, pumps, chemicals and a host of other items, nor can many manufacturing industries exist without the products of the gas system or that of the closely related petroleum system.[4]

The natural gas industry also provides the feedstock from which is made "all or most of the rubber, plastics, fertilizer, paint, industrial solvents, medicines and many other items used daily in the United States. A loss of this [feedstock] . . . would be devastating in time of a national emergency."[5] (Sixty percent of our nation's petrochemical capacity is clustered on the Texas Gulf Coast.)[6] The functioning of the oil and gas industries in turn depends on internal linkages: "the links between segments could be the major frailty."[7]

Oil and gas fields and shipping facilities

The vulnerability of the oil and gas system begins (exploration aside) at the wellhead and in the reservoir. These are exceedingly valuable assets. The oil reserves in the Persian Gulf region, as of October 1980, were worth, at a modest thirty-five dollars per barrel, some thirteen trillion dollars,[8] or more than one Gross World Product-year. Nearly half those reserves lie in Saudi Arabia. The Gulf's estimated ultimately recoverable resources of oil are two or three times as large:[9] at least half the total of all oil that will ever be found in the world. There are few more concentrated assets anywhere. There is no economic motive to extract the oil quickly. A barrel lifted at the beginning of 1974 and sold for eleven dollars would by 1980 have been worth about eighteen dollars if invested in U.S. Treasury bonds, while the same barrel left in the ground could by 1980 have been sold for at least thirty-two dollars.[10] The proprietors of the oil have so far been earning, in this sense, a negative return on their liftings—that is, oil appreciates faster in the ground than in a Swiss bank. But the oil happens to be in the Gulf rather than in Switzerland, and in that unstable region, the Gulf governments understandably worry about whether they will be around to enjoy the future revenues.

The cultural, political, and military volatility of the Gulf[11]—a concern to American military planners since at least 1947—needs no emphasis here. Arab arms orders during 1978–81 totalled about thirty-five billion dollars—more than seventy years' worth of the entire United Nations budget. Even friendly, relatively stable exporters of oil to the U.S. cannot be considered entirely reliable: Canada's provincial/federal tug-of-war in 1980–81, for example, curtailed many Albertan oil and syncrude activities, and price agreements with Mexico do not always seem completely stable.

But present U.S. oil imports are sadly lacking even in the safety of diversity. Nearly a third of the non-Communist world's oil supply comes from the Gulf, and about a third of that comes from the highly congested area at the head of the Gulf.[12] "The sudden loss of Persian Gulf oil for a year," warns former State Department official Joseph Nye, "could stagger the world's economy, disrupt it, devastate it, like no event since the Great Depression of the 1930s."[13]

Within major oil-exporting countries, too, there is astonishing physical concentration. *One* Saudi oilfield, Ghawar, lifts five million barrels per day—more than two Kuwaits, or Venezuela plus Nigeria, or any other *country* except the United States and the Soviet Union. Saudi Arabia lifts about seven to ten million barrels per day from a mere seven hundred wells, whereas the U.S., much further along in its depletion cycle, lifts just over ten million barrels per day (including natural gas liquids) from some six hundred thousand wells.[14] The delivery systems for that concentrated gush of Mideast oil tend to be tightly clustered in groups, linked by some seven thousand miles of exposed pipelines. "The oil wells themselves are obvious targets[;] so are the collecting systems, which pump oil through pipes from the fields to local terminal facilities. [These] . . . , containing gas-separation plants, local refineries, storage tanks, and loading facilities, could also be potential targets. And the pipelines and tankers carrying oil to destinations beyond the Gulf are no less vulnerable."[15] For precisely this reason, military force, even if it succeeded in capturing the oilfields, could not keep them running in the face of a locally based program of sabotage.[16] Just the five hundred-odd miles of pipelines in eastern Saudi Arabia carry about a sixth of the non-Communist world's oil supply. And all the main Gulf oil ports, together with most of the Saudi and United Arab Emirates oilfields, "are within nine hundred miles (a ninety-minute subsonic flight) of the Soviet Union."[17]

Saudi Arabia and the Persian Gulf

These vulnerabilities come to a sharp focus in Saudi Arabia.[18] It provides a quarter of U.S. oil imports (that is, a twelfth of total U.S. oil supplies) from the world's largest oil reserves—at the end of 1980, some one hundred sixty-eight billion barrels. The marine terminals at Ras Tanura and at Ju'aymah handle eighty-five percent of Saudi oil exports. A few minutes' flight inland lie the key facilities in the Master Gas System, which when completed will provide three billion cubic feet of natural gas (and allied liquids) per day. Unfortunately, Ras Tanura and Ju'aymah happen to "lie at precisely the closest geographic point to [Saudi Arabia's] principal military threat, the Iranian air bases at Bushehr and Shiraz"—at most sixteen minutes' flying time away.[19] The Saudis have given Iraqi aircraft safe haven during the recent war with Iran, and, with Kuwait and the United Arab Emirates, have bankrolled Iraq's war effort to the tune of thirty-two billion dollars[20]. The Saudis therefore fear an Iranian attack, whether for revenge or to improve morale at home. They note that leading Iranian mullahs have called for the assassination of King Khalid; that Iran was implicated in the attempted coup in Bahrain in January 1982; that after two warning attacks, Iranian jets on 1 October 1981 set ablaze a major Kuwaiti oil installation at Umm Aysli[21]; and that Iran has fourteen hundred American air-to-ground missiles, together with a fleet of strike aircraft to deliver them (of which perhaps fifteen are still operable).

The delivery of five E–3A Advanced Warning and Control System (AWACS) radar aircraft to Saudi Arabia will make possible sufficient warning of an Iranian attack for Saudi interceptors to make at least one short-range pass and to alert onshore gun and missile defences—providing the Saudis were expecting the attack. (Otherwise they would probably not have an AWACS airborne.)[22] But an attack by small surface vessels, submarines, or frogmen, or even by missile-carrying helicopters (which Iran also has), would be invisible to AWACS, whose sophisticated radar can detect airborne targets only if they move faster than eighty knots.[23] There are several other ways, too, in which Iran could deceive AWACS surveillance.[24] The normal quick-reaction Saudi air cover is "rather 'thin' ";[25] and "even a near miss at Ras Tanura could ignite successive oil tank explosions and damage the basic pumping infrastructure."[26] (Certain key components, without which the Ras Tanura terminal cannot operate, are so unique and hard to make that they could take up to three years to replace.) Sabotage from within is also a concern: "there has been labor and political dissidence in the Eastern Provinces," which contain at least a quarter of a million Shi'ite Moslems, "many of whom are dissatisfied with the [Saudi] regime and have hands-on experience with the oil production equipment and its vulnerabilities"[27]—as was illustrated by damage to "a crude-oil pumping installation at or near Ras Tanura" in 1979.[28]

It is often forgotten that Libya's leverage to begin the oil spiral came from the Suez Canal closure and destruction of a pipeline.[29] In 1977, a fire crippled the oil gathering center at Abqaiq, at the north end of Saudi Arabia's supergiant Ghawar field, cutting off oil exports by the Arab-American Oil Company (ARAMCO) and sending tremors around the world. (Fortunately, temporary repairs bypassed the damage in ten days.) The fire was officially called an accident, but some Saudis think it was an effort by guerrillas, "probably guided by Iraq,"[30] to break Saudi moderation on oil prices,[31] and it was reportedly foreseen in warnings which the Saudi government did not take seriously.[32] "In early 1978 there were reports that Iraq was training frogmen and desert demolition squads, and that Palestinian terrorists had been found on tankers."[33] There have been at least two intelligence alerts,[34] and in early July 1979 a broad hint by Yasser Arafat[35] and Sheikh Yamani,[36] that terrorists might rocket or hijack a supertanker in the twenty-three-mile-wide Strait of Hormuz. In 1979, shortly after two tankers in the Persian Gulf caught fire, security concerns prompted Lloyds of London to propose higher maritime insurance rates for the Gulf.[37]

Outright attacks on Gulf oil facilities used to be fairly rare. When Arab guerrillas cut the Iraq-Haifa oil pipeline in 1936, it was real news.[38] But gradually the psychological barriers against such attacks have eroded to the point where oil plants are becoming almost a standard target for the region's simmering hostilities. Consider a few examples, besides those noted above:

• The South Yemeni Air Force attacked Saudi installations at Sharurah in 1973.[39]

• TAP–Line, a thirty-inch line able to carry a half-million barrels per day for over a thousand miles, has pumped a quarter of all ARAMCO's oil output since it was opened in 1950.[40] But its route from Dharan on the Gulf (where it is fed by the Ghawar and other Saudi oilfields) takes it via the Golan area of Syria to the Zerqa refinery in Jordan and the Zahrani terminal near Sidon in southern Lebanon. All these areas are volatile. The line was repeatedly attacked both by saboteurs and during the Arab-Israeli wars. Its Golan sector was blown up in two places in 1968 and 1969:[41] in May 1969, for example, the Popular Front for the Liberation of Palestine put it out of action for over a hundred days.[42] It was shut at intervals through the 1970s.[43] A thirty-mile stretch of it is currently controlled and patrolled by Israel, whose troops have forestalled several more sabotage missions.[44]

• In July 1981, Israeli damage to a pipeline and partial destruction of the Zahrani refinery (which provides about half of Lebanon's oil needs) led to severe fuel and power shortages in Lebanon.[45]

• Even before the 1980 outbreak of open warfare between Iran and Iraq, Iranian oil facilities had suffered severe damage from sabotage. Poor labor relations, repression of the Arab minority in Khuzistan, and provocation of Iraq had led to frequent bombings of highly vulnerable pipelines[46] and pumping stations,[47] including the destruction of at least fourteen pipelines within three days.[48]

• Similar sabotage, attributed to Shi'ite sympathizers, has occurred in Iraq, including damage to an oil gathering station and a gas liquefaction plant.[49]

• The damage extended to third countries: a third of Iraq's oil exports were halted by sabotage to a Syrian pipeline and "unexplained 'electrical problems'" with a pipeline in Turkey.[50] Similar incidents persist,[51] including highly selective rocket attacks on key pumps.[52]

• Following "fires and explosions, officially called accidents," that "disrupted oil fields in Saudi Arabia and Qatar's natural gas industry," two fires in Sinai oilfields, and the establishment of a "Gulf Battlefield Unit" by the Popular Front for the Liberation of Palestine, seven Arab states and Iran established in 1975 a joint intelligence program to protect their oil and gas facilities. By 1981 a more selective "Gulf Cooperation Council" of Saudi allies was installing "a comprehensive system of electronic surveillance for the oil fields" and was discussing joint air defense systems and a possible Persian Gulf armaments industry.[53]

• As 1982 began, a Lebanese oil tanker was rocketed while loading in Tripoli. The next day, the pipeline carrying Iraqi crude to Tripoli, just reopened after a four-year interruption, was blown up by another rocket attack, shutting it down again and causing a refinery fire.[54] Four days later, the six-hundred-twenty-five-mile pipeline carrying Iraqi oil to Turkey's Mediterranean coast was blown up forty-two miles inside the Turkish border.[55]

Once laden, tankers must run a gauntlet of narrow sealanes where free passage is not always guaranteed. (Egypt, for example, blockaded the Bab-el-Mandeb strait, at the southern end of the Red Sea, in 1973.) About a fourth of the non-Communist world's oil must pass through the Strait of Hormuz. The Panama Canal is less heavily used but very easily blocked. The Straits of Malacca and of Singapore and the Cape of Good Hope are among the other strategic passages. Securing these points, and indeed the shipping lanes on the high seas, is a formidable problem of naval strategy, though one beyond the scope of this book. Even given safe passage, the vulnerability of the huge, lumbering Very Large Crude Carriers needs little emphasis, as they manage now and then to do themselves in without assistance.[56] Oil tankers of various sizes have lately blown up or sunk themselves at a steeply increasing rate—averaging three per month in 1980.[57] They are so slow and so sparsely crewed (about twenty for a one-hundred-thousand-tonner) that during eight months in 1981, twenty-one laden supertankers were boarded at sea or in harbor near Singapore, and their crews robbed of minor valuables, by medieval-style pirates in small native boats.[58] It is therefore not surprising that at the end of 1981 a sizable oil tanker, complete with cargo, was actually hijacked in the Strait of Malacca.

Offshore platforms

Offshore oil facilities are often proposed in the United States and elsewhere as a replacement for oil from the Persian Gulf. But even platforms in a country's own territorial waters are highly vulnerable: sitting ducks laden with highly flammable fuels under pressure.[59] The British Government's five-ship, four-plane task force to patrol North Sea platforms,[60] and a group of commandos trained to protect them,[61] are likely to prove ineffectual. Each platform has a "safety zone" of about sixteen hundred feet, but trawlers have already sailed illegally within a hundred feet because the fishing is richer there.[62] There is nothing to stop them. The platforms are so vulnerable to mere collisions that the Norwegian Government first suspected sabotage (perhaps by a submarine) when a North Sea rig capsized in 1980 with the loss of one hundred twenty-three crew. (The collapse turned out to have been caused by an improperly cut hole in one of the five supporting posts.[63]) In 1980, a gasoline tanker collided with an oil rig in the Gulf of Mexico and burst into flames.[64] Near misses abound.

A single platform may cost upwards of fifty million dollars and carry over forty wells.[65] Junctions of offshore gathering lines frequently bring oil flows of fifty to a hundred thousand barrels a day, or more, into a single, "totally unprotected" line, often in shallow water or in swampy areas where heavy equipment, whether floating or land-based, cannot operate.[66] The Scottish "Tartan Army" demonstrated the vulnerability of offshore platforms' umbilical cord to the mainland when they twice bombed the pipeline which carries North Sea oil one hundred thirty miles to the Grangemouth refinery.[67] (Fortunately, they did not know enough about explosives to cut the line.)

In northern waters, such as the Beaufort Sea and the North Sea, access to platforms for protection and repair may be simply impossible for long periods. Winter waves in the North Sea, for example, average seven feet half the time and exceed fifteen feet a fifth of the time. Winter storms bring hundred-foot waves and hundred-mile-an-hour gusts.[68] In current practice, platforms in and along the Gulf of Mexico must be shut in and deserted during severe storms, as offshore platforms off New England and in the Arctic would surely have to be. This interrupts the filling of natural gas storage, "depended upon more each year for peak load cushions," and might lead to widespread shortages if a late hurricane in the Gulf, for example, coincided with an early cold spell in gas-heated areas.[69]

As of mid-1981 the United States was getting nearly a sixth of its domestic oil from offshore. Yet the federal government had no contingency plans to protect offshore platforms from attack—even in the Gulf of Mexico, where the greatest resources of the oil and gas industry are near at hand to serve both onshore facilities and the more than three thousand platforms.[70] This is a matter of considerable anxiety to the oil industry. The Coast Guard in New Orleans has local plans which could, in good weather, bring a specially equipped vessel to a threatened platform—in eight hours.[71] (Any terrorists who could not destroy a platform in eight minutes would be quite incompetent.) Yet a fire on a platform "is disastrous to the company owning [it] . . . and, if several were started, great economic stress could be placed on the companies involved. These impressive structures appear to be open invitations to terrorists."[72] More than three simultaneous platform fires "would completely overwhelm available control and remedial facilities on the Gulf Coast"—facilities which could all be bottled up by sinking a small barge.[73] Nor is an actual attack on a platform the only way to disrupt its operations. Three North Sea gas platforms and a drill rig have been temporarily shut down by mere hoax telephone threats.[74] Similar threats have been made since May 1981 against drilling rigs in the Santa Barbara Channel.[75]

Primary oil storage

The average barrel of oil takes about three months to get from the well-head to a final American user.[76] Along the way are oil inventories "in the pipeline"—aboard ships, in various tanks, and in pipelines themselves. About three and a third billion barrels of oil worldwide, or nearly two months' world oil use, represent an "absolute minimum unusable quantity" needed to fill pipelines and otherwise keep distribution systems flowing. An additional five hundred million barrels are normally held in stockpiles requiring a political decision for their release. Another eight hundred million barrels are in ships at sea. Thus only stocks which exceed about forty-six hundred million barrels worldwide "can be considered commercially usable inventory."[77] There are normally excess stocks above this level, providing modest "stretch" in the world oil system. But with carrying charges of about six hundred dollars per hour for each million barrels, nobody seems eager to hold "unnecessary" stocks.

In the United States, the minimum operating level (a sort of basal metabolism for the oil industry) is estimated by the National Petroleum Council to be about an eighth of a billion barrels at "primary level": that is, at refineries, major bulk terminals, and pipelines. That sounds like a lot of oil, but in fact it represents only a week's national consumption. The national primary stocks in late 1981, in the middle of an oil glut, were only about eleven days' demand. Of course the total capacity for storing oil at all levels, including retail distribution, is considerably larger. In mid-1981 it was estimated at one billion three hundred million barrels.[78] But even when that storage is completely full, only part of it actually represents usable slack. Thus the oil system is rather "tightly coupled," without large reserves of storage to draw upon in an interruption. This money-saving (but vulnerability-increasing) practice is most striking in the case of refineries, which normally keep only a three to five days' supply on hand[79] and thus wither rapidly if their crude supply is interrupted.

Oil stockpiles represent a valuable, concentrated, flammable target for terrorists. In mid-December 1978, Black nationalists using rockets and tracer bullets burned out a forty-acre oil storage depot outside Salisbury, Rhodesia. The fire destroyed half the complex and nearly half a million barrels of products which the embargoed Smith regime had painstakingly accumulated from Iran and from synthetic oil plants in South Africa. The monetary cost alone, about twenty million dollars, increased the projected national budget deficit by eighteen percent.[80] Though a 1969 attack on a well-prepared Haifa refinery caused relatively little damage,[81] Palestinian Black September terrorists bombed Dutch and German oil tanks in February 1972.[82] Another Palestinian/Red Brigades attack crippled the refinery at Trieste, Italy, burning out four huge storage tanks, in 1972.[83] On 17 July 1981, guerrillas using machine guns and bazookas narrowly failed to blow up oil and gas installations (mainly storage tanks) providing more than half the supplies to Santiago, Chile.[84]

Even the U.S. is not immune: a St. Paul, Minnesota oil tank farm was bombed in 1970,[85] and in 1975, two five-thousand-barrel oil storage tanks in California were bombed with crude high explosives (luckily, the tank nearest the bomb contained only water).[86] For reasons not immediately determined, a tank containing one hundred fifty thousand barrels of jet fuel exploded at a U.S. base near Yokohama, Japan in 1981, causing a huge four-hour fire that forced the evacuation of twenty-eight hundred residents.[87] And six American Nazis were tried for conspiring in 1980 to bomb, among other targets, a gasoline tank farm and a natural gas pipeline in North Carolina.[88]

The Strategic Petroleum Reserve is a federal project for storing crude oil in Gulf Coast salt domes to cushion an interruption of oil imports.[89] It appears to be the only major energy project in the United States which has, from the beginning, paid attention to vulnerability. Siting, stocking of spare parts, and other security measures have been designed with some attention to minimizing the possible damage from an attack. (The project managers did this on their own initiative, not because the responsible government agencies told them to.) Most of the installations, and of course the oil reservoirs themselves, are underground, though there are critical surface installations.

The Reserve is in essence a homegrown, short-lived Persian Gulf. It can supply, for some months until it runs out, a large flow of crude oil—from essentially one place. (Its several sites are relatively close together.) This process requires that not just the Reserve itself but also a farflung network of pipelines, refineries, storage tanks, and distribution systems be functioning normally: otherwise the oil cannot be processed and delivered across the country as intended. For this reason, many oil-industry experts

were dismayed that the United States would invest as its one strategic option for safeguarding this nation [in one set of facilities clustered on the Gulf coast] . . . as opposed to the options that have been taken by our allies in Japan and [in] Europe. These countries have taken a much more dispersed approach to storage . . . of conventional petroleum fuels, ranging from crude oil to refined products.[90]

This approach—spotting relatively small amounts of storage of diverse petroleum products at many sites near the final customers—greatly reduces emergency dependence on pipelines, refineries, and other vulnerable "upstream" facilities which, as will be shown, are at least as vulnerable as a centralized storage depot.

Oil refineries

Oil refineries are typically the most vulnerable, capital-intensive, and indispensible element of the oil system downstream of the wellhead. Since most devices which burn oil are designed to use specific refined products, not crude oil itself, it is not possible to substitute other modes for refining as it is for oil delivery. The refining industry tended to grow up near the oilfields and the major markets. Since three-fourths of domestic oil is lifted in only four states—Texas, Louisiana, Alaska, and California[91]—it is understandable that over half the refinery capacity is concentrated in Texas (with twenty-seven percent in 1978), Louisiana, and California. Including Illinois, Pennsylvania, and New Jersey would account for more than sixty-nine percent of the 1978 national total.[92] Of nearly three hundred major refineries, there were twenty-two sites which each had at least one percent of national capacity, the largest having over three and a half percent. Many of these depend on shared pipelines, ports, and repair facilities.

Local concentrations of refinery capacity and allied plants are remarkably heavy. For example, East Baton Rouge Parish, Louisiana, contains one of the largest U.S. oil refineries (an Exxon unit handling half a million barrels per day, just smaller than the giant Baytown, Texas plant). The same parish contains many petrochemical plants, Kaiser Aluminum, docks, river terminals, and two major river bridges. Through the same area run the Plantation and Colonial pipelines, carrying most of the East Coast's and much of the South's refined products.[93] Thus a nuclear bomb on New Orleans could simultaneously kill most of its inhabitants (including many with unique technical skills), flood the city, destroy control centers for offshore oil and gas operations, destroy many petroleum company headquarters, stop traffic both across and on the Mississippi River (isolating petroleum workers from their homes or plants, depending on the time of day), damage a shipyard and refineries, and destroy port facilities. The Office of Technology Assessment, working with the Defense Civil Preparedness Agency, found that destruction of the seventy-seven largest U.S. oil refineries would eliminate two-thirds of U.S. refining capacity and "shatter the American economy"[94]—as well as destroying, in the assumed eighty-warhead nuclear attack, three to five million lives and many ports, petrochemical plants, and other heavy industrial facilities.

It does not take a one-megaton warhead, however, to destoy a refinery.

A handful of explosives, or sometimes just a wrench or the turning of a valve, will do as well. Refineries are congested with hot, pressurized, highly flammable, and often explosive hydrocarbons. "There are over two hundred sources of fire in an average refinery, so uncontained gases have little trouble finding an ignition source."[95] Heavy pressure vessels may explode if shocked.

> Loosened flange bolts in a hydrogen line, moving a gas that burns with a colorless flame and which even in a small mass, auto-detonates at relatively low temperature, could . . . completely destroy vital segments of a refining process. A broken valve bonnet in an iso-butane line or an overflowing hot oil tank has been known to cause millions of dollars damage.[96]

Some parts of the refinery are essential if it is to work at all; so if a crucial third of the plant is destroyed, output may be reduced to zero, not merely by a third.[97] Refineries involve such complex plumbing and equipment, often custom-made, that repairs are slow and difficult: reconstruction of substantial equipment can take months or years.[98] Thus a simple act of alleged sabotage to a coking unit in a TOSCO Corporation refinery in California, on the first day of a strike, did many millions of dollars' damage and shut down the whole refinery for more than three months. "Physical disaster," reported the company's president, "was narrowly averted" by luck and by the prompt action of supervisory staff.[99]

An authoritative survey lists recent trends which have tended to make refineries more vulnerable:[100]

• the push to enlarge plants within the same boundaries, so increasing congestion;
• localization of capacity, especially in areas "having frequent hurricanes, tornadoes, floods and earthquakes, and by or near tide water";
• making more light products, which require the use of highly explosive hydrogen and make process control more critical and equipment "more sensitive to possible detonations";
• widespread dependence on purchased electricity, even for vital functions;
• reliance on centralized, hard-to-repair computers;
• reduction of the work force, leaving fewer skilled people (or people of any description) on site to cope with emergencies;
• reduced spare parts inventories;[101]
• relatively flimsy construction, especially in control and switchgear houses, cooling equipment, and exposed piping and cables;
• larger storage tanks and supertankers; and
• bigger terminals with higher unloading rates, "resulting in a concentra-

tion of highly combustible products and crude supply into a relatively small area."

To this list might be added a recent structural change in the refining business. The 1980–82 slump in oil demand, and the prospect that it will be permanent because people are using oil more efficiently, has caused an unprecedented rate of permanent closure of surplus refineries,[102] mostly relatively small and dispersed ones near local markets. As a result, reliance on the largest, most centralized, most geographically clustered refineries has increased. The surviving refineries, then, tend to be the largest and newest—precisely those that embody the trends listed above. A more volatile set of trends is hard to imagine, even in the absence of deliberate attacks to exploit these weaknesses.

Nor is refinery sabotage a mere fantasy. Many attacks have occurred in other countries; the world's largest refinery—at Abadan in Iran—has been a key target for Iraqi attack since 1980. Even in the U.S., such incidents are not unknown. In 1970, for example, the "United Socialist Revolutionary Front" caused "millions of dollars" in damage to four units of the Humble refinery in Linden, New Jersey.[103] The national disruption from refinery outages could be maximized by careful selection of the targets, since U.S. refinery flexibility is unusually low.[104] Flexibility could be improved through overcapacity. In fact, this is currently the case—in March 1982, refinery utilization was at an all-time low of about sixty-three percent.[105] But the cost of that inadvertent spare capacity is far higher than the industry would ever incur intentionally.

In the coming decade, too, as the oil-exporting countries sell more of their oil as refined products rather than as crude,[106] their market power will increase and importers' flexibility will decrease. The remaining crude oil will become a more powerful bargaining chip as importers strive to find feedstock for their costly refineries. And of course many new export refineries comparable to Abadan will fatten the list of tempting targets in the Mideast.

Natural gas processing plants

Natural gas processing plants, analogous to (though simpler than) oil refineries, are a similar point of weakness. Some have already been sabotaged. The Black September group blew up two such plants in Rotterdam in 1971.[107] In May 1981, fifty heavily armed rightists also took over, and threatened to blow up, a remote Bolivian gas processing plant owned by Occidental Petroleum Company, but after several days' negotiations they left for Paraguay.[108]

Unlike crude oil refining, gas processing is not an absolutely vital step in the short term, and can be temporarily bypassed.[109] But this cannot be long continued, for three reasons. First, dissolved natural gas liquids can cause transmission problems, and if not extracted, can remain in gas delivered to final users: "[T]he sudden onrush of 'gasoline' out of gas burners could be very dangerous."[110] Second, unextracted water could "freeze and cause considerable damage at low spots in the line,"[111] and makes traces of hydrogen sulfide or carbon dioxide highly corrosive to pipelines.[112] Third, unprocessed gas is more hazardous: it often contains highly toxic hydrogen sulfide, and the presence of even small amounts of higher hydrocarbons having low flashpoints will vastly extend the flammable and explosive limits of gas-air mixtures. Some common impurities are so flammable that the mixture can be ignited by a "static spark or one made by imbedded sand in a person's shoe sole striking the rungs of a steel ladder."[113] Gas processing, then, cannot be omitted for long without grave occupational and public risks.

Yet gas processing plants are at least as vulnerable as refineries, take a year and a half to rebuild "assuming normal delivery of equipment and materials,"[114] and are often centralized. A single plant in Louisiana, the world's largest, provides eleven hundred eighty-five million cubic feet per day to the East Coast. This is the equivalent of the output of more than twenty huge power stations,[115] or about three and a half percent of America's *total* natural gas use (which is in turn a fourth of total energy use). And the gas processing plants are as concentrated geographically as is the gas. Louisiana is to American natural gas as the Persian Gulf is to world oil. An alarming eighty-four percent of all interstate gas either is from Louisiana wells (fifty-three percent) or flows from Texas, mostly via Louisiana (thirty-one percent).[116]

Oil pipelines

Oil pipelines within the United States move about three-fourths of the crude oil used by U.S. refineries and about one-third of the refined products sent from refineries to consumers. These pipelines "are highly vulnerable to disruptions caused by human error, sabotage, or nature. Damage to key facilities on just a few pipeline systems could greatly reduce domestic shipments, causing an energy shortage exceeding that of the 1973 Arab oil embargo."[117] Cutting just the Trans-Alaska, Colonial, and Capline pipeline systems would be equivalent in oil volume to losing

• about the total 1982 level of net U.S. petroleum imports; or

• over one and a half times the maximum U.S. import shortfall during the 1973 oil embargo; or

• about eight times the U.S. imports from Iran when those were stopped in 1978.[118]

If crude oil imports to East Coast refineries were shut off, virtually the only supplies of fluid fuels to the Northeast would come through a single pipeline for refined products—Colonial—and a few natural gas pipelines. All of these could be disabled by a handful of people.

The complexity of modern pipelines is exemplified by the largest and probably the most intricate system in the world—the Colonial Pipeline System from Texas to New Jersey.[119] The largest of its three adjacent pipes is thirty-six inches in diameter. It is fed from ten source points and distributes to two hundred eighty-one marketing terminals. Thirty-one shippers dispatch one hundred twenty varieties of refined products to fifty-six receiving companies. In 1973, after an investment of more than half a billion dollars over eleven years, nearly two thousand miles of main pipe and over one and a half thousand miles of lateral lines, containing a total of over a million tons of steel, were being operated by fewer than six hundred employees. The pipeline takes twelve days to move a product batch from end to end. It is powered by eighty-four pumping stations (totalling over eight hundred thousand horsepower). The pumps use more than two million kilowatt-hours per year—enough to run for a month in 1973 all the houses in Louisiana, Georgia, Mississippi, and South Carolina. Just supplying the valves for this extraordinary engineering project took the resources of ten companies.[120]

An extensive study of American energy transportation stated:

> Pipelines carry huge quantities of energy . . . in continuous operations stretching over thousands of miles. . . . [They] were constructed and are operated with almost no regard to their vulnerability to persons who might . . . desire to interfere with this vital movement of fuel. They are exposed and all but unguarded at innumerable points, and easily accessible even where not exposed over virtually their entire routes. . . . [T]his vulnerability of the most important energy transportation systems of the Nation threatens the national security. . . .
> . . . Although all forms of energy movement are vulnerable to some extent, pipelines are perhaps uniquely vulnerable. No other energy transportation mode moves so much energy, over such great distances, in a continuous stream whose continuity is so critical an aspect of its importance.[121]

While continuity is even more important in electrical transmission, this statement is certainly right to emphasize both the density and the distance of energy flow in pipelines.

By 1975, the United States had installed enough oil pipelines (carrying crude oil or refined products) to reach five times around the Equator. Principal gas pipelines would stretch seven and a half times around the globe. With so much pipeline mileage around, pipeline sabotage is nothing new. Indeed, it is surprisingly old. The first screw-coupling pipeline introduced into the Pennsylvania oilfields in 1865 was dismantled by night by competitive teamsters.[122] In recent years, as pipeline bombings have become common in the Middle East, they have also started to occur more regularly in the United States. A Shell gasoline pipeline in Oakland, California was damaged in 1969, a Puerto Rican pipeline in 1975, and the Trans-Alaska Pipeline in 1977 and 1978 (as described below).[123] A compendium of bombing incidents lists dynamite attacks on twenty gas pipelines (ranging from two to twenty inches) and on two gas-pipeline cooling towers in Kentucky in 1974.[124] And pipelines can be sabotaged by as simple a means as turning valves, most of which are readily accessible.[125] For example, during a refinery strike in Louisiana, someone shut the valves on a twenty-four-inch gas pipeline, causing the gas to be flared through safety valves.[126]

"Little can be done to stop a determined, well-equipped, and knowledgeable saboteur or terrorist" from disrupting a pipeline, since "[I]t would not be feasible to monitor the entire length of a pipeline frequently enough to prevent any action," and virtually "no . . . security precautions were taken in that safer day when most . . . pipelines were built."[127] It is nonetheless important to understand both the potential contributions and the inherent limitations of security measures that can be taken.

Pipeline sabotage and repair

Gas and oil pipelines, ranging up to forty-eight inches in diameter, and frequently laid in parallel groups on the same right-of-way, are welded from steel using special specifications and procedures. They are ordinarily buried in trenches deep enough to protect them from bad weather but not from earthquake or ground shock, as was shown in 1975 when ground shock from a bomb sheared a gasoline pipeline from a tank farm to San Juan, Puerto Rico.[128] Major pipelines in such seismic areas as St. Louis, Lima (Ohio), Socorro (New Mexico), and Salt Lake City appear to be at risk from earthquakes.[129]

The main cause of damage to buried pipelines has so far been mundane—accidental excavation. In a classic 1981 episode, for example, construction drilling in the heart of the San Francisco financial district burst a sixteen-inch gas main, producing a two-and-a-half-hour geyser of gas. The gas got into the ventilation systems of high-rise buildings (luckily, not in explosive concentrations) and forced the evacuation of up to thirty thousand people.[130] The ease of accidentally digging up pipes implies that they could be dug up deliberately too. (It could be done instantaneously with military-type shaped-charge excavating devices.) Corrosion is another enemy: Iranian gas shipments to the Soviet Union were cut off when salty soil and heavy rains caused the failure and explosion of a major Iranian pipeline.[131] Mainly to prevent accidental damage, buried pipelines are clearly marked, especially at road and waterway crossings, as required by law. Extremely detailed maps periodically published by federal agencies and by the petroleum industry—some scaled at one and a half million to one or less—enable anyone to pinpoint pipelines and allied facilities.

Merely penetrating a pipeline may interrupt its flow and cause a fire or explosion. But unless air leaks into a gas line in explosive proportions, the damage will be local and probably repairable in a few days or (if the industry had to cope with several substantial breaks simultaneously) a few weeks. Exposed pipelines can be penetrated or severed using low-technology explosives or thermite. Commercially available shaped charges are used in the oil and gas industry itself for perforating pipe, and have apparently been used against pipelines or tanks by saboteurs.[132]

Even if a pipeline were somehow completely destroyed, it could be relaid at a substantial rate:

> ... under the most favorable circumstances, small-diameter lines of six to eight inches can be constructed as rapidly as three miles or more per day, and large-diameter lines of thirty to thirty-six inches at one mile or more per day. Under extremely adverse conditions the [respective] rates ... are three thousand to four thousand feet per day [and] ... one thousand to fifteen hundred feet per day.[133]

(Rates in swampy areas are often much lower.) But far more vulnerable and less repairable than pipelines themselves are their prime movers—pumping stations for oil, compressor stations for gas—and such allied facilities as interconnections, metering and control stations, and input terminals.

River crossings, either on a bridge or under the riverbed, are similarly vulnerable and complicate repair. (Capline, described below, has a duplicate loop crossing the Mississippi River, but this is far from a universal practice, and adds two vulnerable junction points.) Dropping a bridge can not only sever a pipeline carried on it but can at the same time stop navigation (including tankers and barges associated with an oil terminal or refinery), block traffic, and hinder the delivery of repair equipment.[134] Significant damage at any of these points can reduce or stop fuel flows for a half-year or more.[135] It is not in fact difficult to drop a bridge. Terrorists from Ulster to Uganda do so monthly. Arson in a control house on an abandoned railroad bridge at Keithsburg, Illinois dropped a span that blocked the Mississippi River for a week in June 1981.[136] Three months later, an accidental spill of ten thousand gallons of gasoline from a huge tank farm overlooking the harbor of Portland, Oregon forced the closure of a main bridge and could probably have destroyed it.[137]

"Pipelines are easy to sabotage. A double premium accrues to the saboteur's account—the loss of oil and an extensive fire that might ensue. A trained group of a few hundred persons knowledgeable as to the location of our major pipelines and control stations and with destruction in mind could starve our refineries [for] crude."[138] But would it actually take a few hundred people?

Concentrations of pipeline capacity

A nuclear targeting exercise found that the destruction of eight terminals, sixty-eight pump stations, twenty-seven combined terminal/pump stations, and twenty-three adjacent pipelines would disable all 1968–69 U.S. refined-product distribution pipelines down to and including six inches, isolating the refining areas from agricultural and industrial areas.[139] But in fact, immense mischief could be done by only a few people if they picked the right targets from the copious literature available. For example, only ten hits could cut off sixty-three percent of the pipeline capacity (by barrel-miles) for delivering refined products within the United States. Only six hits could disrupt pipeline service between the main extraction areas and the East and Midwest. Indeed, the concentration is even greater than these figures imply. The General Accounting Office, for example, has pointed out that three pipelines—the Trans-Alaska Pipeline (TAPS), the Colonial system, and Capline—represent less than three percent of American pipeline mileage, but carry about eighteen percent of 1979 U.S. crude oil consumption and twelve percent of refined products.[140] The key role of these three lines merits closer examination.

The Colonial system dominates the U.S. pipeline market for refined products, carrying about half of the total barrel-miles[141] in forty-six hundred miles of pipe spanning sixteen hundred miles. Its products supply more than half the refined product demand in seven states (Virginia, New Jersey, North Carolina, Maryland, Tennessee, South Carolina, Georgia), and between fifteen and fifty percent in five more (Alabama, District of Columbia, Mississippppi, New York, Pennsylvania).[142] "Other pipelines or transportation modes cannot absorb enough" to replace this flow.

Capline is a forty-inch, sixteen-pumping-station pipeline carrying crude oil six hundred thirty-two miles from Louisiana to Illinois at a rate of twelve hundred thousand barrels per day. It provides a quarter of the input to Midwestern refineries and, like Colonial, is irreplaceable. It is the largest of three distribution conduits to be used by the Strategic Petroleum Reserve. The crude oil supplied by Capline and the Trans-Alaska Pipeline totals twenty-four hundred thousand barrels per day—about a fifth of all U.S. refinery runs.

Colonial, Capline, and other U.S. pipelines have been and probably still are startlingly vulnerable to sabotage. In findings reiminiscent of the state of nuclear plant physical security in the mid-1960s, the General Accounting Office's audit in 1979 found appalling laxity—and little managerial consciousness of sabotage risks[143]—at many key pipeline facilities. The main Capline input terminal, for example, described by a company official as a most critical facility, had a catwalk that went over the fence from a public road to the building housing computer controls for the entire Capline system. Entry to the building was uncontrolled during the day, and only a locked door protected the computer itself. Both Capline and Colonial pumping stations have even been burglarized by juveniles (who, fortunately, did not damage or misuse the equipment). Access to many key plants was uncontrolled or poorly controlled. Communications and back-up power were poor. At a major Colonial input station with a peak capacity of one million three hundred thousand barrels per day, for example—equivalent to a tenth of America's total rate of crude oil consumption—the main and back-up power transformers were both accessible and were near each other.[144] "Why there is a total lack of security around such [an electrical] installation . . . is almost beyond comprehension."[145] Simply reducing from afar the line voltage supplied to a facility's motors or electronic systems can cause damage that takes months to repair.[146]

Many supposedly complementary pipelines parallel each other so closely that in practical effect they are co-located and co-vulnerable:

> Some major crude and product lines are extremely close to each other as they extend from Texas and Louisiana . . . northeast. . . . Damage at certain locations . . . could stop the flow of most of the gas and petroleum products now being delivered to the eastern U.S.[147]

> The fact that [the Colonial and Plantation] . . . systems come together at a number of points in their [parallel] route is a built-in weakness from a vulnerability point of view. A nuclear attack [or sabotage] focused at or near certain points of interchange between lines could create a major disruption of the major portions of the entire system. A view of a pipeline map shows flexibility at the intrastate level. It is possible for one pipeline system to sell to another locally. But, once the product is discharged into the interstate system, there is a considerable lack of flexibility.[148]

Further, the buffer stocks of oil downstream of pipelines are generally too small to cope with the duration of interruption that would be expected if an interchange, pumping station, input terminal, river crossing, or control system were damaged (that is, months rather than days). As mentioned earlier, average refinery crude stocks are about three to five days.[149] Typical Colonial receivers' market stocks are also in the range of five to ten days. A two-week interruption of service in 1973, when difficulties arose in repairing a break in a remote area of Texas, "became critical for many Colonial shippers."[150]

Arctic pipelines

The Trans-Alaska Pipeline System (TAPS, not to be confused with the Trans-Arabian Pipeline or TAP-Line) presents unique and daunting vulnerabilities because of its remoteness, length, and special construction. Moreover, there is no known alternative way to move oil from the North Slope to ports and refineries. TAPS is a single forty-eight-inch hot-oil pipeline which cost eight billion dollars. It currently moves twelve hundred million barrels per day—about ten percent of U.S. refinery runs—and displaces oil imports worth nearly five hundred dollars per second. Unfortunately, it also runs through rugged country for seven hundred ninety-eight miles. For four hundred eighteen miles it is held aloft on stanchions above permafrost. It crosses rivers (four by long bridges) accessible to boats and to Alaska's ubiquitous float planes. The five southern pumping stations are also accessible from state highways. The line crosses three mountain ranges and five seismic areas, and passes near four massive but mobile glaciers.[151] Its proprietors annually spend about a thousandth of the line's replacement cost on obvious security precautions. Nevertheless, both they and the government acknowledge that—as a 1975 military exercise showed—it is impossible to prevent determined sabotage which could shut down the line for a year or more.[152]

Major parts of TAPS are invisible and inaccessible to repair crews by air or ground for up to weeks at time in the winter. If pumping were interrupted for three winter weeks, the heated oil—nine million barrels of it at one hundred forty-five degrees Fahrenheit—would cool to the point that it could not be moved, putting the pipeline out of service for six months. It would become "the largest candle in the world" or "the world's biggest Chapstick."[153] (This reportedly happened to an uninsulated Siberian hot-oil pipeline which broke, plugging it with wax for over a year.) The line need not even be damaged to stop its flow: prolonged gales in the Valdez Narrows could halt tanker traffic for longer than the storage tanks at the receiving end of the line could accommodate, as nearly happened in 1979.[154] Damage to certain components at the Valdez terminal could also deprive TAPS of an outlet for up to a year or two.

On 20 July 1977, three dynamite charges exploded under TAPS near Fairbanks without penetrating the pipe wall. Damaged supports and insulation were discovered five days later. A second bombing in February 1978 made a two-inch hole that spilled about fifteen thousand barrels and shut down the line for twenty-one hours,[155] costing over a million dollars to clean up. A deliberately opened valve at Station Three, north of the Yukon River, also spilled three and a half thousand gallons of diesel fuel in September 1977,[156] adding spice to an extortionist's threat. And two short sections of pipe, though their half-inch walls were not pierced, reportedly had to be replaced after being peppered with more than fifty bullets.[157] Despite these incidents, the security manager of Alyeska, the consortium of oil companies that runs TAPS, still "does not perceive a sabotage threat in Alaska."[158]

The line's most vulnerable point may be its eight pumping stations, remotely controlled from Valdez. The impact of losing a station depends on the terrain. Depending on the lift required, the distance between pumping stations on a major oil pipeline can vary from a few miles in mountainous country to nearly two hundred miles on the flats.[159] The engines and pumps are very large—thousands of horsepower—and not a stock item. Especially for Arctic operation, they are special-order items with lead times from a half-year to a year or more.[160] Pending repair, the pipeline may run at reduced capacity or not at all. Damage to successive stations, or to one preceding a high lift, is of course most damaging. On 8 July 1977, operator error blew up the eighth and southern-most TAPS pumping station, in a relatively flat area thirty-three miles south of Fairbanks, killing one worker and injuring five.[161] The station was the least vital and the most accessible of the eight. After ten days, the station was bypassed and pumping resumed, at half the usual rate. Had the failed station been one of those required for pumping over the mountains, pipeline capacity "would have been reduced substantially more, or even curtailed altogether."[162] "Despite an intense rebuilding effort, it took about nine months to rebuild the pump station."[163] In a less favorable location or season, it could have taken much longer.

The gathering lines which feed oil into TAPS, finally, converge into a massive, uninsurably vulnerable labyrinth of pipework called "Hollywood and Vine." It can be built by only one plant—in eight months, plus two to ship from Japan.

A Senate Subcommittee,[164] investigating TAPS's vulnerability in 1977, "was stunned at the lack of planning and thought given to the security of the pipeline before it was built"[165] and urged that the Department of Energy set up an Office of Energy Security. The proposed legislation sank without trace.

Gas pipelines

Natural gas (and LPG) pipelines are vulnerable in about the same ways as oil pipelines, but have the added disagreeable feature that air "makes a 'bomb' out of the line containing an explosive mixture."[166] Instead of pumping stations, gas pipelines have compressor stations spaced about every forty to two hundred miles. Instead of relying on electric motors, as many oil pipeline pumps do, gas pipeline compressors burn some of the gas they transmit—about four percent of it per thousand miles—in gas turbines, which are rugged but inefficient. For this reason and because much of the compressors' work is lost as heat, the pumping energy required is about five times as high for a gas pipeline as for an oil pipeline.[167] The two together, nationally, are a significant energy user: they probably use more energy than either water heaters or aircraft. Very long gas pipelines can have enormous energy needs: the proposed Alaskan gas line would need nearly two thousand megawatts of pumping and gas-conditioning energy, or a twelfth of its own throughput. The use of gas rather than electricity means that gas pipelines can work even in a power failure—provided there is electricity to run their controls and valve motors. On the other hand, it is possible in some cases that a damaged line may not hold enough gas to drive the compressors needed to move enough gas through it to run the compressors, and so forth.

Gas compressor stations, like their oil counterparts, are "virtually unguarded. There is little or no standby equipment. . . . The system can be easily damaged. It is highly vulnerable to almost any hazard either man created or natural. Repair to a damaged segment could take months."[168] Most gas pipelines automatically detect breaks, isolate their sections (generally shorter than the fifty-mile average interval between compressors, as there are valves at each junction and elsewhere), and turn off compressors if necessary. There is little protection, however, for the control and communications links tying all the valves and compressors to a computerized central dispatching system. Because of the total reliance on remote telemetry and controls, "cutting of wires or destroying radio [or microwave] facilities could cause considerable confusion."[169] With widespread disruption of communications "the system could become completely useless." (Interestingly, saboteurs in 1979 blew up a microwave station linking Teheran to the Abadan oil refinery and to Iran's largest port.[170]) Further,

> The operation of complex pulse-time-modulation multiplex micro-wave equipment, telemetering equipment, facsimile units, automatic control systems and voice communication is the responsibility of the communications engineer. In a large terminal area, the engineer might have an assistant or two but as a general rule, one man has responsibility for the equipment over a very large area. . . . [I]t is doubtful that a replacement engineer could come into an [extensively] damaged complex system and make much progress in its early repair. . . . The loss of [key personnel] . . . could cause very significant problems, even though equipment may not be seriously damaged. Even small repairs by one not knowledgeable of the [particular] system can become a major problem.[171]

Gas systems have a further point of vulnerability with no strict analogue in oil systems: the "city gate" station where incoming pipeline gas is metered, odorized, and pressure-regulated. This last function is crucial, since pipeline pressures are vastly greater than retail distribution and end-use pressures. "Should one substantially increase pressure on the service lines serving residences and public buildings, the lines and/or appliances could rupture and the escaping gas could cause fires and explosions. . . . Careful pressure regulation is required in order for gas to be safe."[172] (Centralia, Missouri found this out on 28 January 1982 when an accidentally broken main put high-pressure gas into low-pressure lines, causing dozens of simultaneous fires and explosions all over town.[173]) Conversely, pressure reductions, besides putting out pilot lights, can cause damaging frost heaves near the regulator outlet pipe.[174]

This ability to wreak widespread havoc by remote control through changing distribution pressures has no parallel in the oil system. The thousands of primary and tens of thousands of secondary oil terminals are vulnerable to sabotage,[175] and local oil transportation can also become a target.[176] However, such targets, unlike LNG and LPG cargoes, are unlikely to cause more than locally severe damage unless they endanger some larger target, such as a refinery, tank farm, or reactor, near the site of attack. That is not true of the natural gas system. Its sensitivity to distribution pressure—together with its reliance on pipelines and its relatively limited storage—may exceed even that of the oil system, with its dispersed and diverse routes and with widespread buffer stocks spotted throughout the local distribution system.[177]

Gas grids appear, in partial compensation, to offer better opportunities than oil pipelines for rerouting:

> In the last ten years, many additional interconnections have been added, to the point that, according to industry sources, there is hardly a crossing between two pipelines without an interconnection that could be used if needed. Compression might or might not be needed at interconnecting points to effect deliveries from a line operating at lower pressure than the receiving line, but in general, the technical problems of transferring natural gas within the pipeline network are reportedly not overwhelming. From a practical standpoint, the United States has a natural gas pipeline "grid" which could be used to modify the directions and quantities of natural gas flows substantially.[178]

How far this would remain true if key interconnections or control systems were disrupted is open to considerable doubt, and in any case the *inter*state grid is fairly inflexible.[179] Nonetheless, processed natural gas, unlike oil (crude or specific products), is a relatively homogenous commodity, one unit of which is interchangeable for another within the grid.

Total vulnerability

Both gas and oil grids have recently shown a new form of vulnerability: theft. As prices have risen, "oil rustling" and "gas tapping" have become big business, ranging from the hijacking of a twenty-five-thousand-gallon tank truck to the theft of hundreds of thousands of gallons from Wyoming fields. Perhaps up to a tenth of all Texas oil sold to refineries may be stolen.[180] Every major American port has had oil thefts. Tankers at anchor have even been tapped in New Orleans and Houston. Gasoline has been siphoned out of storage tanks in many Eastern cities. Barges carrying refined products on the Mississippi River have been robbed. Organized crime is implicated in some Southwestern refinery thefts. In an attempt to deal with the problem, the FBI is "spiking" crude oil shipments with chemicals so stolen shipments can be traced.[181] Further,

> The technology for tapping into a pipeline, even a high pressure natural gas pipeline, without causing a leak, explosion, or other major incident revealing the existence of the tap, is published and well-known. In 1975, the [Federal Power Commission] . . . reported one hundred forty billion cubic feet of natural gas as unaccounted for, about half of which was lost during transmission. This gas, which was shown on meters entering the system, but was neither sold to customers, placed into storage, or used in compressors, . . . [was worth at 1975 prices] one hundred ten million dollars. A portion of it may well have been stolen.[182]

Clearly, people knowledgeable enough to steal large amounts of oil and gas from tankers, pipelines, tanks, or other components of the systems are also able to cause serious harm to those systems if they are so minded.

Indeed, the vulnerabilities surveyed in this chapter suggest that three-fourths of America's energy arrives at its destination only because virtually every American does not happen to want to stop it. The United States depends on a highly engineered, inherently brittle oil and gas system designed for a magical world where human frailties and hostilities do not intrude. As a result, we have reached the point where a handful of people in a single night could stop for a year more than three-quarters of the natural gas supplies to the Eastern United States—without ever leaving Louisiana.[183] With a little more traveling, they could cause lasting havoc in the oil system, too. This is not only because nearly three-quarters of the interstate gas originates in only two states, while a similar fraction of the domestic oil is lifted in only four states.[184] It is also an expression of the nature of the processing and distribution technologies used, in the name of economic efficiency, to move those enormous amounts of fuel to its buyers.

A common response to these vulnerabilities—whether identified as broadly as in this chapter or merely as dependence on foreign crude oil—is to propose that oil and gas be replaced by substituting America's most abundant fuel (coal), or uranium, or both, delivered in the form of electricity generated in large, remotely sited power stations. The next chapter shows that this alternative too merely replaces one set of vulnerabilities with another set that is at least as worrisome.

Chapter Ten
Power Stations and Grids

The vulnerability of oil and gas terminals, processing plants, and pipelines is mirrored in central electric systems—only worse. The General Accounting Office recently audited the electrical security of a typical part of the United States; the audit found that sabotage of eight substations could black out the region, and that sabotage of only four could leave a city with no power for days and with rotating blackouts for a year.[1]

The roots of this vulnerability are not hard to find. To start with, electricity, though not itself flammable or explosive, cannot readily be stored. The electric grid provides no "pipeline inventory" of storage between generators and end users (unless they have provided local storage or back-up at their own substantial expense). Thus, in the event of supply or delivery failures, electric power must be rapidly rerouted to prevent widespread and instantaneous failure. This rerouting requires that generating and transmission capacity, switchgear, and control and communications capability all be immediately available.

Throughout the grid, the alternating electric current must change its direction of flow back and forth at an essentially constant rate, which in North America is sixty cycles per second: this constancy is called "frequency stability." Stability of voltage—the amount of electrical "pressure" in the line (as opposed to current, the amount of electrical flow)—is vital to avoid damage to equipment. Power is transmitted over three parallel lines, each bearing a precise time relationship to the others—somewhat akin to singing a three-part round. The "phase stability" among these different lines, and between voltage and current, must also be maintained. And these exacting relationships must be kept in step with each other in all parts of the grid at once ("synchronization").

These problems are considerably more difficult than the analogous requirements to maintain oil and gas purity, pipeline flows, and distribution pressures. In the electric grid, everything happens much faster. Control response is often required in thousandths of a second, not in minutes or hours. Reliance on computerization, farflung telecommunications networks, and specialized skills—already cause for concern in oil and gas grids—is even greater in electric grids, and becoming ever more so.

The electrical and petroleum grids are also vulnerable in many of the same ways. Power lines, like pipelines, are long, exposed, and easily severed by simple means. Like refineries, many vital electrical components depend on continuous supplies of cooling water, pump lubricants, and so forth. Just as refineries have a risk of explosion from hydrogen (used to hydrogenate carbon-rich molecules into light products), so big electrical generators are often cooled with hydrogen (whose small molecules reduce friction). Many key components of electrical systems, ranging from turboalternators to main transformers, are special-order items with long delivery times. Repair of substations and transmission lines has many features in common with repair of pipelines and pumping stations—but the electrical components tend to be costlier, more delicate, and less available than their oil and gas counterparts.

Electrical grids and their components seem to be far more frequently attacked than oil and gas grids—perhaps because power failures are so much more immediate and dramatic than interruptions of oil or gas supply, and offer so few options of substitution in the highly specialized end-use devices. This chapter examines the vulnerabilities—of individual components and of the power grid as an interrelated whole—which make such sabotage tempting and effective.

The major components of power grids are, in their broadest categories,

- power stations;
- transmission lines with their associated switchgear and transformers (which raise generators' output to very high voltages for long-distance transmission, then reduce the voltages again for distribution);
- distribution systems, including further voltage-reducing transformers and switches; and
- the control and communication systems which these components require to work together.

These will now be considered in turn.

Power stations

About twelve percent of the domestically generated electricity supplied to the United States comes from about twelve hundred hydroelectric dams. About three hundred sixty of these produce more than twenty-five megawatts each. Most of the output currently comes from a small number of very large dams, although small dams may, in the coming decades, come to rival the total capacity of the existing large dams. Most dams and their turbines (though not their switchgear and transmission lines) are relatively resistant to interference—luckily, since destruction of a dam often carries a risk of serious flooding. A time bomb containing fifty pounds of dynamite did, however, damage the interior of a government dam in Tennessee in 1978,[2] and the security staff of at least one major Western dam was reportedly infiltrated by potential saboteurs.

About one percent of national installed generating capacity is in nearly a thousand diesel engines, mainly in rural areas and small peaking plants. Another eight percent of the capacity is in about twelve hundred gas turbines, which are run on average only seven percent of the time. Their high fuel cost and low thermal efficiency restrict them to peaking use. About a tenth of one percent of total capacity is in geothermal and wind plants. This fraction is increasing fairly rapidly, especially on the West Coast.

All the remaining power plants—about seventy-eight percent of total installed capacity, supplying about eighty-two percent of the electricity—are the nine hundred-odd major "thermal" (steam-raising) plants. They operate, on average, at just under half their full-time, full-power capacity. In 1980 they generated about fifty-eight percent of their output from coal, twelve percent from oil, seventeen percent from natural gas, and thirteen percent from uranium. (Since then, the nuclear and oil fractions have fallen, the latter sharply. The oil burn, after peaking at over one million seven hundred thousand barrels per day in 1978, plummeted to just over one million in 1981, heading for eight hundred thousand or so by the end of 1982.[3] The main substitutes for oil have been coal and efficiency improvements.) These statistics do not include self-generation of electricity in factories. This "cogeneration" as a by-product of process heat or steam uses combined-cycle steam turbines, diesels, or gas turbines. It provides electricity equivalent to about four percent of central generation, and is often independent of grid operation, providing its proprietors with greater "insurance" against power failures.

The large thermal plants supplying over four-fifths of U.S. grid electricity deserve special attention. They dominate the grid. They are highly centralized. Each plant needs continuous provision of fuel and cooling water, control and communications systems, and outlets for its electricity and effluents. Interruption of any one of these will shut down the plant. On-site fuel stocks can provide a buffer of one or more years for nuclear plants, three months or more for coal-fueled plants, one or two months for oil-fired plants, and days to weeks for dual-fueled gas-fired plants holding oil stockpiles. Single-fueled gas-fired plants, common in such regions as Texas (whose grid is not interconnected with the rest of the country), carry almost no stocks. San Francisco's entire gas storage capacity would last one local gas-fired power plant for only fourteen hours.[4]

Power plants' complex, special-purpose machinery itself is vulnerable to disruption, even by low-technology means. Modern turboalternators, for example, are so big, yet so delicate, that when not spinning they must have their shafts rotated a fraction of a turn several times per hour, by hand if necessary, lest their own weight ruin them by bending the shaft out of true. (On occasion, as during the Three Mile Island accident, this service has been difficult to provide in the face of evacuation requirements.) It is because of this delicacy that an insider using a simple hand tool was able to damage dozens of coils, many beyond repair, on three of the world's largest electric generators (each producing seven hundred megawatts from a rotor sixty-one feet in diameter) in the bowels of Grand Coulee Dam, the world's largest hydroelectric plant.[5]

The vulnerability of central power stations is not a new issue. In 1966, the Defense Electric Power Administration pointed out that

> fewer than two hundred cities and towns of over fifty thousand population contain about sixty percent of the population and associated industrial capacity of the nation. The larger generating facilities tend to be located near[by]. . . . Generating capacity is the most difficult, costly, and time consuming component of an electric power system to replace and also tends to be highly concentrated geographically. If any portion of the power system is to be considered a primary [strategic] target, it would be these large generating plants. . . . Is the concentration of power generation making the industry more vulnerable. . . ?[6]

In the intervening sixteen years, the question has been often repeated. Yet the concentration has increased, with major power plants being drawn to urban areas and probably encouraging urbanization and industrial concentration in their turn. Congress's Joint Committee on Defense Production observed:

> Although there are about three and a half thousand companies involved in generating and distributing electricity, about half of our total electrical capacity comes from fewer than three hundred generating stations. Most of these are located in or near our major urban-industrial areas. The electric utilities therefore present a relatively compact and especially inviting set of targets for a saboteur, a terrorist or an attacker, as well as a lightning bolt.[7]

This concentration is less than that of some other energy facilities such as major pipelines, large refineries, and key smelters.[8] But it is also *uniquely* true of power stations that the loss of substantial generation or transmission capacity can crash the whole grid, shutting down undamaged plants because (as in the New York blackout) they are insufficient to maintain system frequency. The Research Director of the American Public Power Association was recently moved by these trends to remark that "there is considerable evidence that one of our highest national defense priorities should be to insure the continuity and productivity of the United States through aggressive support of decentralized energy supply."[9] Confirming this, attacks on power stations have become almost a routine feature of guerrilla campaigns, ranging from Italy, Iraq, Afghanistan, El Salvador, and Puerto Rico (as noted in Chapter Seven) to Cyprus (1955), Britain (1969, by internal sabotage at Aberthaw and perhaps Fiddler's Ferry), Eire (1974), Chile, India,[10] and even a U.S. Army base in Wisconsin.[11] Far worse may be in store. After a California plant bombing, one power engineer stated that the company had escaped with minor damage only by the saboteurs' fortuitous choice of the strongest point on the strongest station: electric plants, he said, are "terribly vulnerable. Someone who knew anything at all could cause terrible havoc." Other targets in the same area could easily have been "blown over." On 28 August 1981, a few months after those remarks, most of Managua (the capital of Nicaragua) was blacked out when a stray cat wandered into the central power station and caused a short circuit.[12]

Electrical transmission

High-voltage transmission lines carry an astonishing amount of energy, second only to large pipelines. A line rated at five hundred thousand volts (five hundred kilovolts), a common size nowadays, typically handles about two thousand megawatts, the output of two giant power stations.[13] A seven hundred sixty-five kilovolt line handles about three thousand megawatts. Power lines are not easy to site, especially in built-up areas, so as the power grid expands, the larger, newer, and higher-capacity lines tend to be built alongside previous ones, making them vulnerable to the same local events. In some areas, such as New York City and South Florida,[14] geography further squeezes supposedly independent transmission lines into a single narrow corridor. In others, remotely sited plants, perhaps at a Western coal-mine, send their lines over hundreds of miles of remote countryside.

No transmission line can function without switchgear and controls at each end. The vital task of monitoring and dispatching power where it is needed is carried out from computerized control centers, belonging both to individual utilities and to the regional and subregional "power pools" to which they belong. The entire New York-New England power pool, for example, is controlled from a single center near Schenectady.[15] Broadly speaking, the grid of the contiguous U.S. is interconnected within each of three largely separate regions[16]—Texas, the Eastern states, and the Western states, with the demarcation running roughly through Nebraska. Within each region, however, the constituent power pools do not have unlimited capacity to interchange power with each other. That capacity is

heavily dependent on particular extra-high-voltage transmission segments,[17] such as the Wisconsin-Missouri-Illinois intertie—a single corridor carrying seven thousand megawatts.[18] Bulk power transmission also
depends crucially on uniquely vulnerable extra-high-voltage switchgear
and transformers at both ends of the transmission lines[19]—equipment
which, if damaged, often takes a year or more to replace. Despite their key
role in interstate commerce, transmission lines are in general not protected by federal law.[20]

Transmission lines have often been sabotaged. Among the events that
overthrew President Allende of Chile was the blacking out of Santiago, interrupting him in the midst of a televised address, when terrorists bombed
a single pylon.[21] (In an ironic reversal, a military coup failed in El Salvador in 1972 when the principals, having blown up the main power plant
in the capital, could no longer use telephones or broadcasting to communicate with each other or with the public.)[22] Transmission lines to a selected target can be cut, as in a 1975 Irish Republican Army jailbreak attempt[23] or in efforts to cut the power to Colorado military plants.[24] In
1970, the key Pacific Intertie suffered at least three attacks near Lovelock,
Nevada.[25] Fourteen towers in the rugged forests of Oregon were
bombed, and at least six toppled, in 1974 by two extortionists threatening
to black out Portland if they were not paid a million dollars.[26] Pipe bombs
caused minor damage at six California towers in a single night in 1975.[27]
Other attacks on transmission lines occurred in New Jersey in 1978,[28]
Alabama in 1966, Ohio (blacking out parts of Cincinnati) and Louisiana in
1967, Wisconsin in 1968, and California and Washington in 1973.[29]

In the bitter confrontation mentioned in Chapter Four, conservative,
fiercely independent Minnesota farmers caused seven million dollars'
damage during 1979–80 to a direct-current high-voltage line. Nocturnal
"bolt weevils," having perfected a low-technology technique requiring only
a few people and hand tools, have toppled fifteen towers (as of June
1981). An outbreak of "insulator disease," commonly ascribed to rifles (or
even to sophisticated slingshots), has littered the ground with the remains
of over eight thousand fragile glass insulators. The epidemic attacked
three hundred insulators per week in early 1979—sometimes more than
that in a single night.[30] The aluminum wires themselves, an inch and a
half in diameter, proved vulnerable to rifle fire.[31] Guarding just the Minnesota section of line—a hundred and seventy-six miles with six hundred
eighty-five towers, often through farmers' fields far from public roads—is
still, at this writing, proving to be an impossible task. Despite high-speed
helicopters, a reward of one hundred thousand dollars, three hundred
private guards, and extensive FBI activity, not one of the perpetrators has
been caught. It is not likely that they will be, given the depth of their local
support. Nor is it likely that South Africa will discover who is persistently

cutting its transmission lines from the four-thousand-megawatt Cabora Bassa dam in Mozambique (isolating it altogether for two months, then reducing its output by half and causing power shortages in South Africa),[32] or who blacked out Durban by blowing up a substation,[33] or who cut power lines in the Orange Free State,[34] or who simultaneously bombed a substation, a power plant in the Transvaal, and another power plant with Soviet limpet mines.[35]

It is little wonder that an Interior Department expert confirmed that "a relatively small group of dedicated, knowledgeable individuals . . . could bring down [the power grid supplying] almost any section of the country," or could black out "a widespread network" if more widely coordinated.[36] Such attempts have already occurred: just before a Presidential inauguration in Portugal, for example, eighteen coordinated explosions at widely scattered power lines blacked out Oporto and parts of Lisbon and other cities.[37]

Even without interference, transmission lines fail by themselves. Of the twelve worst interruptions in U.S. bulk power supply during 1974–79, six were caused by failures in transmission, six in distribution, and none in generation. Seven were initiated by bad weather, four by component failures, and one by operator error.[38] Among all reported interruptions during 1970–79, however, three-fourths "have been due to problems related to facilities, maintenance, or operation and coordination." Only one-fourth were "initiated by weather or other forces external to the utility." The same is true abroad: the 19 December 1978 blackout of France, the 5 February 1979 blackout of Israel, and the 5 August 1981 blackout of most of southern and southwestern Britain were all caused by cascading transmission failures.[39]

Whatever the causes, failures are rife. On 5 April 1979, a buildup of dust and salt spray on insulators in Florida caused a two-hundred-forty-thousand-volt spark. With no outlet left for the output of three generating stations, blackouts struck the Miami area and much of Fort Lauderdale and West Palm Beach.[40] The Québec transmission grid averages about three major failures per year, chiefly in cold spells which (owing to the intensive promotion of electric heating) coincide with peak demand. In the chilly first week of January 1981, both Hydro-Québec and Ontario Hydro met record peak loads only by importing power: the former had lost nearly two thousand megawatts through transformer failure at the James Bay hydro site, and the latter had lost about one and a half thousand megawatts through emergency shutdowns at two nuclear plants and a coal plant.[41]

On 8 January 1981, a trash fire at the Utah State Prison apparently caused arcing in a major switchyard next door.[42] The resulting quadruple transmission failure blacked out all of Utah and parts of Idaho and Wyoming—some one and a half million people in all.[43] On 24 September 1980, most of Montana was blacked out for about an hour, prompting editorial comment on the vulnerability of "society's electric heartbeat."[44] Both these regions are of special interest because they are officially planned to become a main source of domestic fuel to replace Mideast oil. This plan depends on coal mines, coal slurry pipelines, and synfuel plants, all of which are in turn extremely dependent on reliable electric supplies.

Transmission is usually considered to involve lines carrying at least sixty-nine kilovolts, and bulk power transmision, over two hundred thirty kilovolts.[45] In all, there are more than three hundred sixty-five thousand circuit-miles of overhead transmission lines in the United States.[46] They are all completely exposed to all manner of hazards over great distances. Transmission lines have been interrupted by aircraft accidents (a National Guard helicopter cut a Tennessee Valley Authority line in 1976), explosions, equipment faults, broken shield wires (which run from the apex of one tower to the next), and even flying kites.[47] Southern California Edison Company has experienced extensive damage to wooden-poled subtransmission lines from brush fires; and on occasion, the fiery heat has ionized the air enough to short out high-voltage conductors.[48]

To the vulnerability of the lines themselves must be added that of the key facilities which transform and control their voltage at both ends. As the Defense Electric Power Administration put it:

> Main transmission lines are extremely difficult to protect against sabotage as they are widespread over each state and traverse remote rugged and unsettled areas for thousands of miles. While these facilities are periodically patrolled, ample time is available for a saboteur to work unobserved. It may be comparatively easy to damage this part of a system, but it is readily repaired. Damage to remote controlled or automatic substation equipment could make repairs and operation more difficult.[49]

The analogy with pipelines is clear enough. The line, save in especially awkward locations, is far quicker to repair than its interchanges and operational systems: terminals for pipelines, high-voltage substations for electric transmission. Without those devices, no energy can enter or leave the lines.

Substations and distribution networks

A principal point of vulnerability, though seldom capable of blacking out more than a relatively local area, is the substation, which transforms transmission to lower voltages for distribution over subtransmission lines and over four million miles of retail distribution lines.[50] Lead times for replacing most substation transformers range from weeks to a year. Although some analysts think that damage to substations and distribution networks "would have such a slight effect on the overall system as to make this type of sabotage unlikely,"[51] many saboteurs evidently do not see it that way. There are over four times as many substations handling over ten million volt-amperes (a capacity roughly equivalent to ten megawatts) as there are central power stations.[52] Thus near almost every load center there is a corresponding substation, generally out in the open and next to a public road. Such substations are effective soft targets for highly selective blackouts, and convenient ones for merely symbolic damage. Some attacks can serve both ends at once, as when three fired workers at a strife-ridden naval shipyard were charged in 1980 with plotting to blow up its power transformers.[53]

Both transmission substations (serving mainly large industrial customers at subtransmission voltages) and distribution substations (serving mainly residential and commercial customers) have been attacked by many means. In 1975 and again in 1977, the same Pacific Gas & Electric Company substation was damaged by pipe bombs, interrupting tens of thousands of customers.[54] Four other PG&E substation bombings caused transformer-oil fires and local blackouts in 1977.[55] In the same year, shots fired into transformers did a half-million dollars' damage and blacked out eight thousands customers in four suburban Atlanta counties for up to five hours.[56] The same amount of property damage was done on 28 March 1981 when gunshots and bombs—reportedly showing signs of expertise in explosives—destroyed transformers and damaged a substation at three Florida sites, blacking out parts of Palm Beach and environs.[57] A transformer bombing blacked out eastern Puerto Rico in 1975,[58] and basque separatists bombed a Spanish substation in 1981.[59] In the U.S., additional substation and transformer bombings occurred in California and Seattle in 1975, in Colorado in 1974 (causing a quarter-million dollars' damage), and in Albuquerque in 1977.[60] To simplify the saboteur's task, utility transformers often contain cooling oil that can be released and ignited by standoff methods, including rifle fire. The oil may contain highly toxic PCBs, which greatly complicate repairs and can require difficult cleanup of a substantial area.

During 1972–79, the Federal Bureau of Investigation reported a total of more than fifteen thousand actual or attempted bombings in the United States.[61] Most of these were successful. Over half the successful ones were explosive, the rest incendiary. Public utilities—most of them electrical utilities—represented generally one or two percent of the total targets. This percentage peaked at nearly two and a half percent in 1978, when an American utility was being bombed every twelve days. Since 1979, the campaign has greatly slackened: the number of utility bombings fell to thirteen in 1979 and eight in 1980, with utilities' share of total bombings falling to six-tenths of one percent by 1980. But eight utility bombings a year still represent a level of violence that can do a great deal of damage. Some bombing campaigns, such as the Oregon series in 1974, have posed such a threat to public safety that the government had to institute a massive manhunt, install standby power sources, call for power curtailments, and even consider calling up the National Guard.[62]

Hard-to-trace disruption can be caused simply by using a substation's controls without damaging them. (A novel describes a fictional extortionist who caused blackouts in New York City by throwing under-street transformer switches.[63]) Con Ed's Indian Point substation even caused a blackout on 19 July 1977 when it blew up all by itself. A similar incident on 12 July 1981—one of three Con Ed substation fires in five days—blacked out thirty-nine thousand customers.[64] A recent failure at a single sixty-nine-kilovolt transformer blew it up, ignited three thousand gallons of cooling oil, and halted the supply via thirteen underground cables to substations. Thus a single failure blacked out for four hours six percent of Con Ed's load—much of lower Manhattan, including one of the world's densest concentrations of financial computers.[65] Substations are so vulnerable that they have been shut down by as little as an inquisitive squirrel.[66]

To the end user, it matters little whether a power interruption is in the bulk supply—which accounts for only about fifteen percent of all blackouts—or in distribution (which accounts for the rest).[67] For local or selective disruption, sabotage of distribution is at least as easy to arrange as sabotage of transmission lines or high-voltage switching stations, and it can be just as hard to repair. Attacks on local distribution equipment cannot, of course, affect as many customers, and are much less likely to affect the stability of the entire grid. But they are more certain to black out particular local areas because for distribution, unlike transmission, alternative pathways are often not available unless the utility has mobile equipment for temporary connections.

Control and communications

The ability of power grids to function at all, let alone to reroute power around damaged equipment, *assumes* the operability of most control systems.[68] Control centers must communicate with each other and with field equipment (generators, switches, relays, etc.); otherwise no rerouting or load alterations are possible.

This communication relies on telex, telephone, signals sent over the power lines themselves, radio, and private microwave circuits. Despite battery and standby-generator power supplies, all these links are vulnerable to disruption. With microwaves, for example, "the loss of one base or repeating station can easily make a large portion of the communication system inoperable."[69] Most utility operations can probably be disrupted far more easily by attacks on their communication systems than on generation, transmission, or distribution components. Without instant communication, or at least an army of experts in the field who can manually operate the equipment according to prompt radio instructions, the stability of the grid will be in danger. Such improvised hand operation probably could not protect the grid from sudden, major shocks arising from the loss of major transmission, switching, or generating capacity.

Few utilities have installed comprehensive, reliable systems of underfrequency relays to ensure that if control and synchronicity are lost, the grid will automatically isolate itself into many small islands. This would maintain service where possible and at least prevent serious damage to major equipment. Lacking such automatic "sectionalization," many utilities' only alternative to functioning control and communication systems is system-wide collapse.

Another point of vulnerability is the centralized control centers themselves. Of course, power engineers have tried to make the centers' equipment reliable:

> Because of their vital role in system reliability, the computer facilities in control centers are usually doubly redundant (backed up by a complete set of duplicate facilities); in at least one center they are triply redundant. Their power supplies are "uninterruptable" and are also often doubly redundant.[70]

Yet as simple a thing as a pocket magnet can give a computer amnesia. At a higher level of sophistication, a portable device concealed in a delivery van can produce a credible imitation, on a local scale, of the electromagnetic pulse produced by high-altitude nuclear explosions (Chapter Seven).[71] Done outside a grid control center, this could probably make most of its computers and other equipment permanently inoperable.

Another disturbing possibility, to which no attention appears to have been given, is that rather than merely cutting communications, a saboteur might—like a phone phreak—prefer to use them. Indeed, both private and public telephone lines can be tapped into remotely, as noted in Chapter Two, and many utilities' control computers—not merely their accounting computers—appear to be accessible to phone phreaks. Such codes as are normally used are easily broken by the phreaks' microcomputers. Worse still, despite the encoding used on some utility microwave networks, it is probably well within the capabilities of many electronic enthusiasts to tap into a utility microwave net, using a portable dish, and effectively to take over the grid. Sitting in a van on a hillside somewhere, they could experiment with cutting power plants in and out, changing grid connections, running voltages up and down, or whatever else amused them.

One utility control expert, when asked about these concepts, felt that the diversity of communication links which his company uses, and certain technical features of its microwave and other systems, would make take-over difficult: most likely the company's operators could still maintain control. But he agreed that this result, if true, was not by design but by accident—a result of precautions taken against natural disaster. He also felt that companies less sophisticated than his own (perhaps the best-pre-pared in the country in this regard) might well be worse off. That particu-lar grid is designed to be manually operable from dispersed control cen-ters, but it is not hard to envisage ways in which communications between them could be blocked or spoofed, and the grid perturbed, in ways be-yond the ability of manual control to handle. For most if not all electric utilities, elementary consideration of the published details of communica-tion systems suggests that the vulnerabilities commonly discussed—such as the risk of sabotage to switchyards, transmission lines, and power plants—are just the tip of the iceberg.

Thus all the components of power grids, from the generating plant to the final distribution equipment, and including the control and communi-cation systems which bind all the components together into a functioning whole, lend themselves to easy disruption. But that is not the end of the story. An electrical grid is more than simply a static array of connected devices. It is a finely tuned *dynamic* system. Its dynamic requirements place special obligations on its operators—and provide special opportunities for saboteurs.

System stability

To understand more fully the delicacy of the balance and timing which enable the grid to function, it is helpful to begin by considering, in more detail than in the earlier case study of the 1977 New York blackout, what happens when the steady flows of power in an electrical grid are inter-rupted.

Sudden trips (disconnections) of elements of power systems occur com-monly in the midst of normal operations. If lightning short-circuits a transmission line, for example, automatic circuit breakers open; then they attempt to reclose in a fraction of a second, and again in several seconds if at first unsuccessful. Users are aware only of a brief flickering of the lights if all goes well. If, however, the fault has not cleared (or if the breaker does not work properly), the breaker will remain open. If an alternative transmission path is available (as it normally is), the electrical flow redis-tributes itself within a few cycles—a small fraction of a second. This redis-tribution may overload other lines. They can tolerate substantial overloads for short periods without overheating, and can even be run for up to four hours at their "long-time emergency rating" without damage. But before time and temperature limits on the lines are reached, operators must re-route power or shed (cut off) loads to bring the lines within safe limits.

Similar readjustments may also be needed after the initial rapid redistribution of power flows that accompanies the sudden trip of a loaded generator. Further, the generator itself must rapidly bypass steam from its turbine in order to avoid serious damage from spinning too fast without load. Thereafter the turbogenerator cannot be rapidly reconnected to the grid, but must be brought up gradually from almost zero load.[72]

In practice, the detailed electrical phenomena occurring when normal bulk power flows are interrupted are very complex and demand elaborate mathematical analysis. It is not simply a matter of electricity's flowing or not flowing; rather, the current tends to rush out of some parts of the grid and into others, producing "transients"—abnormally high voltages or currents which can severely damage equipment. The effect is somewhat analogous to what happens when a complex mechanical structure held together by various stiff struts is sharply struck at a single point. A wave of stress propagates through the structure. Depending on the structural details, shocks arriving from different directions may concentrate at single points, doing disproportionate damage to components far from the site of the original blow. How the shocks propagate and focus depends on the relative stiffness and strength of the various members and on how they have been assembled.

Electrical networks have analogous elements and properties. Transient surges of high voltage can break down insulation in a cable or transformer, thereby causing a secondary fault which can itself propagate new transients through the network. A surge of current can likewise trip a protective breaker and needlessly disconnect a circuit. The electrical properties of long transmission lines and (especially) of long underground cables tend to increase transients.

Alternating-current power grids can also become unstable by losing their synchronization:

> In normal operation, all of the [generator] rotors . . . are rotating in precise synchronism. Further, the power output and other electrical quantities associated with each generator are absolutely dependent on this synchronous operation. If a generator is subjected to a sufficiently large disturbance, . . . as . . . from a nearby fault, it may . . . "pull out" of synchronism, even though the original disturbance is momentary. Once synchronism is lost, the power output of the unit drops rapidly. . . .[73]

and it must be instantly taken off-line until ready for exact resynchronization. Steam-driven turbines, if run without load, will ordinarily gain too much speed, so they are normally shut down altogether. They then take twelve hours or more to restart[74] (sometimes days in certain nuclear plants where neutron-absorbing fission products accumulate after shutdown). Restarting time can be reduced to minutes or less by "tripping to house load"[75]—that is, letting the plant continue to meet auxiliary loads in the power station itself while bypassing surplus steam around the turbine. Thus the turbine is not completely shut down and remains ready for rapid reconnection with the grid. This is common practice in Europe and mandatory in Japan, but not universal in American fossil-fueled power stations. The technique could have eliminated the 1977 New York blackout.[76]

If a power grid is more than momentarily subjected to a load larger than it can sustainably supply, and if "spinning reserve" capacity already synchronized with the grid cannot be brought into full production to make good the deficit, the extra energy must come from somewhere. It comes out of the stored rotational energy of the operating generators. They will therefore slow down,[77] and the frequency of the whole interconnected system will be pulled down below the normal sixty cycles per second. This can cause more power to flow toward the deficit area, perhaps further overloading transmission lines[78] and probably tripping protective breakers. (If protective devices did not work properly, different elements of a grid could try to operate at significantly different frequencies, "bucking" each other. This would cause enormous internal stresses and, probably, serious damage.) Some modern turbogenerators of very large capacity (well over a thousand megawatts of electrical output in a single unit) work so close to the yield limits of their materials that they have little safety margin for the stresses generated by loss of synchronization. Some will reportedly suffer gross mechanical failure (e.g., by the shaft's flying apart) if the frequency deviates by one or two percent while they are under full load. Similar cost-cutting savings in generator materials have greatly decreased the rotors' stored energy "and thus increased the probability that synchronism will be lost in the event of a fault."[79]

Instabilities caused by the grid

The stability of a grid depends not only on how its generators can perform relative to their loads and to each other, but also on how well the transmission lines (and their associated switchgear, transformers, and controls) can knit these ingredients together. Transmission lines, because of their electrical properties, are subject to two kinds of limits on how much power they can safely handle: thermal limits, set by how much heat they can dissipate to their surroundings without sagging, and "system stability limits." These arise from the complex electrical properties of transmission lines:

> Transfer of power at a given voltage can be increased only up to a certain level beyond which it becomes impossible to maintain synchronous operation between generators at the . . . ends [of the line]. . . . Following a disturbance, it is possible for a machine to operate momentarily past the stability limit and then

to regain synchronism . . . , but this ability is limited and operating conditions are established to maintain operation within safe limits allowing for the occurrence of some disturbances.[80]

These limits become more stringent at higher voltages and with longer lines—both characteristic of the trend towards larger, more remotely sited generating plants, such as those proposed to use Western coal.

One form of this stability problem was illustrated in microcosm in the 1977 New York blackout. Underground cables, used throughout Con Ed's area, have large distributed "capacitance"—ability to store an electric charge between two separated conductors. This capacitance could produce large voltage transients if not compensated by series "inductances." Inductance is the ability of an electrical conductor—a coil or just a wire— to store energy in its magnetic field. Capacitance and inductance are complementary, and compensating, types of "reactance"—the ability to resist changes in voltage or in current, respectively. Controlling an electrical grid therefore requires not only keeping supply and demand in quantitative balance, but also balancing the reactance of the loads and lines to prevent damaging transients and to ensure that voltage and current do not get badly out of step with each other. That "reactive balancing" is where Con Ed came unstuck.

Con Ed's "black-start" procedures—the sequence of operations for restoring the grid after a complete power failure—relied on the windings of the main, steadily used generators for about two-thirds of the needed inductive reactance. Because circuit breakers had separated those generators from the grid, none of their inductance was initially available for compensation, and inductive compensation in another critical circuit was damaged and unusable.[81] Efforts to restore the grid rapidly in large sections apparently led to series resonance effects—strong electrical oscillations at unexpected frequencies—between the unbalanced inductive and capacitive elements. This in turn caused high-voltage transients, which damaged cables, transformers, and switchgear.[82]

The tripping of the eight-hundred-forty-four-megawatt Ravenswood Number Three generator was also caused by cable capacitance. When load-shedding removed large inductive loads (motors) which had previously compensated for the cable capacitance, the capacitive surge raised voltages to as much as eleven and a half percent above normal. The resulting pathological voltage-current relationships confused the generator's controls so much that it shut off in self-protection. This sealed the fate of the Con Ed grid by dropping system frequency from sixty cycles per second to only fifty-seven and eight-tenths. That frequency was low enough to be sustained by available generating capacity (enough automatic load-shedding already having occurred). But it was too low to keep power plant auxiliaries—fuel pumps, draft fans, feedwater pumps, and so forth—run-

ning fast enough to support the vital functions of the thirty-three generators still operating. The resulting vicious circle of plant failures and further declining frequency crashed the grid in four minutes.[83]

Interestingly, such tight dependence on a stable operating frequency is
not technically essential, especially in a relatively small grid. The Israeli
grid, for obvious geographic reasons, is isolated, not interconnected. It is
so designed that it could have tolerated a frequency drop of at least five
percent, equivalent to only fifty-seven cycles per second. To keep its frequency within five percent of normal, it uses three stages of relays to shed
loads when the frequency gets too low and reconnect them when it gets
too high. (Irrigation pumps are an important part of the sheddable load.)
As a result, Israeli power plants have probably the highest utilization factors in the world. This is in the engineering tradition of the Eastern European power grids, which can tolerate rather wide variations in operating
frequency. The Western European grids have a frequency standard about
five times tighter; the North American, about five times tighter still. The
North American grids, requiring the most rigid frequency control, suffer
the worst collapses if that control cannot be maintained. Yet, because of
the vast distances of many key transmission lines, the electrical properties
of North American power systems make that control most difficult to
achieve.

Brittleness is increasing

Stability problems are not unique to New York's cable system. In various
forms they are emerging nationally. In 1976, the Assistant Director for
Systems Management and Structuring in the U.S. Energy Research and
Development Administration stated:

> It is becoming apparent that the increasing complexities of the nation's elec-
> tric energy system are rapidly outstripping its capabilities. Our interconnected
> electric energy systems seem to be evolving into a new condition wherein
> "more" is turning out to be "different." As they become more tightly intercon-
> nected over larger regions, systems problems are emerging which neither are
> presaged, predicted, or addressed by classical electrical engineering and which
> are no longer amenable to ad hoc solution.

> Up until the past decade the ability of an electrical system to ride out a severe
> electrical disturbance (i.e. to maintain stability) could be evaluated on the basis
> of its ability to remain stable through the first rotor angle swing (about one sec-
> ond) following the disturbance. It is now recognized, however, that this condi-
> tion is no longer sufficient. Instances have occurred wherein systems survived
> for several swings following a disturbance before becoming unstable due to a
> lower frequency phenomenon.

> Accordingly, the industry has been devoting considerable effort to . . . study-
> ing what has become known as the dynamic stability problem . . . [and] it is ac-

knowledged that *the larger, more tightly interconnected system is behaving in a fashion qualitatively different from that of earlier smaller systems.*

A systems problem which was not predicted . . . but which has rapidly become the focus of much . . . attention is . . . subsynchronous resonance. [It was] . . . standard practice [to install] series capacitors to compensate for the inherent inductance of very long lines [i.e., the reverse of Con Ed's requirements]. When this was done in the case of some lines out west, the resonant frequency of the series capacitor-inductance combination was close enough to the natural frequency of the [turbogenerator] shafts of the units involved to set up mechanical vibrations which resulted in shaft failure. The phenomenon is amenable to analysis by available theory, but the necessary tools were not readily available and the problems were not anticipated.

As an example of a future, potentially important problem outside the scope of classical electrical engineering, we point to the fundamental problem of information transfer and decision making in the case of multiple independent control centers, whose decisions affect primarily their own portions of a common interconnected system. In actuality the action taken by any one such center affects the whole. . . . [A]nalyzing . . . effective control strategies . . . is in its infancy.[84]

Today's electric energy system in the United States is one of the most complex technical systems in existence. Unlike most other industries, the individual components do not operate independently but are tied together in an interacting system covering most of the continental United States, wherein deliberate or inadvertent control actions taken at one location can within seconds affect the operation of plants and users hundreds of miles distant. . . . [T]he introduction of complex new technologies into the existing, already-complex system [and the need to consider tighter fiscal and environmental constraints compound] . . . the complexity of the system.

The point of all this is that *there does not yet exist any comprehensive applicable body of theory* which can provide guidance to engineers responsible for the design of systems as complex as those which will be required beyond the next generation. . . . [T]here will be . . . problems of great importance which will be quite different from today's problems, and *the conceptual tools and underlying theory required for their effective solution have not yet been developed.*[85]

There is thus a good deal about the operation of modern large-scale power grids that able engineers are hard pressed to anticipate even in normal operation. In abnormal operation, as Con Ed found, grids can be complex enough to defy prior analysis. This is in itself a source of vulnerability to mistakes, failures, and malice. We may well find, if power systems continue to evolve in their present direction, that they are passing unexpectedly far beyond our ability to foresee and forestall their failures. The ease with which key power-grid components and their control systems can be disrupted is ominous enough without fundamental uncertainties about how grids can behave.

In summary, a small group of people—perhaps one able person in some circumstances—could black out practically any city or region, whether by brute-force sabotage of a key switching or transmission facility or of one of the operational lifelines of giant power plants (such as cooling water or fuel transportation), or instead by an elegantly economical disruption of control and communication systems. With careful selection of targets and of their most vulnerable times (peak loads, options limited by pre-existing outages, unfavorable weather for repair, etc.), it should not be beyond the ability of some technically astute groups to halt most or all of the electrical supply in any of America's three synchronous grid regions. These blackouts can be engineered in such a way as to cause substantial damage to major items of equipment, probably requiring months or years to repair. It is conceivable that similar breakdowns could arise from a combination of natural disasters or technical mishaps, imperfect utility response, and incomplete understanding of the operational dynamics of big grids.

However caused, a massive power-grid failure would be slow and difficult to repair, would gravely endanger national security, and would leave lasting economic and political scars. It is not pleasant to have in the back of one's mind that the next time the lights blink out, they may take an exceedingly long time to come back on again.

Chapter Eleven
Nuclear Power

Nuclear power reactors, which in 1980 provided about a twelfth of world and a ninth of U.S. electrical generation, suffer from the vulnerabilities already described for central electric systems. This chapter explores the following additional, uniquely nuclear vulnerabilities of reactors and their ancillary plants:[1]

• their enormous radioactive inventories, which may be a focus for civil concern and unrest,[2] an instrument of coercion,[3] and a cause of devastation if released by sabotage or war;
• their unusual concentration of interdependent, exotic resources; and
• their facilitation of the manufacture of nuclear bombs which can be used to destroy, among other things, nuclear facilities.

This analysis focuses almost entirely on the first of these three vulnerabilities: how far nuclear facilities can provide an attractive target for sabotage or acts of war.

The large literature on major releases of radioactivity deals almost exclusively with accidental releases. Although these are often claimed to be very improbable,[4] such analyses ignore the possibility that someone might intentionally cause a release. It is common ground, however, that the consequences of a major release by either cause could be unprecedentedly grave. The Atomic Energy Commission's Director of Regulation agreed, for example, that a band of highly trained, sophisticated terrorists could conceivably destroy a near-urban reactor so as to cause thousands, perhaps even millions, of deaths.[5] More recently, his successor in the Nuclear Regulatory Commission agreed that "thousands of lives and billions of dollars" could be lost.[6] Because these consequences are so great, it is important to examine more closely what nuclear terrorism might do and what the consequences—radiological, social, and economic—might be.

141

The chapter also briefly considers the special problems of illicit nuclear bombs and how they make nuclear reactors more vulnerable.

For simplicity, this treatment

- considers only fission reactors—not potential future fusion reactors (which would have analogous but milder safety and waste problems and would also provide routes—though different ones than fission—for spreading bombs).
- largely restricts itself to the type of commercial power reactor used in the United States—light-water reactors (LWRs)—rather than other types such as the Canadian CANDU or the proposed liquid-metal fast breeder. For the purposes of this discussion, these design distinctions do not give rise to important differences of principle. Differences of design between LWRs built in the United States and abroad are also too detailed for treatment here, but do not significantly change the conclusions.
- does not explore the implications of whether or not the spent nuclear fuel is reprocessed; this too does not much affect the conclusions. Basic economics make it unlikely that a commercial American reprocessing industry will develop. However, enough reprocessing plants already exist— for military purposes in the U.S. and for mixed commercial and military use in Europe—to make it worth considering briefly the consequences of releases from those plants' radioactive inventories.
- does not explicitly consider the numerous teaching and research reactors now in operation. It is important to note, however, that both the likelihood and the consequences of sabotage may be comparable for these small reactors and for large commercial power reactors, since the smaller reactors are often in the middle of large cities, take few or no security precautions, and have no containment buildings.
- does not consider in detail certain federal nuclear facilities, damage to which could have serious consequences for public health and for the military nuclear program.[7]

Nuclear terrorism: intentions and incidents

The plausibility of nuclear terrorism is best inferred not only from a study of the technical potential for it, but from what terrorists have said and done. Low-level attacks on nuclear facilities have in fact become so common, and the level of violence is escalating so steadily,[8] that it seems only a matter of time before a major attack is successfully attempted.

International terrorists are directly reported to be showing an increasing interest in nuclear matters. A Europe-wide NATO alert shortly after the assassination of Aldo Moro was reportedly

prompted by an explicit warning from the West German state security officials of possible terrorist plans for atomic blackmail: raids on nuclear bomb depots, kidnapping of specialized NATO officers, hijacked raw materials, occupation of nuclear plants, to name a few possibilities in what the Red Brigades speak of as "a growing sensitization to international security objectives."[9]

In a clandestine interview with the German magazine *Stern*, defected German terrorist Michael Baumann stated: "I do not want to suggest that some group, at this time [1978], has concrete plans or even definite plans [for nuclear extortion]. . . . But nonetheless, this is in the spirit of the times" and has been discussed among terrorists. As governments harden their no-concessions policy against terrorism, terrorists are driven

> to do something that will work for sure, and what else can that be except the ultimate thing? *Q.* Could that mean that they might occupy a nuclear power station? *A.* Sure. These are intelligent people and they have vast amounts of money. They also can build a primitive nuclear bomb. But an attack on a storage depot is more likely. After the killings in Lebach, the Americans noted that in a barracks sixteen half-forgotten nuclear warheads were stored. Only a few German guards were there with their police dogs. *Q.* And how would the . . . terrorists proceed in the course of a nuclear action? *A.* That is, initially, completely without importance. Anyone who has something like that [nuclear weapons] in hand has enough power to make the Prime Minister dance on a table in front of a T.V. camera. And a few other statesmen alongside with him. That is an I.O.U. of ultimate power.[10]

While Baumann's statements are somewhat speculative and cannot be taken as a definitive indication of the intentions of today's hard-core terrorists—he was a somewhat peripheral figure, and defected in the early 1970s—they are nonetheless a useful starting point for further inquiry.

More indirect motives might also be important:

> Given that leftist radicals see nuclear programs as symbols of a corrupt, militarist, capitalist state, they may attempt violent actions against nuclear targets as a way to rally opponents of civilian or military nuclear programs to their cause. . . . [I]t has been reported that in Italy a Red Brigades document urged attacks on nuclear power plants to exploit anti-nuclear sentiment in the country.[11]

Has this interest actually been manifested in overt acts of sabotage and terrorism against nuclear facilities? Unfortunately, the list of such incidents is already long and is growing rapidly. The perpetrators seem no longer to be limited to isolated individual saboteurs and local semi-amateur groups, but increasingly to include more organized and sophisticated international groups with access to a worldwide network of resources. At least two attacks have been made by governments as an open act of war: military aircraft twice bombed an Iraqi "research" reactor. The second attack destroyed the reactor. Lower-level, clandestine episodes are far more numerous. The following list of published incidents (plus the other exam

ples postponed to later sections) give the flavor of the diversity and the
gradually escalating intensity and focus of nuclear terrorism to date. (Incidents not specifically documented are generally given in a compendium
by the British analyst Michael Flood.[12])

Armed attacks and bomb explosions   The Atucha-1 reactor in Argentina,
when nearly built in 1973, was taken over by fifteen guerrillas for public-
ity. They quickly overpowered five armed guards, caused only light damage, and wounded two other guards whom they encountered while withdrawing.[13] The Fessenheim reactors in France sustained peripheral site
damage by fire after a May 1975 bombing. A month later, half the input
terminals at the computer center of Framatome (the French reactor vendor) were destroyed by a carefully placed bomb. Another bomb damaged
Framatome's valve-testing shops. Two months after that, a pair of bombs
set by Breton separatists caused minor damage to a cooling water inlet and
an air vent at the operating gas-cooled reactor at Monts d'Arée, Brittany,
which as a result was closed for investigation. It was the eighth sabotage
attempt in a month by the separatists against utility installations. It was
also the most spectacular, using a boat that crossed the artificial cooling
lake through cut fencing. In early November 1976, a bomb caused extensive damage at the Paris offices of a nuclear fuel manufacturer, and two
more bombs put a French uranium mine out of operation for about two
months by destroying four pump compressors.[14] In 1979, unknown saboteurs skillfully blew up the nearly completed core structure of two Iraqi
"research" reactors at a French factory.[15] The chief scientist of the Iraqi
nuclear program was recently assassinated in Paris (as was a probable wit-
ness), allegedly by Israeli agents.[16] In 1981, four attacks were reported on
uranium prospecting equipment in southern France, while at the Golfech
reactor site in southwestern France, shots were fired and Molotov cocktails
did well over a half-million dollars' damage.[17] And in January 1982, five
Soviet-made shaped-charge rockets were fired at the construction site of
the French Super-Phénix fast breeder reactor, causing only minor damage
but just missing twenty workers and a sodium depot.[18]
    In March 1978, Basque separatists bombed the steam generator of the
Lemoniz reactor, under construction near Bilbao in northern Spain, killing two workers, injuring fourteen, and causing heavy damage.[19] This
was one of ten simultaneous attacks on scattered facilities of the plant's
construction company, Iberduero.[20] In 1981, over a hundred Iberduero
facilities were sabotaged, costing a quarter of a million dollars.[21] Over sixty white-collar workers received death threats; the chief engineer (like the
manager in 1978) was kidnapped, and later killed;[22] Iberduero was
bombed again (killing the fourth victim in three years); more than a doz-

en bomb attacks on Lemoniz and Iberduero occurred in January alone. By 1982, completion of Lemoniz was in doubt.

"There have been armed assaults on nuclear facilities in Spain, and armed terrorists recently broke into a nuclear facility in Italy."[23] Furthermore,

[T]errorists in Spain have kidnapped officials of nuclear facilities for the purpose of interrogating them and taking their keys to place bombs in their offices. The same [Basque] terrorist group has threatened prominent officials in the nuclear industry with assassination if planned nuclear programs were pursued. Terrorists in West Germany have placed bombs at the homes of those charged with the security of nuclear facilities.[24]

The Trojan reactor in Oregon has had its Visitor Center bombed.[25] Electronic controls at the Stanford Linear Accelerator were heavily damaged by two bombs in 1971. Reactor guards at several U.S. sites have been fired upon.[26] On the 1976 Memorial Day weekend, the Nuclear Regulatory Commission issued a security alert to U.S. nuclear plants on the basis of "highly tentative and inconclusive information," the nature of which has not been disclosed.[27] Unexploded bombs have been found at the Ringhals reactor in Sweden,[28] the Point Beach reactor in Wisconsin in 1970, and the Illinois Institute of Technology reactor in 1969. In 1975–76, a person "was arrested for attempting to illegally obtain explosives to use in sabotaging a [U.S.] nuclear powerplant."[29]

Sabotage by insiders   A 1971 fire did between five and ten million dollars' damage to the Indian Point Two reactor in New York. The fire was set in an auxiliary building (housing control panels, cables, and pumps) while Unit Two was fueled but not yet critical and Unit One was operating nearby. The arsonist turned out to be a mechanic and maintenance man at the plant. He had worked for Con Ed for seven years, was an Army veteran, was married with three children, had long lived in the area, turned in the alarm himself, and was among the first to fight the fire.[30] "A series of suspicious fires betweeen June and November 1977 delayed the completion of Brazil's first nuclear power plant at Angra dos Reis";[31] at least five significant acts of sabotage were reported.[32] Worker sabotage has been reported at seven American reactors (in addition to the Indian Point fire): at Zion in Illionois in 1974,[33] Quad Cities in Illinois,[34] Peach Bottom in Pennsylvania,[35] Fort St. Vrain in Colorado, Trojan in Oregon in 1974 (during construction), Browns Ferry in Alabama in 1980 (reportedly including the disabling of closed-circuit TV cameras), and Beaver Valley in Pennsylvania in 1981.[36] A Swiss reactor was also reportedly sabotaged by workers.[37] During a strike against Florida Power & Light Company, there were one hundred one incidents of sabotage damaging equipment offsite, and the FBI was alerted to a rumored plan to sabotage the main generator at the Turkey Point nuclear plant.

Suspected arson has occurred at the General Electric Company's Knolls Atomic Power Laboratory in New York State, at several other U.S. nuclear research facilities, and in 1975 in an equipment storage barn at the West Valley (New York) reprocessing plant. The Winfrith, Wylfa, and Berkeley reactors in Britain have been damaged by sabotage during construction or operation—Winfrith when a mercury compound was poured into the calandria, where it amalgamated with the aluminum alloy, causing serious damage. Two control room workers at the Surry reactor in Virginia were convicted in October 1979 of causing one million dollars' damage "to bring public attention to what they described as lax security and unsafe working conditions at the plant."[38] (Such sabotage was made a federal crime in 1980.)[39] Numerous nuclear facilities of all kinds have received threats, usually bomb hoaxes; during 1969–76, licensed nuclear facilities recorded ninety-nine threats or acts of violence in the United States (seventy-six of them at federal plants), with twenty-three analogous threats at government nuclear plants in the United Kingdom. By 1979–80 the U.S. list had expanded to over four hundred incidents, of which three hundred fifty were telephoned bomb threats to nuclear facilities.[40]

Breaches of security at nuclear facilities   In 1966, twenty natural uranium fuel rods were stolen from the Bradwell reactor in England, and in 1971, five more disappeared at or in transit to the Wylfa reactor. In 1971, an intruder wounded a night watchman at the Vermont Yankee reactor. The New York University reactor building was broken into in 1972. So was the Oconee reactor's fresh fuel storage building in 1973. The fence of the Erwin (Tennessee) plant handling highly enriched uranium was partly climbed in 1974 and fully penetrated in 1975, both times without theft.[41] So was the Kerr McGee plutonium plant in Oklahoma in 1975—where security was reportedly then so lax that five to ten thousand dollars' worth of platinum was stolen and carried home by workers. In 1975 at the Biblis reactor in Germany (then the world's largest), a Member of Parliament carried a bazooka into the plant under his coat and presented it to the director. A Canadian Member of Parliament likewise carried an unchecked satchel into the Pickering plant. In 1977, a Nuclear Regulatory Commission inspector was admitted to the Fort St. Vrain control room unescorted and without having to identify himself.[42] Similar breaches have occurred at other reactors. In recent years, well-organized employee rings have systematically stolen parts and tools from some nuclear plants under construction.[43]

In December 1980, a former employee used a long-out-of-date security pass to enter the Savannah River plutonium production plant, where he stole a truck and other equipment from a high-security area. In 1976 more than a ton of lead shielding was reported stolen from Lawrence Livermore Laboratory, a U.S. bomb design center.[44] In 1974 several tons of unclassified metal were stolen from the nuclear submarine refitting docks at Rosyth, Scotland, apparently through a conspiracy of dockyard employees.[45] (Nuclear submarine fuel, available at the same docks, is highly enriched uranium [HEU], the most easily usable bomb material.) On 5 April 1970, a classified Atomic Energy Commission (AEC) shipment, not fissionable or radioactive, was stolen in an armed robbery from the Railway Express office at Newark Airport.[46] On 14 October 1970, "an AEC courier guarding a truck shipment of nuclear weapons components" was held up and robbed by three armed persons who took his revolver, wallet, walkie-talkie, submachine gun, and keys to the truck, but did not open or take the truck itself.[47] In a bizarre incident in the fall of 1978, the FBI arrested two men for conspiring to steal and sell to the Mafia a berthed nuclear submarine in Connecticut, but prosecutors concluded they only meant to abscond with the down payment.[48] The authorities did not deny that the theft might have succeeded.

U.S. Army blackhat teams are reported to have successfully penetrated and left nuclear bomb storage bunkers without detection, despite armed guards and modern barriers and alarms.[49] Two incidents at a Nike Hercules nuclear missile base outside Baltimore sugggest possible reconaissance by potential bomb thieves. [50] In 1979, journalist Joseph Albright testified that by posing as a fencing contractor he gained an interior tour of two Strategic Air Command bomb depots and their weak points. In late 1977 he came "within a stone's throw of four . . . nuclear weapons" while "riding about five miles an hour in an Air Force pickup truck . . . driven by my only armed escort [with one pistol, and both hands on the wheel. . . . No one] had searched me or inspected my bulky briefcase, which was on my lap." [51] Before publishing the article, he purchased by mail blueprints showing the depots' layout, a method of disabling the alarms, and two unguarded gates through the innermost security fence. Afterwards he received a revised set of blueprints showing "the wiring diagram for the solenoid locking system for the B-52 alert area." Evidently the security of military nuclear bombs still leaves something to be desired.[52]

Nuclear Thefts   In 1978, a ship carrying two hundred tons of natural uranium was hijacked, allegedly to Israel, [53] breaching EURATOM safeguards, but the governments concerned kept it a secret for nearly ten years. In 1974, a uranium-smuggling operation in India to China or Pakistan via Nepal was exposed.[54] There have been numerous natural-uranium-related crimes, some involving thefts of ton quantities [55]. In 1979, an employee at the General Electric Fuel Processing Plant in Wilmington,

North Carolina stole two sixty-six-pound drums of low-enriched uranium, apparently by loading them into the trunk of his car, and used them to try to extort a hundred thousand dollars from the management on pain of public embarassment.[56] Over a period of several years, twenty truckloads of radioactively contaminated tools and scrap metal were illicitly dug up and sold from a waste dump in Beatty, Nevada.[57] "Vast quantities of cannabis resin were smuggled into Britain in radioactive waste drums destined for the Atomic Energy Research Establishment at Harwell," then recovered by asking to have them back for the Pakistani Customs.[58] There is widespread official suspicion that at least a dozen bombs' worth of highly enriched uranium (HEU) was stolen by insiders from a plant in Apollo, Pennsylvania during the mid-1960s [59]: "a knowledgeable insider could quite easily have made off with" it.[60] At the Erwin, Tennessee HEU plant, where employees checked each other for theft under the honor system, [61] suspicious shortages of HEU have persisted for many years,[62] leading the Office of Nuclear Materials and Safeguards at the Nuclear Regulatory Commission to recommend that the plant's license be revoked.[63] Minor amounts of bomb materials—not enough to make a bomb, but enough for materials research or validating a threat—have been stolen from plants in North America on at least three acknowledged occasions, not counting mere inventory discrepancies. [64] In one instance, a six-ounce HEU fresh fuel rod was stolen from Chalk River in Canada.

Miscellaneous human and institutional flaws   A senior general and the former head of the Italian Secret Service were arrested following an announcement by the Italian government, in October 1974,

> that they had discovered a plot by right-wing terrorists to poison Italy's aqueducts with radioactive waste material stolen from a nuclear research center in Northern Italy. The alleged threat was associated with revelations of a planned assassination and political coup by right-wing elements. An engineer at the research center was named as a conspirator, but the allegations were never substantiated. The case became entangled in legal technicalities. Whether the alleged plot, which gained widespread publicity in Italy, was real or not has never been determined.[65]

An analytic laboratory used by the Japanese nuclear industry to monitor effluents was shut down by the government for falsifying and fabricating its test results.[66] In April 1981, a forty-day cover-up of improper effluent discharges was revealed at Japan's Tsuruga reactor. Commonwealth Edison Company (America's most nuclearized utility) and two of its officials were indicted on charges of conspiracy to falsify records "by omitting the fact that protective doors leading to the vital area of the [Quad Cities] plant had been found unlocked and unguarded."[67] Two shift supervisors at Three Mile Island Unit One were found in 1981 to have cheated on their licensing examinations, and some thirty licensed operators had to be retested.[68]

Some three to four percent of the one hundred twenty thousand or so carefully screened military personnel who have the opportuniy to detonate nuclear bombs must be dismissed each year—nearly five thousand in 1976 alone[69]—for reasons ranging from drug abuse (about a third of the total) to mental problems to negligence. Some reports suggest that such problems may be increasing, especially those related to drugs.[70] An Army demolitions officer and seven GIs, all drug smugglers, were arrested in Karlsruhe, West Germany (coincidentally near a German nuclear research center which holds large stocks of bomb materials) after plotting arms thefts and a raid on an Army payroll office.[71] February 1978 press reports describe a Georgia airwoman who broke and removed "four seals to the manual special weapons [i.e., nuclear bombs] terminal handle" at a combat-ready B-52 guarded by soldiers with shoot-to-kill orders.

French scientists testing a bomb in the Algerian Sahara apparently had to destroy it hurriedly lest it fall into the hands of rebellious French generals[72]. During the Cultural Revolution in China, the military commander of Sinkiang Province reportedly threatened to take over the nuclear base there[73].

Malicious use of nuclear materials Many radioactive sources and medical radioisotopes have been stolen,[74] and some shipments of bomb materials have been misrouted, mislaid, or even dropped off trucks.[75] However, only four instances of malicious use of nuclear materials are known so far: a Squibb radiopharmaceuticals worker put radioiodine in another's drink and someone at Brown University put radiophosphorus in two workers' food;[76] a hated supervisor at France's Cap de la Hague reprocessing plant was exposed to gamma radiation from stolen wastes hidden under the seat of his car by a worker;[77] and in 1974 the interiors of some train coaches in Vienna were sprinkled with substantial but nonlethal amounts of radioiodine, contaminating at least twelve passengers.[78] There have been reports that nuclear materials were used in attempted suicide in Europe,[79] and that a thief who tampered with a stolen radioactive source may well have been killed by it.[80] In an apparent case of unintentional suicide, a Tulsa, Oklahoma radiographer died of radiation received from a stolen radio-iridium source.[81]

The foregoing history of actual incidents of nuclear terrorism, sabotage, theft, and related institutional failures shows a diverse group of actors. Most of them breached the security of nuclear facilities for purposes of petty theft or to annoy or embarrass the management. The issue of concern is not so much the acts so far committed—though some of them have caused extensive damage. A greater concern is how much relative amateurs have been able to accomplish at facilities which are claimed to be subject to stringent security precautions. This suggests that if experienced terrorists decide to mount a serious attack, they can do a great deal more damage than has occurred so far. The increasing involvement by terrorists in attacking nuclear facilities, some of whom (notably the Basque group ETA) are believed to have international connections, shows the seriousness of the problem. Further, the review of terrorist resources in Chapter Seven suggests that very considerable firepower can be brought to bear on nuclear facilities. Given these two ingredients, it is worth examining the technical vulnerabilities that might enable terrorist acts (or acts of war) to achieve major releases of radioactivity from nuclear facilities.

The potential for reactor sabotage

More than seventy light-water reactors are operable in the United States, many of them clustered at shared sites. A comparable or larger number of LWRs is under construction. A typical LWR produces about a thousand megawatts of electricity and operates, on average, slightly over half the time. When operating it contains an enormous amount of radioactivity: over fifteen billion curies undergoing nearly six billion trillion disintegrations per second.[82]

The great complexity of such a large reactor arises largely from the many protective devices which are supposed to prevent a major release of the radioactive inventory. This is a formidable task, because even after the nuclear chain reaction has been shut down, the radioactivity continues. It cannot be reduced or controlled in any way. At shutdown the radioactive "decay heat" is six to ten percent of the heat produced at full power—that is, initially hundreds of megawatts. Although that rate slackens, rapidly at first, it remains sufficient for weeks to melt the hundred tons of ceramic (uranium oxide) fuel unless it is carried away by a special cooling system. The total decay heat in that fuel is enough to melt down through a solid iron pillar ten feet in diameter and seven hundred feet long.[83] Even before overheating fuel melts, it is heated further by chemical reactions between its metal cladding and water. Hot fuel also generates steam, hydrogen (which can burn or explode), and carbon dioxide from decomposing concrete, any of which can break open the heavy concrete containment dome. Just the circulating water in a normally operating pressurized-water reactor contains mechanical energy equivalent to the force of two dozen tons of TNT. The water's heat contains about a hundred times more energy than that. All these sources of internal energy, of which the decay heat is the most important, would help, in an accident or sabotage, to release the radioactivity.

All the protective devices are vulnerable in various ways. For example, most of the shutdown, cooling, and control devices cannot work without electricity.[84] Few of these devices have adequate battery storage; instead, they rely on offsite power from the grid, onsite power from the station's own switchyard, or emergency diesel generators (which are not very reliable). Published accident analyses reveal that failure of both offsite and onsite electric power would cause severe and unstoppable meltdowns in which most of the mitigating devices would not work. The operators' instruments, showing what is happening inside the reactor—whether the valves are open or closed and so forth—would not work either, so even manual intervention could not save the reactor.

It is rather easy to cut both offsite and onsite power to a reactor. Low-technology sabotage could disable diesel generators between their periodic tests. A terrorist could then at leisure, before the back-up is fixed, cut the offsite power, which arrives at the station's switchyard via conspicuous transmission lines. One person without special skills could do both, either by gaining access to the site or, in most cases, by standoff attack (since the diesels are often badly protected and sometimes housed in light external sheds). The unstable ex-employee of the Three Mile Island reactor complex who in 1976 drove onto the site, scaled a security fence, entered a protected area next to the Unit One reactor building, and later drove off without being apprehended[85] would have had plenty of time to sabotage the diesels or switchyard or both. Operating power reactors have already experienced accidental failure of all back-up power—fortunately not simultaneous with a grid outage.[86] Operating reactors have also experienced power-grid instability which blacked out the area and shut down the reactor.[87]

More complex modes of attack can be designed with the aid of detailed design information which is publicly available.[88] Attacks can mimic hypothetical accident sequences, as most analyses assume is necessary, or can simplify and shortcut them. One possible approach is to produce a rapid power excursion, beyond the reactor's ability to cool the fuel (a worrisome class of potential accidents, especially in boiling-water reactors). Another approach is simply "interrupting the supply of cooling to a shutdown reactor"[89] so that its decay heat melts the fuel. These types of failure can be arranged from either onsite or offsite; the latter may involve either the use of standoff weapons against the plant or an attack on targets outside the main area of the plant. Such remote targets include transmission lines, related switchyards and transformers offsite, and any cooling-water intake that the plant needs as an "ultimate heat sink"—a source of cooling to carry away the core's decay heat.

For any power plant, but especially for nuclear plants because they need cooling for decay heat after shutdown, "the screenhouse [intake structure] is probably the most vulnerable point of sabotage in steam generating stations."[90] (This may be one of the things that Dr. Bruce Welch, a former Navy Underwater Demolitions officer, had in mind in his widely publicized Congressional testimony that with a few randomly selected military demolition people he "could sabotage virtually any nuclear reactor in the country."[91] A retired Green Beret colonel, Aaron Bank, testified before the same Committee to similar effect about the San Onofre plant, near former President Nixon's house: the intake structures of that reactor are unusually accessible.) Proposals to harden the systems which remove decay heat were long ignored, but after the Three Mile Island accident they are considered a high priority.[92]

Standoff weapons may include mortars, rockets, precision-guided munitions, fixed-wing aircraft, helicopters, or remotely piloted vehicles. Inspection of analyses of the seismic resonances of major reactor structures also suggests that an exotic possibility—standoff attack by infrasound generators tuned to published resonant frequencies—cannot be wholly disregarded. Key control and safety circuitry, as noted in Chapter Seven, may also be vulnerable to intense electromagnetic pulses, which a good physicist could generate locally with a homemade, transportable standoff device.[93]

Onsite overt attacks could be meant to take over the plant. The staff could be subdued or killed with ordinary weapons or by introducing a rapidly lethal gas into the ventilating system. The latter method might be quick enough to prevent operators from raising the alarm, isolating control room ventilation, or shutting down the reactor, and it might be the method of choice for an insider. (It also raises the question, nowhere answered in the literature, of how safe a power reactor would remain if all its staff suddenly dropped dead.) Once the plant has been seized, its security devices and the shielding and life-support systems of the control room would all help to protect its occupiers from both invaders and external radioactive releases. The occupants could then do either of two things, or both in succession, at comparative leisure.

First, they could use their power over the costly plant and its dangerous contents as a basis for political negotiations, as in the plot of a recent James Bond novel.[94] The negotiations might be secret initially, with the threat of disclosure and ensuing public panic used as a bargaining chip. Various concessions could be demanded. Serious damage could be undertaken if the concessions were not forthcoming—or possibly straightaway if the occupiers preferred people dead to people watching, or if they could not competently maintain the plant in safe condition. Such a situation would lead at a minimum to the economic loss of the plant and probable ruin for its owners; at a maximum, to all of that plus major releases of radioactivity.

Two types of deliberate damage, not mutually exclusive, seem possible. Mere demolition is straightforward. Saboteurs wanting to guarantee a major release, and not completely confident that the events they set in motion would cause a major breach in the crucial containment building, could of course blow holes in it; but it would be easier simply to open the dome's personnel airlock doors. (The San Onofre information center used to show every hour a film demonstrating how these doors work.)[95] Mindful of the near miss at Browns Ferry, a low-technology saboteur with an experimental frame of mind might want to see what arson in the cable-spreading room would do. Alternatively, depending on the occupiers' technical knowledge, control systems might be disabled, bypassed, or reversed so as to make the plant destroy itself. Both normal and emergency coolant could be removed or stagnated. In some circumstances, large overpower transients might be achievable, especially with the help of insiders. The occupiers could use, alter, or disable all the electrical systems, controls, cables, valves, pumps, pipes, and so on virtually at will. Even major components are highly vulnerable to commercially available shaped charges, to thermic rods ("burn bars"), and to thermal shock.

Once sabotage had begun, repairs and countermeasures could rapidly become impossible even if the plant's operators quickly regained control of the site. Key parts of the plant could by then already be filled with steam, water, noxious gases, or high levels of radioactivity. It could be impossible even to assess damage. Access to the inside or outside of the plant could readily be prohibited by radioactive releases, chemical poisons, or conventional munitions wielded by defenders from their concrete fortress—which their adversaries would hardly want to damage.

Those adversaries would have to include and coordinate counterinsurgency forces, health physics teams, and reactor engineers. Further, though one can doubtless assume considerable ingenuity and courage on the part of the forces of law and order, the history of major nuclear accidents suggests that one can also expect a full measure of confusion, error, foolishness, and possibly panic. Panic would almost certainly ensue in downwind areas, probably leading to considerable loss of life and property and hindering the arrival of back-up teams. And of course if a meltdown did occur, then events onsite and releases offsite would, by general consensus, be uncontrollable and unstoppable in principle, owing to extreme radiation fields and the formidable temperatures, masses, and chemical properties of the materials involved. Major psychological, political, and economic trauma on a national or world scale would be inevitable. Civil liberties and indeed civil (as opposed to martial) law would probably, as in a nuclear bomb threat, be among the early casualties.[96]

Events at the stricken plant could unfold gradually and inevitably, dominating headlines for weeks. Unlimited resources might not be enough to abate the release. It is often forgotten that once a serious release sufficiently contaminates the plant and its environs that if its staff (if functional) cannot remain to fix the damage or even to prevent further deterioration, a "loss-of-supervision" scenario has begun.[97] Experience at the Seveso chemical plant in Italy, where an accident dispersed so much highly toxic dioxin that not just the plant but the whole valley had to be abandoned, suggests this is far from idle speculation. It was not far from happening when the Browns Ferry control room filled with acrid smoke in 1975,[98] or when a storage tank two miles from the Fort Calhoun, Nebraska nuclear plant spilled one hundred fifty tons of anhydrous ammonia in 1970, forming a thirty-five-foot-thick layer of ammonia that covered some thousand acres.[99] (Nuclear plants do not always have enough breathing apparatus for everyone). Sabotage of the cooling system on a high-level waste tank could lead to boil-off of the water and release of fission products, but this has been officially discounted because it "would take weeks or months, allowing ample time for detection and repair."[100] What if the sabotage has already released so much that nobody can do the repairs?[101] In 1977, workers at the Windscale reprocessing plant in England went on a six-week strike, and a cladding fire was feared when they would not allow liquid nitrogen shipments to cross picket lines. Eventually the (Labour) energy minister had to threaten to call in the Army.[102]

Other types of attacks on nuclear facilities

Possible envelopment by an LNG or LPG fireball, perhaps from a nearby terminal or a stolen gas truck, has already been mentioned as a possible event that could endanger a nuclear facility and disable its operators. Another is airplane crashes. In 1972, a light plane lost in dense fog crashed into the Millstone (Connecticut) reactor complex, disabling the high-voltage supply to the transformer that operates the reactor's shutdown systems, and cutting offsite telephones for three hours. (The plant did not reduce power.)[103] The Big Rock Point reactor in Michigan was apparently such a good landmark that Air Force crews used it for practice bombing runs. (After a B-52 crashed nearby in 1971, the planes were told to stay at least five and a half miles away.) In 1974, the Prairie Island reactor in Minnesota was repeatedly overflown at low altitude by a light plane piloted by a known criminal who appeared to be photographing it. FBI investigations "did not reveal any malevolent intention or violation of the law."[104] In 1975, an Air Force B-52 carrying no weapons exploded in flight and crashed about twenty miles from the Savannah River reprocessing plant.[105] In 1972, three men hijacked a Southern Airways commerical flight to Canada, made the pilot circle over the Oak Ridge complex, threatened to crash the plane into the Oak Ridge Research Reactor or the uranium enrichment plant (the biggest industrial installation in the world), collected a reported two million dollars' ransom, and landed in Cuba.[106]

In view of this history, it is disturbing that most plants are designed to withstand a crash only of a fairly small aircraft. A typical analysis is based on a 1968 census of the civil aviation fleet, before widebody jets.[107] It also considers the impact only of the engines, not of the airframe. Likewise, the official safety report for the proposed Gorleben reprocessing plant in the Federal Republic of Germany considered only crashes by Phantom jets. Yet a jumbo jet travelling slightly slower would produce a peak impact nearly six times as big and lasting more than twice as long.[108] (On Christmas Day 1974, a hijacker was overpowered after threatening to crash a jumbo jet into the center of Rome.) By a lucky irony, the double containment strength that enabled the Three Mile Island containment shell to withstand the hydrogen explosion which occurred during its 1979 accident was designed in because a commerical flight lane for low-level approaches to the Harrisburg airport passes essentially over the plant. But it is unlikely that most reactors or other nuclear facilities are really equipped to handle a crash by well-laden widebody aircraft. The tendency of the jet fuel to cause an after-crash fire about half the time would also complicate shutdown and repair efforts in the stricken plant.

The foregoing selection of examples of potential sabotage has been illustrative, not comprehensive. Many nuclear facilities, for example, are highly vulnerable to reprogramming or disabling of their control computers, resetting of their instrument trip points, biasing of their calibration standards, and so forth, by insiders. It is also possible to attack a plant from a distance in time rather than in space. Now that digital watches with long-lived, low-drain batteries are widely available, along with sophisticated and highly reliable electronics of all kinds, it is feasible to conceal a conventional chemical bomb (or at least to say one has done so) in a reactor under construction. One extortionist recently claimed he had put a bomb in a concrete wall being poured at a German reactor, and it proved very difficult and expensive to find out whether the claim was true: some reports indicate that the wall was torn apart to see. A claim that scrap metal and tools had been incorporated into the molten lead used to cast radiation shields for U.S. Navy reactors required extensive investigation.[109] On occasion, foreign objects considerably more obtrusive than a lump inside a concrete wall have escaped detection for a surprising time: in 1972, for example, Commonwealth Edison reported having retrieved a complete Heliarc® welding rig, complete with a set of cables and hose twenty-five feet long, from inside a malfunctioning jet pump. Substantial foreign objects have even been retrieved from reactor cores. The technical and operational sophistication of the extortionist's bomb that caused three million dollars' damage to Harvey's Resort hotel-casino in Stateline, Nevada on 26

August 1980 (giving rise to hundreds of imitative threats over the follow-ing year)[110] suggests that this sort of threat, skillfully done, could shut down a lot of nuclear capacity virtually at will, simply through fear of the potential consequences if the threat were real.

Other vulnerabilities in the nuclear fuel cycle

Any consideration of potential releases of radioactive material by sabo-tage or war must look at the whole nuclear fuel cycle, not just at reac-tors.[111]

One modest but ubiquitous source, passing through the midst of our largest cities, is casks carrying spent reactor fuel. Dispersal of the contents of one cask could cause, among other consequences, land contamination costing many billions of dollars.[112]

Far more radioactivity resides in the seven thousand tons of spent fuel in storage pools, currently at reactors but perhaps in the future also at centralized pools.[113] The government projects that by the year 2000 there may be a hundred thousand tons of spent fuel in pools. The pools at reac-tors are often badly protected; many are aboveground; and the fuel, espe-cially in its first few months of storage, may require active cooling to keep it from melting.

An even more concentrated source of very-long-lived contaminants is tanks containing high-level reprocessing wastes—the source of two-thirds of the calculated hazard from a major release.[114] Such tanks are essential at reprocessing plants for cooling before any solidification of high-level wastes. They currently contain large inventories at several U.S. sites (West Valley, New York; Savannah River, Georgia; Hanford, Washington; and Idaho Falls, Idaho). The inventories of long-lived isotopes at several of these sites, including West Valley (upwind of most of the cities of the Northeast), are measured in billions of curies—the largest concentrations of radioactivity on earth. Dispersing a substantial fraction of such an in-ventory could make an area the size of Europe or the United States unin-habitable for centuries.

By way of illustration, the Barnwell reprocessing plant partly built in South Carolina (but not licensed, not commercially operable, and recently written off) is designed to reprocess more than three million pounds of spent fuel per year—the output of about fifty reactors. After five years' operation, a one percent release of just seven particularly dangerous ra-dionuclides, mostly radiocesium and radiostrontium, could contaminate tens of thousands of square miles with persistant radiation at rates which would remain far too high for human habitation for generations. Another formulation is that such a plant would in ten years accumulate as much strontium-90 and cesium-137 as would be "released by about eight thou-sand megatons of fission explosions, of the same order as the total fission yield of all the nuclear weapons in the U.S. and Soviet stockpiles."[115]

To make such a release easier to arrange, the reprocessing plant itself, like a reactor, contributes substantial internal energies.[116] Within an operating reprocessing plant are large amounts of flammable solvents, ton inventories of fissionable materials that must be carefully protected from accidental chain reactions, hot reactive acids, thermally and radioactively hot spent fuel and wastes, and such possible accident initiators as "red oil"—a substance, produced by radiation damage to organic solvents, which is not well characterized but is empirically known to be an easily detonated high explosive.

Such a plant separates annually in pure, readily handled form some ten to fifteen tons of plutonium—thousands of bombs' worth. In the course of five years, the plant would separate more fissile material than is present in the entire U.S. nuclear arsenal. The precision with which the plutonium could be accounted for would probably not be much better than one percent, making it impossible to be sure whether ten of bombs' worth per year were present or missing. (For example, the military reprocessing plant at Savannah River, Georgia cannot be sure it is not already missing some three hundred-odd pounds of plutonium.)[117] The presence of such a bomb material and of certain other materials within the plant would permit a saboteur to assemble in the plutonium loading or storage areas, in only a few minutes, a crude nuclear bomb with a yield of the order of tens to hundreds of tons of TNT. Such a bomb would be more than sufficient to disperse virtually the whole plutonium inventory and probably a good deal of the fission-product inventory too. No reprocessing plant's security plan has considered this possibility.

Accidents at the Savannah River reprocessing plant have already released in five days about ten times as much radioiodine as the officially recorded release in the Three Mile Island accident,[118] and nearly half a million curies of tritium—radioactive hydrogen—in a single day.[119] But those releases, however significant,[120] are trivial compared with what a serious accident could do.[121] Such an accident may have been narrowly averted at the Cap de la Hague reprocessing plant in France on 15 April 1980, when a supposedly impossible failure of all power supplies briefly disabled vital cooling and safety equipment. Had the power stayed out longer, a sequence of events could have begun which would have made it impossible for workers to stay at the plant and prevent successively more serious failures and releases.

The potential for widespread harm from facilities that deal with large amounts of radioactive materials was also obliquely illustrated by three accidents in American plutonium-handling plants. In the first, Gulf United Nuclear's plutonium facility, a mixed-oxide fuel fabrication plant at West Pawling, New York, suffered in 1972 a fire and two explosions of unspecified origin; these scattered an undetermined amount of plutonium around the facility, which was then permanently shut down.[122] In the second and third, the Rocky Flats plant, which makes plutonium bomb components fifteen miles upwind of central Denver, suffered two major fires.[123] One in 1957 released at least pounds and possibly hundreds of pounds of plutonium oxide dust. The second, in 1969, appears to have been the costliest industrial accident in U.S. history. General Giller, then the Atomic Energy Commission's Director of Military Applications, testified in Congressional hearings that the 1969 fire was "a near catastrophe" and that "hundreds of square miles" could have been contaminated if the fire had burned through the roof. "If the fire had been a little bigger," he said, "it is questionable whether it could have been contained."[124] The plant probably contained tons of plutonium. The quantity of plutonium known to cause lung cancer, if inhaled into the lung, is much less than a millionth of an ounce. Any facility containing large amounts of plutonium is thus a tempting target for terrorists. Once contaminated by a release, the plant would be very hard to maintain and clean up: deadly plutonium dust could blow around for millenia.

Military attacks on nuclear facilities

Until 1980, nobody had seriously considered the problem of power reactors in wartime.[125] Yet wars are almost ubiquitous. Since World War II, over one hundred fifty armed conflicts have involved more than twenty-five million people.[126] In 1981 alone, thirty-seven armed conflicts were underway, involving more than eight million uniformed people. With nuclear facilities in more than a hundred countries and power reactors operating in more than two dozen countries, it is not surprising that a few countries operating power reactors have had wars on their territory—India, for example. Fortunately, none of these wars has yet involved the reactors. (In Vietnam, the quarter-megawatt research reactor at Dalat was hastily dismantled by retreating American troops, lest its radioactive core be released. Its fuel, only twenty percent enriched, was too dilute to be directly used for bombs.)[127]

If attack threatened, would a country shut down all its power reactors—somewhat reducing vulnerability to attack by reducing the decay heat, but at the expense of power supplies? Swedish officials plan to do this, and therefore privately say that during Sweden's interim use of nuclear power (which Parliament has said must end by 2010) the nuclear share of total capacity should not exceed twenty-five percent—as opposed to the eighty-plus percent sought by France. However, a Finnish nuclear expert said of his own country's plans that "in a state of war the criteria for safety of nuclear power stations would change."[128] Perhaps the French government would make a similar judgment. (Ironically, fallout from a damaged Finnish or French reactor could easily reach Sweden anyway.)

The issue is likely to be taken more seriously following the Iranian (or Iranian-marked Israeli?) bombing of Iraq's Tuwaitha nuclear research center on the outskirts of Baghdad on 30 September 1980,[129] and the destruction of the Osirak "research" reactor at the same site by a major Israeli air raid on 7 June 1981.[130] The deliberate targeting of the sizeable Osirak reactor—fortunately just before it was first loaded with fuel—highlighted the possibility of radioactive releases. Precision bombing with one-ton bombs—just the kind whose effect on a reactor Israeli officials had earlier asked the Nuclear Regulatory Commission about[131]—completely destroyed the reactor.

The bombing was a resounding vote of no confidence in the international safeguards regime. It also showed that ambiguous nuclear facilities are an attractive nuisance inviting preemptive attack: indeed, Colonel Qadafi promptly called for retaliatory bombing of the Israeli "research" reactor at Dimona.[132] And the bombing also suggested that "a belligerent power could use the threat of radioactive contamination resulting from an attack as a means of coercion,"[133] greatly increasingly the military vulnerability of any country having a nuclear facility.

The second raid also gave Iraq an excuse to deny (until mid-November 1981) access to International Atomic Energy Agency inspectors,[134] who wished to satisfy themselves that the twenty-eight pounds of highly enriched uranium (enough for one or two bombs) which France had already delivered,[135] out of a planned consignment of one hundred fifty-four pounds, was not being made into bombs. Senator Alan Cranston stated that he had "been informed by more than one authoritative Executive Branch official [that] . . . the Iraqis are embarked on 'a Manhattan Project-type approach' "[136] to use the French uranium for bombs. (If this was not the case before the Israeli raid, it is very likely the case after it.) The IAEA inspector responsible for that part of the world apparently agreed.[137] Israel also suspected that Iraq planned to use Osirak's neutrons to breed natural uranium (of which Iraq had bought suspiciously large amounts) into plutonium. This could be slowly extracted in the Italian "hot cells" (shielded laboratory-scale devices for handling radioactive materials) at the Osirak site. The status of the "hot cells" after the raid is not publicly known. World consciousness of the link between reactors, bombs, ambiguous threats, and the military vulnerability of nuclear facilities has, however, been considerably advanced.

Attacking reactors with terrorist bombs

The possible use of terrorist nuclear bombs against nuclear facilities must also be considered. Although there are other high-leverage targets for such bombs, nuclear facilities are the only targets that can amplify the radiological damage of the bomb by a thousand to hundreds of thousands of times, contaminating an area the size of Europe or the United States. This could be done by a single bomb, made by "a small non-national group" with "the appropriate technical capabilities"[138] (which are not unduly hard to get),[139] and transportable in the trunk of a car. The amount of bomb material needed would be about the size of a lemon or a grapefruit, depending on its composition and the sophistication of the design. Rule-of-thumb designs with generous safety margins could be used instead of elaborate calculations. Even the most difficult materials-handling operations needed for fancy designs are no harder or more risky than converting morphine base to heroin—a clandestine operation which criminals have done routinely for years.[140] And if terrorists claim in a fashion which is technically credible that they possess bomb materials, or a bomb, they must be taken at their word, since it is statistically impossible to verify the presence or absence of more than twenty tons of bomb materials in the U.S. alone.[141] Inventories are similarly fuzzy abroad, and bombs or materials to make them can be smuggled across national borders as easily as the tens of thousands of tons of marijuana that is smuggled undetected into the U.S. each year.[142]

If terrorists had actually made nuclear bombs, that fact would probably be highly classified. It is known, however, that in the seven years ending in November 1977, forty-nine threats were received in the United States "in which adversaries claimed to possess nuclear material or a nuclear [explosive or dispersion] device and threatened to wreak severe damage with it."[143] By mid-1981 the count was sixty-five and rising.[144] Special procedures, threat evaluation teams, and telephone hotlines have been set up nationally and in some states (notably California) to deal with such threats. At least four threats were deemed sufficiently credible to evoke intensive research by a specially instrumented team[145]—the type of response that raises the most serious civil liberties issues.[146] So far as is publicly known, all threats so far have been treated as bluffs and have actually been bluffs.[147]

The nuclear industry commonly argues that terrorists would not bother to make nuclear bombs because it is easier to steal them from the military.[148] The United States Government owns more than thirty thousand nuclear bombs and plans to build over twenty thousand more during the 1980s. The bombs are stored at up to two hundred sites in more than forty states.[149] The twenty-two thousand tactical bombs include some seven thousand stored in Europe, many small enough to tuck under an arm. Some reportedly weigh less than fifty pounds. Some bombs have been lost,[150] dropped accidentally, or fired accidentally in missiles.[151] Acknowledged nuclear bomb accidents ("Broken Arrows") have so far averaged about one per year or several per thousand bombs.[152] The breaches in bomb storage security mentioned earlier suggest that theft may indeed be credible.

If terrorists did make or steal a nuclear bomb, what could they do with it at a nuclear facility such as a power reactor? This is too complex a question to answer precisely, but a rough idea can be gained from published studies of the effects of nuclear explosions much larger than the kiloton-range yields likely for crude terrorist bombs.[153] The effects of various blast overpressures, and the approximate slant ranges at which ground-burst yields of one and ten kilotons produce those overpressures, are summarized in Table Two.

Bombs yielding one and ten kilotons will also form a crater by vaporizing everything within a fireball range extending to a radius of about two hundred fifty and six hundred feet, respectively. In addition to vaporizing on the order of one thousand and ten thousand tons of material respectively, the bomb will throw out large amounts of rocks and debris at very high speed. These "ejecta" are probably big and numerous enough to do serious damage to the containment dome (let alone to weaker structures) much farther away than the range of damage by airblast.[154] Ground-shock, similar to a heavy earthquake, may do the same. The combination of electromagnetic pulse and prompt nuclear radiation, airblast and groundshock, ejecta, high winds, and fires, all in succession, can be expected to cause worse damage collectively than any of all of them separately.[155]

These considerations strongly suggest that a major release of radioactivity can be guaranteed by arranging a groundburst even of one kiloton within perhaps a thousand feet or more of a reactor. (It is not difficult to obtain such a yield from a crude bomb.)[156] Shortening the range to a few hundred feet would release not just most of the core but virtually all of it.

Table Two   Effects of Various Blast Overpressures

Overpressure (lb./sq.in.)	Range (feet)		Expected effects of blast alone on a typical large pressurized-water reactor
	1 kT[a]	10 kT[b]	
2	4,300	9,500	*Heavy internal damage to cooling towers*
3	3,200	7,100	*Cooling towers collapse, crushing other parts*
12	1,300	2,800	*Control room, auxiliaries, transformers, water tanks severely damaged; meltdown very likely.*
30	720	1,600	*Containment badly damaged; minor damage to primary coolant loop; meltdown within hours.*
150	280	610	*Instant rupture of pressure vessel; at least the volatile fission products released in minutes.*

[a] One thousand tons of TNT equivalent.
[b] Ten thousand tons of TNT equivalent.

SOURCE: U.S. Atomic Energy Commission; Chester & Chester 1976.

Ranges up to the best part of a mile would probably still cause a substantial release. At most reactor sites, a kiloton-range bomb could deliver twelve-pound-per-square-inch overpressure at standoff range from public highways.

Even a fizzle—a tenth of a kiloton or less—may well suffice. Arbitrarily short ranges could probably be achieved in practice by simply driving a truck or van up to the reactor. (Delivery vans which the guards are used to seeing are often simply waved through the gates.) The bomb would not even have to be that close: a thousand feet or less would probably suffice. For example, transmission lines and some diesel air intakes fail at about four pounds per square inch, and this dual failure, unrepaired, could cause a meltdown within hours. It is not realistic to expect prompt repairs, because even a fizzle—say a tenth of a kiloton—produces prompt radiation of five hundred rem (sufficient to kill most of the people exposed to it) at about a thousand feet for gamma rays and fifteen hundred feet for fast neutrons. The same dose would be obtained from an hour's exposure to fallout within about a thousand to three thousand feet of the site of the explosion. Thus within the range of moderate blast damage (three pounds per square inch) from such a fizzle—about a thousand feet—nobody could survive or, having reentered, would want to linger to do repairs.

Of course, major releases could be caused by means other than a nuclear bomb. Military fuel-air bombs can achieve overpressures of three hundred to a thousand pounds per square inch or more at ranges of hundreds of feet.[157] Many munitions available to terrorists (Chapter Seven) could cause a major release at standoff range. So could the more discriminating means of attack, overt or covert, discussed earlier.

Radiological consequences of major releases

What could be the consequences of a major release of radioactivity caused by some of the foregoing techniques and resources? Most of the literature on major nuclear accidents may understate the possible results of successful sabotage. According to the General Accounting Office,[158] a classified Sandia National Laboratory technical assessment of reactor sabotage, for example, found that the consequences could not exceed the maximum calculated in the Rasmussen Report[159] for a major accident. Those effects would include:

- thirty-three hundred prompt deaths,
- fifteen hundred delayed cancer deaths per year for ten to forty years, a total of up to sixty thousand, and
- fourteen billion dollars' property damage.

The Rasmussen Report, however, did not present those figures as the results of a worst possible accident. Worse ones were physically possible but were assigned a lower probability and not considered.[160] A saboteur would be free to *select* all-worst-case conditions—near-urban reactor, mature core, meteorological inversion, wind blowing toward the city—and could disable mitigating systems and breach the containment.

Furthermore, these effects would occur at ranges *up to* tens of miles—a range which, for some reactors such as Zion and Indian Point (but not the "model" reactors assumed in the Rasmussen analysis), includes some of America's largest cities. But at longer range, the radiation dose would be spread among large numbers of people who would receive relatively small individual doses but large collective doses—and thus, by the normal conventions of such calculations, would suffer as many injuries as if fewer people had received larger doses. For this reason, delayed effects, especially land contamination and thyroid damage, "can be a concern more than one hundred miles downwind from an accident and for many decades"—that is, far beyond "the distances for which emergency planning is required by current Federal guidelines."[161] Consider, for example, a major release from (say) Three Mile Island shortly before refueling, in typical weather, with the wind blowing towards population centers. Such a release could occur *with or without a full core meltdown* if the containment failed or were breached deliberately. Over the following seventy-five years, counting *only* ranges *greater than* fifty miles downwind, it would cause up to

- sixty thousand delayed cancer deaths;
- sixty thousand genetic defects;
- four hundred fifty thousand thyroid nodules;
- long-term land contamination of fifty-three hundred square miles; and
- short-term farming restrictions on one hundred seventy-five thousand square miles (an area larger than California).[162]

These long-range consequences should be *added to* the shorter-range consequences quoted above from the Rasmussen Report.

The Rasmussen Report thus understates the possible effects of a major release by ignoring worst-case conditions which a saboteur could deliberately select, and by omitting long-term, long-range effects. Its calculations of consequences have also been severely criticized by many independent reviewers, including an American Physical Society study group, the Environmental Protection Agency, and the Union of Concerned Scientists. Whatever the actual size of the consequences,[163] though, it is common ground that they could be graver than any peacetime disaster, and perhaps any wartime disaster, in recent history.

This point has been tellingly made by comparing the radioactive releases that might be caused by a major reactor accident with the fallout from the explosion at ground level of a one-megaton nuclear bomb.[164] (That is equivalent in explosive force—though its heat and radiation make it more damaging—to one million tons of TNT, or one million World War II blockbusters, or eighty times the twelve-and-a-half kilotons that flattened Hiroshima.) The radioactivity from the bomb is initially more than two thousand times that from the reactor. But the activity of the bomb debris decays far faster, so the two levels become equal after a day. Within five years, the reactor release is a hundred times as radioactive as the bomb debris; after twenty-five years, a thousand times more. Land contamination is caused mainly by this long-lived radioactivity, especially from cesium-137, which emits penetrating gamma rays and takes three centuries to decay to a thousandth of its original strength. For this reason, if the one-megaton bomb were to vaporize and disperse the reactor core, it would interdict ten times as much land after one year as if the same bomb landed on a non-radioactive target.[165] The area seriously contaminated for centuries would be hundreds of square miles, or about forty times the area comparably contaminated by a one-megaton groundburst alone.[166] Taking full account of long-term, long-range consequences makes the damage from a major reactor accident comparable to that from a one-megaton bomb at ranges up to a few hundred miles and even higher beyond about six hundred miles:[167] the reactor can actually expose more people to more radiation than the bomb can.

As noted above, however, hundreds of thousands of square miles could also be lastingly contaminated by breaching a reactor with a bomb "even of relatively small yield, such as a crude terrorist nuclear device."[168] Such a bomb could release the reactor's radioactivity just as effectively as a one-megaton bomb could—in fact, more so, since the weaker explosion would not carry the debris so high into the stratosphere, where it would have more time to decay before the fallout returned to earth. Thus a terrorist with nuclear capabilities or a "determined or desperate combatant can, by waiting for the proper weather conditions, devastate a substantial fraction of the industrial capacity of an opponent with a single nuclear weapon aimed on a reactor":[169]

> ... the possibility of malicious as well as accidental destruction of a reactor core [returns again to] ... the unfortunate links between nuclear power and expanded access to the raw materials of nuclear weaponry. ... For the staggering radiological consequences of destruction of a nuclear reactor by a nuclear weapon ... put the radiologic damage potential of a fair-sized nuclear arsenal into the hands of any nation or terrorist group with a single, ten-kiloton bomb.[170]

As Britain's Royal Commission on Environmental Pollution noted, if nuclear power "had ... been in widespread use at the time of [World War II] ..., it is likely that some areas of central Europe would still be uninhabitable because of ground contamination by [cesium]."[171] Today, scenarios for a NATO/Warsaw Pact conflict on the North German plain curiously overlook the fact that four large reactors have already been built there and could hardly fail to be destroyed, making widespread fallout likely even if no nuclear weapons were used.[172]

Against the sort of catastrophic release considered here, the usual measures meant to mitigate the effects of reactor accidents—remote or underground siting, containment venting filters, evacuation, thyroid blocking,[173] sheltering, air filtration, and the like—would be better than nothing, but still grossly unequal to the task.[174] The Nuclear Regulatory Commission does not seem much interested even in these modest measures,[175] and the nuclear industry seems to feel that mitigation methods are unnecessary or embarrassing. (For example, the Senior Vice President of Philadelphia Electric Company testified in 1980 that "[E]vacuation plans are just the window dressing and the final back-up plan"; that a low population zone some three thousand yards in radius for evacuation planning around Limerick is "more than adequate"; and that "[E]mergencies that will require evacuation will not occur.")[176] Such neglect of even the most basic precautions means that even smaller and less competent acts of sabotage against nuclear plants can still be disastrously effective.

Logistical and financial impacts

Damage to a single nuclear facility can have far-reaching consequences for other, undamaged facilities. Even modest damage to one key plant can bring much of the nuclear industry to a halt because the nuclear fuel cycle is so intricately interdependent. It entails many complex operations whose logistical coordination has remained an elusive goal for several decades. One failure or bottleneck can have unexpected side effects through the rest of the system.[177] And if fuel cycles ever came to depend on reprocessing (as with breeder reactors), about fifty reactors would depend for their fuel on timely deliveries from a single reprocessing plant. At perhaps three to eight billion dollars each, such plants would be too costly to back up. (Breeders would also depend on a few fuel fabrication plants.) Such fuel cycle dependencies create a remarkable vulnerability: a single, otherwise minor problem at a single reprocessing plant—the type of problem that already occurs so often that no reprocessing plant in the world has run on a reliable commercial basis[178]—could idle more than one hundred billion dollars' worth of fast breeders. Ironically, fast breeders have been promoted by successive Administrations as a promising means—in some cases the principal means—of ensuring national energy security.

Although the sheer cost of fixing or replacing a major nuclear plant offers a smaller incentive to sabotage it than the radioactivity within it, costs are not negligible. The cost of replacement energy would be huge for a society that had allowed itself to become dependent on energy from the damaged plant or from others shut down in the wake of the sabotage. The direct costs to the utility concerned can be crippling: just cleaning up Three Mile Island Two enough to be able to *decide* whether to try to get it working again will cost General Public Utilities a billion dollars—with the restoration to service, if this is even possible, not included. The extraordinary capital intensity of nuclear plants (new ones typically will cost several billion dollars each) represents a risk to large blocks of invested capital, as Three Mile Island investors have discovered. Few if any utilities in the world have enough financial safety margin to absorb such a risk, and as Three Mile Island has again demonstrated, institutional preparedness for a multi-billion-dollar loss is also woefully inadequate.

America's capital structure is already at risk because many utilities are insolvent. Their debt and equity—the largest single block of paper assets in the whole economy—is the basis of many highly leveraged institutions.[179] Utility finance, and hence capital markets generally, are currently so precarious—and likely to remain so for many years—that another major loss could trigger cascading bankruptcies on a wholly unmanageable scale. The potential economic consequences of losing a major nuclear asset thus go well beyond a particular utility or its rate-payers or investors. Further, the financial community already perceives substantial risk associated with utility investments in general and nuclear power investments in particular.[180] Any long-term prospects for nuclear finance which may have survived Three Mile Island would certainly not survive a major episode of sabotage anywhere in the world.

Psychological and social impacts

Consequences measured at the crude level of death, disease, land denial, and economic cost may be less important to society than psychological impacts.[181] Whether nuclear sabotage is technically successful or not may even be less important than whether people *think* it may succeed. The psychological impact of a potential release was strikingly confirmed even before Three Mile Island. In Denmark in 1973, a War-of-the-Worlds-type radio drama described a supposed 1982 meltdown in the Barsebäck reactor in Sweden (visible across the narrow straits from Copenhagen), allegedly sending an invisible but deadly plume towards the Danish capital. Residents panicked; some began to flee; some thought their loved ones were dead; and it took hours of repeated assurances that it was all fictitious before people got the message.[182]

Since "large numbers of people in many countries have become acutely concerned"[183] about nuclear risks, it is likely that a major nuclear release will lead to irresistible demands for the shutdown of operating nuclear power plants and, perhaps, of military nuclear plants. In view of deep-seated public attitudes and the many ways which a democracy offers for expressing them, this is not a trivial dimension of vulnerability. It means that regardless of what the government or the investment community may want, a sizeable accident or incident of sabotage anywhere in the world may lead to the loss not of one or two giant plants but of all seventy-odd nuclear plants now operating in the United States. It would almost certainly spell the end of nuclear power here, to say nothing of political fallout in other countries. Already, the discovery of defects common to a certain type of reactor have led to the temporary shutdown of all reactors of that type throughout the U.S.; and with the emergence of such problems as the embrittlement of steel pressure vessels, more serious "generic shutdowns" loom on the horizon. These incidents provide a precedent for shutting down large numbers of reactors by regulatory fiat. Public demand could be a far more irresistible force.

Thus, public attitudes may be the most important motivation for terrorists to acquire nuclear bombs or attack nuclear plants: ". . . the primary attraction to terrorists in going nuclear is not that nuclear weapons would enable terrorists to cause mass casualties, but rather that almost any terrorist action associated with the words 'atomic' or 'nuclear' would automatically generate fear in the minds of the public."[184] This is perhaps the reason to suspect that the maxim "Terrorists want people watching, not people dead"[185] may not mean, as some argue, that nuclear terrorism is implausible. Nuclear targets offer terrorists an opportunity to achieve *both* ends—many people watching, some people dead—either on purpose or because what was meant to be a mere spectacle gets out of control.

People who mean to reassure the public sometimes argue that terrorists are unlikely to make or steal nuclear bombs because other, simpler weapons of mass destruction are more readily available: for example, tankers of chlorine (toxic at fifteen parts per million) or pathogenic bacteria.[186] Extortionists have in fact used both of these in threats, and it is quite true that anthrax spores, mentioned in a German threat[187], are hundreds of times more lethal per ounce than fissionable material in crude bombs[188] —assuming the bombs are not set off near nuclear facilities. The lethality of anthrax could indeed "rival the effects of a thermonuclear device."[189] But it is the psychology, not the technology, of threats that explains why nuclear bomb threats have in fact outnumbered germ warfare threats by better than twenty to one. Furthermore, the existence of non-nuclear means of terrorism does not mean that the nuclear means should not be taken seriously. The existence of one vulnerability in society is not a reason to sustain yet another, but rather to seek to reduce all of them.

Some of the risks described in this chapter, and perhaps earlier, may at first seem far-fetched—just as regional power blackouts seemed until 1965, or the hijacking of three jumbo jets in a single day until 1970, or the bombing of a nuclear reactor until 1981. But given the potential conse-quences, nobody would wish to be in the position of the British intelli-gence officer who, on retiring in 1950 after forty-seven years of service, reminisced: "Year after year the worriers and fretters would come to me with awful predictions of the outbreak of war. I denied it each time. I was only wrong twice."[190]

Chapter Twelve
Forward, Lemmings!

The previous chapters have described the brittleness of America's major energy systems: oil and gas (including LNG and LPG), and central electric power stations—fossil-fueled, nuclear, and hydro—with their grids.[1] Together these energy sources account today for approximately ninety-five percent of our nation's total energy supply. Their vulnerabilities cannot be eliminated by building the same types of devices differently. Cosmetic changes in the details of this system while leaving its basic architecture essentially unchanged would preserve all its major sources of weakness. The vulnerabilities documented in this book are *inherent in the nature of highly centralized energy technologies.*

As if heedless of the risk, the energy industries are spending more than eighty billion dollars per year (and getting over ten billion dollars per year in federal tax subsidies) to build technologies which are still *more* centralized, complicated, and brittle. Industry and government are jointly creating for the twenty-first century an American energy system which not merely embodies but multiplies the same fragilities that threaten our national security today.

The major elements of this ambitious plan for the next twenty years include the following:

• More than doubling national electric generating capacity. The grid would have to be expanded to match; so would devices which use electricity. The new plants, costing over a trillion dollars to build, would burn mostly coal and uranium from Western mines. Compared to today's highly vulnerable central stations, the new plants would be even bigger, clustered in fewer and more remote sites, and linked by longer, higher-voltage transmission lines. More long lines would also be built to import large blocks of power from at least four provinces of Canada.

• Tripling or quadrupling nuclear power capacity. Preparations would

169

be speeded for a shift in the next century to heavy reliance on fast breeder reactors—each fueled with about seven tons of plutonium (over three thousand bombs' worth), and all critically dependent on a very small number of reprocessing and fuel-fabrication plants.

• Vastly expanding the extraction of oil and gas offshore. This would require drilling in high-risk areas, especially in stormy and faraway Arctic waters. Major gathering centers, pipelines, terminals, and conditioning plants would become even more critical to national fuel supplies.

• Building a twenty-seven-billion-dollar Alaskan Natural Gas Transportation System to bring North Slope gas via Canada to the Midwest. The gas would travel a total of four thousand eight hundred miles just to enter the domestic pipeline grid. It would arrive at a daily rate equivalent to between three and six percent of present total U.S. natural gas use. The gas conditioning plant and the forty-eight-inch, seven-hundred-forty-three-mile Alaskan section of pipeline would nearly double the U.S. gas pipeline rate base. There would be no alternative way to deliver the gas.[2]

• Shifting from the historically diverse and dispersed pattern of coal-mining—in 1979, six thousand mines in twenty-six states—towards overwhelming dependence on major strip-mines, mostly in a single Western area. By the year 2000, the Burlington Northern Company's diesel trains would carry out of Wyoming's Powder River Basin three-fourths as much energy as all the oil which the U.S. now imports from all countries. Through a handful of single rail corridors would flow far more coal than is now mined in all the rest of the country put together (as the maps in Figures One and Two illustrate).[3] The terrain is remote and rugged. If the sort of systematic sabotage and bombing of coal trains and railroads which is already endemic in Appalachia[4] were directed against the future flow of Western coal, it could interdict far more energy than an oil embargo could today, and would leave far fewer alternatives.

• Creating—chiefly in remote, arid Western areas—a synthetic fuels industry converting coal and shale into two million barrels per day of expensive liquid and gaseous fuels by 1992. Most of the synfuel plants would use untested technology.[5] Each typical plant would rank among the largest construction projects ever undertaken.[6] A single plant would occupy a square mile, directly employ four thousand workers, and cost several billion dollars. It would be thirty times as large as the largest U.S. pilot plant to date (and several times as large as the South African SASOL One or the 1944 German plants, all of which were such tempting targets that they were destroyed, as described in Chapter Seven). A nominal plant would, if it worked, consume as much energy and water as a sizeable city—both imported from far away. The fluid fuels would be shipped out through long pipelines at a rate of fifty thousand barrels per day. Two such plants would exceed the output of the entire Nazi synfuel program. Forty such

Figure One   Railroad coal movements in 1977

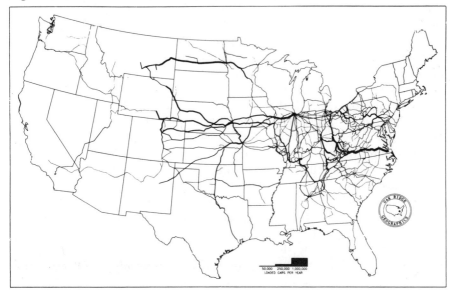

Figure Two   Projected railroad coal movements in 2000

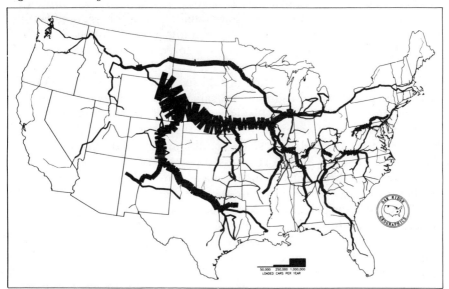

SOURCE: Oak Ridge National Laboratory. Prepared by Dr. Edward Hillsman, Dr. William Eberle, and Mr. Paul Johnson, and made available by Dr. Robert Honea.

NOTE: The 1977 data are from the Interstate Commerce Commission's one-percent waybill sample. The projections for 2000 are based on a coal transportation study done for Oak Ridge National Laboratory by Lockheed. The study assumed no coal exports and used the Series C projections from the Energy Information Administration's 1978 *Annual Report to Congress.* The map for 2000 has about a tenth as many origin and destination ponts as the map for 1977, so it would show more concentrated-looking flows even using the same data. In fact, however, the flows *are* much more concentrated in 2000 than in 1977. The map for 2000 shows total coal-mining of two billion tons per year, Powder River Basin mining of about five hundred million, total minemouth synfuels consumption of six hundred million, Powder River synfuels consumption of about two hundred ten million, and thus Powder River shipments of two hundred ninety million. For comparison, total United States coal-mining in 1977 was slightly under seven hundred million tons, and far more dispersed around the country.

plants—the 1992 goal for which Congress authorized eighty-eight billion dollars' subsidies in 1980—would consume coal at about a third of the rate of all U.S. coal-mining in 1979, yet they would produce the equivalent of only a tenth of present oil consumption. (The Reagan Administration in 1981 cut Congress's target by fourfold—to the equivalent of ten plants, or enough to supply seventy percent of the Pentagon's peacetime energy needs.[7] The military would probably be the only customer willing to pay the very high price which the synfuel companies would have to charge to cover their costs—probably, at retail, about twice the present price of imported oil.)

These enterprises are not a uniquely American phenomenon. Many other countries are following our example. Not to be outdone by the grandiose Alaskan gas pipeline, some key American allies—West Germany, France, Italy, Belgium, and The Netherlands—have agreed to build a fifty-six-inch pipeline to bring upwards of four billion cubic feet of gas per day from Siberia. The gas would supply nearly five percent of Western Europe's total energy needs and almost forty percent of Germany's 1990 gas use.[8] In return, the Europeans would get ten billion dollars in construction fees, a Soviet gas contract, and increased reluctance to upset their Communist suppliers.

The trend towards central electrification produces some unintended side effects in addition to greater vulnerability. For example, doubling the proportion of U.S. electricity used for heating and cooling buildings—the only way to use as much electricity as is forecast—would make demand even more sensitive to weather, with bigger peak loads for air conditioning in heat waves and for heating in cold spells. At these peak periods, the utility load could exceed its minimum value by an even greater factor than the present two- to threefold. Plants would therefore be even less efficiently utilized than they are now (when the average plant stands idle about half the time). More electric space-conditioning would also increase the likelihood of failures in the overstressed power grid.

Since it takes three units of fuel to make a unit of electricity, raising the fraction of energy delivered in the form of electricity from thirteen to as much as nineteen percent by 2000 would have a bizarre, if unintended, result:[9] between fifty-seven and eight-six percent of the additional primary energy used in the United States would be lost in conversion and distribution before it ever got to its final users. That is, two-thirds, perhaps as much as five-sixths, of our nation's energy growth—the very objective of these vast energy projects—would be thrown away in the form of warm water and cooling-tower plumes. Yet so ingrained is the habit of building power stations that such anomalies are hardly noticed.

Is it really good business to create on the Alaskan tundra a new choke-point only four feet in diameter[10]—no less vulnerable than the Trans-

Alaska Pipeline, three and a half times as expensive, yet carrying less than half as much energy? Why recreate in Wyoming an All-American replica of the centralized energy source which seems so critically vulnerable to sabotage when it is located in the Middle East? Do we have no alternative to making Burlington Northern into a new Strait of Hormuz? Will not increasing our already great reliance on central electrification by building over eight hundred more power stations make the power grid even more precarious? Wouldn't this only provide still more ultra-high-voltage temptations to target practice? Is it prudent or necessary to build more than a hundred additional reservoirs of radioactivity upwind of our cities, each containing the fallout equivalent of two thousand Hiroshimas?

The momentum of official and commercial commitments to such projects persists at the very time when national security concerns are becoming more prominent and more urgent in many other areas of public policy. Such inherently vulnerable energy projects—most of them proffered as alternatives to oil imports, the one type of energy insecurity that orthodoxy acowledges—have never received the same security assessment which makes Persian Gulf oil seem so clearly undesirable. Yet once built, the equally brittle systems which now form the basis of national energy policy are supposed to operate until the middle of the twenty-first century. The outlines of the kind of world within which they are supposed to function can already be anticipated. In the coming decades, salient trends that can reasonably be expected to persist or intensify include:

- the nuclear and conventional arms races, now running at a million dollars a minute;
- East-West rivalries;
- North-South tensions, inequities, and conflicts;
- continuing sparks in the Middle Eastern tinderbox;
- global political fragmentation, often expressed as terrorism;
- domestic tensions and political polarization;
- unemployment;
- inflation;
- financial instability, fed by a half-trillion dollars of uncollectable world debt;
- persistent fluctuations in weather and shifts in climate; and
- deepening doubts about the vitality and reliability of global life-support systems.

In such an environment of uncertainty, surprise, unrest, and possible violence, the officially planned, ever-increasing reliance on energy systems with built-in vulnerabilities to all these kinds of disturbances is a weakness

our nation can no longer afford. Still less can we afford energy vulnerabilities which so alter the power balance between large and small groups in
society as to erode, not only our military security, but also the freedom
and trust that underpin our Constitutional government. Least of all can
we afford energy technologies which are prone not only to fail to deliver
energy in these conditions—with all that implies for the potential of catastrophic breakdown in the comity and tolerance of our pluralistic political
system—but to create by their failure hazards to life and liberty as great as
any hazards of war.

It is with this somber background that the following chapters develop,
piece by piece, a message of hope. Alternatives to such vulnerability do
indeed exist. By borrowing the experience of those who study the survival
and stability of ecosystems, and those who seek to make such devices as
computers and aircraft less likely to fail catastrophically, it is possible to
formulate the principles of a design science of resilience. The rest of this
book describes how those principles can be embodied in practical, available energy technologies which can enhance national and individual security, save money, and help all Americans to live better. Taken together,
these inherently resilient energy systems offer a unique opportunity to reverse the unthinking, ominous trend toward ever more brittle power.
They offer instead the power to keep our economy vital, our lives rewarding, and our freedoms undimmed.

Part 3 National Energy Security

Chapter Thirteen
Designing for Resilience

Resilience versus reliability

As we noted at the end of Chapter One, efforts to make the energy system reliable seek to enable it to withstand *calculable, predictable kinds of technical failure.* But subsequent chapters catalogued many incalculable, unpredictable kinds of disruption—by natural disaster, technical failure, or malicious intervention—which most of today's energy systems cannot withstand. Indeed, when those systems were designed, some of the threats which seem most likely today were not even perceived, so energy systems were not designed to withstand them. Those systems were designed rather to work with acceptable reliability in what the Nobel Prize-winning physicist Hannes Alfvén calls a "technological paradise," where "no acts of God can be permitted"[1] and everything happens according to the blueprints. If such a place has ever existed, the world emerging in the coming decades is certainly not it.

Traditional analyses of the reliability of energy supplies have sought to assess the probability and consequences of failure. Unfortunately, for the most serious and unacceptable types of failure, the probability cannot be calculated, especially since it often depends on the unguessable probability of sabotage or attack.

The vulnerabilities of complex systems often cannot be foreseen in detail. It is possible to classify general patterns of failure,[2] but even elaborate schemes of classification cannot predict which particular failures will be most important. A decade ago, intensive efforts sought to identify and to calculate the absolute probability of various kinds of failures in hundreds of aerospace systems.[3] While some useful insights into the relative reliablility of different designs did emerge, the estimates of the reliability of each particular design wildly understated the actual failure rates. Fault-tree and event-tree methods predicted, for example, a failure rate of one per ten thousand missions in the fourth-stage Apollo engine, but the actual rate was about four per hundred. This was not because the analysts were not clever or did not try hard to think of all possible failures; it is because it was simply beyond human ingenuity to think of all possible failure modes. Likewise, about twenty percent of the Apollo ground test failures and over thirty-five percent of the in-flight failures were of types not considered credible until they happened.[4] (Using the same methods which had failed to foresee so many aerospace failures, the Rasmussen Report a decade later did not predict as credible the accidents which still later occurred at Browns Ferry and Three Mile Island.)

The sheer number of possibilities that must be examined makes such analyses intractable. To make it possible to obtain any answer at all, the analysts must severely truncate their work. They must decide to neglect as "insignificant" a very large number of failure modes that they do not have time to study in detail. Unfortunately, even though each of those failures may be unlikely by itself, there are so many of them that they can be *collectively* very important—they may even be the main source of failures. Thus in space rockets as in reactors, most serious failures actually follow one or another of these unexamined, "insignificant" sequences of events.

Another reason such analyses omit many actual causes of failure is that they assume *complete knowledge* of what the system is and how it works. Design or fabrication errors which have not yet been discovered cannot be taken into account. Yet such errors caused a large fraction of the test failures in the Atlas missile program, about half the safety recalls of seven million U.S. cars in 1973, and a significant fraction of reactor mishaps. A recent review of thirty-two major accidents in reactors, aircrafts, ships, trains, and so forth noted pervasive gaps in knowledge about what the failure modes were; how important and likely each one was; how serious its consequences would be; what could cause it; what physical phenomena could occur during the failure; and how it could interact with operating and maintenance errors, the random failure of several components at once, and external events.[5] Thus both gaps in knowledge about how a complex system works and lack of ability to foresee every way it can fail require that precautions against failure be general enough to prevent failure modes that cannot be specifically identified in advance. Such precautions must embody *resilience in the design philosophy*, not merely reliability in the design details.

As highly improbable failures in all kinds of engineered systems illustrate every year, every kind of large-scale failure which is physically possible will occur sooner or later. As time passes, various combinations of circumstances will occur until one fatal to the system happens to turn up. So many "vanishingly improbable" failures are possible that one or another of them is quite probable in a given year. Our foreknowledge of failure is limited only by the fertility of our imaginations, but the limits of our imagination do not affect what happens—only our degree of astonishment.

Traditionally, people have coped with inadequate knowledge by trial and error—the highly successful, if occasionally expensive, strategy of biological evolution and of entrepreneurial economics. The only abilities needed are to generate experiments and to tolerate failures.[6] But in the modern energy system, the cost of major failures is so high that we dare not do this. The impossibility of foreseeing and forestalling all major failures to which the modern energy system is vulnerable—that is, of preventing all surprises—requires that we take a different tack. We must learn to manage surprises and make them tolerable, to incorporate the unexpected in our expectations so that its consequences are acceptable. This requires an analysis of the unexpected: "of the sources of surprise, the perception of surprise and the response to surprise. From that, together with better understanding, come the possibilities of designs and developments that can absorb and benefit from surprise."[7]

For example, this approach would not just make Con Ed's switching relays more reliable in order to prevent an exact repetition of past catastrophic grid failures. Rather, it could seek to organize the grid in such a resilient fashion that system-wide failures became structurally impossible, regardless of the initiating event, the sequence of failures, and whether or not they were foreseen. Equivalently, a strategy of resilience could seek to ensure that if complete grid failure *did* occur, its consequences to energy users would be trivial. From the users' point of view, it is not important whether the likelihood of failures or the social cost of failures is minimized (or both); the point is that neither individuals nor the whole society remain exposed to a significant risk of large-scale failure, whether it is of a type that was foreseen or not.

Passive versus active resilience

This sought-after quality of "resilience" is difficult to define. The word is commonly used to refer only to what the applied mathematician Dr. Edward Kahn calls "ability . . . to withstand large exogenous [i.e., caused from outside] disturbances. The usual power system planning framework does not address itself to the occurrence of droughts, coal strikes or major inter-regional supply deficiencies." "A resilient system absorbs shock more easily than a 'rigid' system; that is, when stressed it gives way gracefully without shattering." "The ability to absorb such shocks gracefully has been called the 'resilience' of a system."

Kahn has studied how energy systems react to surprises. In one of the few quantitative analyses of passive resilience that has been undertaken, he compares the reliability of electrical supply from two hypothetical grids.[9] One grid is powered mainly by central thermal plants, the other by wind turbines. (For simplicity, the role of transmission and distribution systems is ignored in both cases.) Kahn focuses not on the relative size or dispersion of the power plants but rather on the reliability statistics of their "controllability" or intermittence—the extent to which they work or fail. On simplified assumptions (which probably favor the steam plants), the two systems can be made equally reliable if the wind-dominated system is given slightly more storage capacity.

Kahn does not then ask what the probabilities of various detailed failure modes might be, as traditional reliability analysts would do—the "hghly specified network analysis and contingency enumeration approach."[10] Rather, he asks how the reliability of these two systems would change if *each* type of generation worked less reliably than expected. He "perturbs" the system by assuming worse performance all around, such as might be caused by a coal strike, oil embargo, generic nuclear shutdown, drought, or a cloudy or windless period. The absolute *amount* of assumed degradation is the same for both grids. In percentage terms, however, it affects wind generators less than central station generators because the wind generators are *already* more subject to fluctuations: they are already intermittent and cannot get much more so unless weather simply stops happening. Their grid was *designed* to cope with fluctuation and has "bitten the bullet" by providing adequate windpower and storage capacity to maintain the assumed reliability of service anyway. But an equal amount of increase in the failure rate, whatever its cause, is far more serious for the central station system, which was designed on the assumption of high reliability and breaks down rapidly without it. From the utility dispatcher's point of view, degrading reliability by ten percent or more makes the central station grid about five times less reliable than the wind-based grid. Although the central station grid started with relatively less back-up and storage capacity than the equivalent wind grid, the extra storage or back-up which the central stations need to maintain equal reliability zooms up far more steeply and to much higher levels than that of similarly degraded wind plants.[11] Kahn concludes that this "supports the thesis associated with Lovins that the intermittent [sources] . . . produce a more resilient system."[12] Thus "the impact of unusual or extreme circumstances . . . modelled as extra . . . uncertainty . . . [is] smaller . . . on the wind energy system than on the conventional one . . . [showing] a greater ability to absorb risk."[13] The literature on control theory for power systems supports similar conclusions.[14]

A further example compares two hypothetical wind energy systems. What is important to the example is not that these are renewable energy systems, nor how large or centralized the wind machines are, but how they are designed to cope with varying windspeeds. The British Astronomer Royal, Sir Martin Ryle, proposed a system of wind machines[15] that would be more resilient than an alternative wind system designed by the Central Electricity Generating Board.[16] The crucial difference was that Sir Martin's design sacrificed a little performance at high windspeeds in order to be able to operate at low ones, and therefore it could work most of the time. In a long period of low windspeed, that design would still produce power much of the time, while the Board's overdesigned machines would produce none at all, requiring over five times as much storage. Kahn's conclusion that the more "resilient system minimizes the impact of extreme conditions" is just what Sir Martin intended. Such resilience "has important consequences. It means . . . [that surprises from outside] have already been built into the system. Therefore the impact of the marginal risk goes down."[17]

"Resilience," Kahn points out, "incorporates both a passive, behavioral notion and an active feedback control notion." The mechanical description of brittleness versus "bounciness," he continues,

> is a passive characterization. [But the] . . . corrective response to disturbance is an active control notion. In the case of power systems, the corrective response ultimately involves the political economy in which the [technical] system is embedded. Regulatory agencies institute investigations of major disturbances and initiate action to reinforce perceived weaknesses.[18]

While Sir Martin's wind machines themselves display only passive resilience, the mental process that led him to design them to cope with uncertain wind regimes displays active resilience; it is a deliberate effort to become better able to cope with surprises. Thus "passive resilience" describes the mere ability to bounce without breaking; active resilience connotes the further adaptive quality of learning and profiting from stress by using it as a source of information to increase "bounciness" still further. In the spirit of this metaphor, a rubber ball has passive resilience; the nerves and muscles of someone learning to play basketball have active resilience. Systems on which our nation depends need both, but most energy systems currently have neither.

Another way of saying this is that every "existing object or arrangement" tends to remain what it is rather than to become something else.

> Interfere with its existence and it resists, as a stone resists crushing. If it is a living thing it resists actively, as a wasp being crushed will sting. But the kind of resistance offered by living things is unique: it grows stronger as interference grows stronger up to the point that the creature's capacity for resistance is destroyed. Evolution might be thought of as a march towards even more highly articulated and effective capacity for resistance.[19]

It is because of this tendency to resist transformation that efforts to change complex ecosystems often have the opposite effect of the one intended.

Biological systems have the resilient learning and corrective process built in, centered not on ability to predict or avoid stress but on ability to cope with stress. This provides the adaptability that has carried these systems through several billion years in which environmental stresses were so great that all designs lacking resilience were recalled by the Manufacturer and are therefore no longer around to be studied. To understand active resilience so that we can apply it to the design of energy systems—to understand how resilient systems use stress and uncertainty as an essential tool for more fully achieving their ultimate potential—we need to examine the architecture of biological systems that have survived the exacting test of evolution.

This is a central theme of several provocative articles by the Canadian ecologist Professor C. S. Holling. He describes many instances in which the learning qualities of an ecosystem, not just its passive "safety margins" or its redundancy (like having an extra kidney), enable it to emerge strengthened by having experienced stress. Holling's arguments about biological resilience are sometimes framed in the language of abstract mathematics,[20] but at the cost of losing some of his subtler insights, they are summarized here in ordinary terms.

Resilience in biological systems

Chapter Three noted that when the Borneo and Cañete Valley ecosystems were disturbed, unforeseen interlinkages within them were also unwittingly disrupted, causing them to lose their ecological stability. "Stability" in this sense does not mean a static equilibrium, but rather the ability of a system to regulate itself so that normal fluctuation in its populations of plants and animals do not reach the point of either extinction or plague. The system does not remain exactly the same—it is free to vary—but it varies only within one general mode of behavior that is recognizable and coherent.

Self-regulation that works only up to a point is common in biological systems. As the biologist Professor Garrett Hardin has pointed out, our bodies regulate their own temperature at about ninety-eight and six-tenths degrees Fahrenheit.

> If through sickness or . . . dramatic changes in external temperature, the body temperature begins to rise or fall, then negative feedback processes bring [it] back to the equilibrium level. But . . . this regulation occurs only within limits. If the body temperature is forced too high . . . the excessive heat input defeats the regulation, . . . [increasing] metabolism which produces more heat, which produces higher temperatures, and so on. The result is death. The same happens if temperature drops below a critical boundary. We see, therefore, even in this simple system, that stability relates not just to the equilibrium point but to

the domain of temperature over which true temperature regulation can occur. *It is [the breadth of] this domain of stability that is the measure of resilience.*[21]

More complex systems with more variables also have their domains of stable self-regulation or "bounded stability"[22] beyond which they break down. Regardless of the degree of complexity, successful (i.e., surviving) ecosystems "are those that have evolved tactics *to keep the domain of stability, or resilience, broad enough to absorb the consequences of change.*"[23] These systems do not attain the absolute pinnacle of biological efficiency in capturing the energy available from their environment. But by avoiding the extreme specialization this would require, they also avoid the risk of reducing their margin of adaptability to environmental change—in Hardin's language, the risk of "contraction of the boundaries of stability."

Holling describes several possible ways to view these "domains of stability" and hence to judge the resilience of an ecosystem.[24] For example, one mathematically simple and politically comforting view, widely held by non-biologists, is that the domains of stability are infinitely large—that nature is infinitely resilient, tolerant, and forgiving. In this view, no matter how drastically a system is disturbed, it will always bounce back.

The value of heterogeneity   An opposing view holds that nature is so delicately balanced that the domains of stability are infinitely *small*, so that any slight disturbance will lead to extinction. If this were literally true, hardly anything would by now be left alive. But this view is more reasonable if applied only loosely and locally, not strictly and globally, because then temporary extinction in one place can be made up by recolonization from adjacent areas. In this way, the World Health Organization parachuted cats into Borneo to replace those killed by DDT (Chapter Three); American grapes replenished European vineyards devastated by the phylloxera blight in the 1860s; and stocks of disease-resistant seed corn prevented disaster when a 1970 epidemic of mutant fungus destroyed fifteen percent of the U.S. corn crop.[25]

Some classical experiments in population biology illustrate this process. For example,[26] if two kinds of mites, one that eats plants and the other that eats the first kind of mite, are confined so that they can freely move only within a small area, populations of both the predator and the prey will oscillate interactively. The species can be chosen, and the enclosure can be small enough, so that the oscillation becomes unstable and both populations crash to zero as they outrun their respective food supplies. But partitions can be introduced to divide the enclosure into subregions between which either kind of mite can move with some delay and difficulty. Because of slight random variations in population dynamics between one subregion and the next, the population cycle of outbreak and collapse will be out of step among different subregions. Thus even if a type of mite becomes temporarily extinct in a particular subregion, other mites can recolonize it from nearby subregions where they still survive. This recolonization from surplus to deficit areas ensures that someplace in the enclosure, both species will survive.

This experiment—amply confirmed by studies of extinction and colonization on isolated islands[27]—illustrates an important conclusion. What enables the mites to recolonize is that the area of disaster is small; the damage is isolated and local, so it can be repaired. More generally, then, if domains of stability are small—if a system is fragile—it will benefit from being *fine-grained and heterogeneous* in space,[28] having many differing components that vary from one place to another. Failure then does not propagate, and can be repaired from areas that are still functioning. *Local back-up, local autonomy, and a preference for small over large scale and for diversity over homogeneity* all increase resilience in such cases. The scale of the heterogeneity need only be finer than the scale of the disruption, so that an undamaged periphery will remain as a source of repair and regeneration.

There is a possible view precisely between the extremes of supposing nature to be infinitely brittle and infinitely resilient. This is the view that the behavior of ecosystems is neutral, tending toward neither stability nor instability, and neither endangered nor protected by their own general structure. The mathematical formulas (called coupled differential equations) commonly used to represent the interactions between two populations embody this view: they assume that the populations can fluctuate without limit, influenced only by each other.

This view, again, is mathematically convenient but greatly oversimplified. If it is refined by adding any kind of negative feedback (for example, that population outbreaks will be constrained by crowding effects), then collapse becomes—according to mathematical theory—impossible. On the other hand, adding any kind of positive feedback, or time lags in responding to events, creates instability. According to the mathematical theory, collapse then becomes inevitable. Yet both negative *and* positive feedbacks *actually exist* in real ecosystems, leading to a mix of stabilizing and destabilizing properties whose relative dominance varies in time and space. *It is the balance of these stabilizing and destabilizing forces that enables ecosystems to regulate themselves into a semblance of stability—provided they are not pushed too far,* into a region of behavior where the instabilities dominate and cause collapse.

Multiple, shifting domains of stability   In all but perhaps the simplest ecosystems, these mathematical properties create (as both theory and experiment confirm) not just one domain of stability, or region of equilibrium behavior, but *multiple* domains of stability. Each domain represents a "basin" within which the behavior of the system can "slop around" without dramatic change. The greater the deviation from normal behavior, the more steeply the "walls" of the "basin" curve upwards and the greater the resistance to climbing them. But given a big enough disturbance in some key variable, the system can suddenly change into a different "basin" of behavior by "slopping" up over the "ridge" between adjacent "basins."

Eutrophication of a pond is such a change.[29] If more and more nutrients (e.g., phosphates) are added to the water, eventually its limits of tolerance will be reached. With one component allowed to flourish at the expense of others, the pond will suddenly develop an algal bloom, which can lead to rotting of the plant matter and the irreversible creation of anaerobic conditions. The pond can then not support its original species or perhaps any others. As the ecologist Dr. William Clark points out,[30] similarly abrupt transitions, triggered by seemingly small disturbances to critical variables, can occur in fisheries,[31] marine biology,[32] insect ecology,[33] other ecosystems,[34] global climate,[35] and even political and economic systems (as in the Great Depression, revolutions, and similar cataclysms).

If ecosystems have multiple domains of stability and can be easily triggered to switch from one to another, the strategy for avoiding such a transition is to stay far away from the "ridge" separating one domain or "basin" of stability from the next. This is precisely, as Holling remarks, "in the highly responsible tradition of engineering for safety, of nuclear safeguards, of environmental and health standards." But, to add emphasis, this approach

demands and presumes knowledge. It works beautifully if the system is simple and known—say, the design of bolts for an aircraft. Then the stress limits can be clearly defined, these limits can be treated as if they are static, and the bolt can be crafted so that normal or even abnormal stresses can be absorbed. The goal is to minimize the probability of failure. And in that, the approach has succeeded. But in parallel with that achievement is a high cost of failure—the very issue that now makes trial-and-error methods of dealing with the unknown so dangerous. *Far from being resilient solutions, they seem to be the opposite, when applied to large systems that are only partially known.* To be able to identify . . . [safe limits] . . . presumes sufficient knowledge.[36]

Thus the engineering-for-safety approach "emphasize a fail-safe design at the price of a safe-fail one." If the inner workings of a system are not perfectly understood and predictable, efforts to remain within its domain of stability may fail, leading not to safety but to collapse. And if, as is inevitable, the full range of potential hazards is not foreseen, but simple precautions nonetheless give an *illusion* of security by controlling the most obvious and frequent risks, then the ability to cope with major, unexpected risks may well *decrease*. Thus in the case of the *Titanic*, "the new ability to control most kinds of leaks led to the understocking of lifeboats, the abandonment of safety drills, and the disregard of reasonable caution in navigation."[37] And so too in today's energy system, the great reliability of supply most of the time makes designers less likely to take precautions against rare, catastrophic failures which they have not experienced and hence do not consider credible.

The size of a domain of stability, and its relationship to adjacent ones, is not fixed, but rather changes continually (if slowly) under the influence of hidden processes controlled by unseen parameters. These processes may in turn interact with outside influences in ways that may not be perceived in advance. For these reasons, changing the values of key parameters in a well-meant effort to ensure safety may actually create new dangers. Intervention can "shrink" or even "implode" domains of stability, throwing the system unexpectedly into unstable or catastrophic behavior modes—just as spraying pesticides in the Cañete Valley (Chapter Three) made a previously resilient ecosystem too brittle to cope with normal fluctuations in growing conditions.

If the position of each stability boundary could be perfectly known and the distance to it monitored and controlled, safety might be possible. But in the absence of perfect knowledge, efforts at such control are more likely to *shrink* the domain of stability and to *shift* its boundaries in unexpected directions. The World Health Organization (Chapter Three) thought it was using safe levels of DDT in Borneo; it did not think that this intervention, focused on providing a narrow form of safety—eradication of malaria—would so destabilize other interactive predator-prey relationships as to result in plague. "This dynamic pattern of the variables of the system and of its basic stability structure," writes Holling, "lies at the heart of coping with the unknown."[38]

Striving merely for passive resilience—"the property that allows a system to absorb change and still persist"—means striving to stay away from the boundaries of stability. Yet as interventions and environmental changes constantly shift those boundaries, actions that used to be stabilizing may become destabilizing, and far-off boundaries may draw near or be accidentally transgressed. A strategy mindful of the limits of knowledge, therefore, is to strive for active resilience—"a property that allows a system to absorb and utilize (or even benefit from) change." This approach implies very different management methods: for example, environmental standards loosened or tightened according to the needs of the stressed ecosystem. It places a premium on adaptation—on making dangerous changes happen slowly and measures responding to them happen quickly.

Hierarchical structures Ecosystems achieve active resilience partly by their layered structure of successively more complex and specialized organisms. Low-level layers contain a relatively large number of relatively small components with different functions. The integration of these components produces or supports the next higher layer, as in a food chain. Successively higher layers cover a larger area and work more slowly. Within this complex structure, at each level, "the details of operations [among] the components can shift, change, and adapt without threatening the whole."[39]

For example, ecosystems use many overlapping, interchangeable populations to perform the same function, such as primary food production. This is partly a precaution against uncertainty: since sunlight is not uniform, for example, a diverse forest may contain both sun-loving and shade-tolerant plants. "Any particular function represents a role that at different times can be performed by different actors (species) that happen to be those available and best suited for the moment."[40] Thus the primary production by algae in a lake stays essentially constant from one season or year to the next, but the *kinds* of algae doing most of the production can change markedly.[41] The higher organisms in the lake are undisturbed; they simply eat algae and are not finicky about which kinds currently dominate.

The mathematics of such hierarchical structures "allows rapid evolution and the absorption and utilization of unexpected events."[42] It is common to find ten or twenty species able to perform the same basic role (such as primary production in a lake), yet each with a unique variation which makes it better able to exploit a particular opportunity in the changing conditions of the moment. The constant flux of circumstances ensures that this diversity will be retained, since whatever happens "will be at least one species' boat come in."[43] If a long spell of constant, predictable conditions should cause this essential diversity to be lost, the ecosystem might no longer be able to tolerate even modest environmental changes.

The importance of a layered structure, with each level of a system unaffected by substitutions among the elements of another level, is illustrated by H. A. Simon's anecdote about the different working methods of two imaginary Swiss watch-makers:

One watch-maker assembles his watch [by combining] . . . a sequence of [self-contained] subassemblies—a hierarchical approach. The other [merely] . . . builds from the basic elements. Each watch-maker is frequently interrupted by phone calls and each interruption causes an[y incomplete] assembly to fall apart. . . . If the interruptions are frequent enough, the second watch-maker, having always to start from scratch, might never succeed in making a watch. The first . . . , however, having a number of organized and stable levels of assembly, is less sensitive to interruption. The probability of surprise (of failure) is the same for each. The cost . . . is very different [in that one maker is able to finish building watches while the other never can.][44]

There may be a temptation to combine several steps into one in the interests of greater "efficiency." But such skipped steps

> will force bigger steps [which] take a longer time [and] . . . presume the greatest knowledge and require the greatest investment. Hence, once initiated, they are more likely to persist even in the face of obvious inadequacy. Finally, bigger steps will produce a larger cost if failure does occur. To avoid that, the logical effort will be to minimize the probability . . . of surprises or of failures.
>
> For example, . . . a number of watch-makers [might] . . . join together, pool their resources, occupy a large building, and hire a secretary to handle the phone calls. This would control the . . . interruptions and both watch-building strategies would succeed. Without the interruptions, there is not that much to gain by maintaining very many steps in a hierarchy of subassemblies. [Having fewer steps between larger subassemblies] . . . might increase efficiency and produce economies of scale but is totally dependent on complete and invariant control of disturbance. If the secretary were sick for one day production would halt.[45]

Imitating the strategy of successfully resilient ecosystems, then, may not wring out the last ounce of "efficiency" or attain the acme of specialization that might be optimal in a surprise-free world. But in a world of uncertainty, imperfect knowledge, and constant change, such "efficiency," with no slack for adaptations, can be deadly. The more resilient, slightly less "efficient" strategy wins an even richer prize—minimizing unexpected and disastrous consequences which can arise when the causal structure of a real system turns out to be qualitatively different than expected.[46]

Why solutions become problems   The dangers of narrowly "efficient" interventions can be illustrated by five practical examples:[47]

• Spraying to control spruce budworm in eastern Canada. This protects the pulp and paper industry in the short term. But the populations of budworms, their avian and mammalian predators, tree foliage, and other elements of the ecosystem are continually changing anyhow on many different time-scales, with fast, intermediate, and slow variables. Spraying disturbs only the fast variables, sending an intricate web of dynamic relationships into a new behavior mode. The unexpected result of spraying turns out to be reduced tree growth, chronic budworm infestation, outbreaks over increasing areas, and—if spraying stops—high vulnerability "to an outbreak covering an area and of an intensity never experienced before." The sprayers' mental model has one element—that spraying kills budworms, which eat trees, which are worth money—whereas even the simplest successful simulation models of the system have *thousands* of variables.

- Protecting and enhancing salmon spawning on the west coast of North America triggers increased fishing to profit from the larger harvest. But having built more boats, the fisherman must pay for them by catching more fish. This extinguishes the unenhanced (less productive) stocks and leaves fishing "precariously dependent on a few enhanced stocks that are vulnerable to collapse."

- Suppressing forest fires in U.S. National Parks succeeds in the short term, but also allows unburned fuel to accumulate. This leads sooner or later to "fires of an extent and cost never experienced before."

- Transforming semi-arid savannah into productive cattle-grazing systems in parts of the U.S., Africa, India, and Australia also changes the grass composition so as to cause an irreversible switch to woody vegetation. The resulting altered ecosystem is highly susceptible to collapse triggered by drought.

- Some malarial eradication programs have succeeded only long enough to produce DDT-resistant mosquitos and human populations with little immunity, leading in turn to greatly intensified outbreaks.

In each of these examples, like the Cañete Valley spraying mentioned in Chapter Three, a problem was made worse by defining it more restrictively than was consistent with the interactive nature of the ecosystem. Intervention shrank, shifted, or destroyed the original ecosystem's stability domains, making behavior "shift into very unfamiliar and unexpected modes."[48] Some disturbed systems "forgot" their previous history and became "more sensitive to unexpected events that previously could be absorbed."

When ecosystems turn out to be unexpectedly complex, leading to apparently unpredictable side effects, the institutions responsible tend to respond in one of three ways:

First[,] they may try to design away the variability by deliberately simplifying the system and/or its environment [e.g., by seeking to eradicate predators, "pests," or "weeds"—often leading to even more intractable side effects].

Second, they may try to extend the boundaries of definition of the natural system, so as to include "all relevant factors" in their analyses [via elaborate models and large interdisplinary research groups: an approach equally doomed to failure—because the systems are too complex to analyze—but slower to appreciate it]. . . .

Third, they may simply try to find ways to live with high variability. There are at least two design possibilities for living with surprise. First, the institution may attempt to design some means to *stabilize system outputs* without stabilizing system states, by finding some way to *store up outputs* and release them in a more or less steady stream. Individuals hedge against uncertainty by storing money in savings accounts; dams store water for release in dry periods. . . . This design approach is the most promising, in terms of social acceptability, that we have uncovered so far. Finally, the institutions may attempt to spread risks by *disaggregating the system into "operational units," each with a relatively low cost of failure [and minimally interdependent on each other]*. . . . For example, . . . the energy planner must be able to design parallel development . . . options . . . such that failure of one does not drag the others down also.[49]

These two approaches—smoothing, and disaggregating into modular units—are indeed among the "most promising" approaches for making tolerable those surprises that cannot be reduced to expectations.

Toward a design science for resilience

Living systems evolve automatically if slowly towards resilience. Applying the same principles to human affairs, however, requires the integration of biology with engineering. Unfortunately, few engineers know much about biology. This is partly because systems behave differently in biology than in engineering textbooks. Engineers tend to be trained in a mechanistic, Newtonian tradition in which most systems are linear (responding smoothly in proportion to the stimulus), reversible, and predictable. Living systems, on the other hand, are full of delayed, nonlinear, threshold-before-crash behavior, with results as irreversible as the scrambling of an egg. And yet living systems, in all their vast complexity, have survived eons of rigorous environmental stress by virtue of a carefully evolved capacity to bend, adapt, and bounce back even more resilient than before. More precisely, those living systems, and only those, *which are observable today* can be inferred, from their very survival, to be masterpieces of resilience. The brittle systems became extinct. One might therefore expect that such challenging areas of engineering as civil aeronautics, naval architecture, military hardware, nuclear reactor design, and telecommunications would draw heavily on the insights that biological resilience has to offer.

The literature of those and similar disciplines suggests that only a handful of designers have consciously sought to learn from biology. However, the best engineers have long sought to achieve at least passive resilience— to avoid the brittleness of systems that shatter if stressed beyond narrow limits. In this quest they have empirically evolved some interlinked design principles of their own. Unfortunately, few of these have been written down. Classic texts of engineering[50] and of systems theory[51] offer useful illustrations but identify few general rules. A few designers are known by their peers to have a knack for resilient design, but they have not written down the mental process that achieves this result. Popular compendia such as John Gall's *Systemantics* tend to give well-known engineering proverbs rather than new insights.[52]

Nonetheless, certain elements of resilient design can be formulated which seem to embody the principles independently derived, each from a different tradition and in different terms, both by engineers *and* by biologists. These elements can be described qualitatively, but are very hard to pin down in numbers. Some are mutually incompatible, requiring compromise. Living things, which are perhaps most familiar with this process of compromise, are not yet fully satisfied with it after several billion years of evolution towards resilience, so it will doubtless take human analysts a while too. Nonetheless, certain broad principles can be identified which can enable one to design systems (including energy systems) of reasonable cost that can still tolerate failure.

It cannot be overemphasized that the property being sought when one designs a system for resilience is that it be able to *survive* unexpected stress: not that it achieve the greatest possible efficiency all the time, but that it achieve the deeper efficiency of avoiding failures so catastrophic that afterwards there is no function left to *be* efficient. The great mathematician John von Neumann expressed this in seeking biological analogies for the resilient design of automatic systems (called "automata"):

> If you look at automata which have been built by men or which exist in nature you will very frequently notice that their structure is controlled to a much larger extent by the manner in which they might fail and by the (more or less effective) precautionary measures which have been taken against their failure. And to say that they are precautions against failure is to overstate the case, to use an optimistic terminology which is completely alien to the subject. Rather than precautions against failure, they are arrangements by which it is attempted to achieve a state where at least a majority of all failures will not be lethal. There can be no question of eliminating failures or of completely paralyzing [i.e., neutralizing] the effects of failures. All we can try to do is arrange an automaton so that in the vast majority of failures it can continue to operate. These arrangements are palliatives of failures, not cures. Most of the arrangements of artificial and natural automata and the principles involved therein are of this sort.[53]

It is those principles that this section seeks to articulate.

Fine-grained, modular structure　Any system is made of parts. We define a "module" to be a part which is a unit of operation or failure: it is the smallest unit that either works or doesn't work. (Not working may mean doing the wrong thing or doing nothing at all; or these may be synonymous.) Modules can also be the unit of inventory or of growth. A module can be, for example, an organism in a food chain, or a device performing operations within a computer. It can be a device supplying electricity to a grid, or an "island" within that grid, or a city grid which such "islands" make up, or the grid of one utility company, or an entire regional or national grid—depending on the context of the discussion, the level at which one is considering failure.

Modules are connected with each other in some pattern to make up a system. The lines of connection, or *links,* are also possible sources of failure. So are the *nodes* at which links join with each other or with modules. In a power grid, for example, electrical transmission and distribution lines are links; the switchgear, substations, and transformers that join the lines to each other are nodes. Any link or any node can fail, just like any module. (We refer generically to all three of these devices as "components.")

Other things being equal, failures are less serious in small modules than in large modules. That is, a finer-grained structure of modules permits a smaller fraction of the total capacity of a system to fail at one time, so the total functioning of the system is less affected. (Other design properties, discussed below, can isolate the failure of an individual module before it can propagate.) Smaller modules also make repairs easier, spare parts cheaper, and so forth, than if the units were larger and "lumpier." The size of individual modules also affects their cost and performance in many important ways which are discussed in detail in Appendix One.

Early fault detection Individual modules, links, and nodes can fail without serious consequences if the failure is *promptly detected, isolated,* and *fixed.* Prompt detection is easiest with "fail-safe" design—that is, if a component either works right or conspicuously does nothing at all, but at least does not work wrong. This in itself helps to isolate the failure before it can propagate wider failures—in the same spirit as the "dead man's hand" throttle which stops a train if its driver collapses. It is, of course, possible to make a design error which makes a supposedly fail-safe design fail dangerously: in Gall's phrase, "A fail-safe system fails by failing to fail safe."[54] A possible precaution is to back up a fail-safe component with independent means of detecting failures early. That is why, for example, a nuclear reactor will shut down if any of several signals (such as temperature, neutron flux, or the period of the chain reaction) exceeds prescribed limits. The more complex is the equipment for detecting faults, the more it can itself become a source of failure. For example, redundant guidance gyroscopes and/or computers in most spacecraft are reconciled by a "voting" system—best two out of three—which protects against the failure of any one unit. But a failure of the device which compares their readings can disable all the redundant channels simultaneously, leaving the astronauts to make do with a sextant and a hand calculator.

Redundancy and substitutability Individual modules, nodes, or links can fail without serious consequences if other components are available to take over their function right away. This requires redundant, substitutable units. (These, in turn, will be more readily available if they are small and cheap.) Multiple filaments in a light bulb, or spare pumps in a reactor, or leaves on a tree, illustrate redundant modules. The branching veins in a single leaf, intricately connected so that nutrients can still flow through alternative pathways after an insect has chewed the leaf full of random holes, illustrate redundant links. The Bell System's multiple switching centers provide redundant links and (to a lesser extent) redundant nodes to reconnect those links in various patterns.

The telephone analogy shows, on closer study, that redundancy is not a panacea. Telephone trunk transmission is very highly interconnected: long-distance calls are commonly rerouted, even several times per second, without the caller's noticing. If a microwave, satellite, or cable link is lost (through failure of the link itself or of a node that connects it into the network), another can be substituted. But as phone phreaks (Chapter Two) are discovering, this flexibility of rerouting calls actually depends on a relatively small number of key switching nodes. This number is probably only a few. For example, to prevent a single nuclear bomb from paralyzing the nation's telephone system, the Bell system has redundant underground control centers in Georgia, Kansas, and New Jersey.[55] The inference, however, is that three bombs might suffice—or merely a coordinated electronic assault on two or three nodes via the telephone system itself. Some phone phreaks believe that by tying up all the input ports at several critical nodes, perhaps using microcomputer-generated dummy calls, a small group of knowledgeable people could crash the Bell System.

It is indeed the very openness of the telephone system, allowing ready access from innumerable points, that helps to cause this vulnerability. Most people become aware of the fragility of the phone system only if some mishap cuts off their own call—for example, if a tone in their voice happens to be close to the frequencies used by switching equipment to signal a cutoff. But such accidents normally lose only one's own call, not everybody's at once. What may be less obvious is that the multiplicity of relatively open phone links, especially by microwave, facilitate unauthorized access to the phone system. (The Soviet spy agency—the KGB—is widely believed, for example, to intercept virtually all transcontinental phone traffic.) The fewer nodes and links there are, the fewer ways there are to reroute calls and keep a damaged network operating. But the more nodes and links there are, the easier it is for phone phreaks to penetrate and misuse the network.

Interconnected electric power grids give rise to similar compromises. Studies of grid vulnerability show the virtue of a rich structure of interconnections, like the veins of a leaf.[56] They also show the desirability of avoiding big, lumpy nodes or supply concentrations which would tend to focus the probability and consequences of failure. That is, a system made up of a number of energy sources that can route their output using many different paths of roughly equal capacity, diffusing the risk rather than relying unduly on particular sources or conduits, can usually deliver the energy somehow to where it is needed. (A fundamental property of eco-systems is that they tend to spread out their energy flows evenly through a food web in just this way.) Many U.S. power grids, however, lack this property. Their supply is too lumpy or their nodes are too lumpy to spread the risk. On a regional scale, therefore, the apparent flexibility of rerouting power, just as with telephone calls, may well be vulnerable to disruption of just a few key nodes. (Some observers say this is not the case,[57] but they do not appear to have thought very hard about it.)

A grid which *is* well interconnected and distributes its risk among many points is the electrical system of a World War II battleship. Knowing that the ship was likely to get shot up, the designers equipped it with multiple electric supply busses (main power distribution cables), each with spare capacity, which ran through different parts of the ship. They could be hooked up in many different permutations to improvise continued power supplies even after severe damage. Likewise, in the World War II destroy-er, each of the four boilers could be fed into any of the four engines. The extra pipes (links) and valves (nodes) were costly, but greatly increased "survivability." This principle is not consistently followed in some modern destroyers,[58] far less in many giant oil tankers (whose steering and other vital functions depend on unreplicated steam sources)[59] or even in the world's largest passenger liner.[60] Evidently the tried-and-true principles of redundant, substitutable components that naval architects knew two generations ago are now being sacrificed for illusory cost savings. Chapter Nine suggested that the same is occurring in refinery and pipeline design.

Optional interconnection   There are at least four strategies, usable singly or in combination, for isolating failures before they can spread. (Military designers call this practice "damage limitition"; computer designers, "error containment.") The first method is to make each component of a system *optionally autonomous*—able to stand alone at need, so that it can continue to do at least part of its normal work without its usual interconnections. Thus a faulty component could be cut off from the interconnections which otherwise could propagate "sympathetic" failures to other components, yet after the failure was thus isolated, the remaining components could still work.

This is one reason why electric grids have power dispatchers who, if a power station malfunctions, can trip it off the grid (if automatic relays have not already done so), isolate the fault, and call in spare capacity else-where to take its place. (At least that is what is supposed to happen; but as the New York blackout showed, a grid designed to be reliable in the face of defined, predicted kinds of technical failure can lack resilience when confronted with some other kind. As noted in Chapter Ten, today's power grids are brittle in many other respects too.)

Such "selective coupling" is common in biology. Contrary to popular belief, organisms in an ecosystem do not always tend to increase their interdependence wherever possible. In fact, they frequently limit it or make it optional. They also often store up food to "buffer" against an interruption in an accustomed food source.

The key principle here, then, is that modules should be interconnected in a way that normally provides the benefits of cooperation, but in case of failure can be readily decoupled. The federation of modules should be loose, not tight. Thus failures can be confined and repaired without impairing the whole system.

Diversity A second important way to limit damage is to try to ensure that different components will fail in different ways, rather than being mown down *en masse* by a single event. This implies components of diverse (heterogeneous) types. A car's parking brake is not simply a duplicate hydraulic brake; it is coupled differently (mechanically) and redundantly (by a separate linkage) so that even if the normal hydraulic brakes fail, there is a different alternative that does not depend on brake lines, master cyliner, brake fluid, and so on. The parking brake is not designed for routine use to stop the car, but it can serve as an emergency brake at a pinch—because of its diversity of design.

The human body provides numerically redundant kidneys and lungs, plus considerable built-in redundancy (spare capacity) in the unreplicated liver and heart. There need be, however, only one spleen—because certain structures in the liver can gradually take over the spleen's essential functions if needed.[61] Thus the trouble of making a spare spleen is avoided.

Such *functional flexibility* has counterparts in the energy system. The Swedish government, for example, requires that new boilers be able to accept solid fuel (coal, wood, etc.) even if their normal fuel is oil or gas, and requires also that the proprietors keep a fuel stockpile amounting to about nine or ten months' supply. The Norwegian Parliament has asked that government housing loans be usable for ensuring that each new house is equipped with a chimney (no longer usual on electrically heated Norwegian houses), so that a fireplace or stove can later be used if necessary. U.S. planners have developed a Multi-Fuel Program to make military vehicles adaptable to a wider range of emergency fuel supplies. (The Third Reich found such flexibility essential: by March 1944 more than eighty percent of the large German vehicles could burn alternative liquid, gaseous, or solid fuels.[62]

Diversity is a familiar means of increasing reliability. Multiple diesel generators, though numerically redundant, lack diversity. They can be and often are simultaneously disabled by contaminated fuel or by identical errors in design or maintenance. This vulnerability is a source of hazard in U.S. reactors, which depend primarily on either offsite (grid) power or on-site emergency diesel power for safe shutdown and control. In contrast, British designers feel that their own inability to think of a failure mode does not mean the system cannot come up with one. On general principles, therefore, they favor a deliberate diversity of reactor shutdown devices: perhaps centrally supplied electricity in one part of a reactor, local battery power in another, gravity in another, springs in another, and local compressed-air bottles in still another.

By the same reasoning, broadcasting stations and telephone exchanges often back up their emergency diesel or gas turbine generators, not with more of the same, but with banks of batteries. (This also provides buffer storage: once the batteries are charged up, they can "float" on the output of the emergency generator, remaining fully charged for instant use if the generator subsequently fails.) Commercial computer installations, too, tend to have batteries to ensure a few minutes' grace for shutting down without losing data, even where back-up generators are not big enough to operate the air conditioners which the delicate computers require for sustained operation.[63]

A striking example of the value of diversity occurred in 1980 in West Chicago. On the day that an Amoco® gas station powered by an array of solar cells was being dedicated by Department of Energy officials, a violent thunderstorm cut off all power in the area. The solar-powered station was the only one able to pump gas that day.[64] Likewise, the American Petroleum Institute has published an excellent guide to nine emergency methods of dispensing gasoline in a power failure without relying on grid electricity.[65] The diverse methods use motor vehicles, lawnmowers, portable engines, bicycles, or hand-operated cranks. The last two of these methods offer the most diversity, in that they do not depend on the fuel which the pump itself is dispensing.

Such *functional redundancy*—being able to carry out the same function via several physically diverse components—is common also in military hardware. A missile guidance system may use inertial guidance, fluidic, and electronic subsystems so that damage to one of them—for example, by the intense radiation field from a warhead exploding nearby—will not cause total failure.[66] Likewise, nuclear bombs generally have functionally redundant proximity and barometric fuses, backed up by a simple salvage fuse to ensure detonation (or at least destruction to prevent recovery) on hitting the ground.

Diversity need not be purely technological. To enter a Minuteman missile silo, for example, requires two different lock combinations, held respectively by the separate security and maintenance staffs. Many of the former are Oriental in order to make apparent any association with the latter, who are mostly Caucasian. This makes conspiracies for unauthorized entry more difficult and conspicuous to arrange.

Functional redundancy introduces problems of its own. Batteries which back up a diesel generator can eliminate (temporarily) the need to be able to fix a failed diesel, but they also mean that not only diesel spares but also battery parts, distilled water, and so forth must be kept in stock. Thus greater technical diversity can make support logistics more complex.

A functionally redundant back-up system is also one more thing to go wrong, and when it goes wrong, it does so in different ways than the system it backs up. That is the point of diversity, but it can also be a nuisance. In graphite-moderated reactors, for example, some types of accidents might distort the core so that control rods can no longer be fully inserted to stop the chain reaction. The newer British reactors therefore have a last-ditch emergency shutdown device known as the "O Jesus" system, whereby pneumatic hoses can be coupled up by hand to blow neutron-absorbing boron dust into the core. Because this would mean writing off the reactor, the system is well designed to take quite a while to couple up, so that it cannot be used accidentally or thoughtlessly. However, the Fort St. Vrain gas-cooled reactor in Colorado uses hoppers of boronated steel balls which fall down into holes in the graphite moderator block if the current to magnetic latches is interrupted. An accidental activation of this system reportedly left the operators spending the best part of a year vacuuming the balls out again.

The apparent diversity of supposedly independent systems can also be compromised by poorly designed links between them. Westinghouse reactors, for example, commonly activate back-up (safety) systems with the same electrical signals which control normal operation. Interactions via this link have on occasion disabled both systems at once—leading a senior Nuclear Regulatory Commission safety advisor, Dr. Stephen Hanauer, to note that Westinghouse "thinks this [interconnection] is great [because it is cheaper]. I think it is unsafe. This feud has been going on for years." Nor does functional redundancy mean that there are no shared vulnerabilities. For example, the diversity of power stations' fuel supplies permitted the transmission of coal power to oil-short areas in 1973–74, and vice versa during the 1977–78 coal strike.[67] But all the stations, and the grid connecting them, continued to be vulnerable to other threats such as transmission and control failures (Chapter Ten).

Standardization is a well-known way to reduce costs and bother. The ability to plug in common replacement components can make devices far easier to maintain with limited parts and skills. But standardization foregoes the benefits of diversity. If the standardized components incorporate a design or manufacturing flaw, that flaw is then plugged in universally, as has occurred with some automobile spare parts. And even if the individual components of a standardized series do not share a hidden flaw, they lack the diversity to resist simultaneous failures from a single cause.

This dilemma can be partly (but not wholly) evaded by standardizing those features of components that help to make them *interchangeable and mutually compatible,* while making diverse those features that are more likely to be closely related to the causes of failure. For example, the more the components of an electrical grid are designed to work at the same voltage, whatever it is, the fewer transformers (nodes) will be needed to interconnect them and the more kinds of parts will be interchangeable and directly interconnectable. But the more different sources can provide electricity at the standard voltage, the less likely are all the sources to be disabled by a common event (such as a coal strike, oil embargo, or drought). Thus standardizing operating characteristics need not mean standardizing design or losing diversity in design. At the same time, it would be desirable for each component to be able to tolerate a range of operating conditions: that is (to use the same example), to work well over a considerable range of voltage or frequency rather than being finicky.

Dispersion   A third way to isolate failures is to make components *diverse (heterogeneous) in space*—to put them in different places. Military commanders follow this principle by not needlessly bunching up their forces in vulnerable concentrations. Geographic dispersion means that if a mishap occurs in a particular place, it is more likely that some units will be there but less likely that they will *all* be there. The greatest possible simultaneous loss is thus reduced. In the spirit of the von Neuman quotation which opened this section, the aim of the dispersion is not to seize every tactical advantage but to minimize the possibility that a single event will wipe out all one's assets.

By the same principle, wind, being a flow, is always blowing somewhere. Dispersing wind machines therefore means that some of them are more likely to be well placed to capture it. In particular, dispersing wind machines over a large enough area (typically a few hundred miles long) increases the average output of an array of wind machines:[68] although they may not all be exposed to high winds at the same time, neither are they likely to be simultaneously becalmed. Thus the risk of total failure (zero output) is greatly reduced.

Dispersion does not necessarily imply that each unit is small; only that whatever the size of the units, they are not near each other and hence not prone to the failures that can simultaneously affect units at one site. On the other hand, it is also true that a system containing many dispersed modules will be less vulnerable as a whole if each module is relatively small. Since not only modules but also nodes and links are potential sources of failure, the tradeoffs between different kinds of vulnerability can become quite complex. For example, electricity generated by many small sources is more reliable (Appendix One) than equivalent generation by a single, large, equally reliable source.

But whether this advantage helps the final user(s) of the electricity depends also on the structure of the grid. If there is a single user, the single source could be sited at the point of use, eliminating the risk of transmission failure. A single user linked to many small, dispersed sources via a single master transmission line could lose them all if that line failed. A separate line radiating individually from each dispersed source to the user would be far more resilient (and expensive). In a more common situation—many dispersed users—the position would be just the inverse of that of the single user. Dispersed users are most vulnerable to transmission failures if their supply arrives via branches from a trunk line fed by a single source (which would also make the users vulnerable to generator failure). A more richly interconnected grid fed by many dispersed sources would be far more resilient—and somewhat more expensive, though far less so than individually radiating lines from a single source to each user.

Dispersion is possible in other senses than different places on a map. For example, dual diagonal brakelines help to protect cars from brake failure caused by rupture of the brake lines on either side. (The functional redundancy of disc and drum brakes also helps to protect against common-mode failures—e.g., from wet brakes or from wearing out all at the same time.) The lack of spatial separation caused the 1974 crash of a DC-10 airliner near Paris when supposedly independent hydraulic lines were cut by the collapse of the cabin floor after an unlatched cargo door sprang open and depressurized the hold. The lines were numerically redundant and could thus cope with ordinary leaks; but being neither dispersed nor backed up by other, functionally diverse systems located somewhere else, they could not resist the collapsing floor.

Hierarchical embedding A fourth strategy for isolating the effects of failed components is to organize components into a hierarchy in such a way that the larger whole can still work relatively well despite the failure of some of its subordinate parts. This is the strategy cited in the earlier discussion of food webs and of Swiss watch-makers. It also applies, for example, to electric grids in normal operation: the failure of one power plant or transmission line is not supposed to crash the grid in which they are embedded. Selective coupling—the option of autonomous operation for individual portions of the grid—contributes markedly to this ability to keep going despite partial failures. (If there were no relays to disconnect failed power plants from the grid, the failure could propagate instantly.) This feature is examined at greater length below in the context of resilient design for computers.

The ability to isolate and correct faults at the level on which they occur reduces reliance on remote, slow-responding control systems. If the isolation of a failed power station and the substitution of another took place automatically through the action of control devices at the stations themselves, they would not require the intervention of remotely sited control systems linked by fragile lines of communication. The corrective action would be faster and surer.

The same principle applies to organizational design. It can take a long time for information to trickle up a chain of corporate command to senior executives, for them to detect mistakes made by their subordinates, and for corrective orders to trickle back down to the operative level. In contrast, one highly productive Boston stockbroking firm gives its portfolio managers autonomy in choosing what to buy, so that bad investments are made by only one person, not by all of them on central direction. Even more important, that firm relies on the individual managers to detect and correct their own mistakes. They can do this faster for themselves than any superiors could do for them, and without the encumbrance of institutional inertias. By staying fast on their feet in responding to rapidly shifting market conditions, the managers thus avoid the large-scale errors that depress earnings in more traditionally managed firms.

Stability   Resilience involves the ability to take time when you need it. Components should be coupled in such a way that there is *time* for decoupling a faulty unit before others are damaged. An oil refinery, for example, which has very small holding tanks between its stages would have no operational flexibility. If everything worked perfectly, it would have smaller carrying charges on idle in-process inventories than would a plant with bigger tanks. But if all stages did not work at exactly the rate and in the manner planned, there would be no way to bypass a faulty stage, and there would be no grace period—no breathing space—in which to improvise repairs. The whole plant would therefore have to be shut down—at vastly greater cost than that of maintaining a few tanks and their contents. Many refineries are in fact very "tightly coupled"[69] because some narrow-minded accountant wants more "efficiency" in keeping the oil moving, rather than letting it sit in storage between stages. But this greatly increases technical and financial vulnerability to any mishap. Furthermore, in some circumstances having more buffer storage can actually improve economics even in normal operation. For example, the New York City subway system draws so much power in the rush hour that the peak-rate charges for it now justify at least five megawatt-hours of battery storage at the subway system's substations. This storage—being tried out in a new pilot project—would also provide the standby power for safe shutdown in a blackout. Similarly, the two-hour power reserve required by code in high-rise buildings is often supplied by standby generators which can also save money routinely by meeting peak demands.[70]

Many industrial designers have persistently failed to remember that local buffer storage is essential to provide the "slop" or "loose fit" that enables operators to cope with rerouting, fluctuations, modifications, or repairs. General Electric had to write off an entire nuclear fuel reprocessing plant at Morris, Illinois, partly because it was too tightly coupled to allow for normal operational variations among its sequential stages. Likewise, the British car industry, for "efficiency," holds such small buffer stocks of steel that it is often, and promptly, shut down by steel or rail strikes. This is as false an economy as it would be for a hibernating bear to store exactly enough fat to see it through to the *average* date on which its spring food supply would become available.

Another way to make failure-prone systems more stable is to lengthen the "time constants" (the measure of the speed) of their failure, so they "coast down gently" rather than "crashing." A car factory could do this, for example, by keeping bigger stocks of steel on hand or (equivalently) by using them more slowly. A system with this quality of gradual, graceful failure is often called *forgiving*. It fails slowly enough for one to arrange a soft landing. A forgiving system also incorporates sufficiently generous design margins to tolerate the ordinary run of mistakes, variations, and foolishness (even though, as the physicist Edward Teller remarks, no foolproof system is proof against a sufficiently great fool).

For example, the kinds of nuclear reactors which have a large heat-storing capacity and which can heat up only slowly in an accident are more forgiving than the kinds which overheat very quickly and hence require very rapid corrective action. An aircraft which can glide to a safe landing with all engines out is more forgiving than a helicopter which plummets like a stone if one rotor stops, or than aircraft (now proposed by some designers in the name of greater "efficiency") that stay in the air only by virtue of continuous, rapid, computer-controlled adjustments of their flight surfaces. More forgiving than any of these three types of aircraft is, for example, a light plane whose crash speed is slower than that of a person in a parachute.[71]

Forgivingness is often a compromise with peak efficiency. A wire geodesic dome may be impressively "minimal" in how much volume it encloses with how few pounds of wire, but that is little comfort if the removal of a single wire causes the whole dome to collapse. An LNG tanker is unforgiving if (as appears to be the case) a single failure in its inner containment membrane can cause the entire hull to fail by brittle fracture. The particular design of a simple mechanical component can change a forgiving design into an unforgiving one, as in box-girder bridges, a style of construction once popular in Britain. The design techniques and structures (stiffened panels) that they use "are maximally sensitive to imperfections in their manufacture."[72] Therefore even a slight flaw or size deviation in the material can reduce the strength of a panel by a third or more. If one panel buckles, so do the rest. Such failures have cost several deaths and hundreds of millions of dollars in property damage.

Likewise, high-performance jet aircraft engines appear to be highly vulnerable to dust, such as that kicked up by nuclear explosions. This flaw might, in a nuclear attack, disable America's fighters, bombers, cruise missiles, radar aircraft, and airborne command posts (including the President's),[73] for the same reason that the engines of aircraft which flew through the dust cloud from Mount St. Helens caught on fire. Yet simpler, more forgiving engine designs may in many cases entail little sacrifice in performance.[74]

Simplicity Some designs achieve "forgivingness" through simplicity—the elegantly economical use of limited means. Simplicity is sometimes called "the unavoidable cost of reliability." Generations of engineers have enshrined it in the KISS principle ("Keep it simple, stupid"), the Fathy principle ("Don't try to improve on anything that works"), and its cowboy version ("If it ain't broke, don't fix it"). Gall states among the principles of Systemantics:

15. A complex system that works is invariably found to have evolved from a simple system that works.
16. A complex system designed from scratch never works and cannot be patched up to make it work. You have to start over, beginning with a simple working system. (Translation for computer programmers: Programs never run the first time. Complex programs never run.)[75]

Complexity breeds weird failure modes which cannot be foreseen, understood even in hindsight, or fixed. Nobody can see what is wrong. Simplicity, in contrast, provides what designers call "tranparency": anyone can see what is wrong.

Many modern engineers, carried away by the sophistication of their design tools, forget that the more parts there are, the more can go wrong. Boeing-Vertol's first design for a door for Boston subway cars had thirteen hundred parts. The designers had become so sophisticated that they couldn't design a door that was simple enough to be likely to work. (They eventually sweated the design down to three hundred parts, perhaps few enough to work most of the time.) Modern power stations, full of the latest miraculous gadgets, tend to break down far more often than old "tea-kettle" plants full of Victorian cast-iron parts with brass knobs.

The mathematics of elaborate systems is discouraging. A system whose operation depends on *each* of its ten components, each of which works ninety-nine percent of the time, is likely to be out of action ten percent of the time. With one hundred such components, it should be "down" sixty-three percent of the time. With a thousand, it is likely to work an average of only twenty-three minutes per year. And these dismal numbers assume independent failures. Common-mode failures—the way most of the more awkward failures in complex systems actually occur—would make matters very much worse.[76]

Some of the U.S. Navy's most advanced combat ships use the MK-86 fire control system. When it works, it can simultaneously track and destroy multiple incoming missiles. But when it fails, "the ship is virtually defense-less" and can be destroyed by a single shot.[77] The MK-86 is out of action about forty percent of the time.[78] The Navy is having trouble stocking spare parts and training people to install them properly. These reliability and maintenance problems clearly have something to do with the system's having forty thousand components. To be ninety-six percent reliable (for example), a system whose operation depended on *each* of forty thousand parts would have to achieve a component failure rate of one in a million. The average reliability of the MK-86 components is apparently some ten times worse. Common-mode failures may be part of the problem too. There is certainly fertile ground for them, since there are some eight hundred million possible simple interactions between any two of the forty thousand parts, and an astronomical number of possible interactions that involve more components in more complex patterns.

Fortunately, few complex systems depend on the operation of every single part. How far complexity degrades reliability depends not only on how many and how reliable the parts are, but also on how they are organized. If this were not the case, a modern computer, nuclear power plant, or electrical grid would never work at all. Even a very complex system can be passably reliable if its many parts are organized "in such a way that the reliability of the whole . . . is greater than the reliability of its parts" and that "malfunctioning of the whole . . . [can be caused only by malfunction] of a large number of them."[79] This requires the careful use of the architectural principles described in this chapter, together with (in many cases) decentralized control systems acting in parallel.[80]

Despite designers' best efforts to decouple complexity from unreliability, however, a correlation persists. For example, as American fighter planes evolved from the relatively simple (A-10) through the moderately complex (A-7D, F-4E) to the staggeringly complex (F-15, F-111F, F-

111D), not only did the capital cost per plane rise by three- to fourfold, but the time unavailable for missions doubled; the maintenance time per sortie rose two- to four-fold; and the mean flight time between failures fell three- to sixfold, from about seventy minutes to the F-111D's twelve minutes.[81] Clearly the drive for better performance through greater complexity is encountering rapidly diminishing returns. It would not take much more complexity to make the aircraft fail before it even took off.

As important as how often a system fails is how much its failure hurts. If the failure of a MK-86 fire control system results in the loss of a vessel costing thousands of lives and billions of dollars, the complexity of the system bore a high price. Some years ago, there was reportedly a debate in the Pentagon about which of two control systems to buy for a major missile system, supposedly vital to national security: a rigidly hierarchical system which worked only if all its subsystems were in perfect order, or one with less monolithic architecture, designed so that it would work even if about a third of its subsystems had been destroyed. The former was selected because it looked about ten percent cheaper. In the event, the missile was not built anyway. Today, after more experience of oversophisticated, under-reliable weapons systems,[82] one would hope the decision would be different.

Limited demands on social stability   For any system whose collapse bears an intolerable price, the demands placed on reliability are so great as to require a degree of social engineering to protect the fragile technical systems. Whether this is tolerable in a free society is a profound *political* issue, not primarily a technical one. The origin of this concern is worth tracing more explicitly. At some level of complexity and at some level of requirement that failures be extremely rare, reliability ceases to be an engineering problem—the failure rates of pipes, motors, and transistors. It becomes a people problem—the unavoidable fallibility and the occasional irresponsibility, irrationality, or malice of the people who must design, build, run, and maintain the system. Systems designed by geniuses and run by idiots do not always work, nor vice versa. Technologies which require "great vigilance and the highest levels of quality control, continuously and *indefinitely*,"[83] may not get it. Many critics wonder if our society—hardly one that is peopled by angels and robots—is really up to handling such demanding technologies.[84] They are skeptical that enough people can be found to fill positions in which they "must not make serious mistakes, become inattentive or corrupt, disobey instructions or the like . . . : their standard of conduct must differ markedly from historical norms for the general population."[85]

The constraints on the social context which permits and encourages people to behave in this way, and which prevents others from interfering with the highly engineered systems, may imply an unwelcome degree of homogeneity enforced by strict controls. There is a substantial and compelling literature of civil liberties concerns which arise from this root.[86] This literature suggests that the price of some particularly demanding and vulnerable energy technologies may be the very liberties in pursuit of which the United States was founded. Indeed, "after having spent billions of dollars for our [military] nuclear deterrent, our civilian nuclear industry might well accomplish that [political transformation] which our defense system is trying to prevent."[87] Many of the vulnerabilities of non-nuclear energy systems surveyed in the preceding four chapters raise similar concerns. But this makes such systems inferior to "socially stable" energy systems—those which require

> a minimum of social control. It should not be necessary to deploy force to protect [an energy technology. It] . . . should be able to survive and recover from periods of political breakdown, civil unrest, war and acts of terrorism. The system should be unlikely to become a target of protest; should enhance, not threaten social stability.[88]

Accessibility The demands which a technology places upon the society that depends on it are only one of many interactions between people and machines that must be considered in designing for resilience. Another is that the technology be *capable of being understood*, at least in basic outline, by ordinary people, so that they form political judgments about it and use it intelligently even if they cannot necessarily design and build it themselves. This property is a key to *social compatibility*. It is among the main reasons why, "if the United States selected its energy supply systems by a popular vote, there seems no doubt that solar energy would win easily."[89] Understandability helps technologies to be developed, dispersed, and accepted rapidly. An energy technology whose impacts are directly perceivable, patently benign and controllable, and describable in everyday language is more likely to be socially acceptable than one that is mysterious, invisibly threatening, and arcane. Likewise, a technology which equitably allocates its costs and benefits to the same people at the same time, so they can see for themselves how much is enough, is less likely to become embroiled in "energy wars" than a centralized, inequitable system. This too is something which any citizen can understand and act upon.

Understandability is a signal feature of small renewable energy sources (Chapter Sixteen)—so much so that many of the best renewable energy ideas today are coming from people with little or no technical background. A letter recently arrived, for example, from a homesteader in a remote part of Alaska, a man of little schooling and high intelligence, who had invented some novel and useful solar and wind systems to meet his own energy needs. His solar-warmed biogas digester handled normal organic wastes but balked at paper. However, he noticed a moose eating a willow tree, shot the moose, seeded his digester with moose gut (presumably recycling the rest of the moose), and reported that his digester's richer mix of bacteria would now happily digest paper and even sizable chunks of wood. Thus he discovered something quite important, even though he is not Exxon.

Technologies which are *understandable* are also likely to be *maintainable*. This is not the same as being super-reliable, so they do not need maintenance: indeed, such devices may give people too little hands-on experience to be able to fix them when they do fail. Rather, maintainability depends on how well people without arcane skills can understand a device intuitively. Within limits (miniaturized systems can be *too* small to work on), small devices tend to be easier to fix than big ones, partly because they are easier to carry around, experiment with, and cannibalize parts from. Designs that are *scaleable*—able to be built in many different sizes according to the same basic recipe—have further obvious advantages.

Reproducibility without elaborate resources enables many people to make or fix a device even under disrupted conditions. A wind machine simple enough to make in any vocational high school shop, and which can run with virtually no maintenance for twenty or thirty years, is such a "vernacular" technology.[90] If the necessary information and materials are dispersed or stockpiled, such simple, readily buildable and operable technologies can make a profound contribution to energy preparedness. In contrast, technologies which can be built and maintained only by a pool of highly specialized people using unusual skills, processes, and materials are hard to reproduce even in ideal conditions. If there is no longer enough business to keep those technicians continuously employed, well-trained, well-motivated, and recruited at a high level of talent (as appears to be the prospect for the nuclear industry today),[91] then reliability, safety, and maintainability will all decline. The "basal metabolism" of such a complex enterprise requires major resource commitments and tranquil, well-planned conditions just to keep it alive for possible use in the indefinite future. Those resources cannot meanwhile be used in other ways.

Accessibility, reproducibility, and scaleability aid *rapid evolution*, permitting rapid response to new knowledge or new needs—the type of learning required for biological "active resilience." Biological succession, including that of small mammals over dinosaurs, depended on the rapid exchange of genetic information, trial of new designs, and feedback from environmental experience to reject bad designs and improve good ones. While not rapid on a human time-scale, these changes were often very rapid on the time-scale of the earth. Likewise, if an energy technology is sufficiently simple, accessible, and quickly built to undergo many generations of development in the time it takes to build one prototype of a large, complex device, the former is likely to achieve a high level of refinement much sooner, more cheaply, and more surely than the latter. Conversely, the complex technology may reach commercialization only by so compressing its development sequence that the design used for each scaled-up new generation must be committed—"frozen"—before operating experience has had time to reveal the strengths and weaknesses of the earlier units. This process of outrunning real experience greatly increases ultimate costs and risks. Likewise in biological evolution, small, frequent improvements are more likely to survive than abrupt, radical design changes. Organisms whose large gene pool and rapid reproduction encourage many incremental changes can more easily find resilient design solutions than those that can afford only few and infrequent experiments.

By this point many parallels between the principles of biological and of engineering resilience should have become evident. Just as population biology, in the experiment of the mites or in island ecology, reveals the value of being fine-grained and heterogeneous in space, so engineering experience shows a corresponding value in dispersion and in redundant, relatively small modules that can substitute for each other, filling in temporary gaps in function. The selective coupling in food webs, where organisms normally depend on each other but can do without their usual diet and cushion the transition with a buffer stock of stored food if need be, is analogous to the optional autonomy of components—like a householder who normally heats with gas but, at a pinch, can switch to the woodstove and the backyard woodpile. The hierarchy of food chains, where (for example) many different kinds of algae provide primary productivity in a pond interchangeably without worrying about what will eat them in turn, is similar to the redundancy of a grid energized by the similar, interchangeable outputs of different energy sources. The biological adaptability of prolific species is analogous to the ability to evolve a technology quickly through the efforts of many participants. And the compromises inherent in any design for resilience—between standardization and diversity, between autonomy and sharing, between narrow efficiency and broad survivability—are as central to engineering as to life itself.

Analogous universes

Few engineers deliberately design for resilience as an end in itself. If they achieve it, they do so by accident while pursuing other ends. Design philosophy is normally centered around satisfying narrowly conceived regulations or performance/time/cost specifications, rather than around producing an inherently resilient product. This narrowness of objectives was tolerable, if sometimes expensive, in an era when engineers could shrug and go back to the drawing board. In designing an energy system for the decades ahead, that is no longer tolerable.

Even the electric utilities that have thought most about resilience (as they conceive it) agree that such resilience as their grids possess is a side effect of other design considerations (e.g., against earthquakes) rather than having been designed in. Grids are rather like military weapons which are designed only to cope with specified operational threats that can be foreseen and quantified—so much heat, salt spray, neutron flux, shock, vibration, EMP—rather than with unforeseeable threats. In both military and civil hardware, efforts to increase resilience tend to be only (as one Pentagon analyst put it) an "hysterical realization after the fact"—a response to the *previous* failure. And even that narrowly framed response is seldom incorporated into existing equipment, because of cost, inconvenience, and pure inertia. The Nuclear Regulatory Commission recently fined the Tennessee Valley Authority fifty thousand dollars for *still* not having taken basic fire precautions at the Browns Ferry plant, six years after its near-disastrous fire.

Are there fields of design, however, in which the need for resilience has already been so clearly perceived that it has resulted in a coherent, readily identifiable decision to change the architecture of an evolving technical system? Data processing offers such an example. Its lessons have strong parallels, as will be shown, to a desirable direction for the evolution of the energy system; and they emerged in response to similar concerns.

The brittleness of mainframe computers

The past decade has seen a wide-ranging professional debate about whether data processing should become more dispersed ("distributed") or more centralized. As microprocessors have packed more performance into cheaper chips—already more complex than human microcircuit designers can handle[92]—the cost of executing an instruction on a large mainframe computer has come to be equal to or larger than that of doing the same thing on an office microcomputer. But the centralized computers were meanwhile revealing a disagreeable lack of resilience and a high cost of failure. When they broke down, whole corporations, including such time-sensitive ones as airlines and banks, were paralyzed. Airlines would typically lose, in one instant, at least a fifth of a huge computer costing millions of dollars. The computer was typically coupled to about ten thousand terminals and at any given instant would be handling about a hundred different transactions. Eastern Airlines alone could lose twenty thousand dollars in bookings *per minute*.[93] The problems multiplied:

> [D]owntime may balloon to hinder the company's day-to-day operations. For example, one system "crash" may result in an hour of downtime during which the problem is analyzed; perhaps another hour is lost while operations are restored; and finally there is an adjustment phase during which . . . the system again reaches stable on-line operations. All of these delays have significant, and

at times disastrous, impacts on corporate operations. . . . Large monolithic systems still tend to be unwieldy.[94]

Mainframe computers not only failed often and expensively; they also turned out to be harder to understand and repair than small systems. Modifications were painfully slow and often introduced new errors.[95] Since there is no such person as an "average user," all users were in some degree unhappy with the central computer's mismatch to their own needs, and they found in it little flexibility to adapt as those needs changed. The malaise became widespread:

During the 1960s, there was a general thrust toward centralizing all the data processing within an organization in the hope that this approach would serve all users. In fact, it did not serve either the central data processing staff or dispersed users as well as was expected . . . [and attempts at a remedy] resulted in many disappointments as well as some conceptual misdirections in the development of management information systems.[96]

As with the energy system, too, security concerns emerged as the visible vulnerability of the mainframe computers began to attract predators. Fifteen bombings in ten months blasted French computer facilities.[97] It became clear that a major California earthquake could make Visa® and Mastercharge® collapse if computing were not restored within a few days. And the incentives for criminals were high. The first international symposium on computer security[98] heard an American expert "who has so far succeeded in classifying eight hundred types of computer crime" warn that

within ten years the real threat to world stability would not be nuclear [war] . . . but the ability of one nation to enslave another by paralyzing its computers. . . . [In] West Germany . . . an operator had succeeded in stealing twenty-two magnetic [tapes] . . . essential to the operation of a large chemical group. The board hesitated briefly before handing over two hundred thousand dollars' ransom to recover [them]. . . . Many banks are even more vulnerable. . . . Were a big bank to be affected . . . there would be inevitable and serious repercussions on the economy of the country where it was based.[99]

In 1979 alone, six hundred thirty-three cases of computer crime were discovered (three-quarters of them in the United States). In 1981, some eighteen hundred to twenty-seven hundred were forecast just in the U.S.,[100] of which only fifteen percent were expected to be detected. The current cost of computer crime in Europe is estimated at over three billion dollars per year, with the "average holdup of a computer" netting the white-collar criminal "a profit of five hundred thousand dollars compared with only ten thousand dollars for the traditional armed holdup."[101] Evidently with central computers, as with centralized energy systems, sabotage and extortion can threaten commercial and even national survival.

Security of data stored in computers is yet another worry. In one recent fiasco, the file of passwords to the centralized memory banks of one of America's largest time-sharing companies was electronically purloined. Its possessors gained complete access to the private files of more than eight thousand corporations.[102] In a large computer system "it is virtually impossible for a user to control access to his files" and to prevent "subversion of software structure"—unauthorized alteration or erasure of stored programs or data for purposes of embezzlement, spying, or extortion.[103] Every known attempt by competent analysts to "penetrate" and "subvert" a major computer system has succeeded the first time. In one test, systematic exploration disclosed seventy-six promising chinks in the computer's armor.[104] Thirty-five of these were readily confirmed, offering levels of penetration up to and including the option of seizing remote control of the entire computer system. One expert reported, "To my knowledge, no such attack on a 'real' system has ever failed. As an exercise, I just broke into my [company's sophisticated] system after seven minutes' effort." Here too, centralized computers, like centralized energy systems, lend themselves to exploitation by the malicious.

The response: "distributed processing"

Rising concern over these vulnerabilities during the 1970s reversed the ever-greater centralization of computing power. The leaders of the industry, both manufacturers and users, fully participated in the reversal. Major banks, such as Citibank and Bank of America, decided to seek as dispersed a computer network as they could reasonably achieve, putting adequate and autonomous computing power as close as possible to each user. IBM changed its marketing strategy to emphasize more dispersed systems that fail more gracefully. By the mid-1970s, the new conventional wisdom was that

> the solution . . . may be decentralization. In the past few years, advances in . . . technology . . . have made networks of interconnected minicomputers a plausible alternative to centrally oriented operations. At the same time, pressure from dissatisfied users of central systems has speeded the trend toward decentralization. . . . [Decentralized processing meets] an important need for more functionally oriented, more manageable, and more flexible approaches to data processing problems.[105]

The industry's response to the brittleness of centralized computers was

> a new approach to system architecture. New [architectures use] . . . many processors and memory units interlinked by high-speed communications. All processor units are homologous [i.e., can do the same tasks interchangeably] and capable of replacing each other in case of failure [i.e., they are numerically or functionally redundant].[106]

A pioneer in putting these concepts into commercial practice, the Tandem Corporation of Cupertino, California, has had "spectacular success" marketing its own system design, known as NonStop®.[107] This design uses "fail-fast" modules—reliable processors and memories which continuously check themselves so as to detect any errors or failures immediately. Each unit may suffer a failure every few months; but because they are arranged redundantly, in a hierarchy akin to that of the Swiss watch-makers in our earlier example, the whole hardware system will fail much less frequently—typically once in ten years (even longer if desired: it would not cost much more, using the same techniques, to raise the mean time between failures to a thousand years, but that is considerably longer than most users are interested in). In practice, the system fails somewhat more often in actual use, "because of operator errors (about one per year) and application program errors (several per year). These have now become the main limit of system reliability rather than the software or hardware supplied by the manufacturer."[108] The designers, then, have done about all they can do to supply an all but "crashproof" machine to considerably more failure-prone human beings.

The Tandem system doubles up ("duplexes") both modules and links—both the small computers and the communication lines which connect them. If any of these units fails, its "mirror" back-up device returns to the last error-free "save point" and then completes the interrupted operation without a hitch. (This requires careful design to ensure that transactions get properly finished without overlapping.) Tandem typically combines sixteen small, modular computers to make one big machine, or two hundred fifty-six small ones to make a monster one. The unit(s) that can be lost at any one time are thus such a small fraction of total capacity that the loss may not even be noticeable. A loss during intensive use would make the system act a little sluggish; once the faulty component was repaired and reconnected (which is all done during normal operation) it would perk up again. A failure during off-peak use would probably not affect performance at all, since it would only reduce spare capacity. The presence of that capacity also makes the whole system more flexible in handling peak computing loads at which a more monolithic design would balk.

One might expect that the doubled-up units and the general redundancy of the design would greatly increase its capital cost. In fact, the increase is remarkably small.[109] In a typical application such as airline reservations or controlling a large factory, perhaps sixty percent of the cost of computing is labor. Of the forty percent that represents hardware, only a third to a half is in the computer room; the rest is communication systems and peripheral devices (terminals, transducers, etc.). The duplexing or even triplexing of small computers is relatively "inexpensive and [gives] . . . disproportionate reliability increments."[110] For example, while a computer using eight single disk drives could lose one of them about eight times a year, mirrored disks (if they fail independently of each other) reduce the rate of inoperative disk *pairs* to about once per century.[111] Because the units being duplicated are small—some designers refer to their "granular texture"—it is much cheaper to provide back-up for them than for large, expensive units. Thus the cost of the extra hardware in the computer room is only of the order of twenty percent. That extra hardware cost is then so diluted by other, fixed costs that NonStop™ reliability raises the total cost of computing by only about five to ten percent—far less than the benefits. As one of the system's designers summarizes,

> [D]ecentralization may have a positive effect on both availability [being able to operate] and reliability [not making mistakes]. In a loosely coupled system, the failure of one [component] should not affect the [others] . . . . This localization of failures enhances availability. Conversely, by replicating data and programs, [components] . . . may act as backup for one another during periods of maintenance and failure. Lastly, decentralization allows for modular growth of the system. When more storage or processing is needed, it may be justified and added in small [and relatively cheap] units.[112]

Thus this approach offers greater security against failure and error, comparable cost of service, more reliable routine operation,[113] and greater convenience and flexibility to the user.

Dispersed processing can also make "software subversion" more difficult. If data are altered, the correct data are still stored at many other dispersed sites and can be cross-checked and recovered intact. Any individual machine will also probably store less information.[114] Of course, spreading the data among many dispersed, interconnected machines makes it easier for computer "hackers" (the equivalent of phone phreaks) to get unauthorized access and *read* the data, as opposed to erasing or changing them. But this can be combated by putting the data in code. Individual privacy and corporate security will then be as well protected as they would be in a large computer; what matters in either case is that the key to the code be physically secure.

The key to obtaining all these benefits is the *autonomy* of each component in an intercommunicating network. Each minicomputer can serve local users in isolation even if its communication networks fail.[115] The system is therefore able to continue to deliver the services of the computing hierarchy, or most of them, despite the loss of many subsystems. This design principle, and the broader philosophy it reflects, have striking parallels in the design of resilient systems for supplying energy.

The analogy is not exact. The main reason for "duplexing" the Tandem computing and memory units, for example, is that information is not "fungible"—one unit is not interchangeable with another—so each transaction must be protected from error in each device and operation. In contrast, since one unit of electricity fed into a grid (for example) is the same as another, such duplexing of individual power sources would not be required in order to keep the grid working. Another difference is that a thousand hand calculators simply cannot do the same things as one big computer, whereas a user of oil (for example) cannot tell whether it comes from the supergiant Ghawar oilfield or from a large number of small stripper wells.

Despite these differences, the parallel between resilient, distributed data processing systems and resilient, distributed energy systems is illuminating. The design principles that emerge from these two examples and from the earlier discussion of biological and engineering resilience can be summarized thus:

• A resilient system is made of relatively small modules, dispersed in space, and each having a low cost of failure.
• Failed components can be detected and isolated early.
• Modules are richly interconnected so that failed nodes or links can be bypassed and heavy dependence on particular nodes or links is avoided.
• Links are as short as possible (consistent with the dispersion of the modules) so as to minimize their exposure to hazard.
• Numerically or functionally redundant modules can substitute for failed ones, and modules isolated by failed links can continue to work autonomously until reconnected.
• Components are diverse (to combat common-mode and common-cause failures), but compatible with each other and with varying working conditions.
• Components are organized in a hierarchy so that each successive level of function is little affected by failures or substitutions among components at lower levels.
• Buffer storage makes failures occur gradually rather than abruptly: components are coupled loosely in time, not tightly.
• Components are simple, understandable, maintainable, reproducible, capable of rapid evolution, and socially compatible.

The following chapters apply these principles to the problem of designing an inherently resilient energy system.

Chapter Fourteen
Rethinking the Energy System

At a recent conference of people from the Northern Great Plains who had harnessed windpower for their homes and farms, Joe Jodduck reported that at his windpowered home,

> Once I was watching the [television] news and saw that my whole area was blacked out. Sure enough, when I went outside I saw that all my neighbors' lights were off. Then I went back in and watched the rest of the news to see when my neighbors' lights would come back on.[1]

By using an autonomous local energy source—one that normally offered the advantages of interconnection and exchange with the power grid, but could stand alone if the grid crashed—Mr. Jodduck had protected himself against being turned off. Like the Tandem computer designers, he made his module of supply (a wind machine and battery bank) isolatable and independent. He gladly paid a modest extra cost for batteries as insurance against complete failure. His wind machine was embedded within the electric grid, yet buffered from it, so that when the whole grid crashed, his lowly level of the hierarchy could continue to function.

In Finland several years ago, a general strike shut down much of the national electric grid. In the industrial city of Jyväskylä, however, the municipal combined-heat-and-power station (a common fixture in Scandinavian towns) was able to disconnect from the grid and keep the city powered in isolation. The money saved by not having to shut down the local factories for the duration of the strike reportedly paid off the entire capital cost of the power plant.

Similarly, residents of Coronado, California were not even aware that the San Diego grid surrounding them was blacked out in March 1978; their power came from an independent cogeneration plant.[2] And the city of Holyoke, Massachusetts escaped the 1965 Northeast blackout by isolating itself from the regional grid and operating on its own gas turbine—which thereby paid off that turbine's capital cost in only four hours' operation![3]

In the bitter winter of early 1977, the shortage of natural gas in the Midwest became so acute that Ohio and New York factories had to be shut down to help keep the overloaded gas grid from collapsing. Yet in the midst of the same shortage, equally chilly rural New England was virtually unaffected. This was especially true in Vermont, the state (among the contiguous forty-eight) least served by pipeline gas. The explanation: rural New Englanders had always used bottled gas. System-wide failures with loss of pumping pressure or pilot lights could not occur. Not everyone ran out at once, so neighbors could help each other through spot shortages—just as the mites, in the experiment in population biology (Chapter Thirteen), could recolonize areas in which they had temporarily become extinct from nearby areas in which they still flourished.

To be sure, bottled gas (LPG) comes from remote sources—oil- and gas-extracting areas, all far from New England—and LPG distribution is readily disrupted by strikes or bad weather. In the Ohio River Valley in early 1977, for example, at the same time that the gas grid was on the verge of collapse, bottled gas could not always be delivered over poorly cleared and maintained rural roads, even though "extra propane trucks were sought across the Nation" and "every available LPG rail car was purchased or leased."[4] But again, the consequences were less serious. From the gas users' viewpoint, shortages in one building, and at a fairly predictable time, were vastly preferable to simultaneous area-wide failures without warning. Consistently over the years, whenever natural gas or LPG supplies were overstressed, the disruptions were mildest in areas, like northern New England, whose patterns of gas delivery and use were decentralized and unsynchronized. Likewise, Israel does not care if gas pipelines are being blown up all over the Middle East. Although almost every house in Israel has gas, Israel has essentially no pipeline service. The gas comes instead from bottles, whose independent, highly dispersed storage is virtually invulnerable. Israeli military planners like it that way.

These simple examples carry a profound lesson for the design of inherently resilient energy systems. In some sense, energy systems which are more "decentralized" can avoid the large-scale, system-wide collapses to which today's highly centralized, tightly coupled technologies are so prone. But what does "decentralization" really mean? In order to explore the concept, the terminology must first be made more precise.

The semantics of "decentralization"

The term "decentralization" is, as Langdon Winner remarks, a "linguistic trainwreck," defining itself by what it is *not*. Worse, it is ambiguous.[5]

In the literature of appropriate technology, alternative development concepts, and "post-industrial" patterns of settlement, production, and politics, the term "decentralized" has been used to mean everything from "small" to "agrarian/utopian" to "individually controlled." Discussion here, however, is confined to the *energy* system (not to industrial, urban, or governmental patterns). And even in this narrow context, eight dimensions of "decentralization" must be distinguished.

• Unit scale. If "unit" means a device which converts and supplies energy, each unit supplies energy in some form at a rate of so many watts in a particular time pattern, depending on specified parameters. "Scale" in this sense means the size or output capacity of a single unit of supply.

• Dispersion. This refers to whether individual units are clustered or scattered, concentrated or distributed, *relative to each other*. This property—density in space—does not specify how big each unit is, nor whether or how the units may be interconnected.

• Interconnectedness. Separate units can be coupled to each other, stand-alone (connected only to the end-user), or both optionally so as to isolate failures and permit autonomy when needed. Interconnection may increase reliability, and it certainly allows a given amount of supply capacity to meet a somewhat larger amount of scattered demand because not all demands occur at once. Interconnectedness says nothing about unit scale, dispersion, or distance from the user. It may refer to electricity or to other forms of energy (e.g., solar collectors connected by a district-heating grid). It may be simple or complex both in technology and in the intricacy of its pattern.

• Composition (or, as computer designers sometimes call it, "texture"). Different units can be *monolithic* (consisting of inseparable parts) or *modular* (combining multiple subunits). A gas turbine power plant, windfarm, or photovoltaic array is generally modular; a central thermal plant is more monolithic. Proposed "nuclear parks" would be modular but their modules would be individually enormous: composition does not specify unit scale.

• Locality is a concept near the heart of what is often meant by "decentralization," but it is here defined by this different term to avoid ambiguity. Locality is not a technical property of a unit in isolation, but rather expresses *its users' perception of its physical and social relationship to them*. A *remote* unit serves its users via a distribution system which makes the users feel far removed, geographically or politically or both, from that unit. A *local* unit is nearer to its users, linked to them by short supply lines.

This distinction is more subtle than it may at first appear. For example, a large hydroelectric dam serving several large smelters nearby may seem local to their operators; local can be big if the use is correspondingly big. Equally, a collection of small units can be remote. For example, a windfarm with many small wind machines could link them all to its user(s) by a long transmission line; or many solar collectors could deliver their collective heat output via an extensive network institutionally similar to present gas and electric grids. (In principle, a single small unit could also be made remote from its user[s] by putting it at the other end of a long transmission line, but there would generally be no reason to do this.) An assemblage of many solar concentrating dishes may be local if it is either dispersed near scattered users *or* clustered near clustered users. Local does not necessarily mean renewable (for example, locally used natural gas wells or even—in some Swedish proposals—nuclear heat reactors could perhaps be local). Conversely, renewable systems can be centralized, as in "power-tower," ocean-thermal-electric, biomass-plantation, solar-power-satellite, and similar schemes—although it is not obvious why one should wish to gather up an inherently dispersed energy flux (sunlight) into one place in order to be put to the expense of distributing it again to dispersed users. Locality is a property intermediate between the purely technical qualities described above and the more sociologically oriented ones listed below.

• User-controllability. Many energy users are concerned with the extent to which they can choose and control the energy systems important to their lives. This concern extends both to immediate decisions about end-use patterns—for example, being able to turn a light on and off at one's own convenience preserves individual autonomy—and to the wider question of the political process by which decisions about the energy system are made: whether they are participatory and pluralistic or dominated by a central technical elite.

• Comprehensibility. Whether people can control a technology depends partly on whether they can understand it. A system can be understandable to its user even if it is technically very sophisticated. Most people could not build a pocket calculator and do not know exactly what goes on inside it, but for them as users it is a tool rather than a machine: they run it, not vice versa.

• Dependency. The "poles" of this spectrum of economic, political, and psychological relationships might be multinational corporations on the one hand and do-it-yourself, appropriate, or "vernacular" technologies—things that people can do for themselves—on the other. Dependency expresses users' feeling that their own interests may not be identical with those of energy providers. A high degree of dependency might be characteristic of: a "black box" energy source which is designed, made, and installed by some remote and unaccountable institution; an energy source which a user is humiliatingly unable to understand, repair, adjust, or modify; or a source whose presence or price are beyond users' control. Supplying energy oneself or getting it through more familiar (hence usually more local) institutions would incur a different but probably more manageable dependency. Dependency is also related to breadth of choice: buying fuel from one of several competitive local distributors offers a sort of choice, but a narrow one if all those distributors rely on similar wholesalers.

Athough this list characterizes some of these eight qualities by their polar extremes, each has a continuum of values in a spectrum. Those values are relative to each other *and to a particular context of use.* An energy system which is small in the context of running smelters, for example, may be large if the use is running a television. A system which is distributed across the country may nonetheless be clustered in localized clumps, not spread evenly. A device which is comprehensible to farmers may be mysterious to physicists and vice versa. A source which is local in the city may be remote in the countryside (and possibly vice versa). Accordingly, it is important to remember, even in a specific context, that all the dimensions of "decentralization" are relative, not absolute.

Centralization: the root of the problem

Using these concepts, the inherent vulnerabilities surveyed in the first half of this book arise mainly because the energy systems which, for convenience, have been called "centralized"

• consist of relatively few but large units of supply and distribution;
• compose those units of large, monolithic components rather than of redundant smaller modules that can back each other up;
• cluster units geographically, for example near oilfields, coal mines, sources of cooling water, or demand centers;
• interconnect the units rather sparsely, with heavy dependence on a few critical links and nodes;
• knit the interconnected units into a synchronous system in such a way that it is difficult for a section to continue to operate if it becomes isolated—that is, since each unit's operation depends significantly on the synchronous operation of other units, failures tend to be system-wide;
• provide relatively little storage to buffer successive stages of energy conversion and distribution from each other, so that failures tend to be abrupt rather than gradual;
• locate supply units remotely from users, so that links must be long (the "long haul distances" considered in Chapter Four);
• tend to lack the qualities of user-controllability, comprehensibility, and user-independence. These qualities are important to social compatability, rapid reproducibility, maintainability, and other social properties identified in Chapter Thirteen as important in turn to resilience.

Even if one neglects the last point and focuses on purely technical properties, it is clear that the architecture—the basic structure—of today's highly centralized energy systems flies in the face of everything that the previous chapter showed was essential to resilience. As a recipe for disaster, its design could hardly be more expert and comprehensive.

Avoiding the resulting brittleness requires instead an energy system that uses *more dispered, diverse, local, and redundant modules,* incorporating the principles summarized at the end of the previous chapter. But this concept of smaller, more distributed units of energy supply immediately raises serious questions. Indeed, it may conjure up caricatures of (as some critics put it) trying to power an advanced industrial society with billions of backyard windmills. Three questions particularly stand out:

- Is not contemplating the use of smaller, less centralized energy technologies really a covert way of seeking to "decentralize society," leading to fundamental changes in our way of life and to the dissolution of national power?
- Are not small technologies too expensive because they cannot capture economies of scale?
- Are not the potential contributions of small technologies too minor and too slow to meet the needs of a dynamic economy and address the urgent problem of replacing dwindling supplies of petroleum?

This chapter and those following it will examine these questions.

Social "decentralization"?

The first question can be quickly dealt with. The observation that more dispersed, diverse, localized energy technologies are desirable for any reason (such as resilience) often invites the response that one is actually seeking to turn cities into agrarian villages, Congress into town meetings, and (by a further emotive extension) modern technology into primitivism. Whatever the possible advantages or drawbacks of these or any other kinds of broad social changes might be, they are all, as Chapter One made clear, far beyond the scope of this analysis. This book asks only how our *energy* system, through incremental choices of different *technologies,* might be made secure within the framework of our present institutions. This analysis is limited to examining how to construct an energy system with maximal economic and national security benefits to meet the needs of a heavy-industrial, urbanized society—a society, moreover, that is assumed to wish to continue rapid economic and population growth. Exploring what might be the most desirable form of social organization is far beyond the scope of this work.

In point of fact, moreover, neither common sense nor careful study of the actual institutional impact of smaller energy technologies supports the contention that they require people to live, or to manage their affairs, in a less centralized fashion.[6] Smaller technologies actually preserve a complete range of choice in social and political scale,[7] leaving the desirable degree of centralization in these arenas to be chosen individually and through the political process. Indeed, smaller energy technologies are often crititzed by left-wing commentators for *not* automatically producing political changes consistent with those critics' personal agendas. The confusion between the choice of technologies and the choice of patterns of social organization arises in part from sloppy terminology—which the above glossary has sought to clarify—and in part from some advocates' failure to distinguish their technical conclusions from their ulterior political preferences.

The economics of decentralized energy

The second common question about less centralized energy technologies is more complex: aren't they uneconomic? Even if they're more resilient, and even though that is doubtless a desirable quality, aren't they vastly more expensive than the large-scale technologies which meet our needs today? The following two chapters discuss (with the aid of technical appendices) the adequacy and cost of small energy technologies; but first the relationship between their cost and their scale can be considered in general terms.

There is no single "correct" size for energy technologies. The size should depend on the use. Yet despite some preliminary research, for example by the Tennessee Valley Authority, there is no data base anywhere in the world which shows in detail how much of what kind of energy is required, where, and how densely those needs are clustered. Even if such data existed, present knowledge would still not suffice to calculate the best scale of an energy system for a particular application. This may seem surprising, since the energy industries make decisions every day about how big an energy device should be. But those decisions actually ignore many important factors relating scale to cost. More than twenty economies of scale (effects which make bigger devices cost less per unit of output) or diseconomies of scale (which do the opposite) are now known. The diseconomies are far more numerous, and seem collectively larger, than the economies. In principle, all these effects could be added up to find, for a particular technology and application, the size (or sizes—there may be more than one) which will minimize cost. But in practice, no exact theory is yet available to take all important effects fully into account.

The observation that energy is generally supplied today by devices that are enormously larger than the uses to which the energy is put is therefore not conclusive evidence that this large scale is the cheapest. Indeed, the discrepancy of scale between supply and uses is so great that it seems to require more justification than a mere appeal to custom. After all, most of the devices in our daily lives use energy at a rate ranging from watts to thousands of watts. (For comparison, the metabolism of the human body uses somewhat over a hundred watts.) The average heating or cooling load of an inefficient house is typically thousands of watts. Large buildings, and the devices used in most major processes of industrial production, use of the order of hundreds of thousands of watts. Most factories or office buildings use a total of no more than some millions of watts, or in a very few cases a few billion watts.

Yet the scale of modern power plants, refineries, proposed synfuel plants, and the like is *routinely* at or above the highest end of this scale— that is, of the order of billions or tens of billions of watts. Why is it that these energy-supplying technologies are thousands, millions, or more times as large as their typical customers? Does this enormous mismatch of scales actually save money?

A few years ago, it was heretical even to ask this question, let alone to suggest the answer to which dispassionate analysis seemed inexorably to lead: that many of the advantages claimed for large scale in energy systems may be illusory because they are outweighed by less tangible and less quantifiable but perhaps more important disadvantages and diseconomies.[8] Today, however, both question and answer are rapidly becoming more respectable and urgent.

The habit of *assuming* that bigger is always cheaper is still strong, of course. Much of the electric utility industry continues to spend tens of billions of dollars per year building gigantic power plants on this assumption. Furthermore, official studies have observed almost a taboo against testing the assumption with empirical data. Even when the Public Utility Regulatory Policies Act of 1978 mandated that the government assess "the cost effectiveness of small versus large [electrical] generation, centralized versus decentralized generation, and intermittent generation, to achieve desired levels of reliability,"[9] the Economic Regulatory Administration, the agency charged with this study, virtually ignored the call.[10] So did other government studies which were supposed to concern themselves with exactly this problem.[11] Nonetheless, enough evidence is now available to cast the most serious doubt on doctrinaire assumptions that the energy system still has economies of scale available for exploitation.

This does not mean that decisions to build large plants in the past were always irrational. Rather, it means that, taking all relevant economic factors into account, such decisions would no longer be cost-effective in today's altered circumstances. Nor does it deny that big projects may have real economies of scale in *construction cost per kilowatt of installed capacity*. But where this economy of scale exists, it is a gross, not a net, effect. It must be tempered by other effects which may, for example, make each *installed* kilowatt of that capacity *send out* or *deliver* less energy than at smaller scale. Other tempering effects may increase the costs of other parts of the energy system, or they may increase indirect costs or inefficiencies. The object, after all, is to *deliver* energy—or, more precisely, to enable particular services to be performed by using energy—rather than merely to install the *capacity* to put the energy into a distribution system. The goal should therefore be to build the energy system which will perform the desired energy services at the lowest possible economic cost. If bigger technologies decrease construction costs by less than they increase other costs, then the technologies are too big.

A full analysis of the appropriate scale to minimize total economic costs in particular circumstances is inevitably rather complex. The key ingredients of such an analysis are given in Appendix One. It deals with those factors which tend either to increase or to decrease energy costs (especially electrical costs) as a function of scale, classified into ten major categories and based on the best available data from actual experience in several countries. The analysis shows that very large unit scale can typically reduce the direct construction costs (per unit of capacity) by tens of percent—at extreme sizes, even by sixty or seventy percent. But most of the *dis*economies which inevitably accompany that increase in unit size are *each* of that magnitude. Appendix One identifies nearly fifty such diseconomies: for example, a requirement for custom building rather than an opportunity for mass production, more frequent and more awkward failures, generally lower technical efficiency, difficulty of integration to use waste streams efficiently, large costs and losses of distribution, large requirements for back-up capacity, and higher financing costs and risks arising from longer construction times. *Almost any combination of a few of these documented effects could tilt the economic balance toward small scale* for all but the most highly concentrated applications.

Thus there is a *prima facie* case that big energy technologies are not inherently cheaper, and may well be costlier, than those scaled to match their end uses, most of which are in fact relatively small and dispersed. (The next two chapters show that the economic case in favor of smaller devices is even stronger than that.) Of course, there are still tasks for which big systems are appropriate and cost-effective. It would, for example, be almost as silly to run a big smelter with many little wind machines as to heat many houses with one big reactor. Mismatching scale in *either* direction incurs unnecessary costs. What matters is not some mythical "right scale in the abstract" but the right scale *for the particular task*.[12] Even in our highly industrialized society, however, nearly all the enegy-using devices are smaller—most of them are thousands or millions of times smaller—than the billions-of-watts supply systems that have hitherto been *assumed* to be economically essential. It appears that a more sophisticated and comprehensive view of the economics of whole energy systems would lead to a very different balance of sizes between demand and supply.

While that balance is unlikely to be found mainly at a scale of mere watts, or perhaps even mainly thousands of watts, it is most unlikely to be billions of watts. This huge scale is grossly mismatched to all but a tiny handful of specialized applications that are already well provided for by equally large energy supply technologies, notably by existing large hydro-electric dams. Thus the extreme centralization which is at the root of the inherent brittleness of America's energy system is not economically essential and is probably an economic mistake or liability. Conversely, less centralized energy technologies can not only avoid much of this vulnerability; they can also—as later chapters show in more detail—save money.

Can decentralized investments be fast enough?

Even if relatively small technologies are often economic, are they not by their nature (it is often suggested) incapable of making a prompt, major contribution to our nation's energy supplies? Won't they be too little, too late? Can they really provide the rate of growth, in actual units of extra energy per year (or per dollar invested), that the national predicament requires? Aren't they more romantic than practical?

The answer to these questions—the subject of the remainder of this chapter—is again perhaps surprising. Yet it is unavoidable if one simply looks at the data with an open mind. Empirical evidence confirms what, on reflection, one might suspect: that relatively small, simple, accessible technologies are likely to contribute *more* energy *sooner* than conventional large-scale technologies—provided that strong obstacles are not deliberately put in their way. Indeed, as the following data illustrate, individual decisions in the marketplace—decisions to use energy more efficiently and to harness dispersed, sustainable energy sources of relatively small scale—are, in aggregate, providing new energy today about a hundred times as fast as all the centralized supply projects put together.

During 1973–78, the United States got twice as much energy-"supplying" capacity from numerous small energy-saving actions, and got it twice as fast, as synfuel advocates say they can provide at ten times the cost (if, and only if, they are given twenty-two billion dollars' pocket money to get started with). In 1979, ninety-eight percent of U.S. economic growth was fueled by energy savings, only two percent by actual net expansions of energy supply. In 1980, while real GNP stayed constant within better than a tenth of one percent, total U.S. energy use dropped by three and a half percent—the biggest one-year drop in our nation's history. In total, the energy needed to produce a unit of Gross National Product decreased by fifteen percent during 1973–80[13]—that is, at an average rate of two percent per year. By autumn 1981, that rate of improvement had accelerated, with the energy/GNP ratio nearly five percent below its 1980 level.

The United States was not alone in this progress. In the European Economic Community during 1973–78, energy savings supplied more than ten times as much new energy capacity as increased nuclear power. The ratio of energy savings to all expansions of energy supply was nineteen to one.[14] Even the most ambitious nuclear program in the world, that of France, was outpaced three to one by a halfhearted efficiency program with a tiny fraction of the nuclear program's budget and official support.[15] Japan has averaged about four percent annual growth in Gross National Product since 1974, yet at the same time has had almost no growth in total energy use. One source reports that in 1980, Japan increased its inflation-corrected industrial production by four and a half percent and its total economic activity by nearly five percent, while decreasing energy use by ten percent nationally, and by more than twenty percent in industry—all in a single year.[16] Denmark decreased its total direct fuel use by twenty percent just in the two years 1979–80, largely through better thermal insulation of buildings (whose efficiency has improved by thirty percent in about three years).[17] Insulation programs were largely responsible for cutting West Germany's use of heating oil by more than seventeen percent during just the first eight months of 1981 compared to the same period in 1980.[18]

This trend is accelerating in the United States as it is elsewhere. Far from having nearly exhausted the readily available savings, efforts so far have barely scratched the surface (as Chapter Fifteen will show). Investments in saving energy generally repay their investment in less than a year—compared to decades for investments in centralized energy supply. The sums being invested in saving energy are substantial: Americans spent nearly nine billion dollars on small energy-saving devices in 1980, comparable to the total value of imported Japanese cars, and by the mid-1980s this investment is expected to reach tens of billions of dollars per year.[19] Yet far greater investments in higher energy productivity would be worthwhile: energy-saving investments of one hundred billion dollars per year would still be cheaper than new energy supplies.[20] One measure of this advantage is that the nearly nine billion dollars invested just in 1980 to save energy produced immediately a continuing saving equivalent to the output of a synfuel industry that would, on official estimates, take two decades and cost more than fifty billion dollars to build.

The speed of these small technologies has stunned the energy supply industries. Utilities and oil companies had supposed that they, after all, were the experts; nobody could do things faster than they could; and anything they build would take them ten years. They were wrong. The efficiency boom caught them badly off-balance, committed to far more supply capacity than people are willing to buy. Many utilities and oil companies are now suffering financial hardship as their sales unexpectedly decline. There are some silver linings, however: some of Royal Dutch-Shell's most profitable subsidiaries sell energy-saving and energy-managing services. This is proving an extremely high-return enterprise. One American firm of this type, started in 1979, expects a quarter of a billion dollars' turnover in 1983.

Renewable sources: the dark horse pulls ahead

The remarkable speed with which people have bought small devices to raise energy efficiency is not the only energy surprise. Next to efficiency improvements, small-scale renewable sources have turned out to be the second-fastest-growing part of U.S. energy supply.[21]

During 1977–80, renewables gave America twelve hundred trillion British Thermal Units (BTUs) per year of new primary energy, increasing to over seven percent of total U.S. energy supply. Meanwhile, the total contribution from nonrenewables *fell* by six hundred trillion BTUs per year.[22] There is every indication, too, that during 1981 the renewable contribution accelerated while nonrenewables fell further behind, and that this gap is widening further in 1982. A few examples illustrate the rapid emergence of renewable energy as the fastest-growing source of actual energy supplies, outpaced only by more efficient energy use:

• The United States is approaching its millionth solar building, of which half are passive and half those are made by adding greenhouses or other sun-capturing accessories to existing buildings. Many of these were built on the basis of word-of-mouth or information from popular journals, few from officially provided information. In the most solar-conscious areas, about six or seven percent of all space heating in 1980 was solar, and one-quarter to all of the new housing starts in those areas were passive solar designs. Nationally, about fifteen percent of the contractors building tract houses, and virtually all purveyors of prefabricated and package-planned houses, offered thermally efficient, passive solar designs in 1980. By 1981, some of the nation's largest housing developments supplied passive design and active solar water heaters as standard features,[23] and efficient passive designs were moving into the mainstream of construction practice in most parts of the country.

• Despite a depression in house construction, U.S. solar collector production rose twenty-one percent to nearly eleven million square feet in the first half of 1981. Medium-temperature liquid collectors (suitable, for example, for heating domestic hot water) more than doubled in a year in 1981 and for the first time surpassed all other types. The production of high-temperature solar collectors for industry, too, more than trebled in one year to six percent of the market.[24]

• In New England, over one hundred fifty factories have switched from oil to wood, as have more than half the households in many rural (and some suburban) areas. Private woodburning has increased more than sixfold in the past few years. The number of stove foundries has risen from a handful to more than four hundred. By 1981, nearly a tenth of all U.S. homes were heating at least partly with wood, and over eight million wood stoves and furnaces had been sold in a decade (at an annual rate varying from one and a fifth million in 1979 to eight hundred thousand in 1981).[25] In Vermont, the fraction of households heating partly or mainly with wood rose from twenty-two percent in 1978 to fifty-six percent in 1980,[26] and in 1980, for the first time in many years, Vermonters burned more wood than oil. Meanwhile, woodburning, often using advanced processes such as pelletization, gave the forest products industry half its energy, contributing eleven to fourteen hundred trillion BTUs in 1980 in that sector alone.[27] Woodburning also expanded in a wide range of other industries.[28] By 1980, private and industrial woodburning together supplied the U.S. with about twice as much delivered energy as nuclear power did[29]—even though nuclear power had a head start of three decades and over forty billion dollars in direct federal subsidies.[30]

• There are about sixty main companies making wind machines in the United States and many abroad. Commercial windfarms were, by early 1982, competing on utility grids in New Hampshire, Washington, and California, with more being rapidly built to fulfill power contracts probably totalling about ten billion dollars. By late 1981, nearly a hundred U.S. utilities were getting into windpower with either test programs or formal commitments. California, with six windfarms operating by early 1982, expects thirteen hundred machines to be in operation by late 1982, hundreds of megawatts by 1983.[31] Oregon, Montana, and Wyoming will soon have windfarms of their own. In some states, formal windpower targets fully integrate wind into utility supply forecasts: California plans to get one percent of its electricity from wind in 1985 and ten percent by 2000; Hawaii wants to get nearly nine percent of its power from wind by 1985.

• Some ten to twenty thousand megawatts of small hydro capacity was under reconstruction in 1981 (mainly refurbishing old, abandoned dams). A further twenty thousand megawatts at two thousand sites awaited permits in mid-1980[32]—twice the gross nuclear capacity ordered since 1975. (Of these two thousand sites, half had a capacity under five megawatts and two-thirds under fifteen megawatts.) Companies to build microhydro facilities or to gather up and broker their power to utilities are springing up.[33] It appears that the total small hydro capacity ordered during 1979–81 in the United States amounted to more megawatts than the total coal and nuclear capacity ordered during the same period—but the small hydro plants can be completed nearly a decade earlier than their steam plant competitors.

Ethanol is often blended into premium unleaded gasoline. Most states have biomass fuel programs. Fuel alcohol production in 1982 will probably exceed three or four hundred million gallons—approaching only half a percent of the nation's motor fuel use, but an important source in some agricultural areas.

Direct solar and photovoltaic (solar cell) systems were the fastest-growing energy supply technologies between 1975 and 1980, with revenues rising by an average of one hundred fifty-five percent per year. During this period, total U.S. sales of all renewable energy equipment rose by thirty-eight percent per year to the substantial total of more than six billion dollars in 1980,[34] with continued rapid growth in 1981. In some parts of the country, the saturation is astonishingly rapid: in southern Humboldt County, California, for example, the utility reportedly estimates that some eighty percent of all households have disconnected from the grid and installed solar cells instead.[35]

In short, it is hard to find a part of the U.S. that does not have its unique blend of renewable energy ferment. In some, such as oil-dependent Hawaii, a coherent program is emerging: the state plans to get half its energy from renewables by 2000 and eventually to become a net exporter.[36] The California Energy Commission projects that despite rapid population and economic growth, total California energy use will decline by about three-tenths of a percent per year during the remainder of this century; demand for oil and for natural gas will drop by twenty-two and nineteen percent respectively; and renewable sources will by 2000 provide twenty-two percent of total energy supply (compared to five percent in 1980) and seventy-two percent of total electrical generation (compared to twenty-three percent in 1980).[37]

The bulk of today's renewable energy installations, however, are on the scale of single houses, farms, offices, and factories, and have been built not as part of a state program but entirely on individual initiative. Many observers who travel the country remark that although these activities are concealed from governments' view by their dispersion, small *individual* scale, and diversity, they add up to a quiet energy revolution that is reshaping the American energy system with unprecedented speed.

A regional case study

New England offers a particularly informative snapshot of recent national trends in efficiency and renewables.[38] The region is highly reliant on oil. In 1973, oil represented eighty percent of total energy use. In 1980, oil dependence was still nearly seventy-three percent. This dependence made New Englanders acutely aware of interruptions and price increases.

Their response, chiefly at an individual and community level, was dramatic. During the two years 1978–80, New England's population rose seven-tenths of one percent and the region's real personal income rose four and six-tenths percent. But during those same two years, total energy consumption *fell* six and a half percent. Further, renewables grew to supply six and three-tenths percent of total consumption—ranking ahead of coal and just behind natural gas and nuclear power. The renewable energy supply is now expected to double during 1980–85 to about thirteen percent of total regional energy use.

During 1978–80, New Englanders decreased their use of conventional fuels and power by seven and a half percent, or the equivalent of forty-six million barrels of oil per year. They used ten and a half percent less oil and twenty percent less nuclear power. At the same time they increased their use of coal (by five million barrels of oil equivalent per year) and of natural gas (by three). But these increases, plus extra Canadian power imports, were only a quarter as big as the decreases in oil and nuclear. This left a gap between regional energy supply and historic demand. For the first time, that gap was filled by small technologies—renewables—and by more efficient energy use.

Renewables began to play a sizeable role. A drought temporarily reduced New England's hydropower by twenty-two percent, equivalent to utilities' burning an extra two million barrels of oil per year (a deficit made up nearly four times over by increased imports of Canadian hydropower). Meanwhile, however, woodburning displaced nearly five million additional barrels of oil per year. Energy from municipal solid waste, direct solar use, and wind also increased by half a million barrels per year. Net renewable supplies from within the region thus increased by three million barrels of oil equivalent, to a total of nearly thirty-four million barrels per year. In 1980, renewable sources gave New England about forty-six percent more usable delivered energy than nuclear power did. Noteworthy details of this contribution include:

• New England used about twenty-four percent more wood in 1980 than in 1978. Wood made up nearly three-quarters of the total 1980 renewable supply and provided a quarter of northern New England's space heating.

• About forty-three percent of the regional wood use was by industry. A sixth of that was in a wide range of non-pulp-and-paper factories.

• The Department of Agriculture's Pilot Fuelwood project (which helps landowners to manage their woodlots and contract for harvesting) and educational programs by the state energy offices, Maine Audubon Society, and New England Regional Commission helped to expand and improve sustainable wood use.

• The region's eleven thousand solar systems in 1980 are expected to treble by 1985. Hydroelectric capacity should increase thirty percent and energy recovery from municipal solid waste may increase by up to tenfold.

Finally, New Englanders made their greatest progress in harnessing their most abundant energy resource—correctable inefficiencies. During the two-year period, by low-cost/no-cost efficiency improvements and by a slight shift toward less energy-intensive industries, they saved energy equivalent to a twelve percent increase in their total supply. That rate of saving, six percent per year, was nearly twice the national average, and was fourteen times as important as New England's shift from nonrenewable to renewable sources. Yet it relied on even smaller technologies—chiefly weatherstripping and insulation.

Is this a real turning point?

From the vantage point of the five years or so in which the transformation illustrated by the New England example has been well underway, it may seem that the results are meager. But so it must have seemed in 1900 when there were only five to eight thousand cars on U.S. roads, or even in 1908 when there were one hundred ninety-four thousand. Cars became more noticeable in 1911 when the six hundred thousand on the roads caused Standard Oil to sell more gasoline than kerosene for the first time. Two years later there were a million cars; seventeen years after that, in 1930, twenty-three million; today, over a hundred million. In the first decade after World War I, the automobile became sufficiently widespread to transform at first the perceptions of mobility and later, in consequence, the settlement patterns and the whole industrial infrastructure of American society. Yet the car may not at first have seemed so portentous: indeed, on the assumption (common in the early twentieth century) that car drivers would have to pay for their highways just as railroads had had to pay for their roadbeds, the odds seemed stacked against the commercial success of the car. Until the Model A and Model T brought cars to every town, few observers expected rapid success. Thus profound changes in the technostructure of America can creep up on us unawares. Small energy technologies—for efficient use and renewable supply—are likely to repeat the story.

Nobody can say for sure whether they will ultimately work such a transformation. But they certainly have the technical, economic, and social potential to do so. As Congress's Office of Technology Assessment concluded,

> If energy can be produced from on-site solar energy systems at competitive prices, the increasing centralization which has characterized the equipment and institutions associated with energy industries for the past thirty years could be drastically altered; basic patterns of energy consumption and production could be changed; energy-producing equipment could be owned by many types of organizations and even individual homeowners.[39]

The following chapters demonstrate that small technologies for energy efficiency and renewable supply *already* meet the test of "competitive prices." Even in 1979, a panel of government, industry, and academic experts found that

> [D]ecentralized [electricity] generation systems are likely to confer major consumer benefits. These may include shorter lead times in planning and construction, easier siting, reduced capital requirements, greater efficiency in fuel use, and reduced vulnerability to fuel shortages. . . . We find a number of such options are at, or are approaching, a state of technical and economic competitiveness with larger centralized systems.[40]

The panel also found that "on balance, . . . the climate for the development of small, diversified, and dispersed supply and [efficiency] . . . options is likely to improve." By 1980, those improvements had reached the point where the nuclear- and coal-oriented Southern California Edison Company announced that henceforth it would aggressively pursue an efficiency/renewables strategy as the cheapest option for future expansion. A year later, that switch was ahead of schedule. Small, whether beautiful or not, has at least become respectable.

Many countries whose energy problem is even more serious than that of the United States now emphasize decentralized solutions. In oil-dependent Sweden, the energy research and development budget since 1978 has heavily emphasized efficiency (thirty-six percent of the total outlay) and renewable sources (forty percent).[41] The program focuses not only on the long-term goal of wholly renewable supply but also on the short-term goal of reducing oil use, largely by the same means, by one-third during the 1980s. The Swedish Parliament, agreeing with seventy-eight percent of the voters that this goal can be best met by efficiency and renewables, has ratified a plan to emphasize these options and to phase out nuclear power by 2010. Romania, a centrally planned socialist state, has set itself the goal of becoming the world's most energy-efficient country, intending to reduce its energy use per unit of industrial output by forty percent during the 1980s and by a total of sixty-two percent by the year 2000, while also favoring dispersed and renewable sources.[42] In Japan, not only is energy efficiency improving at a sizzling pace, but by 1980 renewable energy already provided more than seven percent of total primary supplies, increasing fast enough to achieve the eight-percent official target for 1990 about eight years early.[43] That seven-odd percent included eight-tenths of one percent direct solar heat, delivered by more than three million solar systems already in place. Over ten percent of Japanese homes will have solar systems by the end of 1982; about twenty-five percent (over eight million units) by 1990.[44] Japanese purchases of solar collectors in 1980 alone totalled over half a billion dollars' worth, including three-quarters of a million systems for water heating and thirteen thousand for industrial process heat. Even in cloudy West Germany, thirty manufacturers installed about a million square feet of solar panels in 1980; Israel, with half a million solar water heaters, requires them on all new houses. France plans to have six hundred thousand such systems by 1985 and to get more than a fifth of its total energy supplies from renewable sources by the year 2000.[45] Clearly, the international market for decentralized energy technologies will not be short of competition.

Why should small technologies be faster?

In many countries, small energy technologies have already achieved more in a few years than governments expected they could do in twenty years. This is no accident. It results not only from economic savings, advantages in safety and resilience, and public acceptance. It reflects also some fundamental *logistical* properties related to *scale and simplicity*. These properties enable such small devices to provide needed energy services faster, per unit of investment, than larger and more complex alternatives. It is important to understand these advantages, for they are the key to the continued rapid growth in smaller and more resilient energy technologies.

First, each unit takes days, weeks, or months to install, not a decade.

Second, those units can diffuse rapidly into a large consumer market—like digital watches, pocket calculators, video games, Rubik's Cubes, and snowmobiles—rather than requiring a slower process of "technology delivery" to a narrow, specialized, and perhaps "dynamically conservative" utility market, as do giant power plants. This is a function of the relative understandability, marketability, and accessibility of the technologies—of their comparative technical and managerial simplicity and the ease with which they can adapt to local conditions. These factors determine the mechanism, and hence the rate, of market penetration.

Technologies that can be designed, made, installed, and used by a wide variety and a large number of actors can achieve deployment rates (in terms of total delivered energy) far beyond those predicted by classical market-penetration theories. For illustration, let us imagine two sizes of wind machines: a unit with a peak capacity of several megawatts, which can be bought for perhaps a million dollars and installed by a heavy-engineering contractor in a few months on a specially prepared utility site; and another of a few kilowatts, which might be bought by a farmer on the Great Plains from Sears or Western Auto, brought home in a pickup truck, put up (with one helper and hand tools) in a day, then plugged into the household circuit and left alone with virtually no maintenance for twenty or thirty years. (Both these kinds of wind machines are now entering the U.S. market.) Most analysts would emphasize that it takes a thousand small machines to equal the energy output of one big one (actually less, because the small ones, being dispersed, are collectively less likely to be simultaneously becalmed).[46] But it may also be important that the small machines can be produced far faster than the big ones, since they can be made in any vocational school shop, not only in elaborate aerospace facilities, and are also probably cheaper per kilowatt. What may be most important—and is hardly ever captured in this type of comparison— is that there are thousands of times more farms than electric utilities on the Great Plains, subject to fewer institutional constraints and inertias. Likewise, California has only four main electric companies, but more than two hundred thousand rural wind sites that can readily accommodate more than ten kilowatts of wind capacity.[47] Not surprisingly, new megawatts of wind machines (and small hydro) are being ordered faster in in California than new megawatts of central power stations.

The third reason for suspecting that many small, simple things should be faster to do than a few big, complicated things is that the former are slowed down by diverse, temporary institutional barriers that are largely *independent of each other*. For example, passive solar may be slowed down by the need to educate architects and builders, microhydro by licensing problems, greenhouses by zoning rules. In contrast, large and complicated plants are slowed down by generic constraints everywhere at once, such as problems in siting major facilities and financing large projects. Because of their independence, dozens of small, fairly slow-growing investments can add up, by strength of numbers, to very rapid total growth, rather than being held back by universal problems. To stop the big plants takes only one insoluble institutional snag; to stop all the diverse kinds of small plants takes a great many. This diversity of renewable and efficiency options is not only a good insurance policy against technical failure; it also helps to guard against specialized, unforeseen social problems in implementation, offering a prospect of alternative ways to solve what problems do arise.

It may still seem counterintuitive to suggest that doing many small things can be faster than doing a few big things. It is certainly contrary to the thrust of official energy policy. It seems to be contradicted by one's sense of the tangible importance of a large refinery or power plant: such a big and impressive installation must surely be the sort of thing of which our nation's industrial sinews are made, whereas a small technology—a bale of roof insulation, a cogeneration plant in a factory, a solar water heater—seemingly has only local and limited relevance. Yet in a deeper sense, the success of the free-market economic philosophy on which American private enterprise has been built depends very directly on the collective speed and efficiency of many individually small decisions and actions by sovereign consumers. It is precisely because those decisions are the fastest and most accurate means of giving practical effect to private preferences that Americans have opted for a market system—one of decentralized choice and action—rather than for a centrally planned economy on the Soviet model. And in energy policy, recent events amply vindicate that choice.

Despite the success of these decentralized energy options, many energy planners are reluctant to rest their confidence in such individual actions. How can we be sure, they ask, that if we do not build our centralized energy plants, people will really insulate their houses and so make our plants unnecessary? After all, such dispersed, individual actions are not under the planners' direct control as a large construction project is (or is supposed to be). Yet exactly the same mechanisms are at work in decentralized actions to increase energy efficiency that have always been invoked as the rationale for forecasting *growth* in energy demand. The many small market decisions which collectively constitute national demand are merely responding to a different set of signals today than they did previously. The bottom line is the proof: small, unglamorous, inconspicuous actions by individuals plugging steam leaks, weatherstripping windows, and buying more efficient cars are collectively increasing total energy capacity about a hundred times as fast as the annual investment of more than sixty billion dollars in centralized energy supply expansions with the combined might of the energy industries and the federal government behind them.

The hypothesis that many small actions can add up to greater speed than a few big actions is thus empirically true; there are good theoretical reasons why it should be true; and it is the approach most consistent with our national traditions. It is one of the reasons, indeed, that a fundamental shift in the architecture of America's energy system is already underway, with profoundly encouraging implications for resilience. For the highly centralized technologies which are being outpaced and outcompeted in the marketplace today are also those whose inherent brittleness so endangers national security. Whatever the reasons for building those vulnerable technologies in the past, those reasons are no longer surviving scrutiny by investors. Highly centralized systems are no longer the only or even the most timely and cost-effective way to meet our energy needs.

Economic and engineering logic, therefore, no longer seems to be automatically on the side of centralization. Rather, it favors a high priority for two types of technologies which, especially in combination, can provide inherent resilience: improved efficiency in using energy, and certain dispersed, sustainable energy sources. The next two chapters explore these opportunities in turn.

Chapter Fifteen

End-Use Efficiency: Most Resilience Per Dollar

One of the principles of resilient design derived in Chapter Thirteen is that the parts of the energy system should be "coupled loosely in time, not tightly," so that failures are slow and graceful rather than rapid and abrupt. This can be done either by providing more storage between successive stages of energy conversion and supply or *by using energy at a slower rate* so that the same amount of storage is depleted more gradually. That is the principle enunciated by the Chinese philosopher Lao-tse two and a half millenia ago:

> In managing affairs there is no better advice than to be sparing.
> To be sparing is to forestall.
> To forestall is to be prepared and strengthened.
> To be prepared and strengthened is to be ever successful.
> To be ever successful is to have infinite capacity.[1]

This chapter shows how applying that simple principle to the energy system can profoundly increase national resilience.

Using energy more slowly need not mean curtailing or doing without the *services* which energy provides—the comfort, light, mobility, ability to make steel or bake bread—which are the motive for seeking energy in the first place. Indeed, some services can be provided without needing to supply *any* energy. Opening office curtains can admit daylight to replace artificial light. A properly designed house can maintain indoor comfort year-round without needing a furnace or an air-conditioner (as will be described below). In such cases, since no energy is required, there is no energy supply to be interrupted, so energy vulnerability has been eliminated. More commonly, the need for energy cannot be wholly eliminated, but it can be reduced by raising the *end-use efficiency* of providing the energy service—that is, by wringing more work out of the energy so that the

235

same service is provided, with unchanged reliability and convenience, in a more clever way that uses less energy.

This is not at all what some people mean by "energy conservation"—driving less, being hotter in the summer and colder in the winter, and shutting down the factories. On the contrary, efficient energy use is a way of driving as much or more, being more comfortable, running the factories at higher capacity, and *yet* using less energy and money. Thus it is not true that the less energy we use, the worse off we are. On the contrary, how much energy we use is—up to a point—a measure not of our affluence but of our carelessness or stupidity, our failure to operate our society with an elegant economy of means. The optimum is rather to use the *amount* (and the type and source) of energy which will provide each desired energy service *in the cheapest way*, balancing the cost of buying more efficiency against the cost of buying more energy instead.

Many energy preparedness planners do not consider energy efficiency as an option. Because they think it is such a slow, gradual process that it cannot help *in* an emergency, they ignore its ability to *prevent* an emergency. Focusing on what can be done immediately *during* a shortage, they restrict their choices to privation and belt-tightening—"saving" energy by simply *doing without* both the energy and the services it provides. Because of this traditionally narrow view, emergency energy planning concentrates on ways to allocate scarce supplies during an emergency so that critical, high-priority needs can be met at the expense of all other needs. Furthermore, shortages are often shared by rationing supplies to a fixed fraction of what they were before the shortage—giving everyone an incentive to ensure ample emergency allocations by "padding" normal rates of usage through continued inefficiency.

Some emergency planners go even further and say that energy efficiency is actually undesirable, for two reasons. First, they argue that fat cut now cannot be cut later—that somehow, if people drove efficient cars all the time, carless Sundays or other means of curtailing driving would become impossible. This is simply a confusion between curtailment and increased efficiency. Both save energy, but only curtailment imposes hardship, even though it saves much less energy than efficiency can.

Second, some people who understand this difference (between saving energy by doing more with less and saving energy by simply doing without) nonetheless suggest that efficiency reduces resilience by trimming flexibility and reserves. In biological systems (Chapter Thirteen), peak efficiency often does mean greater specialization, and hence a reduced ability to cope with changed conditions. But that is not the type of efficiency considered here. On the contrary, the energy systems described in this and the following chapters are more flexible and have more buffer storage built in than today's systems. The argument that, for example, it is wrong to stop a factory's steam leaks now, because that will reduce the scope for doing so later to save energy painlessly during a shortage, reflects a mistaken view of the nature of energy use. The fallacy is often expressed as an analogy: that a society using energy is like a fat person whose reserves of fat can fend off starvation if food becomes scarce. But this analogy is misleading. A leaner energy system, like a healthier person, saves money all the time by needing less energy for normal operation. That saving helps to displace the most vulnerable energy supplies, such as oil from the Persian Gulf, and so reduces the effect (and perhaps the likelihood) of cutoffs in those supplies. A country that uses no foreign oil cannot be blackmailed by a threat of cutoff.

This chapter shows how energy efficiency can yield greater security. Instead of waiting for shortages to occur, we should seek to *reduce or prevent* them by promptly increasing energy efficiency to a level that provides a generous "cushion" of both normal and emergency energy supplies. By doing more with less, it may be possible to avoid altogether having to do without. Insulating the roof may *prevent* freezing in the dark. Efficient cars, by reducing or eliminating the need to import oil, can relieve concerns about interruption of those imports.

More specifically, more efficient energy use can reduce energy vulnerability in at least six ways, described more fully below. Higher efficiency:

- can completely eliminate dependence on the most vulnerable sources;
- enables the most resilient sources to meet a larger fraction of total energy needs—and within a few decades, to replace, largely or wholly, the vulnerable supplies on which our nation now depends (Chapter Sixteen);
- delays and slows down the depletion of fuel supplies (a more efficient factory can run longer on its fuel stockpiles without needing to replenish them);
- can reduce the maximum severity of failures (left without heat, a heat-tight house simply cannot get as cold as a leaky house);
- makes improvised substitute supplies much more effective and leaves enough time to get them working (sources of fuel alcohols which would not do much to help run gas-guzzlers can go far toward running a fleet of fuel-sipping cars); and
- is achieved by technologies which are in general less vulnerable in their own right than technologies which increase energy supply. (Roof insulation and heat exchangers simply cannot be disrupted in the same way as oil tankers and transmission lines; and if they are disrupted, the failure generally affects only a few people for a short period.)

Achieving these benefits may require extra investment in money, brains, or attention.[2] But a purely economic assessment will generally *understate* how much investment is worthwhile, because it will omit the resiliency benefits. If the social cost of vulnerability were put into the economic balance between efficiency and increased energy supply, that balance would shift in favor of efficiency. To make the argument stronger, however, this discussion considers only the narrow economic viewpoint of direct (private internal) costs; and it confines itself to those efficiency improvements which cost less than what increased energy supplies would cost if the efficiency improvements were *not* made. Most of the improvements considered are also cost-effective at present energy prices, which "roll in" costly new supplies with cheaper old supplies and thus understate the "marginal" (incremental) cost of increasing supplies.

By counting only direct economic costs, the economic comparisons in this chapter (and in the following one, which deals with resilient energy sources) implicitly value all risks, vulnerabilities, and side effects at zero. This approach obviously understates how much efficiency is worth buying. It would be a poor basis for national policy, where security concerns must carry great weight. Yet, fortuitously, just doing what saves each individual money in the narrowest sense would *also* dramatically improve the energy resilience of both the individual and the nation.

The resilience benefits of efficient energy use are not only multiple; they are synergistic—that is, they work together in such a way that the total benefit is greater than the sum of its parts. And they are nonlinear—small improvements buy a disproportionate amount of "insurance". The benefits arise at every scale, from the individual user to a whole nation and even the world. The following description of these benefits will show why improving end-use efficiency is the best buy in energy resilience: why, to paraphrase an old Pentagon slogan, it gives the "most bounce per buck."

The state of the art

According to the Energy Information Administration, in 1973, on the eve of the Arab oil embargo, the U.S. imported for consumption (excluding stockpiling and net of re-exports) six million barrels per day of crude oil and refined products. As higher prices failed to keep pace with inflation and "Project Independence" policies favored only grandiose but slow supply projects, net oil imports soared to eight and a half million barrels per day in 1977. Thereafter, price-driven improvements in U.S. energy efficiency[3] were largely responsible for decreasing net oil imports to seven and eight-tenths million barrels per day in 1978, six and two-tenths in 1980, and five and one-tenth (at times below four) in 1981—a forty percent net import decline in just four years. By early 1982, the Organization of Petroleum Exporting Countries (OPEC) was selling the world a third less oil than it had sold a decade earlier, and demand was still falling.

A group of oil industry leaders forecast in 1980 that, contrary to their expectations two years earlier, total U.S. use of refined products would probably stay about constant through the 1980s, with demand for gasoline, home heating oil, and residual fuel oil actually falling.[4] Events so far have outdone even those expectations, undercutting also the still lower demand forecasts issued in 1981. For example, in California—a prosperous state which uses over a tenth of all U.S. gasoline—there were nearly a million more cars in 1980, driven almost ten billion vehicle-miles further, than in 1976; yet gasoline use in 1980 was the lowest since 1976.[5] By March 1981, gasoline demand for the entire United States was the lowest in ten years. Declining oil demand had become the rule, not the exception—so it was news when, in January 1981, unusually cold weather led to the first increase in national oil use in nearly two years.[6] Expectations of unlimited demand growth, so popular in the 1970s, evaporated so quickly that the permanent shutdown of approximately a hundred oil refineries during 1978–82—abandoned because their proprietors do not expect ever to be able to sell that much oil again—passed almost unnoticed. In total, during the period 1973–81, while the Gross National Product grew twenty-one percent beyond inflation, total energy use fell by nearly one percent and total oil use fell by eight percent: each barrel was yielding thirty-one percent more GNP.

These encouraging figures do not by themselves constitute proof that Americans have raised their energy productivity. Such aggregated figures as net oil imports lump together domestic demand with domestic oil extraction and with the substitution of non-oil energy sources. Aggregated demand data also cannot distinguish

- changes in how much energy it takes to provide a service from changes in the *composition* of services provided (since some, like smelting, need far more energy than others, such as banking, and industry in most countries has recently tended to shift its growth into the less energy-intensive sectors);
- changes in efficiency from the effects of economic recessions;
- improved efficiency from degradation of energy services (such as reduced comfort in buildings); and
- better progress in some sectors from worse progress in others.

For these reasons, such aggregated measures as energy/GNP ratios or levels of net oil imports, though a convenient shorthand, can be misleading in comparing true energy efficiencies over time or between countries. These measures cannot reveal either how much end-use efficiency has been improved or how much improvement is still possible and worthwhile. For those purposes, the only practical approach is to assess "technical coefficients"—how much energy is used, in *physical* terms, to provide a precisely specified unit of each energy service: for example, how many BTUs it takes to make a pound of cement or to move a ton of freight for a mile.

In the past few years, a large international literature has assessed, for a wide range of countries and conditions, what those coefficients currently are and what it is economically worthwhile changing them to. Such data can be transferred from one place to another if careful attention is paid to differences of climates, of preferences in the size and performance of cars, in the different kinds of ore fed into steel mills, and so forth. The technical literature on practically achievable efficiency gains is so vast and so fast-moving that a study of this length could not even summarize even all the main results. This has been done elsewhere, most recently in a study originally commissioned by the West German government and incorporating the latest results from a dozen countries.[7] Two authoritative analyses based almost entirely on the U.S. literature have reached similar conclusions in comparable or greater detail.[8] For present purposes, however, it is sufficient to survey typical developments in just a few key sectors. Those not treated here in detail show similar scope for improved efficiency.

Buildings   The eighty million dwellings in the United States account for more than a third of all U.S. primary energy demand. The new buildings added each year, on average, have increased that demand by one percent. If that incremental demand were met half by new power plants and half by synfuel plants, the extra demand would entail the addition of a six-hundred-megawatt power station every thirty days and a large synfuel plant (producing, say, a quarter-billion cubic feet of gas per day) every ninety days[9]—without even counting the need to replace old energy plants, which last only about half as long as the buildings which use their energy.

The present stock of buildings was built mainly before 1970, when real energy prices were low and falling lower. The builders therefore had no incentive to build efficiently. During the 1970s, incentives changed. Air-conditioning bills sometimes came to exceed mortgage payments. Annual household energy costs in New England trebled from three hundred eighty-six dollars in 1970 to thirteen hundred twenty-five dollars in 1980.[10] With this impetus, the average thermal efficiency of all American houses, old and new, improved by twenty to twenty-five percent.[11] In 1970, heating a square foot of floorspace in an average American house through one Fahrenheit degree-day of outdoor coldness required about sixteen BTUs of energy. By 1978, this had dropped to thirteen BTUS.[12] But technological advances meanwhile were making it possible to build cost-effective new houses ten to a hundred times more energy-efficient than that [0013: houses with a space-heating intensity of not thirteen but one and a third BTUs per square foot-degree day, and in some cases much less—even as little as zero.

This astonishing performance can be achieved by various combinations of "superinsulated" tight construction and passive solar gain—capturing and storing solar heat, even on cloudy days, in the fabric of the house itself, for example through windows facing the sun. (Other techniques, such as double-envelope or earth-tempered construction, can do the same thing but are not considered here.) There are at least a dozen general recipes for building a superinsulated house, but most of them built in cold climates have several ingredients in common: typically about a foot of insulation in the walls, two feet in the roof, double or triple glazing, insulated night shutters, and virtually airtight construction. To guard against stuffiness or the accumulation of noxious gases, plenty of fresh air is provided by mechanical ventilation through a small air-to-air heat exchanger. This simple device, commercially available for two to four hundred dollars, can recover about four-fifths of the heat in the outgoing air and use it to prewarm the incoming fresh air (or, in the summer, to prechill it).[14]

These combined techniques reduce the total heat loss through the shell of the house so far that the internal heat gains—from windows, occupants, lights, and appliances—provide most or all of the space heating. Such supplementary heat as may be needed in an especially unfavorable climate is so little—much less than the heat needed for domestic hot water—that it can be provided by slightly enlarging the sun-capturing windows, or taking surplus heat from a slightly oversized solar water heater, or burning a newspaper or a few sticks in a small stove on rare occasion, or keeping one or two forty-watt poodles. Such houses have a lower life-cycle cost (some also have a lower construction cost) than inefficient houses. They can look the same as ordinary houses or can be built in any desired style. They provide a higher than normal standard of comfort—less noise, less dirt, no drafts, excellent temperature stability—and do not, if properly designed, require any significant changes in the occupants' behavior. All the devices which save or produce heat can be as automatic and controllable as present thermostats.

The examples most often cited for such construction are the Saskatchewan Conservation House (considered in more detail below), its hundreds of successors in Canada and the U.S., and the Illinois Lo-Cal design. These and other types are being routinely built by tract-housing contractors.[15] The governments of Canada, Saskatchewan, and Alberta have spread the necessary building information so effectively[16]—over one hundred thousand copies of a builders' manual were distributed by late

1981—that more than a thousand such houses are expected to be finished by the end of 1982, even though the first one was finished only in December 1977.

One reason for this rapid diffusion is economics. Contractors who had already built a few superinsulated houses reported in 1980 that the Saskatchewan design increased the net cost of building a typical frame house by six to eight percent—about twenty-six hundred U.S. dollars or less. At the 1980 world oil price, that investment is recovered through fuel savings in about four years. Moreover, the extra construction cost is falling in real terms as contractors gain experience. Some other designs, though perhaps slightly less efficient, are much cheaper still. For example, the net extra capital cost of the Lo-Cal design is at most fifteen hundred dollars, and in some cases it is reportedly zero or negative: the saving from not having to install a furnace more than pays for the additional insulation and other heat-saving measures.[17] The space-heating fuel needed to maintain comfort in these houses has been measured at two-tenths to eight-tenths of a BTU per square foot-degree day for well-built Saskatchewan designs, and one and one-tenth to one and three-tenths for particular Lo-Cal houses which had zero or negative extra capital cost.[18]

These figures are ten to sixty times better than the U.S. average of thirteen BTUs. They are also better than any present or proposed U.S. building standard. Most government codes call for about ten or eleven BTUs, and this maximum allowable value is often misinterpreted as an optimum. By 1979, many builders were already achieving values below seven BTUs, even though they invested far less in efficiency improvements than would have been economically worthwhile.[19] In 1981, Congress—intensively lobbied by utility companies which said the standard was impracticable—refused to approve a proposed Building Energy Performance Standard (BEPS), proposed in 1979, of about four and a half BTUs, let alone a proposed "strict BEPS" of somewhat over two. Yet houses at least twice as efficient as this "strict" version would probably cost less to build than ordinary houses, and at worst would cut total life-cycle costs (which include both construction and operation) at least in half.[20]

Although these highly efficient designs have most of their window area facing the Equator, and little or none facing away from it, they are not really meant to be good passive solar designs. Passive solar techniques, which are no costlier than superinsulation and may be cheaper, can provide similar or better performance while considerably relaxing the insulation requirements. (Newly developed glazing materials, some of which insulate as well as several inches of plastic foam, should soon make it possible to put substantial window areas even on the sunless side of the house.)

The right combination of thermal efficiency and passive solar gain can reduce net space-heating requirements to essentially zero (less than a tenth of a BTU per square foot-degree day) in climates worse than that of Chicago.[21] The total extra capital cost—at most about two thousand dollars—pays back in under four years at the 1981 world oil price or in under two years at the 1981 average residential electricity price. An added benefit of many passive solar designs is a "sunspace"—extended living space that is bright and comfortable even on cloudy winter days, and in which fresh food can be grown year-round even in severe climates. So many technologies are now available for both superinsulation and passive solar design that the optimal economic balance between them is quite broad, depending on local climate, construction practice, and architectural taste. But the esthetic and psychological benefits of quiet, warm, sunny spaces may outweigh purely economic considerations.

The same measures which reduce heating loads also reduce air-conditioning loads by not letting the house overheat in the first place. Additional cooling methods include window shades and overhangs and coatings, trees, roof ponds, and earth-pipe cooling (a cheap, effective form of passive air conditioning).[22]

Energy savings in buildings are not confined to space heating and cooling. A combination of water-efficient appliances and recovery of waste heat from outgoing "graywater" (from dishwashing, washing machines, showers, etc., but not including sewage) can generally cut the water-heating load in half.[23] Most if not all of these measures are cost-effective at the present world oil price, and all are cost-effective at present electrical or future synfuel prices. In a large-scale New England experiment, as simple a device as a showerhead flow restrictor—a small piece of plastic which turns a shower from a flood into an effective spray—saved large amounts of energy at almost no cost.[24]

Energy-using devices within buildings can also be replaced by more efficient models. Intelligent design of new household appliances would reduce their average use of electricity by at least three-quarters.[25] The technical improvements needed would not change performance or convenience. At the present average price of electricity to U.S. households, the costliest increments of efficiency would pay back in an average of six years.

Refrigerators—the biggest part of the electric bill in most households that do not use electric space or water heating—provide a good example of recent technical advances. In 1975, the average U.S. refrigerator of fourteen to sixteen cubic foot capacity, with top freezer and automatic or semiautomatic defrost, used about eighteen hundred kilowatt-hours a year. In 1981, the best U.S. models used nine hundred to eleven hundred, while the best equivalent Japanese model used five hundred fifty.[26] A California engineer built in 1979 a somewhat unconventional prototype using under three hundred kilowatt-hours per year, and by 1982 he was completing a better, more conventional prototype expected to use only seventy-two—less than a twentieth of the current average.[27] Moreover, in colder climates, even as far south as (for example) New Jersey, it is feasible to substitute a seasonal-storage icebox using no electricity.

The efficiency improvements that can be made in space heating and cooling, water heating, lights, and appliances are often even larger and cheaper in the commercial sector (offices, hotels, churches, schools, hospitals, etc.) than in houses. Many office buildings were designed to be cooled and heated simultaneously. Even in those with a less irrational design, most of the cooling load is still just taking away the heat of overlighting— lighting at headache level. The difference in lighting intensity between offices built in the early 1970s (about four watts per square foot) and in 1980 (two) would by the year 2000 eliminate the need for one hundred fifty giant power plants.[28]

Compared to the total primary energy which the average American office building used in 1978 to space-condition, light, and otherwise operate a square foot of floorspace, Hydro Place, a glass utility headquarters in Toronto, uses half as much; Gulf Canada Square in Calgary, a third; the best office buildings now nearing completion in several countries, less than a thirtieth. Yet all these designs repay their extra cost within a few years. A far larger investment in efficient buildings would be justified. For example, to save just forty percent of the energy to be used in new buildings of all kinds, it would be worth spending nearly fifty billion extra dollars per year on their construction, so as not to have to buy new energy to supply that forty percent instead.[29]

New buildings, of course, are only part of the story. Most of the buildings that the United States will have over the next half-century are already standing, so the main focus must be on retrofitting (fixing up) those existing stocks. Extensive data are available on what retrofits actually cost and how well they work.[30] Most of the techniques described above can be applied, with minor modifications, to existing buildings. Some Canadian builders can remove the siding from a frame house, extend the eaves and casings, add a vapor barrier and superinsulation, and put the siding back on, cost-effectively cutting the space-heating load by ninety percent or more. Where this operation is combined with adding extensions to houses, it could be done for only about two and a half thousand U.S. dollars extra—often less than the cost of enlarging the furnace.[31]

Equally ingenious techniques for retrofit have been developed for a wide range of construction styles. It is common in Europe even to add *exterior* insulation and a new façade onto masonry walls,[32] trapping their large heat-storing capacity or "thermal mass" inside the insulation and so stabilizing the building temperature. Even in countries (such as Sweden and West Germany) which have the world's highest labor costs, specific retrofit costs that are several times those charged in the U.S., and relatively efficient buildings to start with, installing elaborate exterior insulation is still cost-effective at present world oil prices.[33] At least fourteen American manufacturers now offer Outsulation® or its equivalent, and some residential retrofits using such products have saved from sixty to more than eighty percent of heating bills, with payback times of a few years.[34] Alternatively, interior insulated walls can be cheaply inserted.

Retrofitting a building requires that most or all of the holes in it be plugged up even before insulation is installed.[35] (In a typical house, such holes, large enough to leak air, total more than a square yard.) Special techniques, including pressure-testing buildings, can identify even invisible holes, which often account for two-thirds of the total air leakage. In programs that use such techniques, retrofits of U.S. houses or commercial buildings have saved at least two-thirds of the initial space-conditioning energy at a cost of about a dollar per square foot of floorspace—equivalent to saving oil at a price of about fifteen cents per gallon (six or seven dollars per barrel).[36] Even suboptimal programs—such as those which plug only the readily visible leaks, or which use storm windows rather than insulating shades and other cost-effective window treatments—generally cost about forty cents per gallon saved (nineteen dollars per barrel).[37] That is half the price of imported oil at dockside, a third to a fourth of the likely retail price of synthetic oil,[38] and less than a fifth of the price of the heat content of electricity from a newly ordered power plant.

In institutional buildings such as schools, hospitals, and churches, where there has been little profit incentive to control operating costs, the savings are often still cheaper. An audit of forty-eight Eastern hospitals during 1979-81, for example, showed savings exceeding twenty percent available at under twenty-five cents per square foot—a payback time of a year or less. More than one hundred of the nearly nine hundred recommended measures had zero capital cost: they merely required better management of existing equipment.[39] And even in supposedly well-managed buildings, the division of responsibilities and profits between tenants and landlords often lets major inefficiencies go unchecked. The mere installation of a modern control system in a Pennsylvania office building immediately cut power bills in half—prompting the incredulous utility to check whether the meter was working properly.[40] In a California office building, a utility audit and a forty-five-hundred-dollar investment in 1980 saved over a million kilowatt-hours, worth over seventy thousand dollars, in the first ten months.[41]

Transportation   Two-thirds of America's transportation energy, and over half of all U.S. oil use, goes to cars. In 1981 the cars averaged about sixteen miles per U.S. gallon (mpg). Light trucks, about a fifth as numerous, averaged nearer twelve. The state of the art, however, is at least five times better than that.

The average imported car is already more than twice as fuel-efficient as the present American fleet. A Volkswagen diesel Rabbit™ already averages over forty mpg on the road; average 1982-model Japanese cars do slightly better than that. But these are far from the best experimental cars already made. For example, VW has prototyped a turbocharged diesel Rabbit™ which has a sixty-mpg city rating from the Environmental Protection Agency, meets all emission standards, accelerates from zero to sixty miles per hour (mph) in thirteen and a half seconds, and is safe in a forty-mph head-on crash.[42] Even more impressive is an advanced VW diesel with a Rabbit™ body and a three-cylinder engine which turns off on idle or coast, then immediately restarts on acceleration.[43] A prototype of this model was tested by the Environmental Protection Agency in 1981 at eighty mpg city, one hundred mpg highway. Even that does not exhaust the possibilities offered by series hybrid drives (in which a small engine or fuel cell in the car charges a few batteries which run electric drive motors), infinitely variable transmissions (being introduced in 1981–82 by Borg-Warner/Fiat), or the possible use of lightweight but crashproof body materials such as crushable metal foams and plastic foams.

These achievements in the eighty-plus mpg range do not even consider another option—using cars more specialized for their tasks, notably two-seater commuter cars for the vast majority of personal driving. Such cars are selling well in many other countries[44]. Japanese "mini-cars," measuring no bigger than four and a half by ten and a half feet and displacing no more than five hundred fifty cubic centimeters (thirty-four cubic inches), are currently capturing over a fifth of the domestic market in highly urbanized Japan. Some models get on-road efficiencies of fifty-three mpg city, seventy-five highway. (In contrast, the diesel Chevette announced in 1981 by General Motors gets only forty and fifty-five mpg respectively.) Such "minis" offer a good match to the urban driving needs of many Americans, and with modern materials and design they could be safer than conventional cars. Mixing more sophisticated commuter "minis" into the fleet could send fleet averages over one hundred mpg. General Motors has already announced that it is cooperating with two Japanese firms to make and sell mini-cars in the United States.[45]

Government and industry experts have carefully assessed how a large number of individually modest efficiency improvements can add up throughout the engine, drive train, bearings, lubricants, tires, and streamlining. Systematically used in a four-passenger car of about the same size and performance as the average car made in the U.S. in 1981, well-known and presently cost-effective technical improvements would boost efficiency to between eighty and one hundred ten mpg.[46] (Very lightweight body materials and other advanced innovations could improve even on the higher figure.) Improving present U.S. production models only partway— say, to sixty mpg—would increase their cost by an estimated eight hundred to nearly twenty-three hundred dollars.[47] At the 1981 gasoline price, that extra cost would pay back in one to four years. For the nation— which derives social benefits from reduced oil dependence—the payback would be far faster.

Straightforward application of proven and cost-effective technology can reduce the specific energy requirements of heavy trucks and buses by thirty to forty percent and of railroads by about twenty-five percent.[48] New Japanese ship designs have cost-effectively saved about half the normal fuel requirements. Commercial aircraft (seven percent of U.S. transportation fuel use) have raised their fleet efficiency from seventeen and a half passenger miles per gallon in 1973 to twenty-five today. They will reach forty-five passenger miles per gallon once the new generation of aircraft has been fully introduced (Boeing 757 and 767, DC9-80, and advanced L-1011)—a forty-five percent improvement in fuel efficiency. A full, 1982-model jet uses only as much fuel per passenger-mile as an average U.S. car carrying four people used in 1978.[49] Even larger savings are available from new technologies for turbofan engines, special propeller and wing designs, active control technologies, and weight-saving materials; together these promise a saving of about seventy percent from the 1973 norm. High-speed (five hundred fifty mph) turboprops which promise to use fifteen to twenty percent less fuel than turbofans are to be flight-tested around 1986.[50] Lighter-than-air craft also show economic promise,[51] especially for intercity freight hauling. At least one British dirigible design can deliver door-to-door.

Industry　Industry (including agriculture, which uses four percent of industrial energy) uses thirty-seven percent of all U.S. primary energy. During the mid-1970s, industry was responsible for most—probably about two-thirds—of the total energy savings in America. The ten most energy-intensive industries during 1972–79 decreased their energy consumption per unit of product by an average of more than fifteen percent.[52] This was accomplished almost entirely using measures which paid back within one or two years at prices which were well below today's.

Process heat—the heat, generally at moderate to high temperatures, needed to transform industrial materials—accounts for about forty-three percent of all industrial energy. During the 1970s, the efficiency of using process heat improved by about four percent per year. But at least an additional third of the heat could be cost-effectively saved by using better thermal insulation, heat recovery, process controls, heat pumps, cogeneration, and better processes.[53] Alumina smelters can save at least a third of their electrical input by adopting superior processes. Proper sizing, coupling, and controls would save about half of the electricity needs for industrial motors (which use more than a fourth of all industrial primary energy).[54] This one improvement, typically paying back in a few years, would more than displace every nuclear power plant in the country. Alternatively, substituting hydraulic for electric drive can often yield major savings.[55]

Innovative industrial processes which save much more energy than these data indicate are being rapidly developed, such as a new process which saves over three-quarters of the energy needed to make ethylene. A substantial fraction of present industrial energy can also be saved through the more efficient use and re-use of materials.[56] Altogether, stable or declining energy use in U.S. industry could sustain rapid growth in industrial production.[57] The great scope for saving industrial energy even in such already-efficient countries as Sweden[58] offers further basis for confidence.

Micro benefits

The foregoing examples suggest that the energy efficiency of each sector can be more than doubled without approaching practical or economic limits. Any improvement, however—even a much smaller one—would greatly increase energy resilience at the level of individual users as well as for the nation. Large-scale benefits will be considered more fully later in this chapter. At the "micro" scale of an individual household, office, shop, or factory, energy efficiency can increase resilience in three main ways:

• longer time constants;
• limiting extreme behavior; and
• shaving peak loads.

The concept of making failures happen more slowly in order to give more time in which to respond is familiar in preparedness planning. It is the strategy of a person who puts containers of water in the freezer as a "thermal flywheel" so that in a power failure, the freezer temperature will rise only slowly and cannot exceed the freezing point until all the extra ice has melted. It is the strategy of a smelting company that insulates its potlines to slow down their heat loss, so that if the electric current that keeps the alumina and cryolite molten is only briefly interrrupted, they will remain molten. (The alternative—months of work chipping out the pots with chisels—is so unpleasant that it is worth buying a lot of insulation.)

Stretching out failures through more sparing, more efficient energy use is *better* than the traditional strategy of stockpiling fuels to be used during a supply interruption. Maintaining and financing a stockpile costs money, whereas an energy system which *uses fuel more slowly* to provide the same energy services *saves money all the time*, whether there is an interruption or not.

The resiliency benefits of stretching time constants by using energy more slowly can be illustrated on the scale of a single superinsulated house: for example, the Saskatchewan Conservation House, a two-story, two-thousand-square-foot frame dwelling built in 1977 in Regina, Saskatchewan.[59] The site, at sixty and a half degrees North latitude, gets about a tenth less solar radiation per year than the U.S. average. The climate—nearly eleven thousand Fahrenheit degree-days per year—is about half again as cold as Buffalo, New York, Manchester, New Hampshire, or Flagstaff, Arizona. The lowest temperature normally expected is minus twenty-nine degrees Fahrenheit.

The walls of the house use offset double two-by-six-inch studs insulated to an R-value (a measure of resistance to heat flow) of forty. The R-value of the roof insulation is sixty. A heavy, carefully caulked vapor barrier reduces the uncontrolled inward leakage of air (infiltration) to less than five percent of a complete air change per hour. An air-to-air heat exchanger provides three-fifths of an air change per hour—more if desired—while recovering eighty percent of the warmth in the exhaust air. The windows are double-glazed downstairs and triple-glazed upstairs, and are fitted with insulating night shutters. The door, like the foundation slab, is insulated, and there is a double-door "airlock" entryway.

As a result of these highly cost-effective measures, all of which together were repaid from fuel savings within the first few years, the total heat loss through the shell of the house is only thirty-eight watts per Fahrenheit degree of temperature difference between inside and outside when the window shutters are closed, fifty-five with them open. The gross shell loss totals only about forty million BTUs per year—the heat content of just over three hundred gallons of oil. But after allowance for the "free heat" from the windows, people, lights, and appliances, the *net* annual space heating load is only five million BTUs, or fourteen hundred kilowatt-hours—*less than four percent* as big as for an ordinary house the same size in the same city.[60]

Furthermore, all the space and water heating needs of the superinsulated house can be covered, without needing back-up, by a solar system with only one hundred ninety square feet of collectors—less than ten percent of the floor area—together with heat storage in thirteen tons of water (just over three thousand gallons)—less than three percent of the house volume. Most studies would predict that five to ten times this collector area and storage volume would be necessary to cover even two-thirds of the load. Why, then, can the smaller solar system be big enough?

The answer to this question reveals how profoundly the efficiency improvements have changed the basic physics of the house. An ordinary house requires sharp peaks of heat to maintain its inside temperature whenever the weather turns even moderately cold. The rate of supplying heat at these peak periods often exceeds ten kilowatts even in a mild California climate;[61] in an ordinary Regina house they would be many tens of kilowatts. Meeting this peak load would require either a large furnace or an installed electrical generation, transmission, and distribution capacity costing about as much as the house itself. In contrast, the Saskatchewan Conservation House holds in its heat so effectively that even with a temperature difference of ninety-nine Fahrenheit degrees across its shell—seventy degrees inside compared to minus twenty-nine degrees outside—the interior temperature can be maintained with only three and seven-tenths kilowatts of total heat supply if the shutters are closed, or five and a half kilowatts if they are open. A small solar system, a very small stove, or many other types of heat sources can meet such a modest need.

Thus the superinsulation and the air-to-air heat exchanger have reduced the space-heating load from a series of frequent huge peaks to a series of infrequent small blips, superimposed on a steady water-heating load. That water-heating "baseload" is indeed three times as big as the average space-heating load for the whole house, even though the water-heating load has itself been reduced by a third from its normal value through the recovery of heat from graywater. (Water-heating loads bigger than space-heating loads are a common operational definition of a superinsulated house.) It is because the space-heating peaks are much less frequent and less intense—in duration and size—than they would normally be that the solar system can have such a small collector area and storage volume. But whether the house uses a solar system or not (currently it does not), this moderation of the average and peak heating requirements clearly makes it vastly easier to keep the occupants comfortable in both normal and emergency conditions.

Another reason for this inherent resilience is that although the house has "low thermal mass"—it can store heat only in its light frame construction—its thermal "time constant"[62] is about one hundred hours, or about four times as long as for a normal house of similar construction. The Saskatchewan Conservation House stores no more heat than other frame houses, but loses it far more slowly; and for delaying the drop in temperature, this is exactly equivalent.

Thus, such a house provides inherent protection. In zero-degree weather *and in continuous total darkness,* the house would take thirty-four hours to drop to fifty degrees Fahrenheit. Under the December conditions least favorable for passive solar gain through the windows, the house would probably take several weeks to get as low as fifty degrees, and temperatures much below that would be *physically impossible* unless the shell had somehow been seriously damaged. Thus if the house had no working furnace, baseboard heaters, cooking stoves, solar collector, pet, or any other external heat source, an occupant willing to tolerate an English rather than an affluent North American standard of comfort (say fifty-five or sixty degrees in cold weather) could go right through the Canadian winter without even realizing there was no heating system. With slightly more windows on the sunny side of the house, the temperature would stay in the range of sixty-five to seventy-five degrees with no auxiliary heating at all. And whatever else happened, a spell of unusually cold or cloudy weather would be unlikely to last long enough even to cause discomfort if the heating system failed.

This behavior illustrates both the *stretched time constant* of the house—everything happens in slow motion—and its inherent *limitation of extreme behavior.* Any properly built passive solar house cannot get below fifty-odd degrees Fahrenheit, no matter what. Even a badly built passive solar greenhouse, provided it has a reasonable amount of thermal mass (rocks, masonry, drums of water, etc.) for overnight heat storage, will never get below freezing in a Minnesota winter. So robust are insulated passive solar buildings that when vandals broke down the door of one in Massachusetts, leaving a hole of several square yards during the coldest night of the winter, the interior temperature still stayed above sixty. That building did not even have movable insulation under its glazing—a refinement which would have stretched its time constant from days to weeks.

It is also noteworthy that the Saskatchewan house's heat-storing water tank, in cooling off from its highest to its lowest temperature (a range of ninety Fahrenheit degrees), releases enough heat to meet the house's average space- and water-heating load, with no heat input, for four weeks. That is equivalent to having in a normal house a tank containing about three thousand gallons of fuel oil. (The normal inventory of a heating-oil distributor is only ten times that large.)[63] A gallon of the hot water stores less than one percent as much energy as a gallon of oil, but it serves about equally well in a tight house because so much less energy is required to do the same task in that house than would be needed in an ordinary, sievelike house.

A third important result of the Saskatchewan Conservation House's superinsulation is that heat can only diffuse around inside the house—it can hardly get out. The inside of the house is in almost perfect convective and radiative equilibrium. Thus any point source of heat, such as one short section of uninsulated hot water pipe, can heat the whole house evenly without requiring any heat distribution system. In this way an Alaskan superinsulated house is evenly heated by a tiny stove putting out a few hundred watts in one corner. Yet the house has uniform temperatures within about a degree even to its farthest corner, separated by long, labyrinthine corridors. This means that if normal heating fails, a superinsulated house can be amply heated by *any* small, improvised heat source—a small wood-burner, a camping stove, a small lantern, even junk mail burned in a number ten can. The heat thus provided will ensure comfort *throughout* the house, whereas in a normal house with a failed heating system one would have to huddle over a large stove trying to keep a single room habitably warm.[64]

In short, the efficiency of a superinsulated house (whether or not it uses solar energy) makes its occupants virtually invulnerable to failures of the heating system or of its energy supply. Their neighbors, who would be in serious trouble in a few winter hours without heat, can take shelter in the efficient house—and by doing so can provide enough body warmth to heat the whole house. (If there were more than one or two neighbors, excess heat would have to be vented by opening the windows.) If the failure affected the heating sources of all the houses in a region, the occupants of the superinsulated house might find out only from the arrival of their chilled neighbors that anything was amiss. Left to their own devices, they would probably not notice for weeks that their heating system was out of order, and then the signal would be a gradual decline from about seventy to about sixty degrees, not a catastrophic drop to subfreezing or subzero indoor temperatures.

Long time constants have one drawback: they require planning. One Swedish superinsulated house took about two years to attain its design efficiency because its building materials had been left out in the rain. The house needed so little heating that it took two years' heat leakage through the walls to dry out the materials. Likewise, a large seasonal-storage tank for a community district heating system could easily take a year to "charge up" to its normal working temperatures—though once heated, it would "coast" indefinitely thereafter through normal recharging. Thus long-time-constant energy systems must be in place *before* an energy shortage strikes. But if this is done, the systems are likely to outlast the shortage and vastly increase the flexibility of possible responses. Improvised substitutes which would normally be too little and too late become timely and more than adequate.

The ability of either well-insulated buildings with some passive gain or less well-insulated buildings with strong passive gain to protect under all circumstances against low (especially subfreezing) temperatures means that activities such as greenhouse gardening can be guaranteed to work year-round anywhere south of the Arctic Circle. Year-round passive solar greenhouse gardening, even using tropical species, has proven highly successful even in parts of the U.S. that have a three-month growing season outdoors. Another advantage is that even a very crude, unglazed solar water heater—such as a piece of blackened sheet metal attached to a hot-water pipe—can work well inside such a greenhouse to provide water at domestic temperatures. Being always protected from freezing by the thermal mass and solar gain of the greenhouse, the solar water heater needs none of the anti-frost precautions (draindown valves, double antifreeze loops with heat exchangers, etc.) which can make conventional outdoor solar water heaters relatively complex and expensive.

Macro benefits

The foregoing examples have shown how a more thermally efficient house can reduce its occupants' vulnerability by lengthening time constants, preventing extremes of temperature, and making small, improvised sources of heat much simpler, more flexible, and more effective in meeting emergency needs. But the house is only a microcosm for the entire American energy system.

Consider, for example, a car with the average efficiency of a turbocharged diesel Rabbit™—about sixty-four mpg, or about twenty mpg below the best that has been demonstrated for cars of that size and performance. Such a car can be driven four times as many miles or days as a standard car (which gets about sixteen mpg) on the same amount of fuel. The more efficient car can therefore canvas a considerably larger area in search of fuel, or be four times as likely to stay on the road long enough for improvised supplies of liquid fuel to be arranged. Alternatively, since each such car "frees up" three identical cars' worth of fuel, four times as many total car-miles can be driven with a given amount of fuel. Visits to filling stations become four times as infrequent. Fuel stockpiles of all kinds last four times as long. (The April 1982 Strategic Petroleum Reserve of a quarter of a billion barrels, for example, would become sufficient to run the entire fleet of light vehicles for six months; the planned 1989 Reserve, for eighteen months.) Yet this fourfold expansion of effective fuel reserves, far from costing money to maintain, actually incurs *negative* extra carrying charges because once the efficient cars have been bought, their continuing fuel saving generates an immediate positive cash flow.

Suppose now that America's car fleet had an average efficiency of four times its present dismal level. If each car had the same size of fuel tank as today, and if those tanks were, on average, kept as full as they were in, say, August 1979 (sixty-one percent),[65] then the fuel carried by the car fleet itself would total some one and a half billion gallons. That reserve could run the fleet of one hundred thirty million cars and light trucks for seven hundred forty miles each, or a month's driving at the average August 1979 rate. Thus the dynamics of any fuel shortage would be dramatically different than with cars that must be refueled every few days.

With such a fleet, the sudden disabling of several major oil pipelines, refineries, and ports would no longer be an instant calamity. Suppose, for example, that the fuel reserves "in the pipeline" between the wellhead and the gas pump were the same as they are today. (In practice, they might be smaller because the oil industry would have contracted to meet the smaller demand. But a more resilient oil industry would also want to increase the crude and product storage between the various stages of processing and distribution, in order to loosen the very tight coupling noted in Chapter Nine. The shrinkage of the industry should leave ample free storage capacity that could be used for this purpose, partly compensating for the smaller total volume of oil handled.) If, for the sake of argument, the "pipeline inventory" of oil were maintained at its present value, a car fleet that used fuel only a quarter as fast as today's would make that inventory last not for a few months, as it would in a major oil interruption today, but rather for a year or more. That in turn would be long enough to arrange enough improvised biomass liquid fuel supplies to run essential services if not virtually the whole fleet (Chapter Sixteen and Appendix Three). Thus for the first time, stockpiles "in the pipeline" could last for about as long as it takes to repair major damage to pipelines, ports, or other facilities. The nation could therefore withstand considerable destruction of oil facilities without shortages or the need for interim rationing.

Efficient use of electricity would likewise cushion the effects of blackouts. At a micro level, a very efficient refrigerator would protect food from spoiling for longer because of its excellent thermal insulation. It would also need so little electricity to operate that improvising a very small source of electricity or of direct mechanical drive—perhaps using a car or bicycle—within a few days would preserve the food. An electricity-efficient household would need an average power supply of only about thirty watts to maintain the most essential functions (food preservation, lighting, radio),[66] rather than the three hundred to five hundred watts needed today. Such a tiny power demand could be provided for a day by an average half-charged car battery, using a small inverter, such as those found in many boats, to convert the battery's direct current into alternating current for the appliances. Emergency household needs could be met for weeks in this manner if the car were run occasionally; or indefinitely using a very small improvised wind machine or twenty square feet of solar cells.

If electricity were very efficiently used,[67] expedient sources of emergency power that are today unimportant could play a major national role in survival and recovery even from complete breakdown of the power grid, such as might be caused by an electromagnetic pulse (Chapter Seven). For example, the installed generating capacity of generators and alternators in U.S. cars and trucks totals over a hundred thousand megawatts—a sixth as much as all central power plants. If burned-out electronic ignitions could be replaced from stockpiles, those generators—

or standard improvisations such as industrial motors driven backwards by car, truck, lawnmower, and tractor engines[68]—could still operate. Even if no electrical grid survived, such local power sources could be directly connected to vital production machinery and could continue operation pretty much as usual for substantial periods. If community-scale grids were isolated but usable, a local microhydro set or industrial cogenerator normally considered a small fraction of total supply would, with highly efficient use, become able to meet most or all normal needs. If transmission lines survived, they could transfer any remaining steady supplies of power from hydroelectricity or cogeneration over long distances without straining regional interties. Petroleum-dependent peaking plants would not have to be operated; fuel stockpiles for any required thermal plants or cogenerators would be greatly stretched; cogenerators could even run on locally available wastes. The six major steam-using industries, being cost-effective net exporters of electricity, would free up electricity for other, less self-reliant users.[69] In short, efficient use of electricity would provide enough "cushion" of both normal and emergency supplies to enable the nation to survive, and probably to recover from, even a prolonged failure of the entire national electrical system—an event which our economy would otherwise be unlikely to withstand.

A benefit of end-use efficiency which emerges from the previous example is that *it displaces the most costly or most vulnerable energy supplies.* That is, efficiency improvements can provide unchanged energy services not only with less total energy, but with less *in particular* of the energy that comes from the least attractive sources. Thus, decreases in total oil consumption would normally be reflected as decreases in the use of oil from the Persian Gulf. Oil savings can thus provide a disproportionate gain in energy security. Unfortunately, official proposals to save oil by expanding, say, nuclear power are fallacious,[70] both because little oil is used to generate electricity and because much faster and cheaper methods of saving oil are known. For this reason, such misdirected concepts as substituting uranium for oil actually *slow down* oil displacement by diverting resources from more effective measures.

The magnitude of these more effective measures is easily illustrated. U.S. oil imports can be eliminated by about 1990 by two relatively simple measures, neither of which has been seriously considered in federal energy policy. The prescription is distressingly simple: stop living in sieves and stop driving Petropigs. The sieves (buildings) are so leaky that just basic weatherization and insulation of American buildings could save over two and a half million barrels per day of oil and gas by 1990, at an average price under seven dollars per barrel, and a similar additional amount at a similar price during 1990–2000.[71] The Petropigs (gas-guzzling cars and light trucks), however, are a more complex problem.

Gas-guzzlers have such a low trade-in value that they have been trick-ling down to low-income people who can afford neither to run nor to re-place them. Even before high sticker prices and high interest rates devas-tated new car sales during 1980–82, gas-guzzlers were starting to stay in the fleet longer—at the very moment when, to reduce oil dependence, they should be turning over faster. (This is especially damaging because fleet efficiency is a geometric, not an arithmetic, average: a fleet in which eighty percent of the cars get sixty mpg while twenty percent get ten mpg has an average efficiency of thirty, not fifty, mpg.) Just as buildings can be fixed up faster if efficiency loans from, say, utilities relieve people of the up-front capital burden,[72] so gas-guzzlers can be replaced faster if invest-ment that would otherwise go to increase oil supplies were instead loaned or given out for car replacement. For example:[73]

• Rather than spending twenty-odd billion dollars now (plus perhaps six-ty-eight billion dollars later) to subsidize synfuel plants which will probably never compete with oil,[74] the U.S. could save more oil faster by using some of the same money to *give* people diesel Rabbits™ or equivalent—provided they would *scrap* their Brontomobiles to get them off the road. (A gas-guzzler cannot just be traded in, because then someone else might drive it; it must be recycled and a death certificate provided for it.)

• Alternatively, compared with synfuels it would save oil faster to pay people at least three hundred dollars for every mpg by which a new car improves on a scrapped one. (People who scrap a gas-guzzler and do not replace it should get a corresponding bounty for it.) This oil-supplying measure would pay back in fewer than five years against synfuels.

• Instead of merely redirecting synfuel subsidies into better buys, as in the two preceding examples, it would be still better to abolish the subsidies and use a free-market solution. The U.S. car industry plans to spend on the order of fifty billion dollars on retooling during 1985–95.[75] Suppose that the industry spent as implausibly large a sum as one hundred billion dollars extra during the 1980s on retooling, in one giant leapfrog, so that the average car made would get sixty mpg—twenty-odd worse than the best prototypes today. A hundred billion dollars is much too high a figure; it is probably enough to rebuild all of Detroit. A more realistic figure might be only a fifth or a tenth as large. Nonetheless, an extra retooling cost of one hundred billion dollars, spread over a new U.S. fleet of cars and light trucks, would raise the average cost of a vehicle by about seven hundred and seventy dollars. Buyers would recover that cost from their gasoline savings, at the 1981 gasoline price, in fourteen *months.*

The trouble with this last illustration is that Detroit does not have the money. But the oil industry does, and is currently spending it on extreme-ly expensive and risky drilling. If instead Exxon drilled for oil under De-troit by loaning the car-makers money for retooling to state-of-the-art efficiencies, everyone would be better off (assuming some solution to the obvious antitrust problems). Exxon would find under Detroit a vast pool of saved oil, producible (not just extractable) at a rate exceeding five million barrels per day—equivalent to Ghawar, the world's largest oilfield—at a price under seven dollars per barrel, or about a fifth of the 1981 world oil price.

These examples are perhaps a trifle whimsical, but they have a serious point. Switching to a sixty-mpg fleet of cars would save nearly four million barrels of crude oil per day—equivalent to two-thirds of the entire 1981 net rate of U.S. oil imports, greater than the imports from the Gulf, or the same as two and a half Alaskan North Slopes or eighty big synfuel plants. Similar action with light trucks would save a further one and a half million barrels per day, or about one North Slope. Thus just an efficient light vehicle fleet would save nearly five and a half million barrels per day—exceeding the total 1981 net rate of U.S. oil imports. Even if the fleet average reached only forty mpg instead of sixty, the saving would be almost four million barrels per day.[76] That plus the saving from weatherization—two and a half million barrels per day by 1990 (five million by 2000)—would displace about a million barrels per day more than all the net oil which the U.S. imported in 1981, or over two million more than 1982 imports.

In short, just the two biggest oil-saving measures, if pursued for a decade or so to a level well short of what is technically feasible or economically worthwhile, would more than eliminate all U.S. oil imports. They would do this before a power plant or synfuel plant ordered today would deliver any energy whatsoever, and at about a tenth of its cost.[77] And by reviving the depressed housing and car industries, they would be not only economically but also socially efficient—as opposed to the present misallocation of resources, which simultaneously makes boomtowns in the Rockies and ghost towns in Michigan.

Economic priorities

For further illustration, consider the following five ways in which the sum of one hundred thousand dollars could be spent to reduce dependence on imported oil over the next ten years. For each method, the cumulative oil saving during that decade, starting now, is shown for easy comparison. These examples are not meant to be sophisticated calculations—they assume, for example, that real oil prices will remain constant, and they do not discount future savings (dollar amounts are all in real 1980 terms)—but their qualitative point is clear.

1. Use the hundred thousand dollars as seed money to catalyze a door-to-door citizen action program of low-cost/no-cost weatherization in particularly leaky buildings. (Such a program does not involve insulation, but

only plugging obvious holes which let the wind whistle through the house.) Such seed grants totalling ninety-five thousand dollars were in fact made by ACTION, HUD, DOE, and community development block grant programs to the industrial town of Fitchburg, Massachusetts in 1979. With some imaginative red-tape-cutting by ACTION staff, the grants led to the establishment of ten local training centers, each of which, between October and December, ran twenty-five to thirty weekly workshops, each lasting upwards of three-quarters of an hour. (The Boston energy office is now planning to run abbreviated versions on rush-hour subway platforms.) The Fitchburg program was especially directed at low-income people (earning less than fourteen thousand dollars a year for a family of four), living mainly in old, two- or three-family frame houses. Of the fourteen thousand households in town, more than seventeen hundred sent someone to a workshop and received a free retrofit kit; thirteen hundred more took just the workshop. Volunteers helped with installation where needed. Some sixteen hundred forty houses were weatherized with kits in ten weeks, eighty-three hundred ultimately. Each kit-using household saved an average of about one hundred fifty gallons of oil in the first winter. The total oil saving for the town was more than six hundred thousand dollars in the winter of 1979–80 alone. (Using this program and its umbrella organization—Fundamental Action to Conserve Energy—as a model, similar programs were established the following year in several dozen nearby towns.) This example shows that investing a hundred thousand dollars (correcting in proportion from the actual ninety-five thousand dollars) saves, over the first ten years alone, about one hundred seventy thousand barrels of crude oil, at an average cost of about sixty cents per barrel or one and a half cents per gallon.

2. Use the hundred thousand dollars to convert forty-four cars, by replacement, from fifteen to sixty mpg, assuming the highest published cost estimate.[78] Each car will save (if driven an unchanged ten thousand miles per year) five hundred gallons of gasoline per year, equivalent to about thirteen barrels of crude oil per year. The forty-four cars will therefore save, in ten years, a cumulative total of nearly six thousand barrels of crude oil at a cost in the vicinity of nineteen dollars a barrel. This is about the same as for inefficiently executed building retrofits, or about half the price of buying foreign oil.

3. Invest the hundred thousand dollars by buying about three thousand barrels of foreign oil, put the oil into a hole in the ground, and call it the Strategic Petroleum Reserve. While sitting there the oil will perform no direct energy services, but it will presumably cushion against supply interruptions.[79] The *annual* "insurance premium": on the order of one dollar per barrel for storage plus (at late-1981 interest rates) five or six dollars per barrel for carrying charges. After ten years, if the reserve has not been

drawn upon, the three thousand barrels of oil will still be there. They represent an investment cost of thirty-odd dollars per barrel which is probably all recoverable—"probably" because the oil is not yet known to be stable for more than about six years[80]—plus a ten-year storage and carrying cost on the order of sixty or seventy dollars per barrel, which is not recoverable. (If world oil prices rose during storage, the oil would appreciate in value; but so would the value of domestic oil which the two previous options left safely in the ground.)

4. Spend the hundred thousand dollars building a small piece of a plant to make synthetic fuels from coal or shale. Using a reasonable—and most likely conservative—whole-system capital investment of forty thousand dollars per daily barrel, the capacity bought will have the potential, if the technology works, to produce two and a half barrels per day—up to about nine thousand barrels per decade—from the early 1990s to 2020. During the first decade, however, it will have produced nothing. The retail price of its future output will probably be upwards of seventy of today's dollars per barrel.[81]

5. Spend the hundred thousand dollars building a very small piece of the proposed Clinch River Breeder Reactor. After ten years it will have produced nothing. It may thereafter deliver electricity at a price equivalent to buying the heat content of oil at upwards of three hundred seventy dollars per barrel. (The electricity price, twenty-three cents per kilowatt-hour, would be about the same as from presently commercial but expensive solar cells with a cheap optical concentrator—seven dollars a peak watt. The Clinch River Breeder Reactor technology stands no chance of competing even with the costliest conventional alternative—light-water reactors—until well past the year 2050.[82]

It is perhaps superfluous to note that the official energy policy of the United States has lately been to pursue these options almost exactly in reverse order, worst buys first. These inverted priorities have survived several Administrations and are largely bipartisan. They are worst buys in terms not only of money but of ability to produce an immediate, continuing saving in oil imports. One is impelled to wonder whether we might not buy more resilience by stockpiling, not oil, but Fiberglas®, weatherstripping, and other materials for weatherizing buildings.

National least-cost scenarios

How do these arguments apply to all forms of energy throughout the national economy? Two detailed 1980–81 analyses have addressed this question. One was done by a group headed by Roger Sant—a senior energy official under the Ford Administration—at the Mellon Institute's Energy Productivity Center, an industry-supported "think tank" in Arlington, Virginia. (In October 1981 the group metamorphosed into a for-profit enterprise, Applied Energy Services, Inc., at the same address.) Sant and his colleagues began in 1979 with a pioneering analysis of "The Least-Cost Energy Strategy," which "minimizes consumer cost through competition."[83] It showed that if, for about a decade before 1978, Americans had simply bought at each opportunity the cheapest means of providing the energy services which they actually received in 1978, then in that year they would have bought about twenty-eight percent less oil, thirty-four percent less coal, and forty-three percent less electricity than they did buy. They would also have paid about seventeen percent less money for their energy services than they actually did pay. Efficiency improvements would have made up virtually all the difference.

In 1980–81, the same analysts then used an even more detailed model, in which many hundreds of supply and efficiency options could compete freely, to examine the result of economically efficient investments during 1980–2000. They found that even if the size of the economy grew (correcting for inflation) by seventy-seven percent, total primary energy use would rise by only eleven percent.[84] All of that energy growth would be in the industrial sector as other sectors became efficient faster than their activity levels grew. Electricity demand would probably be stagnant for at least the first decade. Efficiency improvements (and some renewable sources) would so dominate the cost-effective choices that investment in conventional supply would virtually cease, and it would hardly be worth finishing building most of the power plants now under construction. The fraction of GNP used to buy energy services would go down, not up, so that far from driving inflation, the energy sector would become a *net exporter* of capital (and jobs) to the rest of the economy. Imported oil—the costliest option except for new synfuel plants and power plants—would rapidly dwindle to about zero, simply because it has already priced itself out of the market. It cannot compete with efficiency improvements (or with most renewables) and will therefore essentially eliminate itself without special attention.

These conclusions have been strongly confirmed by a parallel but independent analysis carried out by dozens of consultants coordinated by the Solar Energy Research Institute (SERI) at the request of then Deputy Secretary of Energy John Sawhill. The SERI draft report was suppressed by the Department of Energy but published by the Commerce Committee of the U.S. House of Represenatives, and is now available commercially.[85]

The analysis assumed that by the year 2000, real Gross National Product will be eighty percent greater than it was in 1977, and that personal income, comfort, and mobility will markedly increase. The study also tested investments in efficiency and renewables against costs for fuel and electricity which, while not as low as Sant's, are still well short of realistic replacement costs. The SERI study embodied many technical conservatisms, and it assumed no technology which is not already in operation in the United States. Yet is showed how total primary energy use could *decrease* to a level thirteen to eighteen percent below the 1980 level. Furthermore, through economically worthwhile investment in presently available renewable sources, the use of nonrenewable fuels would drop by nearly half. At that level, not only would oil imports and most frontier oil and gas become unnecessary, but a good deal of conventional oil and gas in the contiguous forty-eight states could also be shut in as a dispersed "strategic reserve" bearing no extra storage costs.

Total demand for electricity, too, would probably decline. With cost-effective efficiency improvements and onsite solar heating systems, electrical demand would grow during 1978–2000 at an average rate of only a fifth of one percent per year—about a ninth as fast as the utility industry expects. With cost-effective investments in windpower, industrial cogeneration, and onsite solar cells, the "growth" rate would become zero to *minus* one and two-fifths percent per year. Under the former assumption (no wind, cogeneration, or solar cells), national electric supply would be ample even if no new central power plants were commissioned after 1985 and if all oil-fired, gas-fired, and old power plants had been retired by 2000. Under the latter assumption (all cost-effective renewable and cogeneration investments), supply would exceed demand by about a third—more than a sufficient margin to phase out all nuclear plants as well, if desired, and still have national capacity to spare.

Thus the U.S. could enter the twenty-first century with

• a greatly expanded economy;
• zero use of oil, gas, and uranium in power plants;
• total consumption of fossil fuels reduced from about seventy quadrillion BTUs per year in 1980 to only forty or fifty quadrillion BTUs in 2000—a saving of several trillion dollars' worth of fuels that would stay in the ground rather than in the air;
• zero oil and gas imports; and
• ample domestic oil and gas in conventional, accessible sites to last for some further decades of transition to sustainable sources.

What is more remarkable, all this—more than doubling national energy efficiency and making energy supplies at least one-third renewable over the next twenty years—could be done simply by pursuing the policy of using energy in a way that saves money. Indeed, it is easy to calculate that the total investment required for the whole SERI program—of the order of eight hundred billion dollars, or about ten years of the present rate of investment in the energy sector—would more than finance itself through the cash flow generated by its fuel and power savings. Indeed, such an investment would *increase* the funds available in the capital marketplace by several trillion dollars compared with current policy.[86]

Nor is this a peculiarly American result. Similar studies, some in even greater detail, have shown comparable or larger savings for a wide range of other industrial countries, many of which are already more energy-efficient than the United States. These analyses, which have been reviewed elsewhere,[87] show that probably all countries can cost-effectively improve their energy efficiency by severalfold—a fact of considerable importance for the long-term balance of world oil supply and demand. Even Sweden, probably the world's most energy-efficient country, could (at a minimum) improve its energy efficiency by at least two- to threefold over the next few decades.[88]

It is especially encouraging that this could be achieved simply by permitting market forces to achieve the optimal economic balance between investments in efficiency and in new supply. A strategy that minimizes vulnerability and saves oil is thus a least-cost strategy. It is not inimical to national strength, security, and prosperity; rather, it is the very means of obtaining them.

This discussion has not considered the many other advantages of such a policy: in reducing price volatility and price increases, in countering inflation and unemployment, in reducing environmental and social impacts, in moderating tensions and inequities, and in alleviating the global risks of climatic change[89] and nuclear proliferation.[90] All these effects are important. But they, and energy vulnerability itself, need not be considered at all in order to conclude that greatly improved energy efficiency should be a dominant national priority—on economic grounds alone. Indeed, many of the measures described here, despite many artificial distortions of prices and restrictions of opportunity to invest efficiently,[91] are already being implemented through ordinary market mechanisms.

Efficiency is the key to resilience

In any discussion of energy alternatives there is a temptation to succumb to the "gadget syndrome"—to concentrate on supply technologies while short-changing consideration of how the energy supplied can be effectively used. While highly efficient energy use is the cornerstone of any resilient energy strategy, it has never been a serious component of federal energy policy. The government has long *assumed,* as was widely believed a decade ago, that efficiency cannot be improved by much more than ten or twenty percent, and that even this improvement would come only slowly, at high cost, and probably at considerable inconvenience. If this were true, America would need far more energy in the future than in the past, and would have to get much of it by expanding the same kinds of inherently vulnerable energy systems which are of such security concern today.

There would be no alternative to "strength through exhaustion" (of domestic resources). A future of "the past writ large" would mean ever greater domestic vulnerability, with no respite in sight.

The SERI analysis summarized above illustrated a different possibility. It showed how the United States can achieve a strong economy over the next twenty years with—indeed, *by*—investing heavily in energy productivity, so as to achieve a proper balance with energy supply investments. If this were done, the most vulnerable sources (imported oil, LNG, frontier oil and gas, synfuels, nuclear power) could be phased out entirely. Other vulnerable systems (central power stations and their grids, domestic oil and gas pipelines, Western coal), rather than becoming ever more essential to total supply, would become less important than they are now. But a result of even greater importance is that inherently resilient, sustainable energy sources (Chapter Sixteen) could cost-effectively supply up to thirty-five percent of total national needs in the year 2000—and approximately one hundred percent within a few decades thereafter.[92] Sustainable resources, not exhaustion, would then underpin long-term prosperity and security.

Thus greater efficiency has the security advantage that it can rapidly eliminate the most vulnerable (and costly) sources of supply. The remaining demand could also be so reduced—by a quarter in 2000 and by more thereafter[93]—that insecure and dwindling fuels could be readily replaced by almost invulnerable renewable sources. Moreover, these sources, as the following chapter will show, are also the cheapest long-run supply technologies available. Far from being minor, unimportant sources, the many kinds of appropriate renewable technologies could then make a major and soon a dominant energy contribution. Thus a major structural change in energy supply would become both possible and economically preferable. By "being sparing," in Lao-tse's phrase, our nation could "be prepared and strengthened" so as to "be ever successful." Using energy in an economically efficient way can buy the American energy system time in which to complete comfortably the transformation from living on energy capital to living on energy income—and from vulnerability to resilience.

Chapter Sixteen
Inherently Resilient Energy Supplies

The previous chapter showed how highly efficient energy use

- can make some failures of energy supply inconsequential by reducing or eliminating dependence on the most vulnerable energy sources;
- can at least delay and limit those failures which it cannot prevent;
- can, by slowing down the speed of failures, make them happen more gracefully;
- can thereby buy time to improvise substitutes; and
- can, by reducing the amount of replacement energy needed to do a given task, make those substitute supplies better able to maintain normal service.

These achievements embody an important part of the design philosophy of resilience outlined in Chapter Thirteen. But they do not yet address how the energy supply system itself—the energy sources whose output is being used so efficiently—can be designed to be inherently resilient in the first place. The principles outlined in Chapter Thirteen showed that such a supply system should have the following characteristics.

A resilient energy supply system should consist of *numerous, relatively small modules with a low individual cost of failure*. This is quite different from the approach presently followed by most energy companies and governments—vainly trying to build high technical reliability into modules so large that their cost of failure is unacceptable. The philosophy of resilience, on the other hand, accepts the inevitability of failure and seeks to limit the damage that failure can do. For example, rather than suffering a prolonged regional or national failure that can shatter the whole economy, one might occasionally have to tolerate a day or two of reduced production in an individual factory—rather like what happens now when a single fossil-fueled industrial boiler breaks down.

Second, a resilient supply system delivers energy to its users via *short, robust links.* Energy that travels simply and directly from one's own roof-top, or down the street, or across town, is more likely to arrive than energy that must travel hundreds or thousands of miles and be processed and converted in complex devices along the way. Again, this approach recognizes that any individual link, or group of links, is prone to failure. But the wiring which connects the Chicago filling station's solar cells to the motors on its gas pumps (Chapter Thirteen) is less likely to go wrong, easier to fix, and less vital to the whole society than a bulk power grid or a pipeline network.

Finally, such a system should *rapidly detect, isolate, and repair failures.* Rapid *isolation* of failures requires that

- components be combined into larger systems in a hierarchical way, so that local failures do not propagate throughout larger areas;
- successive levels of components be only loosely coupled to each other, so that each stage of operation is little affected by failure or substitution among the devices at earlier stages (for example, failures among many modular alcohol plants only slightly reduce total supplies, whereas failure of one key pipeline feeding an oil refinery can shut it down within days); and
- energy-supplying devices that are isolated by failed links be able to continue serving local needs independently until they are reconnected.

Rapid *repair* of failures requires that

- technical breakdowns be diagnosable and repairable;
- technologies be reproducible with conveniently available resources;
- failures be bridged, pending repair or replacement, in at least one of four ways:
  - simply tolerating the consequences of the failure because they are limited and (thanks to efficient energy use) their onset is gradual;
  - drawing down buffer storage until it can be replenished;
  - if one component suffered a technical failure, substituting a numerically redundant component which is still working; or
  - if the failure was caused by some external event which affected all components of a given type, substituting functionally redundant components whose diversity protected them from failing in the same way.

Substitution of a numerically or functionally redundant component requires that the replacement devices be on hand or quickly deliverable (in the way in which plug-in circuit boards are used to replace failed boards in telephones). If quick replacement is not possible, substitute devices elsewhere must be able to provide energy to the same user through intact interconnections. Obviously, the ability to repair or substitute also requires that components be simple, understandable, and accessible.

This chapter describes a class of energy supply technologies which enjoy these advantages. These technologies are now in or entering commercial service, and most are cost-effective at current fuel and power prices. (In a few cases they are cost-effective only at slightly higher prices, but those are still well below the price of energy obtained by buying new power plants, synfuel plants, or other incremental supplies.) If properly designed and deployed, these technologies can provide a high degree of inherent resilience against all types of disruptions—foreseen or unpredictable, accidental or deliberate, civil or military, local or national.

Sustainable sources

A key feature which helps to make these energy sources resilient is that they are *renewable:* they harness the energy of sun, wind, water, or farm and forestry wastes, rather than that of depletable fuels. This eliminates the need for oil and gas wells, gathering lines, terminals, tankers, pipelines, coal trains, slurry pipelines, and most bulk-transmission power lines. (However, as will be shown below, the electric grid could still have an important role to play in linking dispersed renewable sources.) The renewable nature of these sources also eliminates the need for any technologies analogous to those listed above. Indeed, it eliminates the need for the fuels themselves—oil, gas, coal, or uranium—and hence for dependence on the nations or institutions which extract, process, and sell them.

Also eliminated would be the need for the rest of the vulnerable technologies catalogued in earlier chapters, such as refineries, gas-processing and LNG plants, and steam power stations. True, some of these would have analogues in a renewable energy system: falling water would still have to be converted to electricity in existing and refurbished dams, wind would have to be captured by turbines and sun by collectors, and biomass would have to be converted to fluid fuels by thermal, chemical, or biological plants. But in general (with the exception of the large hydroelectric dams which already exist), all these renewable energy plants would be very much smaller, simpler, and more dispersed than today's giant facilities. For this reason, although they could still fail, the consequences would be smaller. They would still need repair, but the resources needed to fix them would be cheaper, more common, and more locally available. They could still be attacked, but the incentive would be reduced—just as the small, dispersed hydro plants which largely powered Japan in World War II were essentially immune from Allied bombing (Chapter Seven). Even if dispersed renewable sources were destroyed, the consequences would be purely local: knocking over a wind machine could cost someone thousands of dollars (perhaps, with a giant machine, a few million dollars), but only a handful of people, if anyone, would be blacked out. In contrast, knocking over one transmission pylon at the right time and place could black out a city or a region. Likewise, blowing up a farmer's alcohol still, though a calamity for the farmer, is only a private calamity—unlike blowing up Rhodesia's central oil depot or Lebanon's Sidon oil refinery, where the damage disrupted the whole national economy.

Certain of the dispersed plants could still be disabled by a catastrophic event, such as the electromagnetic pulse from a nuclear bomb. But if the electronic circuitry in, say, wind machines and solar-cell inverters had not been hardened to withstand the pulse, it would not be too difficult to plug in new, standardized, cheaply stockpiled circuit boards to place the burned-out ones. (Moreover, the circuitry in these devices could easily be hardened to withstand EMP, since it has not yet been put into mass production.) In contrast, fixing the very large and complex devices which the pulse would disable in conventional power stations and transmission equipment, pipeline controls, and the like could easily take years—even if the factories which made the replacements did not themselves rely on the power and fuel that would no longer be available. Indeed, the relative smallness of the dispersed systems would itself reduce the electronic damage they would suffer, since, other things being equal, the intensity of the electrical pulse induced in a device is proportional to its physical size. It is partly for this reason that electromagnetic pulse would so severely damage the large components in today's power grid.

A simple example illustrates how much renewable sources can simplify the energy system and get rid of its most vulnerable parts. One way (currently the most popular) to obtain light when one flicks the switch is to pay people hundreds of miles away to do the dirty, dangerous job of digging coal out of the ground and shipping it by rail or barge to a power plant somewhere else. There the coal is burned, releasing the energy stored in it by sunlight which fell on a primeval swamp millions of years ago. The flames make high-pressure steam which spins a huge turbine which runs a generator. Giant transformers step up the voltage for transmission over long aerial lines to one's part of the country, where the voltage is again stepped down through several stages of subtransmission and distribution, and eventually brought through a wire into one's home. Proposed "improvements" in the energy system would make this delicate, skill-intensive, computer-controlled system considerably more complicated: for example, by converting the coal into low-quality gas in a synfuel plant before burning it in the power station.

But another alternative is to install on one's roof a device which converts today's sunlight directly into electricity, with no fuel, moving parts, noise, smell, or attention. In various ways which are described below, this electricity can be used to provide light on demand. A still simpler method, for those people who are turning on the lights in the daytime, is to use the sunlight even more directly—by opening the curtains.

Thus renewable sources eliminate at a stroke two of the most fragile parts of today's energy system—the special localities (foremost among them the Persian Gulf) where rich deposits of fuels occur in the earth's crust; and the farflung links which carry raw fuels and deliver processed energy in copious but concentrated flows over long distances. In place of these power transportation systems, renewable sources rely on the automatic arrival of the natural energy flows,[1] direct and indirect, which are distributed freely, equitably, and daily over the entire surface of the earth. This energy flow is not subject to embargoes, strikes, wars, sabotage, or other interference, nor to depletion, scarcity, and exhaustion.

How reliable are renewable energy flows?

"Equitably" does not mean equally. The flow of solar energy fluctuates in time and space, both according to the predictable pattern of the earth's rotation and orbit and according to the variations of weather. Weather variations tend to be random in detail but statistically predictable in general pattern. These variations, moreover, are quite well understood,[2] and a properly designed renewable energy system can cope with them—if coupled with efficient energy use—by using the combination of sources and design parameters suitable to each site and application.[3] Sources can be chosen which tend to work best in different weather patterns: cloudy weather, bad for solar cells, is often good for windpower; droughts, bad for hydropower, are good for solar cells. Existing storage, such as water behind hydro dams, can be provided, as can onsite storage. End-use devices can be designed with long time constants to cope with intermittence. Solar energy can be harvested and converted from vegetation at one's convenience rather than captured daily as direct solar radiation. Sources can be linked together over a geographical area large enough to average out variations in the renewable energy flows or in energy demand. Year-to-year variations in solar and wind energy are less than the variation in water flow of many hydroelectric projects and can be handled by similar planning methods.

The intermittence of renewable energy flows is smaller than one might imagine. A typical wind machine in Denmark needs only ten hours' storage to be as reliable as a typical light-water reactor.[4] In an illustrative array of wind machines on the Pacific Coast, a lull "which reduced power to about a third of the summer mean would last for [no more than] fifteen hours with ninety-five percent probability."[5] Only one percent of the time would the windpower fall below a sixth of the summer mean for as long as ten hours. In contrast, major outages in light-water reactors last an average of three hundred hours, during which no energy whatever can be produced.

Both for this reason and because of the statistical complementarity of wind, hydro, and solar cells (photovoltaics)—especially if they are installed here and there over a sizeable area[6]—a power grid which combines such diverse technologies can actually be *more* reliable than one using fossil- or nuclear-fueled steam plants. This often surprises power station designers. But perhaps they fail to appreciate the unreliability of their own systems. In principle, the need to design for fluctuation is nothing new. Today's energy systems fluctuate too, far less predictably, whenever there is an oil embargo, coal strike, or other such disruption, and this kind of fluctuation must also be guarded against by design. Indeed, it is the failure to do this adequately—to consider the impact of surprises, breakdowns, and deliberate disruptions—that has helped to make today's energy system as vulnerable as it is.

Fluctuations in renewable energy flows are in this sense *better* understood and *more* predictable than those in the supply of conventional fuels and power. The methods used to forecast the path of the sun, or even next week's weather, are considerably more reliable than those which predict reactor accidents or Saudi politics. One can have greater confidence that the sun will rise tomorrow than that someone will not blow up Ras Tanura tomorrow. It can be cloudy for days or weeks (not, as noted below, a serious impediment to solar systems which are designed for cloudy weather), but it is very unlikely that the sun will be totally eclipsed for months, like a complete cutoff of oil imports. Months of utter darkness at a time have not happened since the possible crash of a large asteroid some sixty-five million years ago;[7] and if that happened again, the collapse of agriculture would be a far more serious consequence than shortages of energy.

People who are unused to thinking about the variability of renewable energy flows often assume that the vagaries of weather make renewable sources unreliable unless they are provided with full conventional backup, negating those sources' ostensible saving in conventional capacity. In fact, detailed analyses have shown that the variations in renewable energy flows even in a small geographic area tend to affect different technologies in opposite directions, and to produce briefer, more predictable interruptions, measured in smaller increments, than such interruptions of conventional supplies as technical breakdowns, oil embargoes, or strikes.[8] It is the *conventional* systems that have a serious and so far unsolved energy storage problem.

Reliance on extensive central electrification, in particular, requires vast amounts of very awkward and costly electrical storage.[9] Large power stations require extra back-up capacity (Appendix One), "spinning reserve" (generators kept spinning in synchrony with the grid but at only part of their normal load, ready to step into the breach immediately if a major unit fails), and often hydroelectric pumped-storage systems or other costly ways to reconcile a steady output with a fluctuating load. In contrast, economically efficient use of energy would reduce electrical demand—especially the most fluctuating kinds—so far that present and small hydro capacity would meet most of the total load, not just a modest fraction as they do today. Storage could then be provided at no extra cost simply by closing valves and retaining water behind the dams.[10]

Other forms of renewable energy are even easier to store. Biomass liquid fuels, being produced and used in a rather decentralized pattern, can be stored in tanks which avoid the tempting concentrations of oil terminals. As the example of a superinsulated house showed (Chapter Fifteen), efficient energy use makes the storage of domestic heat for days or weeks straightforward. By using rocks, molten salts or metals, or other suitable materials, heat can be stored even at high temperatures for industrial processes.[11] In all these cases, the energy storage devices, instead of being concentrated in large and vulnerable "lumps," would tend to be relatively dispersed and invulnerable. Most of the stored energy, being at or near the site of end use, could not be cut off at all. In short, a least-cost combination of investments in energy productivity and in renewable energy supply can largely *avoid* the excessive and vulnerable energy storage required for reliable service with highly centralized systems.

Not all renewable sources make sense

This discussion considers only those renewable sources—elsewhere called "soft technologies"[12]—which supply energy at the *scale* and in the *quality* appropriate to the task at hand, so as to provide that energy service at least cost to the consumer. Since this is not the usual approach—most analysts like to consider any and all kinds of renewable technologies, especially those which are large, central-electric, and speculative—it is worth explaining the rationale for this restriction. It is actually quite simple and rests on basic economics. Chapter Fourteen and Appendix One show how a mismatch of scale between source and use can roughly double energy service costs by incurring the costs and losses of a vast distribution network. Proper scale for each task can minimize those costs and losses. Likewise, supplying energy of the right form for each task can minimize the costs and losses of energy conversion.[13]

Thus, for example, the ninety-two percent of U.S. delivered energy which is needed in the form of heat, or as a portable fuel for vehicles, is most economically supplied in those forms—not as electricity, which is cost-effective only for a premium eight percent of all delivered energy needs. This is because electricity is conventionally generated in costly, complex machines which lose two-thirds of the energy in the fuel in order to make a high-quality energy form. If that quality is not used to advantage—if, for example, the electricity is used for space-conditioning—then the whole conversion process was a waste of money and fuel. Because this book takes seriously the economic criterion of providing each energy service in the cheapest way, and because the special uses which can use electricity to advantage are already met twice over by existing power plants,[14] most "appropriate" renewable energy sources provide heat or vehicular fuels rather than electricity. For the same reason, most are well matched in size to the tasks for which the energy is needed.

Renewable sources are often described as "new," "unconventional," or "exotic." None of these labels is accurate. To be sure, many renewable energy technologies have been greatly improved by modern materials and design science. But this is only the latest stage in an evolutionary process stretching back for hundreds, even thousands, of years.[15] Such technologies as passive solar design, windpower, and biomass alcohols were well known in rather sophisticated forms millenia ago. Solar concentrators were used by the Vestal Virgins to light the sacred temple flame in the seventh century B.C., and set the sails of an enemy fleet alight in the Battle of Syracuse (the only significant known military use of solar technology). Flat-plate collectors are two centuries old; photovoltaics and solar heat engines, over a century.

Repeatedly, many solar technologies became respectably mature only to be cut off by the discovery of apparently cheap deposits of fuels, whether wood in the Roman Empire, coal in industrializing Britain, or oil in our own time. Each time, as scarcity and a sense of insecurity eventually returned, the renewable sources were reinvented. The 1970s may become best known to future historians as the time when renewable energy finally re-emerged to stay. The technologies surveyed in this chapter are the fruits of the first decade of modern technologists' serious, concerted attention to the problems and potential of renewable energy.

This analysis has consistently stated that *appropriate* renewable sources— not *all* renewable sources—offer economic and security advantages. Unfortunately, the overwhelming emphasis in federal renewable programs to date has been on the least economic and least resilient renewables, especially the central-electric ones. The historic reasons for this tendency to "make solar after the nuclear model,"[16] as two veteran observers remarked, are rooted not in economic rationality but in mere force of habit. Believing that solar contributions would be small and far in the future, the research managers sought to carry out their self-fulfiling prophecy by emphasizing the least attractive designs, those making the least saleable form of energy. They *assumed* that the desired product was baseload electricity, even though there is no economic market (as utilities are now discovering) for more of this extremely expensive form of energy.[17] Federal energy agencies and their major contractors also assumed, all but universally, that the way to develop renewable sources was to build prototypes—first of megawatt scale, then working up in stages to a scale of the order of a thousand megawatts—just as if the product were a new kind of fission reactor. They apparently assumed that anything else, or anything designed for a market other than utilities, "would fall short of a major contribution."[18]

Thus considerable engineering talent, and contracts probably amounting to tens of millions of dollars, have been devoted to conceptual designs for solar power satellites. Yet the cheap, efficient solar cells which they pre-suppose would deliver far cheaper electricity if put on roofs in Seattle or Boston.[19] In that form they would be virtually invulnerable, whereas in orbit (as the rocketry pioneer Hermann Oberth pointed out a half-century ago), they could be turned into Swiss cheese by anyone who cared to buy a weather rocket and launch a load of birdshot into the same orbit in the opposite direction. There they would meet the vast collector areas of the satellite every half-hour at a combined speed of thirty-six thousand miles per hour.

Likewise, the Department of Energy in recent years spent most of its wind budget on developing multi-megawatt machines with blades like a jumbo jet wing. These machines are enormous, complex, prone to high-technology failures, and useful only to large utilities. Each unit costs millions of dollars and is made, rather like a jetliner, by a highly specialized aerospace firm, then shipped across the country to the site. In contrast, some smaller American manufacturers have independently developed wind machines a hundred to a thousand times smaller. These have simple bolt-on sheet metal blades, no brushes, one bearing, two or three moving parts, and essentially no maintenance requirements.[20] Any handy person can use, if not make, such a machine. Indeed, as will be shown below, some designs this simple are now available at lower costs per kilowatt than the government expects its elaborate designs to achieve in the future.

An anecdote reveals the philosophical divergence. After spending tens of thousands of dollars on computerized electronic sensors to shut down an experimental Department of Energy wind machine if it started to vibrate too much, its designers visited the two-hundred-kilowatt Gedser machine operated decades ago in Denmark. It, too, had a vibration sensor: a saucer containing a large steel ball. If the tower shook too much, the ball would slop out of the saucer and fall down. A string attached to it would then pull a switch. (There is a postscript: the Department's sensors proved unreliable, and had to be supplemented by a closed-circuit television camera monitoring a painted film can hung from a string so the operators could see when the tower shook.)

There is thus a considerable difference between the renewable sources on which most federal attention has been focused and those sources which merit it by their economic and security benefits. This difference is partly in unit scale and simplicity. It is partly in the types of technologies considered: there are few if any cases where central-receiver solar-thermal-electric systems ("power towers"), or ocean-thermal-electric conversion (OTEC), or solar power satellites, or monocultural biomass energy plantations, look economic or necessary. The difference is partly in the basic concept of what energy is for: the central systems favored by most official programs would concentrate a natural energy flow (which was perceived, often wrongly, to be too "dilute" to use directly[21]), then have to redistribute the collected energy to users whose needs were, for the most part, fairly dilute and dispersed in the first place.

Simplified versions

Appropriate renewable sources offer a range of opportunities not shared by any other energy technologies: a range of complexity in design, construction, and operation which can affect cost much more than performance. Anyone who visits community-based energy projects or reads the many journals (*New Shelter, Solar Age, Popular Science, Popular Mechanics,* etc.) dealing with self-help and "vernacular" technology will be aware that many "soft technologies" can—though they need not—be built more simply than normal commercial models. What a high technologist would be likely to do with a steel tower, an aluminum extrusion, a Fiberglas® sheet, or a piece of digital recording electronics can also be done passably well with scrap lumber or lashed saplings, a piece of an old oil drum, a sheet of cloth, or a person with pencil and paper.

High technical sophistication is not inconsistent with cheapness or simplicity: a recently developed digital recording anemometer for analyzing proposed windpower sites is made of a five-dollar Radio Shack® calculator, cups from two Leggs® pantyhose containers, and similar odds and ends, and then calibrated by driving at known speed down a highway on a calm day while someone holds the gadget out the window.[22] It costs in all around ten dollars, but performs about as well as commercial versions costing many hundreds or thousands of dollars. There are tens of millions of Americans who would have no trouble making one. Similarly, the project managers for some costly federal solar projects were amused, on visiting one experimenter, to find that he used a bucket and a stopwatch to measure the flows of water through his solar panels.[23] In their own laboratory, they did the same thing with fancy digital flowmeters. They were less amused to discover that the National Bureau of Standards calibrates those flowmeters with a bucket and a stopwatch.

This is not to dwell unduly on "haywire rigs"—the kinds of technology that can be put together from things that are lying around in virtually any farmyard or town dump in the world. The conclusions of this analysis do not consider such technologies, and the economic comparisons in this book, while offering a few examples, in no way depend on them. But neither can their potential be ignored in favor of the highly refined designs more familiar to well-funded high technologists. Whatever the fancy designers may think of these odd-looking contraptions, they must at least admit that oil refineries, reactors, solar power satellites, or multi-megawatt wind machines are not technologies which lend themselves to production of simplified versions by citizens at greatly reduced cost. That potential for making many renewable technologies in local machine shops or at do-it-yourselfers' workbenches is advantageous enough in normal times; in emergencies it becomes absolutely vital.

This chapter does not suppose that people will be able or willing to make their own energy systems rather than having commercial versions professionally installed (which costs more but is still, as will be shown below, economically attractive). Some people will; but that opportunity is not considered here.

Quality control

This chapter is, however, based on the truism that renewable technologies, like any others, depend on good workmanship and must be the product of intelligent design based on sound economic principles, not on mere habit. Given such good design and sound construction, appropriate renewable energy systems can systematically fulfil their outward promise of being reliable and convenient, as well as very difficult to disrupt or to use so as to cause significant harm. Poorly executed, such systems can fail, with consequences that are relatively localized, but may be replicated many times over.

Without good design, neither renewable nor nonrenewable energy sources, and neither energy supply nor energy efficiency, can make sense. It is, of course, quite possible—as some private and (especially) government programs have shown—to make wind machines which fall down, to use insulation materials which emit poisonous fumes, to install vapor barriers incompetently (causing condensation in the walls, which rots the timbers so that the house collapses), to make solar collectors which rust and leak, to install or maintain wood stoves poorly (setting buildings on fire), or to create biomass harvesting programs which deplete soil fertility. There are always many examples of how not to do things right. For this reason, careful attention to detail, institutionalized quality control, and information feedback to enable people to choose intelligently are absolutely essential to any energy program.

But meticulous quality control is even more vital in large, complex energy systems (with the difference that failures there are more often due to mistakes and overambitious technical efforts than to fly-by-night contractors). Urea-formaldehyde insulation can cost health, money, reputations, and public confidence, but it cannot, given any reasonable alertness, cause the magnitude of damage that might arise from similar incompetence with larger-scale, less forgiving technologies than home insulation. However, this book will not defend anyone's bad engineering. It seeks rather to call attention to the soundest technologies and data sources, which exist in abundance.

System integration

Analyzing dispersed renewable sources is complicated. There are many kinds of technologies, many ways to build them, and many tasks for which they can be used in various ways. Further, they can be combined together into "hybrid" systems which may take on quite a new character, offering the advantages of the parts plus perhaps some additional ones. Chapter Fifteen showed how integrating efficiency improvements (for example, superinsulation in a house) with renewable sources (a domestic active solar system) can greatly improve the performance of both while reducing total costs. Integrating different renewable sources with each other often offers similar benefits. In general, these are available only at the modest scale of localized sources; they therefore have no counterpart in highly centralized technologies. Integration can be as simple as cogenerating electricity as a byproduct of industrial heat or capturing the waste heat from normal electricity generation (options which are described in Appendix One). Or integration can embrace a complex set of interrelationships among, for example, a building, its energy systems, and its food and water supplies. A few examples show the rich variety of ways in which decentralized renewable sources can share, and thus cut, total system costs:

• Successive uses of heat can be linked to cascade heat at successively lower temperatures from one use to the next.

• A dairy farm in Pennsylvania, like many in Europe, uses an anaerobic digester to convert manure to an improved fertilizer (which saves energy) plus methane gas.[24] The methane—homemade natural gas—then runs a diesel generator which powers the farm. (Many such operations produce an exportable surplus of electricity.) The generator's waste heat makes hot water to wash the milking equipment, thus saving more fuel. Waste heat recovered from the washwater is then used to preheat the cows' drinking water, increasing their milk yield. Dried residue from the digester, whose heat kills germs, is used as bedding for the cows; this cleaner bedding leads to a reduction in mastitis, which by itself saves enough money to pay for the digester within a few years. An expansion now being planned will integrate these functions with on-farm production of fuel alcohols from crop wastes, using waste heat for successive processes and sharing other infrastructure, then selling the alcohol or using it to run farm vehicles.

• Another common variation on this theme is to heat the digester in the winter with waste heat from the bulk milk chiller (a giant refrigerator which many state laws require). This often boosts the methane yield so much that one forty-cow dairy farm's output can meet all its own energy needs—before efficiency improvements—plus those of five other farms.

• Still another common pattern integrates the wet or dried residues of alcohol production into livestock feeding: the high yeast content makes the stillage a premium, high-protein feed. The carbon dioxide from fermentation can also be sold to refrigerant or soft drink companies, or used on the farm to raise the food output from a greenhouse. The greenhouse can also provide a productive environment for growing algae or other crops, perhaps partly fed by spare nutrients from the digester.

• Greenhouses can be integrated with other features of a building so as to save energy and money.[25] For example, an attached greenhouse can provide most or all of a house's heating requirements; a frostproof site for a simple, year-round solar water heater; a cheery "sunspace" that extends winter living space; and a place to grow food in all seasons.[26] In such a building, simple sheets of hard plastic can be wrapped into cylinders to form very inexpensive freestanding water-tanks which both store heat and grow fish. In one Cape Cod greenhouse, each tank pays for itself annually through its oil saving (via heat provided by the storage function) *or* through its fish production, with the other output being effectively free. Some houses are now even integrating food production with water recycling or sewage treatment: water hyacinth sewage treatment plants, now commercially available,[27] yield better water quality than costly and energy-intensive tertiary treatment plants, while sequestering heavy metals and providing a feedstock for producing methane and fertilizer.

• Swedish researchers are exploring the use of wood wastes for steel production—not only because wood chips are cheaper than oil (or, in some places, than coal) and contain no sulfur to degrade the quality of the steel, but also because the ironmaking reaction converts the wood into liquid or gaseous fuels which can be recovered and used at virtually no extra cost.

• Where wood wastes are burned for cogeneration, as is now common in the forest products industry, it appears to be possible to cascade process heat to produce methanol—a premium motor fuel—as a cheap byproduct from some of the "junk" wood input. This could also be done in the kind of small wood-fired power station proposed in some parts of the northeastern U.S. and Canada.[28] Indeed, if properly designed, such plants could simultaneously produce, at much reduced total cost, electricity, methanol, *and* district heating, thus replacing all three of the main local uses of oil.

• Solar process heat is increasingly used to raise steam for enhanced oil recovery (encouraged by overlapping tax subsidies for both the technology and its function). Such systems could be designed to cogenerate by-product electricity too. Likewise, many oil refineries, which now cogenerate electricity and find that this newfound independence from the power grid makes them more reliable, could save even more fuel and money with solar cogeneration, which would enable them to export more surplus power during sunny periods. (About seventy percent of U.S. refinery capacity is in the Sunbelt, especially in Texas.)

• Solar process heat can considerably increase the yield of useful liquid or gaseous fuels from a given amount of biomass wastes (an intriguing approach pointed out by Professor Michael Antal of Princeton University).

• Concentrating sunlight with simple reflector or plastic lenses can often save money by reducing the area of costly solar cells needed to produce a given amount of electricity. The concentrated light also heats the cells, from which waste heat can then be recovered. In some circumstances, this heat may be so valuable that the electricity is effectively free. (For household use, this generally requires that both the house and its electrical appliances first be made properly efficient.) On a community scale, the addition of seasonal heat storage and district heating can greatly improve the economics.[29]

These examples show that the integration of two or more renewable energy systems offers a great variety of ways to reduce total costs. So great is this variety that most of the interesting combinations have not yet even been analyzed. It is already clear, however, that the economic advantages of integration often far outweigh the commonly debated differences in price between energy from small renewable and from large nonrenewable technologies.

Linking to the grid: resilience lost?

Conceptually simpler but technically more complex integration issues arise when dispersed sources of electricity, especially renewable sources whose output may vary significantly over time, are connected to an electric grid. The grid must still stay synchronized (Chapter Ten). The electricity, being generated and used in the same instant, must still be closely regulated to balance fluctuating demands and supplies. And the reliability of the grid must not be impaired. Those considerations are well known, if not always well understood, by utility analysts. What is less common is the perspective of designing for resilience (Chapter Thirteen): using more, smaller, less "lumpy" modules of supply; making them diverse, dispersed, intercompatible, and redundant; and ensuring that if isolated they can operate autonomously. Because the requirements of designing large energy systems for resilience have not yet been thought through, resilient renewable sources of electricity, such as small hydro, windpower, and solar cells, are being developed and used before anyone knows how best to integrate them into existing supply and end-use systems.

There is already at least a good beginning on a legal framework for connecting small sources (including nonrenewable ones such as fossil-fueled cogeneration) to existing grids. The Public Utility Regulatory Policies Act of 1978 (PURPA) encourages this. It requires utilities to buy back surplus power from the small generators at the utilities' own "avoided cost"[30]—the amount of money the state regulatory commission thinks the utility saves by this transaction. Some utilities offer technical guidance for how to arrange interconnection.[31] Some, notably in California and Hawaii, are already planning to install many small renewable sources of their own (Appendix Two).

Yet how best to interconnect and use these sources is still controversial. Should they, for example, be integrated into the grid—or isolated from it, providing local storage? Should end-use devices be operated on the hundred-and-fifteen-odd volts of alternating current that the grid supplies, or on low-voltage direct current (such as solar cells supply)? Should houses be wired for alternating current, direct current, or both? These are still largely open questions. There are many possible ways to make dispersed electrical sources, the grid, electricity-using devices, storage systems, and controls all compatible with each other, but no approaches have yet emerged as general standards.

Some previously controversial questions do appear to have been settled, however.[32] For example, adequate methods are now known to ensure that dispersed sources do not endanger utility personnel by energizing supposedly disconnected power lines (for example, by using isolation relays which disconnect the source from the line when the latter becomes de-energized). There are adequate techniques for dispatching dispersed sources (for example, by treating them as "negative loads"—just sending enough power to an area to supply its needs net of its local generation). There are known methods to avoid feeding damaging harmonics—multiples of the proper frequency—into the grid, and to ensure that the electrical characteristics of the dispersed generators do not make the grid unstable or harm utility equipment.

Indeed, recent research suggests that some of these problems are quite the reverse of what had been thought.[33] Many utilities have opposed the interconnection of dispersed generators because, they said, those sources' lower-quality power would "mess up" the supposedly pure waveform of the alternating curent in the grid. But on closer examination, utility power has often turned out to have a "dirtier" waveform than the dispersed generators. The transients and harmonics which small units can introduce are tiny compared to those to which the grid subjects them.[34] The transients, in particular, which occur when utility switching relays open and close, or when branch circuits are interrupted by lightning bolts, tree branches fall-ing on power lines, or cars hitting poles, are so sharp that they are already damaging insulation and utility equipment.[35] The real risk is not that dis-persed sources will damage the grid, but that they will be damaged by it. That is why many of the newer cogeneration installations instantly discon-nect from the grid when a transient comes through it, before the local equipment can be harmed.[36] Engineering standards are badly needed to limit grid transients which could damage dispersed generators.

Although means are available—which also happen to be among the cheapest and simplest technical options (Appendix Two)—for protecting dispersed generators from damage by grid transients, fundamental theo-retical and practical questions remain about whether, and how best, to in-terconnect distributed generators with the grid. These questions are com-plex, because so many different types of technologies can make, use, convert, or interchange electricity, which can be direct current at various voltages or alternating current at various voltages and frequencies. (Ap-pendix Two outlines the main categories of technical options.)

So varied, indeed, is this technological menu that it poses a danger. Amidst the technical debate, a fundamentally important issue is in danger of being overlooked: how best to ensure that the potential resiliency bene-fits of dispersed, renewable sources are actually realized. This is by no means assured. On the contrary, in the name of protecting people who repair de-energized powerlines from being electrocuted by someone's wind machine that happens to start up and feed power into the line, many utilities are encouraging or requiring the use of induction generators so designed that they cannot produce any power without being energized by the line voltage. Similarly, a utility may require the use of inverters (de-vices to convert direct to alternating current) which automatically turn themselves off if the power line to which they are connected goes dead. The result is that if the grid crashes, the renewable source cannot work at all. Not only can it not help to supply other users through the grid, but it cannot even meet an isolated local load. Far from being an adjunct to and, in an emergency, a local replacement for the grid, it becomes a mere slave to it, unable to operate on its own.

But this unattractive result is not necessary for safety or for any other reason. With the safety of utility personnel ensured by isolation relays,[37] ordinary induction generators—the cheapest, most rugged kind—can pro-vide both normal interconnection and local emergency power (Appendix Two). Moreover, this type of generator also happens to be the least sensi-tive to changes in operating conditions and to damaging grid transients and harmonics.

Other design choices whose continued neglect will bear a high price in electrical vulnerability for generations to come include the following:

• There is little effort at standardizing voltages or other operating conditions so that diverse technologies are compatible with each other. This will greatly limit opportunities for interconnection, improvisation, and moving equipment from one site to another in emergencies.

• No effort is being made to make direct-current voltages and wiring details compatible between vehicles and fixed systems (such as houses). If this were done, then the emerging low-voltage direct-current systems, powered for example by solar cells, could be interconnected in emergencies with the hundred thousand megawatts of existing car and truck electrical systems. Household end-use devices could be run temporarily, or battery banks charged, by plugging the vehicle into the house wiring.[38] Even in normal operation, this interconnection could provide considerable economic advantage by providing extra local storage to the grid. Such interconnection would be easiest using twelve-volt systems, though with careful design it can probably be done at the more common twenty-four volts, connecting the higher-voltage bank one-half at a time. Whatever the voltage, making such an interconnection feasible and safe would require standard, foolproof terminals and instructions, perhaps on the outside of a house where standard color-coded jumper cables could be hooked onto them.

• No civilian manufacturers appear to be planning to make inverters, controls, generators, and other renewable energy equipment resistant to electromagnetic pulse. This could be done cheaply today, before many of the devices were built, but would be very difficult to do later after millions have been put into place.

In all these respects, the evolution of the interface between the power grid and its potentially resilient new contributors is disturbingly haphazard. The manufacturers and the engineering profession are quite capable of devising good standards on their own to correct these flaws, and can probably do it better than government agencies could. But so far they have shown no inclination to, and little sign that they even see the problem.

Dispersed renewable sources, properly integrated into the grid, could greatly increase its resilience, mitigating or even preventing cascading failures. A major analysis of the potential of such systems found:

> There is no question that [dispersed sources] . . . would have helped greatly [in the July 1977 New York blackout] *provided* that they had been properly integrated into the power system under conditions of cascading outage. This means that fail-safe procedures must exist to ensure that [the dispersed sources] . . . continue to function . . . and are, in fact, connected to the essential loads, e.g. [vital functions in] buildings, government services, traffic lights, etc. . . . [T]he economic loss caused by the disappearance of these essential services constitut-

ed roughly [eighty-three percent of the estimated direct losses in the New York blackout]. . . . The total demand for essential services is estimated to be in the range of several percent of total demand. Thus, [in New York] several hundred megawatts of [dispersed sources] . . . might have prevented the loss of essential services.[39].

(It was the failure of traffic signals and street lights which "facilitated looting, caused traffic accidents, and immobilized law enforcement.")

The analysis notes that "although major restrictions affecting [conventional] generation resources such as nuclear moratoriums, fuel embargoes, shutdown of all plants having the same design deficiency[,] and strikes" have not been considered in past utility reliability calculations, they may be very damaging "because of the large number of generating units that could be affected simultaneously."[40] Even a rather expensive dispersed source could thus be economically justified.[41] But for it to be

> most useful during a supply emergency, it is essential that there is a priority load allocation scheme as well as supervisory control systems and other hardware to ensure that the system can, in fact, be operated according to this scheme. In the absence of priority allocation, essential loads might be curtailed while non-essential loads continue to be served. In addition, the [dispersed] . . . generator could easily be disconnected from the system by its overload, undervoltage, or underfrequency protections [if it were thus called upon to serve beyond its capacity].[42]

Individual operators of dispersed sources might also need some way to limit their own loads to essential services in order not to overload the generator; but then idle capacity available to the dispersed users might not get into the rest of the grid in its moment of need.[43] This too is another unconsidered design requirement in the control systems for dispersed renewable sources. There is little research even on the theory of such systems.[44] Ultimately, high national levels of end-use efficiency could eliminate these control requirements by allowing the entire grid to depend on inherently resilient, largely local sources. But meanwhile, such sources can contribute most to energy preparedness if they are so deployed that they can be brought into play to serve the most vital needs in an emergency.

Even ignoring all the potential resiliency benefits of integrating dispersed renewable sources into the power grid, however, such integration would be worthwhile on classical grounds of utility economics alone. Several recent studies have shown this in detail.[45] Wind turbines (studied only as government designs ranging from one-fifth to two and a half megawatts), photovoltaics, diesels, and fuel cells "can provide an economic alternative to large-scale central generation if their projected cost goals can be met."[46] (Those goals have already been exceeded by small wind machines,[47] and are likely to be met ahead of schedule, as noted in Appendix Three, for photovoltaics.) The studies also found that dispersed renewable sources of electricity, even if intermittent, would improve the system's generation reliability.[48] They may also add to service reliability by protecting the end user against both grid and generation failures.[49] Roughly half the economic advantage of the distributed sources comes from their displacement of conventional power plant capacity,[50] half from their fuel savings, and a small amount from avoiding grid costs and losses.[51] The total cost saving is not very sensitive to the details of the utility's load or generation mix.[51] Although analysis of renewable systems with dispersed storage is complex,[53] system economics do not seem very sensitive to whether storage is provided. In particular, photovoltaics do not appear to require onsite electrical storage to be economically attractive,[54] as has sometimes been claimed.

In summary: adequate ways exist to integrate available renewable sources of electricity into the power grid, and these methods can save money. More analysis and action are urgently needed, however, to find out

• which methods are best (Appendix Two);
• whether other types of end-use systems would be more advantageous—for example, low-voltage direct current in households (Appendix Two); and
• how to design and organize the dispersed sources to yield the greatest improvement in resilience.

Otherwise, as dispersed renewables emerge into widespread use over the next decade or two, their patterns of use may merely repeat present vulnerabilities so that much of their potential national security benefit is foregone.

Technical status of resilient renewable sources

Appropriate renewable sources and hybrid combinations of them are immensely diverse. They span a large range of complexity and technical sophistication. They are evolving extremely rapidly,[55] often through research outside the channels where energy technologists traditionally communicate.[56] For all these reasons, any assessment of the technical and economic status of these "soft technologies" is bound to reflect only the conditions of the moment. Fortunately, the moving target is moving consistently in a favorable direction—better and cheaper technologies—so not being completely up-to-date usually means omitting the latest good news. It is hard to think of an instance where further research has not disclosed that there were actually more and easier ways to achieve a renewable energy goal than had been suspected. While that happy history is no basis for extrapolating into the future (and this book does not do so), it does suggest that any snapshot of what has been developed in a period of about ten years does not begin to disclose, let alone exhaust, all the promise of renewable energy technologies. What will be considered the best concepts in a decade or two may not even have been thought of yet.

Appendix Two summarizes some of the main directions of recent technical progress in demonstrating and deploying appropriate renewable sources. The details are given there rather than in the text because they are rather technical and not essential to the argument. What does matter is the conclusion: that such renewable technologies are in fact available in great variety. Those already demonstrated, and either on the market today or undergoing product engineering for commercial production in well-proven forms, are ample to contribute, within the next two decades, more than a third of the total energy supplies of the United States.[57] The same technologies, without further technological progress (which is occurring very rapidly), are adequate to meet essentially all of the long-term energy needs of every country so far studied—including not only the United States, but also other heavily industrialized countries which are variously colder, cloudier, farther north, and more densely populated, such as Britain, France, West Germany, Denmark, Sweden, and Japan.[58]

Economic status of resilient renewable sources

Appendix Three first describes some of the pitfalls of economic assessments (especially those which compare renewable with nonrenewable energy sources), and then presents a sample analysis using empirical cost and performance data. The assumptions are consistently weighted against the conclusions, to ensure that those conclusions are durable and do not depend on debatable details. For completeness, the analysis also includes typical prices for efficiency improvements. The data reveal that the best buy will almost always result from combining improved energy efficiency with renewable energy investments—an option which most studies ignore by considering these two ingredients only in isolation from each other.

Leaving the detailed data and their interpretation for the appendix, the general results can be briefly summarized. In all four categories of energy service needs—low-temperature heat (thirty-five percent of all U.S. delivered energy requirements today), high-temperature heat (twenty-three percent), liquid fuels for vehicles (thirty-four percent), and electricity (eight percent), efficiency improvements are the cheapest way of providing the service, followed by presently available renewable sources. These are consistently cheaper than the present world oil price, and in nearly all cases they are also cheaper than domestic oil, gas, coal, or nuclear power. In every case, well-designed renewable sources now available are cheaper in capital cost, and several times cheaper in delivered energy price, than the nonrenewable, highly centralized energy systems which would other-wise have to be built instead to replace the dwindling oil and gas—technologies like synfuel plants, coal-fired or nuclear power stations, or Arctic oil and gas wells.

In general, as the celebrated energy study done at the Harvard Business School found, the best buy in long-term energy sources, after efficiency improvements, is appropriate renewable sources (in their term, "small solar technologies"); the next best after that, synthetic fuels; and the costliest, central power stations.[59] But having not yet fully committed itself to a competitive marketplace in which all these options can compete on their economic merits, the United States, like most other countries, has so far been taking them in precisely the opposite order—worst buys first. The rapidly developing shift of investment priorities described in Chapter Fourteen is a strong hint that these economic realities, long ignored, are at last starting to assert themselves.

External costs and benefits

Economically efficient allocation of social resources requires that energy technologies be left to compete freely with each other and to stand or fall on their economic merits. The analysis in Appendix Three offers insight into those merits, and finds that appropriate renewable sources can be expected to continue their recent successes in competing with centralized nonrenewable technologies.

But neither predicted nor actual market prices reflect, or are meant to reflect, many important social costs and benefits. Even if they did, an economically efficient result might not be equitable. Nor can it be expected always to coincide with the results of the political process, which is designed to reflect and protect a broad range of interests not represented in market processes. A democracy works by "one person, one vote," but the marketplace works by "one dollar, one vote," and the dollars are not evenly distributed among the prople. To increase equity and political compatibility, and to ensure the correct *long*-term distribution of resources (which is not something markets do particularly well), it is therefore important at least to recognize some of the main external costs and benefits of alternative energy technologies.

In economic formalism, it is not correct to count employment as a benefit of any project: it is treated (and must be for theoretical consistency) not as a benefit but as one of the costs of production, in the form of wages, salaries, and benefits whose payment causes some other useful output to be foregone. The amount, duration, location, and quality of work provided by energy projects are nonetheless socially and politically important. Such projects can either increase or decrease total employment. Power stations, for example, are so capital-intensive that each thousand-megawatt plant built destroys about four thousand net jobs by starving other sectors for capital.[60] In contrast, careful and detailed case studies,[61] confirmed by more aggregated calculations,[62] have shown that efficiency and soft-technology investments provide several times as many jobs as equivalent power-station investments, but better distributed by location and occupation[63] and arguably offering more scope for individual responsibility and initiative. It is partly for this reason that many progressive U.S. labor unions (such as the United Auto Workers, Machinists & Aerospace, and Sheet Metal Workers) officially support a "soft energy path."

Another important consideration is the effects of different energy programs on the national economy via spending patterns and interest rates. (Responding effects—how people spend the money they save by using energy more efficiently—are important to the job analyses.) In general, efficiency and soft-technology investments are counterinflationary: once in place, they provide energy services at little or no additional cost, regardless of the price of depletable fuels such as oil. In contrast, purchasing oil and gas, which took only two percent of the Gross National Product in 1973, had soared to more than nine percent by 1981.[64] This worsening hemorrhage drains national wealth away from more productive uses to buy fuel which, once burned, is gone forever, leaving people poorer and the economy weaker.

The relatively short construction time and fast payback of renewable investments, and the direct saving in the money it costs to build them, also tend to reduce pressure on interest rates. An electric utility in financial difficulties can boost the present value of its cash flow severalfold by cancelling long-lead-time plant construction and spending the money instead on efficiency/solar investments, which repay their investment very quickly.[65] Indeed, many utilities—by getting about ten times as much new energy capacity per dollar and getting their dollars back ten times as fast as if they had spent the same money building power plants—will be able to reduce their need for investment capital so far (nearly a hundredfold) that they will no longer need to go to Wall Street to borrow expensive new money. Nationally, the effect would be to increase capital available for all other investments by several trillion dollars over the next two decades or so.[66] Furthermore, the direct saving of money from the operation of those investments is not only immediate and continuous; it is also widely distributed throughout society rather than concentrated in a few sectors or localities.

Efficiency improvements and soft technologies have very much lower and more manageable risks to occupational and public safety and to the environment generally than do competing nonrenewable sources,[67] even if the latter "hard technologies" are operated under stringent controls. Moreover, since the same people who get energy from dispersed sources also get their side effects, they are likely to insist that the technologies be done right. A nonrenewable but local technology offers a striking example. In Heidenheim, West Germany, there is a combined-heat-and-power plant which provides heat and electricity to an apartment complex.[68] It is run by a natural-gas-fired Otto engine (rather like a large car engine) housed in a garage-like structure. The engine is so well soundproofed that its noise cannot be distinguished from the noise of water running underground in the sewers at midnight. It *has* to be that quiet, because there is a house a few yards from the exhaust. The extra cost of the soundproofing, however, is very quickly recovered out of the money saved by having the engine so close to the end users that its waste heat can be distributed.

A combined strategy of efficiency and renewables offers a potent way of avoiding global climatic change and acid rain.[69] And if coupled with recognition of the economic collapse of the utility and nuclear sectors and of the problems posed by the strategic arms race, such an energy policy is also the most effective means so far proposed of limiting or even reversing the spread of nuclear weapons—one of the greatest threats to national security.[70]

Other geopolitical implications of such a strategy are also important. For instance, both directly and by example, it could strongly influence U.S. allies towards a more sustainable energy policy: such countries as Britain, France, West Germany, and Japan all turn out to be able to provide essentially all their long-term energy services using presently available and cost-effective efficiency and renewable technologies.[70] Those and similar countries could, just like the United States, become independent of foreign fuel sources and the associated political pressures.

The attractions of such technologies for developing countries, too, have been extensively documented.[72] The Office of Technology Assessment has noted the special advantages which independence from fuel and technology imports can bring to poor countries, whose most pressing problem is often a balance of trade tipped far into the red by oil imports.[73] "Solar energy is the one energy resource which is reliably available worldwide"—generally in larger and more consistent amounts in most developing countries than in the U.S.[74] Developing countries today pay fuel and power prices often many times those paid in the industrialized countries, making the economic saving from renewables even larger. The advantages of soft technologies for rural-based development, for integration with agriculture, and for simplified versions using locally available materials are especially striking in developing countries. U.S. security would be directly served by helping to relieve dangerous frustrations in the Third World: a defensible America "specializes not in arming or controlling other nations, but in equipping them with the benign technologies that foster stability and self-reliance."[75]

Similar arguments apply within American society itself. Technologies which tend to improve distributional equity, which are equally available to persons of all income levels, which increase individual and community self-reliance and self-esteem, and which by their appropriate scale allocate energy and its side effects more equitably will all tend to reduce the tensions now leading to "energy wars" (Chapter Four). Technologies which are perceived to be relatively benign, whose impacts are directly sensible and understandable by ordinary people, and which are accessible to an accountable and locally responsive political process[76] would increase the likelihood that political conflicts over energy policy would be settled peacefully. And technologies which can be evolved, refined, and selected largely by the processes of the marketplace, rather than by the technocratic mandate of an Energy Security Corporation and an Energy Mobilization Board,[77] are more likely not only to respect our national pluralism and diversity but also to use national resources efficiently. To see the dangers of central crash programs one need look no further than the experience of World War II, when the War Production Board, despite great talent and effort, mandated industrial expansions and conversions "which we could not use and did not need,"[78] diverting precious resources from other uses where they were more urgently needed and failing to use efficiently the considerable capacities of many small manufacturers.[79]

Large, complex technologies built and run by equally large, complex institutions are "inaccessible." They reinforce the supposition that ordinary people should be mere passive clients of remote technocracies. This in turn encourages people to think that if energy supplies are disrupted, "the Government" will take care of it. A basic conclusion of this book, however, is that if energy preparedness is to become a reality, people must feel empowered to use their own skills, solve their own problems, and largely look after themselves. This requires in turn that they have, and know that they have, most of the technological means to do so. The technology and the psychology of self-reliance are two sides of the same coin.

A final consideration important for policy, though difficult to quantify, is the risk of technological failure. It is sometimes suggested that efficiency improvements and soft technologies are uncertain to succeed, and that reliance on them is therefore a risky gamble. On the contrary, such technologies are known to work. (They more often embody the technological principles of the 1890s than of the 1990s, albeit in up-to-date and much improved form. Nearly a third of the houses in Pasadena, California had solar water heaters in 1897,[80] and over the years, Americans have used a cumulative total of some six million wind machines.) The extensions and modifications that would improve the devices are of a modest character:

although interesting to technologists, they are unlikely to present any substantive engineering problems. And the enormous diversity of the technologies and of the policy instruments that can be used to implement them provides many fallback routes to reach the same goals.

In contrast, it is conventional energy supply technologies whose success hangs on adventurous extensions of the present engineering art into wholly uncharted regions where success is far from certain—the conditions of stormy seas, the Arctic, fast-neutron fluxes, shale mining, corrosive hot brines, synfuel processing, outer-space industrialization. It is those same technologies that must overcome formidable sociopolitical obstacles against even longer odds. And it is again those same technologies which stake the energy future on technical, social, and economic breakthroughs far surpassing anything yet experienced.

Those who advocate even greater reliance on such technologies have already brought us the greatest collapse in industrial history: a nuclear enterprise which, after the investment of enormous technical effort and hundreds of billions of dollars, finds itself with no vendor in the world that has made a profit on reactor sales; with at least seventy more reactors cancelled than ordered in the U.S. since 1974; with a similar collapse of prospects throughout the world's market economies;[81] and with America's second-largest reactor vendor (General Electric)—expecting no more U.S. sales for at least the rest of the 1980s and essentially no export market—withdrawing from the market once it has filled its back orders.[82] This unhappy episode underscores the risks of underestimating the challenges of "big engineering,"[83] assuming that capital markets will indefinitely ignore the bottom line, and neglecting the social realities that make it considerably more difficult to achieve a plutonium economy than to insulate houses. It may at first glance appear that the "hard" technologies require merely continuing to do as one has previously done, while the alternatives require striking out into new territory. A pragmatic assessment of what is actually working, however, tells the opposite story. The contrast between one set of technologies, failing to meet the test of the marketplace despite direct federal subsidies exceeding forty billion of today's dollars,[84] and the other, capturing the market despite discriminatory institutional barriers, could not be more complete. Efficiency and renewables are not only the line of least resistance but also the policy of least risk.

Built-in resilience

All the economic and other advantages of appropriate renewable sources described in the past five pages have left out of account their most important national security benefits. Being *inexhaustible* and relying only on domestic energy flows, renewable sources can never place this nation at the mercy of other countries which control dwindling and scarce fuel resources. Similarly, appropriate renewable resources systematically avoid all the twelve sources of vulnerability catalogued in Chapter Four.

• Well-designed systems of dispersed, renewable energy supply are unlikely to bring the user into contact with *dangerous materials* (explosive or radioactive): even renewable liquid fuels such as alcohols tend to be much less hazardous, in flammability and toxicity, than their petroleum-based counterparts.[85]

• Far from having *limited public acceptance*, appropriate renewable sources enjoy an all but complete consensus—generally upwards of ninety percent approval—unmatched by any other category of energy technologies.[86]

• With the exception of existing large hydroelectric dams appropriate for the few concentrated end uses of electricity, such as smelters, sensibly designed renewable sources avoid *centralization of supplies*.

• Because they collect renewable energy flows where they are, rather than mining a fuel elsewhere and transporting it, they do not suffer from *long haul distances*. Their usual range is from inches or feet (in buildings) to miles or perhaps tens of miles in some bioconversion or small hydro systems.

• *Limited substitutability* is seldom characteristic of renewable sources: many bioconversion systems, for example, can cope with an immense range of feedstocks within broad limits of wetness and carbon/nitrogen ratio, and some, like the thermochemical processes (Appendix Two), can make the same widely usable liquid or gaseous fuels from any cellulosic or woody feedstock, regardless of origin. Likewise, efficient solar collectors can be made out of a vast range of materials—glass or plastic or recycled storm doors for glazing, steel or aluminum or wood or paper or plastic film (or even beer cans) for absorbers, rocks or masonry or water-filled oil drums or recycled bottles for heat storage. Or a well-lined hole in the ground and some brine—a solar pond—can be used in lieu of all these components. While the more sophisticated materials and designs will often improve performance, the simpler ones, properly done, usually prove quite serviceable. The range of possibilities is limited mainly by one's imagination. The technologies do not depend on exotic, imported materials.

• Unlike large turbogenerators, renewable sources of electricity are hard to damage if synchronization breaks down. A solid-state grid-interface device can enable them to cope with unusual or rapidly changing electrical conditions which normal electromechanical devices could not handle. Renewable sources integrated into a grid require *synchronization*, but with proper design they can also, unlike other sources, work as well into a local load without synchronization, in isolation from the grid, or even on direct current (Appendix Two).

• Properly designed renewable sources tend to distribute energy in the final forms in which it will be used, such as heat or unspecialized vehicular fuels. This eliminates many of the *inflexible delivery systems* that make non-renewable counterparts so logistically complex.

• The cheapest and most effective renewable designs also tend to avoid *interactions between energy systems* which depend on each other to stay in operation—whether by substituting convective circulation for active pumping in a thermal system or by using wind stirring or solar process heat in bioconversion.

• Although many soft technologies have modestly *high capital intensity*, theirs is considerably lower than their competitors' (Appendix Three).

• They have an even greater advantage in avoiding *long lead times* and *specialized labor and control requirements*.

• Their distribution systems, too, are seldom large enough to make *distribution of noxious materials* a significant concern.

While all these agreeable properties are not a necessary part of a dispersed, renewable energy system, they can be designed into it in ways which a centralized, nonrenewable system does not permit at all. Indeed, doing this will often tend to minimize direct economic costs.

Properly arranged soft technologies also satisfy most or all of the principles of resilient design (Chapter Thirteen). They are mainly *dispersed* to match their uses, capturing inherently dispersed natural energy flows by *diverse* means in many devices each of which serves sufficiently few and local needs to have a *low cost of failure*. Because the devices are *near to and readily understandable by their users*, moreover, *early detection of failure* would be a natural consequence of the "transparency" of the technical system. The energy devices' *large numbers*, diversity, and overlapping end-use functions can offer both *numerical and functional redundancy*—as would be the case if a town chose a blend of a large number of different sources of electricity (wind, microhydro, solar cells, solar ponds with heat engines, etc.) or of biomass liquid fuel technologies, offering built-in back-up in case particular devices or types of devices have trouble. The "fine-grained texture" of the many, relatively small devices tends to confine the effects of failures to local users. As in a biological *hierarchy* (Chapter Thirteen), whether or not a given device works, or is substituted for by another, need not affect energy supplies in a wider area. This is particularly true because electricity-generating technologies (those whose interruption is generally most immediately consequential) can readily be *interconnected* while maintaining *node autonomy*—the ability to stand alone at need. They provide far greater *functional flexibility* in adapting to changes in operating conditions and feedstocks than virtually any "hard technology" could tolerate. Their design can readily incorporate—and often will for economic reasons—

modularity and *standardization* at least to ensure *compatibility* with each other, as in mass production of solar cells or site-assembly of mass-produced collector components. The diversity of people and institutions pursuing them, however, will help to prevent a degree of standardization that might serve to propagate design errors. That safeguard is reinforced by a *speed of evolution* that has already compressed generations of technical development into a few years. Being made of relatively cheap and simple materials and using relatively undemanding processes, soft technologies can readily incorporate *internal decoupling and buffering* without unreasonable extra cost. Their *simplicity* and *forgivingness*, their *accessibility* to and *reproducibility* by a wide range of actors, and their *social compatibility* are among their main hallmarks. There is hardly a quality conducive to resilience which they do not have in abundance; hardly one conducive to brittleness and vulnerability which, with proper design, they cannot avoid.

A final feature of resilient energy technologies which, in these troubled days, cannot be neglected is that they are far easier to protect from harm (as well as to repair, replace, or augment by expedients) than are more elaborate and centralized energy systems. If natural disaster or attack threatens, small devices can be protected "from extremely high blast pressures, and presumably . . . [from] fires and falling debris," by using the same techniques which were developed in the Soviet Union and adapted by Boeing for protecting vital industrial equipment. Considerable protection can be achieved just by placing a device "on shock-absorbing material such as styrofoam blocks, wrapping it in plastic, covering it with crushable materials such as plastic chips or metal shavings, and covering this all with a thick layer of dirt."[87] No similar techniques are applicable to technologies that cover many acres, stand hundreds of feet high, and are in their own right conspicuous, tempting targets—hard to repair, harder to replace, and impossible to shield.

For all these reasons, the widespread use of inherently resilient technologies for supplying energy, in conjunction with highly efficient energy use, can profoundly improve national security. The combination could make impossible many types of large-scale failure of energy supply, and could eliminate the energy systems whose failure could most seriously imperil the public. The option of making America's energy system more efficient, dispersed, diverse, and sustainable offers arguably the greatest national security opportunity in our lifetimes. Technologies now available offer our nation an extraordinary chance to turn a present danger into a new source of security and prosperity.

The next and final chapter considers how actions by governments, private industry, communities and (above all) individuals can together grasp this opportunity, before commitments of resources in less promising directions have foreclosed it. For it will not remain available indefinitely. Our nation's transition to a sustainable energy system must be bridged by the use—the wise, sparing, and brief use—of the fossil fuels with which America still is blessed. Once those fuels have been burned, there is no more bridge. The opportunity to invest the remaining reserves of fuels—and the money and material assets derived from them—in building a secure, lasting energy future only comes once. That opportunity must be seized before it slips away forever.

Chapter Seventeen
Achieving Resilience
(with Alec Jenkins)*

The federal role

From the 1973 oil embargo until 1981 (and thereafter, in all countries except the United States), national governments have considered the energy problem to be primarily *their* problem: one that threatens the security and economic integrity of the whole country, that is debated in the national legislature, and that is to be solved by new laws and regulations. At first, energy efficiency and appropriate renewable sources were scarcely on governments' agendas; such alternatives were more or less politely dismissed in favor of more familiar (but, as it turned out, slower and much costlier) measures to increase domestic energy supplies. But harsh economic realities have markedly changed that dismissive attitude. Support for cost-effective alternatives is nowadays heard even in official quarters not traditionally sympathetic to them. When reservations are expressed, they generally concern questions of degree and speed, not of principle. This change is illustrated by the Canadian government's strategy paper, which reverses previous policy by stating:

> The realities of the energy future indicate the wisdom of accelerated efforts to develop new and renewable energy forms. . . . While most conventional forecasts imply a relatively modest role for renewables, it is clear that many Canadians do not share that view. Indeed, the dramatic surge in the use of wood [as fuel] . . . suggests that these forecasts understate substantially the contribution to be made. Moreover, while forecasts are useful tools for analysis, they can tell us only what will happen under certain conditions. The conditions—the policies—are the keys. Many thoughtful and concerned Canadians believe that we should alter the forecast, that we should decide soon on a preferred energy future, and establish the conditions that will take us there. The National Energy Program envisages a much greater role for renewable energy. The Government of Canada believes that economic realities now favour a range of renewable energy options.[1]

293

The opinions expressed in this chapter are the responsibility of the senior authors.

U.S. policy places greater stress on allowing the renewable share to be determined by the marketplace rather than by social planning, and the Carter Administration's indicative goal of twenty percent renewable supply by the year 2000 has been formally abandoned. (The Department of Energy's estimates are currently under ten percent—barely above the actual 1980 share of seven-plus percent.)

The Reagan Administration has also diluted or reversed most of the substantive embodiments of previous bipartisan commitments to accelerating efficiency and renewable technologies. It has proposed that federal research and development programs be cut in Fiscal Year 1983 to only fourteen percent of the five hundred million dollars that solar energy received two years earlier; and that the energy-efficiency research budget be cut to three percent of its 1981 level of seven hundred twelve million dollars. The proposed 1983 total for efficiency and solar energy, eighty-nine million dollars, would be the lowest since 1974—or just over a third of the proposed 1983 expenditures for the Clinch River Breeder Reactor alone. The main beneficiary would be nuclear power technology, which is slated to receive about one billion dollars in Fiscal Year 1983 and has received since 1954 fifteen times more research funding than solar and efficiency technologies combined. Tax subsidies also favor nuclear power by more than a hundred to one. These discrepancies have been explained by one Department of Energy official thus: "The marketplace will encourage people to use solar energy on their own, but the nuclear industry is weak and requires a government presence to put it on a stronger footing."[2]

Systematic changes in many other federal energy policies, more difficult to quantify but arguably more damaging to industrial progress and investors' confidence, add up to a virtual war against alternative technologies. The effects of some actions, such as the destruction of most of the Solar Energy Research Institute's programs and outreach networks—a remarkable collection of talent that was the envy of the world—will make themselves felt over many years to come. Others, such as proposals (so far rejected by Congress) to repeal solar tax credits, and the impounding of funds appropriated for the Solar and Conservation Bank, are more immediately damaging. These expressions of hostility come despite the Department of Energy's guardedly supportive rhetoric in acknowledging the appeal of alternatives:

> Most "renewables" . . . have little or no public opposition; nor do they pose severe long-term environmental problems. Thus, they are well suited (and may be confined) to any specific regional markets where they make economic sense. The Administration's clear and consistent adherence to free-market principles will remove artificial barriers and provide a major impetus to the development of such technologies.[3]

In giving practical effect to such generalities, several changes of policy would help federal agencies to improve national prosperity and energy resilience.

First, and perhaps most important, federal energy thinking should reflect the comprehensive approach to vulnerability and resilience which the foregoing analysis has developed. This has not been the case since at least World War II (if then). Even such Secretaries of Energy as James Schlesinger, whose background as Secretary of Defense and Director of Central Intelligence might have been expected to heighten his sensitivity to such issues, ignored any energy vulnerability other than cutoffs of oil imports. The Department of Energy's stated desire for a "resilient" energy policy[4] needs to consider a range of disruptions far wider than this traditional and continuing emphasis.[5] Present responses to vulnerability (stockpiling, encouraging dual fueling of certain oil-using devices, developing surge capacity, and international liaison)[6] are well meant. However, they ignore and disguise the tendency of most federal energy policies to *slow down* the displacement of foreign oil and to *increase* other energy vulnerabilities.

Currently, a few federal programs do reflect specific security concerns. The Strategic Petroleum Reserve, for example, has benefitted from vulnerability analyses (done without encouragement from the Department of Energy or much coordination with the Federal Emergency Management Agency). There are also minor utility programs concerned with the integrity of regional grids and with traditional studies of technical reliability, though their future is in doubt under the proposed abolition of the Department of Energy. And finally, there are site- and program-specific nuclear security programs. Yet the focus of all these programs is far narrower than that proposed in this book. The programs tend to focus on the cosmetic treatment of vulnerabilities already created, rather than on selecting alternatives which are not so vulnerable in the first place. The potential contribution which end-use efficiency and appropriate renewable sources can make in enchancing national security—especially in minimizing the consequences of terrorist attacks, a major concern of the current Administration—is thus not being exploited because it is not fully perceived.

Second, the Reagan Administration's free-market approach to energy policy is long overdue and can produce immense benefits in efficient energy investment, but it is not yet being consistently applied.[7] When the Assistant Secretary for Fossil Energy remarked that without the one-and-half-billion-dollar federal loan guarantee given to TOSCO by the Synthetic Fuels Corporation (a huge subsidy fund set up after the 1979 gasoline shortages), even its partner Exxon might pull out of a vast Colorado oil-shale project,[8] that was tantamount to admitting that shale oil cannot compete in a free market. If so, it hardly deserves federal support; conversely, it if can compete, it does not need support. The latter argument is, after all, the rationale being cited for the virtual elimination of federal funding for efficiency and most renewables. And if the competition were unbiased, that argument would be fair enough. The resilient alternatives *can* in fact hold their own in fair competition—but perhaps not against technologies which receive far larger subsidies. As the Executive Director of the California Energy Commission recently testified to Congress, the Reagan Administration has

> banished the energy success stories of the 1970s—conservation measures and the range of solar technologies—to the most distant exile of their holy realm: the so-called free market, [where they are] condemned to "compete" against heavily subsidized fossil and nuclear fuels in the way early Christians "competed" against the lions.[9]

The Christians in this case have in fact done surprisingly well; but in fair combat they would consistently triumph.

The distortion of investment patterns by federal intervention is a continuing impediment to resilient alternatives. It encourages proponents of failed technologies to continue to believe in a Santa Claus who, in the guise of national security, will subsidize and rescue their favorites even after the marketplace has rejected them. In early 1982, for example, representatives of the nuclear and utility industries proposed that a "Federal Nuclear Financing Bank" offer them fifty billion dollars in low-interest loans to bail out, via a "National Nuclear Energy Pool," about twenty nuclear projects that Wall Street is unwilling to finance—all in the name of providing a sort of strategic reserve of electrical capacity.[10] Even if it is currently unsaleable, they argue, we may need it someday. They have presumably not examined the alternative investments which, as earlier chapters showed, would provide far greater security, sooner, at a tenth of the cost.

From a preparedness perspective it is regrettable that recent budget shifts have tended to maintain or increase support to the costliest, most vulnerable, and most heavily subsidized technologies while reducing support to the cheapest, least vulnerable, and least heavily subsidized. Eliminating *all* the subsidies would be better economics and would speed recent trends toward resilient systems. At least providing "market parity"—equal subsidies, if one must have any at all—is a prerequisite for efficient investment. Attacking subsidies to resilient technologies while augmenting those for the most vulnerable technologies is a course that can only damage national security.

There is also a strong case for compensatory programs (such as the Solar and Conservation Bank) which help the most vulnerable members of society to achieve lasting energy self-reliance. Such one-time investments, replacing perpetual welfare payments for fuel assistance, typically pay back in a year or so. It is odd that such programs do not find the same support in the White House, which ostensibly is concerned to make people less dependent on handouts, that they enjoy in Congress. (Likewise, the Residential Conservation Service Program, whereby utilities offer energy-saving advice, has survived budget-cutting only to be gutted by proposed administrative changes.)

Cost-effective federal non-subsidy programs to hasten the refinement and use of the most resilient technologies are also deserving. Such opportunities—many already endorsed by the Department of Energy's industry-dominated Energy Research Advisory Board—include industrial efficiency programs, appliance efficiency labeling and a wide range of other consumer information programs, analysis of institutional barriers to least-cost investments, the implementation studies and programs of the Solar Energy Research Institute and its regional branches (including, for example, research into the behavioral determinants of energy use),[11] and work on second-generation photovoltaics. The last of these is, like refrigerators, a prime example of a vast market likely to be captured by Japan if U.S. industry concentrates—as it would tend to do if not helped to take a longer view—on first-generation technologies soon to be rendered obsolete. Recent slashes in the programs listed above, and similarly rewarding ones, are short-sighted and prolong America's energy vulnerability.

Third, in order to make federal energy policy more coherent, and to direct it towards achieving energy resilience as soon as possible, far greater efforts are needed to ensure the conditions that enable the marketplace to work efficiently. Price deregulation will indeed provide even greater *incentive* for energy efficiency and renewables.[12] But failure to remove market imperfections will result in a frustrating and persistent lack of *opportunity* to respond to price signals.

For example, vigorous enforcement and strengthening of the Public Utility Regulatory Policies Act of 1978, which seeks to replace restrictive utility practices with a competitive market in generation, would encourage entrepreneurial programs of dispersed electric generation. Yet the Federal Energy Regulatory Commission, rather than urging states to set full avoided-cost buyback rates, is overlooking derisory rates and defending the Act only weakly from legal and political attack by special interests which do not want to be exposed to competition. The Federal Energy Regulatory Commission is also rapidly increasing subsidies to central-station generation—effectively locking up money which, in an efficient capital marketplace, would go to cheaper and more resilient alternatives which would improve utilities' financial integrity.[13] Likewise, most federal programs to help states and localities modernize their building codes, provide information on cost-effective technologies, and otherwise remove barriers to least-cost investment are being eliminated from the federal agenda. The resulting federal energy policy is inconsistent not only with the Administration's free-market preferences, but also with its stated preparedness objectives.

Fourth, renewable technologies and technologies to increase efficiency are evolving very rapidly. Some key technical issues require early analysis and federal policy action—such as the preparedness aspects of grid integration and the encouragement of multifuel capability in cars (Chapter Sixteen and Appendix Two). Without proper handling of these issues, many of the potential preparedness benefits of efficiency and renewables programs will not be realized. The few analytic groups that had begun to consider such questions, notably at the Solar Energy Research Institute, have been disbanded, along with many of the best solar programs at the National Laboratories. The private sector has no incentive to take over such research on national preparedness.

Making policy coherent

More broadly, the patterns and processes of federal thinking about energy need to be leavened by a greater awareness of the nature of vulnerability and how to combat it. The best federal energy preparedness planning today appears to be in the Department of Defense—as exemplified by impressive efficiency and renewables programs at some military bases—but the details and rationale of this work are not well known to civilians, even in the Department of Energy. (The improper diversion to other programs of up to a quarter of a billion dollars earmarked for energy-saving programs during the 1979 and 1980 Fiscal Years[14] implies that such programs face opposition even within the Pentagon.) The Department of Defense proposed some years ago to have a liaison in the office of the Secretary of Energy to ensure that vulnerability got proper attention, but this was never done. Over the years, diverse Secretaries of Energy have continued, incrementally and unknowingly, to increase the vulnerability of America's energy system, apparently assuming that the Armed Forces will somehow be able to defend whatever systems are built.

National energy preparedness also demands better coordination among the Departments of Energy, Interior, and Commerce and the Federal Emergency Management Agency to ensure that the concerns which are FEMA's statutory responsibility receive due weight in, and are not undercut by, other agencies' decisions taken on other grounds. (For example, recent Department of Energy decisions have largely removed federal authority for ensuring that military fuel needs can be met in an emergency.) It would also be worthwhile to improve liaison with those members of Congress who have shown particular expertise and interest in energy resilience (as in Senator Percy's study of a possible National Defense Alcohol

Fuel Reserve). Currently, in both the executive and legislative branches, the programs and plans which affect energy vulnerability—in either direction—tend to be specialized, scattered, and uncoordinated.

In summary, the most fruitful federal role in promoting energy preparedness would be to raise the consciousness, expertise, and public accountability of those federal agencies whose decisions are increasing energy vulnerability; to identify and coordinate federal action on the detailed gaps in federal planning (such as grid integration); and to spread information on the specifics of achieving greater energy resilience, especially by encouraging locally based programs addressed to local security and economic concerns, drawing on the experience described below. Distributing, as did FEMA's predecessor, instructions on how to use a truck as an improvised electric generator[15] is useful if all else has failed. But distributing instructions on how to make buildings and factories efficient, harness renewable sources in the service of energy preparedness, improvise efficiency and renewable technologies out of locally available materials, and integrate alternative energy devices in the pattern that is most supportive of preparedness goals would not only save energy and money all the time, but would also be the best insurance against ever having to hook up that truck generator. At present, such federal energy preparedness programs as still exist are concerned with managing curtailments. To go further—to offer Americans the informational tools they need in order to *prevent* curtailments by building each day an ever more resilient energy system—will require a basic reorientation in government thinking. It will require that, instead of relying on a Federal Emergency Management Agency to help pick up the pieces after a disaster, we seek to equip the nation so that energy emergencies needing management are unlikely to arise.

It will also require a healthy skepticism toward the dogma that a national problem can only be solved at a national level. In a country as large and diverse as the United States, any issue aggregated to a national level tends thereby to become all but unmanageable. Much of the current federal trend towards devolving choice back to a state and local level wisely recognizes that unique local circumstances can often be best dealt with by people who know them in detail—if the will and the resources to do so are there. This may not work for every social problem. But the evidence of recent years is that it works very well in energy policy. The energy problem is already being solved from the bottom up, not from the top down, and Washington will be the last to know. This is not surprising, for the national energy problem is made of billions of small pieces which are mainly perceived, chosen, and regulated at a local level. Institutional barriers—ten thousand obsolete building codes, obsolete lending regulations and utility practices, and the like—are generally at the state, county, or local level. The rest of this chapter, therefore, is devoted to the best-proven and most promising approach to achieving energy resilience: state and local implementation programs.

State programs

Some state governments are already doing pioneering work on energy preparedness, equalling or surpassing in quality that of federal agencies. California is widely regarded as the leader—perhaps just ahead of oil-dependent Hawaii—in analyzing and preparing for interruptions of oil supply (and, to a lesser extent, of natural gas and electricity). This approach and expertise are in part an outgrowth of the high expectation of a major earthquake, and of state experience in managing drought. On paper, the state's oil prospects have been analyzed at a sophisticated level.[16] The California Energy Commission's Energy Contingency Planning Staff, led by Commissioner Varanini, has summarized in a memorable 1981 wall chart ("Oil Crisis Regulation") the labyrinth of present arrangements—international, federal, state, and local—for coping with an oil crisis. A 1980–82 series of well-argued papers, consequence models, and conferences has revealed that those arrangements would be largely unworkable even if executed with perfect competence. The state is therefore seeking, with little federal help, to develop—at least for itself—a policy that might work.

Some authors have proposed "energy emergency districts"[17] as a basis for an inventory and "mobilization" of local energy sources and skills, and for demonstrating the potential of local renewable sources for improving resilience.[18] ("Mobilization" may be the wrong word, with its connotations of wartime mandates; in this context it refers to voluntary community-based programs that can be equally coherent and effective.) The California effort does not go that far: it is still largely directed towards managing shortages, not with the more fundamental shifts in strategy needed to make the probability and consequences of shortages very small. To be sure, California's energy policy has been among the leaders in promoting efficiency and renewables, especially by local action; yet in the senior authors' view, that policy seems to have little connection with the efforts of Varanini and others to improve energy preparedness, conceived of as short-term responses to conventional types of supply interruptions. Thus, although those preparedness efforts are arguably the best of their kind at a state level, they are no substitute for a more comprehensive view of energy resilience. They can only help to provide a framework for political leadership to encourage and coordinate local actions that would most quickly accomplish that shift.

It is therefore especially unfortunate that the same federal budget cuts which crippled many local energy programs are also leading to the dismantling, during 1981–82, of most of the state energy offices. The cuts have come just as the state offices were hitting their stride and becoming effective facilitators of local action. Without such substitutes as the Energy Management Partnership Act (proposed federal legislation which was not enacted), much of the present capability for coordinating state energy preparedness measures—for both preventing and responding to energy emergencies[19]—is slated to disappear. Such state efforts, like corresponding ones at county and municipal scale (e.g., in Los Angeles[20]), should on the contrary be strengthened as a cheap way to achieve local goals which also add up to national resilience.

Regardless of national or state policies, there is a widespread perception, especially among county and municipal leaders around the country, that when energy supplies are next seriously disrupted—an event which most experts believe is virtually certain to occur within ten years—federal programs, with the best will in the world, will not be able to do much for most people. It will be every community for itself. The experience described in the rest of this chapter shows that people are generally prepared to accept that their best protection against the resulting inconvenience or hardship is to get busy *now* with what they can do for themselves to develop efficiency and renewables—not to wait for what others might do for them many years in the future. This approach responds both to people's well-founded anxieties about energy security and to their equally shrewd suspicion that there is a great deal they can do to increase their personal and community energy security while saving money meanwhile. Such programs can certainly be encouraged and helped by federal and state actions, but their main impetus can only come from within communities themselves. The rest of the chapter, therefore, discusses the basis and technique of such locally based programs.

Why act now?

Communities, like people, tend to wait until a crisis is at the door before taking a new and unfamiliar direction. Democracies, as the late physicist Dennis Gabor remarked, respond magnificently to great dangers but are not so good at responding to smaller, creeping dangers. Energy, however, may well be different, because relatively small interruptions of supply— gasoline lines, natural gas shortages, regional blackouts—should already have prepared Americans psychologically to understand the vulnerabilities described in this book, and because the economic burdens of buying energy are visible daily. If those two reasons do not goad communities into action, it may be too late: options that exist before a major failure of energy supply rapidly vanish during it, because of uncertainty, capital shortages, and hardware shortages.

Uncertainty In an energy shortage, whether from traditionally considered causes such as an oil embargo or from the types of system failures on which this book focuses, the members and leaders of any community will be asking themselves: How serious is this emergency? How long will it last? Who will help us? Without good answers—indeed, being bombarded by conflicting answers from all sides—people will tend to wait and see, doing as little as will give the appearance of muddling through. The ambiguity that stalls action is not only a lack of information; it is real. The federal government currently says it will adopt a laissez-faire, free-market attitude, but it is not reckoning with public pressures if gasoline reaches five or ten dollars a gallon and many people cannot afford it. Communities will then look to the federal government to impose rationing or release its reserves.

But just as the International Energy Agency has worked hard on three occasions to ensure that its oil-sharing agreement was not triggered, so there are reasons to think the Strategic Petroleum Reserve would not be used except in extreme emergency. Federal and state contingency plans, where they exist, are generally in disarray. Nobody knows whether they would be used, or, if used, whether they would work. Who will pay for their implementation is a completely open (and politically delicate) question. In localized failures in the past, states and regions have proved reluctant to pay for making up each other's deficits. Local administrators who hope that these uncertainties will somehow be resolved in a crisis, presenting them with clear options that nobody can see now, are likely to be badly surprised.

Capital availability Efficiency and appropriate renewables are already attractive investments even before an energy emergency. The knowledge that demand for them may rise steeply during an emergency adds a further and more speculative attraction. During an emergency, however, that speculative character is more likely to tempt short-term profit-takers to buy stockpiles of fuels, or shares of companies which hold such stockpiles. Thus the glittering profits to be had by speculating in oil at hundreds of dollars a barrel may quickly dry up the flows of capital that can be much more productively used to save oil. In just this way, tens of billions of additional dollars per year are already flowing into heavily subsidized oil and gas drilling rather than going into better but less familiar investments in saving those same fuels.

Furthermore, most energy-saving and resilience-improving investments must be made in millions of little pieces, not in the huge chunks with which capital markets are accustomed to deal. Yet energy emergencies limit the jobs, disposable income, and local revenues which provide precisely these local flows of capital. To the extent that federal funds are available, they are more likely to be used to bail out conspicuously hard-hit major industries, to supplement transfer payments to the unemployed and needy (notably to help pay their increased fuel bills), to increase military spending, or to rescue bankrupt cities, than to weatherize individual buildings. Energy emergencies also provide the purveyors of the slowest, costliest, and least competitive, but highly visible, supply technologies with a vocal argument for more federal bailouts. All these pressures on the Treasury tend to raise taxes or interest rates or both, and to crowd the smallest borrowers, who have the fastest and cheapest energy-saving opportunities, out of the capital market. The difficulty today of financing many small investments rather than a few big ones is a warning that under the pressure of an emergency, this imbalance of investments will worsen.

Hardware availability America has shown, in past national emergencies, a remarkable ability to increase total industrial production: after Pearl Harbor, for example, production grew about fivefold in two years.[21] The capacity to produce and distribute the specific equipment needed to replace vulnerable energy supplies with resilient ones may well behave in the same way: in principle, it should be even easier to expand because the devices are generally smaller, simpler, and able to be made by a wider range of industries. But it does take time and money to expand the capacity to produce anything, including caulking guns, insulation, and greenhouse glazings. No systematic study has been done on where bottlenecks might arise, if an energy emergency induced people to buy a great many such items all at once, and how these bottlenecks might be anticipated and forestalled.[22] (Dr. Abbie Page and Alec Jenkins wrote various proposals for several years to make such a study, but no federal agency seemed interested.) Some preliminary data are available, however, from historic examples and from telephone surveys made by Roy Pitts (wind and hydro) and Carolyn Danahy (insulation). The data deal mainly with the purely logistical problem of expanding factories; they do not address the managers' problems in deciding how reliable the expanded market will be or in raising capital to finance the expansion.

In 1977, a surge in demand led to a six-month shortage of glass fiber insulation, which accounts for ninety percent of the insulation used in new houses and is also widely used for retrofits. By August, the shortage was stalling projects for half of all builders.[23] The insulation-making industry actually had excess capacity in place, but it takes about a month to bring the production processes up to their working temperature and two months to move supplies from the factories to the retail distributors. A similar shortage today, when glass fiber factories are working at only fifty or sixty percent of capacity (because of the depressed building industry), could likewise start to be met within three months, though it would take months more to work off the backlog of orders. Actually building new insulation plants would take two or three years. Capacity to produce cellulose insulation, however, could probably be built up faster. Hundreds of plants, scattered around the country, can shred newspaper and treat it with fire retardant. The plants are simpler, smaller, and less capital-intensive than equivalent glass fiber plants, although the product may be somewhat less effective and durable.

The rate of expanding production of energy-supplying equipment is subject to a variety of constraints. For example, based on seven responses from a survey of thirty-two small-hydro turbine makers, it appears that they could readily double their production rate. But there may be delays in putting new factories into full service, the limited number of experienced designers could become overworked, and other steps in the process (such as finding good sites and installing the equipment) could well take longer than making the turbines. Current delivery times for turbines range from a few weeks to seven months for standardized units (up to one or two hundred kilowatts), most of which are made in underused factories; plants in the low megawatt range are non-standard and take about fifteen months to deliver.

A small sample of wind machine manufacturers, most of whom assemble parts made by other industries, similarly showed delivery times ranging from a few weeks to five months for small machines; seven to ten months for those from forty to six hundred kilowatts; and typically two years or more for machines in the megawatt range. Though these times are shorter than those for any thermal power plants, they still show the importance of ordering before an actual emergency. In principle, it should be possible for a wide range of manufacturers, including car factories, to tool up to mass produce very large numbers of wind machines in less than a year; but this would require standardized designs, standardized installation and interconnection methods and an assured market.

The U.S. solar cell industry made cells totalling about four megawatts of peak capacity in 1981, but had the ability, working multiple shifts, to make probably five or six times that much in 1980.[24] As larger, more automated plants come into operation during 1982–83, bringing down costs, the actual and potential production rates will probably rise steeply. Some second-generation processes lend themselves to very rapid production and increases in production; vacuum-sputtered films and amorphous silicon, for example, or other thin films deposited by wet chemistry, could be integrated with plastic-film-making machines which discharge their product at tens of miles per hour. Some such processes are now in advanced pilot development.

Recent reports indicate that major Japanese manufacturers of solar water heaters (mainly passive thermosiphon designs) have a spare production capacity of a hundred thousand units per month, and that they are planning to use it to enter the U.S. market in 1982–83. Such manufacturing lends itself to rapid expansion, using a wide variety of techniques and materials.

In summary, most of the main technologies for improving energy efficiency and harnessing renewable energy flows could be produced at a much increased rate with less delay than corresponding centralized technologies, where tooling up often requires years and installation a decade. But such acceleration of the production rate would be more efficient and more certain if it took place smoothly, through continued market expansion before an emergency, than if it were attempted under all the uncertainties, capital shortages, and (of course) energy shortages that would complicate all industrial activity during an actual energy emergency.

For all these reasons, a community seeking to replace vulnerable energy systems with resilient ones will find its task greatly simplified by mobilizing its resources in advance, so as to prevent an emergency rather than respond to it. Fortunately, such anticipatory action also reaps the economic rewards of cheaper energy services, relieving a present burden of which most communities are acutely aware.

What energy dependence costs the community

Indeed, it has often been the economic benefits of a more resilient energy strategy, not its preparedness advantages, that have attracted the most notice, support, and action. While the specter of blackouts and oil cutoffs is at the back of people's minds, the reality of day-to-day energy costs is at the front. The importance of reducing those costs is most visible not at a national level, where oil import bills of thousands of dollars per second are too big to visualize, but at a local level, where household energy bills are all too obvious.

At a local level, too, the problem and solution can be stated in concrete and memorable terms, and specific opportunities for and obstacles to such a policy can be most directly identified and dealt with: most building codes, zoning regulations, and the like exist and can be changed locally. Finally, such community concerns as strengthening the local government revenue base and the business climate, providing sustainable jobs, and reducing the drain of buying outside energy are all addressed by more efficient energy use and more local supply.

The imperatives that drive communities toward more local and resilient sources of energy can be easily illustrated. The financial drain of buying energy can be almost as damaging as the shock of having it cut off. For example, Wooster, Ohio, a city of ninety-six thousand people, is close to the national average in having spent in 1980 about three and a half thousand dollars per household for energy used at home and in the commercial sector[25] (whose energy costs were reflected in the price of goods and services to the community). About ninety percent of that energy cost leaves Wooster—the equivalent of losing a local payroll of about seven thousand jobs. A ten percent increase in energy prices costs Wooster residents an extra eleven million dollars a year—the equivalent of losing another seven hundred fifty jobs. Every year, as Wooster imports ever-costlier energy, the economic lifeblood of the city drains away. On a national scale, thousands of Woosters add up to an economy in which, by 1981, over nine percent of the Gross National Product was disappearing down the rathold of paying for oil and gas.[26] This represents an enormous and continuing drain of wealth away from citizens, communities, regions, and our entire nation—money no longer available for more productive and more permanent investments. The coming deregulation of natural gas toward prices more representative of its long-run replacement value will only increase this capital outflow.

Wooster is not atypical. Santa Cruz County in California imports eighty-five percent of its energy—equivalent to three times its net income from an extensive tourist trade.[27] Humboldt County, further north, has great hydroelectric and wind resources, yet imports eighty-five percent of its energy,[28] and finds this burden ever harder to support as the local mainstay, the forest products industry, suffers a continuing depression. Springfield, Illinois spends eighty-five percent of its energy dollars on imports—the equivalent of losing eleven thousand jobs in 1980.[29] The state of Iowa imports ninety-eight percent of its energy;[30] Massachusetts, ninety-seven percent.[31] Nor do the dollars respent by local workers in the energy industries do much to redress this imbalance. Of every dollar Iowans spend on petroleum, only fifteen cents stays in the state economy; of every dollar spent on coal, only seven cents is retained.[32]

Of course, this is not to say that every town, county, or state should strive for a rigid economic independence; rather, that imports and exports should be based on comparative advantage. There is no point paying other far away for what one can get more cheaply and more securely close to home. Local energy sources, made and installed using local skills and resources, keep money in local circulation—sustaining community jobs, businesses, and disposable income and perhaps capitalizing more opportunities to export goods and services for cash. Even where vulnerable and costly imports are not completely displaced, local sources create local income which can help to pay for remaining imports.

Table Three summarizes the main costs which communities as a whole, local governments, and local industry must bear for expensive energy *both* when it is routinely delivered *and* when its flow is interrupted. Table Three shows why communities are being challenged to create a new economic base: one which, rather than continually eroding as the price of imported fuel and power rises, offers a firm foundation for sustainable development. For many communities, energy efficiency and renewable sources are a prerequisite for economic survival and a centerpiece of economic revival. This—more than volumes of data showing the unimaginable hundreds of billions of dollars (thousands of dollars per household) that our nation could lose in say, a major oil interruption—speaks to people and communities in their own language.

It is therefore not surprising that community energy planning based on efficiency and appropriate renewable sources is now underway in hundreds, perhaps thousands, of towns, cities, and counties across America. In fact, enough such efforts have been successfully undertaken in the past few years that it is now possible to distill from experience the main elements which make such programs work.

Creating a sustainable local economy

A concerted program to make a community's energy supplies more affordable and resilient depends above all on shared public sentiment. Informed community feeling engenders an irresistible excitement, an integrity and purpose, which make it possible to overcome differences and obstacles for a common goal. Guided by sentiment, people can do difficult, even heroic, things that they have never thought of doing before. They can pick up new skills, take responsibility, stretch themselves, and take credit for success. Fully harnessing American communities' remarkable resources of voluntarism and expertise requires that the program's leaders, whatever their position and style, first establish a sense of certainty about the direction and outcome of the effort. It also requires a deliberate inclusion of the most diverse possible views and talents, striving for the widest participation by all sectors of the community. The ideas and the impetus should come from within the community, not be laid on it by outsiders.

Communities have used many different organizing techniques for energy action. Some of the more successful include:

• A community energy analysis giving a clear picture of where the community's energy comes from, how it is used, the present economic effect of energy costs, expected trends, and the community's vulnerability to energy shocks. It is often helpful if the larger employers in the community take part in these assessments, calculating their own energy expenditures as a percentage of their profits, and estimating how energy shortages would effect their operations and employment.[33] Participation by a wide range of stakeholders is indeed essential if the results of the analysis are to be both technically and politically credible. The key ingredient is one or more people who think clearly, have access to community data, and can do arithmetic. (Several methods for such analysis have been developed, and specific computational patterns and worksheets are available.[34]) The analysis provides insight into the community's present energy situation,

**Table 3   Major Economic Costs to Communities
of Expensive Energy and Interruptions in Energy Supply**

	EFFECT ON COMMUNITY	EFFECT ON LOCAL GOVERNMENT	EFFECT ON LOCAL INDUSTRY
DIRECT EFFECTS OF HIGH ENERGY PRICES	*Reduces disposable income for all, margin of survival for the poor. May completely offset economic growth, since typically 80–95% of energy expenditures leave the community. Will worsen with gas deregulation. Closure of marginal factories likely: New England lost 22% employment, Southwest gained 27%, in energy-intensive industries in recent years.[a]*	*Reduces funds available for services and adds pressure to raise taxes or go deeper into deficit. Energy is the second largest item of expense for 50% of cities and 43% of counties.[b] Pressure of current energy expense defers investments that could reduce it.*	*Reduces profitability and capital available for new products and improved processes. Energy costs rose from 19% of pretax profits in 1968 to 39% in 1980, more today.[c] High oil and gas prices may divert capital from local investments into speculative drilling elsewhere.*
EFFECTS OF AN ENERGY PRICE SHOCK	*Higher prices for all goods. Economic stress may raise interest rates or taxes. After initial burst of inflation and unemployment, sustained reduction in output (recession) likely as in 1975 and 1980.*	*Economic slump reduces tax base and tax revenues. Magnitude of loss is illustrated nationally by estimates that the 1973–74 and 1979 oil shocks reduced consumption and investment by a total of about $821 billion[d]—equivalent to local revenue losses of many billions of dollars.*	*Ripple effects of depression in cars, airlines, etc. as consumer preferences change. Discretionary outlays by non-energy industries reduced 16% ($35 billion) in 1980, delaying productivity gains.*
VULNERABILITY TO ENERGY SHORTAGES	*Unemployment rises immediately; affected businesses may relocate to areas with more secure supplies or may close permanently. Local hardship: in the 1976–77 South Carolina gas shortage, 1.5 million workers were laid off in a few weeks; three counties lost $4.7 million disposable income; alternative fuels cost $12 million extra.[e]*	*Budgets strained by need for emergency services, added welfare payments, alternative fuels, etc. Ambiguous federal and state role: little federal support is either planned or, in widespread shortages, even feasible. Almost no plans for interruptions of gas or electricity—only of oil.*	*Vulnerable to loss of own energy supplies and of vital materials and processes outside local control. Concern that private fuel stocks may be confiscated in emergency. May lack energy for worker commuting or for delivery of supplies and outputs.*

Table 3 **Major Economic Costs to Communities**
of Expensive Energy and Interruptions in Energy Supply *(Continued)*

	EFFECT ON COMMUNITY	EFFECT ON LOCAL GOVERNMENT	EFFECT ON LOCAL INDUSTRY
COSTS OF ENERGY INTERRUPTIONS	*The U.S. has not yet experienced a really serious or prolonged supply disruption. Market allocations broke down in shortages of a few percent. Foreign and domestic vulnerabilities could produce much larger and longer shortages, multiplying prices manyfold.*	*Required government responses are costly and generally unbudgeted, coming just as revenues plummet. Breakdown of vital services could incur very large social costs. Localities likely to bear the brunt of coping with allocating scarce supplies, keeping order, and handling family/neighborhood emergencies. Stress could equal or exceed the worst in the Great Depression,[f] with added medical costs, crime, etc.*	*Plant closures—very costly and disruptive. The 1976–77 gas shortage shut 4,000 factories; others were willing to pay 25–50 times normal gas/electricity price to stay open. Future shortages could involve several energy forms at once.*

[a] Tsongas 1981; Clark 1981a:6.

[b] Data from International city Management Association, quoted in Woolson & Kleinman 1981

[c] Schaffer 1981a.

[d] Mork & Hall 1980, 1980a (converting 1972 to 1980 dollars by multiplying by 1.774).

[e] Jennings 1980:1, 48.

[f] Deese & Nye 1981. Much of the damage might be slow or impossible to reverse: Comptroller General of the U.S. 1981b:II:8.

how energy could be better used, what supply alternatives are locally available, and what the economic consequences of "business as usual" might be. From this base of information, communities generally do not find it hard to reach consensus on what they should do next.

• A moment for telling the truth, when community leaders and citizens are presented with the results of the assessments and urged to participate in further programs.[35] The early participation of diverse interests will have helped to build a political base for continued and broadened participation as the effort moves from a paper study to suggested actions. Specific events, such as town meetings, workshops, specialized presentations, and advisory group meetings can help to focus that participation and provide a forum. "Energy fairs"—like those already held (generally under private sponsorship) in over a third of California's cities and counties[36]—can help to raise awareness.

• Creation of an energy task force or commission—an arm of local government—by formal resolution of elected officials. The number of members generally varies between five and fifteen, representing key constituencies to draw on the community's diversity, ensure broad credibility, and guard against domination by any interest group.[37] Task forces have been successfully used in such diverse areas as Los Angeles, California; Franklin County, a mainly rural area in western Massachusetts; Seattle, Washington; and St. Paul, Minnesota.

By these and similar means, communities bent on using their own energy resources more effectively tend to seek an early consensus on these principles:

• Community economic development is in substantial part an energy issue, and the use of energy efficiency and renewable sources is a prime strategy for economic development.[38]

• The community should be building a local market for new energy manufacturing and service businesses, since local economic activity is entwined with the developmemt of energy and economic resilience. Such markets need to be attractive and to offer the confidence and reasonable certainty that come from durable, widely shared community values.

• The community may well need to use one of a number of institutional innovations to make enough private capital available to finance the front-end costs of energy development. Some of these approaches (described below) can also increase local government revenues.[39]

• It is appropriate to apply the powers of local government to create a new set of rules—openly, democratically, and equitably—for helping to determine the community's energy future,[40] and to ensure that practices left over from the era of cheap oil, which today are hindering efficient choices within the community, are corrected.[41]

Community energy action programs also generally require a team including:

• at least one political figure with the commitment and strength of character to push the enterprise to completion;

• a dedicated city or county staffperson able to provide accurate technical information; and

• a community outreach person and a community-based task force willing to devote the many hours necessary to build a constituency for the program.[42]

Two further requirements for success are:

• some agreement among the business community, and with the local utility or utilities, that the key principle of the program—community choice
of cheaper and more resilient patterns of energy use and supply—is desirable (this agreement will usually, though not always, ensure active cooperation); and

• an understanding that speed is essential if enough progress is to be made
before the local economy's ability to respond is further damaged by high
energy prices or by interruptions of supply.

Some local governments have appointed an energy coordinator to help
provide leadership for local efficiency-and-renewables programs. About
two-fifths of the cities and counties in California, for example, have such a
person.[43] Energy coordinators have shown they can stimulate local governments to practice greater energy efficiency themselves (which sets a
good example and visibly improves local finances); to link with citizen and
business groups; and to initiate energy programs for action by local legislative bodies, administrators, and community groups. In some cases, very
sophisticated long-term energy programs have resulted.[44] Coordinators
can also help diverse government agencies to keep in touch and can serve
as troubleshooters to help keep the energy plan on track. Thus Santa Barbara's coordinator monitors the progress of efficiency improvements in
each government department and advises each department head annually
on new goals.[45] Over sixty percent of California cities and counties, generally through the efforts of an energy coordinator, have analyzed how
they use energy in government buildings, and nearly seventy percent
monitor the local government's own energy use.[46] Where the climate is
not yet ripe (as in the early stages of the work in Franklin County, Massachusetts), the coordinator may be unable to take concrete action without
first building an internal consensus among county commissioners, department heads, and staffs, and setting up a community energy information
center to stimulate informed discussion.[47] But where institutions are
ready to act, an energy coordinator can repay his or her salary quickly
through energy savings—as the one in Santa Clara County, California did
by saving the country one hundred fifty to two hundred thousand dollars
in her first two years.

Getting started

The process of agreeing on, pursuing, and achieving greater local energy self-reliance and resilience can be started in many ways. One of the
most promising is to invite citizens to a session of energy brainstorming
and planning. This is the approach developed by Joel Schatz, formerly en-

ergy coordinator for the state of Oregon. His "Energy Futures Conference" concept has been applied in Salem, Oregon; Boulder, Colorado; and Missoula, Montana. A conference coordinator brings together local leaders, chosen both as occupants of key positions and as innovative thinkers, without regard to their initial agreement on appropriate energy policies. After a provocative evening session on the community's energy problem, a day-long session focuses on energy and contingency policy through sectoral workshops (residential, commercial, industrial, transportation). The challenge to the participants in each workshop is to assume that the community has agreed to move rapidly toward resilient systems, and to figure out how to do this. Processes have evolved for focusing this question on specific actions that can be taken during one, six, and twelve months, and on setting priorities among those actions.[48]

In practice, this process has tended to produce reasonable consensus that the hypothetical goals and actions were in fact a good idea. Accordingly, the actions recommended at the Salem conference were integrated into an energy plan sent to the City Council for approval. The Boulder conference's output went not only into the city's planning policies but also into Colorado's state energy contingency plan. A group of pro- and anti-nuclear residents even formed a coalition to improve their communication with each other, and cooperatively made a joint presentation on energy to the City Council. The Missoula conferees developed several major policy recommendations for city and county governments—spurred by the announcement, during the conference, that the City Council in Billings had just resolved to try to make their city the most energy-efficient in Montana by 1982.

A sample of the communities that have conducted their own energy analyses and from them drawn a consensus on new policy directions includes: Madison, Wisconsin; Geneva County, Alabama; Fulton, Missouri; Philadelphia, Pennsylvania; Cambridge, Massachusetts; Carbondale and Springfield, Illinois; Humboldt County and Santa Cruz, California; the Southern Tier Region of New York State. These studies broadly confirmed that most energy expenditures (eighty to ninety-five percent) leave the community to pay for energy imports; that continuing this pattern is economically impossible; and that efficiency and renewables offer an escape from the ever-worsening poverty that would otherwise occur.

Among the best examples of how to analyze and present the energy needs of a community, and how to develop a political process giving that analysis substantive form, is one of the earliest such efforts. It took place in Franklin County, the poorest county in Massachusetts: cold, cloudy, economically depressed, and almost wholly dependent on imported oil. Several years ago, a group of citizens with a thirty-thousand-dollar Department of Energy grant drew on a range of community resources and participation to analyze the county's energy future.[49]

They began with a dismal energy present. Every year, the average Franklin County household was sending out of the county more than thirteen hundred dollars to pay for energy. At an informal "town meeting" to discuss the study's findings, someone held up a bucket with a hole in it, to dramatize the drain of twenty-three million dollars per year from Franklin County, mostly to Venezuela, in 1975. That drain was the same as the total payroll of the *ten largest employers* in the county. (The total county energy import bill for all sectors was about forty-eight million dollars in 1975. By 1980 it had risen to one hundred eight million current dollars—of which fifty-two million dollars was just for households.)

The analysts next showed that if the *lowest* official forecasts of energy needs and prices in 2000 became reality, people would become four times worse off, paying over fifty-three hundred dollars per year (not counting inflation) to buy household energy from outside the county and, generally, outside the country. To keep *that* leaky bucket full, the biggest single employer in the county would have to clone itself every few years for the rest of the century. This prospect made the Chamber of Commerce and utility people blanch: the future, presented in such terms, was simply not possible.

The study group had, however, worked out what could be done instead: making the buildings heat-tight, using passive and active solar heat, running vehicles on methanol from the sustained yield of some unallocated public woodlots, and meeting electrical needs with wind or microhydro within the county. Local machine shops, with skilled workers unemployed, could make all the equipment. The cost of paying it off would be about the same as what the county was then paying for household energy— about twenty-three million dollars per year. But the leaky bucket would thereby be plugged up. The money, the jobs, the economic multiplier effects would stay in Franklin County, not go to Venezuela.

Before the 1973 oil embargo, a dollar used to circulate within the county some twenty-six times before going outside to buy an import; today, it circulates fewer than ten times. Franklin County is hemorrhaging money. A fair consensus developed, as a result of this analysis, that the only hope for economic regeneration would be to stop the bleeding by promoting local energy efficiency and self-reliant renewable supply. As a result, what was a paper study is now the Franklin County Energy Project. With various fits and starts—and considerably delayed by the sudden loss of its modest federal funding—it is starting to be implemented.[50] Once the energy problem was so presented that people could see it as *their* problem, and one not just of convenience but of economic survival, they were motivated to start solving that problem on their own. This is in the best tradition of local self-help and self-determinism. As Ronald Reagan remarked in a nationally syndicated 1979 newspaper column, the study found that

> a carefully planned transition to renewable energy sources would not be difficult, would probably yield actual increases in the local standard of living and would cut back sharply on air and water pollution. . . . I suspect quite a few communities and counties across the country are going to undertake the kind of study that the people in Franklin County have pioneered. . . . They can act in their own communities to take charge of their own future.
>
> That's a spirit worth bottling and spreading around.[51]

Occasionally an analysis whose motivation originates outside a community can still have a valuable influence within it. For example, the study *Jobs and Energy*,[52] organized by Jim Benson and others under the auspices of the Council on Economic Priorities, made important methodological advances in calculating the economic and employment benefits of meeting energy needs by greater efficiency (and a few solar measures) rather than by building two proposed nuclear plants on Long Island. This comparison had long been the subject of speculation, but had not previously been carefully analyzed. It turned out that redirecting the four-billion-dollar nuclear investment toward more cost-effective (and resilient) options would save Long Island energy users between seven and eleven billion dollars and would create ten to twelve thousand more new jobs in the two-county area than would the nuclear project.

Sometimes an energy emergency provides the spur for mobilizing community sentiment.[53] For example, when the Arab oil embargo curtailed nearly all the expected 1974 oil deliveries to the Los Angeles Department of Water and Power, the Department issued stern warnings and proposed phased restrictions on electricity use, including eventual rolling blackouts.[54] Concerned about likely layoffs, Mayor Bradley appointed a blue-ribbon panel—three representatives from business and industry, three from labor, and three from city government—who, after working almost continuously for six days, emerged with a plan which the Mayor endorsed to the City Council. It was adopted with little change and received extensive press coverage. It called for two phases of reduction in energy use in each sector, with stiff penalties for customers failing to meet targets for their sectors, but few specific uses were proscribed. Community response was overwhelming. In Phase One, the residential, commercial, and industrial sectors, targeted to save ten, twenty, and ten percent respectively, actually saved eighteen, twenty-eight, and ten. The city's total use of energy fell seventeen percent in the first two months, compared with the twelve hoped for. An eleven-percent drop occurred just in the first four days. The proposed penalties were never needed and were eventually suspended. Indeed, electricity use did not rebound to its 1973 level until 1976, suggesting that customers had not found the savings (from "good house-keeping measures," not even efficiency gains) particularly burdensome.

Buoyed by that success, a citizen's commission appointed by the Mayor, and supported by one of the federal grants given to seventeen cities for comprehensive energy management planning, devised during 1979–81 an attractive plan which the City Council is to consider in 1982. The Energy/ L.A. Action Plan is expected, during 1981–90, to turn the officially pre-dicted growth in electricity demand into a decline, save a fifth of projected demand (worth nearly half a billion dollars in 1990 alone), and create nearly ten thousand new construction jobs in the 1980s and fourteen thousand permanent jobs thereafter.[55] Economic development was a similar motive in Fresno's Project Energy Independence, a joint city/coun-ty plan expected to enrich the local economy with annual utility savings of twenty-five million dollars.[56]

These examples suggest that large numbers of people can be motivated to individual action by an obvious community problem. Giving citizens credit for maturity is often rewarded—as when the government of Nova Scotia, distressed by oil deficits, simply gave every household a check for several hundred dollars, asked that it be spent on weatherization, and de-cided that policing whether the money was so spent would cost more in money and (more importantly) in public confidence than it was worth. Most of the money *was* well spent—after all, people were themselves bur-dened by their oil bills—and at least half of the houses had been weather-ized within the first year. (Some other Canadian provinces later did even better.) Enabling people to benefit directly from actions for the communi-ty can also elicit much help: a southern school district which told students that they could have half of the money they saved by simple "energy mon-itoring" (such as turning off lights in empty rooms) reportedly had to pay them forty thousand dollars in the first year.

Some communities have found that planning against energy emergen-cies saves so much money at once that they cannot understand why they did not tap this source of revenue earlier. In 1973, for example, Dade County, Florida, disappointed with chaotic federal responses to the oil em-bargo, set up its own office of energy management. Metro-Dade County's energy management now embraces more than seventy program activities which have saved millions of tax dollars. The energy coordinator manages a county-wide reporting system of energy use and savings; identifies local energy resources; develops policies and programs to promote their use; promotes energy efficiency as a component of community economic de-velopment; strengthens the county's energy management abilities; and de-velops county-wide energy contingency plans. Already, the Fuel Manage-ment Program has increased the efficiency of forty-six hundred county vehicles, set up better accounting controls that since 1973 have saved the county more than thirteen million gallons of motor fuel, established priorities if fuel becomes scarce, and stockpiled enough fuel to run essential services through a complete cutoff of several months. The county's energy management program carefully integrates crisis management measures with efficiency and renewables programs meant to prevent crises from happening.[57] In 1981, when federal contracting for such things was cut off, county officials were developing curricula and workshops to train other local officials in this broad approach to energy preparedness.[58]

While Dade County's approach to energy resilience is not as broad or as deep as that of this book, its integration of preventive measures with crisis management measures illustrates the key concept that energy preparedness consists of much more than having a paper plan to ration gasoline. If Florida's energy supplies are seriously disrupted, Dade County—knowing how its energy is used and having procedures in place for orderly maintenance of vital services—will be better off than most other areas. County officials' experience of the value of their own programs has led to their belief, as the program's Deputy Director expressed it, that energy preparedness "is a critical issue of national security that ought to be a top priority of the United States Department of Defense."[59] Local officials are taking national needs so much to heart not only out of patriotic concern, but also because of the tangible local benefits.

Concerted action

Many communities are rediscovering that they can take significant action to create their own energy futures. Sometimes these actions seem almost a cry of joy or an exuberant competition—a celebration of people's commitment and capability. In other cases, the task has been a fight for economic survival. Whatever the motive and form, the human energy generated has been extraordinary.

Six New England states and five maritime provinces of Canada recently held a competition to save energy. Because the program was very short-term, the savings were achieved by curtailment rather than by efficiency, but the community processes revealed are illuminating. Monterey, representing Massachusetts, began its competition with a blast from a fire engine and a parade down the main street. For the next three days, encouraged by a round of social events, the people of Monterey strove to reduce their use of electricity by more than their counterparts in the ten other participating towns. The Monterey Selectmen appointed a coordinator who, with volunteers throughout town, tried to make energy saving the only thing on people's minds. One volunteer personally sewed some twelve hundred small yellow flags bearing the town's motto, "Monterey Lights the Way." The local utility took several readings before the event to establish a baseline for judging the saving—only to find that attention focused on the coming competition had already reduced electrical use by fifteen percent in the preceding month. The additional saving during the competition was fifteen and six-tenths percent—just behind the winner, St. Stephens (New Brunswick), with a seventeen and a half percent reduction.[60]

In California, the Pacific Gas & Electric Company uses oil, mostly imported, to supply about sixty percent of its summer power. To save money, PG&E offered to pay three cities ten thousand dollars each for every one percent of peak power reduction during the summer of 1980, subject to a maximum payment of one hundred thousand dollars per city. Each of the three won the maximum. One of the towns, Chico, held a seminar of two hundred businesspeople, who reported that they felt tremendous support when they observed neighboring businesses saving energy. Nine hundred schoolchildren competed for prizes for signing up the most pledges to save energy. By the end of the summer, Chico had become energy-conscious, and reduced its peak power load by seventeen percent.[61] The second town, Merced, saved over thirteen percent over the previous summer;[62] Davis, the third participant, which was more efficient (and more energy-conscious) to start with, saved over twenty-two percent.[63]

In early January of 1980, the Mayor of St. Paul, Minnesota announced with maximum fanfare that the city was about to undertake an Energy-MOBILIZATION. The announcement created a good deal of confusion. Was a mobilization the same as an audit? Was the city conscripting troops, or was this a volunteer army? A few irate citizens thought the mayor was going to come and turn down their thermostats. The Mayor's office had, however, two objectives—raising energy consciousness and collecting city-specific data—and hoped to pursue them by giving people information on energy savings and a few convincing words about how saving energy could save them money. The original concept was to do an energy "audit" in each household. "Audit" turned out to be an unfortunate word with connotations of tax collectors. So the audits became surveys, and were mailed to one hundred fifteen thousand residents and small businesses and then collected by volunteers. Better press releases and more comprehensive information converted the wary and skeptical, and the program began. To get attention and to mobilize three thousand volunteers, the Mayor closed City Hall for three days in mid-February; most city workers volunteered to be among the three thousand. Businesses fed the volunteers, donated energy information kits and prizes, staffed energy hotline telephone banks with their own experts, and donated vans to move the volunteers to their survey areas. Other firms donated computer time to process the data from the ninety-two percent of the building occupants that were contacted. By the end, St. Paul had not only the data—perhaps the most detailed energy profile in the nation—but also the community awareness and excitement needed to sustain longer-term action on what the data showed.

A year later, a Caulkmobile was still out in the residential neighborhoods with free caulk and demonstrations of how to use it. An Energy Park had been conceived and was being planned in hundreds of hours of meetings with community groups. The city was analyzing energy use in its one hundred eleven buildings. Zoning ordinances had been changed to promote energy efficiency and renewables, and to encourage fixing up old buildings rather than tearing them down. The city and the regional private utility, the Northern States Power Company, had submitted a proposal for a City Energy Resource Center and a one-stop financing center for weatherization and related measures. Since that time, the Center has been set up, and the first phase of the program is funded with six hundred and twenty-five thousand dollars in deferred loans from the utility and one million dollars in city tax-exempt bonds from St. Paul. Loans are being offered at seven percent interest, and need not be repaid until the house is sold.[64]

Fitchburg, Massachusetts has provided one of the best-known examples of mobilizing a community for rapid and extensive weatherization (as was mentioned in Chapter Fifteen). The program was backed by ACTION and several other federal antipoverty programs, most of which are now defunct. During the central three months of the program, five hundred people volunteered time—in some cases over twenty hours a week—to be trained and to help their neighbors implement low-cost/no-cost efficiency improvements. Sixty percent of the city's fourteen thousand households participated. The average program cost for materials and salaries, paid for by the federal grants, was nineteen dollars per retrofit kit. But for each household joining a workshop, almost two more were eventually weatherized by the later diffusion of the information and skills gained. Thus the average cost of weatherizing a household was much lower, for an average first-winter saving of seventy-three dollars. Those with kits saved fourteen percent of their heating oil, worth one hundred forty-six dollars per household, in the winter of 1979 alone.[65] At least twenty other communities have adapted the techniques pioneered in Fitchburg.

In some communities, volunteer neighborhood groups have organized grassroots weatherization and solar services. The three-year-old Urban Solar Energy Association in Somerville, Massachusetts is a formal organization with directors and members. Through committees it is active in tenant/landlord issues, solar access, legislative initiatives, and other issues. It provides workshops for homeowners and tenants, helps do-it-yourselfers upgrades energy professionals through its Technical Assistants/Professionals Committee, and helps community groups with educational programs and technical advice.[66]

Neighborhood energy work can be sustained even at the street level. The Rowell Energy Group in Boston was started by a Rowell Street resident, Steve Kropper, who set out to show himself and his neighbors that investing in energy saving in a triple-decker home delivers "as handsome a return as a Texas wildcatter" (an independent driller of speculative oil wells). Now, the group provides workshops on superinsulation retrofits. Kropper is planning to form a local energy services corporation to fix up buildings and share the savings with local institutions such as community libraries and churches.[67]

Some neighborhood groups have also organized energy co-ops for bulk buying of materials at wholesale cost, have replaced Tupperware™ parties with "housewarming parties" where weatherization methods are demonstrated, and have arranged block meetings to discuss energy issues.[68] The bond between people who already know each other can enable knowledge and motivation to spread quickly.[69]

The deterioration of America's urban areas over the past few decades has begun to lead public and corporate interests in sound local economies to a new convergence. The declining quality of life and rising price of energy in the cities has limited recruitment of able staff, while many cities' dwindling tax base has put pressure on corporations to pay a higher share of taxes. Some corporations have responded to these forces by supporting community programs for energy efficiency and renewables. Corporate objectives—assured supply, minimized costs, and a fair return—are at least as well served by these programs as by more traditional investments. Thus in Hartford, Connecticut, several local companies donated the services of advertising and marketing experts to help the city "sell" (successfully) an energy assistance program.[70] Volunteer advertising executives helped city officials in Portland, Oregon to develop a multi-media campaign publicizing the then-proposed Portland Energy Policy.[71] Los Angeles worked with local businesses to develop the nation's largest ride-sharing program, encouraging carpooling with special lanes and other incentives. By arrangement with the city, companies that convince employees to carpool or use mass transit can provide fewer parking spaces than local codes normally require and can use the scarce land for other, more productive purposes.[72]

Businesses also have at hand immediate opportunities for energy efficiency, and not only in their own factories—where, for example, a recent survey showed that sixty-nine percent of businesses which had installed automated energy management controls were planning to buy more of them within the next year.[73] Employee drivers of business fleets are being trained in safe, energy-conscious driving through workshop programs being offered by community colleges and by the Atlantic Richfield Company. Driver education easily saves ten percent of fleet fuel, but some businesses have reported savings as high as forty-six percent.[74] Vanpooling is another money-saver: not only in fuel (a fully loaded van gets the equivalent of a one-hundred-fifty-mpg car), but also in saved parking spaces worth about two thousand dollars per commuter.[75] Los Angeles County even provides free vans, fuel, and insurance for certain private vanpooling schemes, because the reduced traffic saves the county even more money in highway construction and maintenance, air pollution, and other public costs. Some farsighted businesses, finally, now treat energy services to their employees as a fringe benefit—cheaper to the company than high salaries, but yielding the employees a much larger increment of tax-free income, plus more comfortable houses, greater resilience against energy shocks, and good models for the neighbors to emulate. For example, Rodale Press provides its seven hundred-plus employees with a full-time staff expert who does energy surveys and provides a written report and consultation on request. Some ninety percent of eligible employees requested this service to save energy and money in their own homes.

Some remarkable examples of organized efficiency improvements have come from large corporations and bureaucracies. The Migros chain of department stores in Switzerland, for example, has systematically improved its energy efficiency by several percent per year since 1973, paying for successively costlier measures with the proceeds from savings generated by cheaper ones. The National Aeronautics and Space Administration developed in 1976 a ten-year energy-saving program which, after its first three years, had already saved three times as much as it cost, and which was expected by 1982 to have saved a cumulative total of two hundred thirty-nine million dollars, rising by over fifty million dollars per year.[76] When CalTech's Jet Propulsion Laboratory was threatened with loss of its vital energy supplies in 1973–74, ad hoc committees of practical technicians explored about a dozen possible alternatives, ranging from small hydro and wind to various solar electric systems and repowering existing diesel generators with methane from landfills or digested cow manure. Although the crisis eased before any of the proposals was acted upon, it appears that each of the concepts explored was technically feasible and that most of them would be economically attractive.[77]

Crisis response

Some communities do not have the leisure to undertake carefully planned programs of analysis and step-by-step implementation: they are suddenly thrown in off the deep end, and must improvise a way out of an instant energy crisis. The energy disruptions described in earlier chapters are still the stuff of everyday life whenever several things go wrong at the same time. In the January 1981 cold spell, for example, schools and some businesses in several eastern Massachusetts communities had to close because a storm off Algeria had sunk an LNG tanker on 28 December 1980,[78] causing Massachusetts gas companies to deplete their stockpiles when pipeline capacity proved inadequate to import gas they had stored in Pennsylvania. Such incidents remain fairly common, and the only response local officials can make is curtailment: turn down thermostats, huddle over wood stoves, shut down factories, and listen to emergency broadcasts. Yet in some communities that have none of the access to sophisticated management and resources that might be expected in Massachusetts, energy shortages have already led to remarkably effective responses.

One such instance is fairly well known: in a dispute over prices in the late autumn of 1977, the natural gas supply of Crystal City, Texas was shut off.[79] Low income and the imminence of the brief (two months) but cold Texas winter forced the townspeople to work with what materials they had. They did so well with weatherization, mesquite stoves, and simple improvised solar water heaters costing eighty-five dollars each that many are still using and indeed expanding those "stopgap" measures, reinforcing their energy independence. Thus responses developed expediently served to introduce people to energy options of which they had previously been unaware and whose economic advantages they then wished to receive routinely.

A less well known but equally impressive case comes from the San Luis Valley in southern Colorado—a sunny but cold plateau, nearly as large as Delaware, at an elevation of eight thousand feet. The traditional Hispanic community in the valley heated with firewood, cut on what they thought was their commons land from old Spanish land grants. A few years ago, a corporate landowner fenced the land and started shooting at people who tried to gather wood. The crisis was unexpected and immediate. Some of the poorest people in the United States, they could not afford to buy wood or any commercial fuel. But a few people in the community knew how to build very cheap solar greenhouses out of scrounged materials, averaging under two hundred dollars each. Through hands-on greenhouse workshops, somewhat akin to old-fashioned barn-raisings, the word spread quickly. In a few years, the valley has gone from a documented four to over eight hundred greenhouses—which not only provide most or all of the space heating but also extend the growing season from three months to year-round, greatly improving families' winter nutrition and cash flow. Now there are solar trailers, a solar Post Office, even a solar mortuary. Baskin & Robbins has installed a high-technology solar system on its ice-cream parlor, and other renewable sources are starting to spread. Wind machines are springing up, and some farmers are building an ethanol plant fed with cull potatoes and barley washings and powered by geothermal process heat. The valley is on its way to energy self-reliance because, under the pressure of a supply interruption, people found they were too poor to use anything but renewables.[80]

Tools for such local action are becoming widely available. There have been two national conferences on community renewable energy systems.[81] Publishers have responded to the growing public interest by releasing books of case studies,[82] how-to books,[83] guides to county energy analysis,[84] indices to local resources,[85] technical compendia on regional renewable resource bases,[86] and introductions to community planning for resilience.[87] Among the most valuable ways of putting tools in people's hands has been the free Department of Energy periodical *The Energy Consumer*, whose special issues—on such subjects as solar energy,[88] alcohol fuels,[89] community energy programs,[90] and energy preparedness[91]—include comprehensive state-by-state indices of key people and programs to help local action. In 1981, unfortunately, publication of *The Energy Consumer* and public distribution of its back issues were suspended and its staff was disbanded, so this effective source of self-help information was lost.

Meanwhile, however, several concerned citizens have developed techniques for involving community leaders in efficiency-and-renewables mobilizations on the lines described above. In particular, Fran Koster, previously a prime mover in the Franklin County Energy Project and then director of the Tennessee Valley Authority's solar programs, has conducted community energy training sessions.[92] Alec Jenkins, in his capacity as a Division Chairman of the American Section of the International Solar Energy Society (AS/ISES), has organized several programs to explore ways in which communities can anticipate and prevent energy shortages through voluntary "mobilization."[93] Jenkins, Koster, and their associates are intent on evolving a technology of community transformation, a process and a set of tools by which people and their institutions can move rapidly and with certainty to develop local energy resilience. They hope to coordinate this work with the programs already undertaken by some major industries trying to improve their own energy resilience.

What local governments can do

Once a community-based process has determined that a more efficient and renewable energy system will save money and vulnerability, and there is a consensus in favor of moving rapidly to implement such a policy, what should be done next? Some means of implementation are probably beyond the scope of a locality. Federal tax and price subsidies, for example, or even state regulation of utility tariffs, are usually beyond local control,[94] though not immune to local influence. But many policies that can either encourage or discourage a more resilient energy system are already made at a local level, and can be systematically examined to ensure that they are acting in the desired direction.

New buildings Communities enacted energy-conscious building codes before states or the federal government took much interest in the subject. The best-known early example is the code which Davis, California developed in 1974 and adopted in 1975—the nation's first comprehensive energy-saving code designed, with active participation by many citizens, for a particular microclimate.[95] A careful economic-engineering analysis which showed that any extra cost of compliance would pay back within three years at energy prices far below today's. Together with land use and retrofit ordinances, the code has helped Davis to save thirty percent of all energy used in buildings compared with the 1973 level, even though the population has meanwhile increased seven percent. Further improvements and new initiatives are continuing.[96] Partly through the example set by Davis, the California Energy Commission was able to gather enough support to enact in 1978 a building standard for new houses which, compared to 1975 norms, saved half the energy and, over thirty years, would save householders between eight and seventeen thousand dollars in net costs. But as technologies evolved and energy prices rose, even that standard soon became too lax. In July 1982, revised standards will reduce energy use in new houses by a further sixty percent. (The standards specify performance, and provide several prescriptive options for achieving that performance in each of sixteen climatic zones, so that builders do not have to do elaborate calculations themselves.) The economics are very attractive: in mild San Diego, for example, the buyer of a passive solar house meeting the new standard will pay an extra hundred dollars down and fifty-three dollars on the annual mortgage bill, but will receive a state tax credit (for the south-facing glazing) of one hundred seventy dollars plus a first-year fuel saving of about fifty dollars.[97]

Existing buildings Local governments have authority to require the upgrading and retrofit of existing buildings in the public interest. In 1979, the City Council of Portland, Oregon adopted a retrofit ordinance meant to reduce the city's energy use by thirty percent by 1995, requiring that houses sold in or after 1984 be brought up to specific efficiency standards. In 1980, several California communities passed similar requirements to take effect sooner. Eugene, Oregon followed in 1981 with an ordinance requiring that all housing be brought up to a stated standard by 1985, with compliance checked whenever there is a change in the electrical service.[98] By September 1981, twelve percent of California's population lived in jurisdictions which had adopted or were considering retrofit ordinances. The Local Government Commission of California's SolarCal Council (a Governor's advisory group which develops and advances innovative programs for faster solar implementation) has published a handbook on the preparation and adoptions of such rules. The California Energy Commission estimates that retrofits could save California households half a billion dollars per year in 1985 and by 2000.[99]

Retrofit ordinances usually include such measures as attic insulation, caulking, weatherstripping, blankets for water heaters, flow restrictors, duct insulation, hot water line insulation, and sometimes shading. They usually require compliance at time of sale; some require it within ten years in any event. Many require on-site inspection: the Davis checklist takes one person a total of about fifteen minutes. Some ordinances place a limit on costs (for example, one-half to one percent of the house's sale price), so that lower-income people do not have to spend as much as higher-income people. Some, like a state law in Minnesota, are aimed especially at ensuring that rented housing, which is often occupied by low-income people with little control over it, is retrofitted.

Retrofit ordinances are only part of a comprehensive program. Eugene, for example, couples retrofit requirements with low-interest financing. New York has a "truth-in-renting" law requiring that prospective renters be entitled to inspect past utility bills. Some localities are considering house efficiency labeling—perhaps a nominal "gallons-per-year" rating shown on the For Sale or For Rent sign.[100]

Programs to guard against fraud and ensure quality control are also very important. Simple methods which can be quite effective include:

- a toll-free number from which one can ascertain if there are any complaints on record against a contractor, including any previous incarnations in which that contractor might have done business;
- a periodically published survey of performance and complaints, compiled by a knowledgeable person at a local or state consumer affairs agency (knowledge that such a survey will be published tends to deter shoddy work);
- a provision in financing contracts that the contractor is not entitled to payment for labor until a competent inspector of the buyer's choice has found that the work was indeed properly done;
- consumer education programs to increase sophistication in what to look for; and
- ways for people to advise each other of their experiences.

Information feedback appears to be the cheapest form of protection, though others may also be needed.

Land use planning   Local governments have reflected energy concerns in land use controls in several ways:[101]

- making a policy statement on energy, as fifty-five cities and fourteen counties in California have already done;[102]

- including an energy element in a comprehensive master plan;
- removing or changing land use regulations which hinder energy efficiency or development of renewables;
- providing incentives;
- mandating energy-efficient development through subdivision or other ordinances; and
- providing a procedure for protecting solar access for existing buildings and for new buildings in developed areas.

Among California cities and counties surveyed in 1981, energy-saving land use policies were already in place in twenty-two percent and pending in twenty-eight percent; solar access in new subdivisions was protected in twenty-four percent and pending in twenty-eight percent; and solar orientation was ensured by subdivision layout policies in thirty-three percent and about to be in a further twenty percent.[103] Some jurisdictions are even more advanced: New Mexico, for example, is the first state to have protected solar access by state law.

Many older types of local ordinances restrict or forbid—often unintentionally—energy-efficient building designs and passive solar measures. Davis, California, for example, had to change its ordinances to allow clotheslines and the more flexible design of overhangs for summer shading. Davis and some other communities permit narrower streets to reduce the energy needed for materials and construction; encourage bicycling and the planting of trees to reduce summer overheating; and facilitate earth-sheltered buildings.[104] Richmond, British Columbia adopted a zoning bylaw in 1980 which allows builders of multi-family developments to increase housing densities by ten to fifteen percent if a certain fraction of the buildings' energy is supplied renewably.[105] Pitkin County, Colorado has policies to encourage proper building orientation, to protect solar access, and to make some local automobile traffic unnecessary.[106] Some communities judge alternative development proposals competitively according to their energy efficiency or use of renewables, and allow a density bonus of up to one-fourth for renewable energy supply.[107] Nearly four-fifths of California communities are implementing bicycle circulation systems; three-fifths, dial-a-ride systems and synchronized traffic signals.[108] Mixed zoning, so that people can walk to shopping districts and jobs or can raise food around or between houses or other buildings, is also a popular way to reduce transportation needs. And longer-term prevention of unthinking sprawl can reduce a community's energy needs by as much as one-half.[109]

Regulation   Mandatory action, such as a retrofit ordinance, is a community's trump card. Certainly, removal of institutional barriers to voluntary action and provision of ample information, capital, and choice of services can and should come first. But some communities, after careful economic assessments, have chosen also to use their innate powers to protect public health, as they do in present building and zoning regulations, to require certain efficiency or renewable energy actions. Such regulatory actions can arouse mixed reactions within the solar community. But they are a part of the energy picture, an available policy option, that cannot be ignored.

For example, several California communities have passed ordinances requiring solar water heating in new construction.[110] The first, a bipartisan measure passed in San Diego County in 1978, required solar water heating instead of electric ones in new all-electric buildings put up in unincorporated areas, and was extended to all areas of the county in 1980. It appears to have helped sustain a healthy pattern of development for the local solar industry, providing enough market stability for one manufacturer to install automated machinery for making collector boxes,[111] and has held solar prices steady during 1978–81. Kauai County, Hawaii, has a similar requirement for solar water heaters in new residences.[112] Soldiers Grove, Wisconsin, which relocated out of a flood plain and in the process made itself solar-based and energy-efficient, requires that new non-residential buildings be at least half solar-heated.[113] New Jersey's Energy Commission has asked the Township of Washington to revise its local zoning and site ordinances to require proper solar building orientation and the use of solar water heaters in new construction.[114] Similar ordinances are often a local part of larger energy programs which include state tax incentives, consumer protection, utility services, and public information.[115] In some instances, abatement of air or water pollution may also be part of efficiency and renewable energy development plans.[116]

Renewable energy development   Under a unique venture guided by local government and funded by private investors, Oceanside, California has begun leasing solar systems to energy consumers via its Municipal Solar and Conservation Utility. The customers pay a small deposit; city-approved dealers own and maintain the devices. Fifty-five percent of the customers' municipal utility bills qualify for the state solar tax credit, which is available for privately purchased equipment or for equipment leased through a municipal solar utility. Although Oceanside is a small city, the three leading syndicates initially approved under the program have capitalized it with twenty million dollars—perhaps the nation's largest concentration of capital for solar installations. The leasing companies raised the money by marketing investment packages in California and elsewhere. The city charges a ten percent fee on gross revenues collected. After the first thousand installations, the program will generate a net revenue stream for the city.[117]

Fairfield, California negotiated as part of its economic development program the move of a semiconductor plant to its area. At the last minute, however, the deal collapsed when the Pacific Gas & Electric Company would not commit the needed power. To avoid a repetition, Fairfield is developing a windfarm and a municipal wind utility, and is opening industrial parks powered by cogeneration. In coordination with neighboring communities, Fairfield has been leasing windfarm sites and negotiating machine deliveries. The city is now seeking to attract wind-machine manufacturers to locate in the city.[118]

In sunny Los Angeles, whose electricity is generated mainly from oil (a main contributor to smog, acid fog, and high utility rates), photovoltaics are potentially attractive.[119] An aerial study showed that solar cells on no more than half of the available south-facing roofs in the San Fernando Valley could supply over half of the present (inefficiently used) annual electric needs of that sixty-five-square-mile area.[120] (Similar studies have been done in such disparate areas as Denver and several Swedish cities, with results at least as encouraging.) Certain time-of-day features of the electricity tariff would make solar electricity even more valuable. Los Angeles has become a center for research and development on solar cells, fledgling manufacturers are locating there, and the Mayor is a strong supporter of solar energy. The Municipal Solar Utility study at Oceanside[121] and an analysis of third-party financing for the San Diego area[122] have shown that third-party financing of distributed systems is quite plausible. These ingredients led the then Energy Coordinator of Los Angeles, Mark Braly, to propose a photovoltaic buyers' cooperative to help reduce purchase prices.[123] As photovoltaic prices drop over the next few years (Appendix Two), these building blocks for a solar Los Angeles may well be picked up.

Speeded by these and similar local initiatives, California cities and counties reported in 1981 that energy production plans were active or pending for solar heating in forty-two percent of their jurisdictions, methane from sewage in twenty-three percent, small hydro in eighteen percent, windpower and alcohol fuels in seventeen percent, biomass fuel in at least fourteen percent, methane from landfills in thirteen percent, cogeneration or geothermal in ten percent, and district heating in eight percent.[124] The jigsaw of diverse, dispersed, renewable energy sources is beginning to fit itself together in California as in many other states. The examples in this chapter include perhaps a disproportionate number of California examples; but that is largely because the state government has not only encouraged but surveyed and described these local efforts as a guide and example to communities that have not yet grasped the extent of their own energy opportunities.

Some unique partnerships are also emerging between local governments and private industry. For example, St. Paul, Minnesota is developing a mixed residential/business/industrial park of one hundred fifty-five acres, planned as a model of a energy-efficient urban neighborhood. It is to be built by the city and Control Data Corporation, which has committed eighteen million dollars to the project. Energy management systems, daylighting, earth sheltering (a popular Minnesota development), and super-insulation will facilitate the use of various active and passive solar systems and district heating. The park's theme and reduced costs are expected to attract energy-related firms and to create about six thousand new jobs.[125]

Soft-energy industrial development is not only the prerogative of industrialists and governments. In Colton, near San Bernadino, California, Valerie Pope Ludlum and several other welfare mothers bootstrapped a small federal grant into a multi-million-dollar-per-year business, hiring neighborhood youth to build and install weatherization and solar equipment. Under this program, the economic and security benefits of using that equipment, and the jobs and incomes that flow from making and selling it, remain in the Black community—a striking example of the power of locally made, locally usable energy technologies as a tool for community development.

Financing

Excellent guides to new approaches for financing energy efficiency and renewable sources have been published.[126] Investor-owned and public utilities, insurance companies, banks, industries, and private investors are increasingly eager participants, seeking the high rates of return or the reductions in their own risks: Denver banks started to give solar loans after Susan Carpenter pointed out that otherwise many people's utility bills would exceed their mortgage payments, and the bankers would get stuck with houses nobody could afford to live in.

Municipal programs   Minneapolis, Minnesota raised two and three-quarters million dollars privately through local banks to start training and financing for homeowner weatherization programs. A local utility, Minnegasco, handles the paperwork through its billing system, and gives participants an incentive bonus of ten percent of the loan, up to a hundred dollars. The ten-year loans cost eleven percent per year, or one point above the city's cost of capital. The second phase of the "Energy Bank" program will begin in summer of 1982 with the sale of nearly seven million dollars in municipal bonds through an underwriter.[127]

To ensure that the Energy Bank is known and used throughout the city, the Minneapolis Energy Coordination office sends trained organizers into areas, each of about sixty blocks, to locate a key person on each block who will take responsibility for being the "inviter" who spreads the word. The "inviters" are trained in weatherization and how to sign up their neighbors. An all-day Saturday workshop is scheduled in each five- or ten-block area with about seventy-five invitees. After morning instruction, these recruits go home and do a self-audit, then come back by lunchtime with a list of needed materials (typically worth about forty dollars), which Minnegasco then provides at no cost. The participants then return home and install the materials, advised by a roving "house doctor" from the city's Energy Office. People who want a more extensive building treatment (in the range of several hundred to several thousand dollars) are visited by a Minnegasco specialist who offers an Energy Bank loan. This process has become a social event, with a participation rate of about half the households in each neighborhood—a target which the "inviters" strive for. In about ten workshops, the neighborhood is weatherized. The five thousand blocks of Minneapolis should thus be weatherized, and residential energy use reduced by thirty percent, by 1985. Administrative costs, now covered partly by an Innovation Grant from the federal Department of Housing and Urban Development, will be fully covered by combining the neighborhood programs into the Residential Conservation Service currently carried on by Minnegasco, which has operated at higher costs and with less success than the city's program.

Palo Alto, California, through its municipal utility, is operating a solar loan program with eight percent annual interest, no down payment, and a payback period of five to ten years. The utility's reserves provided six hundred fifty thousand dollars of initial capital to get the program running. That process took about three months, and the first loans were issued in eight months—about a third of the time expected. The reserves will be replenished and the loan program expanded through tax-free municipal revenue bonds, so that fifteen thousand installations can be made at the rate of ten per week. The loans cover the entire bid cost of each system up to thirty-five hundred dollars each. The city expects the program to stimulate the private financing and installation of another fifteen hundred systems. The loan program, which grew out of a study by six local governments of the feasibility of a municipal solar utility, includes consumer protection measures and system design and installation standards, developed in workshops with seventy-six local businesses before loans were issued.[128] Altogether, seven California cities, starting with Santa Clara, have already set up municipal solar utilities. California's Alternative Energy Source Financing Authority, a new state agency, offers further options.

Utility financing Years ago, Michigan Consolidated Gas Company loaned its customers money to insulate over a hundred thousand roofs around Detroit, because it was cheaper, even then, to insulate than to find more gas. Heating oil dealers in parts of Canada and New England have similar programs for similar reasons. In the past few years, hard-pressed electric utilities—typically driven to borrowing to pay dividends—have discovered the economic advantages of efficiency loans. Since efficiency investments typically decrease both the capital intensity and the payback time of energy investments by about three- to tenfold compared to building new power plants, their combined effect is to reduce the need for investment capital by about ten- to a hundredfold. This can largely or wholly eliminate the need to go to Wall Street for costly new capital to supplement that which is generated internally (for investor-owned utilities, somewhat over two billion dollars per year). Properly arranged loans can thus provide enormous cash flow advantages for utilities while eliminating the capital burden on their customers.[129] For this reason, by 1980 upwards of forty percent of U.S. generating capacity belonged to utilities that were doing or about to do efficiency loans (though often not in the most advantageous way). Many, especially on the West Coast, even loan at zero interest, and do not require repayments to start for ten years or until the sale of the house.[130]

There are many variations on this theme. Utilities in Texas, Arizona, Florida, and Minnesota now buy "saved power" from their customers just as if it were cogenerated or renewably generated power: a customer, for example, who is getting a more efficient appliance (of certain specified kinds) receives a voucher worth as much money as the purchase saves the utility. (Ideally, such a voucher should be applicable to the purchase "up front," not just to the utility bill later.) William Appel, bond counsel in Seattle, has proposed that utilities could also buy "peak load easements," whereby building proprietors undertake not to use more than a certain amount of peak power. In principle, such easements, so far as state real property law permits, could become a marketable commodity which a utility could use in its own resource planning or which industries could buy and sell, much as abatements of air pollution are marketed today.

More conventional programs already abound. The Tennesseee Valley Authority has an extensive program of financing and installing efficiency and solar measures. Some utilities give away weatherization materials because doing so saves them so much money. The Pacific Gas & Electric Company, among others, finances the dozen most cost-effective efficiency measures without requiring an energy audit. Zero-interest loans, available for further measures after audit, are repaid over fifty or a hundred months, depending on tax credit treatment. Utilities typically report that efficiency improvements cost them three to ten times less than new supply—somewhat worse than the best-managed programs, whose margins of advantage are generally ten- to a hundredfold, but still an excellent buy.

Third-party financing   This traditional way of buying "hard technologies" has been made more attractive for dispersed systems by 1981 tax law changes. Many new energy management/shared-saving systems, and solar devices in commercial and industrial buildings, are now being financed by a new entrepreneurial system. Limited partners who seek both cash flow and tax shelters team up with a general partner who manages the investment and with project developers and operators (these may also be the general partner). For example, the National Conservation Corporation obtains third-party financing for a mass of individual projects. The company identifies an unexploited market in energy saving which will save somebody money. It can negotiate with a utility, under independent arbitration, to determine how energy can be saved, how much, at what cost, and at what financial saving to the utility. Once the company reaches agreement with the utility (approved by the state regulatory commission), the company makes audits and installs efficiency improvements free of charge, then gets repaid by the utility out of its own monetary savings until the company's investors have been paid off. All parties—shareholders, ratepayers, and building occupants—thereby benefit; the financial benefit is split among them. National Conservation has started such a pilot program in a thousand homes in New Jersey, with completion scheduled for mid-1982.[131] Some energy-intensive industries are already seeking similar ways to get relatively cheap energy by making or financing energy-saving investments and splitting the savings either with the building owners directly or with the utility.

Energy services delivery

A few years ago, one of the recognized barriers to building energy resilience was the lack of "outreach"—information on what opportunities were available and help in implementing them. The above examples, and the success of specialized "energy management companies" (such as Energy Clinic, Inc.), "house doctors," and other private services, suggest that "outreach" is rapidly emerging as a profitable venture. It also appears to be focusing less on simply providing information and more on delivering a complete "packaged" service to reduce the "hassle factor" of making detailed arrangements to choose, install, and check unfamiliar technologies. Some such services are also emerging in the public sector, such as Portland Energy Conservation, Inc. (PECI), established by the city of Portland, Oregon as a one-stop "efficiency shopping center" for businesses and householders.

An even simpler and more fundamental approach is beginning to change profoundly the nature of the utility business. Its premise is that people want energy services such as comfort, light, and mobility, rather than electricity, oil, or natural gas. Consequently, those services can be sold directly by an Energy Service Corporation, which would take responsibility for determining the cheapest method of providing them. If conventional utilities do not evolve in this direction, they can expect increasing competition from private firms which cater specifically to customers' exact needs and which have no innate preference for supplying more energy rather than improving energy productivity.[132]

Other institutional innovations are bound to emerge to meet the need of fixing up and solarizing our nation's stock of buildings and equipment, just as they have emerged in the past when it became necessary to change large capital stocks relatively quickly. For example, decades ago many of our cities, such as Los Angeles, changed the voltage or frequency of their electrical system. Metropolitan Toronto and Montréal did it with fleets of specially equipped vans which retrofitted each neighborhood in turn: one van contained hundreds of clocks from which householders could choose replacements to swap for their clocks designed to run at the old frequency; another contained a machine shop for rewinding motors and rebuilding controls; all were staffed by resourceful people who had used the vans to clean up after the Normandy invasion. Other technical and social innovations enabled Holland to switch many boilers from oil and coal to Groningen natural gas; enabled Britain to switch, over a decade or less, to North Sea gas and smokeless fuel, and in about a year to decimal coinage; enabled Sweden to switch to right-hand driving during a single night in 1967 (the main expense was recutting the bus doors); and are today enabling Sweden to change its cities from single-building oil furnaces to district heating in about ten years. These and other examples of how a society can organize itself for constructive change offer rich lessons for the changes that can, in the coming decades, create energy security for America.

Resilience begins at home

The foregoing sections have shown why *community-based action is the fastest and surest way to build a resilient energy system.* Support for such local analysis and action—reinforcement of what is already a rapidly growing national trend—is our most important recommendation.

This chapter has described the peculiar vividness and social effectiveness of efficiency-and-renewables programs built by local institutions with local resources to respond to local needs. (Readers are urged to communicate other such examples to us.) It has shown, too, how local governments—state, county, and municipal—have extensive powers and opportunities to hasten the transition to a more efficient, diverse, dispersed, renewable, hence resilient energy system. But governments at any scale are not the only or even necessarily the most important ingredient of that transition. A multitude of organizations—women's groups, labor unions, churches, professional societies, farm groups, business and fraternal groups, specialized societies—are already emerging as leaders in this creation of a more lasting basis for national security. The Daughters of the American Revolution have written and sponsored an excellent program of high school assemblies dealing with the need for energy efficiency and appropriate renewables. The League of Women Voters has taken a leadership role in informing public opinion. Chambers of Commerce, environmental groups, physicians, Rotaries, many religious groups, several key unions—all are now working, perhaps for different reasons, for a common goal in energy policy: one that can transform vulnerability into resilience.

A danger inherent in any issue of public policy, debated in the national political arena, is that people will suppose that answers must come only, or mainly, from governments—forgetting that it is the people who *are* the government. Too much emphasis on what governments can do can sap people's impulse to do for themselves. Government programs can help, but above all they must not hinder—logistically, economically, or psychologically. The Fitchburg program would not have worked if "laid on people" by outsiders from Washington. It worked because, having cut some crucial pieces of red tape, the Washington initiators went home and left the local people to get on with the job. No government program, even at a state level, could have brought to every sizeable town in Montana the depth of information and action that the Local Energy Organizers (LEOs) of the Alternative Energy Resources Organization, a low-budget private group, have done—nor commanded the same trust. Nobody but neighborhood people in the Bronx could have made the Frontier Project and the People's Development Corporation a reality. The personal energies, the ideological diversity, and the sense of self-reliance that have made hundreds of such projects blossom across the nation are precious resources. They can be nurtured, but they must not be stifled, homogenized, or robbed of their self-respect.

The remarkably rapid reorientation of American energy development in the past few years has taken place not reluctantly through cajoling by federal leadership, but eagerly and despite federal obstruction. It reflects the wisdom of countless individual citizens who are concerned about the cost and insecurity of their own energy supplies: in aggregate, the supplies that fuel the nation. It reveals their ingenuity and commitment in solving that problem with the means at hand. These assets can be harnessed, and the transition can be greatly smoothed and speeded, by governments at all levels. This will require sensitivity to local needs, and a philosophy of encouraging grassroots initiatives rather than imposing requirements from afar. It will require observance of Lao-tse's remark two and a half millenia ago:

Leaders are best when people scarcely know they exist,
not so good when people obey and acclaim them,

worst when people despise them.
Fail to honor people, they fail to honor you.
But of good leaders who talk little,
when their work is done, their task fulfilled,
the people will all say: "We did this ourselves."[133]

Harnessing that kind of leadership can yield a great reward: a sustainable foundation for national prosperity; an energy system that contributes to that prosperity and to preparedness, rather than sapping them; and a tangible basis for regaining a sense of security in our lives and freedoms.

Choosing a more resilient energy future and then making that vision into a reality will not be easy. It will only be easier than not doing it. It is pragmatically achievable; but it will take trial, error, and hard work. It is presented here for the consideration of our fellow citizens in the spirit in which the physicist Theodore Taylor—a nuclear bomb designer turned solar designer and community energy organizer—recently remarked that it is better to strive with all our hearts to achieve a future that may seem too good to be true than to continue to drift towards one that is too dreadful to contemplate.[134]

Appendix One
Scale Issues

Chapter Fourteen summarized the conclusion that if all relevant economic factors are taken into account, the cost of supplying energy services to relatively dispersed users—that is, to most users—can be minimized by building energy supply systems on a relatively small scale. This appendix outlines the technical basis for that finding.

Electrical supply in the 1970s accounted for two-thirds or more of the capital invested in the U.S. energy sector and in federal energy research and development. (By 1981 it accounted for about a third of the former and over three-fourths of the latter.)[1] Better data on scale effects are available for electric than for other energy systems. For both these reasons, the examples in this appendix are mainly (though not exclusively) electrical, even though this form of energy accounts for only twelve percent of U.S. delivered energy and for eight percent of current U.S. delivered energy needs.[2] Similar arguments apply to other energy forms, to other classes of energy technologies, and probably to at least some ranges of unit size outside the span to which most of the data directly apply.

Doctrinaire belief in economies of scale—the bigger, the cheaper per unit—has long dominated energy investment decisions, especially in the electric utility industry. This belief made the capacity of the largest turbogenerators, for example, double every six and a half years through a size range of over ten thousandfold.[3] Since the total capacity of the electric grid doubled slightly more slowly (about every seven years until the 1970s), this meant that the physical centralization of generating electricity steadily increased.

Indeed, ever since the world's first central power station was commissioned in 1882 at Appleton, Wisconsin, the scale of all kinds of electrical generating and transmission components has grown at a rate which, until the past decade, has been remarkably inexorable and consistent. This trend contributed, until about the 1960s, to real economic savings in the cost of new power stations (Figure A.1). But as the stations got bigger, they also moved farther from their customers, making grid failures a more important source of blackouts than power plant failures and introducing the new types of control and grid-stability problems described in Chapter Ten. In 1900, sixty percent of the nation's electricity was generated on-

Figure A.1 Evolution of U.S. central electric technology (maximum generator size and maximum transmission voltage) and of average delivered electricity price (1968 dollars)

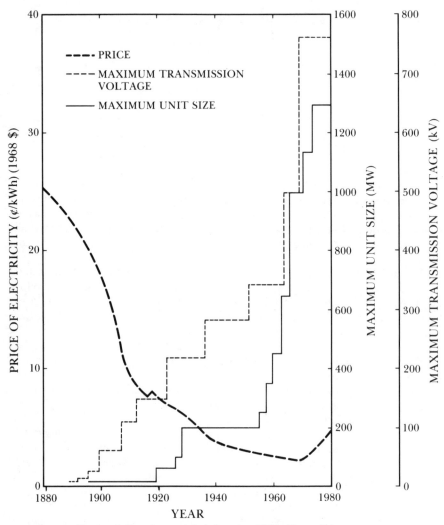

SOURCE: Economic Regulatory Administration 1981: Figure 2.1.

site. By 1920, the portion had fallen to twenty percent. Today it has bottomed out at approximately four percent and is beginning to rise again as traditional economies of scale reverse themselves.

Figure A.1 illustrates the relentless growth of scale in electrical supply equipment over the past century. The largest generating unit produced an output of only a thirteenth of a megawatt in the earliest days of pressure-staging turbines.[4]

By 1903, the biggest generators produced five megawatts. By 1930, engineering advances had raised the maximum size to two hundred megawatts, where it stayed for more than twenty-five years. It then rose rapidly to about thirteen hundred megawatts by the late 1970s—though, as we shall note below, it is far from clear that the increase from two hundred megawatts was economically worthwhile. Maximum steam pressures, too, rose from two thousand pounds per square inch in the 1940s to over five thousand by the 1960s, then fell back to about two thousand four hundred as it became "clear that some of these technological trends had been extrapolated prematurely."[5] And as generating units became larger, more units were clustered at a single site. This trend led the average size of power plants to increase two-thirds faster, during 1938–57, than the average size of the generating units in those plants.[6]

Maximum transmission voltages also rose more or less exponentially during the hundred-year history of central electrification, from a few kilovolts (thousands of volts) in the 1800s to seven hundred sixty-five kilovolts in the late 1960s. (Experimental lines in the megavolt—million-volt—range are encountering such difficulties that seven hundred sixty-five kilovolts may represent a saturation level.) The increased voltage offered, at least at first, considerable economies, since electricity "can be transmitted over a seven-hundred-sixty-five-kilovolt line for three hundred miles as effectively as over a one-hundred-thirty-eight-kilovolt line for ten miles."[7] This trend significantly promoted concentration of utility ownership and made possible the siting of power plants hundreds of miles from their loads.

It is widely accepted in the utility industry today that many of these technical developments have gone about as far as present technology permits (and in some cases further). Enormous increases of scale which were pursued more or less blindly—as if the size of anything could keep on doubling indefinitely—are now slackening. But those increases are normally examined only from the narrow standpoint of engineering feasibility for a single plant, not in the broader context of whether they improve the economics of building and operating the *whole* electrical system. In this wider perspective, might not the increases of scale have gone, not just up to, but well beyond an optimal level? An answer to this question may lie in a list of the effects which utilities considered when they ordered ever-larger components and plants—and the more numerous and important effects which they did not consider but should have.

Direct construction costs

Claimed economies of scale in direct construction costs arise mainly from two factors. First, in large projects, the fixed costs—those of setting up a project regardless of its size—become small relative to the variable costs—those which are proportional to size. Total costs per unit of capacity should thus become smaller at large sizes as the fixed costs are diluted. Second, the costs of the materials and labor needed to build anything depend in part on geometrical relationships: for example, the cost of building a vessel depends mainly on its surface area, while its capacity depends mainly on its volume. Since volume increases more rapidly with size than does surface area, a classical rule of thumb holds that for chemical plants, power stations, and so forth, cost per unit of capacity tends to rise only as approximately the six-tenths power of plant size,[8] so that doubled capacity increases total cost by only about half. But in practice this geometrical saving is mostly exhausted by the time a power plant is as big as a hundred megawatts, and becomes at best trivial above a few hundred megawatts.[9]

Several reasons for this departure from the industry's expectation of unlimited economies of scale can be readily identified. First, a quarter or more of the total construction cost of large projects is the interest paid on construction capital before commissioning. "Economy of scale is nonexistent in interest rates":[10] bankers charge essentially the same interest rate on a large loan as a smaller one, so as interest becomes a larger component of total construction cost, the "scaling exponent" of total cost should rise from six-tenths toward seven- or eight-tenths or more. This reduces the savings from larger sizes. Longer construction times, considered separately below, intensify this effect because interest payments increase both in absolute size and as a fraction of total costs.

Second, building large plants may "involve more complexity, greater precision, smaller margins of error, and new engineering problems" compared to building smaller plants.[11] It may even introduce wholly new designs and requirements. Thus the increase in pressures and temperatures accompanying the modern shift from subcritical to supercritical steam conditions made the specifications on coal plants far more stringent. As nuclear plants became larger, they lost the ability to remove their post-shutdown decay heat passively by natural convection of their cooling water after shutdown. They therefore developed new potential accident modes not characteristic of small plants, requiring new safety analyses and devices to ensure active cooling.

Larger facilities also tend to need more onsite fabrication. This method of construction is costlier and more prone to error than prefabrication of subsystems that can be transported whole to the site. And large plants may require "custom design and custom construction. In these cases," remarks the former Chairman of Con Ed, "a consequent increase in the eighty percent of the plant costs represented by field labor and overhead—most of which are time dependent—make[s] the total cost of a larger plant comparable to an equivalent number of smaller facilities"[12] —that is, it eliminates net economies of scale.

Another implication of this requirement for more or less custom-building large plants is that they cannot benefit significantly from economies of mass production. In contrast, with smaller units "it becomes possible to standardize a design and replicate a large number of identical units." According to a senior official of the [U.S.] General Electric Company, "this opens up the possibility of a new dimension in scale economy" which "may be of considerable significance."[13] The saving from mass production can so outweigh traditional scale economies in construction that the optimal turbogenerator size would be the *smallest,* not the largest, that can be made for specified steam conditions, opening up "an entirely new and profoundly different avenue for reducing the capital cost of generating capacity."[14]

The possible magnitude of cost savings from mass production can be illustrated by a simple analogy. Mass-produced car engines cost only a few dollars per kilowatt of shaftpower, while the engines that drive power stations cost hundreds of dollars per kilowatt. Car engines could be made as durable as power-plant prime movers at an extra cost that is very much smaller than their initial cost difference. For equivalent durability, the remaining net saving from mass production would be at least tenfold. This is not to say that power plants should be replaced with large numbers of car engines; but it does give some idea of the potential savings which custom-built large devices inevitably forego.

The combined result of these phenomena (except perhaps for mass production, which is seldom relevant at the large unit sizes considered) is revealed by an exhaustive statistical analysis of the entire body of U.S. experience with commercial coal and nuclear power stations.[15] For nuclear plants, the scale exponent is not six-tenths as hoped but rather exactly eight-tenths. As a result, the actual cost data show that doubling the size of a nuclear plant reduces its direct construction cost per installed kilowatt by only thirteen percent, rather than by the twenty to thirty percent *assumed* in all industry and government cost studies. (Even the existence of the decline is also statistically less certain than that of most of the other explanatory variables.) As will be mentioned below, construction time also increases with unit size, and the resulting extra interest costs decrease the apparent cost saving of thirteen percent with doubled capacity to only ten percent. While not trivial, a ten percent saving is two or three times smaller than was assumed in the official studies which sought to show that nuclear power is attractive.[16] Those studies, on close examination, proved to be only theoretical; they ignored the real data.

Coal plants show an even smaller economy of scale in construction costs. Although it is normally presumed that doubled size reduces cost per kilowatt by ten to fifteen percent, there is in fact *no* statistically significant correlation between size and cost. At most, there might be (at only eighty-two percent statistical significance) a gross cost saving of three percent—reduced to only two percent net saving by the longer construction time.[17]

Operating costs

The money saved by building a bigger plant may be more than made up by the extra costs of operating it routinely or of repairing it when it fails. The following four categories of scale effects are concerned with running costs. (Later categories consider broader system effects which raise the cost of delivering the energy sent out by the plant, or the cost and risk of financing the project, or the cost of doing separately some other energy task which, in an integrated project design, could be done jointly.)

Although no detailed data are yet available on operating and maintenance costs as a function of unit size, it is clear from operating experience with all kinds of power stations that larger ones tend to have more numerous and complex failure modes, longer downtime, more difficult repairs, higher training and equipment costs for maintenance, higher carrying charges on spare parts inventories, and higher unit costs of spare parts made in smaller production runs. Conversely, there "may be a reduction in maintenance personnel [per kilowatt] for smaller units because of their higher reliability"[18] (discussed further below). Large units may be more able to attract and equip the specialized maintenance cadres they require, but may also become disconcertingly more vulnerable to those cadres' whims, as noted in Chapter Four.

A survey of the general problem of repairing large industrial plants notes that high interest rates have "made it more important than ever to keep plants operating," and the high cost of financing inventories has forced manufacturers to live within tight production schedules: any equipment breakdown is bound to anger customers and likely to cost a company business. Yet while costly money has increased the pressure to avoid breakdowns, it has also made them more likely. Many companies believe they are forced to cut corners when building new plants, either by eliminating backup equipment or going without spare capacity. "It used to be that you'd install a spare pump at every critical point in a refinery. You can't afford to do that willy-nilly now," says [a senior officer of a construction firm]. . . . Moreover, neither equipment manufacturers nor their customers can afford to keep a wide range of spare parts in stock. This is due not only to the high cost of financing the parts, but also to the cost of the parts themselves. Westinghouse Electric Corp. has managed to sell about one hundred spare power-plant turbine-rotors in the past five years by persuading utilities that they can save seven days of costly outage by having parts on hand. But for many utilities the cost of these spares, currently one to seven million dollars, is prohibitive.[19]

Just installing them is a risky and demanding operation: "We're dealing with things that are extremely heavy and yet extremely delicate," said a Con Ed official.[20] Dropping a rotor could cost millions of dollars in an instant.

The logical consequences of these considerations is that big plants tend to have smaller safety margins built in, less redundancy, fewer spare parts, and hence more frequent and serious failures. In contrast, since smaller plants are often simpler than big plants, lower skills and standards of maintenance may suffice; the plants are more comprehensible to their staff; and for technical reasons they often tend to fail more gracefully. All the extra costs of maintenance for larger plants then operate in reverse.

A possible economy of scale in operation is that it may be simpler to arrange delivery of fuel, or conversion from one fuel to another, for a single large plant than for multiple smaller plants. This argument does not apply, however, to comparisons between conventional power stations, which require fuel, and renewable energy sources, which do not.

Availability

A low cost per kilowatt of installed capacity is useless if that capacity is not available to provide energy. Since about eighty percent of the cost of generating nuclear electricity (or about forty percent for coal-fired electricity) is the capital cost of the plant itself, the cost of electricity, even after adding the cost of delivering it, is quite sensitive to the reliability of the plant. Unfortunately, the reliability of large power stations has in fact been generally disappointing. As Robert Mauro of the American Public Power Association remarked,

> . . . the disappointing availability record of many large units has diminished, if not entirely dissipated [,] the theoretical savings expected from bigness. . . . [It is ironic that] many small . . . electric utilities, which have been jeered at for operating "obsolete" plants with "tea-kettles," have had fewer problems in maintaining adequate power supply than some larger systems with modern large-scale units.[21]

The reasons for the greater unreliability of large plants are simple and fundamental. A five-hundred-megawatt boiler has approximately ten times as many miles of tubing as a fifty-megawatt boiler, so "a tenfold improvement in quality control is necessary to maintain an equivalent standard of availability for the larger unit."[22] A large turbine has high blade-root stress, often forcing the designer to use exotic alloys with unexpected characteristics: highly skilled turbine designers in several advanced industrial nations have watched their turbines explode because the metal did not behave as hoped. (Giant wind machines show similar stress and vibration problems, making their design complex and costly. As a result, no net economies of scale have yet been demonstrated for wind machines bigger than tens of kilowatts.) A more complex control system runs up against the discouraging mathematics of unreliability (Chapter Thirteen). Even on the scale of such simple components as nuclear pumps and valves, detailed assessments show that larger units are less reliable.[23] In general, the technological evolution needed to meet ever more stringent performance standards exhibits diminishing returns to money and talent invested. Rapid scaling-up often outruns engineering experience, especially in long-lead-time technologies. This is true of all types of engineering.

The combined effect of the greater unreliability of more and bigger components in more complex plants has recently been quantified by analyzing the capacity factor (actual output as a fraction of output if the plant ran at full rated power all the time) of U.S. power plants.[24] For all commercial nuclear reactors through June 1980, the capacity factor averaged sixty-six percent for the twenty-three plants (one hundred seventy-three plant-years) with electrical output capacities under eight hundred megawatts. But for the thirty-nine larger plants (one hundred eighty-eight plant-years), the capacity factor averaged only fifty-four percent—nearly a fifth worse. Sufficient experience is available, according to the nuclear industry, to distinguish statistically the effects of age from those of size. There is now no doubt that if all other variables are held constant, the larger plants are less reliable.[25]

An equally striking correlation between size and unreliability holds for U.S. coal plants.[26] During 1961–73, average unit size increased by seventy-seven percent while capacity performance (a measure of reliability) fell by thirteen percent. Coal plants of between four hundred and eight hundred megawatts were about eight percentage points less available than plants half as big. And for all U.S. coal- and oil-fired power plants during 1967–76, the forced outage rate (fraction of the time the plant was broken down) ranged from a tiny two and a half percent for plants under one hundred megawatts to sixteen percent for plants upwards of eight hundred megawatts,[27] rising proportionately in between.[28] It is partly for this reason that the average size of newly installed coal plants *fell* from about seven hundred megawatts in 1971 to four hundred megawatts in 1978; three hundred megawatts is now a common size for new utility orders. The frequent breakdowns of large plants are simply proving to be more than utilities can afford.

Similar experience abounds worldwide. As the Federal Energy Administration was castigating the dismal reliability of large new power plants in the U.S.,[29] similar evidence was already accepted in Europe as showing that a fundamental mistake had been made in investment strategy. A German/British conference in 1973, for example, had already found that poor availability had cancelled out the expected economies of scale in coal plants. The larger plants took longer to "mature"—to overcome their "teething troubles"—and never did become as reliable as the smaller units. After four years' operation, availability ranged from about eighty-two percent for sixty-megawatt units (which had already levelled off at their "mature" availability) to only about fifty-two percent for five-hundred-megawatt units, which were still far from maturity. Intermediate sizes fitted this pattern corresponding-ly.[30]

Reserve margin

The unreliability of large units is worse than appears at first sight. The possibility that a large unit might fail requires the provision of an equally large block of back-up capacity to protect the grid. Conversely, a larger number of smaller units provides better protection because they are not all likely to fail at the same time.[31] Hence the smaller units would need less reserve margin to achieve the same reliability. In other words, "the enhanced reliability contribution of small generating units arises because the failure of a single large unit is more likely than the simultaneous failure of two smaller units equalling the same capacity."[32]

For this reason, several studies of typical interconnected grids show that building several power plants of three or four hundred megawatts each, rather than a single plant of a thousand megawatts, would provide the same level and reliability of service with about a third less new capacity.[33] Thus a thousand megawatts of new nuclear capacity should, in such a grid, be compared in costs and impacts with only about seven hundred megawatts of coal plants, because the latter can come in smaller units. For still smaller units, such as ten-megawatt fuel cells sited at distribution substations, the savings in extra capacity to do the same task may exceed sixty percent because of the added protection from grid failures.[34] (This initial rate of savings diminishes as dispersed sources are successively added to a typical grid.) Conversely, big, "lumpy" units require disproportionately large back-up capacity, especially if they are unreliable or not thoroughly interconnected.[35]

Thermal efficiency

Power plant engineers have devoted immense ingenuity to trying to increase the amount of electricity derived from each unit of fuel. By the 1960s, average thermal efficiencies (the fraction of the fuel's energy that is converted into electricity) had improved from less than twenty-three percent to about thirty-four percent. Part of this progress was achieved simply by making plants bigger: larger scale both permitted more ambitious engineering designs and improved, for example, the ratio of boiler combustion volume to heat-losing surface area. But despite more rigorous engineering and the pure geometric advantages of scale, the average efficiency of U.S. power plants has slightly *decreased* in recent years. This is partly because larger plants, built in the hope of wringing another few tenths of a percentage point out of the thermal inefficiency, proved less reliable.[36] Their frequent stopping and starting greatly increased heat losses—having to heat up the boiler and plumbing afresh with each restart—and entailed more operation at partial load, also reducing efficiency.

Thus in Britain, among stations of the same size (five hundred megawatts), thermal efficiency ranged from twenty-three or twenty-four percent for plants with a capacity factor of only five or ten percent (out of order nearly all the time) to thirty-four or thirty-five percent for relatively reliable plants (capacity factors over sixty percent).[37] For all plants upwards of four hundred fifty megawatts in output capacity, the correlation was equally strong[38]—lower reliability meant lower thermal efficiency. Based only on availability, thermal efficiency, maintenance cost, lead time, and direct capital cost, the optimal size for such a plant was calculated to be between two hundred and three hundred megawatts. The British electrical authorities, however, adopted five hundred megawatts as the standard size. Because these larger plants proved to be less reliable and less efficient than smaller ones, the choice of an excessive standard size led to a sixteen percent overbuilding of U.K. generating capacity[39]—a mistake costing more than ten billion dollars.

U.S. data confirm that bigger or newer power stations are, on the whole, no more efficient than smaller or older ones.[40] The ten most efficient power plants operated in 1974, for example, had thermal efficiencies around thirty-seven to thirty-nine percent. They ranged in size from two hundred thirty-eight to nine hundred fifty megawatts, and in vintage from 1958 to 1970. The quintupling of the size of the largest plants during 1958–74, and all the technological progress of those sixteen years, did not improve thermal efficiency.

The same lesson applies in many other energy systems. For example, efficiency (and energy cost) bear no necessary relation to unit scale or degree of centralization in most technologies for generating electricity from high-temperature solar heat[41] or even in machines that capture energy from the wind. With these technologies as with conventional power stations, bigger is not necessarily more efficient, and may cost more, too.

Waste-heat integration

Using fuel to raise steam to drive turbines to generate electricity inevitably loses about three-fifths or more of the fuel's energy in the form of warm water used to cool the steam condenser. But this heat need not be wasted, as it normally is in U.S. power stations. Instead, it can be used to heat buildings or greenhouses via a combined-heat-and-power station. Such an integrated "total-energy system" can raise to eighty percent or more the efficiency with which useful work is extracted from the fuel, saving money correspondingly. This can be done particularly well on a small scale because it is more difficult to transport low-temperature heat for long distances than electricity.

Neighborhood- or building-scale total-energy systems are especially attractive.[42] Devices which use small engines to generate electricity and provide heat for a building and its domestic water supply are commercially available. Some achieve about ninety percent overall efficiency,[43] use standard automotive engines burning a wide range of liquid or gaseous fuels, and are suitable for a single apartment house.[44] The current price of a typical total energy system such as the Fiat TO-TEM℠ is about ten thousand dollars for an output capacity of fifteen kilowatts of electricity plus thirty-eight kilowatts of heat[45]—easily competitive with centralized supplies, despite the limited engine lifetime. Fuel cells, which convert fuels directly into electricity plus heat without fumes, noise, or moving parts, can be similarly economical. Models now being field-tested by the Gas Research Institute are expected to achieve overall efficiencies from eighty to ninety-five percent.

Total-energy systems can distribute waste heat at the scale not only of a building or neighborhood but even of a whole city. This is commonly done in Europe, and especially in the Soviet Union and Scandinavia. District heating, for example, warms forty percent of all Danish households. Sweden, widely regarded as the leader in district heating technology, is halfway through a ten-year program of converting all cities of over one hundred thousand people to district heating (Stockholm will take twice as long). The conversion process involves both technical and institutional innovations. The former include highly insulated flexible pipes which can be laid rather cheaply to carry pressurized hot water throughout large areas, even at low suburban housing densities. (Steam systems are usually considered obsolete.) Many Swedish boilers for district heating can burn a wide range of fuels, including municipal wastes or wood chips. Cheap back-up boilers are commonly provided to ensure reliable service, and there is usually redundant water-pumping capacity. An experimental boiler at Enköping, Sweden uses fluidized-bed combustion to burn virtually any combustible material efficiently and cleanly.

Not content with present fuel flexibility, the Swedish District Heating Association even recommends that new district heating systems be so designed that they can later be easily converted to solar district heating. Several solar district heating systems are in operation or under construction, mainly in Scandinavia.[46] Geothermal district heating systems are already operating in parts of Lassen County and elsewhere in California, in Boise, Idaho, and in Klamath Falls, Oregon (which also uses the hot water for air conditioning and industrial process heat).[47] Three Minnesota towns and the city of St. Paul are currently installing modern fossil-fueled district heating systems.

Not surprisingly, most modern power stations are too big to take advantage of district heating opportunities. A thousand-megawatt power station produces about two thousand megawatts of warm water—far too much to use conveniently. The largest readily manageable combined-heat-and-power systems operating in Sweden are only half this size, serving the heat and power needs of a city of one hundred thousand; and that system took seventeen years to build up. Considerably smaller systems, typically tens of megawatts and downwards, offer more flexibility, are faster to build, and need less back-up to ensure reliability.

Another kind of integration between electrical and heating systems is industrial "cogeneration"—making electricity in a factory as a byproduct of heat or steam that is already being used for an industrial process. The most common way to do this is to use a slightly higher temperature than normal, use it to drive a steam or gas turbine, then use the exhaust heat (still quite hot) for the industrial process. Such cogenerated electricity can cost about half as much in capital investment and use half as much fuel as would be the case if the same amounts of electricity and process heat were made separately.[48] In effect, cogeneration replaces two separate boilers—one at the factory and another at the power plant—with a single unit that costs little more to build and operate.[49] Not just a third but about three-fourths of the energy in the fuel can then be harnessed. Further byproducts can include air conditioning and desalination.[50] The proprietor of cogeneration equipment also gains a reliable power source that can work in isolation—an advantage that the publishers of the computer-intensive *Los Angeles Times* found irresistible.[51] California alone expects to have over six thousand megawatts of cogeneration capacity by 1990[52]—about a third as much as currently operates in the United States. One team of four California engineers recently identified a hundred megawatts of attractive cogeneration projects embracing virtually every sector of industry, yet generally small enough to have escaped prior notice. Some inventors believe that cogeneration may be attractive even on as small a scale as a home furnace, using a tiny gas or steam turbine to produce household electricity and then distributing the waste heat.[53]

Many forms of system integration besides the use of waste heat are feasible and economically very attractive at small scale. This important advantage of decentralized systems is described more fully in Chapter Sixteen.

Transmission and distribution costs

If an energy-supplying device is much larger and more concentrated than its customers, its energy must be distributed to them through a costly network. The costs and losses of that distribution are a diseconomy of excessive scale.

The extent of this mismatch is illustrated by U.S. private electric utilities in 1965–71.[54] Their demand was very diffuse; it averaged only three hundredths of a watt per square meter of land area—up to tenfold more or less in extreme cases. The density of demand by nonindustrial users was only half this great—only about a twelve-thousandth of the average density of solar energy on the earth. In contrast, a thousand-megawatt power plant which (with its coal depot or nuclear exclusion area) occupies an area of several square miles represents a source whose power density is about a thousand watts per square meter, the same as bright sunlight at noon—some thirty thousand times as great as the average density of demand. Therefore, to spread out the highly concentrated electricity to its relatively dispersed users, it must be hauled an average of about two hundred miles or more. Even in the denser European grid, this distance is typically around sixty miles. That is, to reach enough customers to be able to *use* the output of a single modern power plant often entails covering a large area with a transmission and distribution network. This is expensive.

In 1972, the last year for which a detailed analysis is available, the cost of building and maintaining that grid accounted for about seventy percent of the cost of delivered U.S. electricity[55]—more than twice the cost of generation. That is, only about thirty percent of what we paid for electricity in 1972 actually bought electricity; the rest paid for getting it from the plant to us. Similarly, natural gas systems are so concentrated that in 1976, transmission and distribution accounted for sixty-five percent of the delivered gas price; wellhead gas accounted for only twenty-nine percent.[56]

In recent years, galloping escalation in the cost of energy plants has shifted these ratios. By 1980, for example, U.S. private electric utilities were spending sixty-nine percent of their total investment on generation and twenty-six percent on the grid, compared with fifty percent for generation and forty-seven pecent for the grid eleven years earlier.[57] But the grid also loses nine percent of the electricity sent through it, and the cost of operating and maintaining the grid (currently four billion dollars a year) is probably even greater than the capital charge for all the transmission lines.[58] Thus even the 1980 investment pattern suggests that about a third of the price of electricity from newly ordered plants will be for delivering it, not for generating it. This is a significant diseconomy of large scale in central generation. Clearly, both costs and losses could be greatly reduced by better matching the scale of supply to that of end use.

Several studies have tried to estimate how much money is saved by putting smaller generators near the users so that less grid investment is needed. Five studies with widely varying assumptions found "dispersion credits" ranging from eight dollars to one hundred sixty-five dollars per kilowatt of dispersed generating capacity.[59] (The latter figure is roughly what a kilowatt of generating capacity *cost* ten years ago.) However, none of these studies counted the saving from eliminating underground cables, which are used in most new primary distribution circuits and can cost ten to forty times as much as overhead lines. The actual saving is therefore even larger.

Several of the same studies allowed a credit for more reliable service. This arises because a source sited at the substation, or even closer to end users, protects them from transmission failures—the main cause of blackouts—and can thus improve reliability ten- or twentyfold.[60] This is in addition to any gain in reliability from the possible use of a different generating source that is inherently more dependable than a central station.

Construction time and indirect costs

As cost of money and escalation of real capital cost take a larger share of total construction costs—due to the interrelated increase of capital intensity, scale, technical complexity, perceived impacts,[61] and lead times—total economies of scale decline because only physical, not financial, quantities become cheaper with size.[62] But the reality appears to be worse than that. There is some evidence that for very large units, economies of scale in capital cost per installed kilowatt actually become *negative*. Figure A.2, for example, shows this effect for a sample consisting of half of the thermal power stations commissioned in the United States in a two-year period during 1972–74. Plots of the capital cost per kilowatt of installed generating capacity (squares) or per kilowatt available to be sent out (triangles) as a function of unit size reveal that unit capital cost in this sample is *less* for a small plant than for a very large one—just the opposite of the usual economies-of-scale theory.

A possible explanation for this unexpected result arises from differences in construction times as a function of scale.[63] Although it might seem intuitively that doubling the size of a plant will double its construction time, utilities have traditionally expected any increase in construction time to be negligible. The actual data, however, show that doubling the size of a nuclear plant in fact increases its construction time by twenty-eight percent, or of a coal plant, by thirteen percent, simply because of the sheer volume of materials and labor whose use must be coordinated.[64] (These increases refer only to actual construction time, not to licensing. There is no statistically significant correlation between licensing duration and reactor cost.[65]) Two Los Alamos researchers, who also consider the process of siting and licensing, find even stronger scale effects on construction time.[66]

Although all parties to utility construction projects tend to blame each other for delays, it is indisputable that the complexity of large projects is at the heart of the difficulty. The Federal Power Commission reported that during 1967–76, utilities themselves cited vendor-related problems (late delivery, unacceptable quality, etc.) as being responsible for thirty-seven percent of their plant delays; poor site labor productivity and other labor-related problems for thirty-four percent; regulatory problems for thirteen percent; utility-related problems (chiefly finance) for nine

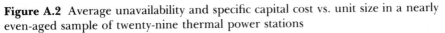

Figure A.2 Average unavailability and specific capital cost vs. unit size in a nearly even-aged sample of twenty-nine thermal power stations

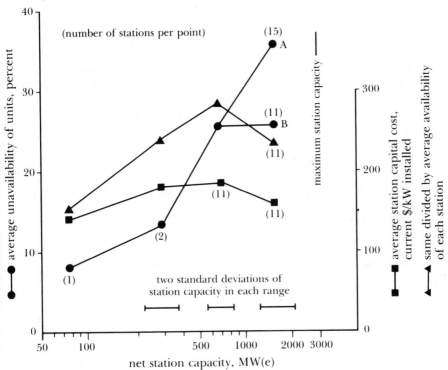

SOURCE: Data from *Electrical World* 1975, replotted in Lovins 1977b:92.

NOTE: The sample includes seventeen or eighteen coal-fired, two to four nuclear, three gas-fired, two gas- or oil-fired (dual-fuel), and one or two oil-fired stations—a total of twenty-nine plants, built in every region except New England. Point A on the graph is from the original source's graph; point B is from its tabular data, which omit the [apparently high] unavailability of four very large plants included in the graph. The right-hand triangular point is calculated using the lower value (B). Komanoff's (1981) smallest reactor has a capacity of four hundred fifty-seven megawatts—between the second and third groups in the graph—so his finding of a positive economy of scale is not inconsistent with the graph, which shows a reversal of the sign only for plants below about a hundred megawatts. *Electrical World*'s corresponding data for 1980 (Friedlander 1982:76–77) are consistent with the graph for 1974, but the numbers and types of stations in the 1980 survey provide sparse data for the lower size ranges.

percent; and bad weather, legal challenges, and all other causes for eight percent.[67] The more ambitious the project, the more important all these problems become and the greater the delays.

Longer construction times increase the indirect costs of construction in at least seven ways, some of which are difficult to quantify but all of which can be important. Longer lead time

• increases exposure to real cost escalation;[68]

- increases the absolute and fractional burden of interest payments during construction;[69]
- makes the utility's cash flow less favorable, reduces the self-financing ratio, increases the debt/equity ratio, reduces the interest coverage ratios, and generally increases the utility's financial risk and hence its cost of money in the capital marketplace;[70]
- increases the project's exposure to regulatory changes during construction[71] and to technological progress that can alter the design criteria or even make the project obsolete;
- may increase the incentive (and bargaining power) of some construction unions to demand very high wages, or to stretch out construction still further, or both (as occurred on the Trans-Alaska Pipeline);
- may arise from siting problems provoked by the large scale and hence the more obtrusive impacts of the plant[72] (this may in turn lead utilities to try to maximize installed capacity per site, making the project so big and problematical that the plant becomes a worse neighbor than it should have been, so the next site becomes that much more difficult and time-consuming to find, and so on exponentially); and
- exposes the builders to high financial risk because of uncertainty. This last point deserves further discussion.

"The greater time lags required in planning [and building] giant plants mean that forecasts [of demand for them] have to be made further ahead, with correspondingly greater uncertainty; therefore the level of spare capacity to be installed to achieve a specified level of security of supply must also increase."[73] Longer lead time increases both the uncertainty of demand forecasts and the penalty per unit of uncertainty. Some analysts have tried to show that the financial penalty for underbuilding is greater than the penalty for overbuilding;[74] but their recommendations—to overbuild baseload plants—are actually artifacts of flaws in their models.[75] More sophisticated simulations show on the contrary that (at least for utilities which do not carry unfinished plants in their rate base) if demand is uncertain, the low-financial-risk strategy is deliberately to *under*build large, long-lead-time plants.[76] There are three reasons for this:

- it costs less to use short-lead-time stopgap plants more than expected (even gas turbines burning petroleum distillate) than it does to pay the carrying charges on giant power stations that are standing idle;
- short-lead-time plants have a shorter forecasting horizon and hence a greater certainty of being needed; and
- short-lead-time plants can be built modularly in smaller blocks,[77] responding more closely to short-term perceptions of need and straining a utility's financing ability far less. That is, adding a plant to a hundred similar small ones rather than to two similar big ones causes an incremental capitalization burden of one percent, not thirty-three percent.

These qualities all reduce the financial risk and therefore the utility's cost of money.[78] Therefore, as a *Business Week* article remarked, "Utilities are becoming wary of projects with long lead times; by the time the plant is finished, demand could be much lower than expected. If you're wrong with a big one, you're really wrong. . . . Uncertainty over demand is the main reason for the appeal of small plants."[79]

Control of residuals

It is often claimed that centralization simplifies control of residuals, such as air pollutants released by burning coal. But this is not obvious in view of the many counterarguments:

- Smaller scale may reduce the total load of residuals by permitting the use of combined-heat-and-power plants or of inherently more flexible and benign processes (for example, fluidized-bed combustion of coal, now commercially available at thermal capacities of tens or hundreds of megawatts but not of thousands of megawatts).
- Smaller scale lowers both the risk and the cost of failure in individual pollution control installations: less will get out than in the case of failure at a large plant, and there is less fiscal incentive to bypass a defective scrubber than if the alternative were shutting down a major power station.
- Smaller scale in certain kinds of installations makes it possible to turn residuals from pollutants into useful nutrients and byproducts, as in the case of ethanol stillage.[80]
- Smaller scale, by siting the plant near its users, also gives them a direct incentive to insist that it run cleanly and quietly—as is illustrated by the German block-heating plant cited in Chapter Sixteen.[81] Conversely, when a large plant is rurally sited, often because politically stronger urban residents do not want it near themselves, agrarian politicians are often impotent to enforce environmental standards in the face of its overwhelming economic power. The result is often inequity, giving rise to tensions and perhaps to violence.[82]

Other issues of scale economies

Large plants may make it easier to use and finance the best technologies *currently* available. On the other hand, smaller plants with shorter lead times may, at each stage during rapid technological evolution, have less capital sunk in inflexible infrastructure, and may reflect a shorter institutional time constant for getting and acting on new information. Thus less capital is sunk at one time in any particular technology that may soon become obsolete, and a larger fraction of capacity at any time will use up-to-date designs.

Small plants may be perceived as so benign, and fit so well onto existing sites near users (such as the sites of old municipal power stations), that they have few siting problems: they offer far greater siting flexibility than large plants,[83] and this in turn saves transmission costs and losses, increases the scope for total-energy systems, and encourages the use of inherently superior sites.[84]

A social or psychological perspective suggests many further scale effects.[85] Some, like users' perceptions of dependency or oligopoly, are beyond the scope of this work.[86] Others are of a more technical character. For example, large technologies tend to submerge, but small ones to emphasize, individual responsibility and initiative. This may improve the quality of work and decisions. Furthermore, large technologies, as the physicist Freeman Dyson has remarked, are "less fun to do and too big to play with." [87] They are so complex and expensive that their design is fixed by committees, not changeable by a single technologist with a better idea. The kind of fundamental innovation which evolved cheaper and more effective energy systems in the past has often depended on the technologies' accessibility to a multitude of tinkerers.[88] (This emerges clearly from the relative speed of innovation in large vs. small wind machines or in mainframe vs. microcomputers.) The ability of a single person to understand a technology and make a basic contribution to it is of fundamental importance: there is, so far as we know, nothing in the universe so powerful as four billion minds wrapping around a problem. It is for this reason that many of the most exciting solar developments, as noted earlier, are the work of individuals, often without the trappings and inertias of "big science."

The scale of an energy system can also change its basic physics and its potential performance in ways that are rather subtle and unexpected. For example, several analyses have found that solar district heating should be able to cut the delivered price of active solar heat roughly in half.[89] There are good physical reasons for this:[90]

- A large water tank, shared between tens or hundreds of dwellings, provides (compared to the small tank in a single house) a large ratio of volume to surface area, hence low heat losses.
- The large tank has a favorable ratio of variable to fixed costs, and it is relatively cheap to increase the size of an already large tank.
- One can therefore afford to use a big enough tank to provide true seasonal (summer-to-winter) heat storage.
- This in turn provides a full summer load, improving annual collector efficiency.
- The large tank also permits further efficiency gains by separating the storage volume into different zones with the hottest water near the center and the coolest near the periphery: this improves collector performance and further reduces heat losses from storage.
- With true seasonal storage, collectors can face east or west with relatively little penalty, rather than only towards the Equator, so such a system would be more flexible to site, especially in a city.

The net result of all these effects is a marked cost reduction—probably to a level well below the oil prices of the mid-1970s[91]. Incorporation of solar ponds or ice ponds[92] or both[93] would cut costs still further, and would incorporate energy collection and energy storage into the same device.

This example illustrates how sensitively optimal scale depends on technological concept and on the proposed use. (It will certainly depend, for example, on how much heat the buildings require, and on the local climate.) It may well turn out that active solar heating is cheaper at some intermediate scale than at the scale of a single house or a whole city. And it may also very well turn out that active solar heat at any scale is uncompetitive with simpler, smaller measures to make buildings more heat-tight and to increase their passive solar gain. The question of optimal scale for a particular device is therefore not the only important question to ask; one must also determine whether that sort of device is worth building at all.

Finally, to make this analysis of scale issues at all tractable, it has excluded such questions as the appropriate *organizational* scale of energy systems. (For example, solar district heating may be technically cheaper than single-building active solar heating, yet cost more in practice because of the greater *social* costs of organizing a joint project among many people.) The organizational patterns of the energy system are a vast and important subject. It is important for some purposes, for example, to know that of the roughly three and a half thousand U.S. electric utilities, the largest ten own about twenty-five percent of the total capacity, the largest thirty own fifty percent, and the largest hundred own eighty percent.[94] (The concentration before the Great Depression was even greater: in 1932, eight holding companies produced three-quarters of America's electricity, although several of them then went bankrupt as sales declined.[95]) The quintupling of the size of steam-electric generating stations during 1950–75 submerged the authority of localities, states, and even individual utilities themselves beneath that of regional power pools.[96] But although the nature and scale of utility ownership, control, and regulation undoubtedly affects somehow the economics of the hundred-billion-dollar-a-year utility industry, no effort has been made here to determine how. This analysis also neglects the sociopolitical effects of scale (many of which were mentioned in previous chapters), because while they are undoubtedly important—some would say dominant—in the way the United States actually makes public policy decisions about energy, nobody knows how to quantify those effects.

What is the net result?

This appendix has listed ten broad classes, and nearly fifty specific types, of competing effects of scale on the economics of energy systems. Large scale affects direct construction costs through the ratio of fixed to variable costs, geometrical factors, construction techniques, technical requirements and complexity, and scope for mass production of components. Some of these effects are economically favorable, at least at first, while others tend to be adverse. Scale alters operating costs in many ways and probably in both directions. Large scale affects (generally adversely) technical reliability, reserve needs, opportunities for thermal and other types of system integration, and distribution costs and losses. Scale and concomitant effects (notably availability) can affect thermal efficiency. And large scale is intricately (and generally adversely) related to construction time and, via at least seven pathways, to ultimate cost.

Clearly, then, it is not good enough to look only at one or two economies of scale—such as a saving on the direct construction cost of a power plant per kilowatt—and ignore nearly the nearly fifty diseconomies identified here. Yet it is by such defective reasoning that America has come to rely on huge and brittle energy technologies. The same habit of thought has led many energy technologists to assume that smaller technologies, lacking those economies of scale, must be uneconomic. Yet on the contrary, it is partly by avoiding the *dis*economies of large scale that many small energy technologies are in fact able to compete economically with conventional large technologies, as is demonstrated in the next two appendices.

The dispute over the economics of scale would be easier to settle if one could cite a careful economic comparison between big and small technologies which focused solely on scale as the key variable. Unfortunately, small systems also tend to differ from big ones in many respects other than scale: they may, for example, be total-energy or renewable systems, and these fundamental differences tend to submerge the importance of their different scale. There is, however, a detailed analysis by two Los Alamos scientists which shows how scale alone can give an economic advantage to the smaller of two otherwise identical systems—big versus very big coal-fired power plants.[97] That analysis is only peripheral to the broader case developed here. Whereas Part Three of this book is concerned mainly with small technologies, the Los Alamos study deals only with two different sizes of a technology which are *both* many thousands of times larger than any small technologies. The importance of the example lies rather in showing that by considering eight scale effects rather than only one, the conventional wisdom of the utility industry (very big power stations are cheaper per kilowatt than big ones) can be reversed.

The Los Alamos scientists' calculation used empirical cost and performance data to compare coal-fired power station projects in two different sizes: four plants each generating seven hundred fifty megawatts; and nine plants, each only a third as large. Because the larger plants are less reliable and can "drop out" more capacity at once, they would need a third more total capacity to do the same job. This puts the larger plants at an initial disadvantage. In addition, the smaller plants would save money by being nineteen percent more reliable, by taking five years to build instead of nine, and by having a forced outage rate fifty-nine percent lower than the big plants. The money saved by these advantages would more than make up for the smaller plants' economic disadvantages: fifteen percent worse thermal efficiency, eleven percent higher capital cost per kilowatt, and slightly higher costs for coal transportation and electricity transmission. Balancing all these effects, the total cost (discounted to present value) of building the smaller plants would be less than that of the larger plants by one percent in operating costs, seventeen percent in construction costs, and six percent in total lifetime electricity price. The smaller plants would thus save electricity consumers a total (in 1977 value) of two hundred twenty-seven million dollars compared to the bigger plants.

The Los Alamos calculation is especially impressive because it finds an advantage for the smaller plants—within the size range in which economies of scale are supposedly best known to operate—even though it leaves out approximately forty diseconomies of large scale identified earlier in this appendix. Its assumptions, too, consistently favor the larger plants. For example, it supposes that in practice, the hoped-for gains in thermal efficiency at larger scale will not be reversed by higher forced outage rates. It assumes economies of scale in construction four times as large as those (if any) actually observed for all U.S. coal plants. It ignores the likelihood that the better cash flow associated with shorter lead time would reduce the utility's effective cost of money. It does not account for possible reductions in grid costs and losses from siting the smaller plants closer to the users. Most importantly, it does not count the potentially very large savings that could be achieved through district heating or other forms of system integration—opportunities that could completely change the design and purpose of the project if the plants were, say, two hundred fifty kilowatts rather than a thousand times larger. Yet despite its narrow focus, the study finds that taking a few competing diseconomies into account gives the smaller plants a cost advantage larger than many on which utilities now base their investment choices.

The evidence cited earlier for additional advantages of much smaller scale, and especially for total-energy systems and other forms of system integration (treated in Chapter Sixteen), suggests that a much stronger economic case could be made for making the plants even smaller and more local than the case study assumes. And in the case of renewable sources—which tend to have greater integration opportunities, which can generally be sited directly at the point of use so as virtually to eliminate grid costs and losses, and which have no cost of fuel delivery—the economic advantages of small scale, for uses of normal (relatively low) density, should be even greater.

By now, in short, the evidence of compensatory diseconomies of large scale which favor smaller technologies is so overwhelming that no rational decision-maker can ignore it. However these many competing effects are balanced, it is difficult to imagine a way—save in the most centralized applications, such as operating a giant smelter—that they can yield lower net costs of delivered energy services at very large scale than at moderate, and often quite small, scale. Thus the relatively small, dispersed modules of energy supply required for a genuinely resilient energy system do not appear to be incompatible with reasonable cost, and may indeed be one of the simplest ways of achieving it.

Appendix Two
Technical Progress in Appropriate Renewable Sources

The state of the art in inherently resilient energy sources has been treated in detail in recent primers for lay audiences,[1] for scientists,[2] and for policy-makers.[3] It is not possible in a book of this length to do justice to those fundamentals. Rather, this appendix highlights some recent technological advances, not described in earlier chapters, which seem especially promising for making the U.S. energy system less vulnerable.

Heat

Passive solar design Passive solar techniques—capturing and storing solar energy in the fabric of the building itself—are now known to be the best buy (after, and in combination with, efficiency improvements) for space-heating both new buildings and retrofits. Passive devices requiring no pumps can also heat domestic water cheaply (Appendix Three). Sophisticated design tools[4] and packaged design kits have been tailored for use in many climates.[5] These now permit the performance of any combination of passive elements in any climate to be accurately simulated and optimized on a hand calculator. In general, passive design has turned out to be simpler and more effective than expected. Annual national and international passive solar conferences have refined and propagated these techniques with remarkable speed. Successful passive solar houses are now being built or retrofitted[6] at a rate of hundreds of thousands per year, even in the least favorable solar climates.[7]

New materials New materials with unusual properties are becoming available for both passive and active solar use. Transparent insulation and heat-reflecting glazings (including Heat Mirror®) are now in commercial production. An experimental glass-plastic-argon glazing with an R-value of nineteen—as good an insulator as nearly two and a half inches of foam—has been developed in Germany. Some new plastic-film glazing materials, such as 3M's Flexigard®, transmit better than window glass at visible wavelengths, are nearly opaque in the infrared, and show no signs of degradation after twelve years' weathering in bright sun.[8]

Solar plastics Tough, highly durable plastic films have been proposed by T.B. Taylor and developed by Brookhaven National Laboratory as materials for active solar collectors at least ten times cheaper than conventional ones. Such collectors have for several years been sold in Switzerland,[9] and could easily be site-assembled just as plastic-film greenhouses are now. (Stockpiling appropriate films and instructions could indeed be an important element of any solar mobilization.) Active solar collectors molded from up to four different polymers, each suited to its task, are now being sold. Micropolished reflective films are proving highly resistant to weathering and are starting to reduce dramatically the price of concentrating collectors.

Simple concentrating collectors So diverse are the designs of active solar collectors—now being made by more than three hundred fifty U.S. companies—that it is not yet clear whether flat-plate or concentrating collectors are superior for supplying heat below the boiling point of water. The Office of Technology Assessment found that the cheapest collector on the 1977 market (other than rollable plastic mats and other unconventional designs, some of which are quite effective) was a concentrating parabolic trough.[10] Very simple automatic tracking mechanisms have been developed. They can be quite reliable, as attested by the performance of military and airport radar trackers. Robert Stromberg of Sandia National Laboratory, who has sold thousands of sets of plans for a homemade concentrator of the type used on his own house, argues with some justification that even in a climate as cloudy as Boston, the extra efficiency of a concentrating collector when exposed to direct sunlight can more than make up for its inability to capture the diffuse light which may be at too low an intensity to reach the flat plate's operating threshold. This argument has particular merit for photovoltaic cogeneration systems (described below). Moreover, compound parabolic (Winston) collectors can achieve concentrations of several suns—in some cases approaching ten suns—without needing to track the sun at all, or with only a few adjustments of their orientation each year. Such collectors can combine the advantages of concentration in direct sunlight with respectable performance as flat-plate collectors on cloudy or hazy days, and can be cheaply mass-produced from molded plastic.

Selective surfaces A response to the argument for concentrating collectors is that in a cloudy climate, "conventional" flat plates—those with a flat-black absorbing surface—are the wrong choice. A "selective" surface, which absorbs visible wavelengths well but radiates infrared badly, is far preferable. A surface which absorbs visible light about five times as well as it emits infrared (a "selectivity" of five) can be made simply by brushing a lampblack-water slurry on a metal absorber plate and letting it dry to a thickness which removes the metallic luster but is still gray, not black. A selectivity around eight to ten can be achieved by many kinds of electrochemical coating processes and some special paints. Adhesive selective foils (such as SunSponge®) can boost even the performance of Trombe walls—passive, glazed masonry walls—by about a third, more cheaply than equivalent night insulation.

For about thirty cents per square foot, a selectivity-eight foil can be applied, perhaps by stretching it over a slightly convex absorber, to an active collector. This simple modification produces remarkable results. Since the diffusely scattered light on a cloudy day, although somewhat reduced in intensity, is still energy of extremely high quality—its effective color temperature is over five thousand degrees Fahrenheit—a selective surface, suitably insulated, will attain very high equilibrium temperatures. Thus a single-glazed selectivity-eight collector—a selectivity achieved in many commercial U.S. and Japanese flat-plate collectors—has been demonstrated to heat domestic water by a highly satisfactory fifty-four Fahrenheit degrees—that is, to a final temperature well over a hundred degrees—with forty-five percent efficiency on a cloudy winter day in Hamburg.[11] (The total solar radiation per square foot was equivalent to a fifth of the level obtained on a clear summer day at noon. Raising this to three-tenths increased the efficiency to fifty-seven percent.)

Higher selectivity would make the collector even less sensitive to cloudiness. A selectivity in excess of fifty can be obtained by sputtering thin films using well-established high-vacuum techniques similar to but less demanding than those used in coating optical lenses. A selectivity-fifty surface in a hard vacuum will serve a process heat load at upwards of a thousand degrees Fahrenheit on a cloudy winter day in Juneau. If the liquid-metal coolant in such an absorber should stop flowing, the metal absorber plate would probably melt.

Medium-concentration-ratio collectors In contrast, only direct sunlight can be used to operate conventional collectors. Commercial line-focus systems, of which more than a million square feet were made in the U.S. in 1980, go up to about five hundred degrees Fahrenheit, and sold in 1980 for about thirty or forty dollars per installed square foot[12]—a price competitive with oil today, and certainly with new synfuels or electricity (Appendix Three). Point-focusing dish collectors can achieve higher temperatures. General Electric prototype dishes twenty-three feet in diameter recently supplied heat at seven hundred fifty degrees Fahrenheit with seventy-one percent collection efficiency.[13] (That temperature is adequate to supply essentially all the process heat needed by the food, paper, and chemical industries, plus most of the needs of oil refining.) Point-focus systems for loads up to about fifteen hundred degrees Fahrenheit are beginning to enter the market at attractive prices. For example, Power Kinetics Corporation, of Troy, New York, offers for thirty-seven thousand dollars an eight-hundred-sixty-square-foot dish with a peak output capacity of fifty-nine kilowatts and a measured efficiency of seventy-four to seventy-nine percent. It is calculated to pay for itself by saving oil in the Northeast within three to ten years[14]—similar to the economics estimated in the Solar Energy Research Institute's "conservative" mass-production case shown in Table A.2 in Appendix Three, and competitive today with most fuels in most parts of the United States. Another dish has heated gas to twenty-two hundred degrees Fahrenheit steadily, twenty-six hundred maximum.[15]

High-concentration-ratio collectors Large dish concentrators can achieve concentration ratios up to about a thousand suns—enough to vaporize any material. For achieving very high temperatures, however, it is more common (though not yet proven to be cheaper) to focus sunlight on central receivers by using large fields of tracking mirrors (heliostats). Such systems, now under development in many countries, can achieve essentially any concentration ratio. One Italian firm sells small heliostat fields.[16] Heliostats operate megawatt-range solar power plants in Japan, Spain, and France. Southern California Edison Company proposes to build by 1988 a hundred-megawatt solar peaking unit instead of oil-burning gas turbines. Edison believes that modest heliostat production—about a hundred megawatts of electrical capacity per year for five to seven years—would make such solar-thermal systems economic for repowering oil-fired plants in the Southwest.[17] The biggest application of heliostat technology, however, will probably be in high-temperature direct process heat. In that market it will have some stiff competition from lower-technology solar collectors. As an example of what can be achieved even with devices simple enough for a tinkerer to make at home, one dish concentrator built by Doug Wood in the cloudy Olympic Peninsula of Washington State provides forty kilowatts of steam at a new-materials cost less than half the cost of heat from burning 1981 world oil in an eighty-percent-efficient boiler. Even a commercial replica of this simple dish (made of sections of pipe and cheap sections of mirrored glass) would compete handily with today's oil prices (Appendix Three).[18]

Solar ponds Among the most rapidly emerging solar technologies during 1980–82 has been the solar pond—a passive device for cheaply supplying heat year-round, day and night. Although there are several types of solar pond, the most common is a hole in the ground with an impervious liner, filled with concentrated brine— various kinds of salts can be used—and preferably with a darkened bottom. Both direct and diffuse solar radiation heat up the bottom of the pond, but because the hotter water there dissolves more salt and is thus denser, convective heat transfer to the surface is suppressed. (The proper geometry can enable the salt to form a self-stabilizing gradient of optical bending power which helps to concentrate light on the bottom.) A layer of fresh water on top, which stays fairly well segregated, acts as a transparent insulator. Other forms of translucent insulation can also be added. A simple heat exchanger, such as some pipes near the bottom, can extract heat at nearly the boiling point: solar ponds in sunny areas can boil by late summer, as a pond near Albuquerque did in 1980. The large thermal mass of the pond provides built-in heat storage, although it may take some months to come up to its full working temperature. Good ponds convert twenty to thirty percent of the total solar radiation into usable heat. They may cost fifty cents to a dollar per square foot if salt is available onsite, as near many mines and factories; three dollars or more per square foot if the hole, liner, and salt must be specially provided.

Solar ponds were originally expected to work only in desert climates, but the successful operation of a nearly half-acre pond by the City of Miamisburg, Ohio since 1978 has dispelled that notion. Even with ice on the surface, the bottom temperature in the cold spell of February 1978 was still eighty-three degrees Fahrenheit. The total cost, mostly for eleven hundred tons of salt and for the liner, was three dollars twenty cents a square foot. Maintenance cost is very small. The delivered heat price, as noted in Appendix Three, is just over nine dollars per million BTUs.[19] That is equivalent to burning seventy-five-cent-a-gallon oil (hard to find these days) in a seventy-percent-efficient free furnace, or to running a baseboard heater with electricity costing three and a tenth cents per kilowatt-hour (about half the national average residential price). Recent reports indicate that the heat was stored for two or three months rather than for six, and thus did not quite match the load, but a larger or better-lined pond would provide longer storage. Other pond projects, including some to provide district heating, are being pursued in cloudy northern climates.[20]

Solar pond research and demonstrations being pursued by the CalTech Jet Propulsion Laboratory, Los Alamos National Laboratory, California Energy Commission, Southern California Edison Company, and others should lead in the next few years to the sort of "cookbook" understanding of pond design already obtained for passive solar techniques. Solar ponds are a robust, nearly invulnerable heat source: even an event which disturbed the salt gradient and reduced collection efficiency would still leave weeks' worth of recoverable heat.

Ice ponds Another and in some ways even more exciting development, seasonal storage ice ponds,[21] can store winter coolth through the summer, offering reliable air-conditioning at a tenth of the usual energy cost. T.B. Taylor has demonstrated that high-density ice can be formed on a chilly winter day in Princeton, New Jersey, simply by spraying water from a garden hose into a hole in the ground. Insulated by straw (or more elaborate materials), such a block of ice can supply thirty-two-degree meltwater for chilling a building right through the summer. (A large building using this principle is now under construction in Princeton with funding by an energy-conscious insurance company, Prudential.) A combination of ice ponds with solar ponds,[22] taking advantage of the economics of seasonal storage noted in Appendix One,[23] can provide heating, cooling, and—via a low-temperature heat engine—electricity at prices which look very attractive today.

Vehicular liquid fuels

Enough liquid fuels can be sustainably produced from farm and forestry wastes (not special crops) to run an efficient vehicle fleet.[24] (Biomass-derived chemical feedstocks also show considerable promise.)[25] The sustainable use of biomass wastes will require careful management and integration with basic reforms of cultural practice which should be undertaken in any case to protect soil fertility—now eroding faster than during the Dust Bowl.[26]

Primers on biomass liquids have been published elsewhere.[27] The main types of liquid fuels available from biomass include pyrolysis "oil" made by heating woody substances with little air; such "oil" slurried with char produced in the same process; diesel fuel or gasoline refined from pyrolysis "oil"; methanol; ethanol; butanol; and blends of various alcohols. These can be burned neat or blended with oil-based fuels; Gasohol®, for example, is a blend of ten percent anhydrous ethanol with ninety percent gasoline. Other liquids also show promise: for example, alcohols and inedible vegetable oils can be reacted in a simple solar-heated catalytic device to form esters which are reportedly superior to oil-based diesel fuel.[28]

Use in vehicles Some of these fuels are usable directly in unmodified car engines; others need minor modification which costs up to several hundred dollars for retrofit or nothing at the factory.[29] (These modifications must, however, be properly done; inadequate attention to such details as making fuel-system gaskets insoluble in alcohols and preventing alcohols from becoming contaminated by water has led to well-publicized problems in Brazil's ethanol fuel program.) The range of some fuel-engine combinations can be extended by changing the engine design: alcohols, for example, burn well in spark-ignited diesels with proper lubrication. The high compression ratios obtainable from such designs can enable alcohols, especially methanol, to burn much more efficiently than gasoline—one of the reasons why methanol has long been used as a premium fuel by racing drivers.

It would enhance energy preparedness if car makers routinely used methanol-proof components in fuel systems, and provided carburetors with a switch for easy conversion between gasoline, gasoline/alcohol blends, and pure alcohol. (At least one U.S. automaker has reportedly developed such a device.) Brazilian automakers owned by Ford, General Motors, Chrysler, and Volkswagen are already making pure-ethanol cars and converting about ninety thousand gasoline cars to ethanol each year.[30] Despite some teething troubles, Brazil's program is expanding. In California, some cars are being commercially converted to burn neat methanol (cheaper and cleaner than gasoline), with the conversion cost being almost entirely covered by the renewable energy tax credit.

Dispersed ethanol production Excellent manuals on commercial ethanol production from crops are available,[31] though analogous guides are not yet available for other, more promising, feedstocks, processes, and products. Extensive grassroots training programs in ethanol still construction and operation are provided by a wide range of groups, especially in the Midwest.[32] Given that knowledge, a still big enough to fuel a car can be built from commonly available materials in a few days and operated from almost any sugary or starchy feedstock. Although this approach, using traditional still designs, is not energy-efficient, it does provide a premium fuel from what may otherwise be waste materials. Small- and medium-sized ethanol plants of more formal design also offer interesting advantages for integration into farm operations[33] and are attracting special interest as a community economic development tool at small Black colleges.[34]

Whether ethanol is produced in small stills or (preferably) a wider range of fuels is produced by more efficient methods from non-crop feedstocks (especially cellulosic wastes), the potential contribution from many small plants, both routinely and in an emergency, could be very large. As an analogy, in the United States today about eleven million cows, in herds averaging sixty cows each, produce fifteen billion gallons of milk per year. That is about a fifth as many gallons as the gasoline used annually by American cars, or about the same as the number of gallons that those cars would use if they were cost-effectively efficient (Chapter Fifteen). Yet much of that milk "is efficiently supplied by small-scale decentralized operations"[35]—at far lower cost than if all the milk were produced, say, in a few giant dairy farms in Texas and then shipped around the country. Likewise, "the average stripper well produces about two and eight-tenths barrels of oil per day, which is about one-seventh of one one-thousandth of a percent of what we consume in oil every day, . . . but . . . the cumulative effect of all our stripper wells [is] . . . twenty-one percent of continental oil [extraction]."[36]

A special advantage of alcohol or other liquid-fuel production from farm and forestry wastes is that it would tend to be concentrated in the mainly agricultural, rural areas which have disproportionate, highly dispersed needs for mobility fuels.[37] These regions are at the end of conventional supply lines: some North Dakota farmers today must drive hundreds of miles to get to a gas station, making it hardly worthwhile to fill up. But without adequate fuel, those rural areas cannot grow food for export to the cities. Of the two and a half quadrillion BTUs used in American agriculture in 1978, about ninety-three percent was oil and gas.[38] Most of that ran farm equipment and dried crops. In a shortage, and especially in a war, farms could no longer compete in the marketplace for very costly mobility fuels— especially if agricultural exports had also been interrupted, making grain prices plummet at the very time when oil prices were skyrocketing, probably to several dollars a gallon. In these dire circumstances, farmers could continue to feed the nation only if they had the means to convert crop wastes (and perhaps even surplus grains at a pinch) into alcohol fuels. It is for this reason that Admiral Moorer, former Chairman of the Joint Chiefs of Staff, noted "the valuable contribution of a highly dispersed, self-contained liquid fuel production system to serve the vast U.S. farming community in developing the strategic defenses of the United States."[39]

Other biomass-to-liquids alternatives Many people think only of corn-based ethanol when biomass liquids are mentioned. A million tons of corn did in fact provide about one hundred of the hundred and five million gallons of fuel alcohol made in 1980.[40] If earlier federal commitments had been honored, grain ethanol plants producing nearly six hundred million gallons per year would have been built by the end of 1982.[41] But corn ethanol is far from the only important feedstock, process, or product, and—especially with the inefficient, oil- or gas-fired stills commonly used—is among the least attractive. Other processes, notably thermochemical ones, have better economics and at least equal technical simplicity.[42]

Feedstocks for pyrolysates or alcohols abound, even in urban areas: just the pure, separated tree material sent each day to Los Angeles County landfills, not counting mixed truckloads, is four to eight thousand tons, with an energy content of the order of a thousand megawatts. At a nominal conversion efficiency of seventy percent, a thousand megawatts (thermal) of tree wastes would yield fuel equivalent to nearly half a million gallons of gasoline per day—enough to drive a sixty-mpg car more than ten miles per day for every household in the county. Sacramento is spending three and a half million dollars to build a fluidized-bed gasifier, expected to repay that cost within six years, which will consume twenty thousand tons per year of tree, lawn, and garden trimmings—a third of the City's total trimmings now sent to landfill. On completion in late 1982, the gasifier is to provide sixteen megawatts of heat at eighty-five percent efficiency, replacing half the natural gas now used in the boilers that heat and cool the Capitol and seventeen large state office buildings.[43] Similarly, Gold Kist, Inc. expects a three-year payback for the four-million-dollar boiler installed in 1981 at its soybean processing plant, and fired with peanut hulls and pecan shells. Diamond/Sunsweet, formerly having to dispose of a hundred tons of walnut shells per day, is now getting a three-year payback by burning them in a four-and-a-half-megawatt cogeneration plant. And the Boeing Company's huge production complex in Everett, Washington is building a plant which will burn cartons and other factory wastes to raise steam for space-heating and powering manufacturing processes.[44]

Most parts of the United States have some similarly rich source of biomass wastes whose premium use, in general, is not combustion for heat or electricity, but rather conversion to mobility fuels. The cotton-gin trash currently burned or dumped in Texas is enough to run every vehicle in Texas at present efficiencies. The distressed grain in an average year in Nebraska would fuel a tenth of the cars in Nebraska at sixty mpg. At that efficiency, the straw burned in the fields of France or Denmark each year would fuel every car in those countries. Feedstocks range from walnut shells and rice straw in California to peach pits in Georgia and apple pumice (left after squeezing cider) in Pennsylvania. None of these wastes by itself is nationally significant. But numerous small, localized terms, of which the largest is logging wastes, add up to quite enough to fuel, even with expended travel, the entire American transport system if it is run at cost-effective levels of efficiency.[45]

Appendix Three shows that some of the processes available today can provide liquid fuels from biomass wastes at prices competitive with oil products. Some other processes and feedstocks are not quite competitive with today's oil, though they are much cheaper than the synthetic fuels which are proposed (with huge federal subsidies) to be made from coal or oil shale. To bring the full range of bioconversion processes from promising pilot-scale tests to competitive market availability will require three main types of technical developments. The first, most important, and least supported is reform in farming and forestry practice to make these activities sustainable by protecting soil fertility while at the same time providing residues for fuel conversion.[46] This is an intricate biological, social, and economic question which no federal program addresses; but without it, Americans will not long remain able to feed themselves.

The second need is rapidly being met: the final product engineering and wide deployment of improved processes to ferment sugars or starches into ethanol. For example, a few years ago it took fifty to a hundred thousand BTUs to distill a gallon of ethanol to one hundred ninety proof. Today some commercial processes use twenty-five thousand BTUs to go all the way to dried (anhydrous) ethanol,[47] and the best demonstrated processes have reduced this to only eight or ten thousand BTUs, using advanced distillation or critical-fluid processes.[48] Innovative water-alcohol separation processes include freezing (New England applejack and Appalachian moonshine were long fortified by leaving the kegs out to freeze), chemical extractants, hydrophobic plastics, cellulosic adsorbants,[49] and—just emerging—synthetic membranes.[50] Good process efficiencies, in mass yield from feedstock to alcohol, are now typically forty-six to forty-eight percent for glucose fermentation to ethanol—some ninety to ninety-five percent of the theoretical limit on efficiency. These processes are likely to become widely available at all scales over the next few years.

The third and technically most exciting line of development is the evolution of new processes (or refinement of old ones—acid hydrolysis has been in use for over a century) to convert cellulosic wastes, the most versatile and abundant kind, into alcohols. Acid hydrolysis can break down cellulose to glucose with virtually complete yields, providing a mass yield of over forty percent from cellulose to ethanol.[51] Cellulose and hemicellulose can also be converted directly into ethanol by special bacteria at mass yields of better than twenty-five percent[52]—a figure that is being improved upon.

Thermochemical processes Thermochemical processes can yield methanol by the routine catalytic "shift reaction"[53] of steam with synthesis gas (a hydrogen/carbon-monoxide mixture produced by oxygen gasification of biomass). Using modified coal-conversion technology, which is not optimal for biomass, the efficiency of the whole process is about forty to forty-eight percent, or about as good as the main processes for making synthetic fuels from coal.[54] A new downdraft gasifier has increased the methanol yield to an astonishing eighty-three percent, while another gasifier design can directly produce gasoline.[55] Pyrolytic "oil" production has at least a fifty percent conversion efficiency[56]—typically sixty to eighty percent including the slurried char, even in small plants that can fit on the back of a pickup truck and go to where a pile of logging wastes, mill sawdust, or other feedstock happens to be available.[57]

Most thermochemical processes are better suited to producing methanol than ethanol. As mentioned earlier, methanol has long been considered a premium fuel for its high performance, cleanliness, and safety; in a high-compression-ratio car (say, fourteen or more to one), it burns so efficiently that even though it contains only half as much energy per gallon as gasoline, it can supply only a fifth to a quarter fewer miles per gallon. Methanol/ethanol/*tert*-butanol blends and other combinations of several types of alcohol can be even more advantageous.[58] Since cellulosic feedstocks are the most widespread and the easiest to convert and use efficiently in small, dispersed plants using low technology, the emerging cellulosic conversion processes seem particularly advantageous for building a nearly invulnerable national capability for dispersed, sustainable liquid fuel production.

Gaseous fuels for road vehicles As still another option, cars can burn gaseous hydrocarbons with little modification except in the fuel tanks. Although hydrogen-burning cars are still fairly rare, other gaseous fuels are becoming quite popular. Canada has a program of conversion to compressed natural gas (CNG), at a capital cost of about seventeen hundred dollars per car for retrofits or at most a few hundred dollars at the factory. Although the limited gas capacity of the steel gas bottles reduces the range of the cars to about forty-five miles per standard welding-gas-sized tank, the bottles can be kept in the trunk without taking up all the luggage space, and the normal gasoline tank can be kept connected to the fuel line too. Thus the car can remain duel-fueled, enjoying both the long range of gasoline and the reduced engine wear, lower emissions, and lower costs of CNG (especially in urban driving). Upwards of twenty thousand American and a quarter-million Italian drivers have already switched to CNG. They usually refill their gas bottles in a few seconds at compressor stations (many of which are at gasoline filling stations). Methane suitable for CNG cars can also be made from biomass wastes and compressed on the farm. Congress recently passed a Methane Transportation, Research, Development and Demonstration Act to encourage CNG applications.

Another alternative vehicular fuel now gaining ground is LPG (Chapter Eight)—chiefly propane stored as a pressurized liquid and vaporized on demand by a small heat exchanger warmed by the vehicle's exhaust. About three million LPG carburetors have been sold in the U.S. since 1969, and the rate of conversions is rapidly increasing as fuel costs and taxes rise. Renault and Peugeot sell LPG production cars.[59] Ford offers a 1982 propane model in production Granadas and Cougars.[60] Many fleet operators already use LPG. The fuel tank is arguably more dangerous than a gasoline tank in a crash, though the safety experience so far is not bad. With CNG—already gaseous rather than liquid, and contained within half-inch steel tank walls—no tank ruptures have been reported in one hundred eighty rear-end collisions.

A million portable wood gasifiers ran European cars during World War II. Extensive data are available on their design and performance.[61] Although they take about an hour a day to fuel and care for, and consume about twenty-two pounds of dry wood per gallon gasoline equivalent, they are such a robust substitute in heavily wooded regions that Sweden is considering stockpiling gasifiers in case of severe gasoline shortage. Direct-combustion Stirling engines may also be attractive.[62] The Boat Division of Chalmers in Sweden has even burned wood flour directly in diesel engines. Wood itself (and sawdust, peat, etc.) is easy to store, ship, and handle in pelletized form: one version, Woodex℠, is cleaner than coal, at least as cheap, and made by at least twelve plants in seven states.

Electricity

The most commonly discussed renewable electrical sources are microhydroelectricity, wind electricity, and photovoltaics (solar cells). (Others, such as solar cogeneration in dish concentrators supplying industrial process heat, or electric-only "power towers" using large fields of heliostats, will not be treated here.) Wind and small hydro can also be used for pumping water or heat, for direct mechanical drive, for compressing storable air to run machines, or even for refrigeration.[63] At least one small hydro operation in upstate New York is also reported to be using its surplus off-peak output to electrolyze water; the resulting hydrogen, a premium gaseous fuel, could of course be stored under pressure or in solid hydrides and used to operate clean vehicles at high efficiency. Surplus electricity from solar cells or other sources could be similarly used. Although pure-electric cars cannot compete in principle with very efficient fueled cars, some of those, such as series hybrids, lend themselves to partial operation by cheap solar cells (perhaps installed on the car itself) or other renewables.

Low-temperature solar thermal electric systems A little-known option may, in favorable sites, be the cheapest known source of new baseload electricity: a solar pond with a low-temperature heat engine, especially if it works into an ice pond as suggested by T.B. Taylor. The large heat capacity of the pond would provide weeks or, in large ponds, many months of built-in storage. Israel has operated a hundred-fifty-kilowatt-electric solar pond/Rankine-engine combination of this type since 1979. There are plans to expand this to five megawatts, at a cost of about two thousand dollars per electric kilowatt, in 1983. Israel also plans two thousand megawatts (the equivalent of two giant power stations) in floating solar ponds in the Dead Sea by 2000, and projects that a proposed Southern California Edison Company plant in the Salton Sea—officially projected to generate electricity at about seven to ten cents per kilowatt-hour (competitive with central coal or nuclear plants)—could actually be built to run at four to seven cents a kilowatt-hour.

Small hydro Small hydro—variously defined as less than one-tenth, five, or twenty-five megawatts per site—is being intensively exploited by entrepreneurs.[64] Many of these projects merely revive older ones that had fallen into disrepair. By 1976–77,[65] innumerable small dams, including over ten thousand in New England alone, had been abandoned: just in the past twenty years, more than three thousand working hydroelectric plants totalling some three thousand megawatts had been taken out of service, considered a nuisance by utilities that preferred to manage a few big plants instead. (Many existing large dams were also left with empty turbine bays.[66]) The National Hydroelectric Power Study by the Army Corps of Engineers has identified still more opportunities, but has tended to ignore many of the best ones, such as canal locks.

There are more than fifty thousand dams over twenty-five feet high, plus many which have a lower head but are still potential power sites (heads as low as five feet,[67] or essentially zero-head run-of-the-river sites, can be used). Some of these sites are environmentally or institutionally unsuitable,[68] but many others can be refurbished and some developed from scratch without doing much harm. The technologies are generally straightforward and highly cost-effective.[69] A do-it-yourself manual and several excellent periodicals are available.[70]

The rate of progress in installing small hydro equipment is hard to measure because many utilities seem to underreport their hydro projects. For example, Pacific Gas & Electric and Southern California Edison reported one hundred seventy megawatts of hydro in the January 1981 *Electrical World* survey of capacity additions underway, but the California Energy Commission's staff report on the proposed Allen-Warner Valley coal project lists, for these two companies respectively, seven hundred seventy and eleven hundred fifty megawatts of hydropower as "reasonably expected to occur" and about fifteen hundred and seven hundred fifty megawatts as "additional, but not counted." Thus those two companies' hydro projects already underway, most of them with permits filed for, total eighteen hundred fifty-seven megawatts—over ten times what the *Electrical World* survey, the utility industry's standard source, reflects.[71]

A further barrier is that the Federal Energy Regulatory Commission is inundated with license applications: twenty-six hundred applications averaging eight megawatts each were submitted in the two years ended July 1981[72] (including some applications apparently filed by a few companies that intend to sit on them or resell them at "scalper's" profits). In that one month alone, the Commission issued more small hydro permits than it used to do in a whole year; but it also received new applications at a rate averaging ten per day, so the backlog grew.

Despite these impediments, the impact of small hydro is already substantial in some areas.[73] Nationally, over the next few decades small hydro should approach the same total capacity as existing large-scale hydroelectricity, but far more evenly distributed around the country. New York State alone envisages two to three thousand megawatts of small hydro by the mid-1990s, the equivalent of three or four major power stations.[74] Similar programs are underway abroad, even in countries noted for their devotion to large hydroelectric plants: Sweden, for example, plans to have built two hundred and fifty small plants by 1982, while New Zealand has sixty and plans to build more.[75]

Small hydro should be speeded by new companies providing a "no-hassle" turnkey development service, such as Energenics Systems, Inc. Among the new hardware, too, is a range of Chinese turbines designed by American engineers a half-century ago and ruggedly built for export at prices well below those of American and European manufacturers. China, as mentioned in Chapter Seven, now gets more than seven thousand megawatts from over ninety thousand local microhydro sets (few of them grid-connected[76]) ranging from six hundred to a hundred thousand watts, and usually with heads of only zero to sixteen feet. This adds up to at least a third of all Chinese electricity outside the cities,[77] and powers much of the dispersed light industry—an important element of Chinese civil defense planning.

Windpower Windpower has the disadvantage (compared to flat-plate photovoltaics) of moving parts, but the considerable advantage of being able, in decent sites, to collect a great deal of energy from a relatively small machine. A machine which extracts only thirty percent of the power in the wind—reasonable performance for a good design without fancy equipment (tipvanes, shrouds, variable pitch, etc.)—can extract nearly twice as much power from a square yard of area swept through an eighteen-mile-per-hour wind as a square yard of ten-percent-efficient solar cells can extract in bright sunlight.[78] Furthermore, the average U.S. sunlight (direct plus diffuse) averaged over the day and year is only a sixth as strong as bright noon sunlight on a clear day, whereas strong winds can blow at any time, and tend to be especially common in cloudy winter weather. Accordingly, a simple wind machine in a good site, such as many parts of New England, the Great Plains, or the Pacific coasts and islands, can capture mechanical work very cheaply.

A few examples give the flavor of the machines now commercially available and of those now being tooled up for series production. Designs like the very simple one mentioned on page 232 in Chapter Fourteen are now on the market and will become much cheaper when mass production supplants model-shop opeations.[79] Even with hand production of only twenty per month, each with a peak capacity of only one kilowatt, those Bergey machines sold in 1981 for twenty-five hundred dollars FOB factory (five hundred more for a synchronous inverter). In a windy site on the Great Plains, such a machine can produce electricity at prices as low as five to eight cents per kilowatt-hour. Professor Otto Smith, a Berkeley engineer, has made at home, for fifteen hundred dollars (1980 value), a seventeen-and-a-half-kilowatt (at thirty-eight mph) Chalk-wheel turbine, looking like a giant bicycle wheel, which he estimates could be commerically produced for sixty-seven hundred dollars, or under four hundred dollars per peak kilowatt[80]—an excellent bargain. (The electrical output capacity of wind machines is normally rated at a particular speed, generally lower than Smith's figure, and the cost of that capacity is expressed per kilowatt peak [kWp] at that rated speed.) The Borre sailwing design[81] is on the market in an eighteen-kilowatt version for about six hundred fifty to six hundred ninety dollars per peak kilowatt,[82] producing power in good sites at about five cents per kilowatt-hour. Machines made by U.S. Windpower of Burlington, Massachusetts, and designed around commonly available, mass-produced components, are selling (complete except tower, FOB factory, 1981) for six hundred ten to seven hundred dollars per peak kilowatt in the twenty-five- and thirty-seven-kilowatt sizes (models CA and CB respectively).[83] A refined prototype can probably be made for about half that much.[84] The late Terry Mehrkam of Hamburg, Pennsylvania recently built a very large (one-megawatt) machine for a local factory at a total labor-and-materials cost of four hundred twenty-five dollars per installed kilowatt—roughly half the expected mass production cost of the more complex megawatt-range machines developed by government programs with aerospace companies.

The roughly sixty U.S. manufacturers of small machines are listed in indices published by *Wind Power Digest*, the American Wind Energy Association, and the Rockwell International wind test program at Rocky Flats. (There are also many manufacturers abroad, including more than two dozen in Denmark alone.) Basic guides to selecting wind machines[85] and their sites[86] are bringing the technology into common currency. New "wind prospecting" methods include satellite observation of inversion-layer breakups (University of Alaska) and detailed computer simulation of windflow over digitized terrain (Lawrence Livermore Laboratory). Although one might suppose that an art as ancient as wind machines has already had all possible technical refinements, basic improvements continue, especially in blade aerodynamics and in designs for applications other than electric generation. For example, the Wind Baron Corporation (Phoenix, Arizona) reports that its design, by using adjustable weights to counterbalance the water column, can pump up groundwater from three hundred feet down in winds as low as five mph—a speed which occurs ninety percent of the time over ninety-four percent of the earth's surface.

Large-scale commercial wind projects are springing up. Southern California Edison Company has agreed to buy the output from eighty-two megawatts offered by entrepreneurs and is negotiating for several hundred more—over twice its target for the year 2000. A three-hundred-fifty-megawatt project by Windfarms™ of San Francisco, contracted in January 1982 for construction during 1983–89 thirty miles northeast of that city, is to cost over seven hundred million dollars and serve four hundred fifty thousand people. It is to supply nearly a billion kilowatt-hours per year at a real price of three and a half cents per kilowatt-hour[87]—probably less than half the likely incremental cost which California utilities face if they order a coal or nuclear plant. Another company, U.S. Windpower, is currently installing an array of two hundred machines, each with a peak capacity of fifty kilowatts; in all, the company seeks to have six hundred such machines supplying ninety million kilowatt-hours per year by mid-1983. The same firm built twenty machines of fifty kilowatts in New Hampshire within five months of first contacting the site owner, and hooked them to the grid in late 1980 in a mutually profitable symbiosis.[88] This is about twenty-five times as fast as central-station capacity can be built—clearly a way both to reduce utilities' forecasting and financial risks (Appendix One) and to replace power plants in an emergency.

The Hawaiian Electric Company has offered to buy eight and a half percent of its electricity from wind machines starting in 1985. This could be supplied by building twenty large machines at a site (Kahuku Point, Oahu) with twenty-mph minimum winds eighty percent of the time. Plans to finance such a project collapsed in 1982, but the opportunity remains. At least one California city has an operating municipal windpower utility.[89] The Bonneville Power Administration is operating three multi-megawatt wind machines on its grid in the Columbia River Gorge in Washington State. A private entrepreneur reportedly built more than a hundred sailwing gyromills of twenty-five to thirty kilowatts each, priced at eighteen thousand dollars, to run a bleach plant in Dalhart, Texas.[90] Other private projects abound.

Interest in windpower is rapidly rising abroad as well. The Dutch government, for example, is expected to approve a plan for eleven hundred wind machines each providing about three megawatts and all generating, in conjunction with lagoon pumped storage, about nine billion kilowatt-hours per year, or about twelve percent of projected national electricity demand in the year 2000.[91] The Dutch wind array would be completed one-third at a time (by 1990, 1995, and 2000), at a cost of about nineteen hundred million dollars, or just over two cents per kilowatt-hour—a fifth of typical European electricity prices today.

Photovoltaics Photovoltaics are extremely durable, reliable, and simple to use:[92] when placed in the sun, they produce direct current, needing no maintenance unless they have a tracking concentrator. There is no chemical reaction inside them; nothing decays, discharges, or is consumed or given off. These qualities have long commended them for such applications as powering buoys, highway signs, Forest Service towers, microwave relay stations, and remote military bases (part of the rationale for proposed Defense Department purchases[93]). Indeed, solar cells are considered a strategic device whose export is restricted by law.

As with transistors in the 1950s and 1960s and integrated circuits in the 1970s, the cost of solar cells has been falling dramatically. Even conventional, first-generation cells (silicon wafers cut from cylindrical single crystals melt-grown by the Czochralski process) have shown a steep price drop. Czochralski silicon array prices fell from about thirty dollars per peak watt in late 1976 to seven to ten dollars per peak watt in 1979–80. (Photovoltaics are rated in peak watts [Wp] of direct-current output in full sunlight of one thousand watts per square meter.) Such single-crystal silicon cells are now made and sold in many countries: Brazil will even begin exporting them in 1982. There is a consensus among the managers of the very competently run federal photovoltaics program that implementing proven technologies for producing such cells in a more automated fashion, without the thirty-odd hand operations now needed, can reduce the array price to about two dollars and eighty cents per peak watt (in 1980 dollars) by late 1982, corresponding to an installed whole-system price of about six to thirteen dollars per peak watt for flat-plate systems.[94] This is already a sufficiently interesting price that Citicorp has announced plans to install photovoltaics on the slanting roof of its New York City headquarters; the Sacramento Municipal Utility District plans a hundred-megawatt array next to the Rancho Seco nuclear plant; and the European Economic Community in November 1980 authorized the construction of approximately twenty photovoltaic pilot plants in Europe, ranging from thirty to three hundred peak kilowatts.[95]

It is highly likely that several of the second-generation processes already demonstrated and in advanced commercial development—silicon web or ribbon growth, coarse polycrystalline silicon, amorphous silicon films (which can be very cheaply vacuum-deposited on anything, including plastic films), or other materials—will achieve, on or ahead of schedule, the Department of Energy's 1986 array-price goal of seventy cents (1980 dollars) per peak watt, corresponding to a whole-system price of a dollar sixty to two dollars and sixty cents per peak watt and to electricity prices comparable to or lower than those from a newly ordered central power station.

American firms recently invested about two hundred million dollars in photovoltaic risk capital in a year and a half.[96] Solarex, a pioneering firm in Rockville, Maryland, plans by late 1982 to be operating an advanced and automated silicon wafer plant entirely powered by cells which it produces (which should settle the spurious net-energy question once and for all). Westinghouse, Mobil-Tyco, and others report progress with advanced processes for making fairly cheap single-crystal silicon in large amounts. Several American firms have announced the development of amply efficient amorphous materials which they expect to market by about 1985 at about seventy cents per peak watt or less. One such material, developed by AMETEK,[97] can be applied by a simple wet-chemical process similar to electroplating; is already about eight percent efficient; has a materials cost of forty cents per peak watt; and may be applied to the absorber plate of an AMETEK flat-plate solar heat collector to produce electricity as a byproduct. Collector glazings can also be used as nonfocusing concentrators by dispersing a fluorescent dye in the glazing material so that the fluorescence is internally reflected to a photovoltaic strip along one unsilvered edge: a small cell area could thus produce byproduct electricity.

Some of these cheaper designs may be delayed in coming to market by the 1981 cancellation of federal funding for the higher-risk, second-generation cells. A more serious concern is that the longer-term competitive edge in photovoltaics will probably shift to other countries. In Japan, for example, Sanyo has already invested fifty million dollars in a factory for commercial production of amorphous silicon cells.[98]

It is not yet clear how the recent cuts in federal funding for photovoltaics will affect the timetable for achieving the Department of Energy's goal of seventy-cent-a-peak-watt arrays by 1986. If American firms miss that date, however, it will be only by a few years; and foreign competitors are likely to be ahead of schedule. It is therefore important to note that, according to detailed economic calculations, this confidently expected 1986 price—which assumes no further technological breakthroughs—will permit solar-cell electricity to compete on utility grids in most of the United States.[99] (Solar-cell power without a cogeneration heat credit would probably, however, be unable to compete with electricity from wind and small hydro in good sites.) Accordingly, the Department of Energy's Solar Photovoltaics Energy Advisory Committee stated in February 1981 that, due to a combination of rapid technical advances, PURPA buyback provisions (which help to create a competitive market in generation), and higher marginal cost estimates for conventional sources, it is likely that central station photovoltaics will compete around 1986.[100] This means that well-designed cogeneration versions should have become competitive around 1980–81 on a residential scale and in the late 1970s on a community scale.[101] In seeming confirmation, many small firms are now springing up to offer packaged photovoltaic cogeneration systems, which concentrate sunlight on a small cell area and capture the waste heat for domestic use. Such a system is reportedly being installed in a San Diego hotel[102]; another (a costly federal demonstration) is operating in a Kauai hospital.

Many photovoltaic experts expect that by the late 1980s it will probably be fairly common for new houses (and some old ones) to be net exporters of electricity. Already, using only the relatively expensive single-crystal silicon wafers, at least hundreds of houses had installed stand-alone photovoltaic systems with battery storage by the end of 1981.[103] By 1982, thousands of photovoltaic houses were operating in the U.S., of which the greatest concentrations occur in certain remote parts of California. The California Energy Commission expects photovoltaics to supply eleven percent of the state's peak electrical demand by the year 2000.[104]

New technical developments, now in the "breakthrough-a-month" stage, may indeed outdo even these prognoses in helping devices to move rapidly from laboratory achievements to mass-marketed products. Conscious of the need to make photovoltaics easy for builders and homeowners to use, General Electric is developing photovoltaic shingles which would cost little more than normal shingles but produce electricity too. They would be hooked up by nailing them onto the roof. Texas Instruments is developing a clever photovoltaic-hydrogen system with on-site hydrogen storage and a fuel cell. Technical developments in this field are moving, as is the way of semiconductors, too quickly even to report. This adds urgency to the need to plan for the long-term shape of renewable source integration into the power grid (Chapter Sixteen). The photovoltaics revolution is indeed already upon us. We should start getting used to the idea and figuring out how best to use these rugged, almost invulnerable devices to increase the resilience of national electrical supply.

Interconnection with the electric grid

There are many possible ways to connect dispersed renewable sources of electricity to the grid.[105] Which is the best method depends in part on which type of electricity the source generates. Fuel cells, solar cells, or special types of shaft-driven devices make direct current, whose flow is steadily in one direction. Batteries, the most commonly available electrical storage device, can be charged with, and when discharged provide, direct current. So far so good: direct current, with proper wiring, is a safe, simple, and robust way to deliver electricity throughout a building. Once delivered, direct current can operate incandescent lights and certain types of motors. Direct current at the proper voltage is also required by electronic circuitry and some industrial processes such as electroplating. Today, direct current for these purposes is often obtained by "rectifying" alternating current from the grid, then smoothing out its "ripple" to a semblance of a constant flow. Thus almost any electronic device—a television or stereo, for example—contains a rather bulky, heavy, and costly power supply to convert line-voltage alternating current to low-voltage direct current. If this were no longer necessary—if direct current were supplied to start with—a good deal of money, weight, and copper could be saved, provided that the equipment manufacturer offered a direct-current option. This is already the case with many types of appliances which are already available in direct-current versions (typically at twelve or twenty-four volts) for marine use and for recreational vehicles. Before rural electrification, thirty-two-volt direct-current appliances, such as washing machines, were also commonly sold for use on farms with direct-current wind systems and battery banks. This type of market is now re-emerging.

Historically, a main reason for standardizing the power grid to use alternating current was that it can be readily changed from one voltage to another by using a transformer (an iron core wound with two coils having different numbers of turns). That reason, however, is no longer valid, since modern solid-state circuits can convert one direct-current voltage to another very efficiently. Other new circuitry can operate ordinary alternating-current motors (which tend to be cheaper) on direct current over varying loads with better-than-normal efficiency. These conversion devices broaden the opportunities for using direct current without having to replace all of one's appliances.

Inverters Alternatively, or additionally, direct current can be converted into alternating current by a device called an "inverter." Old inverters used rotating motor-generator sets, but most today use solid-state switching electronics. Small inverters, such as are used to operate normal alternating-current appliances from the direct current available in a car or boat, are widely available. Larger ones, less commonly available, enable a house wired for direct current to interconnect synchronously with the alternating-current grid. Alternatively, the house itself can remain wired for, and operate its appliances on, alternating current, but connect the internal wiring via an inverter to its own solar cells or other local sources of direct current (typically via a battery bank or other storage device). A household source of direct current can thus connect to alternating-current appliances, to the grid, or both.

There are several kinds of inverters with different electrical properties, complexity, price, and reliability.[106] Some particularly useful inverters are sold in Japan, for example by Hitachi: they use a microcomputer to make a ninety-nine-percent-plus pure sine wave which changes in a fraction of a cycle to respond to the size and reactance of the load. The Sandia National Laboratory experts who design inverters for the firing circuits of atomic bombs have also been applying their skills to devising simple and reliable inverters for renewable energy sources. Most of the inverters now on the market were designed for use with wind machines, and do not operate as well with solar cells. Solar cell companies and special "packaged-system" consultants, however, are starting to provide complete combinations of compatible components—all the way from cells through inverters and other control equipment to end-use devices. Though this type of "balance-of-system" requirement is still the weakest point in solar-cell equipment, the available range of efficient, versatile inverters, compatible with a wide range of sources and uses, is likely to increase rapidly in the next few years as solar cells become more economic and widespread.

An inverter which connects a direct-current supply to the alternating-current grid must of course be synchronized with the grid. Some inverters take their cue from the grid itself but cannot work without it; some process the line voltage through a microcomputer for greater responsiveness; some maintain roughly the right frequency on their own even if disconnected from the grid; and some rely on radio signals for synchronization. Among the relatively old and unsophisticated designs in common use with wind machines today, the "line-excited" inverters are the most common.

Alternating current Alternating current can by directly generated by any source of shaftpower, using an ordinary generator.[107] There are two main types. A "synchronous" generator, the type used in nearly all large power plants, must have its shaft turned at a constant speed—thirty-six hundred revolutions per minute, divided by the number of pole pairs in the generator—if it is to produce sixty-cycle output. It can operate, and supply local loads, in isolation from the grid, but will not produce the correct frequency unless properly regulated (which is quite easy to do). It cannot be connected to the grid at all unless its speed, voltage, and phase are first matched to those of the grid: otherwise, both the generator and utility equipment could be seriously damaged.

A simpler and somewhat cheaper type of generator is simply an induction motor turned around backwards. An induction motor connected to the grid will turn at a particular speed determined by the voltage fed into it. If, instead, the motor's shaft is turned—for example, by a wind turbine—slightly faster that it would run of its own accord, then instead of consuming power from the grid, it feeds power back into the grid ("induction backfeed"). An induction generator can be connected to the grid at any speed down to and including zero. It is in general more "forgiving," especially of irregularities in the pattern of voltage and current, than a synchronous generator.

Induction generators Many people assume that induction generators cannot start up by themselves ("self-excite") when disconnected from the grid, or when connected to a grid that is not energized—for example, during a blackout. This feature is indeed often relied upon to ensure the safety of people repairing power lines. But in fact, many induction generators use series capacitors to compensate for their inductance and ensure the correct relationship between voltage and current. If those capacitors are sited near the generator, it can in some circumstances "self-excite" in isolation. Ordinarily, it would then generate at a frequency and voltage different from its normal output, and this could damage certain end-use devices connected to it. A "spike" of high voltage can be limited in duration, but not in intensity, by overvoltage relays, since it occurs very rapidly. For this reason, the interconnection criteria of (for example) the Southern California Edison Company state that where self-excitation is possible,

> special service arrangements will be required such as two-line loop service or subtransmission service in order to avoid the induction generator['s] becoming isolated with small amounts of load [which could cause voltages high enough to burn out the load devices]. In many cases, the addition expense for such special load service methods may outweigh the cost savings associated with induction generators.[108]

Such criteria, in practical effect, require that if induction generators are used, they be used in such a way that they cannot function at all without the grid. Their ability to serve an isolated local load is therefore outlawed.

Induction generators' outwardly disagreeable ability to self-excite with their own compensating capacitors, however, can be turned to advantage. By *deliberately* providing enough capacitors near the generator to self-excite it, then switching those capacitors (typically with fast-acting thyristor controls) to stabilize the voltage and frequency generated, it is possible to obtain the constant output conditions of a synchronous generator with a simpler, more rugged, and probably cheaper induction generator whose voltage/current relationship is almost ideally matched to the grid. (Isolation relays could ensure the safety of utility personnel.) Induction generators have long been used in some remote hydroelectric sites—the North of Scotland Electricity Generating Board, for example, has approximately twenty-seven megawatts of them on its thirty-three-kilovolt grid,[109] and Southern California Edison Company itself has operated one (apparently without capacitors) since 1951[110]—but the concept of controlling with switched capacitors is apparently new,[111] having been practiced, for example, in 1980 and 1981 installations by the Metropolitan Water District of Southern California.[112] The concept appears useful even in large central-station generators.[113] Applied to smaller, more dispersed sources, it has the subtle advantage that induction generators are far less likely than synchronous generators to be damaged by harmonics and switching transients which arrive through the grid. Thus, with modern control circuitry, induction generators can go a way towards solving, at reasonable cost, the dilemma posed in Chapter Sixteen—how to protect both the utility's and the end user's equipment while remaining able to supply local loads in an emergency. The use of such systems, however, will probably require utilities to rethink their restrictions on dispered self-excitable induction generators.

Unusual frequencies Whichever type of alternating-current generator is used, it need not operate at sixty cycles per second if it is not connected to the grid at the time. This expands still further the number of ways in which renewable sources can generate electricity. Many alternating-current motors can, within limits, tolerate a "wild" frequency from a unregulated generator, though synchronous clock motors will of course run at the wrong speed.[114] Some devices normally operated on alternating current are quite indifferent to frequency—incandescent lights, for example. Fluorescent lights normally operate at more or less sixty cycles per second but do not require an exact frequency match. As a further complication, some new types of high-efficiency fluorescent lights operate at much higher frequencies: hence the high-pitched whine from portable camping lanterns. Indeed, to save power and weight (high-frequency transformers and motors contain less metal), aircraft often operate on four hundred cycles per second or more. Thus sixty-cycle alternating current and direct current are not necessarily the only two interesting options. The only restriction is that whatever is connected to the grid must be synchronized and at sixty cycles.

If, as appears likely, solar cells become important sources of dispersed supply, it appears that the near-monopoly of alternating current in end-use devices and in local wiring may be broken. A challenge facing electrical engineers and renewable energy designers is to devise the most flexible possible ingredients for an inter-compatible system—from end-use devices to patterns and hardware for household wiring to inverters and (if any) utility interconnections—that will both save the customer money and preserve, for that customer and for the grid, the potential resiliency benefits of essentially uninterruptable sources. The case of the induction generator, described above, offers hope that these goals may prove mutually compatible. But above all, the present procedure—setting interconnection and wiring requirements purely out of habit without even considering resilience—must be changed before unconsidered standards, emerging *de facto,* sacrifice the security gains that the resilient technologies could have offered.

Summary

Five years ago, analysts who suspected that appropriate renewable energy sources might well offer cost-effective ways to replace dwindling fossil fuels tended to be dismissed as enthusiasts. Technologists conditioned by dismal experience with complex, large-scale energy systems told them that it would take decades just to develop renewable sources from a laboratory curiosity to a useful commercial form, and many decades more to disseminate them throughout society. But since then, despite the normal quota of trial and error, actual developments in the field have produced more, better, and cheaper renewable options than anyone thought possible. Experience has also shown that the expected decades of research and engineering could be—indeed, in many cases have been—telescoped into a few years, because the devices were so simple and small that each generation took only days or months to build and test, not ten years.

In many cases, adequate and cost-effective renewable sources sufficient to provide for most or all of the needs of a major sector are already on the market. In some other cases, such technologies are available but not yet optimized: processes are in use (for example, for certain cellulose-to-alcohol conversions or high-temperature uses) which work and which can compete but which are likely to be markedly improved in the next few years. And in other cases, such as solar cells, technologies which are now cost-effective only in certain uses or places are virtually certain to become generally economical very quickly—sooner than a centralized plant could be built—as processes now being perfected in many countries move into intensive production. This book, in concluding that today's best renewable sources are economic and ample, does not assume such future progress; but the new developments are very likely to happen anyhow, and it is only prudent to get ready for them and seek to capture their security benefits.

The pace of development is continuing to accelerate so quickly that any snapshot of the state of the art, including this one, is bound to be out-of-date before the ink is dry. But already, so many solid technological achievements have been reported that many renewable energy experts suspect that they had guessed wrong about what their main problem would be over the next five to ten years. The problem they had feared was that there might not be enough attractive renewable sources to meet the needs of an advanced industrial economy. The problem they are actually encountering, however, is that there are too many. The range of choice is so wide, and so quickly expanding, that the hardest part of many renewable energy projects is deciding which of many inviting opportunities to grasp first. A wider appreciation of how those opportunities can reduce energy vulnerability can only speed up this process.

Appendix Three
Economic Assessment of Appropriate Renewable Sources

Comparing the calculated costs of energy services delivered by renewable and nonrenewable sources (or by renewables vs. each other or vs. efficiency improvements) is an easy process to describe but a very difficult one to do properly. In principle, the economic value of renewables depends both on the price of the energy they deliver and on the price of the energy they replace. Both are highly uncertain. Both can be evaluated only with reference to a particular energy service delivered to a final user. Market price reflects some "internal" costs but excludes others ("externalities"), such as unregulated forms of pollution, vulnerability, or other costs paid by neighbors or by society as a whole, not specifically by the buyer (Chapter Sixteen). While a complete cost comparison should include these factors, this appendix considers only internal costs that are private to the purchaser/operator of the energy device. This biases the results in favor of the centralized, nonrenewable technologies, because they tend to have larger external costs than appropriate renewable sources do.

Renewable energy systems have no fuel cost (except for the feedstock to bioconversion systems and, perhaps, water rights for some hydro). If well designed and built, they also tend to have low operating and maintenance (O&M) costs. (Long-term economic performance can be quite sensitive to those costs.) The price of energy from renewable sources thus depends mainly on:

• their initial capital cost. This depends strongly on

  • the simplicity, cleverness, and durability of design. These can vary enormously and may bear no relation to the designer's formal credentials: indeed, highly qualified designers may produce the most gratuitously complex designs.

  • the marketing structure. A "packaged" flat-plate solar collector system whose price is marked up three or four times—by the manufacturer, wholesaler, retailer, and installer (if different from the retailer)—can end up costing its user several times as much as an otherwise identical "site-assembled" system with one mark-up.[1] Most analyses assume only the "packaged" method.

  • how efficiently the delivered energy is used. This affects, as the Saskatchewan Conser-

- vation House example in Chapter Fifteen showed, the size of the renewable system (which can be reduced by tenfold), its performance, and its complexity (as in the replacement of a heat distribution system by natural convection). Such synergisms can be examined only on a micro design level.

These effects can together change unit prices by factors ranging from *ten to perhaps a thousand.*

- the cost of financing them over their lifetimes. This depends on

  - real interest rates, which depend on perceived risk and should therefore be lower for many renewables[2]—but may not be in practice if the lending agency is unfamiliar with the technology.

  - working capital requirements. These are related to capital intensity by construction time, payback time, and shape of cash flow, and again should be more favorable for soft technologies.[3]

  - projected operating lifetime, which may be difficult to estimate. (Some wind machines and flat-plate solar collectors have worked well for decades with little or no maintenance. Badly built, they could have failed in a few months or years. Some designs are much more forgiving of mistakes and environmental insults than others.)

- the amount of energy supplied annually. This depends on

  - quality of design, construction, operation, and maintenance.

  - patterns of energy use. A mismatch between supply and demand patterns could leave some demand unmet or lead to the "dumping" of surplus supply (such as unneeded waste heat in the summer).

  - variations in weather and climate.

  - appropriateness of design to local conditions and use patterns. Some large corporations have been unable to compete in the solar collector market with some small businesses, not only because the latter had better innovation and lower overheads, but also because they could achieve better performance by matching designs to local weather, building styles, and so forth—rather than making a "cookie-cutter" product which is designed for a hypothetical average house and is therefore suboptimized for any actual particular house.

- the amount and type of storage required, if any. This depends on the three factors just listed and on the nature and degree of integration with other renewable or nonrenewable sources (Chapter Sixteen).

This may seem, and it is, more complex than one might have expected. To make matters worse, the price of competing nonrenewable energy is equally imponderable. It depends mainly on

- general and sector-specific inflation in the cost of goods, services, and money, both during construction and afterwards for the project's operating lifetime.

- the relationship between historic and marginal capital costs. (The latter have generally exceeded the former since about 1970.)

- the difficulty of obtaining fuels from ever more remote and awkward places.

- the economic and political policies of fuel-exporting countries interacting with a complex world market and with unforeseeable political exigencies.

- national and local policies regarding trade, legal structures, inflation control, employment, environment, and a host of other factors.
- the degree of technical reliability and resilience desired.
- tax and accounting conventions, tariff structures, and subsidies. Subsidies to the U.S. energy system total over two hundred fifty-two billion 1978 dollars historically.[4] Those to nuclear power alone suffice to cut the cost of nuclear electricity, as seen by consumers, about in half.[5] Tax and price subsidies are currently continuing at a rate approaching one hundred billion dollars per year[6]—enough to reduce average energy prices by over a third and nuclear electricity prices by more than half again.[7] Direct tax subsidies currently favor supply over efficiency by eight to one and hard over soft technologies by between ten and twenty to one.
- salvage values. (For nuclear facilities and wastes these are negative—that is, the plant will cost money to decommission—but of unknown size.)

Renewable/nonrenewable comparisons are further complicated by the following problems:

- great variation in price quotations even for one product in one market. Identical gas-fired water heaters in identical Southern California apartments differ by a factor of two in retail price and by nearly a factor of three in installed price. Price scatter is larger in solar markets, which are less mature and have more diverse product lines and marketing structures.
- extremely rapid technical change, especially for renewables, much of it outside official programs and traditional information channels.
- uncertainty about how far, or how, to internalize important externalities (many of which are considered in Chapter Sixteen).
- what depletion value to put on nonrenewable fuels and other resources. Their cost was traditionally assumed to be only the cost of mining them, as if that mining did not make their future replacement cost more.
- the many imponderable (e.g., psychological and political) factors which help to determine how far and how fast different available technologies can be put into use.
- economies and diseconomies of scale (Appendix One).
- the inability of most simulation models used by energy policy analysts to cope properly with diverse, relatively dispersed renewable sources or with their nontraditional processes of market penetration (Chapter Fourteen). Models attuned to centralized and nonrenewable technologies tend to give results that favor those technologies.
- the need to match any renewable source to its climate, site, applications, and users, in order to achieve best performance at least cost.
- the difficulty of comparing the storage and back-up requirements of complete energy systems containing renewable or nonrenewable components, to achieve a

given level of reliability to final users, when there is not a fully satisfactory reliability theory for either type of system, let alone for both in combination.

the potential for total-energy systems which provide electricity and heat (and perhaps liquid fuels) and for other types of hybrids (Chapter Sixteen and Appendix One).

the opportunities offered by many renewable sources (but only rarely by nonrenewables) for sharing functions and costs through integration into shelter, food, water, or other systems (Chapter Sixteen). Such opportunities, however, can be identified only by a highly localized and disaggregated analysis which goes beyond the energy sector itself.

the sensitivity of economic comparisons to minor changes in accounting for inflation, "levelizing" varying costs over the life of a project, discounting the future, and so on. Small, seemingly innocuous changes in real discount rate are a commonly used method of reversing the outcome of renewable/nonrenewable comparisons.

In view of these complications, it is not surprising that virtually no renewable/nonrenewable cost comparison will prove satisfactory to everyone. Experts often disagree about basic data by factors of severalfold, depending on their familiarity with recent developments and willingness to accept an example of what exists as an "existence proof" for what can be done more widely. They differ in their assessment of the state of the art or the applicability of certain methodologies. They do not accept other experts' views on how far particular case studies are more widely applicable. Thus a large number of energy experts, laid end to end, will probably never reach a conclusion about the economics of renewable sources. The only recourse is to make assumptions and data sources explicit enough so that cost calculations are transparent, scrutable, and easily compared.

It must also not be expected that the unit cost of any technology can be represented by a single number. How much a thing costs depends on how many of them you want. Economic theory indeed requires that each technology (or aggregate of different technologies) be subject to a "supply curve" in which unit price rises with increasing supply. That this is the case for conventional utility power plants, owing to a complex series of political-regulatory relationships reflecting a social desire to hold constant the perceived social costs of expanding coal and nuclear sectors, is nicely illustrated in Figure A.3. It plots as supply curves the data obtained by a detailed statistical analysis of historic costs,[8] which explains ninety-two percent of the observed variation in the real cost per installed net electric kilowatt of forty-six nuclear plants and sixty-eight percent for one hundred sixteen coal-fired plants.

Renewable sources too have supply-curve costs rather than point costs, though the shape of the curve will differ from one technology to another. For example, solar heat collectors which are small enough to fit onto a building usually cost less than those which need extra land, and those so small that they can be integrated into the structure of a building cost still less. How big a collector is needed depends on how efficient the building is. Likewise, if biomass fuels are efficiently used, not much will be needed, so the feedstock can be wastes which are cheap (or

Figure A.3 Plant construction cost (1979 steam-plant dollars per net electric kilowatt of installed capacity, without interest during construction)

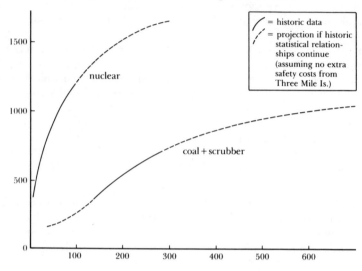

Thousands of megawatts of net electric capacity (of each type of plant)
built or being built

which may even have a negative cost because converting them to fuel saves a disposal cost). Less efficient use, hence higher demand, may require the use of more expensive feedstocks such as grains; higher demands may entail the growth of special "fuel crops"; higher still, irrigation for that purpose. This raises costs, as can be illustrated by the schematic sketch in Figure A.4 (not meant to be exact, since complete data do not yet exist). Buying efficient vehicles—because their efficiency costs less than fuel—means that the nation needs substantially less fuel; therefore it is relatively cheap (near the lower left corner of the graph). Underinvesting in efficiency requires the nation to buy a large amount of fuel which rapidly becomes expensive (near the upper right corner of the graph). Most studies assume the latter and hence find that biomass fuels are costly. This book, however, is concerned with a more nearly optimal economic balance between investments in energy supply and in energy productivity, represented by the "market clearing price" at which the supply and demand curves cross in equilibrium. This example illustrates why, even though the price estimates for renewable sources are discussed below as points or narrow ranges, each estimate is only part of a supply curve which cannot be analyzed independently of competition between increased energy supply and increased efficiency.

Despite all the generic uncertainties of renewable/nonrenewable cost comparisons, four broad principles can often simplify economic choices. First, investment decisions should be based not on projected small differences of marginal cost (which are often well within the uncertainty of tne data) but rather on how sensitive those costs will be to changes in key variables such as oil price. Basing decisions on sensitivities enables one to "play safe" in an uncertain world. In general,

Figure A.4   Illustrating schematic supply curve for biomass liquid fuels.

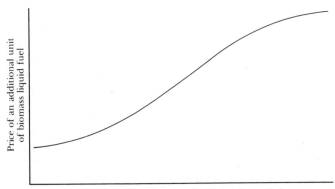

Total amount of biomass liquid fuel demanded

the variations of greatest policy interest, such as high world oil prices or high inflation, tend to improve the competitive position of renewables still further. Yet soft technologies do not (as the data below will show) need such assumptions for their attractiveness, since they can generally compete with present oil prices with considerable room to spare.

Second, differences of internal cost may be less important to many nations than differences not captured in that cost—implications for resilience and self-reliance, employment, equity, balance of trade, and so forth.[9] Third, in general, the real costs of fossil and nuclear energy are likely to rise and those of most renewable sources to fall. The relative speeds of change in both cases are the subject of great uncertainty and dispute, although the directions of change are empirically undeniable and the fundamental reasons for those changes are all but certain to persist.

And finally, renewable sources in general offer far greater scope than non-renewables for simple, low-technology adaptations suitable for local construction with limited skills and common materials. Such simplified versions cost far less than those normally analyzed; they are more analogous to the improvisations commonly made by individuals at a grassroots level. It is difficult to capture the enormous range of costs reported for such self-help projects, especially those done by low-income people who do not cost their own labor or who do cooperative projects. But in general the real costs to the users are far less—even orders of magnitude less—than for conventional, industrially supplied hardware, and the performance is often broadly comparable and sometimes better. This important point is explored under "Simplified versions" in Chapter Sixteen.

Subject to these caveats and uncertainties—the last, the immense range of technical complexity and costs over which many renewable options can be built, being perhaps the most difficult to analyze—illuminating comparisons of renewable/nonrenewable economics are in fact possible. Dispassionate evaluations yield a result which, though it seemed surprising a few years ago, is now becoming widely accepted: that if one chooses good designs and shops carefully for best buys, many renewable energy systems already offer a pronounced economic advantage over present fuels, and virtually all appropriate renewables are cheaper than the incremental cost of nonrenewable, centralized supply technologies. The renewables' advantage is generally increased by doing the still cheaper efficiency improvements first. This economic ranking of marginal sources—efficiency improvements cheapest, *then* appropriate renewables, *then* nonrenewables (synfuels and power plants)[10]—holds true even if one ignores (as this book does) all external costs and benefits not currently reflected in market prices, including differences in vulnerability or resilience. If those important nonmarket considerations were included, the results would favor efficiency and renewables by an even more lopsided margin.

A responsible analysis of renewable energy economics, however, must be internally consistent. Data derived by different analysts often cannot be directly compared because they use different assumptions and accounting conventions. This appendix therefore uses consistent conventions. Furthermore, to ensure that the results are robust and cannot be overturned by minor changes in the assumptions, those assumptions are consistently weighed in the sense least favorable to the conclusions. An earlier comparison of this type, for example, assumed:[11]

• no real cost escalation for any source after ordering in 1976 (whereas in fact the capital cost of nonrenewable technologies continues to escalate steeply, while that of most renewables is declining);

• generously low prices for nonrenewable systems;[12]

• no cheap designs (such as passive solar systems, solar ponds, community-scale or roof-integrated collectors, collectors made of such materials as plastic films or extrusions, other low-technology designs and devices);

• the same fixed charge rate (which converts an initial capital cost into an annual capital charge against output) for renewable as for nonrenewable systems, making no allowance for the renewables' more favorable cash flow due to shorter lead time and faster payback time;[13]

• a high fixed charge rate[14] for both systems (this discriminates against those with a high ratio of capital to operating costs, such as renewables, whose operating cost is virtually nil);

• for heating applications, an unrealistically efficient heat pump (two hundred fifty percent efficient even on the coldest winter day) operated by baseload (rather than average or peaking) electricity; and

• subsidies included for hard technologies but excluded for efficiency improvements and soft technologies.

Such multiple "conservatisms" help to ensure that the severalfold price advantage shown for the soft technologies over their nonrenewable, centralized competitors is not an artifact of arguable assumptions but a firmly defensible conclusion—one on which many analyses have lately converged.[15] Most of the same conservatisms are preserved in the present analysis. Although a few simplified designs are included to reflect more fully the wide range of technical complexity among systems actually being bought in the marketplace, the economic advantage found for soft technologies generally does not depend on these simplified versions; it is merely stronger in their case. As in the earlier analysis, subsidized nonrenewable systems are compared in price with *un*subsidized renewable systems, to emphasize the advantage which the latter actually display.

Tables A.1 through A.4 compare the delivered price of an energy form or service in each of four service categories: heat below the boiling point of water (thirty-five percent of U.S. delivered energy needs); heat above that temperature (twenty-three percent); vehicular liquid fuels (thirty-four percent); and electricity (eight percent). The measured or calculated prices shown are documented in the tables, using a wide variety of sources, but care has been taken to normalize the results to the same assumptions so they are comparable. While this comparison cannot be definitive, it does support the broad conclusion that soft technologies are cheaper than competing hard technologies, summarized below in each sector. For consistent comparison, all prices are normalized to the same units: constant 1980 dollars per million BTUs (or, approximately, per billion joules) of energy—heat, liquids, or electricity—delivered to the final user. With a few noted exceptions, all the cost calculations use the same fixed charge rate: ten percent per year in real terms, or ten percent plus the assumed inflation rate in nominal (current-dollar) terms. Thus a device with a capital cost of one thousand dollars per kilowatt is assumed to incur each year a capital charge of one hundred dollars per kilowatt. The sum of that charge plus any operating costs equals the total cost of providing the energy. The fixed charge rate used here has been chosen to be comparable to or slightly greater than that used by most energy companies today in their own cost calculations.

Table A.1 shows that low-temperature heat provided by burning today's fuels in a seventy-percent-efficient furnace (better than many) will cost, with the very temporary exception of natural gas pending its decontrol, around fifteen dollars per million BTUs, or about twice as much as (subsidized) average 1981 electricity used in an extremely efficient heat pump. Synthetic gas from coal is no better. Electricity from a newly ordered nuclear (or coal) central station is about the same or worse—in round numbers, twenty-five dollars per million BTUs if used in resistance heaters, or perhaps as little as ten dollars if used in a super-efficient heat pump.

In contrast, efficiency improvements cost typically zero to three dollars per million BTUs saved—at most five dollars among the measures shown, the full achievement of which should keep the nation well provided with savings opportunities for the next decade or two. Passive solar measures are similarly cheap. With careful shopping, active solar space and water heating for a single house (generally costlier than a multi-family dwelling or a neighborhood-scale system) is in the range of eight to ten dollars per million BTUs, competing with deregulated fuels and power today. The real price of conventional packaged active systems is widely expected to continue falling by two to three percent per year,[16] and some simplified designs shown in Table A.1, whether do-it-yourself or commercial, have already dropped prices even faster, empirically achieving about four to six dollars per million BTUs even with commercial fabrication. The empirical cost (nine dollars per million BTUs) of heat from a municipally operated solar pond in Ohio (Appendix Two) also competes with oil or electric resistance heat at today's prices, and competes even with electric or gas heat pumps at their marginal prices. Community solar heating systems,[17] using conventional collectors or solar ponds, can drop heat prices down into the range of passive solar or the costlier efficiency improvements—about four to six dollars per million BTUs. For providing heat,

Table A.1 Illustrative delivered prices, in 1980 dollars, for heat below two hundred twelve degrees Fahrenheit. The prices shown reflect the effect of subsidies only for the hard technologies (save in the one solar case shown in parentheses).

Technology	Remarks	Source	1980 $ per million BTUs
HARD TECHNOLOGIES:			
Oct. 1980 controlled natural gas	*subsidized fuel & power prices for comparison*	*SERI 1981:II-96*	4.0
#2 heating oil @ $1.10/gallon	*70%-efficient free furnace*	*Green 1980*	13.7
propane @ 80¢/gallon	*70%-efficient free furnace*	*Green 1980*	13.4
electricity @ 5.5¢/kW-h	*70%-efficient free furnace*		16.1
same (Jan. 1981 av. resid. price)	*free resistance heater*		6.8
	$250/kWe, 250%-efficient heat pump, 1% O&M		
Alaskan gas	*70%-efficient free furnace, 1% O&M*	*Linden 1981:37*	16.6
marginal syngas (first generation)	*same*	*same*	12.3–16.6
same (second generation)	*same*	*same*	11.5–15.2
same (second generation)	*$300/kWt input, 130%-eff. heat pump, 2% O&M*	*Ross & Williams 1981:306*	11.5–13.6
marginal nucl. elec. @ 8.4¢/kWh	*free resistance heater*	*see Table A.4*	24.7
same	*electric heat pump as above*	*see Table A.4*	10.3
EFFICIENCY IMPROVEMENTS:	*3%/y real discount rate, 10-year time horizon*	*SERI 1981:II*	
retrofitted direct-fueled houses	*save over 50% of heat*	*:12–13*	2.7
same	*save over 75% of heat*	*same*	5.0
retrofited elec.-heated houses	*save over 50% of heat*	*same*	5.0
retrofited commercial buildings	*save over 35% of space conditioning*	*:70*	1.3–2.2
superinsulated new houses	*save over 90% of heat*	*Leger & Dutt 1979; Shick, Shurcliff 1980*	negative
same	*save ca. 100% of heat*	*see Chapter Fifteen*	ca. 0–1.1

SOLAR TECHNOLOGIES:

passive house retrofit (empirical)	"best buys" examples	SERI 1981:II:94, 204–5	1.5–2.2
same	"average" (DIY & Solar I)	same	3.5–7.8
active house retrofit (empirical)	"best buys" examples	same	8.2
same	"average" (DIY & Solar I)	same	9.5
1980 commercial water heater	typical packaged system, no tax credit	:186–7	9.4–32.5
(same)	(same with 40% tax credit)	(same)	(5.6–20.4)
1990 same, expected	no tax credit	:186–7, 175	5.0–25.5
ca. 1982 Teagan water heater	simple design	Popular Sci. 1981a	ca. 6–7
1980 breadbox water heater	batch; 10-year lifetime	Green 1980; see also Shapiro 1980	2.2–6.2
1981 breadbox water heater	batch; CETA-installed @ $85 complete	Fisk 1979	2.7
1978 site-assembled air collector system	see also SERI 1981:II:172, Godolphin 1981, Shapiro 1980	Green 1980; Worcester Poly. 1978	4.1–11.4
1990–2000 low-cost collector program goals	average installed hot-water system (projected)	SERI 1981:II:177	5.3
1980 inflatable greenhouse	10-year horizon, 8¢/kW-h fan	Solar Flashes 1980	ca. 0.6
1980 solar pond	Miamisburg, Ohio municipal operation built from scratch	Soft Energy Notes 4(1):18–20 (1981)	9.2
same if it were bigger	estimated from empirical data		8.0
community solar systems, flat-plate	calculated	Schurr et al. 1979: Ch. 11	3.8–6.4
same, concentrator	calculated	same	5.1
wood @ $70–90/cord	20 million BTUs/cord, 50%-efficient stove	Green 1980	7.0–9.0

therefore, well-designed and presently available renewable sources are clearly the best buy after efficiency improvements.

Table A.2 shows a similar result. Synthetic gas burned in an industrial boiler to provide process heat will deliver even costlier heat (twelve dollars per million BTUs) than residual oil at market prices does now (nine dollars), though still cheaper than marginal electricity (twenty-five dollars). Even expensive wood wastes can deliver the same clean heat via commercially available gasifiers[18] for three or four dollars, or more cheaply (if perhaps less conveniently) via direct combustion. Simple solar concentrators at temperatures adequate for nearly all industries other than ceramics/bricks/glass and primary metals (which need higher concentrations or indirect forms of solar energy)[19] now deliver heat at prices competitive with syngas or OPEC oil or both. It is for that reason that an Israeli-American entrepreneur can make a profit by offering to supply a specified fraction (normally fifteen to thirty percent) of any factory's steam needs for twenty years at a price ten percent below what the factory now pays. He simply builds parabolic trough collectors, sells their steam, and pockets the ample difference. By late 1981, such schemes were under construction at three textile mills, involving over two hundred thousand square feet of collectors which, over the twenty-year contract period, will save the equivalent of over one billion cubic feet of natural gas.[20]

Homemade concentrating collectors (costing only materials, not labor) can achieve two dollars per million BTUs even in cloudy areas—a remarkable bargain. As the prototype commercial concentrators now on the market are replaced by mass-produced models,[21] their heat prices over the next few years should fall to about three to six dollars per million BTUs—well below present oil prices—through normal scaling-up of what are now model-shop operations. As noted in Appendix Two, several solar process heat systems in their initial production runs were already selling for prices comparable to those listed in the "conservative" projection in Table A.2—prices competitive with oil anywhere (especially in Europe),[22] and with most domestic fuels in most parts of the United States today. The only fossil fuel that can probably compete with the best solar concentrators today is coal in areas that have a good distribution infrastructure. The *average* coal price today (which conceals wide variations), with a clean and efficient boiler, can undercut almost any commercial solar concentrator (but not, as Table A.3 shows, homemade ones). As the average coal price rises above twenty dollars per barrel equivalent (about eighty dollars a ton, compared to the present thirty-odd) over the next two decades, commercial solar process heat costs will fall. The two costs should cross sometime during 1982–85 in much of the United States and by 1990 in virtually all parts.

Table A.3 shows that many renewable liquid fuels—especially those from thermochemical processes fed with farm or forestry wastes—are likewise cheaper than synthetic fuels. This is partly because woody materials have much more favorable chemical reaction kinetics than coal: they break down faster, at lower temperatures, with little or no tar formation, and they contain virtually no corrosive sulfur. Both the energy and the capital requirements are accordingly lower, and the yields generally higher, than for equivalent coal liquefaction. Some renewable liquids, especially those emphasized by current policy, are slightly costlier per BTU than

Table A.2 Illustrative delivered prices, in 1980 dollars, for heat above two hundred twelve degrees Fahrenheit. The prices shown reflect the effect of subsidies only for the hard technologies.

Technology	Remarks	Source	1980 $ per million BTUs
HARD TECHNOLOGIES:			
1980 average coal	subsidized fuel & power prices for comparison 70%-efficient free boiler, 3% O&M	Linden 1981:32	2.5
2000 average coal (DOE est.)	same	same	5.9
$40/barrel residual oil	80%-efficient free boiler, 2% O&M		8.7
syngas (first generation)	same; delivery cost $1 per million BTUs	Linden 1981:37	8.9–12.8
#2 fuel oil from coal syncrude	same; delivery & marketing 77¢/million BTUs	same	12.5–13.7
marginal nuclear electricity	8.4¢/kW-h, free resistance furnace	see Table A.4	24.7
SOLAR PROCESS HEAT:			
30"-dia. parabolic dish built by Doug Wood (Fox Island WA)	new-materials-only cost; average U.S. site would have 50% greater insolation	Soft Energy Notes 2:97 (Dec. 1979)	2.2
mass-produced Fresnels including storage @$1/GJ	$2.6–5.3/sq ft + installation (semiempirical prices), U.S. av. insolation, 63% eff.	Ross & Williams 1981: 331; OTA 1978	3.6–4.5
1980 handmade parabolic troughs including storage @ $1/GJ	$45/sq ft, 60% efficient, in climatic range equivalent to New Mexico to New Hampshire	SERI 1981:II: 623, 630	6.4–12.5
mass-produced collector goals	"conservative" (same range)—commercial 1981	:634	3.7–6.9
same	"expected" (same range)—mid 1980s estimate	same	3.2–5.6
same	"optimistic" (same range)	same	2.3–3.8
570°F Winston collector including storage @ 50¢/GJ	$17.7/sq ft calculated installed price, U.S. av. insolation, 44% eff., 2% O&M	Grimmer & Herr 1977	9.8
Sandia 1985 projection	up to 600°F; well above best 1981 prices	Energy Insider 1980a	10.0
OTHER RENEWABLE SOURCES:			
wood @ $20/green ton, 65% eff.	different fixed charge rate than this table	Hewett et al. 1981:150	2.3
same, gasified	same	same	3.6
retrofitted wood gasifier	30%/y nominal fixed charge rate; $30/dry ton; 80%-efficient free boiler, 2% O&M	OTA 1980:II:138	3.4–3.7
same	different fixed charge rate; $20/dry ton	SERI 1979:I:29	3.8
manure biogas	500 cu ft active volume; same boiler	OTA 1981:99	7.8

385

Table A.3 Illustrative delivered prices, in 1980 dollars, for vehicular liquid fuels. All tax credits excluded except the present subsidies to nonrenewables. All BTUs counted as equal in value (thus underestimating the value of fuel alcohols in appropriate blends and engines in which they can do more work per BTU than petroleum-based fuels).

Technology	Remarks	Source	1980 $ per million BTUs
HARD TECHNOLOGIES:			
1980 untaxed regular gasoline	subsidized fuel & power prices for comparison	Linden 1981:39	7.2–8.0
1980 taxed regular gasoline	regional price range		11.2
gasoline from shale oil	$1.35/U.S. gallon	same	10.4–12.4
same	$12.50/bbl marketing & distribution mark-up	OTA 1980a	12.3–13.3
gasoline from coal	same; likewise omits recent cost overruns	Linden 1981:39	12.4–13.4
#2 diesel oil from shale oil	same	same	9.2–10.2
#2 diesel oil from coal	same	same	11.2–12.2
EFFICIENCY IMPROVEMENTS:			
efficient light vehicles	see Chapter Fifteen	see Chapter Fifteen	under 3.5
THERMOCHEMICAL BIOCONVERSION:			
portable pyrolyzer	free, half-wet sawdust; semi-empirical	Tatom et al. 1976	1.0–1.4
pyrolysis "oil" from muni. wastes	empirical	Benemann 1977	6.0
same from wood & cellulosic wastes	empirical	Green 1980	6.9–12.6
methanol from all sources	empirical; mostly from wood	SERI 1981:II:591	ca. 16
methanol from muni. wastes	empirical and calculated	Green 1980	3.9–8.1
methanol from forestry wastes	hybrid Canadian processes; estimated	InterGroup 1978	ca. 10–13
methanol from wood, $20/green ton	large scale (2000 tons/day); different fixed charge rate than this table	Hewett et al. 1981:150	4.1
methanol from wood, oxygen-gasified	$10–30/dry ton; calculated	OTA 1980:II:173	11.5–22.8
BACTERIAL & ENZYMATIC BIOCONVERSION:			
homemade ethanol from wastes	empirical; no crop or labor cost	Amer. Homegrown Fuel Pye & Humphrey 1979	5.7
ethanol from wood & cellulosic wastes @ $11.25/dry ton	enzymatic; estimated from lab results		ca. 10–11
ethanol from grains (empirical)	conventional large-scale distillation	OTA 1980:II:165	11.3–15.7
same	same; wet milling	Flaim & Hertzmark 1981:99	14.9–16.0
same	same, various processes	SERI 1980a:84	15.8
ethanol from cellulosic wastes	same; projected	OTA 1980:II:173	12.2–17.0
ethanol from lignocellulose	Emert process; projected	SERI 1981:II:581	ca. 16
same	other processes in development; projected		ca. 6–10

386

present gasoline prices if they are inefficiently produced or made from specially grown crops. But a comparison of cost per BTU does not count the credit due to fuel alcohols for burning (in properly designed engines) more cleanly and efficiently than oil. A recent methanol-powered cross-country flight in a light aircraft by former Astronaut Gordon Cooper and by President Reagan's former pilot[23] not only dramatized methanol's potential for greatly improving the airlines' parlous finances; it also demonstrated that in piston engines at altitudes above about ten thousand feet, methanol is more powerful per gallon than aviation fuel, even though it has only about half as many BTUs per gallon. Its advantage in low-altitude cars, though less, is still enough to tip many of the close comparisons in Table A.3 in favor of fuel alcohols.

Finally, Table A.4 shows that a wide range of renewable sources—small hydro, wind, simple solar-thermal engines, even some photovoltaic cogeneration systems—can deliver electricity at about two to six cents per kilowatt-hour. This competes handily with the delivered price from newly ordered central power stations (in the vicinity of eight cents or more in most areas: Southern California Edison Company estimates about twelve cents or more). Many of the presently available renewables also compete with the present average (rolled-in) price seen by the consumer, or with the roughly equivalent fuel and operating cost *alone* for oil-fired stations (typically from five to seven cents or more). Virtually any of the renewables would be attractive today in high-price areas, such as New York City (where in late 1980 the regular taxed price was fifteen cents per kilowatt-hour—twenty-five cents at peak periods), Alaskan villages and remote military bases (typically upwards of forty cents), and rural areas of developing countries (thirty to ninety cents).

Table A.4 confirms that well-designed smaller technologies tend to deliver cheaper electricity than the centralized ones (Appendix One). It also illustrates the great diversity of options available for cost-effectively generating renewable electricity. Although it is sometimes claimed that solar energy, while an effective source of heat, cannot economically make electricity, Table A.4 shows that on the contrary there is an embarrassing surplus of ways to do so, without even counting solar cells. Photovoltaic prices, as noted in Appendix Two, are dropping so quickly that the Department of Energy now expects them, even in central-station applications, to compete with average grid prices by 1986 using demonstrated technologies;[24] but microhydro and wind, and perhaps other renewable sources, have *already* achieved this with hardware now on the market. The same cannot be said of the centralized solar electric systems—multi-megawatt wind machines, power towers, ocean-thermal-electric conversion, centralized biomass plantations to fuel thermal power plants, solar power satellites, and so on. (Unfortunately, it has been these centralized technologies that have received most of the federal solar budget for the past decade.) For comparison, there is not even a credible prospect of *ever* competing with appropriate renewables via the nuclear fusion program, the second-biggest component of the federal energy budget,[25] nor (as Table A.4 shows) via fission.

In summary, in every category of end-use need (heat, vehicular liquid fuels, and electricity), there are already several varieties of dispersed renewable sources which compete handily with present fuel and power prices—let alone with the far

Table A.4 Illustrative delivered prices, in 1980 dollars, for electricity. The prices shown reflect the effect of subsidies only for the hard technologies. Electricity prices converted to heat prices at 3413 BTUs per kilowatt-hour of electricity.

Technology	Remarks	Source	1980 $ per million BTUs
HARD TECHNOLOGIES:			
Jan. 1981 av. U.S. residential price	subsidized fuel & power prices for comparison 5.5¢/kW-h	Russell 1981	16.1
New York City 1980 av. taxed price marginal price: light-water reactor commissioned 1988 (8.4¢/kW-h)	15.3¢/kW-h (peak rate 24.9¢/kW-h) GNP deflator applied to earlier calculation done at 12%/y real fixed charge rate	Lovins 1977b, 1978a, 1979a, 1981c	44.8 (72.6) 24.6
same recalculated: 7.6¢ with 1979 ordering, ca. 8.6¢ with 1981 ordering; same methodology	updated data on reactor, decommissioning, fuel-cycle, and O&M costs; updated grid & fuel-cycle facility costs	Komanoff 1981; Bechtel (Lovins 1979a: nn20,21); 1979–80 GNP deflator	22.2–25.2
marginal nuclear electricity price (GNP-deflated from 1982)	Southern California Edison Co. levelized life-cycle cost estimate (12¢ in 1982 $)	F.A. McCrackin, personal communication, 1 Dec. '81	29.1
EFFICIENCY IMPROVEMENTS: typically 0–1.5¢/kW-h	see Chapter Fifteen	SERI 1981; Lovins 1982	0–4.4
SMALL HYDRO	2–8¢/kW-h; highly site-specific	SERI 1981:II:958	5.9–23.4
WIND MACHINES: 10-kWp Millville, 13 mph @ 40', calculated from empirical data assuming mass produc. (5.1¢/kW-h)	privately owned, 1% O&M, no extra grid or land costs; innovative installation & 95% learning curve would yield 3.4¢/kW-h	SERI 1981:II:191	14.7
best small comm'l models, 1980–81	empirical ca. 4–6¢/kW-h in excellent sites	see Chapter Sixteen	11.7–17.6
1-MWp Mehrkam machine, empirical	0.3 capacity factor, 2% O&M	see Chapter Sixteen	4.8

2.5-MWp Boeing Mod II high-tech, 0.3 capacity factor, $15,000/y O&M @ 4.6¢/kW-h)	projected 100th-unit price ($809/kWp inst'led + 10% contingency); $85/kWp land; $100/kWp grid; 4% grid losses	*SERI 1981:II:935–9*, GNP deflator	13.0
Mod II machines in Columbia Gorge, $1720/kWp, 1981	preliminary empirical busbar price (ca. 4¢/ kW-h) plus ca. 2¢ for grid + losses + O&M		ca. 18

SOLAR-THERMAL-ELECTRIC:

homemade 30' dish/steam engine (generates @ 3.2¢/kW-h)	new-materials-only cost; average U.S. site would have 50% greater insolation	*Soft Energy Notes 2:97 (Dec. 1979)*	9.3
high-tech power tower (7.4¢/kW-h)	Phoenix; $7.9/sq ft heliostats, projected	*Solar Thermal Rpt. 1981*	21.7
same, dish design (ca. 16¢/kW-h)	1985, no cogeneration credit	*SERI 1981:II:943*	46.9
same, 1990 projection (5.2¢/kW-h)	25,000/y production rate	Ibid.	15.2

PHOTOVOLTAIC:

community cogeneration, heat credit, municipal utility ownership	$15/Wp array, 18% eff. @ 20°C; $7.4–12.6/ sq.ft; diesel back-up; 1976–80 GNP deflator	*Ross & Williams 1981:170–179*	24.1–28.3
best 1981 components, cogen., 4 Wt/ We, heat credit $13.7/million BTUs	$14/Wp system including 3-sun Winston con- centrator; Phoenix/Seattle climatic range	*Henry Kelly, pers. com., 1981; calculated*	5.3–66.5
Martin-Marietta Fresnel concentrator	1981 technology @ 50 MWe order; offered price $1.6–2.2/Wp system; utility buyback @ 50% of average price; delivers @ 5.9–8.1¢/kW-h	*Maycock 1981:42 Russell 1981; DOE 1980a; JPL 1980; AMETEK 1979*	17.6
1986 flat-plate DOE goal or AMETEK estimate; no cogeneration			17.3–23.7
1990 flat-plate (11¢/kW-h)	conservative So. Cal. Edison Co. estimate	*Ca. Energy Comm. 1980a:176*	32.2

higher replacement prices which new power plants, synfuel plants, frontier oil and gas systems, or other such systems would incur. In each category there are also new renewable energy processes and devices which can be confidently expected to progress over the next few years from pilot-scale engineering to fully commercial products, and which will widen still further their price advantage over centralized, nonrenewable energy sources. Even ignoring these imminent developments, just the economically attractive renewable options already on the market are so numerous and diverse that claims that renewable energy is uneconomic are increasingly confined to the uninformed.

Notes

Notes to Chapter One

1 This hastened the decline of reliance on coal; the rate of mining had already peaked in 1910. Meanwhile, the demand for oil was skyrocketing, especially after the 1901 discovery of the Spindletop field near Beaumont, Texas launched the intercoastal oil trade. In World War I, as Lord Curzon remarked, "the Allies floated to victory on a sea of oil"—most of it American. See Congressional Research Service 1977:I:165ff.

2 Ibid. : 7–9.

3 This was due not only to inadequate preparation but also to panic buying and to some mistakes in trying to manage the allocation of scarce oil.

4 Lovins & Lovins 1981b.

5 Brown 1977.

6 Deese & Nye 1981; Yorke 1980; Alm 1981; *Emergency Preparedness News* 1980; Marshall 1980; Rowen & Weyant 1981; Senate Committee on Energy & Natural Resources 1980; Aspen Institute 1980; Comptroller General of the U.S. 1981b; California Energy Commission 1981c.

7 The production and distribution of food are currently so centralized, with small buffer stocks and supply lines averaging thirteen hundred miles long (Becker 1982:21), that bad weather or a truckers' strike can put many retail food stores on short rations in a matter of days. This vulnerability is especially pronounced in the Northeast, which imports over eighty percent of its food (Serrin 1981). In a disaster, "the lack of regional self-sufficiency both in food production and food storage would cause havoc [but] . . . no one is planning for such possibilities." (ibid.) The important Cornucopia Project (whose report is available from Rodale Press, Emmaus PA) found much the same. The promotion of greater self-reliance in food production as between regions of the country (Sing 1981) and between urban and rural areas could make important contributions to national preparedness. In some instances, such as Alaska, such essential self-reliance used to exist but was systematically dismantled during the 1950s and 1960s in order to generate a lucrative dependence on a long supply line (in that case from Seattle). A few weeks' shipping strike in Seattle today would bring Alaska near to starvation; yet Alaska can easily be a net exporter of food, and holds many national records for vegetable growing. Both for these reasons and on other grounds (such as regional economics, inflation-fighting and nutritional quality) there is good reason to examine more closely the national security dimensions of America's agricultural structure; but that is beyond the scope of this book.

8 The Joint Committee on Defense Production (1977:II:34, 42–45) notes that American industry is tailor-made for easy disruption. Its qualities include large unit scale, concentration of key facilities, reliance on advanced materials inputs and on specialized electronics and automation, highly energy- and capital-intensive plants, and small inventories. (It is

small comfort that the Soviet economy has similar vulnerabilities and bottlenecks [Katz 1981:326ff].) The Committee found that correcting these defects, even incrementally and over many decades, could be very costly. But the cost of *not* doing so could be even higher—a rapid regression of tens or even hundreds of years in the evolution of the American economy, should it be suddenly and gravely disrupted.

9 Joint Committee on Defense Production 1977:I:vii.

10 Lovins & Lovins 1981b.

11 Bucknell et al. 1979:16.

12 Ibid. 18–20.

13 Ibid. 21.

14 Ibid. 22.

15 Ibid. 23.

16 Ibid. 25.

17 Congressional Research Service 1978:44.

18 Moreland 1979; Freiwald 1980; Bucknell et al. 1979; Collins & Mark 1979.

19 Cooper 1978:244; Brown 1977a; Wilson 1980.

20 Hoover 1979; Moreland & Bucknell 1978.

21 Hoover 1979; Moreland & Bucknell 1978; Taylor 1976; Hermann 1977; Bucknell 1979; Brown 1977a; Barnet 1980, 1981; Joint Committee on Defense Production 1979:I:3–4, which summarizes the expanded agenda of national security thus: "Even for security against physical threats to American life or property, armies no longer fully suffice. . . . The security of life and property is . . . more than defense against enemy invasion or coercion. This is not to underrate the significance of armies. It is rather to give full meaning to the idea of securing the general good of the populace."

22 Collins & Mark 1979; Christman & Clark 1978.

23 Brown 1978:26–27.

24 The term "defense" merits careful use. Some analysts (e.g., Boston Study Group 1979) argue that because of geography, there is no significant military threat to the territory of the United States that can be defended against. Apart from minor incursions handled by the Coast Guard and border patrols, the only overt external risk is from strategic nuclear attack, which cannot be defended against, though it may be deterred. (A modest Poseidon fleet would do this: each of the thirty-one Poseidon submarines has sixteen missiles, each capable of carrying ten to fourteen independently targetable warheads. This total of between one hundred sixty and two hundred twenty-four warheads per submarine corresponds to roughly one for each of the two hundred eighteen Soviet cities with a population of at least one hundred thousand people. Each Poseidon warhead has a nominal yield of about forty kilotons—three Hiroshimas—and would kill roughly half the people in an area of the order of fifteen square miles. Even a single large land-based missile, of which the U.S. has over a thousand, packs in its ten to fifteen warheads more firepower than all the bombs dropped in World War II—an equally formidable deterrent.) In this view, the United States itself could be adequately defended with some three percent of its 1978 military budget. The other ninety-seven percent of that budget (recently much increased to a rate of about ten thousand dollars per second) pays for general-purpose forces to project American power into disputes in other parts of the world, including U.S. allies and trade routes, to protect perceived national interests. While both this thesis and the concept of nuclear deterrence itself (Dyson 1981) can be argued with, it is indisputable that the development of the world's nuclear arsenal—over one and a half million Hiroshimas' worth and rising fast—has not increased anyone's national security. Until such weapons were developed, American territory was, in military terms, virtually invulnerable, whereas today it is entirely exposed to devastation (Schell 1982).

25 Dresch & Ellis 1966.

26 Lovins & Lovins 1981b.

27 The Defense Civil Preparedness Agency also commissioned our friend Wilson Clark to conduct a parallel and slightly earlier study (Energy & Defense Project 1980) independently of this one. It conveys broadly similar concerns and provides a readable survey of many resilient energy supply technologies. Its popularized version (Clark & Page 1981) has done much to draw these issues to public attention. More recently, the Division for Studies of Society and Total Defense in Forsvärets

Forskningsanstalt (FOA, the Swedish Defense Research Establishment in Stockholm), under the leadership of Dr. Peter Steen, has conducted a preliminary study closer in scope and method to our own. His group's first findings, which we understand resemble ours in a more specifically Swedish context, will become available in spring 1982. Some related inquiries were also begun in late 1981 at the U.S. National Defense University (R. Hayes, personal communication, December 1981). We have been unable, however, to find anywhere in the world an analysis comparable in scope and detail to this one.

Note to Chapter Two

1 Glassey & Craig 1978:330.

2 *Los Angeles Times* 1981. Somewhat better protection may become available if it becomes possible—as some authorities think it already is—to give "suspicion" warnings a few days in advance of a disaster such as an earthquake. Such a capability, however, also raises thorny legal and political questions.

3 Even if foreseen, a major natural disaster can send shock waves through the economy. There is currently federal concern, for example, that when the expected Richter eight-plus earthquake strikes Los Angeles or San Francisco, parts of the insurance industry may not survive paying for the damage—predicted at upwards of eighty billion dollars (Smith 1980).

4 Joint Committee on Defense Production 1977:I:17–20.

5 Ibid.:17.

6 Stephens 1970:13.

7 Ibid.:23.

8 Chronic bad weather can have curiously indirect side effects. The salt spread on New England roads to combat ice, for example, speeds corrosion not only of vehicles (which in consequence suffer more structural failures) but also of bridges and underground pipelines. Salt also gets into the water table, apparently causing epidemic high blood pressure in some Massachusetts towns.

9 Joint Committee on Defense Production 1977:II:22, which describes why the patterns of weather and farming make it infeasible to evacuate Soviet cities at most times of the year.

10 Congressional Research Service 1977:III:189.

11 Quirk & Moriarty 1980:90–91.

12 Congressional Research Service 1977:III:189

13 Ackermann 1979; Subcommittee on Energy & Power 1979:17.

14 Congressional Research Service 1977:III:191.

15 Kellogg & Schware 1981:63.

16 Quirk & Moriarty 1980:90–92.

17 Ibid.:94.

18 Ibid.:97.

19 Kirtland 1981.

20 Quirk & Moriarty 1981:90–91.

21 Lorenz 1976; Study of Man's Impact on Climate 1971.

22 Glassey & Craig 1978:335–336.

23 If, as appears likely, the climate is becoming more severe and erratic, plant breeders will be hard pressed to adjust. Most of today's hybridized crops were specially bred to grow best in conditions which seemed normal at the time but are now known to be the mildest since the Ice Age. Furthermore, the genetic base of major crops has been deliberately narrowed; many adaptable, primitive strains have been lost (Myers 1981); and government seed banks are rapidly losing their stock of viable germ plasm (Crittenden 1981).

24 For example, under the extreme conditions of a post-nuclear-war environment, insects are likelier to survive than higher organisms that eat them, because insects can tolerate far more radiation (National Academy of Sciences 1975). Plagues of crop pests are a plausible result. Already, the milder stress of pesticides has induced similar "differential selection," causing considerable pest outbreaks. Antibiotics can similarly select the most virulent and resistant pathogens to prey on dense monocultures of people.

25 Mieher 1980.

26 Joint Committee on Defense Production 1977:II:37–38.

27 See Chapter Nine and Note 29 to this chapter for references to the high degree of concentration in U.S. and Soviet refining capacity.

28 These include hydraulic facilities (dams, locks, pumping stations, canals) needed to irrigate or drain four million square miles of otherwise barren farmland, and factories making bulldozers and tractors. (Over eighty percent of Soviet tractors are made in nine factories.) Joint Committee on Defense Production 1977:II:65–68.

29 The Soviets shared that problem even in 1948–49, when a U.S. targeting plan for one hundred fifty nuclear weapons gave top priority to refineries, especially those producing aviation fuel (Joint Chiefs of Staff 1949/1978). Soviet refining is still highly concentrated (Arms Control & Disarmament Agency 1978; Office of Technology Assessment 1979a; Katz 1981:317ff).

30 Stephens 1970:74.
31 Dumas 1976, 1980.
32 Coates 1980.
33 Wentzel 1979:4.
34 Ibid.:7.
35 Perlman & Hastings 1981; Kolata 1982.
36 Lyons 1981.
37 Hsu 1981.
38 Dumas 1980: 18ff.
39 Schultz 1980.
40 Friedman 1980.

Notes to Chapter Three

1 Dresch & Ellis 1966:3, emphasis added.
2 Ford 1982:25–26.
3 Hoover 1979:53. The "comprehensive study of reactor safety" referred to was the "Rasmussen Report" (NRC 1975), whose risk assessments were subjected to such stinging criticism that the Nuclear Regulatory Commission, four years later, found they were "no longer considered reliable."
4 Okrent & Moeller 1981:73.
5 Our argument does not depend on this sometimes forced distinction, which is drawn by, among others, Solomon & Salem 1980.
6 Epler 1970.
7 Pollard 1979: failure of power supply, 17; transformer failure, 28; incorrect installation, 30; incorrect manufacture, 70, 73; inproper soldering, 48, 65; leaking floats, 50; wiring errors, 51; water damage, 57; contaminated oil, 61; clogged strainers, 62; miswired thermostat, 63; origin unknown, 11.
8 Ibid.: control rods, 17; relays, 22.
9 Cooper 1973; Manned Spaceflight Center 1970, 1970a.

10 Clark 1978:7.
11 Holling & Goldberg 1971:222, from whom the example is paraphrased.
12 Ibid.:223.
13 Ibid.:224.
14 Ibid.:227–228.
15 Clark 1978:11–12.
16 Belady & Lehman 1976.
17 Vacca 1974.
18 Wentzel 1979:2.
19 Lovins 1977b:10–11
20 Jackson 1980; Jackson & Bender 1981.
21 Clark 1978:6–17.
22 Isaksen 1980.
23 Boeck et al. 1975.
24 Campbell & Martin 1973.
25 Kerr 1981.
26 Park & Helliwell 1978.
27 Clark 1978:8.
28 Ibid.:10.
29 A.B. Lovins wrote the list in the course of consultancy in the early phases of the MIT Workshop on Alternative Energy Strategies. He is still looking for his copy.

Notes to Chapter Four

1 We do not treat here the additional, longer-term problem that the fossil and nuclear fuels on which today's energy system largely depends are finite and therefore exhaustible (Hubbert 1969; Bartlett 1981). The alternatives proposed in Part Three, however, do not have this drawback.

2 Foley 1979.
3 Stephens 1970:69, 96.
4 West 1976.
5 *Los Angeles Times* 1981b. The tank held six hundred eighty cubic meters.
6 Congressional Research Service 1977:I:13.

7 Stephens 1973:34–35.

8 *Los Angeles Times* 1981t.

9 Joint Committee on Defense Production 1977:I:29.

10 Casper & Wellstone 1981; Gerlach & Radcliffe 1979; Lovins 1979, 1980a.

11 Foley & Lönnroth 1981:25.

12 Bass et al. 1980.

13 Casper & Wellstone 1981; see also Chapter Ten.

14 Gerlach 1979; Gerlach & Radcliffe 1979.

15 Burwell et al. 1979; Nuclear Regulatory Commission 1976b; IIASA 1981.

16 Energy & Defense Project 1980:11.

17 Congressional Research Service 1977:I:62–63, 77.

18 Ibid. I:2.

19 Glassey & Craig 1978:330–331.

20 *Los Angeles Times* 1981v.

21 Patterson & Griffin 1978. A fluidized bed consists of a layer of sand, ceramic pellets, or other inert, heat-proof particles, buoyantly suspended by air blown up from below through a porous plate. Fuel is added to the bed. Its combustion keeps the particles red-hot. The turbulent motion and enormous surface area of the particles make combustion very efficient, whether the fuel is gaseous, liquid, or granular. The nature of the fuel is immaterial, and only simple changes in fuel-handling gear are needed to switch to a different type.

22 Economic Regulatory Administration 1981:I:4–12.

23 NERC 1979:7.

24 Stephens 1973:14.

25 Deese & Nye 1981:40.

26 Subcommittee on Energy & Power 1977:116–117.

27 Kalisch 1979.

28 Congressional Research Service 1977:I:84–89.

29 Ibid.:171–172.

30 Stephens 1973:114.

31 Congressional Research Service 1977:I:198–200.

32 Ibid.:14.

33 Ibid.:178, 181.

34 Ibid.:255.

35 Subcommittee on Energy & Power 1978:18.

36 Ibid.:9.

37 *Public Power Weekly* 1981.

38 Nevin 1969; Pickering 1969.

39 Stephens 1970.

40 Stephens 1979:206.

41 Stephens 1973.

42 Energy & Defense Project 1980:77.

43 Congressional Research Service 1977:I:75.

44 *New York Times* 1981e.

45 Egushi et al. 1981.

46 Lovins 1977b, 1978.

47 Quirk & Moriarty 1980:93.

48 Holusha 1981a.

49 *Los Angeles Times* 1981b.

50 As an example of the complexity of managing a large pipeline system (Chapter Nine), just a temperature change of three Fahrenheit degrees throughout the thirty-six-inch Colonial pipeline, or a change in pressure by only ten atmospheres, would change the volume of the pipeline by some ten thousand barrels, worth several hundred thousand dollars (Congressional Research Service 1977:I:200–201).

51 Stephens 1973:34.

52 Ibid.:114.

53 *New York Times* 1981q.

54 Gage 1978.

55 *New York Times* 1978f.

56 *Daily Mail* 1979.

57 *Los Angeles Times* 1981n.

58 *Straits Times* 1980.

59 *Business Week* 1976.

60 *New York Times* 1973, 1973a.

61 *Wall Street Journal* 1977.

62 *New York Times* 1978d.

63 *New York Times* 1978e.

64 *New York Times* 1981u.

65 Actual or threatened contamination of mass-marketed food has been a fairly frequent ploy of extortionists. In late 1981, eyedrops and nasal sprays marketed by Southern California chain stores were contaminated with corrosive acids (Malnic 1981), leading to a massive product recall; but no extortion attempt was reported, leading to speculation that the act was purely malicious. Ironically, it appears that the Strategic Petroleum Reserve has already been contaminated (though probably not irreversibly) by the deliberate substitution of up to nine million barrels of waste oil for high-grade crude. This substitution, de-

tected only after the "bad oil" had been added, was not meant for extortion, but arose
from pure venality (*New York Times* 1982).
    66 Billiter 1981.
    67 ERAB 1980:65.
    68 D. Goldstein (University of Texas at

Austin), personal communication, 4 January
1981.
    69 *Houston Chronicle* 1977.
    70 Davis 1981. See also Chapter Nine, Note
177.
    71 Stephens 1970:149.

Notes to Chapter Five

1 Federal Power Commission 1977:26.
2 *Electrical Construction and Maintenance*
1965.
3 Congressional Research Service 1979:142.
4 Federal Energy Regulatory Commission
1978:1.
5 Subcommittee on Energy & Power
1977:34, 149–154; 1978a:44, 95.
6 Clapp 198:10.
7 Subcommittee on Energy & Power
1977:32, 100–101.
8 Subcommittee on Energy & Power
1978:53.
9 Boffey 1978. Copyright 1978 by the
American Association for the Advancement of
Science.
10 Clapp 1978:22, 23, 25.
11 Ibid.:39.
12 Joint Committee on Defense Production
1977a:23.
13 Corwin et al. 1979.
14 Subcommittee on Energy & Power
1977:53–65.
15 Federal Energy Regulatory Commission
1978:139.
16 Subcommittee on Energy & Power
1977:46.
17 Clapp 1978:59–60.

18 Boffey 1978:995.
19 NERC 1979:13–14.
20 Joint Committee on Defense Production
1977a:5.
21 Federal Energy Regulatory Commission
1978:49.
22 Park 1978:45.
23 Federal Energy Regulatory Commission
1978:45.
24 Subcommittee on Energy & Power
1977:26–27.
25 Subcommittee on Energy & Power
1978a:139.
26 Federal Power Commission 1977:20, 46.
27 Economic Regulatory Administration
1981:6–9ff.
28 Federal Energy Regulatory Commission
1978:21.
29 Joint Committee on Defense Production
1977a:105.
30 *Newsweek* 1977:20.
31 Federal Energy Regulatory Commission
1978:55.
32 *Evening Standard* 1979.
33 Kihss 1981.
34 Federal Energy Regulatory Commission
1978:55.

Notes to Chapter Six

1 Defense Electric Power Administration
1962:28.
2 Joint Committee on Defense Production
1977a:108.
3 Ibid.
4 Chenoweth et al. 1963:8.
5 Stephens 1970:49, 53.
6 Stephens 1973:58.
7 Ibid.:142.
8 Lambert 1976:56–60.
9 Ibid.:60.

10 Chenoweth et al. 1963:38–41.
11 Stephens 1973:20, 34, 96.
12 Ibid.:iv.
13 Ibid.:150; Fernald 1965.
14 Energy & Defense Project 1980:7.
15 Goeller 1980:81–84. Many of the concepts developed in this book apply also to
non-fuel minerals. Among the more useful introductions to this enormous field are Fishman 1980; Broad 1980; Barnet 1980; Stanley
1977; Goodman 1978; Joint Committee on

Defense Production 1977:I:87–97; Office of Technology Assessment 1979; Ayres & Narkus-Kramer 1976; Krause 1981; Kihlstedt 1977; Lovins 1973.

16 Katz 1981; Joint Committee on Defense Production 1977:II:42–44.

17 Dresch & Ellis 1966:11–12.

18 Katz 1981 (in the context on nuclear attack).

19 Economic Regulatory Administration 1981:Ch. 4

20 Lovins 1977; Junger 1976.

21 Katz 1981:48–50.

22 Crittenden 1981.

23 Economic Regulatory Administration 1981:Ch. 5.

24 Alec Jenkins, personal communication, 15 January 1982. We are grateful to him for calling our attention to the following two references.

25 EPRI 1979.

26 EPRI 1979a.

27 This is the usual basis for estimates such as the one (Aspen Institute 1980:62) that the 1976–77 oil interruptions cost America about twenty billion dollars, or many others (e.g.,

Rowen & Weyant 1981) that future interruption of oil exports from the Persion Gulf would cost hundreds of billions of dollars. Such calculations assume, without economic basis, that GNP is a useful surrogate for welfare.

28 *Newsweek* 1977.

29 Subcommittee on Energy & Power 1978:3.

30 Congressional Research Service 1978a.

31 Subcommittee on Energy & Power 1978a:142.

32 Subcommittee on Energy & Power 1977:69.

33 Congressional Research Service 1978a:3.

34 Subcommittee on Energy & Power 1978a:16.

35 *Newsweek* 1978:18.

36 Subcommittee on Energy & Power 1978a:11.

37 *Newsweek* 1978:18.

38 Podgers 1980.

39 Goldman 1981.

40 Emshwiller 1980.

41 *Newsweek* 1977.

Notes to Chapter Seven

1 Joint Committee on Defense Production 1977:I:99.

2 Ibid.:II:75–77.

3 Energy & Defense Project 1980:19–29. We are indebted to Wilson Clark for calling these World War II examples to our attention.

4 McIsaac 1976:VI:49; Clark & Page 1981:50–51.

5 Clark & Page 1981:3.

6 SIPRI 1974:142–145.

7 Masselli & Dean 1981:17 (*cf.* Energy & Defense Project 1980:22–24.

8 Ramberg 1980:15.

9 Energy & Defense Project 1980:19–29; Clark & Page 1981:52–54.

10 Energy & Defense Project 1980:19–29; Clark & Page 1981:52–54.

11 Barnet 1981:67.

12 Smil 1981; Taylor 1981a.

13 Clark 1981.

14 Smil 1981; Taylor 1981a.

15 *New York Times* 1969.

16 Hofmann 1979.

17 Burns 1980, 1980a; *Los Angeles Times* 1980c.

18 Peel 1980.

19 Peel 1980a.

20 *Los Angeles Times* 1980d; *Wall Street Journal* 1980b.

21 Rose 1981.

22 *Los Angeles Times* 1981s, w.

23 de Leon et al. 1978:22.

24 *New York Times* 1976b.

25 *New York Times* 1969.

26 *New York Times* 1980e.

27 *Los Angeles Times* 1979e.

28 *New York Times* 1981m.

29 *Far Eastern Economic Review* 1976.

30 Tanner 1978.

31 *Anchorage Times* 1980; *New York Times* 1980d.

32 *Los Angeles Times* 1981x.

33 *Atlanta Journal & Constitution* 1981.

34 *Boston Globe* 1981; *Los Angeles Times* 1981m, 1982h.

35 *New York Times* 1981v.

36 *Los Angeles Times* 1981bb.
37 *Newsweek* 1981b; *Los Angeles Times* 1982c.
38 Caputo 1980:42.
39 *Le Monde* 1978, 1978a; *New York Times* 1978, 1978a.
40 Comité d'Action pour le Solaire 1981:78–79.
41 Holmberg 1981.
42 Chenoweth et al. 1963; Lambert 1976.
43 Lerner 1981:42.
44 King et al. 1980.
45 Lambert 1976:51; Lerner 1981:42ff.
46 Broad 1981.
47 Lerner 1981:42ff.
48 Ricketts et al. 1976.
49 DCPA 1973.
50 Nelson 1971.
51 Lerner 1981:46.
52 Dircks 1981.
53 Even if shutdown and cooling systems are still operable, the operators may be unable to prevent a meltdown if their instruments have failed, since they will have no way of knowing internal conditions, valve and pump status, etc.
54 Lerner 1981a; Energy & Defense Project 1980:305.
55 Dircks 1981.
56 Ibid. Preliminary results will become available in mid-1982. The research project, involving a variety of government and industrial contractors with EMP and nuclear engineering expertise, initially applies only to a particular design of pressurized-water reactor. For this reason, and because such analyses are extremely complex and subject to many fundamental uncertainties, the NRC study, however carefully done, is unlikely to prove definitive.
57 Broad 1981a.
58 Clark & Page 1981:30.
59 E.g., Wagner 1977.
60 E.g., Turner et al. 1970.
61 RAND 1980:12.
62 Kupperman & Trent 1979:5.
63 Eschwege 1974:2; Subcommittee on Energy & the Environment 1977:204.
64 Rosenbaum et al. 1974:S6623; Cochran 1977.
65 Office of Technology Assessment 1977a:197.
66 de Leon et al. 1978:42.

67 Ibid.:19.
68 Ibid.:vi.
69 Ibid.:12; Burnham 1975:57–59.
70 Burnham 1975:59.
71 Prugh 1981.
72 Ibid.
73 *Los Angeles Times* 1981h.
74 de Leon et al. 1978:13ff; Bass et al. 1980:17.
75 de Leon et al. 1978:14.
76 Bass et al. 1980:17.
77 de Leon et al. 1978:13.
78 Satchell 1973.
79 Comptroller General of the U.S. 1977:8.
80 *Editor & Publisher* 1980.
81 *New York Times* 1980b.
82 Comptroller General of the U.S. 1977:9.
83 E.g, *New York Times* 1979a.
84 *Boston Herald American* 1980. Similarly, after eighteen security guards at the Surry reactor ran afoul of rules against marijuana (*Electrical World* 1982a), a bag of it was found in the control room (*Los Angeles Times* 1982f), but the utility could not determine which of a hundred employees was responsible.
85 Smith 1978:Encl. 2:App. J #8.
86 Emshwiller 1980a:13.
87 Comptroller General of the U.S. 1977:15.
88 Beard 1981.
89 *New York Times* 1979b.
90 Jenkins 1975a:14.
91 Burnham 1975:69.
92 Aspin 1975.
93 Jenkins 1975a:14.
94 Aspin 1975.
95 Kupperman & Trent 1979:56; Gervasi 1981:249.
96 Burnham 1975:69.
97 Kupperman & Trent 1979:83.
98 Jenkins 1975a:13.
99 Kupperman & Trent 1979:30–31. Similar antiaircraft and antitank missiles were recently seized from Red Brigades terrorists (*Los Angeles Times* 1982i), but three days later a Red Brigades team took two sixty-millimeter morters, two bazookas, various machine guns, and so forth from an armory (ibid. 1982j).
100 Jenkins 1975a:14.
101 Kupperman & Trent 1979:55.
102 Walker 1981:41.
103 Jenkins 1975a:14.

104 Ibid.
105 *Los Angeles Times* 1980e.
106 *Guardian* 1975a.
107 Bass et al. 1980:25–26.
108 *Evening Standard* 1976.
109 Kupperman & Trent 1979:5.
110 *Evening Standard* 1976; *Ottawa Citizen* 1976.
111 Kupperman & Trent 1979:65.
112 Ibid.
113 *New York Times* 1977b.
114 Pike 1972.
115 Burnham 1975:50.
116 E.g., Powell 1971 (reprinted. 1980).
117 *Los Angeles Times* 1981gg, ee.
118 Burnham 1975:49.
119 de Leon et al. 1978:35.
120 Cooley 1978.
121 McCullough et al. 1968.

122 Endicott 1979; Turner 1977.
123 Gervasi 1981.
124 Ramberg 1980:66.
125 Walker 1981:45.
126 Clark & Page 1981:57. We are grateful to Wilson Clark for kindly supplying this information. Unfortunately, in supplying the table to Senator Percy's office, the Department of Energy declined to supply any source or documentation for it. It appears that in some categories the table lists more incidents than are documented in this book; in other categories, fewer. Without knowing the specific incidents to which the Department's list refers, it is not possible to determine whether either data base is incomplete or whether (as is more likely) the Department has listed incidents which were not considered significant enough to list here.

Notes to Chapter Eight

1 More precisely, one cubic meter of LNG weighs four hundred sixty-five kilograms and has an energy content of twenty-five billion joules, two hundred thirty-eight therms, or twenty-four million BTUs, equivalent to about four and a quarter barrels of crude oil. There are six and three-tenths barrels, or thirty-five and a third cubic feet, in a cubic meter.
2 Comptroller General of the U.S. 1978; Davis 1979; Office of Technology Assessment 1977.
3 Fay 1980:89.
4 Williams 1971, 1972.
5 GAO I:12–15.
6 Hardee et al. 1978.
7 GAO I: exec. summ. 25.
8 Thomas & Schwendtner 1972; Dobson 1972.
9 Fay 1980:96.
10 GAO I:exec. summ. 25–27.
11 Ibid. I:10–8.
12 Ibid. I:10–11.
13 Ibid. I:exec. summ. 27.
14 Ibid. I:12–17.
15 Aronson & Westermeyer 1981:24.
16 Ibid.:21.
17 Ibid.:5.
18 GAO; Fay 1980:90.
19 GAO:2–7.
20 Fairley 1975.

21 GAO; Davis 1979.
22 Aronson & Westermeyer 1981.
23 GAO I:6–10, 6–11, 6–59, 6–60.
24 Ibid. I:9–21.
25 Ibid. I:9–20.
26 *Times* 1981.
27 Davis 1979.
28 BBC 1981.
29 A normal flight pattern could, at that time, have brought in planes as low as a hundred feet above an LNG tanker's masts (GAO I:6–39ff), but the Federal Aviation Administration now plans to suspend landings that would do so.
30 GAO I:exec. summ. 8. About five percent of all earthquakes have occurred in areas with little known seismic history or active faulting. Boston experienced a major quake of this kind in 1755. Others at Charleston, South Carolina in 1876 and in New Madrid, Missouri in 1811–12 were felt over an area of two million square miles; the latter changed the course of the Mississippi River and were felt as far away as Boston. The origin of such quakes is not known (GAO I:3–12ff), though at least the Missouri quakes may be related to a newly discovered rift that runs seventeen hundred miles from Washington State to the southern tip of the Appalachian Mountains (*Los Angeles Times* 1981jj).

31 GAO I:Ch. 5.

32 Ibid. I:exec. summ. 8.

33 A crack that exceeds a certain "critical" length will propagate very rapidly, causing total failure of the tank. The Columbia LNG Corporation estimates that for a large, fully loaded tank made of the normal nine percent nickel alloy steel, this critical crack length is between four and a half feet and eight and a half feet. The General Accounting Office estimates it is only one foot to one and a half feet, but points out that the actual value could be smaller, since there have been no detailed calculations or experiments to determine it (GAO).

34 GAO I:9–3.

35 Ibid.:9–12ff.

36 Ibid.:exec. summ. 10ff.

37 Fay 1980:91.

38 GAO:exec. summ. 16.

39 Poland & White 1981.

40 GAO I:7–1.

41 Ibid.:7–7.

42 Ibid. I:9–17.

43 Ibid. I:7–9.

44 Ibid. I:9–19.

45 Ibid. I:exec. summ. 18.

46 Ibid. I:exec. summ. 16.

47 Ibid. I:7–6.

48 Ibid.:7–7ff.

49 Ibid.

50 Ibid.:7–11.

51 Ibid. I:exec. summ. 17, I:7–10ff.

52 Ibid.:I:7–11

53 Marshall 1981.

54 GAO I:9–6.

55 de Leon et al. 1978:22.

56 At sixty degrees Fahrenheit, propane liq-uefies at about one hundred ten pounds per square inch, butane at forty. At atmospheric pressure, they liquefy at about minus forty-four and plus thirty-one degrees Fahrenheit respectively. See Congressional Research Service 1977:III:406.

57 GAO I:exec. summ. 5.

58 Davis 1979.

59 GAO I:7–13.

60 Ibid.:7–12.

61 Ibid.:7–13.

62 Walls 1963.

63 GAO I:7–14.

64 Fay 1980:100. GAO (I:8–1) reports that about a hundred thousand railcar loads of LPG were shipped in the U.S. in 1977.

65 Williamson & Mann 1981.

66 Sharry & Walls 1974.

67 GAO I:8–3.

68 Ibid. I:exec. summ.:19. In addition, see generally Davis 1979.

69 GAO I:8–14.

70 *Los Angeles Times* 1974b.

71 Ibid.:1979i, j.

72 Ibid.:1979h.

73 Ibid.:1978b.

74 Narvaez 1981.

75 GAO I:9–18.

76 Ibid.:2–11.

77 Fairley 1975; Mostert 1974:325–326.

78 GAO I:21–6ff.

79 Ibid.:9–16.

80 Ibid.

81 Williamson & Mann 1981.

82 GAO I:exec. summ. 8.

83 Ibid. I:7–8.

84 *Los Angeles Times* 1981c.

Notes to Chapter Nine

1 Stephens 1973:62.

2 Stephens 1974:87.

3 Wilburn 1981.

4 Stephens 1974:79–80.

5 Ibid.:4.

6 Office of Technology Assessment 1979a:69.

7 Stephens 1973:136.

8 Office of Technology Assessment 1980b:17.

9 Ibid.:25.

10 Foley & Lönnroth 1981:7.

11 Deese & Nye 1981.

12 Rosen 1980.

13 Deese & Nye 1981:3.

14 Taylor 1980:304.

15 Kemp, in Deese & Nye 1981:370.

16 Cranford 1981.

17 Comptroller General of the U.S. 1979:3.

18 Senate Committee on Foreign Relations 1981.

19 Ibid.:16, 18. The time could be cut at

least in half by deception.

20 Ibid.:14, says fifteen; the higher figure, for 1981, is from James Akins.

21 *Los Angeles Times* 1981q.

22 Senate Committee on Foreign Relations 1981:23.

23 Ibid.:60.

24 Ibid.:23.

25 Ibid.:25.

26 Ibid.

27 Ibid.

28 *New York Times* 1979e.

29 Deese & Nye 1981:9.

30 Rand 1981. This view is not canonically received.

31 If so, it does not appear to have succeeded.

32 *New York Times* 1977c.

33 Stobaugh & Yergin 1979:40.

34 *Times* 1975a; *Los Angeles Times* 1979b.

35 *Los Angeles Times* 1979a.

36 *Newsweek* 1979.

37 *New York Times* 1979c. The proposal was later withdrawn. It would not have significantly affected oil prices.

38 Schmidt 1974.

39 Senate Committee on Foreign Relations 1981:24.

40 Broder 1977.

41 Ibid.

42 Schmidt 1974:163.

43 SIPRI 1974:55; Congressional Research Service 1977:III:169.

44 Broder 1977.

45 *New York Times* 1981b.

46 Ibrahim 1979; *Los Angeles Times* 1979c; *New York Times* 1979d.

47 Deese & Nye 1981:66.

48 *New York Times* 1980a, i.

49 *New York Times* 1980h.

50 *New York Times* 1980g.

51 *Los Angeles Times* 1980b, e; 1981ff.

52 *Wall Street Journal* 1980a.

53 Cooley 1978; Meadows 1982; *Los Angeles Times* 1982d. Meadows (1982) reports that the destruction of Iraqi pipelines in 1981 dissuaded Saudi Arabia from building an alternative oil export route (a six-hundred-mile pipeline from Ras Tanura to the Oman coast) or giant oil storage depots.

54 *Los Angeles Times* 1982.

55 *Los Angeles Times* 1982a.

56 Mostert 1974.

57 *Economist* 1980.

58 Beech 1981. The IRA has also boarded and blown up two British coal ships (*Los Angeles Times* 1982m).

59 Kessler 1976; Kupperman & Trent 1979:72.

60 Donne 1975; Middleton 1976.

61 *Houston Chronicle* 1981.

62 Faux 1981.

63 Apple 1980; *Washington Post* 1981.

64 *Los Angeles Times* 1980a.

65 Stephens 1979:208.

66 Stephens 1973:34.

67 *New York Times* 1975c.

68 Middleton 1976.

69 Congressional Research Service 1977:III:193.

70 Stephens 1979:209.

71 *Houston Chronicle* 1981.

72 Stephens 1981:208–209.

73 Stephens 1974:93.

74 *Guardian* 1975b.

75 *Houston Chronicle* 1981.

76 Marshall 1980.

77 *Petroleum Intelligence Weekly* data, quoted in Federation of American Scientists 1980:6.

78 Comptroller General of the U.S. 1981b:I:16.

79 Stephens 1979:208.

80 *New York Times* 1978b, c.

81 *New York Times* 1969.

82 Schmidt 1974:186.

83 Bass et al. 1980:44; Sterling 1978:41.

84 *New York Times* 1981p.

85 Burnham 1975:122.

86 Comptroller General of the U.S. 1978:II:App. IX.

87 *Los Angeles Times* 1981p.

88 *New York Times* 1981n.

89 Davis 1981.

90 Subcommittee on Energy Conservation & Power 1981:23.

91 Stephens 1979:210.

92 Ibid.:208; Katz 1981:164.

93 Stephens 1973:148–149, 52.

94 Office of Technology Assessment 1979a:64. The Soviet concentration is even heavier, with only about sixty operating refineries in the 1980s, though they are less clustered geographically: Arms Control & Disarmament Agency 1978; Katz 1981:317ff; OTA

1979b:2, 4, 13.
95 Stephens 1973:52.
96 Ibid.:101.
97 Ibid.:141.
98 Stephens 1970:105.
99 *Wall Street Journal* 1980.
100 Stephens 1970:vii.
101 Cowan 1979.
102 Rempel 1982. The number of operating refineries, about three hundred in 1978, might be fewer than two hundred by the end of 1982. The concentration of capacity—in 1978, the thirty-seven largest refineries had half the total national capacity (OTA 1979: 14)—is thus bound to increase.
103 *New York Times* 1970.
104 Deese & Nye 1981:40.
105 Martin (1981) describes the distress caused by sixty-eight percent utilization a year earlier.
106 Fesharaki & Isaak 1981.
107 Energy & Defense Project 1980:15.
108 *Los Angeles Times* 1981i; Occidental Petroleum Co. telephone inquiry.
109 Stephens 1974:27.
110 Ibid.:15.
111 Ibid.
[0112 Ibid.:24. Bacteria can cause similar corrosion in oil pipelines (Cranford 1981).
113 Stephens 1974:87, 90.
114 Ibid.:27.
115 Stephens 1973:149.
116 Stephens 1979:211.
117 Comptroller General of the U.S. 1979:i.
118 Ibid.:34.
119 Congressional Research Service 1977:I:198–200.
120 Stephens 1973:115.
121 Congressional Research Service 1977:III:159–160.
122 Ibid.:I:162.
123 Energy & Defense Project 1980:16.
124 Comptroller General of the U.S. 1978:II:App. IX. FBI 1979:22–23 also notes four attacks, including one bombing, on the natural gas supply to an industrial plant in Arkansas.
125 Congressional Research Service 1977:III:163.
126 *New York Times* 1975b.
127 Congressional Research Service 1977:III:166–167.

128 *New York Times* 1975.
129 Congressional Research Service 1977:III:195.
130 *New York Times* 1981h.
131 Ibid. 1980j.
132 Stephens 1973:142.
133 Goen et al. 1970:60–70. An analogy arose in July 1981 when four youthful vandals opened a valve on a New Jersey aqueduct. This burst two huge pipelines, tore away a hillside carrying them, and spilled a hundred million gallons of water. With Newark and four towns cut off and facing water reserves of five to six days, round-the-clock crews laid a double forty-eight-inch replacement pipe more than eight hundred feet long within a week. They shortcut the usual month for manufacturing by scavenging an unusual pipe surplus elsewhere (Hanley 1981, 1981a-f). Interestingly, neither of New York City's two water tunnels (built in 1917 and 1936) can handle the full flow, so neither can be cleaned or inspected, but a long-proposed third tunnel remains in limbo (Meislin 1981a).
134 Stephens 1973:46, 96, 101.
135 Stephens 1974:v, 91; Comptroller General of the U.S. 1979:15.
136 *New York Times* 1980o.
137 *Los Angeles Times* 1981o.
138 Stephen 1973:34.
139 Goen et al. 1970:62–64.
140 Comptroller General of the U.S. 1979.
141 Goen et al. 1970:62. (The data are over a decade old.)
142 Comptroller General of the U.S. 1979:15, iii.
143 Ibid.:30.
144 Ibid.:29.
145 Stephens 1974:91.
146 Ibid.; Comptroller General of the U.S. 1979:23.
147 Stephens 1973:iv.
148 Ibid.:58.
149 Stephens 1979:208.
150 Stephens 1973:38.
151 Pryor 1975.
152 Ibid.; Endicott 1979; *New York Times* 1977a.
153 Pryor 1975.
154 Endicott 1979.
155 Comptroller General of the U.S. 1979:30.

156 *New York Times* 1977d.

157 Ponte 1977. Earlier the line had had a stormy construction history; at one point "elite Army troops had to be called out in Fairbanks . . . to help quell a riot by dissatisfied pipeline welders" (Pryor 1975).

158 Comptroller General of the U.S. 1979:30.

159 Goen et al. 1970:60.

160 Comptroller General of the U.S. 1979:22, 24.

161 Turner 1977; Endicott 1979.

162 Comptroller General of the U.S. 1979:39.

163 Ibid.

164 Senate Judiciary Committee 1977.

165 Congressional Research Service 1977:III:169.

166 Stephens 1974:v.

167 Fulkerson 1981:58.

168 Stephens 1974:v.

169 Stephens 1973:34.

170 *Los Angeles Times* 1979g.

171 Stephens 1974:45.

172 Stephens 1974:46. There are an estimated forty-three million retail distribution lines (Atallah 1980).

173 *Los Angeles Times* 1982e.

174 Atallah 1980.

175 Stephens 1973:112; for an example, *Los Angeles Times* 1979d. Other oil company buildings have been bombed, e.g., in Pittsburgh in 1974 and San Francisco in 1975; a live mortar round was discovered at an oil company facility in New York City in 1977 (Comptroller General of the U.S. 1978:II:App. IX).

176 As when Japanese opposing Narita Airport firebombed a heavily guarded train carrying jet fuel to it (*Los Angeles Times* 1981d) and cut a bridge on the same rail line (*Los Angeles Times*:1981hh).

177 Lerner et al. 1967; Grigsby et al. 1968; Boesman et al. 1970. Most of the dispersed oil stocks however, are in or near urban areas, and would therefore be lost in any general disaster such as a nuclear attack (Katz 1981:267 ff). Furthermore, distillate stocks must be cycled through storage. If left dormant they may oxidize, or grow bacteria or fungi at the water-oil interface at the bottom of the tank. Both processes can irreversibly make the fuel unusably gummy; it may clog lines, filters, and burner tips. Oxidation and biological decomposition reinforce each other. Both make more water, improving the habitat for microorganisms. These eat oil and excrete acids and water. These products speed tank corrosion. Metals eaten away from the tank catalyze faster oxidation. So do metals left over from new, highly efficient cracking processes: modern refineries, seeking to maximize their yield of higher distillates, are producing products which are less stable in storage than they used to be (Alec Jenkins, personal communication, 15 January 1982).

178 Congressional Research Service 1977:I:16.

179 Stephens 1979:213.

180 Sisk 1981. See also Soble & Tumulty 1982.

181 O'Toole 1981.

182 Congressional Research Service 1977:III:165.

183 Kupperman & Trent 1979:73.

184 Stephens 1979:210–211.

Notes to Chapter Ten

1 Comptroller General of the U.S. 1981a.

2 FBI 1979:28. The bomb damaged pipes and pumps and caused some internal flooding, but caused no structural damage to the dam. In a somewhat analogous incident, the UNITA guerrilla group "claims to have mined the South African-run hydroelectric project on the Cunene River inside Angola" (McColm & Smith 1977), but it is not clear whether this refers to the dam, turbines, or exterior switchgear and lines, nor how much damage was done.

3 Taylor 1980a.

4 Goen et al. 1970:75.

5 Shaw 1978.

6 Defense Electric Power Administration 1966:13A.

7 Joint Committee on Defense Production 1977a:1.

8 Goen et al. 1970:71.

9 Robert Mauro, quoted in Holmberg, 1981.

10 *New York Times* 1977.

11 *New York Times* 1970a. A plant in Missouri was also bombed in 1981 as cover for robberies (*Miami Herald* 1981a:23).

12 *New York Times* 1981j.

13 Congressional Reseach Service 1977:I:357.

14 Joint Committee on Defense Production 1977a:7–8. It is mainly in urban areas like New York City that underground transmission—about one percent of total U.S. transmission mileage—occurs.

15 Joint Committee on Defense Production 1977:II:36.

16 Congressional Research Service 1977:I:365.

17 For examples, see Economic Regulatory Administration 1979:II:181–216.

18 Metz 1977. There are more than fifty-five thousand miles of extra-high-voltage lines in the United States. (Kupperman & Trent 1980:71).

19 Kupperman & Trent 1980:71–72, 106.

20 Joint Committee on Defense Production 1977a:8. See also Notes 37 and 75 to this chapter. Draconian legislation proposed in 1981, however, would make damage to most energy facilities a federal felony. The organizers of a peaceful demonstration would become liable as conspirators if, for example, *agents provacateurs* in their midst later caused any damage.

21 Howe 1973. Other attacks at the same time blacked out Valparaiso and Roncagua. The army was sent to guard power installations (Howe 1973a), and foiled a repeat attack four months later.

22 Buckley 1981.

23 *New York Times* 1975b.

24 A participant in the Colorado bombings spent nearly six years on the FBI's "ten most wanted fugitives" list (*New York Times* 1975a). Seeking to prosecute him under federal law, the government won a conviction under the Sabotage Act of 1918, which was allegedly activated by an unrepealed 1950 declaration of a State of Emergency by President Truman during the Korean War. This use of the Act was later rejected on appeal (*New York Times* 1977e).

25 *New York Times* 1970b.

26 *New York Times* 1974.

27 Comptroller General of the U.S. 1978:II:App. IX.

28 Energy & Defense Project 1980:16.

29 M. Flood, personal communication, 1977.

30 Casper & Wellstone 1981:284, 285.

31 Ibid.:277.

32 *Los Angeles Times* 1981e; *Financial Times* 1981; *Newsweek* 1981c; Peel 1981.

33 *Los Angeles Times* 1981g.

34 Foisie 1981.

35 *New York Times* 1981i; *Los Angeles Times* 1981gg.

36 Joint Committee on Defense Production 1977a:87.

37 *New York Times* 1972.

38 Economic Regulatory Administration 1981:4–4, 4–5.

39 *Le Monde* 1978, 1978a, and *New York Times* 1978, 1978a; Hoffman 1979; *New York Times* 1981f. Winter storms repeated the southern and western British blackout four months later (*Los Angeles Times* 1981u) and again in January 1982—still only because of transmission failures, since Britain has an enormous surplus of generating capacity.

40 *International Herald Tribune* 1979.

41 Claridge 1981.

42 *Electric Light & Power* 1981.

43 *New York Times* 1981.

44 *Great Falls Tribune* 1980.

45 Congressional Research Service 1977:I:349.

46 Economic Regulatory Administration 1981:2–9.

47 Clapp 1978:41.

48 Chenoweth et al. 1963:34. In 1981, Greek terrorists set forest fires (*New York Times* 1981d).

49 Defense Electric Power Administration 1962:25–26.

50 Defense Electric Power Administration 1969.

51 Defense Electric Power Adminstration 1962:26.

52 Goen et al. 1970:79.

53 Nussbaum 1980.

54 Joint Committee on Defense Production 1977a:61.

55 FBI 1978:17, 20, 25.

56 *Atlanta Constitution* 1977.
57 *Miami Herald* 1981, 1981a.
58 *New York Times* 1975.
59 *Philadelphia Inquirer* 1981.
60 Comptroller General of the U.S. 1978:II:App. IX.
61 FBI 1973–80.
62 *New York Times* 1974a; Congressional Research Service 1977:III:159. The perpetrators, an Oregon couple, were eventually caught when FBI direction-finding equipment pinpointed the transmitter from which they radioed coded demands blown on a duck-call. Federal jurisdiction arose because the lines attacked belonged to the Bonneville Power Administration.
63 Chastain 1979.
64 Gargan 1981.
65 Kihss 1981, 1981a. New transformer coolants may eliminate the fire and PCB hazards (Kaplan 1982:68).
66 *New York Times* 1981g.
67 Economic Regulatory Administration 1981:4–10.
68 Lambert & Minor 1975.
69 Defense Electric Power Administration 1962:31.
70 Economic Regulatory Administration 1981:2–8.
71 Dircks 1981.
72 Federal Energy Regulatory Commission

1978:15–16.
73 Ibid.:16–17.
74 Park 1978:40.
75 Ibid.:44.
76 Ibid.:45.
77 Federal Energy Regulatory Commission 1978:37. How fast the rotors slow down depends on their "inertia constant"—their ratio of stored angular momentum to output rating—and on the extent to which the change in line frequency also changes the load. The latter effect can be quite complicated.
78 Ibid.:17.
79 Park 1978:40.
80 Economic Regulatory Administration 1981:I:2–5. It is largely because of system stability limits that some key long lines, generally including those from Canada, use direct current which is converted from and back to alternating current using special equipment at each end. This equipment is not only very expensive; it is also special-purpose, easy to disrupt, and slow to replace.
81 Federal Energy Regulatory Commission 1978:47–48.
82 Ibid.
83 Ibid.:37–38; Clapp 1978:17.
84 Fink 1976; emphasis added. We are grateful to *Professional Engineer* for permission to reproduce this copyright material.
85 Ibid.; emphasis added.

Notes to Chapter Eleven

1 For fuller discussion and documentation of the subjects of this chapter, see Lovins & Price 1975 and Ford 1982 (mainly on safety), and Lovins & Lovins 1980 (mainly on proliferation).
2 Ramberg 1978, 1980.
3 Ramberg 1978, 1980; Norton 1979.
4 E.g., NRC 1975.
5 Dye 1973.
6 Subcommittee on Energy & the Environment 1977:8.
7 IEAL 1980:I:2–10ff.
8 Bass et al. 1980:77.
9 Sterling 1978:38.
10 Kellen 1979:61ff.
11 Bass et al. 1980:6.
12 Flood 1976.
13 Burnham 1975:32.

14 de Leon et al. 1978:29.
15 Lewis 1979.
16 Marshall 1980a.
17 *Los Angeles Times* 1981ii; *Nucleonics Week* 1981.
18 *Los Angeles Times* 1982b; Marshall 1982. The rockets were reportedly early-1960s forerunners of the modern RPG-7. One entered an opening in the reactor building but missed the vital components inside. The others' shaped charges only made four-inch-deep holes in the reinforced concrete because they were designed to penetrate homogeneous material like armor plate, not heterogeneous material. There are, however, other types of warheads designed to penetrate hardened concrete structures or to spall high-velocity debris off their inner walls.

19 Bass et al. 1980:11.

20 *Times* 1978.

21 *Nucleonics Week* 1982, 1982a; *International Herald Tribune* 1981.

22 Toth 1981.

23 Bass et al. 1980:74.

24 Ibid.

25 Kupperman & Trent 1979:36.

26 E.g., Subcommittee on Energy & the Environment 1977a:247.

27 *Los Angeles Times* 1976.

28 de Leon et al. 1978:29.

29 Comptroller General of the U.S. 1977:2.

30 Bass et al. 1980:40.

31 Ibid.

32 *Latin America* 1978.

33 Emshwiller 1980a.

34 *Los Angeles Times* 1979f.

35 *Wall Street Journal* 1979.

36 *Nucleonics Week* 1982b.

37 Bass et al. 1980:74.

38 *New York Times* 1979.

39 *New York Times* 1980f.

40 Bass et al. 1980:53. Among the most recent of these threats (to the Zion plant in Illinois) was delivered by videotape (Green & Rempel 1982; *Los Angeles Times* 1982g). The list omits nuclear-related military incidents—such as eleven cases of arson in three months (killing one worker and injuring more than thirty sailors) aboard the nuclear-capable carrier *John F. Kennedy,* perhaps set by a sailor seeking to delay her sailing (Bass et al. 1980:43), or twenty incidents of sabotage aboard the carrier *Ranger* in summer 1972 (*Los Angeles Times* 1973).

41 Smith 1978:Encl. 2:App. J. #18, #29.

42 Subcommittee on Energy & the Environment 1979:46. This type of reactor uses highly enriched, bomb-grade fresh fuel.

43 Beard 1981.

44 DeNike 1975.

45 *Times* 1974a; *Hansard* 1974.

46 Smith 1978:Encl. 3:2.

47 Ibid.:3.

48 Bass et al. 1980:15.

49 Barnaby 1975.

50 O'Toole 1974.

51 Dumas 1980:19.

52 E.g., Comptroller General of the U.S. 1980.

53 Bass et al. 1980:75.

54 *Times* 1974.

55 Smith 1978:Encl. 2:Att. A #4; Bass et al. 1980:14–15.

56 Subcommittee on Energy & the Environment 1977:4–5; Bass et al. 1980:15.

57 NRC 1976a.

58 *Times* 1975.

59 Fialka 1979; Burnham 1979.

60 Subcommittee on Energy & the Environment 1979:7.

61 Burnham 1979b.

62 As of January 1978, the limit of error had been exceeded in eight of the previous twelve inventory periods (Subcommittee on Energy & the Environment 1979:7). This is not unusual: for U.S. bomb materials accounting as a whole, the statistical alarm bells have been ringing at least a third of the time (Marshall 1981b), but the facilities are apparently considered too important to shut down.

63 NRC 1978.

64 NRC 1979; Smith 1978:Encl. 2:App. J. #47 and cover letter:2; R. Rometsch, remarks to Institute of Nuclear Materials Management, 20 June 1975, reprinted in Committee on Government Operations 1976:1214–1217.

65 de Leon et al. 1978:30.

66 *Nuclear Engineering International* 1974a.

67 *New York Times* 1980c.

68 NRC 1981.

69 Aspin 1977.

70 Dumas 1980.

71 Ibid.

72 Brennan 1968.

73 Ibid.

74 E.g., Finley et al. 1980:App. I; AP 1974; *Nuclear News* 1974; *Los Angeles Times* 1974, 1974a; de Leon et al. 1978:30.

75 Finley et al. 1980:H–4.

76 E.R. Squibb & Sons, Inc. 1971 (the thyroid uptake was estimated at just under four millionths of a curie of iodine-131); *Los Angeles Times* 1982n.

77 *Daily Mail* 1979a; *Not Man Apart* 1981. The exposure was quite large, since the gamma radiation (from three stolen plugs from a graphite-moderated reactor) was measured to be ten to fifteen rads per hour at the car seat, and the plugs were under the seat for six months before they were discovered.

78 de Leon et al. 1978:30. The isotope used was iodine-131.

79 Bass et al. 1980:77.

80 AP 1974.

81 *New York Times* 1981a.

82 Holdren 1974.

83 Morrison et al. 1971.

84 Okrent & Moeller 1981:71–72.

85 NRC 1976.

86 Pollard 1979:42.

87 Ibid.:46.

88 Subcommittee on Energy & the Environment 1977:215.

89 Ibid.:14.

90 Bisset 1958.

91 Joint Committee on Atomic Energy 1974.

92 Okrent & Moeller 1981:74.

93 Dircks 1981.

94 Gardner 1981.

95 Schleimer 1974:27n8.

96 Ayres 1975.

97 Gorleben International Review 1979:Ch. 3.

98 Comey 1975.

99 Pollard 1979:26.

100 Chester 1976.

101 Gorleben International Review 1979:Ch. 3.

102 AP 1977. Strikes frequently shut down nuclear construction projects, though a recent no-strike agreement has usually been observed. In summer 1981, strikes shut down the Y-12 nuclear weapons component plant at Oak Ridge for seven weeks (*New York Times* 1981c). Non-union workers maintained normal operations at the Georgia Power Company, a major nuclear utility, during a 1981 strike.

103 Pollard 1979:39.

104 Smith 1978:Encl. 2:App. J. #10.

105 *Washington Post* 1975.

106 Burnham 1975:124.

107 Wall 1974.

108 Hatzfeldt et al. 1979:92.

109 Nussbaum 1980.

110 *Los Angeles Times* 1981f.

111 There are also non-nuclear hazards in the nuclear fuel cycle. For example, heavy-water plants, operating at Savannah River and in Canada, have enormous inventories of hydrogen sulfide, whose toxicity limit is five hundred parts per million. Some official British calculations suggest that a major release of this noxious gas could be about as hazardous as a modest reactor accident; and the plants have far less protection than a reactor.

112 A three-element shipment cooled for one hundred fifty days contains several million curies, including a half-million curies of radiocesium. Dispersal in New York City of a shipment totalling only two hundred thousand curies is calculated to contaminate two billion dollars' worth of land (Finley et al. 1980:65–66.) This is not a worst case. For example (ibid.), dispersal of just eighteen ounces of plutonium oxide into the air is conservatively calculated to cost two billion dollars in land contamination and to cause more than two thousand deaths. Dispersal of one hundred forty-four curies of polonium-210 (a fairly common alpha-ray source) would cause scores of deaths and nine billion dollars' contamination. All these isotopes, and more, are shipped in comparable quantities through America's largest cities, though some, notably New York, have had some success in retaining authority to prohibit this practice.

113 Dinneen et al. 1980.

114 Chester & Chester 1976:337.

115 Taylor 1981.

116 Gorleben International Review 1979:-Ch. 3.

117 Burnham 1980.

118 Marter 1963.

119 South Carolina Department of Health & Environmental Control 1974.

120 Alvarez 1980; Johnson 1982 (a compact review of releases from all U.S. nuclear weapons facilities).

121 Gorleben International Review 1979; Hatzfeldt et al. 1979:79–98.

122 Cochran & Speth 1974:10–17.

123 Johnson 1981.

124 Committee on Appropriations 1970.

125 Ramberg 1980.

126 Gervasi 1981:3.

127 *Guardian* 1975.

128 Flood 1976:33.

129 Marshall 1980a; *Boston Globe* 1980.

130 Kempster 1981; *Los Angeles Times* 1981r; *Newsweek* 1981a; Marshall 1981d.

131 *Oakland Tribune* 1981. Unconfirmed reports from the *Sunday Times* of London (*New York Times* 1981w) suggest that the bombing might merely have provided cover for demoli-

tion by charges placed deep inside the reactor by Israeli sappers. Israel has declined comment. In view of the precision of the bombing, such a tactic hardly seems to have been necessary.

132 *Boston Globe* 1981a.

133 Ramberg 1980.

134 Koven 1980.

135 Marshall 1980a. France had tried to change to non-weapons-grade fuel, but Iraq had refused. (In 1982, France agreed to rebuild the reactor only if it were redesigned not to use HEU [Smith 1982], so perhaps France will ask for the return of its delivered HEU, for which Iraq can have no legitimate further use.) Of course, French HEU exports to Iraq, Chile, etc. are much smaller than U.S. exports, which total tons of HEU (and other material directly usable for bombs), to such countries as Argentina, Brazil, Iran, Israel, Italy, South Korea, Pakistan, Spain, Taiwan, and South Africa. The HEU currently held (in quantities sufficient for one or more bombs) in Spain and Italy is presumably liable to seizure by terrorists in those countries.

136 Hume 1981.

137 Marshall 1981d; Richter 1981. Compare, however, Fainberg 1981.

138 Gossick 1977.

139 Lovins 1980; Lovins & Lovins 1981.

140 Taylor 1973:182.

141 O'Toole 1977. This imprecision is unlikely to improve much, for fundamental reasons which undercut international safeguards (Moglewer 1981).

142 Hsu 1981. The late Nobel Laureate in chemistry, Harold Urey, foresaw early that bombs could be smuggled into the U.S. anonymously (Urey 1945).

143 Bass et al. 1980:55.

144 Leader 1981.

145 Singer & Weir 1979.

146 Royal Commission on Environmental Pollution 1976; Ayres 1975; Barton 1975; Grove-White & Flood 1976; Justice 1978; Sieghart 1979.

147 It is, however, theoretically possible that our government, or some other government, has in fact capitulated to a non-hoax nuclear threat and is implementing, in the guise of normal incremental policy shifts, concessions dictated by an extortionist. The de-

gree of openness and public trust associated with governmental affairs, at least in the United States, makes this hypothesis seem very unlikely, but it cannot be altogether excluded. Certainly there is a lingering air of suspicion about apparent efforts, as the Comptroller General of the United States saw them (Burnham 1979a), to block a full investigation into alleged thefts of bomb material in the mid-1960s.

148 Could terrorists get a stolen military bomb to explode when they wished? Modern U.S. bombs, including all those in Europe (Miller 1979:59), are equipped with "Permissive Action Link" (PAL) devices. These require the entry of electronic authorization codes before the bomb becomes armed. Repeatedly entering the wrong code irreversibly scrambles the electronics so that the bomb cannot be detonated without first repairing the circuitry. This outwardly reassuring scheme raises three questions which cannot be answered from open literature:

• Is it true that PAL-equippped bombs cannot be set off without a currently authorized code, even by the more than fifty thousand people with up-to-date PAL training? Retired Admiral Gene LaRocque has stated, in paraphrase (DeNike 1975a), that "existing PALs malfunction often enough during practice drills that getting around them has become a regular practice. On any nuclear-armed U.S. Navy ship [some seventy percent of U.S. warships, according to the Admiral], there are four or five technicians trained to do this." If so, PAL is hardly tamperproof.

• Can a military bomb be carefully dismantled so as to recover its core? (And perhaps its other main components: any arming and firing circuits, and indeed everything else up to the detonators, could be readily replaced by an electronics expert.) It is possible to detonate the high-explosive components of a military nuclear bomb in an asymmetrical way which disperses the fissionable core beyond recovery but does not produce a nuclear explosion. It would be technically possible to arrange for this to happen automatically if the bomb is tampered with. For safety reasons, however, most if not all U.S. bombs apparently do not embody this precaution. (Military commanders do not want high explosives going off and scattering highly toxic plutonium around their magazines, ships, and aircraft.) Defense Secretary Schlesinger stated in 1974 (Miller 1979:62) that "emergency destruction devices and procedures have been developed so that nuclear weapons may be destroyed without producing a nuclear yield in the event that enemy capture is threatened." But that is clearly not the same as an *automatic* anti-tampering safeguard.

• What are the corresponding safeguards in bombs made by other countries? It seems implausible that some, especially developing countries, will have developed the elaborate and very costly mechanisms used in modern U.S. and British bombs for command, control, and operational safety (including "one-point safety"—designing bombs so that a single detonator can fire inside them without causing a nuclear explosion: developing this feature reportedly cost billions of dollars).

149 Talbot & Dann 1981.

150 Several are in swamps or under the ocean and have not been recovered (SIPRI 1978).

151 In 1961, for example, the U.S. Air Force accidentally dropped on North Carolina a twenty-four-megaton bomb—equivalent to three Vietnams or twelve World War IIs. It failed to explode because one, and only one, of its six safety devices worked. Some bombs now in service allegedly contain unstable high explosives which tend to go off when dropped only a few feet (Solomon 1981). A nuclear air-to-sea missile was reportedly fired by accident by an American F-102 over Haiphong Bay in the mid-1960s (SIPRI 1978, citing the *Washington Post*) owing to "a crossed wire in the firing safety mechanism." The missile was apparently not recovered from the hostile waters.

152 Talbot & Dann 1981; SIPRI 1978:63–82, which also documents some corresponding Soviet, British, and French incidents.

153 Chester & Chester 1976:329. Weapons effects are described in detail in such government handbooks as *The Effects of Nuclear Weapons*, which comes supplied with the Atomic Energy Commission's handy "Nuclear Bomb Effects Computer."

154 Fetter 1981.

155 Ibid.

156 Lovins 1980.

157 Gervasi 1981:207.

158 Comptroller General of the U.S. 1977:6.

159 NRC 1975.

160 Kendall et al. 1977:61.

161 Beyea 1980. Ramberg (1980:33–35) cites similar results. It is by disregarding long-term, long-range effects that an Atomic Industrial Forum spokesman was able to say (Dembart 1981) that a large nuclear bomb would cause "hundreds, maybe thousands" of times as much radioactive release as a reactor breach that it caused.

162 Beyea 1980. He assumed that less of the core would escape than would be the case if a bomb exploded near the reactor.

163 Most commentators have uncritically accepted contentions by the Sandia group (whose supporting analysis, if any, is unavailable to the public), in the Rasmussen Report itself (which supplied none—it nowhere considered sabotage), and elsewhere that sabotage could not cause worse consequences than a serious accident. That finding has never been justified in open literature and "is very likely untrue" (Kendall et al. 1977:61).

164 Fetter & Tsipis 1980, 1981.

165 Fetter & Tsipis 1980, 1981.

166 Ramberg (1980) cites other sources with similar or worse conclusions.

167 Holdren 1981.

168 Fetter & Tsipis 1980:29.

169 Ibid.

170 Holdren 1981.

171 Royal Commission on Environmental Pollution 1976.

172 Ramberg 1980:81.

173 Solon & Rosenberg 1981; *Nucleonics Week* 1981a (Swedish implementation).

174 Ramberg 1980:44, 134–141.

175 Beyea 1980.

176 Kostmayer & Markey 1980.

177 For example, reactors can become constipated if there is no place to store their spent fuel (a problem that has lately required the hasty "densification" of many spent-fuel storage pools), or if there are not enough special casks in which to ship the spent fuel elsewhere. A reprocessing plant can likewise become constipated if spent fuel arrives faster than technical breakdowns allow it to be processed. This is currently the cause of a serious

and worsening problem at the British and French plant for reprocessing spent fuel from gas-cooled, graphite-moderated reactors. The magnesium-alloy cladding of those reactors' metallic natural-uranium fuel corrodes in a matter of years when stored (as it normally is) in water. Persistent problems at both reprocessing plants have led to an increasing backlog of rotting fuel in storage pools. This increases operational problems and occupational hazards, leading to still more breakdowns and, on occasion, to strikes. At the French plant at Cap de la Hague, this cascading slowdown has diverted much of the capacity originally meant for handling oxide (LWR) fuel. This in turn has so reduced the plutonium output from La Hague that France must buy British plutonium to fuel the Super-Phénix fast breeder.

178 See Gorleben International Review 1979:Ch. 1.

179 Lovins 1982.

180 See e.g., Emshwiller 1980, 1981; Hershey 1981; Bupp 1981; O'Donnell 1981; Marshall 1981a; Parisi 1981; Shearson Loeb

Rhodes, Inc. 1981:4–9; Allison et al. 1981.

181 E.g., Lifton 1967; Del Tredici 1980; Perelman 1979. The official analyses of the Three Mile Island accident, though they appear to have seriously underestimated the amount of radioactivity released and hence the health effects from it, concluded that the major effects were psychological.

182 *Nuclear Engineering International* 1974.

183 Ramberg 1978:4; Farhar et al. 1980. Polls in 1981 showed higher anxiety.

184 Jenkins 1975:7.

185 Jenkins 1975. An argument often linked with this one is that nobody would actually want to cause mass destruction, even in war. There are, however, many precedents for such behavior (Ramberg 1980:18–19); both U.S. and Soviet strategic doctrines are based on it; and anyhow the destruction can accidentally be far greater than was intended.

186 Kupperman & Trent 1980:46.

187 Ibid.

188 Ibid.:57.

189 Ibid.:46, 65–68.

190 Drobnick & Enzer 1981.

Notes to Chapter Twelve

1 Coal, which provides a fifth of U.S. primary energy, has been treated in less detail by the earlier discussion of its transportation and labor problems, and implicitly by Chapter Ten, since most of the coal is burned in large power stations.

2 There are several other ways to deal with the estimated twenty-six trillion cubic feet of North Slope gas. First, keeping it where it is permits it to be repeatedly recycled through the oil reservoirs, greatly increasing the fraction of the oil resource that is ultimately recovered—and still making it possible to recover the gas afterwards. Second, keeping it there until it is *economically* worth bringing to market (there is currently every prospect it would prove unsaleably costly despite the subsidies given it) will prevent a costly misallocation of resources. The proper question is not how we could better use the gas than piping it south, but rather how we could better use the *money* which this would cost. Third, there may be an attractive technical alternative: converting the gas onsite to methanol, a portable vehicular

fuel. Apparently there are some technical difficulties in shipping methanol through the existing oil pipeline, but it is not yet clear how serious these are, and Congress was not given the opportunity to find out. It is quite likely that despite the extensive 1981 package of waivers of existing law, Wall Street will nevertheless refuse to finance the project and it will therefore not be built. Interestingly, one of the many competitors that makes the pipeline of North Slope gas grossly uneconomic for the next few decades, if not forever, is the burgeoning discovery of new gas fields in many parts of the United States which now import virtually all of their gas from Texas and Louisiana (e.g., Byron 1981; Pennino 1981). This trend, if continued, promises to disperse U.S. gas extraction and reduce dependence on long-distance pipelines—a goal which, decades ago, was met by dispersed town-gas plants (Stephens 1974:80). The contrast in vulnerability between Ohio or Pennsylvania gas brought from a well within tens of miles and Alaskan gas shipped about five thousand miles could not be more complete.

3 Fulkerson 1981:48, 169.

4 *Los Angeles Times* 1978, 1978a; FBI 1979:16–17, 28–29; FBI 1980:19. Kentucky coal-related bombings in particular have exceeded one per month during 1977–80, chiefly in connection with strikes and labor-management tensions.

5 Masselli & Dean 1981. This is more true of technologies to make synthetic liquid fuels than of those which make gas, especially gas of low or intermediate heat content. Some of those technologies are relatively well proven. Whether they can compete with more efficient energy use, some renewable sources, or conventional natural gas is another matter (Appendix Three; Linden 1981).

6 Perry & Landsberg 1981:234.

7 The peacetime rate of energy use of America's military establishment in 1979 was estimated at about seven hundred thousand barrels of oil equivalent per day (Maize 1980),

mostly in the form of premium liquid fuels for vehicles.

8 Marshall 1981c; Burns 1981. It is not yet clear whether the agreement will be affected by developments in Poland. It may at least be impeded by the U.S. embargo on export of turbines for the compressor stations. The gas contracts reportedly exact hefty hand-currency penalties from the Soviets if they do not deliver the gas on time, and at least in the medium term the main customers have arranged non-Communist back-up supplies.

9 Data from DOE 1981a:21. The losses arising in the synfuels industry are relatively small, since DOE has reduced the production target to half a million barrels per day by 1990 (Ibid.:23).

10 Since compact objects are easier to defend than long, slender objects, one measure of physical vulnerability is the ratio of length to breadth. For the Alaskan section of ANGTS this ratio would be one million.

Notes to Chapter Thirteen

1 Alfvén 1972.

2 Manley et al. 1970:100–103.

3 Bryan 1974; Comptroller General of the U.S. 1974.

4 Bryan 1974; Comptroller General of the U.S. 1974.

5 Solomon & Salem 1980.

6 Clark 1978:18. We are grateful to Dr. Clark for his helpful comments and writings on resilience.

7 Holling et al. 1979:2.

8 Kahn 1978:3, 19.

9 Kahn 1978.

10 Ibid.:19.

11 Alternatively, if the reliability requirements were somewhat relaxed, the renewable grid could take more additional load than the central station grid (ibid.:20), or equivalently would show a greater saving in back-up or storage capacity.

12 Ibid.:3.

13 Kahn 1979:343–344.

14 Citations in Kahn 1979.

15 Ryle 1977.

16 Leicester et al. 1978; Anderson et al. 1978.

17 Kahn 1979:344.

18 Kahn 1978:19.

19 Welch 1965:20. The concept of resilience has long roots in Taoist philosophy.

20 There is a new branch of mathematics known as "catastrophe theory" (Thom 1975; Stewart 1975; Woodcock & Davis 1978) dealing with discontinuous changes in the state of complex systems. It is able to classify these changes—which can be, for example, only of seven basic kinds in a system controlled by four variables—and can describe them by geometrical analogies. (Strictly speaking, the style of mathematics is more akin to that of topology, which deals with the most general properties of geometrical forms, such as how many holes they have through them, without being concerned with their exact size or shape.) Holling's results do not rely on the theorems of catastrophe theory, but initially borrowed some of its terminology. Readers with good mathematical intuition are urged to read Holling in the original (1978; Holling et al. 1979). Related mathematical developments (May 1976; Feigenbaum 1980) offer a further useful counterpoint to Holling's work.

21 Holling & Goldberg 1971:225; emphasis added.

22 Clark 1978:29.

23 Holling & Goldberg 1971:225; emphasis added.

24 Holling 1978:99–104

25 National Academy of Sciences 1972; Walsh 1981.

26 Huffacker et al. 1963.

27 Citations in Clark 1978:35.

28 MacArthur 1972; Levin 1974.

29 Vollenweider 1970; Bazykin 1975.

30 Clark 1978:32.

31 Beeton 1969; LeCren et al. 1972.

32 Russell et al. 1974; Platt et al. 1977.

33 Southwood 1975.

34 Sutherland 1974.

35 Lorenz 1976.

36 Holling 1978:102ff.

37 Clark 1978:50.

38 Holling 1978:104.

39 Ibid.:105–106.

40 Ibid.

41 Clark 1978:40.

42 Holling 1978:106.

43 Clark 1978:42.

44 Holling 1978:105–106, taken from Simon 1973.

45 Ibid.

46 Holling & Goldberg 1971:229.

47 Holling et al. 1979.

48 Ibid.:27.

49 Holling et al. 1979; emphasis added.

50 E.g., Thompson & Beckerley 1964–70.

51 E.g., Weinberg 1975.

52 Gall 1978.

53 von Neumann 1966.

54 Gall 1978:132.

55 Vicker 1981.

56 E.g., Lambert & Minor 1975.

57 E.g., Joint Committee on Defense Production 1977a:72–73, 116–117.

58 Comptroller General of the U.S. 1981:61.

59 Mostert 1974.

60 *Los Angeles Times* 1981cc.

61 Altman 1980.

62 Energy & Defense Project 1980:23.

63 Meislin 1981.

64 *Energy Insider* 1980:4.

65 FEMA 1979:22–23.

66 Weingart 1977:29.

67 NERC 1979:7.

68 Kahn 1979:320; Sørensen 1979.

69 Stephens 1970:105; 1973:34, 112.

70 Fowler 1981; Choi et al. 1982.

71 A Helio Courier® short-takeoff-and-landing (STOL) design has this agreeable property. Accordingly, military personnel using it are not supposed to wear parachutes.

72 Stewart 1975:450.

73 Broad 1981b.

74 Shifrin 1981.

75 Gall 1978:130.

76 If the potential for common-mode failures is somehow related to the number of possible interactions between any two components, and if those interactions can be of only one kind, then the number of interactions among n components is $n(n-1)/2$: that is, the number of simple interactions rises as the square of the number of components. If interactions can be of more than one kind or can involve more than two components, the number of possibilities rises much faster and quickly becomes utterly unanalyzable.

77 Comptroller General of the U.S. 1981:6.

78 Ibid.

79 von Neumann 1956.

80 Šiljak 1978; Barstow & Proschan 1975.

81 Hill 1981.

82 Comptroller General of the U.S. 1981; Fallows 1981; Kaldor 1981.

83 Kneese 1973.

84 Weinberg 1973; Edsall 1974; Lovins & Price 1975:15–18.

85 Lovins & Price 1975:15.

86 Barton 1975; Ayres 1975; Royal Commission on Environmental Pollution 1976; Grove-White & Flood 1976; Justice 1978; Sieghart 1979.

87 Speth et al. 1974.

88 Hoover 1979:24.

89 Simmons 1981:25.

90 This term is due to Illich (1980).

91 U.S. nuclear vendors have already lost approximately half—probably the best half—of their staff as the nuclear capacity forecast for the year 2000 has declined by more than eightfold. Recruitment of able nuclear engineering students is an increasing problem despite high salaries. According to *Business Week* (1981c), market prospects are so dim that many key suppliers of reactor components

may soon stop bothering to renew their federal certification as qualified nuclear suppliers, making it much harder to find suitable parts.

92 Shaffer 1981.

93 *Business Week* 1981b.

94 Drexhage & Whiting-O'Keefe 1976:6.

95 Belady & Lehman 1976. Their tactful phraseology is due to the awkward fact that they are describing the operating system of their employer's flagship computer—the IBM System/360.

96 Drexhage & Whiting-O'Keefe 1976:1.

97 Kessler 1981.

98 Murray 1981.

99 See Schultz 1981.

100 *Los Angeles Times* 1981dd.

101 Murray 1981.

102 McLellan 1981.

103 Lorin 1979:595.

104 Attanasio et al. 1976.

105 Drexhage & Whiting-O'Keefe 1976:1.

106 Ibid.

107 *Business Week* 1981b.

108 Gray 1981:6.

109 Jim Gray, personal communication, 7 December 1981. We are much indebted to Dr. Gray for editorial suggestions on this chapter.

110 Lorin 1979:591.

111 Gray 1981:4.

112 Gray 1979:5.

113 Alsberg & Day 1976; Lamport 1978.

114 Drexhage & Whiting-O'Keefe 1976:5.

115 Katzman 1977; Bartlett 1977; Highleyman 1980; Gray 1977; Tandem 1981.

Notes to Chapter Fourteen

1 *AERO Sun-Times* 1981, quoting from *Alternative Sources of Energy*.

2 Larue 1981.

3 *Electrical Construction and Maintenance* 1965.

4 Congressional Research Service 1977:III:190.

5 Hyman 1981. This is partly because the concept has been widely (if loosely) used in the literature of political economy. The sociopolitical implications of energy centralization, though beyond the scope of this book, are important and controversial (Lovins 1977, Nash 1979).

6 Messing et al. 1979.

7 Ibid.; see also Hyman 1981.

8 Lovins 1977:86.

9 In section 209.

10 Economic Regulatory Administration 1981.

11 E.g., Asbury & Webb 1979.

12 Persons acquainted with the work of the late economist E.F. Schumacher only by the title of his best-known book, *Small Is Beautiful*, are often surprised to find that he emphasized this point, stating explicitly that it is just as wrong to be addicted to universally small as to universally large scale.

13 Schipper 1981.

14 St. Geours 1979.

15 Lovins & Lovins 1981a, calculating from Ministry of Industry data.

16 *Chikyu no Koe* 1981.

17 Schipper 1981.

18 *New York Times* 1981s.

19 *Business Week* 1981.

20 Sant et al. 1981.

21 RTM 1981.

22 Ibid. RTM's estimates of the energy savings from geothermal, municipal solid waste, cogeneration, and waste-heat recovery are omitted from these data. The nonrenewable decline was largely in oil and gas. Coal mining increased by less (a still impressive seventeen hundred trillion BTUs per year). Fuller accounting for nonmarket wood use, or counting delivered rather than primary energy, would make the renewable increment exceed even this addition from coal.

23 Weintz 1981.

24 *Solar Age* 1981b.

25 Brown 1981:205; Gouraud 1982:4 (who also points out that some two million kerosene heaters were sold in 1981).

26 *New York Times* 1981k; *Los Angeles Times* 1981z.

27 ERAB 1981a:15.

28 Hewett et al. 1981:142.

29 Lovins & Lovins 1981:66n144. The delivered energy (in terms of heat content) from nuclear power was eight hundred trillion BTUs; the delivered energy from wood, con-

servatively assuming average consumption efficiencies of forty percent in households and seventy percent in industrial boilers, was a bare minimum of thirteen hundred trillion BTUs, more likely about twenty-one hundred, and quite possibly twenty-five hundred. The uncertainty arises mainly from nonmarket wood transactions, which are difficult to estimate.

30 Bowring 1980.

31 See California Energy Commission 1981b for manufacturers; and for plans, ibid. 1981, Park & Obermeier 1981, and O'Reilly 1982.

32 Ron Corso (Federal Energy Regulatory Commission), personal communication, 4 August 1981. Competing applications for the same sites are not double-counted.

33 Siegel 1981.

34 *Energy Daily* 1981, based on RTM data.

35 Larry Schlussler, personal communication, December 1981. Many of the households are remote and produce special crops which the householders are reluctant to expose to the gaze of meter-readers. This alters the perceived economics of photovoltaics.

36 Shupe 1981; Lubenow 1981; Shupe & Weingart 1980.

37 California Energy Commission 1981c. The estimates are conservative.

38 Katz et al. 1981.

39 OTA 1978.

40 Aspen Institute for Humanistic Studies 1979:Summ.:2. See also Southern California Edison Company 1980.

41 Delegationen för energiforskning 1980. In addition, three percent of the budget is for district heating (solar or fossil-fueled) and seven percent is for system studies, basic research, and overheads. Thus only the balance of fourteen percent is for nonrenewables, chiefly for prior commitments in fusion and in nuclear waste management.

42 Ursu & Vamanu 1979:18.

43 Tsuchiya 1981.

44 *Solar Age* 1981.

45 Ibid.; Comité d'Action pour la Solaire 1981:10.

46 Kahn 1979; Sørensen 1979.

47 Congressional Research Service 1979:113.

Notes to Chapter Fifteen

1 In *Tao Te Ching* 59.

2 This book assumes, however, technologies that require no more attention from their *user* than present centralized systems. It would be possible to make energy devices more "fiddly" so that they would require more intervention by the user. Such sytems would be cheaper than the "hands-off" ones assumed here.

3 Hershey 1981a; Schipper 1981. Data from EIA's *Monthly Energy Review*, ending in 1981 in November for oil use and in the third quarter for GNP.

4 *Los Angeles Times* 1980.

5 Billiter 1981a; *Los Angeles Times* 1981j. The decline continued in 1981 (*Los Angeles Times* 1982o).

6 *Los Angeles Times* 1981k.

7 Lovins et al. 1982.

8 Sant et al. 1981; SERI 1981.

9 Bullard 1981:199.

10 *Washington Post* 1981a.

11 Schipper 1980; Schipper et al. 1981:14.

An average of twenty percent was saved in residential space heating with natural gas (American Gas Association 1981); and during 1978–81 alone, demand for heating oil plunged eighteen percent (Martin 1981a).

12 Rosenfeld et al. 1980. This assumed a seventy percent efficient furnace. Actual furnace efficiencies are often lower, and some are higher—Lennox sells ninety-two percent efficient pulse-combination gas furnaces—but this should be analyzed separately from the efficiency of the house itself.

13 Department of Energy 1981b.

14 Shurcliff 1982.

15 Meyer & Sieben 1982.

16 University of Saskatchewan 1979.

17 Rosenfeld et al. 1980; Shurcliff 1980; Leger & Dutt 1979; Shick 1980; Department of Energy 1981b; *Superinsulated Building*.

18 Rosenfeld et al. 1980; Department of Energy 1981b. The Lo-Cal examples referred to are the Phelps and Leger houses respective-

ly (Leger & Dutt 1979; Shick 1980; Shick, personal communications, 1981).

19 O'Neal et al. 1981; Bullard 1981:202–203.

20 Department of Energy 1981b.

21 SERI 1981:I:31. (Pagination in references to this source refers to the original two-volume edition by the House Commerce Committee.)

22 AS/ISES 1982.

23 Carter & Flower 1981; Nelson 1981.

24 Department of Energy 1980c.

25 Nørgård 1979, 1979a. The saving is somewhat larger than he shows because his refrigerator efficiency target has already been overtaken by a further factor-of-four improvement.

26 Holt 1982, referring to the most efficient equivalent Toshiba model.

27 Dr. Larry Schlussler PE, 725 Bayside Drive #6, Arcata CA 95521.

28 SERI 1981:I:54–55.

29 Bullard 1981:209–210.

30 See e.g., SERI 1981; Carhart et al. 1980.

31 Palmiter & Miller 1979.

32 Holland 1981.

33 Lovins et al. 1982.

34 Holland 1981; *Solar Age* 1981a; Riemers 1980.

35 Rothchild 1981; Wilson 1981; Socolow 1978.

36 SERI 1981:I:24–27, 65.

37 Ibid.:27.

38 Congressional Research Service 1981: OTA 1980a; Masselli & Dean 1981.

39 Stelson 1981.

40 Shoskes 1981.

41 Ruben 1981.

42 VW of America 1980.

43 Seiffert & Walzer 1980.

44 Boyle 1981; Lehner 1980; *Japan Automotive News* 1980; Dexler 1981.

45 *New York Times* 1981r.

46 SERI; Gray & von Hippel 1981; TRW 1979; Shackson & Leach 1980.

47 Shackson & Leach 1980; Gorman & Heitner 1980; SERI 1981.

48 Lovins et al. 1982; Samuels 1981.

49 Schipper 1981.

50 Shifrin 1981.

51 Feder 1981.

52 *Energy Insider* 1981. See generally, for technical discussions of potential industrial energy savings, SERI 1981; Sant et al. 1981; Lovins et al. 1982; Chiogioji 1979; Ross 1981; Steen et al. 1981.

53 Ross 1981. Case studies of specific plants often reveal even larger savings. For example, British analyses show economically worthwhile savings of two-thirds of total energy use in a light engineering factory (Chase et al. 1978), forty-five percent in aluminum extrusion (Ladamatos et al. 1979a), and values spanning that range in three heavy enginerring plants (Ladamatos et al. 1979).

54 Ross 1981:381. The saving is documented in Lovins et al. 1982.

55 Ladamatos et al. 1979. Olivier et al. in England (cited in Lovins et al. 1982) found nationally significant savings from this shift.

56 See Krause's analysis in Lovins et al. 1982.

57 Ross 1981.

58 Steen et al. 1981.

59 Besant et al. 1978; Dumont et al. 1978; Dumont & Orr 1981.

60 Besant et al. 1978; Dumont et al. 1978; Dumont & Orr 1981. In 1978–79, the actual net load was twelve and a half million BTUs (Besant et al. 1979; Rosenfeld et al. 1980), owing to air leakage around the shutters and the net heat loss from about a thousand visitors per week. By late 1981, the load had been reduced below its design value of five million BTUs (Meyer & Sieben 1981).

61 Kahn 1979:316.

62 This measures the time required for the inside temperature to fall exponentially a certain fraction (about two-thirds) of the way to the outside temperature if no heat is provided from any source.

63 Congressional Research Service 1977:I:248.

64 Even in a house as inefficient as two or three BTUs per square-foot-degree day, the heating capacity needed would be less than a tenth the size of the smallest central furnaces sold today (Bullard 1981:204ff). It is also noteworthy that although the earlier experimental house at Aachen, West Germany is four times less efficient than the Saskatchewan Conservation House, its inside temperatures

are physically incapable of falling below fifty-five degrees Fahrenheit in an average winter even if no space heating whatever is supplied.

65 Energy Information Adminstration 1981.

66 Goen et al. 1970:83.

67 See Lovins et al. 1982 and Lovins 1982.

68 Foget & Van Horn 1979; Black 1971.

69 Ross 1981:409n. These six sectors include oil refineries, which would not only save money but also eliminate their dependence on the power grid. Such reliable, steady sources could also meet a larger fraction of public demand if peak demands were deliberately reduced—a goal which efficient buildings would go far toward achieving. Additional institutional mechanisms proven in the past few years include peak-shaving cooperatives (Energy & Defense Project 1980:156), power brokerage among utilities (successful in Florida), and utility payments to communities which shave their peak loads (successful far beyond expectations when offered as an incentive by Pacific Gas & Electric Company—see page 317). New mechanisms are emerging, including utility-purchasable (perhaps remarketable) peak-load easements and third-party efficiency investments (which can split the financial benefit with the utility). Since aluminum, enriched uranium, and other electricity-intensive products are easier to store than electricity itself, plants which make them can contribute to load management, as government enrichment plants did when they shut down and saved three thousand megawatts during the 1977–78 coal strike.

70 Lovins & Lovins 1980; Taylor 1980a.

71 Ross & Williams 1979; SERI 1981. This assumes a rate of implementation slower than could be achieved by using special mechanics to speed up retrofits; see page 332.

72 Lovins 1981, 1982. These can both eliminate the capital burden on the owners and make the utilities financially healthier.

73 The supporting calculations are set out in Lovins 1981b. The present version assumes a retail synfuel price of seventy dollars per barrel (1981 dollars), though the general conclusions are rather insensitive to the exact value.

74 Congressional Research Service 1981.

75 von Hippel 1981:101. Government estimates for 1981–82 are about eighty billion dollars.

76 Ibid.:95.

77 The United Auto Workers and several private analysts have proposed accelerated scrappage of inefficient cars for at least seven years. The federal government has not yet paid attention. The one officially sponsored study (Energy & Environmental Analysis 1980) uses such artificially restrictive assumptions that the calculated savings were small and costly. The Department of Energy's supposedly encyclopedic survey of major oil-saving options (DOE 1980) does not even mention accelerated scrappage. By November 1980, DOE's senior oil-saving analysts had not done even back-of-the-envelope arithmetic about it. Even Gray & von Hippel (1981) omit the possibility from their otherwise excellent survey, although they expect that normal market forces alone will improve the fleet average to about sixty mpg by 2000 anyhow.

78 That is von Hippel's estimate of nearly twenty-three hundred dollars per car (SERI 1981); the actual value is almost certainly lower (Shackson & Leach 1980; Gorman & Heitner 1980). The oil saving will actually be somewhat less than assumed here, because the average car *sold* in the U.S. in 1981—the one that would presumably be displaced by the sixty-mpg version—had an on-road efficiency of about twenty mpg, not fifteen. In partial compensation, however, new cars tend to be driven more miles per year than old cars, so introducing new cars yields a disproportionate oil saving for the fleet.

79 Deese & Nye 1981; Davis 1981.

80 Davis 1981:620.

81 Congressional Research Service 1981; OTA 1980a; Masselli & Dean 1981. In late 1981, the plant-gate price of shale oil (in 1981 dollars) was estimated at about forty-five dollars a barrel. Early–1982 estimates were substantially higher. The mark-up for refining, marketing, and distribution would normally be over twelve dollars per barrel, plus a five-dollar premium because shale oil is harder to refine than natural crude. See also page 000.

82 Stockman 1977; citations in Lovins & Lovins 1980:70ff.

83 Sant 1979.

84 Sant et al. 1981.

85 SERI 1981.

86 Lovins & Lovins 1982.

87 Lovins et al. 1982.

88 Steen et al. 1981.

89 Lovins et al. 1982.

90 Lovins & Lovins 1980.

91 Ibid.:91–125.

92 Sørensen 1980; Lovins et al. 1982.

93 Sørensen 1980; SERI 1981; Lovins et al. 1982.

Notes to Chapter Sixteen

1 This book does not consider geothermal energy or tidal power (moonpower), since neither is renewable in principle. In the right sites and with due attention to their considerable potential for environmental damage, however, both could, where economic, be locally important for providing heat and electricity respectively.

2 Sørensen 1979.

3 Metz 1978.

4 Sørensen 1976, 1979.

5 Kahn 1978:33.

6 Kahn 1979:319ff.

7 Kerr 1981a.

8 Kahn 1978, 1979; Sørensen 1976, 1979; Systems Control 1980; Diesendorf 1981.

9 Ryle 1977.

10 There could be modest changes in the optimal ratio of the dams' storage volume to their peak output (Kahn 1978, 1979).

11 OTA 1978.

12 See Lovins 1977b, 1978, for a fuller definition and discussion.

13 See Lovins 1977b, 1978, and the Appendix Three tabular data on converting electricity or fuels into heat as compared with supplying heat directly.

14 Before efficiency improvements, eight percent of U.S. delivered energy needs—the premium, non-thermal applications (Lovins 1977b)—can economically justify such a costly form of energy as electricity. However, thirteen percent of delivered energy is supplied in the form of electricity, and sixteen percent would be if many power plants were not standing idle, unable to sell their output. Thus five-thirteenths of the electricity supplied is already spilling over into uneconomic uses—space-conditioning and water heating (Lovins 1982).

15 Butti & Perlin 1980.

16 Hammond & Metz 1977.

17 Lovins 1982.

18 Hammond & Metz 1977.

19 Foreman 1981.

20 For example, see Bergey 1981. The goal is for the maintenance instructions to say, "Once a year, go outside on a windy day and look up at the wind machine. If the blades are turning, it is OK."

21 Caputo (1981:29) points out that even with assumptions unfavorable to solar energy, energy output can be practically harnessed from an average square foot of land area at about the same rate at which energy can be obtained by burning, over the course of a century, the ultimately recoverable oil and gas underneath that square foot. In this sense too, solar energy is not too dilute.

22 Leckie et al. 1981.

23 M. Lillywhite (Domestic Technology Institute, Evergreen CO 80439), personal communication, 1979.

24 Simmons 1981:25ff. The Mason-Dixon Farm is near Harrisburg.

25 Department of Energy 1980; California Energy Commission 1980.

26 OTA 1981; Yanda & Fisher 1980.

27 OTA 1981.

28 The municipal utility in Burlington, Vermont has already substituted some wood chips for oil and is currently building an entirely wood-fired fifty-megawatt power plant. We do not advocate such plants, however, as there are usually even cheaper sources of saved and renewable electricity which could reserve wood wastes for producing premium liquid fuels.

29 Hollands & Orgill 1977; OTA 1978; Lovins 1978:492; Ross & Williams 1981:170–179.

30 *Promoting Small Power Production* 1981. The avoided costs so far set by state commissions range from more than eight cents per kilowatt-hour down to practically nothing. The Federal Energy Regulatory Commission is supposed to ensure that the rates are fair, but shows no signs of wanting to do so.

31 Sun*Up 1981; see also the technical guidelines published by Southern California Edison Co., San Diego Gas & Electric Co., and others.

32 Systems Control 1980, 1980b.

33 We are indebted to E.R. Baugh PE for calling our attention to this literature.

34 Shipp 1979; Linders 1979.

35 For example, there is concern that the transient torque loads on turbogenerator shafts may be fatiguing them and reducing their lifetime: Jackson et al. 1979; Dunlop et al. 1979; Walker et al. 1981.

36 Daley (1982) gives an example from Sea World in San Diego.

37 Various relays are also important for protecting the generator itself: Breedlove & Harbaugh 1981.

38 Conversely, flat car batteries could be recharged from the house. In the long run, if cars using series hybrid drive trickle-charged their batteries during the day through cheap photovoltaic arrays on their roofs, the interconnection would benefit the householder still further. Various opportunities on these lines are envisaged in Cullen 1980.

39 Systems Control 1980:5–50.

40 Ibid.:5–51. The same argument has been made in almost identical language (Falcone 1979:4) for strengthening interregional power transmission capacity. This approach has the drawback, however, that it may increase grid instabilities and propagate failures: "The more we have interconnected, the more we have the chance that [the grid] will topple due to the interconnecting effects" (Lewis 1979a:18).

41 For example (Systems Control 1980:5–51), if the failure of a class of generators all at once caused the expected outage rate to rise from one day per decade to one week per decade, a standby source with an annual cost of sixty dollars per kilowatt (about as costly as many central fossil-fueled power plants today) could well be justified, because the outage costs might well exceed its break-even point of about eleven dollars per kilowatt-hour.

42 Ibid.:5–52.

43 Ibid.

44 Systems Control, Inc., is continuing research on priority load allocation for whole power grids, but not on the scale on which a dispersed source might be used and controlled; and the work is very far from practical realization.

45 Systems Control 1980, 1980a, 1980b, 1980c; Boardman et al. 1981. The studies assumed that new central power plants are far cheaper than they really are and that electricity demand will be very insensitive to rising real prices (thus avoiding changes in the shape of the grid: Diesendorf 1981). These assumptions strengthen the conclusions.

46 Systems Control 1980:Summ.:3.

47 Appendix Three; Lovins 1978.

48 Systems Control 1980:5–52.

49 Ibid.:5–53.

50 Diesendorf 1981.

51 Systems Control 1980:3–4: the grid savings are typically about a tenth as large as the capacity and fuel savings.

52 The Systems Control analysis (1980) shows that the distributed sources' economic advantage declines as their fractional contribution to the grid rises. One calculation (Lee & Yamayee 1980) suggests that under pessimistic assumptions the extra spinning reserve requirements for "unreliable" dispersed sources may limit the economic use of certain renewables to a few percent of the total load (Systems Control 1980). But the assumed methodology appears to treat dispersed renewable sources and central nonrenewable sources differently by not counting such a penalty for the latter, even though they can fail in much larger blocks. The cost and outage data used for nonrenewables also appear to be unrealistic. This conclusion therefore cannot be considered reliable. If the problem were real, a cheaper solution could be available in the form of system storage, since one kilowatt of storage "can provide up to two kilowatts of spinning-reserve and load-following capability" (Systems Control 1980c:14). This whole subject is being explored further at Systems Control and elsewhere. It is, however, a very intricate problem, since it also depends on price-induced shifts in demand.

53 E.g., Ma & Isaksen 1979.

54 Systems Control 1980c. Onsite storage may, however, increase the end user's resilience enough to warrant paying a large premium for it.

55 For example, a state-of-the-art review

(Lovins 1978) drafted in November 1977 had to have half its data revised by March 1978, and a quarter re-revised by May 1978, simply because new and better data were coming in so quickly.

56 *Soft Energy Notes* (1978–) is arguably the best effort so far to shortcut the delays in circulating this information worldwide.

57 SERI 1981.

58 See national studies cited in Lovins et al. 1982.

59 Stobaugh & Yergin 1979.

60 Hannon 1976. Up-to-date data would probably raise this figure.

61 Schachter 1979; Buchsbaum et al. 1979.

62 Rodberg 1978; Brooks 1981:154–167.

63 Congressional Research Service 1978:212–219.

64 Richards 1982.

65 Kahn et al. 1980.

66 Lovins & Lovins 1982.

67 Holdren et al. 1980. The National Audubon Society (950 Third Ave., New York NY 10022) is extending this research in its "Side Effects of Renewable Energy Sources" project.

68 Hein 1979.

69 Lovins et al. 1982.

70 Lovins & Lovins 1980.

71 See national studies cited in Lovins et al. 1982.

72 Ibid.; Lovins & Lovins 1980; Reddy 1981.

73 OTA 1978, quoted in Congressional Research Service 1978:199–209.

74 Ibid.:204.

75 Becker 1981a. See generally Congressional Research Service 1978:208ff; Reddy 1981; Lovins et al. 1982; Lovins & Lovins 1980.

76 Lovins 1977b.

77 Lovins 1980a.

78 Congressional Research Service 1978:310–329.

79 Ibid.:377.

80 Butti & Perlin 1980.

81 Lovins & Lovins 1980, 1981.

82 *Electrical World* 1982.

83 Bupp & Derian 1978.

84 Bowring 1980.

85 Methanol—wood alcohol—is quite toxic, although workers and the public could be straightforwardly protected by the addition of odorants and the consistent use of locking fittings (like those used for fueling aircraft) on filling-pump spouts to contain fumes and prevent spills. Another exception often cited is that certain types of solar cells can be made with small amounts of cadmium, arsenic, or other highly toxic materials. The burning of a house which used such cells could release these materials to the environment in ounce or (conceivably) pound quantities. But highly efficient and probably superior cells can also be made from other materials which are usually cheaper and which are nontoxic (or have such high melting and boiling points that it is hard to imagine how much of them could be dispersed).

86 Russell 1982.

87 Joint Committee on Defense Production 1977:II:45.

Notes to Chapter Seventeen

1 EMR 1980:65.

2 Quoted by Harding 1982, who collated most of the data in this paragraph.

3 DOE 1981a:9.

4 Ibid.:1.

5 Ibid.:2.

6 Ibid.:13–14.

7 Lovins & Lovins 1980a.

8 *Oil Daily* 1981.

9 John Geesman, quoted in Harding 1982.

10 Omang 1982. Similar trends may emerge from the revival of dormant utility emergency-planning groups set up by the 1950 Defense Authorization Act (*Inside Energy* 1981).

11 ERAB 1981:6.

12 DOE 1981a.

13 Lovins 1981, 1982.

14 *Los Angeles Times* 1982k.

15 DCPA 1977:App. G.

16 California Energy Commission 1981.

17 Energy & Defense Project 1980; Clark & Page 1981.

18 Jenkins 1980.

19 *Energy Consumer* 1980b:32–45.

20 Los Angeles Energy Management Advi-

sory Board 1981.

21 Seib & Harris 1981:1.

22 Iklé 1979.

23 Brookhaven National Laboratory 1978:1–42.

24 California Energy Commission 1981e:22.

25 Benson 1981.

26 Richards 1982.

27 Stayton 1981:9, 16.

28 Humboldt County Energy Advisory Committee 1981.

29 Data from Professor Al Cassella, Sangamon State University, Springfield, Illinois; see Benson 1981.

30 Stanek 1981:30.

31 Tsongas 1980.

32 Stanek 1981:30.

33 Colorado Office of Energy Conservation 1981:71.

34 E.g., Okagaki & Benson 1979. See also Gorenflo et al. 1981; Schaefer & Benson 1980; Lovins's primer in *Soft Energy Notes,* May 1978; and Randolph 1981.

35 Pomerantz et al. 1979; SERI 1980c.

36 Tomasi et al. 1981:8.

37 Colorado Office of Energy Conservation 1980:70.

38 Alschuler 1980.

39 National League of Cities 1981.

40 Randolph 1981; Corbett & Hayden 1981; Morris 1980.

41 For a short list of barriers and solutions, see Lovins & Lovins 1980:115–119.

42 SERI 1980c.

43 Corbett & Hayden 1981:960.

44 Tomasi et al. 1981:3.

45 For example, Los Angeles Energy Management Advisory Board 1981. The program does not list and exhaust all cost-effective technical options, but it is clearly conceived and presented.

46 Corbett & Hayden 1981:957.

47 Tomasi et al. 1981:3–4. Significantly, over two-thirds of the jurisdictions surveyed consider energy costs as a separate line item in their budgets.

48 Pomerantz et al. 1979. (Other barriers and pitfalls are discussed in *Soft Energy Notes* 1982.)

49 Pomerantz et al. 1979. The program has also been the subject of two excellent televi-sion specials by Bill Moyers. (Purists may point out that Franklin County is a net export-er of energy—on paper—because it contains the Yankee Rowe nuclear plant, whose power is exported to Berkshire County. From the viewpoint of county residents, however, that does them no good. Most of their energy is oil and comes from outside the county, state and—usually—country.)

50 For example (Clark 1980:99), more than ninety percent of county residents polled in 1980 said they had reduced their energy use since 1974; nearly half used or planned to use wood for heating. Weatherization projects had cut energy use in half in more than two hun-dred homes, and energy audits saved an aver-age of five hundred sixty dollars per audited home per year. Total energy use in the county did not grow during 1976–78. Recent pro-gress is probably even greater, though many of the original principals in the program, with their small federal grants cut off, are now back at their factory jobs and can devote only even-ings and weekends to analysis and leadership for the Project. In mid-1981, the twenty-three town energy committees and the county task force were still active, though funds for the two-person county energy staff were running out.

51 E.g., *Greenfield* [MA] *Recorder* 24 August 1979.

52 Buchsbaum et al. 1979.

53 Koster 1978. See also Orange County 1981.

54 Wheeler et al. 1975.

55 Los Angeles Energy Management Advi-sory Board 1981.

56 Tomasi et al. 1981:1.

57 MetroDade 1980, 1980a.

58 Leslie Brook, Deputy Director of the Dade County program, personal communica-tion, 18 May 1981.

59 Ibid.

60 Alan Silverstein, telecon to Alec Jenkins, 25 February 1982. See also Delmasto 1980.

61 Details are available from John Sutthoff & Betty Dean, Center for Business & Econom-ic Research, California State University at Chico.

62 California Energy Commission 1981d.

63 Ibid.

64 St. Paul Energy Office 1980, 1982a; Al-

ice Murphy & Gary Dodge, personal communications to Carolyn Jane Danahy. The Office closed at the end of 1981. Its publications are available from Mayor Latimer's office.

65 Department of Energy 1979; see also 1981c.

66 Urban Solar Energy Association 1981.

67 Fitzpatrick 1980; Morton 1980.

68 McRae 1981.

69 Morris & Reiniger 1981.

70 Academy for Contemporary Problems 1980:A–18.

71 Ibid.:A–19.

72 Ibid.:A–20.

73 Baum & Colby 1981.

74 Atlantic Richfield Company; GasCAP.

75 Department of Energy 1979a.

76 NASA 1976.

77 John Newton and Dick Baugh, personal communications, 1982.

78 Knight 1981.

79 *Energy Consumer* 1980b:23. Among the relevant technologies are solar water heater kits developed at the National Solar Water Workshop. A community college workshop process which lends itself to rapid replication is available from the same contact: Stan Mumma, Arizona State University at Tempe. See also Fisk 1979.

80 Maria & Arnie Valdez (Rt. 1, Box 3-A, San Luis CO 81152), personal communications, 1980–81.

81 SERI 1980b, 1981a.

82 Center for Renewable Resources 1980; Becker 1981; Coates 1981; Morris 1979, 1980; Hampshire College 1979; Vine 1981; Ridgeway 1979; Randolph 1981; Corbett & Hayden 1981.

83 Talbot & Morgan 1981; Conference on Alternative State and Local Policies 1981, 1981a, 1981b; Freedberg 1981. More specialized materials include Conference on Alternative State and Local Policies 1981c; Okagaki 1981; Alschuler 1980; Jones & Ford 1980; Freedberg & Slavet 1981; Wilson 1981; Reif 1981; Morrison 1979; *Alternative Sources of Energy*.

84 Woolson & Kleinman 1981; Okagaki & Benson 1979; Schaefer & Benson 1980; Gorenflo et al. 1981. (Jim Benson's organization, the Center for Ecological Policies, PO Box 442, Merrifield VA 22116, has an extensive

national network of localities doing such studies, as does the Conference on Alternative State and Local Policies, 2000 Florida Ave NW, room 407, Washington, DC 20009.

85 Department of Energy 1980a; Woolson & Kleinman 1981; Tomasi et al. 1981.

86 Glidden & High 1980. Pliny Fisk is doing exciting bioregional work on these lines, mainly in Texas. Mr. Fisk can be reached at the Center for Maximum Potential Building Systems, 8604 F.M. 969, Austin TX 78724.

87 Previous reference plus Corbett 1981, Portland Energy Office 1980, *Ways and Means*, and the regional appropriate-technology newsletters, notably *New Roots*, *RAIN*, and *A.T. Times*.

88 *The Energy Consumer* 1979.

89 Ibid. 1980.

90 Ibid. 1980a.

[0089] Ibid. 1980b.

92 Mr. Koster can be reached at 2341 Cedar Shore Circle, Jacksonville FL 32210.

93 *Energy Consumer* 1980b:13ff.

94 Clark Bullard has suggested, however, that the law of some states may permit municipalities to impose their own taxes on sales of electricity or fuels, and in principle those taxes could be so structured as to result in whatever tariff structure to the end-user the municipality wished. This concept would require legal research before it was tried.

95 Hunt & Bainbridge 1978; Vine 1981; Corbett 1981.

96 Marshall Hunt, personal communications, 1980–82.

97 Tomasi et al. 1981:21–22.

98 Randolph 1981:266.

99 California Energy Commission 1981c:136; SolarCal Local Government Commission 1981.

100 Congressman Richard Ottinger's committee has conducted useful hearings on building efficiency labeling.

101 Randolph 1981:267; California Energy Commission 1981f.

102 Tomasi et al. 1981:4–5.

103 Ibid.

104 Randolph 1981:267; Corbett 1981; Vine 1981.

105 Notkin 1982.

106 Colorado Office of Energy Conservation 1981:99.

107 Randolph 1981:268.
108 Tomasi et al. 1981:6.
109 President's Council on Environmental Quality 1974:13.
110 California Energy Commission 1979, 1979a; San Diego County Board of Supervisors 1978; Hedgecock 1980.
111 Bates 1981.
112 Randolph 1981:265.
113 Bohan 1981; Becker 1981.
114 *Financial Times* 1981a.
115 Hamrin 1980; California Energy Commission 1980b, c, d.
116 TERA 1982.
117 Terry 1981; Rinard 1981; Forster 1981; Saitman & Garfield-Jones 1981.
118 J.I. Lerner (consultant, Fairfield Department of Public Works), personal communication to Alec Jenkins.
119 Los Angeles Energy Management Advisory Board 1981:65.
120 Angelici et al. 1980.
121 California Solar Utility Development Authority 1981.
122 Department of Energy 1981d.
123 Braly 1980.
124 Tomasi et al. 1981: 8.
125 Alschuler 1980.
126 National League of Cities 1981; Center for Renewable Resources 1982; Adams 1981; Shawnee Solar Project 1981; Oberg 1981;

Freedberg 1981.
127 Sheldon Strom (Director of the Minneapolis Energy Coordination Office), personal communication to Alec Jenkins, 9 February 1982.
128 Saitman, 1980, 1980a, 1982; Saitman & Garfield-Jones 1981; McClure 1981; Braly 1979; Doyle & Duenwald 1981. For a cautionary tale, see *Soft Energy Notes* 1982.
129 California Public Utilities Commission 1980; Lovins 1981, 1982; Bryson & Elliot 1981.
130 Pacific Power & Light, Puget Power & Light, Portland General Electric, Pacific Gas & Electric, and Southern California Edison are among the pioneers. Among these, only Puget Power seems to be giving serious attention to loans for the commercial sector, which tends to have even larger and cheaper saving opportunities than the residential sector.
131 J.H. Paster (President, National Conservation Corporation) and J.C. Anderson (Manager, Environmental Affairs, Jersey Central Power & Light Co., Morristown NJ), personal communications to Alec Jenkins.
132 Sant et al. 1981; Merrill Lynch 1981. The California Energy Commission is revising a staff report on energy service corporations.
133 In *Tao Te Ching* 14.
134 Taylor 1981.

Notes to Appendix One

1 The three-fourths figure is for Fiscal Year 1982 (ERAB 1981b:17). The proposed fraction for FY1983 is considerably higher—perhaps the highest in the world. Meanwhile, instead of increasing to about thirty-nine billion dollars as expected, total investment in the U.S. electric utility industry fell in 1981 to the mid-twenties of billions of dollars, and appears to be continuing to fall.
2 Lovins 1977b.
3 Marchetti 1975.
4 Messing et al. 1979:3.
5 Ibid.
6 Ibid.:17.
7 Congressional Research Service 1979:12.
8 Comtois 1977.
9 Huethner 1973; Messing et al. 1979:204–206.

10 Comtois 1977:52.
11 Messing et al. 1979:206.
12 Quoted ibid.
13 Fisher 1979:10.
14 Ibid.:12.
15 Komanoff 1981.
16 Ibid.:200.
17 Ibid.:220.
18 Fisher 1979:10.
19 Petzinger 1981.
20 Ibid.
21 Messing et al. 1979:209.
22 *Electrical Times* 1975.
23 Procaccia 1975; see also Knox 1977.
24 Komanoff 1981.
25 Ibid.:248.
26 Ibid.:253–257.
27 Ford & Flaim 1979:35.

28 Anson 1977.

29 *Weekly Energy Report* 1975.

30 *Electrical Times* 1973.

31 Ouwens 1977.

32 Economic Regulatory Administration 1981:7–4ff.

33 E.g., Kahn 1977; Wisconsin PSC 1977.

34 Peschon 1976. The exact value depends on details of the grid.

35 Peschon et al. have calculated (personal communication, 1978), for example, that for a loss-of-load probability of one day in ten years—the normal U.S. standard for grid reliability—and a forced outage rate of four percent, generating units equivalent to two percent of the peak load require reserves of only five percent of the peak load; units providing ten percent require about an eleven-percent reserve; units providing twenty percent need about twenty-three percent; and units providing fifty percent need about sixty-five percent. That is, the bigger and "lumpier" the unit, the bigger—disproportionately—its reserve requirements. This becomes much worse with a higher forced outage rate, say fifteen percent: the reserve requirements at the same unit sizes then become respectively about twenty-two, forty-three, sixty-two, and one hundred fifty percent. In fact, forced outage rates of fifteen percent or more are quite common for large power plants. For isolated grids, see Galloway & Kirchmayer 1958.

36 *Electrical World* 1975.

37 *Electrical Times* 1973.

38 Abdulkarim & Lucas 1977:226.

39 Abdulkarim & Lucas 1977.

40 Messing et al. 1979:10, 14.

41 E.g., Caputo 1977; OTA 1978.

42 Hein 1979.

43 Energy & Defense Project 1980:167–169.

44 Landsbaum 1981.

45 *Popular Science* 1981.

46 Margen 1980; Gleason 1981, 1981a, 1981b. The largest, being built in Uppsala, is to use a hundred thousand metric tons of seasonal water storage in a rock cavern (BFR 1980). Solar district heating could provide four billion kilowatt-hours of heat to Sweden annually by 1990. The Self-Reliance District Heating Group (1717 18th St. NW, Washington DC 20009) provides access to these and si-

miliar technological developments.

47 University of Arizona 1981:VI–16; Tomasi et al. 1981:61; Megida 1981.

48 Williams 1978. Payback times of a few years have been reported (Klock 1982). OTA will publish a cogeneration study during 1982.

49 Williams 1978; Klock 1982; Machalaba 1979.

50 *Diesel & Gas Turbine Progress* 1973.

51 Larue 1981.

52 Ibid. The California Energy Commission provides excellent publications.

53 *Los Angeles Times* 1981aa; Larue 1981.

54 Baughman & Bottaro 1976.

55 Ibid.

56 AGA 1977.

57 Economic Regulatory Administration 1980:Exec. Summ.:9; 1980 data from Edison Electric Institute.

58 Baughman & Bottaro (1976) show explicitly that this was true in 1972. Costs have escalated about as fast since then for operation and maintenance of the grid as for building it.

59 Systems Control 1980:Summ.:43–44. Bell (1981:4764) cites eighty-seven to one hundred fifty dollars' credit per kilowatt of dispersed fuel cells, but omits the waste heat credit, which could be worth many hundreds of dollars.

60 To procure the greatest benefit, the dispersed source should be as close as possible to the user, since an estimated eighty-five to ninety-five percent of outages are due to failures in distribution, not in the bulk generation/transmission system (Systems Control 1980:Rpt.:5.47; Systems Control 3–7; *cf.* Economic Regulatory Administration 1981:4–10).

61 Komanoff 1981.

62 Comtois 1977.

63 As Peter Bradford notes (personal communication, 7 January 1982), this effect has a long and curious history. The financier J.P. Morgan felt that Thomas Edison was mistaken in proposing to build the Pearl Street Generating Station in New York City. Construction, Morgan believed, would take too long, idling capital which could be more profitably used building smaller, decentralized generators in individual buildings. Later, as new markets and alternating-current technology switched the economics in Edison's favor, Morgan

changed sides in forming the General Electric Company (from which Edison was bought out). Ironically, today's economics are again reversing the trend and so hurting General Electric's sales of large power plants.

64 Komanoff 1981:208–209, 224.

65 Mooz 1978, 1979; Komanoff 1981:205. This finding has been consistently ignored by those anxious to "streamline" nuclear licensing.

66 Ford & Flaim 1979.

67 Messing et al. 1979:207. The Nuclear Regulatory Commission concurs.

68 Komanoff 1981; Mooz 1978, 1979.

69 Comtois 1977.

70 Kahn & Schutz 1978; Wiegner 1977.

71 Komanoff 1981.

72 Ford & Flaim 1979. The feedback loop was pointed out by H.R. Holt.

73 Cantley 1979.

74 Cazalet et al. 1978; Stover et al. 1978.

75 Ford 1978; Ford & Yabroff 1978; Lovins 1981.

76 Ford & Yabroff 1978; Ford 1978, 1979a; Boyd & Thompson 1978; Ford & Polyzou 1981.

77 Hoag & Terasawa 1981.

78 Kahn 1978:333ff; Lovins 1981, 1982.

79 *Business Week* 1980.

80 Carioca, Arora, & Khan 1982.

81 Hein 1979.

82 Gerlach 1979; Gerlach & Radcliffe 1979; Casper & Wellstone 1981.

83 Fisher 1979:10.

84 Some instances of siting problems with small units have been reported, such as a total-energy system for the Harvard Medical School and wind machines in Cape Cod and in Riverside County, California. In general, these problems have arisen from failure to let the local community participate in decisions.

85 Carioca, Arora, & Khan 1982.

86 Lovins 1977b.

87 Dyson 1979:104–106; personal communication, 1979.

88 This does not imply that end users *need* to be tinkerers. Recognizing that many do not wish to be, this analysis assumed technologies that are at least as convenient, reliable, and "hands-off" as the centralized systems in use today.

89 Hollands & Orgill 1977; OTA 1978.

90 Lovins 1978:492.

91 Hollands & Orgill 1977.

92 McPhee 1981a.

93 Taylor & Taylor 1981.

94 Economic Regulatory Administration 1980:Ex. Summ.:8.

95 Congressional Research Service 1979:11.

96 Morris 1981:114.

97 Ford & Flaim 1979.

Notes to Appendix Two

1 E.g., Energy & Defense Project 1980.

2 Sørensen 1979; Simmons 1981; Lovins 1978.

3 Metz & Hammond 1981; SERI 1981; *Soft Energy Notes*.

4 Department of Energy 1980.

5 E.g., California Energy Commission 1980.

6 Reif 1981.

7 E.g., Maine Office of Energy Resources 1980; Woychick 1981.

8 King 1979; Kensil 1981.

9 Ener-Nat 1979.

10 OTA 1978.

11 Raetz 1979, 1979a.

12 Simmons 1981:11.

13 *Sunworld* 1980.

14 Barden 1981. By mid-1981, ten U.S. dish designs were in detailed engineering de-

velopment, of which three were ready for production (ibid.).

15 *Solar Thermal Report* 1981a.

16 Ansaldo (Genoa), cited in OTA 1978.

17 F.A. McCrackin, personal communication, 1 December 1981.

18 *Soft Energy Notes* **4**(1):18–20 and personal communications, 1979-81.

19 Wittenberg & Harris 1980; Nielsen 1980.

20 Bessell 1981.

21 McPhee 1981a.

22 Taylor & Taylor 1981.

23 Hollands & Orgill 1977; Lovins 1978:492; OTA 1978.

24 SERI 1981; OTA 1980.

25 Lipinsky 1981; Palsson et al. 1981.

26 Jackson 1980.

27 SERI 1981; OTA 1980; Energy & Defense Project 1980; Lovins & Lovins 1981.

28 J.D.B. Carioca & H.A. Arora, University of Cearà, personal communication, November 1981.

29 OTA 1980:II:201ff.

30 Cals (undated).

31 SERI 1980, 1980a.

32 *Energy Consumer* 1980.

33 Patterson 1980.

34 Billingsley 1980.

35 Hobson 1980.

36 Hallberg 1981.

37 Hallberg 1980.

38 Flaim & Hertzmark 1981:89n.

39 Holmberg 1981.

40 ERAB 1981a:28.

41 Ibid.:31.

42 Illustrating the potential for simplicity, John Tatom PE (4074 Ridge Road, Smyrna GA 30080) has designed effective pyrolyzers for developing countries, made of old oil drums, rocks, and pieces of pipe.

43 *Energy Task Force Newsletter* 1981.

44 These three cases are described respectively by Deans 1981, Murnane 1980, and Murnane 1980a, and were called to our attention by Alec Jenkins.

45 SERI 1981; OTA 1980. Such a transport system would use about five or six quadrillion BTUs of liquid fuels per year, compared with the present eighteen.

46 Lovins & Lovins 1981; Jackson 1980.

47 Flaim & Hertzmark 1981:94; BioSynthetics 1981.

48 Ferchack & Pye 1981. For a summary of recent developments, including pilot processes using below four thousand BTU/gallon, see Pacific Northwest Laboratory 1981.

49 Ladisch et al. 1978.

50 Ferchack & Pye 1981.

51 Ladisch et al. 1978; *Biotechnology Newswatch* 1981.

52 Wang et al. 1979.

53 SERI 1981:II:583ff.

54 OTA 1980.

55 SERI 1981:II:585; Simmons 1981:27.

56 Lindström 1979.

57 Tatom et al. 1976; Hewett et al. 1981:147.

58 Tom Reed (SERI), personal communications, 1980–81.

59 *Los Angeles Times* 1981ee.

60 Jedlicka 1982. LNG cars have also attracted some interest (and safety concerns). Another, more exotic cryogenic possibility that may be interesting is to fuel a car with liquid air; the temperature difference between it and ambient would operate a heat engine.

61 Ingenjörsvetenskapsakademien 1950; Datta & Dutt 1981.

62 Ortegren 1981.

63 Franklin 1980. This is a pressing need in many developing countries.

64 McPhee 1981; Shenon 1981.

65 Congressional Research Service 1978:48–128.

66 Ibid.:129–136.

67 Schneider Corp. 1980.

68 Franklin Pierce Energy Law Center.

69 Energy & Defense Project 1980:178–184; SERI 1981.

70 The manual is Alward et al. 1979. The California Office of Appropriate Technology publishes a guide to federal and state programs, *Small-Scale Hydro;* the California Department of Water Resources supplies a newsletter, *Small Hydro News;* and the Idaho National Engineering Laboratory publishes the *Small Hydro Bulletin.*

71 Jim Harding (FOE), personal communication, 19 May 1981.

72 Ron Corso (FERC), personal communication, 4 August 1981.

73 McPhee 1981.

74 Dionne 1981.

75 Gouraud 1981.

76 Energy & Defense Project 1980:178.

77 Smil 1981. The figure was formerly over two-thirds (Lovins 1977b:124). Taylor (1981a) gives an excellent account of the program.

78 Sørensen 1979a:6.

79 Most wind machines now on the market are handmade, with tooling costs spread over production runs of tens to hundreds. Small and medium-sized wind machines, however, lend themselves to mass production of the kind now practiced in appliance and car manufacturing. Karl Bergey, personal communications, 1980–81; Bergey 1981.

80 Lovins 1978:496.

81 Ibid.

82 Carter 1978.

83 Stoddard 1981.

84 Ibid. Stoddard was U.S. Windpower's chief designer.

85 Park 1981. See also the listing in California Energy Commission 1981b.

86 Wegley et al. 1978.

87 Frank 1981.

88 Graves 1981.

89 Tomasi et al. 1981:65.

90 *Energy Research Reports* 1979.

91 *Business Week* 1981a.

92 Maycock & Stirewalt 1981; Watts et al. 1981; Smith 1981.

93 Congressional Research Service 1978:223–274.

94 JPL 1980; Smith 1981.

95 Friedman 1981; Treble 1980.

96 Friedman 1981.

97 AMETEK 1979; personal communications, 1981.

98 Maycock 1981.

99 Russell 1981.

100 Adler 1981.

101 Ross & Williams (1981) present strong arguments to this effect.

102 Larue 1981.

103 McNary 1981.

104 Tomasi et al. 1981:69.

105 Systems Control 1980, 1980b; Cox 1981; Smith 1979; Watts et al. 1981.

106 Smith 1979; Cox 1981; Watts et al. 1981.

107 Systems Control 1980:5–16ff.

108 Southern California Edison Company 1981:5.

109 Hodges 1981:3.

110 Ibid.

111 de Mello & Hannett 1981. We are indebted to E.R. Baugh PE for bringing the concept and references to our attention.

112 Hodges 1981:4–5.

113 de Mello & Hannett 1981.

114 In an era of cheap digital electronics, it no longer makes sense to use the grid as a universal clock. Yet large turbogenerators requiring extremely stringent standards of frequency and phase stability are locking us into a grid of clocklike precision for decades to come. This may make interface with large numbers of dispersed renewable sources more difficult, and certainly imposes extra costs for little benefit. (If "stiffer" frequency and phase stability were needed in a renewable-based grid, one solution might be to insert motor-generator sets with large flywheels: angular momentum is cheap.) Similar considerations apply to voltage stability and to reliability. For example, present standards of grid reliability certainly exceed an economically worthwhile value (Telson 1975). Rather than giving everyone maximal reliability, it would be cheaper for customers needing it to get it from local storage or standby capacity, as telephone exchanges, hospitals, etc. do now, while others get—at reduced cost—slightly less reliable supplies. This would improve still further the economics of intermittent renewable sources (Kahn 1978:338ff).

Notes to Appendix Three

1 Worcester Polytechnic Institute 1978; Godolphin 1981.

2 Kahn et al. 1980.

3 Ibid.

4 Cone et al. 1980.

5 Bowring 1980; Omang 1981.

6 Lovins 1981a.

7 Chapman 1979.

8 Komanoff 1981.

9 Quantifying these externalities rigorously, however, may not be possible. The serious theoretical and practical obstacles to such calculations are beyond the scope of this book but have been surveyed elsewhere: Lovins 1977; Junger 1976; Council for Science and Society 1979.

10 E.g, Stobaugh & Yergin 1979.

11 Lovins 1978.

12 Lovins 1978a, 1979a; Nash 1979.

13 Kahn et al. 1980.

14 The rate used in Lovins (1978) was twelve percent a year in real terms—chosen to be several percentage points higher than was justified by the actual cost of capital in 1978, in order to discriminate against renewables. The rate is not nearly so unrealistic, however, in the light of actual 1981–82 market conditions (Lovins 1981c).

15 E.g, Stobaugh & Yergin 1979; Southern California Edison Co. 1980; SERI 1981.

16 SERI 1981:II:175. This considers, of course, only technological costs, not the effects of tax credits.

17 Gleason 1981, 1981a; Taylor & Taylor 1981; Hollands & Orgill 1977.

18 OTA 1980:II:154–55; SERI 1979. Direct combustion, as noted earlier, is another option being taken seriously: in new sales of solid-fueled industrial boilers, wood ranks only slightly behind coal as the main fuel.

19 This is discussed in the context of the steel industry by Lovins et al. 1982.

20 The company is LUZ International, which is based in California but sells equipment made mainly in Israel (and installed about fifty thousand square feet of parabolic troughs there in 1981 under similar arrangements): Pospisil 1981.

21 This is starting to happen: *Solar Thermal Report* 1981b.

22 Caputo 1981 confirms that solar process heat is economic there.

23 Cooper & Paynter 1981.

24 Adler 1981; Maycock 1981; Russell 1981.

25 The Reagan Administration's budget proposals for Fiscal Year 1983 include eight hundred thirty million dollars for civilian nuclear power, four hundred forty-five million for magnetic fusion (not counting inertial-confinement fusion, which is in the military budget), seventy-three million for solar, and nineteen million for efficiency.

Bibliography

Note: The references are listed under the surname of the senior author or (failing that) the name of the publication or organization. Listings are alphabetical in the form cited: if in doubt, look for organizational listings under both name and common abbreviation. (Cross-references are provided.) Listings under the same surname or equivalent are chronological, not alphabetical by initials: Jones, Z. 1975 comes before Jones, A. 1980. Listings are repeated by a dash, which refers to the name or names most recently listed; thus in

> Jones, A. 1975
> — 1976
> — & Smith, B. 1972
> — 1981

the last listing refers to Jones & Smith 1981, not to Jones alone.

ABDULKARIM, A.J., & LUCAS, N.J.D. 1977: "Economies of Scale in Electricity Generation in the United Kingdom," *Energy Research* 1:223–231.

ABRAHAMSON, D.E. 1973: "Nuclear Power: Its Hazards and Social Implications," Centre Party / School for Adult Education Symposium on Energy, Development, and Future, Stockholm, 25–26 November.

ACADEMY FOR CONTEMPORARY PROBLEMS 1980: "Establishing a National Community Energy Management Center," Washington DC, November.

ACDA: see Arms Control & Disarmament Agency.

ACKERMANN, J.A. 1979: "The Impact of the Coal Strike of 1977–1978," *Industrial and Labor Relations Review* 32(2):175–188, January.

ADAMS, M.R. 1981: "Tax Study Enhances Prospects for Commercial Solar Sales," *Solar Age*, pp. 14–15, June.

ADLER, A.W. 1981: 5 February memorandum to Energy Research Advisory Board, U.S. Department of Energy, re "Status Report, U.S. DOE, Photovoltaics Program."

AERO SUN-TIMES 1981: "Wind Machine Owners Talk," 8(11):13, late November, Alternative Energy Resources Organization, 424 Stapleton Building, Billings MT 59101.

AGA: see American Gas Association.

ALFVÉN, H. 1972: *Bulletin of the Atomic Scientists* 28(5):5, May.

ALLISON, G., CARNESALE, A., ZIGMAN, P., & DEROSA, F. 1981: "Governance of Nuclear Power," 25 September report to Nuclear Safety Oversight Committee (Governor Bruce Babbitt, Chairman).

ALM, A. 1981: "Energy Supply Interruptions and National Security," *Science* 211:1379–85, 27 March.

ALSBERG, P.A., & DAY, J.D. 1976: "A Principle for Resilient Sharing of Distributed Resources," May, Center for Advanced Computation, University of Illinois at Urbana-Champaign.

ALSCHULER, J.H. JR. 1980: "Using Local Energy Programs for Economic Development," in *Energy and Economic Development Management Report*, International City Managers Association, Washington DC.

ALTERNATIVE SOURCES OF ENERGY, 107 S. Central Ave., Milaca MN 56353.

ALTMAN, L.K. 1980: "The Doctor's World: Loss of Spleen Demonstrates The Body's Ability to Adapt," *New York Times*, p. C1, 1 April.

ALVAREZ, R. 1981: "Report on the Savannah River Plant Study," Radiation Health Information Project, Environmental Policy Institute, 317 Pennsylvania Ave. S.E., Washington DC 20003.

ALWARD, R., EISENBART, S., & VOLKMAN, J. 1979: "Micro-Hydro Power: Reviving an Old Concept," DOE/ET/01752–1, 1 January report to USDOE by National Center for Appropriate Technology, PO Box 3838, Butte MT 59701, $1.75.

AMERICAN GAS ASSOCIATION 1977: "Monthly Gas Statistical Report," November, Statistics Directorate, Data Analysis, AGA, Arlington VA 22209.

—1981: "A Survey of Actual and Projected Conservation in the Gas Utility Industry: 1973–1990," 20 March, AGA.

AMERICAN HOMEGROWN FUEL CO. 1981: brochure, 864–B Haight St., San Francisco CA 94117.

AMETEK 1979: 22 October press release, plus 1981 briefings by photovoltaics researchers, AMETEK Corp., Station Square 2, Paoli PA 19301.

ANCHORAGE TIMES 1980: "Sabotage suspected in massive Puerto Rico electrical outage," AP story, p. A7, 12 April.

ANDERSON, J., & WHITTIER, L. 1976: "Pipeline Sabotage Worries CIA," *Washington Post*, p. D15, 31 December.

ANDERSON, M.B., NEWTON, K., RYLE, M., & SCOTT, P. 1978: "Short-term storage and wind power availability," *Nature* **275**:432–434.

ANGELICI, G.L. ET AL. 1980: *Urban Solar Photovoltaics Potential: An Inventory and Modelling Study Applied to the San Fernando Valley Region of Los Angeles*, August, JPL–80–43, Jet Propulsion Laboratory, Pasadena CA.

ANSON, D. 1977: "Availability Patterns in Fossil-Fired Steam Power Plants," FP–583–SR, Electric Power Research Institute, Palo Alto CA.

AP [ASSOCIATED PRESS] 1974: "Nuclear Device Threatens Thief," 8 June story datelined Deerfield Beach, Florida.

—1977: "Nuclear Strike," 13 March morning story.

APPLE, R.W. JR. 1980: "137 Feared Lost in Collapse of North Sea Platform," *New York Times*, pp. 1 & 4, 29 March.

ARMS CONTROL & DISARMAMENT AGENCY 1978: *An Analysis of Civil Defense in Nuclear War*, December.

ARONSON, J.D., & WESTERMEYER, W. 1981: "Public and Private Regulation of LNG Transport," School of International Relations, University of Southern California, Los Angeles, in press in *Marine Policy*, October.

ASBURY, J.G., & WEBB, S.B. 1979: "Centralizing or Decentralizing? The Impact of Decentralized Electric Generation," ANL/SPG–16, March, Special Projects Group, Energy & Environmental Systems Division, Argonne National Laboratory, Argonne, Illinois.

AS/ISES 1982: *Proceedings of the Passive Cooling '81 Conference*, in press, American Section of the International Solar Energy Society, Killeen TX 76451.

ASPEN INSTITUTE FOR HUMANISTIC STUDIES 1979: "Summary Report: Decentralized Electricity and Cogeneration Options," Second Annual Energy R&D Priorities Workshop, 13–17 July, Aspen (R.W. Fri & J.C. Sawhill, Co-Chairmen), AIHS, Aspen, Colorado.

—1980: *Petroleum Interruptions and National Security*, Summary Findings of a Conference at Wye Plantation, Maryland, 9–11 May 1980 (Al Alm, Chairman), AIHS, New York.

ASPIN, CONGRESSMAN L. 1975: "Aspin: Enough Weapons Stolen from Army to Arm 8000 Men," press release, 2 September.

—1977: "Aspin: U.S. Defense Personnel Purged from Access to Nuclear Weapons," press release, 9 August.

ASSOCIATED PRESS: see AP.

ATALLAH, S. 1980: "Distribution System Safety," *Gas Research Institute Digest* **3**(3):4–5, August, Gas Research Institute, Chicago.

ATLANTA CONSTITUTION 1977: p. 1, 24 July.

ATLANTA JOURNAL & CONSTITUTION 1981: "Sabotage Blast Darkens Major El Salvador City," "Weekend" section, p. 3–A, 7 February.

ATLANTIC RICHFIELD COMPANY: "The Drive for Conservation," ARCO, PO Box 30181, Los Angeles CA 90030.

ATTANASIO, C.F. *et al.* 1976: "Penetrating an operating system: a study of VM/370 integrity," *IBM Systems Journal* **1**:102–115.

A.T. TIMES: from NCAT, PO Box 3838, Butte MT 59701.

AYRES, R. 1975: *10 Harvard Civil Rights — Civil Liberties Law Review* 369ff.

AYRES, R.U., & NARKUS-KRAMER, N. 1976: "An Assessment of Methodologies for Assessing National Energy Efficiency," 76–WA/TS–4, American Society of Mechanical Engineers.

BARDEN, F. 1981: "New Solar Concentrating Dish Tailored for Industrial Use," *Solar Age,* pp. 23–24, August.

BARLOW, R.E., & PROSCHAN, F. 1975: *Statistical Theory of Reliability and Life Testing,* Holt, Rinehart & Winston, New York.

BARNABY, F. 1975: *New Scientist* **66**:494f, 29 May.

BARNET, R. 1980: *The Lean Years,* Simon & Schuster, New York.

—1981: *Real Security: Restoring American Power in a Dangerous Decade,* Touchstone/Simon & Schuster, New York.

BARTLETT, J.F. 1977: "A Non-Stop™ Operating System," January 1978 Hawaii Conference of System Sciences, available from Tandem (*loc.cit.*).

BARTLETT, A. 1981: "Forgotten Fundamentals of the Energy Crisis," typescript, Physics Department, University of Colorado at Boulder (also on videotape).

BARTON, J.H. 1975: "Intensified Nuclear Safeguards and Civil Liberties," 21 October report to U.S. Nuclear Regulatory Commission, Stanford Law School.

BASS, G., JENKINS, B., KELLEN, K., KROFCHECK, J., PETTY, G., REINSTEDT, R., & RONFELDT, D. 1980: "Motivations and Possible Actions of Potential Criminal Adversaries of U.S. Nuclear Programs," February report to Sandia Laboratories, R–2554–SL, RAND Corporation, Santa Monica CA 90406.

BATES, J. 1981: March comments in California Energy Commission Docket 78CON–1.

BAUGHMAN, M.L. & BOTTARO, D.J. 1976: "Electric Power Transmission and Distribution Systems: Costs and Their Allocation," *IEEE Transactions on Power Apparatus and Systems* **PAS–95**(3):782–790.

BAUM, D., & COLBY, L. 1981: "69% of EMS Owners will Buy Another Within 12 Months," *Energy User News,* p. 1, 13 April.

BAZYKIN, A.D. 1975: "Elementary Model of Eutrophication," at 197–201 in H.R. Grumm, ed., *Analysis and Computation of Equilibria and Regions of Stability,* CP–75–8, International Institute for Applied Systems Analysis, Laxenburg, Austria.

BBC 1981: British Broadcasting Corporation television news reports, evening of 26 January.

BEARD, B. 1981: "Break-in expert boasts perfect score on nuclear plants," *Arizona Republic,* pp. C–1 & C–6, 25 October.

BECKER, W.S. 1981: *The Making of a Solar Village,* Wisconsin Energy Extension Service, U. of Wisconsin—Extension, 437 Extension Bldg., Madison 53706.

—1981a: "War and Peace in the Solar Age," *Solar Age,* p. 96, November.

—1982: "The Indefensible Society," Lorian Press (PO Box 147, Middleton WI 53562).

BEECH, K. 1981: "Pirates Raiding Supertankers," *Los Angeles Times,* pp. I:1 & 14, 27 November. See also "Oil Firm Takes Steps to Thwart Tanker Pirates," *id.*I:2, 12 November.

BEETON, A.D. 1969: "Changes in the Environment and Biota of the Great Lakes," in *Eutrophication,* National Academy of Sciences, Washington DC.

BELL, R.A. 1981: "The Electric Utility 4.5 MW Fuel Cell Power Plant—An Urban Demonstration," *IEEE Transactions on Power Apparatus & Systems* **PAS–100**:4760–4764, 12 December.

BENEMANN, J.R. 1977: "Bioconversion: An Assessment," September, Electric Power Research Institute, Palo Alto CA.

BENSON, J. 1981: "Getting on the Right Path:

Constituency Building Through Energy Planning," *Alternative Sources of Energy*, pp. 20–24, May/June.

BERGEY, K. 1981: "Development of High-Performance, High-Reliability Windpower Generators," Bergey Windpower Co., 2001 Priestley Ave., Norman OK 73069.

BESANT, R.W., DUMONT, R.S., & SCHOENAU, G. 1978: "The Saskatchewan Conservation House: Some Preliminary Performance Results," Dept. of Mech. Engineering, U. of Saskatchewan, Saskatoon S1N 0W0, Canada.

—1979: "The Saskatchewan Conservation House: A Year of Performance Data," paper to Charlottetown Annual Conference of Solar Energy Society of Canada.

BESSELL, R. 1981: "Inventing the Solar Pond," *New Roots*, pp. 23–26, May/June, Greenfield MA 01301.

BEYEA, J. 1980: "Some Long-Term Consequences of Hypothetical Major Releases of Radioactivity to the Atmosphere from Three Mile Island," Report PU/CEES #109 to President's Council on Environmental Quality, Center for Energy & Environmental Studies, Princeton University, Princeton NJ 08540.

BFR [BYGGNADSFORSKNINGSRÅDET] 1980: *Swedish Building Research News* 3, BFR, International Secretariat, S:t Göransgt. 66, S–11230 Stockholm.

BILLINGSLEY, A. 1980: 30 October letter, with accompanying report on Community-Scale Renewable Fuels System, to Secretaries of Energy and Agriculture, from Morgan State University, Baltimore MD 21239.

BILLITER, B. 1981: "PCB Found in Natural Gas Systems; U.S. Will Test Households for Contamination," *Los Angeles Times* I:27, 14 March.

—1981a: "California Records Decline in Gasoline Use," p. I:3 & 28, 26 February.

BIOSYNTHETICS 1981: brochure, 25 E. Church St., Frederick MD 21701.

BIOTECHNOLOGY NEWSLETTER 1981: "General Electric affiliate will try to derive sugars from hardwood cellulose," p. 4, 6 July, McGraw-Hill, New York.

BISSET, G. 1958: "Sabotage Threat in the Electric Utility Industry," *Industrial Security*, October.

BLACK, R.H. 1971: *Improvising Electric Power*

from Induction Generators During Prolonged Power Outages, September report to Office of Civil Defense, Office of Secretary of the Army, from URS Research Corp., San Mateo CA.

BLAIR, B.G., & BREWER, G.D. 1977: "The Terrorist Threat to World Nuclear Programs," *Journal of Conflict Resolution* 21(3):400ff, September.

BOARDMAN, R.W., PATTON, R., & CURTICE, D.H. 1981: "Impact of Dispersed Solar and Wind Systems on Electric Distribution Planning and Operation," ORNL/Sub.–7662/1, February, Oak Ridge National Laboratory, Oak Ridge TN.

BOECK, W.L., SHAW, D.T., & VONNEGUT, B. 1975: "Possible consequences of global dispersion of krypton 85," *Bulletin of the American Meterological Society* 56:527.

BOESMAN, W.C., GRIGSBY, J.W., & MANLY, R.P. 1970: "Vulnerability of the Petroleum Distribution System: Detroit, Michigan," Checchi & Co., Washington DC 20006.

BOESMAN, W.C., MANLY, R.P., & ELLIS, R.A. 1972: *Total Resource System Vulnerability: Development and Application of a General Model*, September final report to Defense Civil Preparedness Agency, Work Unit #4342A, Accession #AD 749–804, Checchi & Co., Washington DC 20006.

BOFFEY, P.M. 1978: "Investigators Agree N.Y. Blackout of 1977 Could Have Been Avoided," *Science* 201:994–998, 15 September.

BOHAN, P. 1981: "Soldiers Grove Sees the Light," *Environmental Action*, pp. 10–15, July.

BOSTON GLOBE 1980: "Iran planes attack Iraq nuclear center," p. 1, 1 October.

—1981: "Salvador guerrillas' push," p. 12, 12 June.

—1981a: "Khadafy calls for raid against nuclear facility," p. 9, 12 June.

BOSTON HERALD AMERICAN 1980: exposé of nuclear security lapses, 3 & 10 April.

BOSTON STUDY GROUP 1979: *The Price of Defense*, Times Books, The New York Times Book Co., New York.

BOWRING, J. 1980: "Federal Subsidies to Nuclear Power: Reactor Design and the Fuel Cycle," March pre-publication draft, Financial & Industry Analysis Division, Office of Economic Analysis, Assistant Administrator for Applied Analysis, Energy Information

Administration, U.S. Department of Energy, Washington DC 20585; see also Omang 1981.

BOYD, R., & THOMPSON, R., "The Effect of Demand Uncertainty on the Relative Economics of Electrical Generation Technologies With Differing Lead Times," Division of Environmental Studies, University of California at Davis, and California General Services Administration, Sacramento.

BOYLE, P. 1981: "Some Americans Seeking an Automobile Built for 2," *Los Angeles Times*, p. VI:1/3, 22 February.

BRALY, M. 1979: "Solar Utilities: The Third Phase of Public Power," at 81–84 in *To Will One Thing: Solar Action at the Local Level*, ON THE RISE Program of the 1979 Annual Meeting, American Section of the International Solar Energy Society, Killeen TX.

—1980: "A Proposal to Examine the Feasibility of and to Organize a Solar Photovoltaic Buyers' Co-operative in Los Angeles," Office of the Mayor of Los Angeles, December.

BREEDLOVE, H., & HARBAUGH, J.R. 1981: "Protection of the Induction Motor/Generator," IEEE PCI–81–13.

BRENNAN, D.G. 1968: "The Risks of Spreading Weapons: A Historical Case," *Arms Control & Disarmament* (Pergamon) 1:59–60.

BROAD, W.J. 1980: "Resource Wars: The Lure of South Africa," *Science* 210:1099–1100.

—1981: "Nuclear Pulse," *id.* 212:1009–1012.

—1981a: "Military Grapples with the Chaos Factor," *id.* 213:1228–1229.

—1981b: "Threat to U.S. Air Power: The Dust Power," *id.* 213:1475–1477.

BRODER, J. 1977: "Why Israelis protect 'Arab' oil line," *Chicago Tribune*, p. 4, 10 July.

Brookhaven National Laboratory 1978: "An Assessment of Thermal Insulation Materials and Systems for Building Applications," June, BNL–50862.

BROOKS, D.B. 1981: *Zero Energy Growth for Canada*, McClelland & Stewart, Ltd., Toronto.

BROWN, H. 1977: Statement of 4 May to the Ad Hoc Committee on Energy, USHR, 95th Cong., 1st Sess., *Hearings on the National Energy Act*, pp. 69–72, USGPO, Washington DC.

—1978: *Annual Report, Fiscal Year 1979*, Department of Defense, 2 February.

BROWN, L.R. 1977a: "Redefining National Security," Worldwatch Paper 14, Worldwatch Institute, Washington DC.

—1981: *Building a Sustainable Society*, Worldwatch Institute/W.W. Norton, New York.

BRYAN, W. 1974: testimony to Subcommittee on State Energy Policy, Committee on Planning, Land Use, and Energy, California State Assembly, 1 February; reprinted *Not Man Apart* 4(5):1, Mid–May.

BRYSON, J.E., & ELLIOT, J.F. 1981: "California's Best Energy Supply Investment: Interest-Free Loans for Conservation," *Public Utilities Fortnightly* 108(10):19–23, 5 November.

BUCHSBAUM, S. *et al.* 1979: *Jobs and Energy*, Council on Economic Priorities, New York.

BUCKLEY, T. 1981: "Letter from El Salvador," *The New Yorker*, pp. 41ff, 22 June, at 50.

BUCKNELL, H. III 1979: "Energy and National Security: A Midwestern Perspective," 27 April talk to Army & Navy Club; Energy and National Security Project, Ohio State University, Columbus.

—, BAILEY, R., & RASK, N. 1979: "National Security, Mobility Fuels, and the Defense Production Act," 9 March report for Subcommittee on Economic Stabilization, Committee on Banking, Finance & Urban Affairs, USHR; Energy & National Security Project, Ohio State University, Columbus.

BULLARD, C.W. 1981: "Energy Conservation in New Buildings," *Annual Review of Energy* 6:199–232.

BUPP, I.C. 1981: "The actual growth and probable future of the worldwide nuclear industry," *International Organization* 35(1):59–76, Winter.

—& DERIAN, J.-C. 1978: *Light Water: How the Nuclear Dream Dissolved*, Basic Books, New York.

BURNHAM, D. 1979: "The Case of the Missing Uranium," *The Atlantic*, pp. 78–82, April.

—1979a: "GAO Says 2 U.S. Agencies Impeded A-Fuel Inquiry," *International Herald Tribune*, 23 March, Paris.

—1979b: "U.S. Urged to Revoke License of Nuclear Fuel Plant," *International Herald Tribune*, p. 1, 24 December, Paris.

—1980: "G.A.O. Finds Government Safeguards on Plutonium Thefts Inadequate," *New York Times*, p. A24, 20 March.

BURNHAM, S. (ed.) 1975: *The Threat to Licensed*

Nuclear Facilities, MTR–7022, MITRE Corporation (Washington Operations) report to NRC, contract #AT(49-24)-0129, Project #2770, Dept. W-50, September.

BURNS, J.F. 1980: "South African Rebels Attack 3 Fuel Plants," *New York Times*, pp. A1 & 8, 2 June.

—1980a: "South African Saboteurs: An Evolution to Violence," *id.*, p. A14, 4 June.

—1981: "Soviet Speeding Pipeline Deal," *id.*, p. D15, 6 August.

BURWELL, C.C., OHANIAN, M.H., & WEINBERG, A.M. 1979: "A Siting Policy for an Acceptable Nuclear Future," *Science* **204**:1043ff, 8 June.

BUSINESS WEEK 1976: "Argentina . . . ," p. 69, 22 November.

—1980: "The Utilities Are Building Small," 17 March.

—1981: "Energy Conservation: Spawning a billion-dollar business," cover story, pp. 58–69, 6 April.

—1981a: pp. 42L–N, 7 September.

—1981b: "The push for fail-safe systems," pp. 81–83, 7 September.

—1981c: "The U.S. nuclear power industry cries for help," pp. 70–71, 31 August.

BUTTI, K. & PERLIN, J. 1980: *A Golden Thread: 2500 Years of Solar Architecture and Technology*, Cheshire/Van Nostrand Reinhold, New York.

BYRON, C. 1981: "Seeking New Oil in Old Fields," *Time*, p. 58, 6 April.

CALIFORNIA ENERGY COMMISSION 1979: *Solar Energy Economics for the County of Santa Barbara*, September, CERCDC, 1111 Howe Ave., Sacramento CA 95825.

—1979a: *Solar Energy Economics for Santa Clara County*, July.

—1980: *Passive Solar Handbook*, 28 January, Sacramento.

—1980a: *Electricity Tomorrow: 1980 Preliminary Report*.

—1980b: *Status of Solar Energy Proposals in Cities and Counties Responding to the OAT Survey of June 1980*, December.

—1980c: *Adopted California Local Government Solar Energy Ordinances: Summaries and Texts*, November.

—1980d: *Local Government Energy Programs: Status, Opportunities, and Recommendations for State Support*, December.

—1981: *California & World Oil: The Strategic*

Horizon, 17–19 July 1980 USC symposium proceedings, January.

—1981a: "Wind Energy: Investing in Our Energy Future," brochure, July.

—1981b: *California Wind Directory*, July.

—1981c: *Energy Tomorrow, Challenges and Opportunities for California: 1981 Biennial Report*.

—1981d: *Moving Toward Security—Strategies for Reducing California's Vulnerability to Energy Shortages*.

—1981e: "Presentation on the Potential Role of Solar Photovoltaics in California," 20 November presentation, Docket 80–BP–3.

—1981f: "Planning Solar Neighborhoods," April.

CALIFORNIA PUBLIC UTILITIES COMMISSION 1980: *Energy Efficiency and the Utilities: New Directions*, July, CPUC, San Francisco.

CALIFORNIA SOLAR UTILITY DEVELOPMENT AUTHORITY 1981: "Oceanside MSU: The Plan for the City of Oceanside," January report to California Energy Commission.

CALS, C. (Brazilian Minister of Mines and Energy), undated, ca. 1980: "The Brazilian Energetic Policy." No publisher shown; 36 pp.

CAMPBELL, W.J., & MARTIN, 1973: "Oil and Ice in the Arctic Ocean: Possible Large-Scale Interactions," *Science* **181**:56–58.

CANTLEY, M.F. 1979: "Questions of Scale," pp. 4–5, *Options '79*, #3, International Institute for Applied Systems Analysis, Laxenburg, Austria.

CAPUTO, R. 1977: *An Initial Comparative Assessment of Orbital and Terrestrial Central Power Systems*, 900–780, CalTech Jet Propulsion Laboratory, Pasadena, California, at p. 4–22.

—1980: February interview with H. Durand, Commisariat à l'Énergie Solaire (Paris), reported at p. 42 in M. Messenger & R. Caputo, "A Spot Check Survey on European Solar Research from an International Perspective," February, International Institute for Applied Systems Analysis, Laxenburg, Austria.

—1981: "Solar Energy for the Next 5 Billion Years," PP–81–9, IIASA.

CARHART, S.C., MULHERKAR, S.S., RENNIE, S.M., & PENZ, A.J. 1980: "Creating New Choices: Innovative Approaches to Cut Home Heating and Cooling Costs," Rpt. 3, Energy Productivity Center, Mellon Institute, Arlington VA 22209.

CARIOCA, J.O.B., ARORA, H.L., & KHAN, A.S. 1982: "Technological and Socio-Economic Aspects of Cassava-Based Autonomous Minidistilleries in Brazil," *Biomass—An International Journal*, in press.

CARTER, J. 1978: "The Windflower," *Wind Power Digest*, pp. 30–32, Fall.

— & FLOWER, R.G. 1981: "The Micro-Load," *Solar Age*, pp. 2–9, June.

CASPER, B.M., & WELLSTONE, P.D. 1981: *Powerline: The First Battle of America's Energy War*, University of Massachusetts Press, Amherst.

CAZALET, E. *et al.* 1978: "Costs and Benefits of Over/Under Capacity in Electric Power System Planning," EA–927, October report by Decision Focus Inc. to Electric Power Research Institute, Palo Alto, California; see also "Planning for Uncertainty," *EPRI Journal*, pp. 6–11, May.

CENTER FOR RENEWABLE RESOURCES 1980: *Shining Examples: Model Projects Using Renewable Resources*, CRR, 1001 Connecticut Ave NW, Washington DC 20036.

—1982: *Resource Directories*, in press.

CHAPMAN, D. 1979: "Nuclear Economics: Taxation, Fuel Cost and Decommissioning," Report A.E.Res. 79–26 to California Energy Commission from Dept. of Agricultural Economics, Cornell University, Ithaca, New York.

CHASE, J., LUCAS, N.J.D., MURGATROYD, W., & WILKINS, B.C. 1978: "Industrial Energy Use—II. Energy Use in a Light Engineering Factory," *Energy Research* 2:375–388.

CHASTAIN, T. 1979: *High Voltage*, Doubleday, Garden City, New York.

CHENOWETH, J.M., HOH, L.A., HURT, R.C., & McCAMMON, L.B. 1963: "A Method for Predicting Electrical Power Availability Following a Nuclear Attack," Vol. I, April report #SN 108–1 to Office of Civil Defense, U.S. Department of Defense, Contract #OCD–OS–63–15, National Engineering Science Co., 711 S. Fair Oaks Ave., Pasadena, California.

CHESTER, C.V. 1976: "Estimates of Threats to the Public from Terrorist Acts Against Nuclear Facilities," *Nuclear Safety* 17(6):659–665.

— & CHESTER, R.O. 1970: "Civil Defense Implications of a Pressurized Water Reactor in a Thermonuclear Target Area," *Nuclear Applications and Technology* 9:786–795, December.

—1974: "Civil Defense Implications of an LMFBR in a Thermonuclear Target Area," *Nuclear Technology* 21:190–200, March.

—1976: "Civil Defense Implications of the U.S. Nuclear Power Industry During a Large Nuclear War in the Year 2000," *Nuclear Technology* 31:326–338, December.

CHIKYU NO KOE 1981: "Progress and Tradition in Energy Conservation," pp. 11–13, November, from Chikyu no Tomo, 1–51–8 Yoyogi, Shibuya-ku, Tokyo 151.

CHIOGIOJI, M.H. 1979: "Industrial Energy Conservation," Marcel Dekker, Inc., New York.

CHOI, S., HIRSCH, J., & BIRDSALL, B. 1982: "Peak Saving in Buildings Through Use of a Diesel Engine-Driven Emergency Power Generating System," *ASHRAE Journal*, pp. 33–37, January.

CHRISTMAN, D.W., & CLARK, W.K. 1978: "Foreign Energy Sources and Military Power," *Military Review*, pp. 3–13, February.

CLAPP, N.M. 1978: "State of New York Investigation of New York City Blackout July 13, 1977," January report to Governor Carey.

CLARIDGE, T. 1981: "2 Electricity giants had shortage scares during deep freeze," *The Globe and Mail*, p.4, 8 January, Toronto.

CLARK, W.C. 1978: "Managing the Unknown: An Ecological View of Risk Assessment," W–26, January, Institute of Resource Ecology, University of British Columbia, Vancouver.

CLARK, T. 1980: "Western Massachusetts: Land of Dissenters and Dreamers," *Yankee*, pp. 94ff, September.

CLARK, W. 1981: "Power from waste," *Asia 2000* 1(1):12–16.

CLARK, J. 1981a: "Building an Energy Consensus: Key Issues for the Eighties," Northeast-Midwest Institute, 530 House Annex #2, Washington DC 20515.

CLARK, W., & PAGE, J. 1981: *Energy, Vulnerability, and War: Alternatives for America*, W.W. Norton, New York.

COATES, J. 1980: "False war alerts result in reforms," *Chicago Tribune*, p. I:5, 2 November.

COATES, G.S., ed. 1981: *Resettling America—Energy, Ecology and Community*, Brick House, Andover MA 01810.

COCHRAN, T.B. 1977: "Design Basis Threat," 2 August, Natural Resources Defense Council, Washington DC, reprinted at 254–260 in Subcommittee on Energy & the Environment 1977a (*op. cit.*).

—& SPETH, J.G. 1974: "NRDC Comments on WASH–1327, ... GESMO," Natural Resources Defense Council, Washington DC, 30 October.

COLLINS, J.M., & MARK, C.R. 1979: "Petroleum Imports from the Persian Gulf: Use of U.S. Armed Force to Ensure Supplies," Issue Brief IB79046, 4 June, Congressional Research Service, Library of Congress, Washington DC.

COLORADO OFFICE OF ENERGY CONSERVATION 1981: *Renewable Resources in Colorado: Opportunities for Local Government*, November, Denver.

COMEY, D.D. 1975: "The Incident at Browns Ferry," Friends of the Earth, 1045 Sansome St, San Francisco CA 94111, 8 pp., 1975.

COMITÉ D'ACTION POUR LE SOLAIRE 1981: *Politique Energetique, Les Voies du Solaire*, La Documentation Française, Paris.

COMMITTEE ON APPROPRIATIONS 1970: *Hearings on the Supplemental Appropriations Bill, 1971*, USHR, 1 October.

COMMITTEE ON GOVERNMENT OPERATIONS 1976: *Hearings on the Export Reorganization Act of 1976*, U.S. Senate, USGPO #71–259.

COMPTROLLER GENERAL OF THE U.S. 1974: "Review of Reliability Data on Weapon and Space Systems," **120** *Congressional Record* S20775–76, 9 December.

—1977: *Security at Nuclear Powerplants—At Best, Inadequate*, EMD–77–32, 7 April, U.S. General Accounting Office, Washington DC 20548.

—1978: *Liquefied Energy Gases Safety*, 3 vols., EMD–78–28, 28 July.

—1979: *Key Crude Oil and Products Pipelines Are Vulnerable to Disruptions*, EMD–79–63, 27 August.

—1980: memorandum B–197458 (EMD–80–48), 19 February.

—1981: *Effectiveness of U.S. Forces Can Be Increased Through Improved Weapon System Design*, PSAD–81–17, 29 January.

—1981a: *Federal Electrical Emergency Preparedness Is Inadequate*, EMD–81–50, 12 May.

—1981b: *The United States Remains Unprepared for Oil Import Disruptions*, EMD–81–117, 29 September, 2 vols.

COMTOIS, W.H. 1977: "Economy of scale in power plants," *Power Engineering*, pp. 51–53, August.

CONE, B.W. *et al.* 1980: *An Analysis of Federal Incentives Used to Stimulate Energy Production*, PNL–2410 Rev. II, Battelle Pacific Northwest Laboratory report to U.S. Department of Energy, February; summarized in Cone, B.W., & Bezdek, R.H. 1980: "Federal incentives for energy developments," *Energy* 5:389–406 (Pergamon).

CONFERENCE ON ALTERNATIVE STATE AND LOCAL POLICIES 1981: *Energy Planning and Education: A Handbook for Community Leaders*, CASLP, 2000 Florida Ave NW, room 407, Washington DC 20009.

—1981a: "Innovative Energy Policies: A Briefing Book."

—1981b: *Citizen Involvement in Community Energy Planning*.

—1981c: *New Initiatives in Energy Legislation: A State by State Guide 1979–1980*.

CONGRESSIONAL RESEARCH SERVICE 1977: *National Energy Transportation*, 3 vols., report to U.S. Senate Committees on Energy & Natural Resources and on Commerce, Science, and Transportation, May, USGPO #95–15.

—1978: *The National Energy Plan: Options Under Assumptions of National Security Threat*, April report for Subcommittee on Energy & Power, Committee on Interstate & Foreign Commerce, USHR, 95th Congr., 2nd Sess., USGPO.

—1978a: "The Cost of an Urban Blackout: The Consolidated Edison Blackout, July 13–14, 1977," June report to Subcommittee on Energy & Power, USHR Committee on Interstate & Foreign Commerce, USGPO.

—1979: "Centralized vs. Decentralized Energy Systems: Diverging or Parallel Roads?," May report for Subcommittee on Energy & Power, Committee on Interstate & Foreign Commerce, USHR, 96th Congr., 1st Sess., Print #96–ICF 17, USGPO.

—1981: "Costs of Synthetic Fuels in Relation to Oil Prices," March report for Subcommittee on Energy Development & Applications, Committee on Science & Technology, USHR, 97th Congr., 1st Sess., Serial B, USGPO.

COOLEY, J.K. 1978: "An 'Interpol' for oil formed in Middle East," *Christian Science Monitor*, p. 3, 2 May.

COOPER, H.S.F. Jr. 1973: *Thirteen: The Flight That Failed*, Dial, New York.

COOPER, R. 1978: quoted at 11 in [Hoover 1979] from 244, W. Rostow, "Competing for Resources in a Two Trillion Dollar Economy," *Proceedings of the Fifth National Security Affairs Conference 1978*, National Defense University, Fort McNair, Washington DC.

COOPER, COL. G. & PAYNTER, W. 1981: written testimony to US Senate Government Affairs Committee, Subcommittee on Energy, Nuclear Proliferation and Government Processes, 24 March; also submitted to Senate Energy & Natural Resources Committee, Subcommittee on Energy Research & Development, 3 April, and to USHR Committee on Energy & Commerce, Subcommittee on Fossil & Synthetic Fuels, 25 March.

CORBETT, M.N. 1981: *A Better Place to Live: New Designs for Tomorrow's Communities*, Rodale Press, Emmaus, Pennsylvania.

— & HAYDEN, T. 1981: "Local Action for a Solar Future," *Solar Law Reporter*, pp. 953–969, January/February.

CORRADI, A.Q. 1979: "Energy and the Exercise of Power," *Foreign Affairs*, Summer, pp. 1144ff.

CORWIN, J.L., MILES, W.T., & WALLDORF, S.P. 1979: "Synthesis of Regional Electric Reliability Council responses to the recommendations issued by the Federal Power Commission following the 1977 New York City blackout," Systems Control, Inc. (Palo Alto CA) report to U.S. Department of Energy, DOE/ERA/6359-2, December.

COUNCIL FOR SCIENCE & SOCIETY 1979: *Deciding about Energy Policy*, J. Ziman, Chm., CSS, 3/4 St. Andrew's Hill, London EC4.

COWEN, E. 1979: "Unrest Raises Doubts on Iran Oil," *New York Times*, pp. A1 & 20, 6 December.

COX, C.H. III 1981: "Power-Producing Homes: Making the Utility Connection," *Solar Age*, pp. 39–47, December.

CRANFORD, C.L. 1981: "Oil Technicians Fighting Rust in Saudi Arabia's Vast Fields," *Los Angeles Times*, p. X:11, 26 November.

CRITTENDEN, A. 1981: "U.S. Seeks Seed Diversity as Crop Assurance," *New York Times*, pp. 1 & 28, 21 September.

CULLEN, J. 1980: *How To Be Your Own Power Company*, Van Nostrand Reinhold, New York.

DAILY MAIL 1979: "Power men warn of blackout chaos," p. 2, 10 April, London.

—1979a: "Radio-active death bid," p. 4, 28 April.

DALEY, J.M. 1982: "San Diego's Sea World Reduces Costs With Cogeneration," *Electrical Consultant*, pp. 22–26, January-February.

DALY, H. 1980: *Steady-State Economics*, W.H. Freeman, San Francisco.

DATTA, R., & DUTT, G. 1981: "Producer Gas Engines in Villages of Less-Developed Countries," *Science* **213**:731–736.

DAVIS, L.N. 1979: *Frozen Fire: Where Will It Happen Next?*, Friends of the Earth, San Francisco.

DAVIS, R. 1981: "National Strategic Petroleum Reserve," *Science* **213**:731–736.

DCPA: see Defense Civil Preparedness Agency.

DEANS, R. 1981: "Georgia Firm Fuels Boiler With Peanut Shells," *Energy User News*, p. 8, 25 May.

DEESE, D.A., & NYE, J. S. 1981: *Energy and Security*, Harvard Energy & Security Project/ Ballinger, Cambridge MA 02138.

DEFENSE CIVIL PREPAREDNESS AGENCY 1973: *DCPA Attack Environment Manual*, CPG 2-1A4, Ch. 4, Panel III, Department of Defense, Washington DC.

—1977: *Energy Emergencies*, CPG 1–28.

DEFENSE ELECTRIC POWER ADMINISTRATION 1962: "Protection of Electric Power Systems," June, Research Project 4405, Dept. of the Interior, Washington DC 20240.

—1966: *Civil Defense Preparedness in the Electric Power Industry*, March, Dept. of the Interior.

—1969: "Vulnerability Analysis of Electric Power Distribution Systems: Albuquerque, New Mexico," Dept. of the Interior.

DELEGATIONEN FÖR ENERGIFORSKNING 1980: *Energi i Utveckling—Program För Forskning Utveckling och Demonstration inom Energiområdet 1981/82–1983/84*, EFUD 81, SOU 1980:35, Sveavägen 9–11, 9 tr., 11157 Stockholm.

DELMASTO, R.T. 1980: "Monterey, united in state effort, practices energy tightfistedness," p. 1, *The Berkshire Eagle,* 23 October.

DEL TREDICI, R. 1980: *The People of Three Mile Island,* Sierra Club, San Francisco.

DE MELLO, F.P., & HANNETT, L.N. 1981: "Large Scale Induction Generators for Power Systems," *IEEE Transactions on Power Apparatus & Systems* **PAS-100**: 2610–2618.

DEMBART, L. 1981: "Vulnerability of U.S. A-Plants Cited," *Los Angeles Times,* p. I:24, 11 June.

DENIKE, L.D. 1975: KFWB Radio (Los Angeles) report quoted at p. 22 in Subcommittee on Energy & the Environment, USHR Committee on Interior & Insular Affairs, serial #94-16, Part VI, USGPO.

—1975a: "Nuclear Terror," *Sierra Club Bulletin,* November/December.

DEPA: see Defense Electric Power Administration.

DEPARTMENT OF ENERGY 1979: "Final Evaluation Report: Fitchburg Action to Conserve Energy (FACE)," October/December.

—1979a: "Vanpooling—Update," September, DOE/CS-0031/1.

—1980: *Passive Solar Design Concepts,* 2 vols., DOE/CS-0127/1, Assistant Secretary for Conservation and Solar Energy, Office of Solar Applications for Buildings, DOE, Washington DC 20585.

—1980a: "National Photovoltaics Program Multi-Year Program Plan," 30 September draft.

—1980b: *Renewable Energy Development: Local Issues and Capabilities,* DOE/PE/0017, January, Office of Solar Policy, Asst. Sec. for Policy & Evaluation.

—1980c: "The Low Cost/No Cost Energy Conservation Program in New England, An Evaluation," DOE/CS/21366-01, July.

—1981: *Reducing U.S. Oil Vulnerability: Energy Policy for the 1980's,* DOE/PE/0021, Asst. Sec. for Policy & Evaluation.

—1981a: "Securing America's Energy Future: The National Energy Policy Plan," DOE/S-0008, July.

—1981b: *Superinsulated Houses: Least Cost Methods for Space Heating in New Home Construction,* review draft, Office of Policy, Planning, & Analysis.

—1981c: "Community Energy Projects: How to Plan Them, How to Run Them," Community Energy Project report to Office of

Conservation and Renewable Energy, July.

—1981d: *San Diego County: A Case Study of Opportunities for Grid Connected Photovoltaic Power Systems,* Office of Solar Power Applications for Buildings, April.

DEXLER, P. 1981: "The Micros Are Coming! The Micros Are Coming!," *Motor Trend,* pp. 59–63, July.

DIONNE, E.J. JR. 1981: "Water Power Being Rediscovered," *New York Times,* p. B1, 7 August.

Diesel and Gas Turbine Progress 1973: "Pre-Tested Energy Plant," May.

DIESENDORF, M. 1981: "As Long As the Wind Shall Blow," *Soft Energy Notes* 4(1):16–17, February/March.

DINNEEN, P.M., SOLOMON, K.A., & TRIPLETT, M.B. 1980: "Away-From-Reactor Storage of Spent Nuclear Fuel: Factors Affecting Demand," R-2558-DOE, October RAND Corporation, Santa Monica CA 90406.

DIRCKS, W.J. 1981: "Electromagnetic Pulse (EMP)—Effects on Nuclear Power Plants," 5 November memorandum to Commissioners, SECY-81-641, Nuclear Regulatory Commission, Washington DC 20555.

DOBSON, R.J.C. 1972: "Problems in the design and construction of liquefied gas carriers," Paper 7, LNG/LPG Conference, London, 21–22 March 1972, *Shipbuilding & Shipping Record.*

DOE: see Department of Energy.

DONNE, M. 1975: "Special fleet will guard oil and gas installations," *Financial Times,* 12 February, London.

DOYLE, M., & DUENWALD, M. 1981: "Palo Alto Finances Solar, Hopes to Cut Gas Use by 5 Percent," *Solar Age,* pp. 12–13, August.

DRESCH, F.W., & ELLIS, H. 1966: *Methodology for Assessing Total Vulnerability,* Stanford Research Institute report to Office of Civil Defense, Office of the Secretary of the Army (Contract OCD-PS-64-201, Work Unit 4341A), August, SRI, Menlo Park CA 94025.

DREXHAGE, K., & WHITING-O'KEEFE, P. 1976: "The Promise of Distributed Processing," SRI Business Intelligence Program Guidelines, Report #10, December, Stanford Research Institute, Menlo Park CA 94025.

DROBNICK, R., & ENZER, S. 1981: "Future Environments of International Trade: A Summary and Report of the Fourth Twenty Year Forecast Project," F-42, March, Center for Futures Research, Graduate School of Business Administration, University of Southern California, Los Angeles 90007.

DUMAS, L.J 1976: "National Insecurity in the Nuclear Age," *Bulletin of the Atomic Scientists*, pp. 24–35, May.

—1980: "Human fallibility and weapons," *Bulletin of the Atomic Scientists*, pp. 15–20, November.

DUMONT, R.S., BESANT, R.W., & KYLE, R. 1978: "Passive Solar Heating—Results from Two Saskatchewan Residences," Dept. of Mech. Engineering, U. of Saskatchewan, Saskatoon S1N 0W0, Canada.

DUMONT, R.S., & ORR, H.W. 1981: "Cost of Energy Conservation Measures for New Housing," September, Division of Building Research, National Research Council of Canada, Ottawa.

DUNLOP, R.D., HOROWITZ, S.H., PARIKH, A.C., JACKSON, M.C., & UMANS, S.D. 1979: "Turbine-Generator Shaft Torques and Fatigue: Part II—Impact of System Disturbances and High Speed Reclosure," *IEEE Transactions on Power Apparatus & Systems* **PAS-98**:2308-2314 and discussion, *id.*:2314–2328.

DYE, L. 1973: "Nuclear Energy: Great Hopes, Great Problems," *Los Angeles Times*, 17 December.

DYSON, F. 1979: *Disturbing the Universe*, Harper & Row, New York.

—1981: "The Quest for Concept," draft typescript, Institute for Advanced Study, Princeton NJ 08540.

ECONOMIC REGULATORY ADMINISTRATION 1979: *The National Power Grid Study*, September, 2 vols., DOE/ERA-0056-1/2, Office of Utility Systems, U.S. Department of Energy, Washington DC 20461.

—1981: *The National Electric Reliability Study*, February draft, Vol. 1, DOE/RG-0055, Office of Utility Systems.

ECONOMIST 1980: p. 52, 12 April, London.

EDITOR & PUBLISHER 1980: p. 11, 9 February.

EDSALL, J.T. 1974: *Environmental Conservation* **I**(1):32, Geneva.

EGUCHI, R.T. *et al.* 1981: "Earthquake Performance of Natural Gas Distribution Systems," at 1096–1104 in *Preprints of the 1981 International Gas Research Conference*, GRI/

AGA/DOE, Government Institutes, Inc., Rockville MD 20850.

EIA: see Energy Information Administration.

ELECTRIC LIGHT & POWER 1981: "Utah Governor Blacks Out Data on State-Wide Energy Outage," **59**(3):1 & 6–7, March.

ELECTRIC POWER RESEARCH INSTITUTE: see EPRI.

ELECTRICAL CONSTRUCTION & MAINTENANCE 1965: "The Case for Emergency Power," December, McGraw-Hill, New York.

ELECTRICAL TIMES 1973: "Thermal efficiency hangs on availability," p. 21, 10 May, London.

ELECTRICAL WORLD 1975: "Nineteenth Steam Station Survey," pp. 43–58 (esp. graph, p. 51), 15 November.

—1982: Editorial (p. 3) and "GE winds down its reactor business," pp. 26–27, January.

—1982a: "Thirteen nuclear-plant security guards . . .," p. 11, January.

EMERGENCY PREPAREDNESS NEWS 1980: **4**(19):7 (9 October), reporting findings of the Environment, Energy & Natural Resources Committee, Government Operations Committee, USHR.

EMR 1980: *The National Energy Program*, Energy, Mines & Resources Canada, Ottawa.

EMSHWILLER, J.R. 1980: "Generating Doubt: Some Investors Shun Nuclear-Powered Utilities, Jeopardizing Funds to Build New Atomic Plants," *Wall Street Journal*, 20 November, p. 56.

—1980a: "Nuclear Safety: Sabotage by Insiders: How Serious Is Threat to Atomic Facilities?" *id.*, pp. 1ff, 3 September.

—1981: "Plunging Power: Big Financial Problems Hit Electric Utilities; Bankruptcies Feared," *id.*, 2 February, p.1.

ENDICOTT. W. 1979: "All Flows Smoothly for Alaska Pipeline," *Los Angeles Times*, pp. 1 & 11, 1 April.

ENERGY & DEFENSE PROJECT 1980: *Dispersed, Decentralized and Renewable Energy Sources: Alternatives to National Vulnerability and War*, December report to Federal Emergency Management Agency (Contract DCPA 01-79-C-0320, FEMA Work Unit 2314-F), distributed by Environment Policy Center, Washington DC. See also the popularization (Clark & Page 1981).

ENERGY & ENVIRONMENTAL ANALYSIS, INC.

1980: "Energy Impacts of Accelerated Retirement of Less Efficient Passenger Cars," 17 October report to Office of Policy & Evaluation, U.S. Dept. of Energy, Washington DC 20585, contact #DE-AC01-79PE-70032, from EEA, Inc., 1111 N. 19th St., Arlington VA 22209.

Energy Consumer 1979: August/September special issue on solar energy, Office of Consumer Affairs, U.S. Department of Energy, Washington DC 20585.

—1980: January special issue on alcohol fuels.

—1980a: February/March special issue on community programs.

—1980b: December 1980 / January 1981 special issue on energy preparedness.

Energy Daily 1981: "Solar Sales Spurt By 155 Percent A Year," p. 4, 3 November.

Energy Information Administration 1981: "Energy Fact Sheet: Fuel Use by Motorists—Summer of 1979," 15 January, DOE/EIA-0240/07, U.S. Dept. of Energy.

Energy Insider 1980: "Area Power Failure No Problem For Solar-Powered Gas Station," 3(19), 15 September, U.S. Department of Energy.

—1980a: "Combination of Fossil and Solar Pushed for Industrial Process Heat," p. 3, 8 December.

Energy Research Advisory Board: see ERAB.

Energy Research Reports 1979: "Toward commecial wind power: 3 big projects financed privately," 5(11):1–3, 4 June, Advanced Technology Publications Inc., 1001 Watertown St., Newton MA 02165.

Energy Task Force Newsletter 1981: pp. 4–5, October, California Department of General Services, Room 590, 915 Capitol Mall, Sacramento CA 95814.

Ener-Nat SA, case postale 69, CH-1880 Bex, Switzerland.

Environmental Action Foundation 1981: *Power and Light: Political Strategies for the Solar Transition,* Pilgrim Press, New York.

Epler, E.P. 1970: "The ORR Emergency Cooling Failure," *Nuclear Safety* 11:323-27 (July–August 1970).

EPRI [Electric Power Research Institute] 1979: "Evaluating Energy and Capacity Shortages—The 1976–1977 Natural Gas Shortage," EPRI EA-1215, November, Electric Power Research Institute, Palo Alto CA.

—1979a: "Power Shortage Costs and Efforts to Minimize: An Example," EPRI EA-1241, Interim Report, December, p. 16.

ERA: See Economic Regulatory Administration.

ERAB [Energy Research Advisory Board] 1980: "Research and Development Needs in the Department of Energy: Interim Report of the Research and Development Panel, Energy Research Advisory Board," 5 September, U.S. Department of Energy, Washington DC 20585. See also ERAB 1981b.

—1981: "Annual Report of the Energy Research Advisory Board Conservation Panel," final draft, 23 February.

—1981a: "Biomass Energy," November.

—1981b: "Federal Energy R&D Priorities," November.

E.R. Squibb & Sons, Inc. 1971: 24 November letter to USAEC Division of Complicance regarding overexposure of worker due to criminal act, ORNL NSIC accession #34092, NRC Public Document Room.

Eschwege, H. 1974: 16 October letter B-164105 to Chairman Ray, USAEC, U.S. General Accounting Office, Resources & Economic Development Division, Washington DC 20548.

Evening Standard 1976: "Killer nerve gas plot foiled by police," p. 10, edn. 6, 8 November, London.

—1979: p. 6, col. 6, 12 January, London.

Fainberg, A. 1981: "Osirak and international security," *Bulletin of the Atomic Scientists,* pp. 33–36, October.

Fairley, W.B. 1975: "Evaluating the 'Small' Probability of a Catastrophic Accident from the Marine Transportation of Liquefied Natural Gas," September, reprinted at 331–354 in Fairley, W.B., & Mosteller, F., eds., *Statistics and Public Policy,* Addison-Wesley, Reading MA, 1977.

Falcone, C.A. 1979: "The National Power Grid—Issues and Problems," at 3–6 in *The National Grid: A Solution Or a Problem?,* Power Engineering Society, IEEE, Piscataway NJ 08854.

Fallows, J. 1981: *National Defense,* Random House, New York.

Far Eastern Economic Review 1976: "The Taiwan Bombers," p. 6, 3 December.

Farhar, B.C., Unseld, C.T., Vories, R. & Crews, R. 1980: "Public Opinion About Energy," *Annual Review of Energy* **5**:141–172.

FAUX, R. 1981: "Navy guards oil rig from illegal trawlers," *The Times*, London, p. 3, 26 January.

FAY, J.A. 1980: "Risks of LNG and LPG," *Annual Review of Energy* **5**:89–105.

FBI [Federal Bureau of Investigation] 1973–81: *Bomb Summary 1972* through *1980*, Uniform Crime Reports, FBI, Washington DC.

FEDER, B. 1981: "Surveillance Blimp Stirs New Interest," *New York Times*, p. D1, 28 September.

FEMA [Federal Management Agency] 1979: "Energy Emergencies—Checklist for Local Government," 20 June preprint from "Disaster Operations: A Handbook for Local Governments," CPG 1–6.

FEDERAL ENERGY REGULATORY COMMISSION 1978: *The Con Edison Power Failure of July 13 and 14, 1977*, June final staff report, USGPO.

FEDERAL POWER COMMISSION 1977: "Supplement to Staff Report on July 13–14, 1977 Electric System Disturbance on the Consolidated Edison Company of New York, Inc., System," 4 August.

FEDERATION OF AMERICAN SCIENTISTS 1980: *F.A.S. Public Interest Report* **33**(9), November.

FEIGENBAUM, M.J. 1980: "Universal Behavior in Nonlinear Systems," *Los Alamos Science*, pp. 2–27, Summer, Los Alamos [NM] National Laboratory.

FERC: see Federal Energy Regulatory Commission.

FERCHACK, J.D., & PYE, E.K. 1981: "Utilization of Biomass in the U.S. for the Production of Ethanol Fuel as a Gasoline Replacement— II. Energy Requirements, with Emphasis on Lignocellulosic Conversion," *Solar Energy* **26**: 17–25.

—1981a: *id.*: "I. Terrestrial Resource Potential," *loc. cit.*:9–16.

FERNALD, O.H. 1965: *Critical Industry Repair Analysis: Petroleum Industry*, Advance Research, Inc., Wellesley Hills MA, October report to Office of Civil Defense, CIRA-4, OCD Subtask 3311A.

FESHARAKI, F., & ISAAK, D.T. 1981: "OPEC Downstream Processing—A New Phase of the World Oil Market," October, Resource Systems Institute, East-West Center, Honolulu.

FETTER, S. 1981: *The Vulnerability of Nuclear Power Reactors to Attack by Nuclear Weapons*, May B.Sc. thesis, Physics Department, Massachusetts Institute of Technology, Cambridge MA 02139.

—& TSIPIS, K. 1980: "Catastrophic Nuclear Radiation Releases," Report #5, September, Program in Science & Technology for International Security, Department of Physics, Massachusetts Institute of Technology.

—1981: "Catastrophic Releases of Radioactivity," *Scientific American* **244**(4):41–47, April.

FIALKA, J.J. 1979: "The American Connection: How Israel Got the Bomb," *Washington Monthly* **10**(10):50–58, January.

FINANCIAL TIMES 1981: p. 4, 4 March, London.

—1981a: *World Solar Markets*, December, London.

FINK, L.H. 1976: "Systems Engineering Challenges Emerge as Electric Energy Network Increases in Complexity," *Professional Engineer* **47**(12):20–21, December.

FINLEY, N.C. *et al.* 1979: *Transportation of Radionuclides in Urban Environs: Draft Environmental Assessment*, SAND 79–0369, NUREG/CR-0743, Sandia National Laboratory report to Nuclear Regulatory Commission, Albuquerque.

FISHER, J.C. 1979: "Optimum Size of Subcritical Fossil Fueled Electric Generating Units," paper presented to June workshop, "Size and Productive Efficiency: The Wider Implications," International Institute for Applied Systems Analysis, Laxenburg, Austria (proceedings in press as *The Scale in Production Systems* and summarized by Cantley 1979).

FISHMAN, L.F. 1980: *World Mineral Trends and U.S. Supply Problems*, R-20, Resources for the Future, Inc., Washington DC 20036.

FISK, P. 1979: "A Conceptual Approach Toward the Development of Appropriate Technologies," paper to 1978 AAAS Annual Meeting; see also "Appropriate Community Technology," Center for Maximum Potential Building Systems, 8604 F.M. 969, Austin TX 78724.

FITZPATRICK, J. 1980: "Drilling for Oil At Home," *Boston Herald American*, 23 September.

FLAIM, S., & HERTZMARK. D. 1981: "Agricultural Policies and Biomass Fuels," *Annual Review of Energy* **6**:89–121.

FLOOD, M. 1976: "Nuclear Sabotage," *Bulletin of the Atomic Scientists*, pp. 29–36, October.

FOGET, C.R., & VAN HORN, W.H. 1969: *Availability and Use of Emergency Power Sources in the Early Postattack Period*, August report to Office of Civil Defense, Office of Secretary of the Army, OCD Work Unit 3311B, rep. #URS 710–4, from URS Research Co., 1811 Trousdale Dr., Burlingame CA 94010.

FOISIE, J. 1981: "Sabotage Jolts South Africa's Republic Day," *Los Angeles Times*, pp. I:1 & 24, 26 May.

FOLEY, G. 1979: "Economic Growth and the Energy Future," report to December seminar at Ljubljana (Yugoslavia) of Senior Advisors to ECE Governments on Environmental Problems, "Alternative Patterns of Development and Lifestyles," U.N. Economic Commission for Europe, Geneva, ENV/SEM.11/R.21, 1 November.

—& LÖNNROTH, M. 1981: "The European Transition from Oil: Mapping the Landscape," overview of 49th Nobel Symposium, in press in *European Transition from Oil—Societal and Institutional Constraints on Energy Policy*, Academic Press, New York, 1981.

FORD, A. 1978: "Expanding Generating Capacity for an Uncertain Future: The Advantage of Small Power Plants," LA-UR-79-10, December, Los Alamos Scientific Laboratory, Los Alamos NM 87545.

—1979: "A New Look at Small Power Plants," LASL-78-101, January.

—1979a: direct and surrebuttal testimony of 30 March to New Mexico Public Service Commission, Santa Fe, case #1454.

—& FLAIM, T. 1979: *An Economic and Environmental Analysis of Large and Small Electric Power Stations in the Rocky Mountain West*, LA-8033-MS, October.

FORD, A., & POLYZOU, A. 1981: "Simulating the Planning Advantages of Short Lead Time Generating Technologies Under Irregular Demand Growth," 3 July paper to Western Economic Association Conference (San Francisco), Economics Group, Los Alamos National Laboratory.

FORD, A., & YABROFF, I.W. 1978: "Defending Against Uncertainty in the Electric Utility Industry," LA-UR-78-3228, December.

FORD, D.F. 1982: *Three Mile Island: Thirty Minutes to Meltdown*, Viking and Penguin, New York.

FOREMAN, J. 1981: "Terrestrial Photovoltaics Compared to SPS Reference System," 3 February briefing paper, Naval Research Laboratory.

FOWLER, G. 1981: "State Tests Use of Batteries on Subway Trains," *New York Times*, p. 67, 4 October.

FPC: see Federal Power Commission (succeeded by FERC).

FRANK, A.L. 1981: "Windmill Clusters and Giant Turbines Log Many Ups, One Down," *Solar Age*, p. 17, June.

FRANKLIN, R. 1980: "Wind-Driven Refrigerator Project," Dept. of Chem. & Physics, Westmar College, Le Mars IA 51031.

FRANKLIN PIERCE ENERGY LAW CENTER 1980– : reports of comprehensive project on microhydro, White St., Concord, New Hampshire.

FREEDBERG, M. 1981: "Meeting Local Energy Needs: Resources for Self-Sufficiency," Conference on Alternative State and Local Policies (*q.v.*).

—& SLAVET, J. 1981: *Energy Conservation and Low-Income Consumers: Options for State and Local Governments*, available *id.*

FREIWALD, D.A. 1980: "Use of Non-Petroleum Fuels to Reduce Military Energy Vulnerabilities," LA-UR-80-3445, Los Alamos Scientific Laboratory.

FRIEDLANDER, G.D. 1982: "Twenty-second steam station cost survey," *Electrical World*, pp. 69–84, January.

FRIEDMAN, R. 1980: "The Dalton Gang's Computer Caper," *New York* magazine **13**:65–75, 8 December.

FRIEDMAN, T.L. 1981: "Industry Starts Smiling on Photovoltaics," *New York Times*, p. 22E, 20 September.

FULKERSON, W. 1981: *Energy Division Annual Progress Report for Period Ending September 30, 1980*, ORNL-5740, November, Oak Ridge National Laboratory.

GAGE, N. 1978: story datelined Teheran, N.Y. Times News Service, 2 November.

GALL, J. 1978: *Systemantics: How Systems Work and Especially How They Fail*, Kangaroo/Pocket Books, New York.

GALLOWAY, C.D. & Kirchmayer, L.K. 1958:

"Comment," *Transactions of the American Institute of Electrical Engineers* **39**:1142–1144.

GAO [General Accounting Office]: see Comptroller General of the U.S. 1978.

GARDNER, J. 1981: *License Renewed,* Richard Marek Publishers, New York.

GARGAN, E.O. 1981: "Blackout on S.I. Ended, Power Restored to 39,000, *New York Times,* p. B1, 13 July.

GARON, P.A. 1981: "Major Industries Continuing Trend to Energy Efficiency," *Energy Insider* **4**(1):1, 19 January, U.S. Department of Energy.

GASCAP [Gasoline Conservation Awareness Program]: West Valley Community College District, 14000 Fruitvale Ave, Saratoga CA 95070.

GERLACH, L. 1979: "Energy Wars and Social Change," in Abbot, S., & van Willigan, J., eds., *Predicting Sociocultural Change,* Southern Anthropological Society Proceedings #13, University of Georgia Press, Athens; available from author at Department of Anthropology, U. of Minnesota, Minneapolis MN 55455.

—& RADCLIFFE, B. 1979: "Can Independence Survive Interdependence?", *Futurics* **3**(3):181–206.

GERVASI, T. 1981: *Arsenal of Democracy II,* Grove Press, New York.

GLASSEY, R. & CRAIG, P. 1978: "Vulnerability of Renewable Energy Systems," at II:330–38, in Craig, P. *et al.,* eds., *Distributed Energy Systems in California's Future,* Interim Report for USDOE, University of California, HCP/P7405–02.

GLEASON, J. 1981: *Efficient Fossil and Solar District Heating Systems: Preliminary Report,* draft, Consultant Agreement #CA-0-0156-1, April, for New England Sustainable Energy Project (Jim Ohi, Project Manager), Solar Energy Research Institute, 1617 Cole Blvd., Golden CO 80401.

—1981a: *Report on District Heating: I. Energy Sources and Technologies,* draft for Solar Cities Project, Center for Renewable Resources, Suite 510, 1001 Connecticut Ave NW, Washington DC 20036.

—1981b: "District Heating: Choice Between 'Hard' and 'Soft' Path Technology," *Self-Reliance* **25**:1f, January-February, Institute for Local Self-Reliance, 1717 18th St NW, Washington DC 20009.

GLIDDEN, W.T. JR., & HIGH, C.J. 1980: *The New England Energy Atlas,* Resource Policy Center, Thayer School of Engineering, Dartmouth College, Hanover NH 03755.

GODOLPHIN, D. 1981: "Automation Streamlines On-Site Construction," *Solar Age,* pp. 10–11, June.

GOELLER, H.E. 1980: "Future U.S. Energy Supply: Constraints by Nonfuel Mineral Resources," ORNL-5656, December, Oak Ridge National Laboratory.

GOEN, R.L., BOTHUN, R.B. & WALKER, F.E. 1970: *Potential Vulnerabilities Affecting National Survival,* Stanford Research Institute report to Office of Civil Defense, OCD Work Unit 3535A, Contract DAHC 20-69-C-0186, September.

GOLDMAN, J.J. 1981: "Con Ed Ruled Grossly Negligent in 1977 New York City Blackout," *Los Angeles Times,* p. I:20, 20 November.

GOODMAN, A.E., "The Threat from the Third World," *Proceedings of the Fifth National Security Affairs Conference 1978,* August, National Defense University, Fort McNair, Washington DC.

GORENFLO, L., GREGG, D., & WEAVER, D. 1981: *Farm and Rural Energy Planning Manual,* Institute for Ecological Policies, PO Box 442, Merrifield VA 22116.

GORLEBEN INTERNATIONAL REVIEW 1979: *Bericht des Internationales Gutachten Gorleben für das Niedersächsische Sozialministerium,* Hannover, April.

GORMAN, R., & HEITNER, K.L. 1980: "A Comparison of Costs for Automobile Energy Conservation *vs.* Synthetic Fuel Production," TRW Energy Systems Group, 8301 Greensboro Drive, McLean VA 22102.

GOSSICK, L.V. 1977: "Operating Assumption on Clandestine Fission Explosives," 8 August memorandum, USNRC, reprinted at pp. 211–214, Subcommittee on Energy & the Environment 1977a (*op. cit.*).

GOURAUD, J.S. 1981: *Energy Clinic News* **2**(4):3, April, 722 Post Rd. E., Westport CT 06880.

—1981a: "Purpa 210," *id.* **2**(6):3, June.

—1982: "Catalytic Stoves" and "Kerosene," *id.,* January–February.

GRANT, S. 1981: "Wood Chips Used to Battle High Oil Cost," *Los Angeles Times*, pp. X:3–4, 10 December.

GRAVES, A. 1981: "Private Wind Farm Generates 1 MW," *Solar Age*, p. 14, April.

GRAY, C., & VON HIPPEL, F. 1981: "The Fuel Economy of Light Vehicles," *Scientific American*, pp. 48–59, May.

GRAY, J.N. 1977: "Notes on Data Base Operating Systems," Research Report RJ2188-(30001)2/23/78, Summer, IBM Research Laboratory, San Jose CA 95193, available from IBM Thomas J. Watson Research Center, Distribution Services, PO Box 218, Yorktown Heights NY 10598.

—1979: "A Discussion of Distributed Systems," Research Report RJ2699-(34594)9/13/79, IBM Research Laboratory, *loc. cit.*

—1981: "The Transaction Concept: Virtues and Limitations," TR 81.3, September, Tandem Computers, Inc., 19333 Vallco Parkway, Cupertino CA 95104.

GREAT FALLS TRIBUNE 1980: "Society's electric heartbeat," editorial, p. 6-A, 26 September, Great Falls MT.

GREEN, B.D. 1980: "Comparative Energy Costs," draft, Community & Consumer Branch, Analysis & Applications, SERI (*q.v.*), Golden CO 80401.

GREEN, L., & REMPEL, W.C. 1982: "Nuclear Plant 'Attack' Taped," *Los Angeles Times*, p. I:10, 29 January.

GRIGSBY, W.J., MANLY, R.P., BOESMAN, W.C., & JOHNSON, J.M. 1968: "Vulnerability of the Local Petroleum Distribution System: Albuquerque, New Mexico," Checci & Co., Washington DC 20006.

GRIMMER, D.P., & HERR, K.C. 1977: "Solar Process Heat from Concentrating Flat-Plate Collectors," LA-6597-MS, Los Alamos Scientific Laboratory.

GROVE-WHITE, R., & FLOOD, M. 1976: "Nuclear Prospects," Friends of the Earth / Council for the Protection of Rural England / National Council for Civil Liberties, London.

GUARDIAN 1975: "Vietnam reactor immobilised," 1 April, London.

—1975a: 13 May, cited in Flood [1976: 36n29].

—1975b: 27 August.

HALLBERG, D. 1980: "Security and Renewables: A Natural Combination," pp. 18–19, *The Energy Consumer*, December 1980/January 1981, Special Edition on Preparedness, Office of Consumer Affairs, U.S. Department of Energy.

—1981: statement to Energy Policy Task Force, U.S. Department of Energy, at p. 147 in transcript of 30 April meeting.

HALLORAN, R. 1981: "U.S. Discloses 5 Accidents Involving Nuclear Weapons," *New York Times*, p. A16, 26 May.

HAMMOND, A.L., & METZ, W.D. 1977: "Solar Energy Research: Making Solar After the Nuclear Model?" *Science* **197**:241–244, 15 July.

HAMPSHIRE COLLEGE 1979: *Energy Self-Sufficiency in Northampton, Massachusetts*, DOE/PE/4706, from National Technical Info. Service, Springfield VA 22161.

HAMRIN, J. 1980: "Rapid Transitions," at Vol. 3.2, pp. 1159–1165, in *Proceedings of the 1980 Annual Meeting*, American Section of the International Solar Energy Society, Killeen TX.

HANLEY, R. 1981: "Rupturing of Reservoir Pipelines Imperils Newark's Water Supply," *New York Times*, pp. 1 & B2, 8 July.

—1981a: "Water Importing Begins in Newark," *id.*, pp. A1 & B2, 9 July.

—1981b: "Water Concerns Eased in Newark As Pipe Arrives," *id.*, pp. B1 & B16, 10 July.

—1981c: "4 Seized in Cutoff of Newark Water," *id.*, pp. 1 & 48, 11 July.

—1981d: "First of 2 Newark Pipelines Finished," *id.*, pp. B1 & B3, 13 July.

—1981e: "A New Leak Ruptures Newark Water Pipeline," *id.*, p. B2, 14 July.

—1981f: "Newark Cuts Red Tape To Rush Water Repairs," *id.*, p. B3, 16 July.

HANNON, B. 1976: "Energy and Labor Demand in the Conserver Society," Center for Advanced Computation, University of Illinois at Urbana-Champaign.

HANSARD 1974: written answer by Secretary of State for Defence, pp. 276–277 (19 July).

HARDEE, H.C., LEE, D.O., & BENEDICK, W.B. 1978: "Thermal hazard from LNG fireballs," *Combustion Science & Technology* **17**:189–197.

HARDING, J. 1982: "Reagan's New Cuts: Renewables, -86% / Conservation, -97%," *Not Man Apart*, p. 17, February/March, Friends of the Earth, San Francisco.

HATZFELDT, H., HIRSCH, H., & KOLLERT, R. 1979: *Der Gorleben-Report,* Fischer, Frankfurt/M, FRG.

HEDGECOCK. R. 1980: "Local Leadership for Solar Energy in San Diego County," at 175–179 in SERI 1980b, *op. cit.*

1982: *The Third World Nuclear War,* William Morrow, New York, in press.

HEIN, K. 1979: *Blockheizkraftwerke,* C.F. Müller Verlag, Karlsruhe, FRG.

HERMANN, C.F. 1977: "Are the Dimensions and Implications of National Security Changing?", Autumn *Quarterly Report,* Mershon Center, Ohio State University, Columbus.

HERSHEY, R.D. JR. 1981: "Can Reagan Lift The Cloud Over Nuclear Power?", *New York Times,* 8 March.

—1981a: "Winning the War on Energy," *id.,* pp. 3:1 & 17, 11 October.

HEWETT, C.E., HIGH, C.J., MARSHALL, N., & WILDERMUTH, R. 1981: "Wood energy in the United States," *Annual Review of Energy* 6:139–170.

HIGHLEYMAN, W.H. 1980: "Survivable Systems," esp. Part 4, "Survivability," reprinted from *Computerworld* by Tandem Computers, Inc. (*q.v.*)

HILL, W. JR. 1981: "The Case for a Defensive Air-to-Air Fighter," *Astronautics and Aeronautics,* pp. 28–36, November, at T-2, p. 32.

HOAG, J., & TERASAWA, K. 1981: "Some Advantages of Systems With Small Module Size," JPL 900-990#8, June review draft, Economics Group, CalTech Jet Propulsion Laboratory, Pasadena CA 91109.

HOBSON, T. 1980: "Alcohol Fuels: A Path to Reconciliation," at p. 35 in *Energy Consumer* 1980 (*q.v.*).

HODGES, D.A. 1981: "The Induction Generator in Cogeneration Applications," paper to Cogeneration Workshop, San Luis Obispo CA 20–21 May, available from author at (209) 798-1963.

HOFMANN, P. 1979: "Israel Suffers Extensive Blackout," *New York Times,* p. A3, 6 February.

HOLDREN, J.P. 1974: "Radioactive Pollution of the Environment by the Nuclear Fuel Cycle," Paper XXIII-2, Pugwash (Aulanko), revised & reprinted in *Bulletin of the Atomic Scientists* **30**(8):14ff.

—1981: Letter to the Editors, *Scientific American,* 27 March, Energy & Resources Group, University of California at Berkeley.

—*ET. AL.* 1980: "Environmental Aspects of Renewable Energy Sources," ERG-80-1, Energy & Resources Group, 100 T-4, University of California, Berkeley CA 94720. See also *Annual Review of Energy* 5:241–291 (1980).

HOLLAND, E. 1981: "Insulation Moves Outside," *Solar Age,* pp. 22–27, November.

HOLLANDS, K.G.T., & ORGILL, J.F. 1977: *Potential for Solar Heating in Canada,* 77–01, Project 4107-1,2, report by University of Waterloo Research Institute, Waterloo, Ontario, to Division of Building Research, National Research Council of Canada, Ottawa.

HOLLING, C.S. 1978: "Myths of Ecological Stability: Resilience and the Problem of Failure," Ch. 4 in Smart, C.F., & Stanbury, W.T., eds., *Studies on Crisis Management,* Butterworth for the Institute for Research on Public Policy, Montréal.

—& GOLDBERG, M.A. 1971: "Ecology and Planning," *Journal of the American Institute of Planners* **37**(4):221–30, July.

HOLLING, C.S., WALTERS, C.J., & LUDWIG, D. 1979: "Surprise in Resource and Environmental Systems," typescript, Institute of Resource Ecology, University of British Columbia, Vancouver.

HOLMBERG, W.C. 1981: "Decentralized energy systems needed for national security," *Public Power,* pp. 104–107, January–February, American Public Power Association, Washington DC.

HOLT, H.R. 1982: "High Efficiency Refrigerators: Recent Developments," January memorandum, Office of Policy, Planning, and Analysis, U.S. Dept. of Energy.

HOLUSHA, J. 1981: "Americans Are Back on Roads, but Gas Prices Are Shortening their Trips," *New York Times,* p. A14, 11 August.

—1981a: "Remote Gander Is Storm Center on Flight Control," *id.,* p. 12, 13 August.

HOOVER, P.S. 1979: "National Security Implications of the Soft Path Approach to Energy Futures," draft, Program for Energy Research, Education and Public Service, Ohio State University, Columbus.

HOUSTON CHRONICLE 1977: p. 21, 16 October.

—1981: p. III:20, 12 July.

Howe, M. 1973: "Allende Cabinet Orders Strong Steps To Curb Violence and End Truck Strike," *New York Times*, p. 10, 15 August.

—1973a: "Military Trying to Placate Chile," *id.*, p. 11, 16 August.

Hsu, F. 1981: advertisement, *id.*, p. E7, 2 August.

Hubbert, M.K. 1969: in National Academy of Sciences, *Resources and Man*, W.H. Freeman, San Francisco.

Heuthner, D. 1973: "Shifts in Long Run Averge Cost Curves: Theoretical and Managerial Implications," *Omega* 1(4).

Huffacker, C.D., Shea, K.P., & Herman, S.S. 1963: "Experimental Studies in Predation: Complex Dispersion and Levels of Food in an Acarine Predator-prey Interaction," *Hilgardia* 34:305–330.

Humboldt County Energy Advisory Committee 1981: 26 April report to County Board of Supervisors.

Hume, E. 1981: "Cranston Sees Iraq, Pakistan A-Arms Peril," *Los Angeles Times*, p. I:1, 17 March.

Hunt, M., & Bainbridge, D. 1978: "The Davis Experience," *Solar Age*, May.

Hyman, B., ed. 1981: *Decentralized Electricity for Washingtn*, Program in Social Management of Technology, U. of Washington (in collaboration with House and Senate Committees on Energy & Utilities. Washington State Legislature), May, U. of Washington, Seattle WA 98195, especially Ch. 4.

Ibrahim, Y.M. 1979: "Khomeini Supporter Is Killed in Teheran by Moslem Radicals," *New York Times*, p. A1, 9 July.

IEAL [International Energy Associates Ltd.] 1980: *Consequence Risk Analysis of Sabotage at DOE Facilities: Phase I*, 2 vols., IEAL-181, 15 December final report for Sandia Laboratories, IEAL, 600 NH Ave NW, Washington DC 20037.

IIASA: see International Institute for Applied Systems Analysis.

Iklé, F.C. 1979: "Could We Mobilize Industry?", *Wall Street Journal*, p. 6, 26 December.

Illich, I. 1980: "Vernacular Values," *CoEvolution Quarterly* 26:22–49, Summer.

Ingenjörsvetenskapsakadamien 1950: *Generator Gas—The Swedish Experience From 1939–1945*, as translated by SERI (*q.v.*), SERI/SP-33-140, 1979.

Inside Energy 1982: "Industry Help to Be Sought in Reviving Energy Emergency Groups at DOE," p. 7, 29 January.

InterGroup Consulting Economists Ltd. 1978: *Liquid Fuels from Renewable Resources: Feasibility Study: Summary and Conclusions*, May report to Interdepartmental Steering Committee on Canadian Renewable Liquid Fuels Program Options, Ottawa, by IGCE, 704-283 Portage Ave, Winnipeg, Manitoba.

International Herald Tribune 1979: "Blackout Hits Miami Region," p. 5, 6 April, Paris.

—1981: "ETA Bombs Atom Plant, Killing One," p. 2, 31 Jan.–1 Feb., Paris.

International Institute for Applied Systems Analysis [IIASA] 1981: *Energy in a Finite World*, Vol. 1, February, Ballinger Publishing, 17 Dunster St., Cambridge MA 02138.

Isaksen, I.S.A. 1980: "The Impact of Nitrogen Fertilization," pp. 257–268 in Bach, W. *et. al.*, eds., *Interactions of Energy and Climate*, Reidel, Dordrecht (The Netherlands).

Jackson, M.C., Umans, S.D., Dunlop, R.D., Horowitz, S.H., & Parikh, A.D. 1979: "Turbine-Generator Shaft Torques and Fatigue: Part I—Simulation Methods and Fatigue Analysis," *IEEE Transactions on Power Apparaus & Systems* **PAS-98**:2299–2307.

Jackson, W. 1980: *New Roots for Agriculture*, Friends of the Earth, San Francisco.

—& Bender, M. 1981: "American Food: S/oil And Water," pp. 3–6, and "Saving Energy and Soil," p. 7, in *Soft Energy Notes* **3**(6), December 1980/January 1981 (*q.v.*).

Japan Automotive News 1980: "Again, Mini in the Limelight," p. 10, 1 September.

Jedlicka, D. 1982: "Ford to Produce Propane-Powered Fleet Autos in February," *Denver Post*, p. 3G ("Wheels"), 8 January.

Jenkins, B.M. 1975: "Will Terrorists Go Nuclear?", Discussion Paper 64, California Seminar on Arms Control & Foreign Policy, P.O. Box 925, Santa Monica CA 90406.

—1975a: "High Technology Terrorism and Surrogate War: The Impact of New Technology on Low-Level Violence," P-5339, RAND Corporation, Santa Monica CA 90406.

Jenkins, A. 1980: "Community Energy Mobilization: Prosperity in Spite of Shortage," at 13ff in *The Energy Consumer* 1980b, *op. cit.*

Jennings, D.M. 1980: "Socioeconomic Impacts of Natural Gas Curtailments: A Study of the Textile Industry in the Southeastern United States," January final report to Department of Energy from JBC Scientific Corporation, Contract #EM-78-C-01-4139.

JET PROPULSION LABORATORY: see JPL.

JOHNSON, C.J. 1981: "Cancer Incidence in an Area Contaminated with Radionuclides Near a Nuclear Installation," *Ambio* 10(4):176–182.

—1982: "Evaluation of Environmental and Health Effects of Nuclear Weapons Development and Production," paper to Session 20 (Arms Control and Security), Annual Meeting, American Association for the Advancement of Science, January, Washington DC.

JOINT CHIEFS OF STAFF 1949/78: Joint Outline War Plan ("Harmon Report," codename Trojan), JCS 1953/1, 12 May 1949, declassified with deletions 3 November 1978.

JOINT COMMITTEE ON ATOMIC ENERGY 1974: testimony of 28 March (at 285ff) in *Hearings on Possible Modification or Extension of the Price-Anderson Insurance and Indemnity Act*, 93rd Congr., 2d sess., USGPO.

JOINT COMMITTEE ON DEFENSE PRODUCTION 1977: *Civil Preparedness Review*, 2 vols., Joint Committee Print, U.S. Congress, 95th Congr., 1st Sess., February, USGPO.

—1977a: *Emergency Preparedness in the Electric Power Industry and the Implications of the New York Blackout for Emergency Planning*, 10–11 August hearings, U.S. Congress, 95th Congr., 1st Sess., USGPO.

JONES, A.H., & FORD, D.L 1980: *Community Energy Planning: The Basic Elements*, Colorado Office of Energy Conservation, Denver.

JPL [CalTech Jet Propulsion Laboratory] 1980: "National Photovoltaics Program" briefing documents, 27 October, JPL, Pasadena, California.

JUNGER, P.D. 1976: "A Recipe for Bad Water: Welfare Economics and Nuisance Law Mixed Well," *27 Case Western Reserve Law Review* 3–335, Fall.

JUSTICE [UK Section, International Commission of Jurists] 1978: "Plutonium and Liberty," London.

KAHN, E. 1977: testimony on reliability planning to New Jersey Board of Public Utility Commissioners, Newark NJ, docket 762–194.

—1978: "Reliability Planning in Distributed Electric Energy Systems," LBL-7877, Lawrence Berkeley Laboratory, Berkeley CA 94720; most of this material is in Kahn's "Reliability Planning for Solar Electric Power Generation," *Technological Forecasting & Social Change* 18:359–378 (1980).

—1979: "The Compatibility of Wind and Solar Technology With Conventional Energy Systems," *Annual Review of Energy* 4:313–352.

—, DAVIDSON, M., MAKHIJANI, A., CAESAR, P., & BERMAN, S.M. 1976: "Investment Planning in the Energy Sector," LBL-4474, Lawrence Berkeley Laboratory, Berkeley CA 94720.

KAHN, E. & SCHUTZ, S. 1978: "Utility Investment in On-Site Solar: Risk and Return Analysis for Capitalization and Financing," LBL-7876, *id.*

KAHN, E. *et al.* 1980: "Commercialization of Solar Energy by Regulated Utilities: Economic and Financial Risk Analysis," LBL-11398, *id.*

KALDOR, M. 1981: *The Baroque Arsenal*, Hill & Wang, London.

KALISCH, R. 1979: telecon from American Gas Association to G. Gorenstein, 18 December.

KAPLAN, G. 1982: "Power systems," *IEEE Spectrum*, pp. 65–68, January.

KATZ, A.M. 1981: *Life After Nuclear War*, Ballinger, Cambridge MA 02138.

KATZ, R., PAWLICK, L., & SPENCER, B. 1981: *Energy in New England: Transition to the '80s*, 22 June, New England Congressional Institute, 53 D St SE, Washington DC 20003.

KATZMAN, J.A. 1977: "A Fault-Tolerant Computing System," January 1978 Hawaii International Conference of System Sciences, revised January 1979, available from Tandem [*loc. cit.*].

KELLEN, K. 1979: "Terrorists—What Are They Like? How Some Terrorists Describe their World and Actions," N-1300-SL, November RAND Note for Sandia Laboratories, RAND Corporation, Santa Monica CA 90406.

KELLOGG, W.W., & SCHWARE, R. 1981: *Climate Change and Society*, Westview Press (Boulder, Colorado) and Aspen Institute for Humanistic Studies.

KEMPSTER, N. 1981: "Israeli Planes Destroy Iraqi Nuclear Plant," *Los Angeles Times*, p.

I:1ff, 9 June.

KENDALL, H.W. *et. al.* 1977: *The Risks of Nuclear Power Reactors,* Union of Concerned Scientists, 1384 Massachusetts Ave., Cambridge MA 02238.

KENSIL, D. 1981: "A Guide to Greenhouse Glazing," *New Roots* **16**:33–35, May/June, Greenfield MA 01302.

KERR, R.A. 1981: "Pollution of the Arctic Atmosphere Confirmed," *Science* **212**:1013–1014.

—1981a: "Impact Looks Real, the Catastrophe Smaller," *id.* **214**:896–898.

KESSLER, C.J. 1976: "Legal Issues in Protecting Offshore Structures," Professional Paper #147, June, Center for Naval Analysis, Arlington, Virginia.

KESSLER, F. 1981: "French Computers Under Heavy Guard As Attacks Continue," *Wall Street Journal,* p. 6, 2 February.

KIHLSTEDT, G. 1977: "Samhällets Råvaruförsörning under Energibrist," IVA-112, Ingenjörsvetenskapsakademien, Stockholm.

KIHSS, P. 1981: "A Con Ed Explosion and Blaze Disrupt Lower Manhattan," *New York Times,* pp. 1 & 16, 10 September.

—1981a. "A Faulty Transformer Switch Tied to 4-Hour Power Failure," *id.,* pp. 1 & B2, 11 September.

KING, N.J. 1979: " 'Flexigard' Brand Protective Film as a Glazing Material for Solar Collectors, Storm Windows and Greenhouses," pp. B-15–B-19, *Proceedings of the 1979 Topical Conference on Solar Glazing,* Mid-Atlantic Solar Energy Association, Philadelphia.

KING, M.A. *et al.* 1980: "An Overview of the Effects of Nuclear Weapons on Communications Capabilities," *Signal,* January, Armed Forces Communications and Electronics Association.

KIRTLAND, R.R. 1981: " 'Weather Trauma' of '70s and '80s Normal Historically, U.S. Climatologist Says," *Los Angeles Times* I-A:5, 13 March.

KLOCK, P. 1982: "Winery Shuts Down Boiler and Cogenerates Power," *Electrical Consultant,* pp. 14–21, January/February.

KNEESE, A.V. 1973: "The Faustian Bargain," *Resources* **44**:1, September, Resources for the Future, Washington DC 20036.

KNIGHT, M. 1981: "Fuel Shortage Disrupts Life in Massachusetts Town," *New York*

Times, p. 1, 13 January.

KNOX, R. 1977: *New Scientist* **73**:458.

KOLATA, G. 1982: "Students Discover Computer Threat," *Science* **215**:1216–1217.

KOMANOFF, C. 1981: *Power Plant Cost Escalation,* Komanoff Energy Associates, 333 West End Ave, New York NY 10023.

KOSTENMAYER, P.H., & MARKEY, E.J. 1980: 4 June letter to Chairman Ahearne, U.S. Nuclear Regulatory Commission, from Congressman Kostenmayer's office, USHR.

KOSTER, F. 1978: "Why People Don't Listen to Warnings / With Discussion of Implications for Futurists," University of Massachusetts manuscript, 3 April, from Mr. Koster, 2341 Cedar Shore Circle, Jacksonville FL 32210.

KOVEN, R. 1981: "Baghdad Blocks Inspection of Its Nuclear Reactors," *Washington Post,* p. A1, 7 September.

KRAUSE, F. 1981: "The Industrial Economy—An Energy Barrel Without a Bottom?", Second International Conference on Soft Energy Paths, January, Rome; available from IPSEP, 1045 Sansome St, San Francisco CA 94111.

KUPPERMAN, R., & TRENT, D. 1980: *Terrorism: Threat, Reality, Response,* Hoover Institution Press, Stanford University.

LADISCH, M.R. *et al.* 1978: "Cellulose to sugars: new path gives quantitative yield," *Science* **201**:743–745.

LADOMATOS, N., LUCAS, N.J.D., MURGATROYD, W., & WILKINS, B.C. 1979: "Industrial Energy Use—III. The Prospects for Providing Motive Power in a Machine Tool Shop from a Centralized Hydraulic System," *Energy Research* **3**:19–28.

—1980: "Energy Use in Industry—V. Energy Use in a Heavy Engineering Workshop," *id.* **4**:377–383.

LAMBERT, B.K. 1976: "Electric Power Systems Vulnerability Methodology," August final report to Defense Civil Preparedness Agency, Work Unit #4334B, Defense Electric Power Administration, Dept. of the Interior.

— & MINOR, J.E. 1973: "Vulnerability of Regional Electric Power Systems to Nuclear Weapons Effects," May final report to Defense Civil Preparedness Agency, Work Unit #4334B, Defense Electric Power Administration.

—1975: "Vulnerability of Regional and Local

Electric Power Systems: Nuclear Weapons Effects and Civil Defense Actions," July final report to Defense Civil Preparedness Agency, Work Unit #4334B, Accession #AD-A-014431, Defense Electric Power Administration.

LAMPORT, L. 1978: "The Implementation of Reliable Distributed Multiprocess Systems," *Computer Networks* **2**(2):95–114, June.

LANDSBAUM, M. 1981: "First Backyard Power Plant Set Up," *Los Angeles Times*, p. I:1, 2 July.

LARUE, S. 1981: "Cogeneration May Be New Wave in Energy Efficiency," *San Diego Union*, pp. A1 & A3, 26 December.

LATIN AMERICA 1978: p. 86, 17 March.

LEADER, L. 1981: "The day S.F. was held for $100 million ransom," *San Francisco Examiner*, pp. 1 & A20, 24 July.

LECKIE, J., MASTERS, G., WHITEHOUSE, H., & YOUNG, L. 1981: *More Other Homes and Garbage*, Sierra Club, San Francisco.

LECREN, E.D., KIPLING, C., & McCORMACK, J.C. 1972: "Windermere: Effects of Exploitation and Eutrophication on the Salmonic Community," *Journal of the Fisheries Research Board of Canada* **29**:819–832.

LEE, S.T., & YAMAYEE, Z.A. 1980: "Load-Following and Spinning-Reserve Penalties for Intermittent Generation," paper #80 SM 582-7 to IEEE Power Engineering Society meeting, 13–18 July, Minneapolis.

LEGER, E.H., & DUTT, E.S. 1979: "An Affordable Solar House," 4th National Passive Solar Conference, Kansas City; available from Vista Homes, PO Box 95, E. Pepperell MA 01437.

LEHNER, U.C. 1980: "In Japan, Car Owners Think Even Smaller When Gas Costs Rise," *Wall Street Journal*, p. 32, 14 October.

LEICESTER, R.J., NEWMAN, V.G., & WRIGHT, J.K. 1978: "Renewable energy sources and storage," *Nature* **272**:518–521.

LEITENBERG, M. 1969: "Accidents of Nuclear Weapons and Nuclear Weapon Delivery Systems," in *Yearbook of World Armaments and Disarmament, 1968/69*, Stockholm International Peace Research Institute, Humanities Press, New York.

LE MONDE 1978: numerous articles, p. 1, 20 December.

—1978a: numerous articles, p. 39, 21–22 December.

LERNER, E.J. 1981: "Electromagnetic pulses: potential crippler," *IEEE Spectrum*, pp. 41–46, May.

—1981a: "EMPs and nuclear power," *IEEE Spectrum*, pp. 48–49, June.

LERNER, H.A., GRIGSBY, J.W., & JOHNSON, J.M. 1967: "Vulnerability of the Local Petroleum Distribution System: San Jose, California," Checchi & Co., Washington DC 20006.

LEVIN, S.A. 1974: "Dispersion and Population Interactions," *American Naturalist* **108**:207–228.

LEWIS, F. 1979: "France Blacks Out News on Blast At Plant Building Atomic Reactors," *New York Times*, p. A19, 11 April.

LEWIS, W. 1979a: comment at 16 in *The National Grid: A Solution Or a Problem?*, Power Engineering Society, IEEE, Piscataway NJ 08854.

LIFTON, R.J. 1967: *Death in Life: The Survivors of Hiroshima*, Random House, New York.

LINDEN, H.R. 1981: *U.S. Energy Outlook— 1981*, October, Gas Research Institute, Chicago.

LINDERS, J.R. 1979: "Electric Wave Distortions: Their Hidden Costs and Containment," *IEEE Transactions on Industry Applications* **IE-15**:458ff.

LINDSTRÖM, O. 1979: "Bio-fuels make Sweden independent of oil and nuclear energy," October, Dept. of Chemical Technology, Royal Swedish Institute of Technology, 10044 Stockholm.

LIPINSKY, E.S. 1981: "Chemicals From Biomass: Petrochemical Substitution Options," *Science* **212**:1465–1471.

LORENZ, E.N. 1976: "Nondeterministic Theories of Climate Change," *Quarternary Research* **6**:495ff.

LORIN, H. 1979: "Distributed processing: An assessment," *IBM Systems Journal* **18**(4):582–603.

LOS ANGELES ENERGY MANAGEMENT ADVISORY BOARD 1981: *The Energy/LA Action Plan*, July, Energy Office, Office of the Mayor, Room 1401, MS376, City Hall, Los Angeles CA 90012.

LOS ANGELES TIMES 1973: "Sailor Found Not Guilty of Sabotage," p. I:18, 13 June.

—1974: "Radioactive Plates Stolen From Lab," 3 October.

—1974a: "Radioactive Needle Sought After

Theft Suspect Is Arrested," 28 November.
—1974b: "Security officer. . .," p. I:2, 24 April.
—1976: "Explanation for A-Plant Alert Sought," 1 June.
—1978: "Strike-Related Sabotage Continued in Coalfields," p. I:5, 21 February.
—1978a: "Bomb Detonator Fails; Coal Mine Escapes Blast," p. I:5, 21 February.
—1978b: "Chlorine Deaths Laid to Sabotage," p. I:1, 4 March.
—1979: "High winds caused the . . .," p. I:2, 9 February.
—1979a: "PLO May Block Key Waterway, Arafat Hints," p. I:8, 4 July.
—1979b: "The State Department . . .," p. I:2, 20 July.
—1979c: "Pipeline in Iranian Arab Province Blown Up; Incidents 2nd in 4 Days," p. I:8, 12 July.
—1979d: "6 Sought in $50,000 Blaze at Long Beach Oil Plant," p. II:2, 31 August.
—1979e: "Underground Group Says It Blew Up Power Lines to Sections of Uganda," p. I:13, 6 February.
—1979f: "A-Plant Sabotage Attempt Suspected," 23 December.
—1979g: "Saboteurs struck . . .," p. I:2, 1 October.
—1979h: "Derailment of Train Blamed on Sabotage," pp. II:1 & :3, 9 October.
—1979i: "With no new talks . . .," p. I:2, 4 September.
—1979j: "Twenty-year-old John Woods . . .," p. I:2, 2 November.
—1980: "Rising U.S. Demand for Oil Will Stabilize, Panel Says," p. IV:2, 11 December.
—1980a: "Divers with television . . .," p. I:2, 24 August.
—1980b: "Iran Threatens Western Nations With Oil Reprisal," p. I:2, 16 January.
—1980c: "Blasts in S. Africa Rip 3 Refineries," p. I:1, 2 June.
—1980d: "Oil Firm Sabotaged," p. I:1, 12 August.
—1980e: "Saboteurs Blast Iran Oil Depot, Attack Patrol," p. I:2, 11 June.
—1981: "Be Prepared," lead editorial, II:10, 12 February.
—1981a: "Strike Will Force Britain to Close Airspace Monday," Reuters story, p. I:4, 7 March.

—1981b: "Alcohol Fuel Tank Explodes in Brazil," p. I:3, 7 March.
—1981c: "The lower Florida keys . . .," p. I:2, col. 4, 4 March.
—1981d: "Suspected radicals . . .," p. I:2, 17 March.
—1981e: "All power . . .," p. I-2, col. 2, 16 April.
—1981f: "$6.5-Million Threat Empties N.J. Casino," p. I:4, 9 March.
—1981g: "Blast Disrupts S. African City," p. I:2, 22 April.
—1981h: "2 in A-Plant Incident Seized in Miami with Bomb," p. I:14, 15 April.
—1981i: "Troops Secure Bolivian Plant," p. I:29, 5 May.
—1981j: "Californians used less . . .," p. I:2, 16 April.
—1981k: "Cold Raises Demand for Oil; First Hike in Nearly 2 Years," p. I:16, 21 February.
—1981m: "Rebels Reportedly Move Toward Key Salvadorean Dam," p. I:9, 20 March.
—1981n: "Israeli power . . .," p. I:2, 27 May.
—1981o: "10,000-Gallon Fuel Spill Closes Bridge," p. I:22, 13 October.
—1981p: "2,800 Flee Explosion in Japan," p. I:2, 14 October.
—1981q: "Iran Accused of Air Attack on Major Kuwaiti Oil Installations," p. I:9, 2 October.
—1981r: "New Mideast Dangers Feared," p. I:1, 9 June.
—1981s: "Angola's state. . .," p. I:2, 14 December.
—1981t: "Sabotage could have . . .," p. I:2, 20 December.
—1981u: "Fierce Winter Storms Cause Chaos in Britain," p. I:4, 14 December.
—1981v: "River Reopened as Barge Burns," p. I:8, 12 December.
—1981w: "Saboteurs set fire . . .," p. I:2, 2 December.
—1981x: "Puerto Rico's Macheteros . . .," p. I:2, 29 November.
—1981y: "Nearly 100 utility companies . . .," p. I:2, 1 December.
—1981z: "Vermont Residents Favor Wood for Winter Heating," p. X:15, 26 November.
—1981aa: "Home Furnaces Proposed as Power Plants," p. VIII:3, 26 November.
—1981bb: "El Salvador's. . .," p. I:2, 25

December.

—1981cc: "A boiler-room fire . . .," p. I:2, 28 December.

—1981dd: "Computer Crimes Costs Predicted," pp. IA:2, 26 December.

—1981ee: "Motorists Switch Cars to Liquid Petroleum Gas," p. IA:2, 26 December.

—1981ff: "Explosions Wreck Iranian Oil & Gas Pipelines," p. I:20, 20 May.

—1981gg: "Sabotage in S. Africa," p. I:1, 21 July; see also p. I:2, 22 July.

—1981hh: "Controversial Tokyo Airport," p. I:14, 12 May.

—1981ii: "Saboteurs Blast French Drilling Rig," p. I:6, 11 September.

—1981jj: "Geologists Find Big Crack Across Face of America," p. I:1 & :9, 17 December.

—1982: "Lebanese oil . . .," p. I:2, 4 January.

—1982a: "An Iraqi oil . . .," p. I:2, 8 January.

—1982b: "Rockets Hit French Atom Plant Project," p. I:1, 19 January.

—1982c: "Leftist guerrillas . . .," p. I:2, 27 January.

—1982d: "Saudi Arabia. . .," p. I:2, 27 January.

—1982e: "Dozens of Fires Flare Up in Town as Gas Main Breaks," p. I:1, late final edition, 28 January.

—1982f: "A bag of marijuana . . .," p. I:2, 4 February.

—1982g: "Greenpeace of Chicago Staged 'Nuclear' Attack," p. I:25, 30 January.

—1982h: "Salvadorean troops . . .," p. I:2, 7 February.

—1982i: "The Red Brigades . . .," p. I:2, 7 February.

—1982j: "Red Brigades Terrorists Seize Weapons in Raid," p. I:4, 10 February.

—1982k: "Between $78. . .," p. I:2, 2 February.

—1982m: "IRA 'Pirates' Seize, Destroy British Ship," p. I:11, 24 February.

—1982n: "Two Brown University . . .," p. I:2, 24 February.

—1982o: "California drivers . . .," *id.*

LOVINS, A.B. 1973: *Openpit Mining*, Earth Island Ltd. (London); available from FOE, 1045 Sansome St, San Francisco CA 94111.

—1977: "Cost-Risk-Benefit Assessments in Energy Policy," *45 George Washington Law Review* 911–943, August.

—1977a: "Resilience in Energy Policy," op-ed, *The New York Times*, 24 July, IV:17.

—1977b: *Soft Energy Paths: Toward a Durable Peace*, Ballinger, Cambridge MA 02138; republished 1979, Harper & Row (Colophon paperback), New York.

—1978: "Soft Energy Technologies," *Annual Review of Energy* **3**:477–517.

—1978a: "Lovins on Energy Costs," *Science* **201**:1077–1078.

—1979: "Is 'Red Tape' a Code Word for Law?", *The Washington Post*, op-ed, 3 August.

—1979a: "Energy: Bechtel Cost Data," *Science* **204**:124–129.

—1980: "Nuclear Weapons and Power-Reactor Plutonium," *Nature* **283**:817–823 and typographical corrections *id.* **284**:190.

—1980a: "Democracy and the Energy Mobilization Board," *Not Man Apart*, pp. 14–15, February, Friends of the Earth, San Francisco.

—1981: "Electric Utility Investments: *Excelsior* or Confetti?", March 1979 E.F. Hutton paper, reprinted in *Journal of Business Administration* **12**(2): 91–114, spring 1981, Vancouver.

—1981a: Supplementary information provided for the record, 3 April 1981 hearings, *Energy Production vs. Energy Efficiency in the Utility Industry*, Subcommittee on Energy Conservation & Power, Committee on Commerce, USHR.

—1981b: 1 January letter to Hon. David Stockman, reprinted in *Congressional Record* E2512, 21 May.

—1981c: surrebuttal testimony to Pennsylvania Public Utility Commission, Limerick Investigation, 14 August, docket #I-80100341.

—1982: "How To Keep Electric Utilities Solvent," *The Energy Journal*, International Association of Energy Economists (Tucson), in press.

— & LOVINS, L.H. 1980: *Energy/War: Breaking the Nuclear Link*, Friends of the Earth, San Francisco, and Harper & Row Colophon paperback, 1981.

—1980a: "Reagan's Energy Policy: Conservative or Ultraliberal?", *Washington Post* op-ed, p. A21, 24 November.

—1981: see LOVINS, L.H., & LOVINS, A.B. 1981, below.

—1981a: "What Is the Energy Problem?," paper to September Paris colloquium of the Groupe de Bellerive (122 rue de Lausanne, 1202 Geneva), in press, reprinted in *The Ecologist* [UK] **11**(6):302–313, December.

—1981b: *Energy Policies for Resilience and National Security*, final report to the President's Council on Environmental Quality for the Federal Emergency Management Agency, released 13 November, Contract #DCPA-01-79-C-0317, FEMA Work Unit 4351C, Defense Technical Information Center accession #A108263.

—1982: "Electric Utilities: Key to Capitalizing the Energy Transition," Mitchell Prize essay, The Woodlands Conferences, The Woodlands, Texas, in press.

LOVINS, A.B. & L.H., KRAUSE, F., & BACH, W. 1982: *Least-Cost Energy: Solving the CO_2 Problem*, Brick House Publ. Co., 34 Essex St., Andover MA 01810.

LOVINS, A.B., & PRICE, J.H. 1975: *Non-Nuclear Futures: The Case for an Ethical Energy Strategy*, Harper & Row Colophon, New York, 1980.

LOVINS, L.H. & A.B. 1981: "Biomass fuels: Options and Obstacles," typescript to be published, available from IPSEP, 1045 Sansome St, San Francisco CA 94111.

LUBENOW, G.C. 1981: "Saying Aloha to Oil," *Newsweek*, p. 79, 28 September.

LYONS, R.D. 1981: "Illegal Hookup: Silent Foe of a Cable Television Line," *New York Times*, p. B1, 3 August.

MACARTHUR, R.H. 1972: *Geographical Ecology*, Harper & Row, New York.

MACHALABA, D. 1979: "Cutting the cord: Idea of Producing Own Power Intrigues Many Companies; Utilities Are Alarmed," *Wall Street Journal*, p. 46, 1 March.

MAGIDA, A.J. 1981:" 'District Heating' Being Reborn in U.S.," *Los Angeles Times*, p. IA:7, 31 October.

MAINE OFFICE OF ENERGY RESOURCES 1980: *Maine Solar Architecture: A Building Inventory*, State House, Station #53, Augusta ME 04333.

MAIZE, K. 1980: "Why DOD Wants $5.4 Billion More for Fuel," *Defense Week*, p. 15, 7 April.

MALNIC, E. 1981: "Contaminated Eye and Nose Products Found at Five Stores," *Los Angeles Times*, p. II:1 & 12, 12 December.

MANLY, R.P., LERNER, H.A., & GRIGSBY, J.W. 1970: "Petroleum Distribution, Gross National Product, and System Vulnerability: Methods of Analysis," report 5D-11101-4361B-04 to Office of Civil Defense, Office of Secretary of the Army, OCD Work Unit 4361B, by Checchi & Co., Washington DC 20006.

MANNED SPACEFLIGHT CENTER 1970: *Apollo 13 Mission Report*, MSC-02680, September, National Aeronautics & Space Administration, Houston.

—1970a: *Apollo 13 Cryogenic Oxygen Tank 2 Anomaly Report*, MSC-02545, June, *id.*

MARCHETTI, C. 1975: "Geoengineering and the energy island," at pp. 220–244 in W. Häfele, ed., *Second Status Report on the IIASA Project on Energy Systems*, RR-76-1, International Institute for Applied Systems Analysis, Laxenburg, Austria.

MARGEN, P. 1980: "Economics of Solar District Heating," *Sunworld* **4**(4): 128–134 (Pergamon).

MARSHALL, E. 1980: "Planning for an Oil Cutoff," *Science* **209**:246–247.

—1980a: "Iraqi Nuclear Program Halted by Bombing," *id.* **210**:507–508.

—1981: "Solving Louisville's Friday the 13th Explosion," *id.* **211**:1405.

—1981a: "Utilities Lose Power on Wall Street," *id.* **211**:461–464.

—1981b: "Nuclear Fuel Account Books in Bad Shape," *id.* **211**:147–150.

—1981c: "United States Objects to Soviet Gas Deal," *id.* **214**:1004–1005.

—1981d: "Fallout from the Raid on Iraq," *id.* **213**:116–117 & 120.

—1982: "Super Phenix Unscathed in Rocket Attack," *id.* **215**:641.

MARTER, W.L. 1963: "Radioiodine Release Incident at the Savannah River Plant," *Health Physics* **9**:1105–1109.

MARTIN, D. 1981: "Oil Industry Hurt By Drop in Demand," *New York Times*, pp. D1 & D6, 31 March.

—1981a: "With Fall's Fuel Bounty The Forecast Is 'Pleasant'," *id.*, p. E7, 4 October.

MASSELLI, D.C., & DEAN, N.L. JR. 1981: *The Impacts of Synthetic Fuels Development*, National Wildlife Federation, 1412 16th St NW, Washington DC 20036.

MAY, R.M. 1976: "Simple mathematical models with very complicated dynamics," *Nature* **261**:459–466.

MAYCOCK, P. 1981: briefing to energy Research Advisory Board, U.S. Department of Energy, 5 February, from official transcript.

—& STIREWALT, E.N. 1981: *Photovoltaics: Sunlight to Electricity in One Step*, Brick House, Andover MA 01810.

McCLURE, R. 1981: "Palo Alto encourages Solar Energy," pp. 11–13, *Solar Energy: Northern California Solar Energy Association Newsletter*, March.

McCOLM, B., & SMITH, D. 1977: "Guerrillas Growing Threat in Angola," *Washington Post*, pp. A1 & A10, 8 January.

McCULLOUGH, C.R., TURNER, S.E., & LYERLY, R.L. 1968: *An Appraisal of the Potential Hazard of Industrial Sabotage in Nuclear Power Plants*, SNE 51, July, Southern Nuclear Engineering, Inc. report to U.S. Atomic Energy Commission.

McISACC, D., ed. 1976: *United States Strategic Bombing Survey*, Garland, New York.

McLELLAN, V. 1981: "Case of the Purloined Password," *New York Times*, p. F4, 26 July.

McNARY, D. 1981: "Photovoltaics: A Small Boom in Home Systems," *Solar Age*, pp. 48–49, August.

McPHEE, J. 1981: "Reporter at Large: Minihydro," *The New Yorker*, pp. 44ff, 23 February.

—1981a: "Our Far-Flung Correspondents: Ice Pond," *id.*, pp. 92ff, 13 July.

McRAE, G. 1981: "Building a Solar Network in Philadelphia," *New Roots*, pp. 34–37, Holiday.

MEADOWS 1981: "OPEC Ministers Will Have Many Middle East Topics to Discuss in Abu Dhabi," *The Oil Daily*, pp. 1 & 6–7, 7 December, at 7.

MEISLIN, R.J. 1981: "Computers Lose Data Capability in Power Failure," *New York Times*, p. B9, 10 September.

—1981a: "City Is Urged to Reconsider Building 3d Water Tunnel," *id.*, p. 26, 2 August.

MERRILL LYNCH 1981: "The Outlook for Alternative Generation: Financial Techniques in Public Power," Utility Research Group, Merrill Lynch, Pierce, Fenner & Smith, Inc., New York, September.

MESSING, M., FRIESEMA, H.P., & MORRELL, D. 1979: *Centralized Power: The Politics of Scale in Electricity Generation*, Oelgeschlager, Gunn & Hain, Publishers, Cambridge MA 02138.

METROPOLITAN DADE COUNTY 1980: "Energy Contingency Management Workshops for Local Government Officials: Concept Paper," 10 November submission to Emergency Conservation Programs, U.S. Dept. of Energy, by Office of Energy Management, Suite 2302, 44 W. Flagler St., Miami FL 33130.

—1980a: "Compendium of Energy Management Activities," from same address.

METZ, W.D. 1977: "New York Blackout: Weak Links Tie Con Ed to Neighboring Utilities," *Science* **197**:441–442, 29 July.

—1978: "Energy Storage and Solar Power: An Exaggerated Problem," *id.* **200**:1471–1473.

—& HAMMOND, A.L. 1978: *Solar Energy in America*, American Association for the Advancement of Science, Washington DC.

MEYER, J., & SIEBEN, C. 1982: "Super Saskatoon," *Solar Age*, pp. 26–32, January.

MIAMI HERALD 1981: "Power firms worried," p. 1ff, 30 March.

—1981a: p.VI:22, 6 April.

MIDDLETON, D. 1976: "Britain Prepared to Use Warships To Protect Oil Fields in North Sea," *New York Times*, p. 2, 30 December.

MIEHER, S. 1980: "Power Plants Suffer Shell Shock as Clams Begin to Mussel In," *The Wall Street Journal*, p. 1, 12 August.

MILLER, VICE-ADM. G.E. 1979: "Existing Systems of Command and Control," at pp. 50–66 in Griffiths, F., & Polanyi, J.C., eds., *The Dangers of Nuclear War*, Pugwash Symposium, University of Toronto Press.

MILSTEIN, J.S. 1978: "Soft and Hard Energy Paths: What People on the Street Think," March unpublished internal report, Office of Conservation and Solar Applications, U.S. Dept. of Energy, Washington DC 20461.

MOGLEWER, S. 1981: "IAEA safeguards and non-proliferation," *Bulletin of the Atomic Scientists*, pp. 24–29, October.

MOOZ, W. 1978: "Cost Analysis of Light Water Reactors," R–2304–DOE, RAND Corporation, Santa Monica CA 90406.

—1979: "A Second Cost Analysis of Light Water Reactors," R–2504–RC, RAND Corp.

MORELAND, W.B.1979: "Energy and National

Security: A Question of Mobility Fuels for the Military," August, Energy & National Security Project, Ohio State University, Columbus.

—& BUCKNELL H. III 1978: "Energy and National Security: Implications for the Future," Spring *Quarterly Report,* Mershon Center, Ohio State University.

MORK, K.A., & HALL, R.E. 1980: "Energy Prices and the U.S. Economy in 1979–1981," *The Energy Journal* 1(2):41–53.

—1980a: "Energy Prices, Inflation and Recession, 1974–75," *id.* (3):31–63.

MORRIS, D. 1979: *Planning for Energy Self-Reliance: A Case Study of the District of Columbia; Baltimore: Solar and Conservation Potential by the Year 2000,* Institute for Local Self-Reliance, 1717 18th St NW, Washington DC 20009.

—1980: "Putting It All Together: The City As Energy Planner," at Vol. 3.2, pp. 1166–1174, in *Proceedings of the 1980 Annual Meeting,* American Section of the International Solar Energy Society, Killeen TX.

—1981: address at 113–122 in *Energy Utilities: The Next 10 Years,* California Public Utilities Commission, San Francisco.

MORRIS, W.S., & REINIGER, C. 1982: "New Mexico Solar Greenhouse Study," *Passive Solar Journal* 1(1), in press, January.

MORRISON, D.L. *et al.* 1971: "An Evaluation of the Applicability of Existing Data to the Analytical Description of a Nuclear-Reactor Accident—Core Meltdown Evaluation," BMI–1910, U.S. Atomic Energy Commission.

MORRISON, J.W. 1979: *The Complete Energy-Saving Handbook for Homeowners,* Harper & Row, New York.

MORTON, S. 1980: "City Housing: Superinsulation, Community Heat," *Whole Life Times,* September/October.

MOSTERT, N. 1974: *Supership,* Knopf, New York.

MURNANE, T. 1980: "Walnut Shells Fuel Firm's Cogeneration," *Energy User News,* p. 7, 1 December.

—1980a: "Boeing Waste Plant to Supply Steam Needs," *ibid.,* p. 10, 27 October.

MURRAY, I. 1981: "Vision of computer-enslaved world," *Times,* p. 6, 29 January, London.

MEYERS, N. 1981: "The Exhausted Earth," *Foreign Policy,* Spring (#41), pp. 141–155.

NARVAEZ, A.A. 1981: "Chemical Fire in Newark Rail Car Routs Hundreds and Jams Traffic," *New York Times,* pp. A1 & B4, 28 July.

NATIONAL ACADEMY OF SCIENCES 1972: *Genetic Vulnerability of Major Crops,* NAS, Washington DC.

—1975: *Effects of Multiple Nuclear Explosions Worldwide,* NAS, Washington DC.

NATIONAL AERONAUTICS & SPACE ADMINISTRATION 1976: "Energy Management Multiyear Action Plan," NASA HQ BX77, January.

NATIONAL LEAGUE OF CITIES 1981: *Financing Local Energy Programs: A Resource Guide for Local Officials,* September, NLC with the National Community Energy Management Center, Washington DC.

NELSON, D.B. 1971: "A Program to Counter the Effects of Nuclear Electromagnetic Pulse in Commercial Power Systems," ORNL–TM–3552, August, Oak Ridge National Laboratory, Oak Ridge TN.

NELSON, G. 1981: "Greywater Heat Recovery," *Solar Age,* pp. 50–53, August.

NERC (National Electric Reliability Council) 1979: *1978 Annual Report,* NERC, Research Park, Terhune Rd, Princeton NJ 08540.

NEVIN, R.L. 1969: "Vulnerability of the Albuquerque Water Supply System," Stanford Research Institute, Menlo Park CA 94025.

NEW ROOTS: from PO Box 548, Greenfield MA 01301.

NEWSWEEK 1977: "Heart of Darkness," pp. 16–30, 25 July.

—1978: "Night of Terror," p. 18, 20 February.

—1979: "Yamani on Oil—and Israel," p. 21, 9 July.

—1981: "A Solar Energy Breakthrough," p. 68, 7 September.

—1981a: cover story on Israeli raid on Osirak, pp. 20–33, 22 June.

—1981b: " 'Not Winning Is Losing'," pp. 63–64, 23 November.

—1981c: p. 21, 14 September.

NEW YORK TIMES 1969: "Saboteurs Halt Power to Settlements in Negev," p. 15, 6 July.

—1970: p. 1 col. 5 and p. 56 col. 4, 27 January.

—1970a: "Three Explosions Damage an Army

Base in Wisconsin," p. 39, 27 July.
—1970b: UPI story, p. 39, col. 2, 27 July.
—1972: "Power In Lisbon Is Cut By Blasts," p. 5, 10 August.
—1973: "Strike in Puerto Rico Reduces Electricity and Water Service," p. 44, 10 July.
—1973a: "One of Two Major Strikes Is Ended in Puerto Rico," p. 18, 11 July.
—1973b: "Chile Reports 5 Men Killed In Attack on Power Line," p. 5, 23 December.
—1974: "Coast Couple Plead Guilty in Bomb Plot," p. 50, 14 November.
—1974a: p. 67, 10 November.
—1974b: p. 15, 21 October.
—1975: "Two Blasts Damage Rockefeller Banks," p. 36, 1 January.
—1975a: " 'Wanted' Fugitive Arrested," p. 50, 13 March.
—1975b: "Refinery Picketing Quiet," p. 31, 30 January.
—1975c: "Flow of Oil from North Sea Into Britain Is Inaugurated by Queen," pp. 47 & 49, 4 November.
—1975d: "Dublin Embarrassed By I.R.A. Jailbreak Attempt," p. 2, 19 March.
—1976: p. 16, 21 November.
—1977: "India Tightens Security After Suspected Sabotage," p. 6, 28 November.
—1977a: "Alaska Pipeline Sabotage Held Impossible to Stop," p. 10, 11 March.
—1977b: "Ex-Pentagon Researcher Says the Army Waged Mock Attack on Nixon," p. 10, 11 March.
—1977c: "Fire Halts Oil Flow in Major Saudi Line," pp. 1 & 5, 13 May.
—1977d: "Alaskan Pipeline Leak Attributed to Sabotage," p. 16, 21 September.
—1977e: "Conviction Reversed for Antiwar Activist in Power Line Blast," p. 8, 7 May.
—1978: "Power Blackout spreads Disruption Across France," p. 2, 20 December.
—1978a: "French Power Failure's Cost Is Estimated at $1 Billion," p. 10, 21 December.
—1978b: "Smith Calls Oil Sabotage A Setback for Rhodesia," World News Briefs, 14 December, AP story.
—1978c: "A Fiery Setback For Smith Regime," p. 2E, 17 December.
—1978d: "Bomb Blasts Knock Out Power in San Juan," p. A10, 20 January.
—1978e: "San Juan Electrical Union Votes to End Long Strike," p. 20, 20 April.

—1978f: "Prime Minister Links Iranian Strife to 'Saboteurs,' Not True Moslems," p. 12, 6 December.
—1979: "Defendent in Sabotage Case Says Action Was Worth a Prison Term," p. A18, 18 October.
—1979a: "Guards Charge Security Is Lax at Indian Point," p. B2, 17 October.
—1979b: "U.S. Sells Booklets on A-Plant Security," p. II:16, 29 November.
—1979c: "Oil Insurance," p. 22, 29 August; see also "Lloyd's of London," *Los Angeles Times*, p. I:2, 27 September.
—1979d: "Saboteurs Blow Up Four Iranian Oil Pipelines," p. A6, 19 October.
—1979e: "Envoy tells Uneasy Americans in Saudi Arabia They'll Be Safe," p. A20, 6 December.
—1980: "Most of Israel Is Struck By Power Breakdown," p. A8, 4 June.
—1980a: "Iran Expects More Oilfield Sabotage," p. A12, 10 March, Reuters.
—1980b: "Judge Won't Bar Nuclear Articles," p. A19, 5 February.
—1980c: "Largest Nuclear Utility in Nation Indicted on Breaches of Security," p. 1, 27 March.
—1980d: "A Power Surge Caused Puerto Rico Blackout, Governor Announces," 16 April.
—1980e: "Afghan Regime Said to Broaden Its Base by Including Past Foes," p. 4, 13 March.
—1980f: "Senate Passes Bill on Nuclear Safety," p. IV:17, 17 June.
—1980g: "Iraq Reported to Halt Oil Deliveries through Pipelines to Mediterranean," p. 10, 19 December.
—1980h: "Oil Installations in Northern Iraq Are Said to Be Sabotage Targets," p. 14, 14 September.
—1980i: "Oil Output in Iran Falls Again," p. 27, 8 March.
—1980j: "Iran Pipeline Explodes, Cutting Gas to Soviet," p. 10, 24 February.
—1981: "Power Failure in 3 Western States Closes Schools, Stores and Offices," p. 12, 9 January.
—1981a: "Radiation Poisoning Kills a Former Radiographer," p. A12, 30 July.
—1981b: "Fuel Shortage Afflicts Lebanese," p. A3, 7 August.
—1981c: "Atomic Workers Expected to Ratify

Pact, Ending Strike," p. A17, 6 August.
—1981d: "Fires Set by Extremists Still Burning in Greece," p. A6, 6 August.
—1981e: "Gas Fire Forces Evacuation of Jersey town," p. B2, 6 August.
—1981f: "Power Disrupted in England," p. A21, 6 August.
—1981g: "Power Cut to 1,400 in Jersey," p. A12, 10 August.
—1981h: "Thousands Evacuated After Coast Gas Line Bursts," p. A17, 26 August.
—1981i: "South African Power Plant Bombed," p. A3, 22 July.
—1981j: "Cat Cuts Off Managua Power," 29 August.
—1981k: "Wary of Fuel Prices, Vermonters Heading for the Woodsheds," p. 73, 4 October.
—1981m: Iran Says It Bombed Iraqi Hydroelectric Plant," p. A2, 20 July.
—1981n: "Jurors Screened in Trial of Nazis On North Carolina Bombing Plot," p. A23, 14 July.
—1981o: "Barge Shipping Resumes Around Collapsed Spans," p. A14, 1 July.
—1981p: "Guerrillas Attempt to Blow Up Santiago Oil and Gas Plants," p. A2, 20 July.
—1981q: "New Orleans Blackout Halts Electrical Service to 250,000," p. A6, 20 July.
—1981r: " 'Mini-Car' Deal Entered by G.M., Suzuki, Isuzu," p. 25, 13 August.
—1981s: "German Oil Use Down," p. D16, 6 October.
—1981t: "Oil Cleanup," p. IV:3, 3 November.
—1981u: "Bomb Explodes in San Juan," p. A13, 12 November.
—1981v: "Power Failure in El Salvador Blacks Out a Third of Country," p. 8, 5 November.
—1981w: "Paper Links Saboteurs to Raid on Iraqi A-Plant," p. 5, 12 October (quoting the London *Sunday Times* of the same date).
—1982: "Edwards Says 'Bad Oil' Could Be in Reserve," p. A14, 6 April.
NIELSEN, C.E. 1980: "Nonconvective Salt Gradient Solar Ponds," at 30–31 July Non-Convecting Solar Pond Workshop, Desert Research Institute, University of Nevada; obtainable from author at Physics Department, Ohio State University, Columbus.
NØRGÅRD, J.S. 1979: *Husholdninger og Energi*, Polyteknisk Forlaget, København (in Danish); English translation unpublished, U.S.

Dept. of Energy. See also the popularization by Nørgård, J.S., & Christensen, B.L., Energihusholdning / Husholdning / Holdning, 1982, Faellesforeningen for Danmarks Brugsforeninger, 2620 Albertslund.
—1979a: "Improved Efficiency in Domestic Appliances," *Energy Policy* [UK], March, pp. 43–56.
NORMAN, L. 1981: "Renewable Power Sparks Financial Interest," *Science* **212**:479–481.
NORTON, A.R. 1979: "Terrorists, Atoms and the Future: Understanding the threat," *Naval War College Review* **460**:6ff, 30 August.
NOTKIN, J.T. 1982: "Solar and Energy Conservation Zoning Incentives in Richmond, B.C.: The Carrot Versus the Stick," in press in *Proceedings of the 1982 Annual Meeting*, American Section of the International Solar Energy Society, Killeen TX.
NOT MAN APART 1981: "Man Irradiates Boss, Gets Stay on Sentence," p. 5, June.
NRC: see Nuclear Regulatory Commission.
NUCLEAR ENGINEERING INTERNATIONAL 1974: p. 11, January.
—1974a: "Fiddling the figures," p. 123, March.
NUCLEAR NEWS 1975: "Cesium sources stolen, found; damage reported," p. 59, February.
NUCLEAR REGULATORY COMMISSION 1975: *Reactor Safety Study*, WASH–1400 / NUREG–75/014, October.
—1976: "NRC Staff Cites Pennsylvania Utility for Noncompliance with Physical Security Requirements; Proposes Fine," Press Release 76–64, 17 March.
—1976a: *Report to Congress on Abnormal Occurrences*, January–March 1976, NUREG–0090–3.
—1976b: *Nuclear Energy Center Site Survey—1975*, NUREG–0001, January.
—1978: "Preliminary Notification of Safeguards Event," PNS–78–03, 13 January.
—1979: *Safeguards Summary Event List (SSEL)*, NUREG–0525.
—1981: Press release 81–121, 6 August.
NUCLEONICS WEEK 1981: "An Antinuclear Demonstration. . . ," p. 8, 8 October.
—1981a: "Potassium Iodide Will be Distributed to 30,000 Households Near Sweden's. . . ," p. 10, 10 December.
—1982: "Iberduero Pushes On, Despite Plant Delays and More Terrorist Threats," pp. 9–10, 4 February.

—1982a: "Iberduero Says It Is On Brink Of Terminating Lemoniz," pp. 3–4, 18 February.

—1982b: "In An Apparent Disagreement with the FBI, NRC Has Concluded. . . ," pp. 3–4, 11 February.

NUSSBAUM, P. 1980: "New Tests Set for N–Shields on Navy Ships," *Los Angeles Times*, pp. II:1 & :2, 19 September.

OAKLAND TRIBUNE 1981: "NRC suspected attack after briefing Israeli engineers," UPI story, 20 June, Oakland CA.

OBERG, K. 1981: *Community Energy Cooperatives: How to Organize, Manage and Finance Energy Cooperatives*, Conference on Alternative State and Local Policies (*q.v.*).

O'DONNELL, P. 1981: "Energy Crisis: Fate of Nuclear Power In U.S. Could Depend on Troubled Project," *Wall Street Journal*, p. 1, 8 January.

OFFICE OF TECHNOLOGY ASSESSMENT: see OTA.

OIL DAILY 1981: p. 1, 8 October.

OKAGAKI, A. 1981: "State and Local Solar Energy Policy: Meeting Low-Income Needs," Conference on Alternative State and Local Policies (*q.v.*).

—& BENSON, J. 1979: *County Energy Plan Guidebook: Creating a Renewable Energy Future*," available *id.*

OKRENT, D., & MOELLER, D.W. 1981: "Implications for Reactor Safety of the Accident at Three Mile Island, Unit 2," *Annual Review of Energy* 6:43–88.

OMANG, J. 1981: "Nuclear Energy Subsidy Estimate Slashed by DOE," *Washington Post*, p. A9, 8 April.

—1982: "Nuclear Industry Asks $50 Billion in U.S. Loans," *Washington Post*, p. A1, 4 February.

O'NEAL, D., CORUM, K., & JONES, J. 1981: "An Estimate of Consumer Discount Rates Implicit in Single-Family Housing Construction Practices," ORNL/CON–62, Oak Ridge National Laboratory.

Orange County 1981: *Fuel Shortage Contingency Workshop Proceedings*, Orange County Board of Supervisors and Transportation Commission, 26 June.

O'REILLY, R. 1982: "Wind Energy Plans Weather the Storms," *Los Angeles Times*, pp. II:1ff, 21 February.

ORTEGREN, L. 1981: "Biomass Conversion Technologies," *Science* 214:864.

OTA [Office of Technology Assessment] 1977: *Transportation of Liquefied Natural Gas*, September, OTA, U.S. Congress, Washington DC 20510.

—1977a: *Nuclear Proliferation and Safeguards*, July.

—1978: *Application of Solar Technology to Today's Energy Needs*, 2 vols.

—1979: *Technical Options for Conservation of Metals*, September.

—1979a: *The Effects of Nuclear War*, May, OTA–NS–89.

—1979b: "Case 2: Small Attacks on U.S. and Soviet Energy Production and Distribution Systems," unpublished 27 February working paper for OTA 1979a.

—1980: *Energy From Biological Processes*, 2 vols., OTA–E–128, September.

—1980a: *An Assessment of Oil Shale Technologies*, June.

—1980b: *World Petroleum Availability 1980–2000*, OTA–TM–E–5, October.

—1981: *An Assessment of Technology for Local Development*, OTA–R–129, January.

O'TOOLE, T. 1974: "2 Break-ins Suggest Thieves Eye A-Arms," *Washington Post*, p. A3, 28 July.

—1977: "U.S. Missing Weapons-Grade Uranium," *Washington Post*, p. A–12, 9 August.

—1981: "FBI 'Spiking' Crude Oil Shipments in Effort to Trace Stolen Fuel," *Los Angeles Times*, p. I:16, 17 February.

OTTAWA CITIZEN 1976: "Austrian police nab poison-gas producers," 2 March.

OUWENS, K.D. 1977: "Beschikbaarheids- en belastingsfactoren," April memorandum, from author, Montgomerylaan 481, Eindhoven, The Netherlands.

PACIFIC NORTHWEST LABORATORY 1981: "Preliminary Evaluation of Alternative Ethanol/ Water Separation Processes," summarized in *Alcohol Update*, 27 April.

PALMITER, L. & MILLER, B. 1979: "Report on the October 13–14, 1979 Saskatchewan Conference on Low Energy Passive Housing," National Center for Appropriate Technology, Butte MT 59701.

PALSSON, B.O. *et al.* 1981: "Biomass as a Source of Chemical Feedstocks: An Economic Evaluation," *Science* 213:513–517.

PARISI, A.J. 1981: "Hard Times for Nuclear Power," *New York Times Magazine*, 12 April.

Park, R.H. 1978: "Hardware and software for system protection," *IEEE Spectrum,* pp. 40–45, May.

Park, C.G., & Helliwell, R.A. 1978: "Magnetospheric Effects of Power Line Radiation," *Science* **200**:727–736, 19 May.

Park, J. 1981: *The Wind Power Book,* Cheshire Books, Palo Alto CA 94301.

—& Obermeier, J. 1981: *Common Sense Wind Energy,* California Energy Commission and California Office of Appropriate Technology, Sacramento.

Patterson, D. 1980: "Fuel Alcohol Production in the United States: A Status Review and Evaluation," in Joint Economic Committee, U.S. Congress, *Farm and Forest Produced Alcohol: The Key to Liquid Fuel Independence,* USGPO.

Patterson, W.C., & Griffin, R. 1978: *Fluidized Bed Energy Technology: Coming to a Boil,* INFORM, 25 Broad St., New York NY 10004.

Peel, Q. 1980: "Sabotage campaign fear after Sasol plants are hit," *Financial Times,* p. 1, 3 June, London.

—1980a: "Sabotage bids stress S. African vulnerability," *id.,* p. 4, 3 June.

—1981: "Power cuts threat in South Africa," *id.,* p. 4, 4 March.

Pennino, W. 1981: "Backyard Gas Drilling Boom on Horizon as Heating Fuel Prices Continue to Increase," *Los Angeles Times,* p. I-B-2, 13 March.

Perelman, L. 1979: "Social Dynamics of the Nuclear Power Program," typescript, Cal-Tech Jet Propulsion Laboratory, Pasadena CA 91103.

Perlman, J., & Hastings, D.A. 1881: "Raiders Proliferate With Computers," *Los Angeles Times,* pp. II:1, :3, & :8, 6 December.

Perry, H., & Landsberg, H.H. 1981: "Factors in the Development of a Major US Synthetic Fuels Industry," *Annual Review of Energy* **6**:233–266.

Peschon, J. 1976: "Regulatory approaches for handling reliability and reserve margin issues and impact on reserve margin of dispersed storage and generation systems," 28 July testimony to California Energy Commission, Sacramento, from Systems Control, Inc., Palo Alto CA 94304.

Peskin, A., & Pittenger, C. 1978: "Blackouts and brownouts and their effect on computer operation," BNL–24960, Brookhaven National Laboratory, Upton NY.

Petzinger, T. Jr. 1981: "Out of Order: Avoiding Plant Failure Grows More Difficult For Many Industries," *Wall Street Journal,* p. 1, 8 January.

Philadelphia Inquirer 1981: "Corporal is injured in Basque explosion," p. 6–A, 9 November.

Pickering, E.E. 1969: "Inter-Systems Relationships: Local Vulnerability of Utilities, San Jose," Stanford Research Institute, Menlo Park CA 94025.

Pike, E.A. 1972: *Protection Against Bombs and Incendiaries for Business, Industrial and Educational Institutions,* C.C. Thomas Co., Springfield IL.

Pine, G.F. 1981: "Energy Consumed in 2010 by an Energy Efficient Building Sector," ORNL–5772, November, Oak Ridge National Laboratory, Oak Ridge TN.

Platt, T. *et al.* 1977: "Modeling the Productivity of Phytoplankton," in E. Goldberg, ed., *The Sea: Ideas and Observations on Progress in the Study of the Seas. Vol. VI,* Wiley, New York.

Podgers, J. 1980: "Blackout Riot Damages Sought from N.Y. Utility," *American Bar Association Journal* **66**:1353, November.

Poland, S.S., & White, J.G. Jr. 1981: "Report on the Status of Liquefied Natural Gas Imports," *Natural Resources Law Newsletter* **13**(4):17ff, American Bar Association, Chicago.

Pollard, R.D., ed. 1979: *The Nugget File,* Union of Concerned Scientists, 1384 Massachusetts Avenue, Cambridge MA 02238.

Pomerantz, D., Koster, F., Wagshal, P. *et al.* 1979: *Franklin County Energy Study: A Renewable Energy Scenario for the Future,* Franklin County Energy Project, Box 548, Greenfield MA 01301, $12 (summary $2); also summarized at 421–451 in Coates, G., ed., *Resettling America,* Brick House, Andover MA 01810, 1981.

Ponte, L. 1977: "Target for Terrorists," *National Observer,* pp. 1 & 13, 4 July.

Poposil, R. 1981: "3 Mills to Save 10% on Fuel Costs With Solar Steam," *Energy User News,* 31 August.

Popular Science 1981: "Co-generator pro-

duces heat and electricity," p. 59, April.
—1981a: "Solar water heat—no pumps, no tanks," p. 20, April.

PORTLAND [OREGON] ENERGY OFFICE: "Portland Energy Information Package," 1220 SW 5th Ave, room 405, Portland OR 97204.

POWELL, W. 1971/80: *The Anarchist Cookbook*, Lyle Stuart Co., Secaucus NJ 07094.

PRESIDENT'S COUNCIL ON ENVIRONMENTAL QUALITY 1974: *The Costs of Sprawl: Detailed Cost Analysis*, April.

PROCACCIA, H. 1975: "Probabilité de défaillance des circuits de refroidissement normaux et des circuits de refroidissement de secours des céntrales nucléaires," IAEA–SM–195/13, at pp. 351–372 and 392 (esp. Figs. 6–9) in *Reliability of Nuclear Power Plants*, International Atomic Energy Agency, Vienna.

PROMOTING SMALL POWER PRODUCTION: IMPLEMENTING SECTION 210 OF PURPA 1981: February monograph by Center for Renewable Resources, Environmental Action Foundation, Institute for Local Self-Reliance, Natural Resources Defenses Council, and Solar Lobby, all in Washington DC.

PRUGH, J. 1981: "13 Mercenaries Arrested Near Nuclear Plant," *Los Angeles Times*, p. I:1, 21 March.

PRYOR, L. 1975: "The 'Invaders'—A Test for the Pipeline," *Los Angeles Times*, pp. I:1, :18, & :21, 18 November.

PYE, E.K., & HUMPHREY, A.E. 1979: "Production of Liquid Fuels from Cellulosic Biomass," pp. 69–75 in *Proceedings of the Third Annual Conference on Biomass Energy Systems*, SERI/TP–33–285, National Technical Information Service, Springfield VA 22161.

PUBLIC POWER WEEKLY 1981: "Endicott generator will burn methane from sewage treatment," p. 4, 27 July.

QUIRK, W.J., & MORIARTY, J.E. 1980: "Prospects for Using Improved Climate Information to Better Manage Energy Systems," pp. 89–99 in Bach, W. *et al.*, eds., *Interactions of Energy and Climate*, Reidel, Dordrecht (The Netherlands).

RAETZ, K.-H. 1979: "Konvex-Sonnenlichtkollektor," *PTB-Mitteilungen* **89**:217–218, März, Physikalisch-Technische Bundesanstalt, Braunschweig.
—1979a: "Der Konvexkollektor," *TAB* IX.79;

available from author, Gassnerstr. 12, 3300 Braunschweig, FR Germany.

RAIN: from 2270 NW Irving, Portland OR 97210.

RAMBERG, B. 1978: "Destruction of Nuclear Energy Facilities in War: A Proposal for Legal Restraint," World Order Studies Program, Princeton University.
—1980: *The Destruction of Nuclear Energy Facilities in War*, Lexington Books (D.C. Heath), Lexington MA.
—1981: "The Real Gamblers Are the West's Nuclear Salesmen," *Los Angeles Times*, pp. V:1 & :6, 14 June.

RAND, C.T. 1981: "Politics of Oil," *New York Times*, p. A21, 7 August.

RAND 1980: "Security and Subnational Conflict Research Program," September, RAND Corporation, Santa Monica CA 90406.

RANDOLPH, J. 1981: "Comparison of Approaches for Developing Community Energy Plans," at **6**:471–475, *Proceedings of the Sixth National Passive Solar Conference*, American Section of the International Solar Energy Society, Killeen TX.

REDDY, A.K.N. 1981: "A Biomass-Based Strategy for Resolving India's Oil Crisis," November typescript updating articles in *Current Science* **50**:50–53 and *New Scientist*, 9 July; Indian Institute of Science, 560 012 Bangalore. See also —1980, "Alternative Energy Policies for Developing Countries: A Case Study of India," at 289–351 in Bohm, R.A. *et al.*, eds., *World Energy Production and Productivity*, Ballinger, Cambridge MA 02138, 1980; —, ed., 1981, *Rural Technology*, Indian Academy of Sciences, 560 080 Bangalore.

REIF, D.K. 1981: *Solar Retrofit*, from *Solar Age*, Harrisville NH 03450.

REMPEL, W.C. 1982: "Oil Refineries Shutting Down at Rapid Pace," *Los Angeles Times*, pp. I:1, :8, & :9, 11 January.

RICHARDS, D.K. 1982: "Hope for World's Economic Recovery Rests With Lower OPEC Prices," *Los Angeles Times*, pp. V:3 & :9, 31 January.

RICHTER, R. 1981: "Testimony from a former safeguards inspector," *Bulletin of the Atomic Scientists*, pp. 29–31, October.

RICKETTS, L.W., BRIDGES, J.E., & MILETTA, J. 1976: *EMP Radiation and Protective Tech-*

niques, Wiley-Interscience, New York.

RIDGEWAY, J. 1979: *Energy-Efficient Community Planning,* JG Press, Emmaus PA.

RIEMERS, R. 1980: "Micro-load Retrofit," *Alternative Sources of Energy,* pp. 3–6, May/June.

RINARD, A. 1981: "Oceanside to Offer Solar Leasing Plan: Unique Program Links Consumers, Private Marketers of Equipment," *Los Angeles Times,* 21 October.

ROCKY MOUNTAIN NEWS 1981: "Contract signed for wind power," p. 24–H, 29 August.

RODBERG, L. 1978: *The Employment Impact of the Solar Transition,* Joint Economic Committee, U.S. Congress, USGPO #052–04915–4.

ROSE, J. 1981: "U.S. Oil Firms in Angola Cooperate With a Regime Washington Won't Recognize," *Los Angeles Times,* pp. I-B:4–6, 17 December, at 6.

ROSENBAUM, D.M., GOOGIN, J., JEFFERSON, R., KLEITMAN, D., & SULLIVAN, W. 1974: "A Special Safeguards Study," *Congressional Record* S6623–7, 30 April.

ROSENFELD, A.H. *et al.* 1980: "Building Energy Use Compilation and Analysis (BECA): An International Comparison and Critical Review. Part A: New Residential Buildings," LBL–8912 Rev., Preprint, November, Lawrence Berkeley Laboratory, Berkeley CA 94720.

ROSS, M.H. 1981: "Energy Consumption by Industry," *Annual Review of Energy* 6:379–416.

—& WILLIAMS, R.H. 1979: "Drilling for Oil and Gas in Our Buildings," PU/CEES–87, Center for Energy & Environmental Studies, Princeton University, Princeton NJ 08540.

—1981: *Our Energy: Regaining Control,* McGraw-Hill, New York.

ROTHCHILD, J. 1981: *Stop Burning Your Money: The Intelligent Homeowner's Guide to Household Energy Savings,* Random House, New York.

ROWEN, H.S. 1980: "Western Economies and the Gulf War," reprinted in *The Energy Consumer,* pp. 4–5, December 1980/January 1981, special issue on energy preparedness, U.S. Department of Energy, Office of Consumer Affairs.

—& WEYANT, J.P. 1981: "Oil and National Security," *Annual Review of Energy* 6:171–198.

ROYAL COMMISSION ON ENVIRONMENTAL POLLUTION 1976: *Sixth Report,* Cmnd. 6618, HM Stationery Office, London, esp. ¶¶185–6, 321, 325, 331–3, 505–7.

RTM 1981: *Alternative Energy Data Summary®* for the United States, Vol. 1, 1975–80, Resource & Technology Management Corp., 714A S. 15th St., Arlington VA 22202.

RUBEN, P. 1981: "Audit, Building Conversion Save $72,000," *Energy User News,* p. 6, 22 June.

RUSSELL, M.C. 1981: "A Summary of Residential Photovoltaic System Economics," 6 January, MIT Lincoln Laboratory, Lexington MA 02173.

RUSSELL, C. 1982: "A-Policy May Backfire, Study Shows," *Washington Post,* 5 January.

RUSSELL, B.C., TALBOT, F.H., & DOMM, S. 1974: "Patterns of Colonization of Artificial Reefs by Coral Reef Fishes," *Proceedings of the 2nd International Symposium on Coral Reefs* 1:207–215.

RYLE, M. 1977: "The economics of alternative energy sources," *Nature* 267:111–117.

ST. GEOURS, J. 1979: "In Favour of an Energy-Efficient Society," report to the Commission of the European Communities, Brussels, Annex 2, p. 1 (cf. p. 2).

ST. PAUL ENERGY OFFICE 1980: "Saint Paul Energy Mobilization: A History," May. See also "Saint Paul Energy Mobilization: City-Wide Survey Results," *Ibid.*

—1982: "The Saint Paul Energy Project: Challenge, Direction, Action—A Report," January, from Office of the Mayor, 347 City Hall, St. Paul MN 55102.

SAITMAN, B. 1979: "A Case for Solar Municipal Utility Districts," pp. 8–10, *Solar Energy: Northern California Solar Energy Association Newsletter,* March.

—1980: "Development of Municipal Solar Utilities in California: An Infrastructure for the Future," in SERI 1980b, *op. cit.*

—1980a: "Commercializing Solar Energy Through Municipal Solar Utilities (MSU)," at Vol. 3.2, pp. 1361–1365, *Proceedings of the 1980 Annual Meeting,* American Section of the International Solar Energy Society, Killeen TX.

—1982: "Municipal Solar Utilities: A Final Report," in press in *Proceedings of the 1982 Annual Meeting, Ibid.*

—& GARFIELD-JONES, S. 1981: "Municipal Solar Utilities in California: A Status Report," at Vol. 4.2, pp. 1356–1360, *Proceedings of the 1981 Annual Meeting, AS/ISES, Ibid.*

SAMUELS, G. 1981: *Transportation Energy Requirements to the Year 2010,* ORNL–5745, April, Oak Ridge National Laboratory, Oak Ridge TN.

SAN DIEGO COUNTY BOARD OF SUPERVISORS 1978: *Solar Ordinance Feasibility Analysis for San Diego County,* 21 November.

SANT, R. 1979: "The Least-Cost Energy Strategy: Minimizing Consumer Cost Through Competition," Energy Productivity Center, Mellon Institute, Suite 1200, 1925 N. Lynn St, Arlington VA 22209; summarized in *Harvard Business Review,* pp. 6ff, May–June 1980.

—*et al.* 1981: "Eight Great Energy Myths: The Least-Cost Energy Strategy—1978–2000," September, Energy Productivity Center, *loc. cit.*

SATCHELL, M. 1973: "Ex-AEC Aide Put on Probation," *Washington Star-News,* 21 February.

SCHACHTER, M. 1979: *The Job Creation Potential of Solar and Conservation: A Critical Analysis,* DOE/TIC–10250, Office of Policy Evaluation, U.S. Dept. of Energy, Washington DC 20585.

SCHAEFER, E., & BENSON, J. 1980: *Energy and Power in Your Community,* available from Conference on Alternative State and Local Policies (*q.v.*).

SCHAFFER, R.A. 1981: "Complexity of Circuits Tests Designers of Microelectronics," *Wall Street Journal,* p. 27, 20 February.

SCHAFFER, P. 1981a: "Energy Pressure on Profits Eyed," *Energy User News,* p. 27, 14 September. See also "Nonenergy Investment Maimed?", *Ibid.,* pp. 17–18, 1 June.

SCHELL, J. 1982: *The Fate of the Earth,* Alfred Knopf, New York.

SCHIPPER, L. 1981: "Progress In More Efficient Energy Use: The Importance of Keeping Score," October paper to International Conference on Energy Use Management (Berlin), Lawrence Berkeley Laboratory, Berkeley CA 94720.

—, MYERS, S., & KETOFF, A. 1981: "Progress in Residential Energy Conservation—A Multi Country Perspective," LBL–11701, April, Lawrence Berkeley Laboratory.

SCHLEIMER, J.D. 1974: "The Day They Blew Up San Onofre," *Bulletin of the Atomic Scientists,* pp. 24–27, October.

SCHMIDT, D.A. 1974: *Armageddon in the Middle East,* New York Times Survey Series, John Day (Intext), New York.

SCHNEIDER CORP. 1980: brochure, 5310–D Power Inn Rd., Sacramento CA 95820.

SCHULTZ, B. 1981: "Analyst's $20,000 'Times' Ad Slams MX Missile Program," *Computerworld,* 24 August.

SCHURR, S.H. *et al.* 1979: *Energy in America's Future: The Choices Before Us,* Resources for the Future/John Hopkins U. Press, Baltimore.

SEIB, G.F., & HARRIS, R.J. JR. 1981: "In Military Buildup, Big Contractors Face Supplier Bottlenecks," *Wall Street Journal,* p. 1, 21 August.

SEIFFERT, U., & WALZER, P. 1980: "Development Trends for Future Passenger Cars," August preprint, 5th Automotive News World Congress, from Research Division, Volkswagenwerk AG, Wolfsburg, FRG.

SENATE COMMITTEE ON ENERGY & RESOURCES 1980: *The Geopolitics of Oil,* November staff report; Executive Summary reprinted *Science* **210**:1324–27.

SENATE COMMITTEE ON FOREIGN RELATIONS 1981: "The Proposed AWACS/F–15 Enhancement Sale to Saudi Arabia," September staff report, USGPO.

SENATE JUDICIARY COMMITTEE 1977: "The Trans-Alaskan Pipeline—Problems Posed by the Threat of Sabotage and the Impact on Internal Security," Subcommittee to Investigate the Administration of the Internal Security Act and Other Internal Security Laws, 95th Congr., 1st Sess., USGPO.

SERI [Solar Energy Research Institute] 1979: *A Survey of Biomass Gasification,* 3 vols., SERI/ TR–33–239, July (I & II) and April 1980 (III), SERI, 1617 Cole Blvd, Golden CO 80401.

—1980: *Fuel from Farms—A Guide to Small Scale Ethanol Production,* SERI/SP–451–519, February.

—1980a: *A Guide to Commercial-Scale Ethanol Production and Financing,* SERI/SP–751–877, November

—1980b: *Community Energy Self-Reliance,* SERI/ CP–354–421, July.

—1980c: *Planning an Energy Futures Conference*

for Your Community, SERI/SP–744–923.

—1981: *A New Prosperity: Building a Sustainable Energy Future*, draft, preprinted (#97–K) by Committee on Energy & Commerce, USHR, 2 vols., April, USGPO, out of print; republished by Brick House Publishing Co., 34 Essex St, Andover MA 01810.

—1981a: Proceedings of the 1980 [Seattle] Second National Conference on Community Renewable Energy Systems (CRES–II), in press.

SERRIN, W. 1981: "New York Area's Reliance on Imported Food Grows," *New York Times*, p. I:3, 26 July.

SHACKSON, R.H., & LEACH, H.J. 1980: "Using Fuel Economy and Synthetic Fuels to Compete with OPEC Oil," Energy Productivity Center (*q.v.:* Sant 1979).

SHAPIRO, M. 1980: "Boston Solar Retrofits: Studies of Solar Access and Economics," E-80-11, December, Kennedy School, Harvard University.

SHARRY, J.A., & WALLS, W.L. 1974: "LPG-Gas Distribution Fire," *Fire Journal*, January.

SHAW, G. 1978: "3 Large Power Generators Sabotaged at Coulee Dam," *Los Angeles Times*, pp. I:1 & :21, 10 November.

SHAWNEE SOLAR PROJECT 1981: *Municipal Solar Utility: A Model for Carbondale Illinois*, Conference on Alternative State and Local Policies (*q.v.*).

SHEARSON LOEB RHOADES INC. 1981: "Equity Research: Monthly Utility Service," March.

SHENON, P. 1981: "Hot Times in Hydropower," *New York Times*, pp. F6–7, 12 July.

SHICK, W. 1980: article on Phelps house, 16 June, in press, *New Shelter*, Rodale Press, Emmaus PA 18049.

SHIPP, D.D. 1978: "Harmonic Analysis & Suppression for Electrical Systems Supplying Static Power Converters and Other Nonlinear Loads," *IEEE Transactions on Industry Applications* **IA-15**:453–458.

SHUPE, J.W. 1981: "The Role of Renewable Energy in Hawaii's Energy Future," 30 September paper to International Energy Symposium II, 1982 World's Fair, Knoxville, from Hawaii Natural Energy Institute, U. of Hawaii at Manoa.

—& WEINGART, J.W. 1980: "Emerging Energy Technologies in an Island Environment: Hawaii," *Annual Review of Energy* **5**:293–333.

SHURCLIFF, W. 1980: *Superinsulated Houses and Double-Envelope Houses*, Brick House Publishing Co., 34 Essex St, Andover MA 01810.

—1982: "Air-to-Air Heat Exchangers for Houses," *Solar Age* **7**(3):19–22.

SIEGEL, B. 1981: "Hydro Boom: Towns Seek Own Power From Water," *Los Angeles Times* p. I:1 & :14, 16 April.

SIEGHART, P. 1979: Chapter 4.4 in *Report of the Gorleben International Review* submitted to the Governor of Lower Saxony, Niedersächsisches Sozialministerium, Hannover, April (in German); summarized in H. Graf Hatzfeldt *et al.*, eds., *Der Gorleben-Report*, Fischer, Frankfurt/M.

ŠILJAK, D.D. 1978: "Dynamic Reliability Using Multiple Control Systems," at 173–187 in *Proceedings of the Second Lawrence Symposium on Systems and Decision Sciences*, 3–4 October 1978; available from the author at University of Santa Clara, California.

SIMON, H.E. 1973: "The Organization of Complex Systems," at 1–28 in Pattee, H.H., ed., *Hierarchy Theory*, Braziller, New York.

SIMMONS, M.K. 1981: "Solar Energy Technology—A Five-Year Update," *Annual Review of Energy* **6**:1–42.

SING, B. 1981: "State Too Successful at Farming?," *Los Angeles Times*, pp. I:1 & :19, 16 December.

SINGER, M., & WEIR, D. 1979: "Nuclear Nightmare: Your Worst Fears Are True," *New West*, pp. 15–34, 3 December, Southern California Edition.

SIPRI 1974: *Oil and Security*, Stockholm International Peace Research Institute, Humanities Press, New York.

—1978: *SIPRI Yearbook 1977*, MIT Press, Cambridge MA.

SISK, M. 1981: "Texas Wages War Against Oil 'Rustlers,' " *Los Angeles Times*, p. IX:10, 18 December.

SMIL, V. 1981: "Energy in Rural China," November paper to International Energy Symposium II, 1982 World's Fair, Knoxville, from U. of Manitoba, Winnipeg.

SMITH, C.V. JR. 1978: "Response to Recommendation from the OIA/OGC 'Inquiry into the Testimony of the Executive Director for Operations,' Volume 1, Summary Report, Dated February 1978," document to Commissioners, U.S. Nuclear Regulatory Commission, #SECY-78-425A, NRC Public Document Room.

SMITH, D.F. 1979: *Workshop on Power Conditioning for Alternative Energy Technologies,* Sandia Laboratories, Albuquerque NM.

SMITH, P. 1980: "Findings of National Security Council Ad Hoc Committee on Assessment of Consequences and Preparations for a Major California Earthquake," memo to Governor Brown, NSC, The White House, 29 August.

SMITH, J.L. 1981: "Photovoltaics," *Science* **212:**1472–1478.

SMITH, R.J. 1982: "France Toughens Position on Reactor for Iraq," *id.* **215:**483.

SOBLE, R.L., & TUMULTY, K. 1982: "Thievery in Oil Fields Easy," *Los Angeles Times,* pp. I:6 & :10, 22 January.

SOFT ENERGY NOTES 1978– : bimonthly from IPSEP, 1045 Sansome St, San Francisco CA 94111; #1–7 are reprinted by USDOE as DOE/OE-0016/1, October 1979.

—1982: "Solar Skirmishes: The Carbondale Case," pp. 176–177, January/February.

SOCOLOW, R.H., ed. 1978: *Saving Energy in the Home,* Ballinger, Cambridge MA.

SOLAR AGE 1981: "Commerce Is the Focus of ISES Solar World Forum," p. 17, November.

—1981a: "Low-Cost Fix for a Turn-of-the-Century Home," pp. 12 & 14, December.

—1981b: "First Half Collector Production Soars Despite Softening Economy," p. 49, December.

SOLARCAL LOCAL GOVERNMENT COMMISSION 1981: *Local Ordinances to Improve Energy Efficiency of Existing Housing: A Guide for Local Governments,* September, California Energy Commission *(q.v.).*

SOLAR ENERGY RESEARCH INSTITUE: see SERI.

SOLAR FLASHES 1980: "An Inflatable Greenhouse," pp. 1ff, May, San Luis Valley Solar Energy Assn., 512 Ross, Alamosa CO 81101.

SOLAR THERMAL REPORT 1981: "Mass Production Predicted to Slash Heliostat Costs," p. 2, Winter, SERI, Golden CO 80401.

—1981a: "Three Parabolic Dish-Compatible Receivers Tested," p. 8, May.

—1981b: "1983 Goals," p. 11, May.

SOLOMON, N. 1981: "Unstable explosive still on sub warheads called a very serious danger," *San Francisco Sunday Examiner & Chronicle,* p. A18, 18 October.

SOLOMON, K.A., & SALEM, S.L. 1980: "Understanding Our Limitations in Predicting Technological Risk: An Issue Paper," November typescript, RAND Corporation, Santa Monica CA 90406.

SOLON, L.R., & ROSENBERG, K. 1981: "The release of radioiodines in a nuclear emergency," *Bulletin of the Atomic Scientists,* pp. 54–56, October.

SØRENSEN, B. 1976: "Dependability of Wind Energy Generators with Short-Term Energy Storage," *Science* **194:**935–937.

—1979: *Renewable Energy,* Academic Press, New York.

—1979a: UN Nairobi conference background paper on wind.

—1980: "An American Energy Future," August report to SERI *(q.v.)*; available from author at Roskilde Univ. Center, Energy Group, Bld. 17-2, IMFUFA, PO Box 260, 4000 Roskilde, Denmark.

SOUTH CAROLINA DEPARTMENT OF HEALTH & ENVIRONMENTAL CONTROL 1974: "Report on Accidental Release of Tritium Gas at the Savannah River Plant," Division of Radiological Health, 2 May.

SOUTHERN CALIFORNIA EDISON COMPANY 1980: 17 October press announcement by Chairman William Gould, and his 16 October memorandum to employees (reprinted in *Soft Energy Notes* 3(6):29–30, December 1980 / January 1981), SCE, Rosemead CA.

—1981: "Guidelines for Operating/Metering/Protecting/Relaying for Co-Generators and Small Power Producers," June.

SOUTHWOOD, T.R.E. 1975: "The Dynamics of Insect Populations," in Pimentel, D., ed., *Insects, Science and Forestry,* Academic Press, New York.

SPETH, J.G. *et al.* 1974: *Bulletin of the Atomic Scientists* **30**(9):15ff.

STANEK, E.J. [director of the Iowa Energy Policy Council] 1981: testimony in Clark 1981a, *op. cit.*

STANLEY, T.W. 1977: "Resources and Geography in the North-South Dialogue," *Proceedings of the National Security Affairs Conference 1977,* July, National Defense University, Fort McNair, Washington DC.

STAYTON, R. 1981: "Santa Cruz: A Community Developed Energy Plan," *Solar Energy: Northern California Solar Energy Association Newsletter*, pp. 9 & 16, June.

STEEN, P., JOHANSSON, T.B., FREDRIKSSON, R., & BOGREN, E. 1981: *Energi—till vad och hur mycket?*, LiberFörlaget, Stockholm.

STELSON, J. 1981: *Energy-Use Data for Audited Hospitals*, February, Oak Ridge Associated Universities, Oak Ridge TN.

STEPHENS, M.M. 1970: *Minimizing Damage to Refineries from Nuclear Attack, Natural and Other Disasters*, February report to Office of Civil Defense, Industrial Participation, Department of the Army, by Office of Oil & Gas, Dept. of the Interior.

—1973: *Vulnerability of Total Petroleum Systems*, May report to Defense Civil Preparedness Agency, Washington DC, #DAHC20-70-C-0316, DCPA Work Unit 4362A.

—1974: *Vulnerability of Natural Gas Systems*, June report to Defense Civil Preparedness Agency, #OCD-PS-66-100, DCPA Work Unit 4334C (with J.A. Golasinski, Consultant).

—1979: "The Oil and Natural Gas Industries: A Potential Target of Terrorists," pp. 200–223 in Kupperman & Trent 1979 *(op. cit.)*.

STERLING, C. 1978: "The Terrorist Network," *The Atlantic*, pp. 37–47, November.

STEWART, I. 1975: "The seven elementary catastrophes," *New Scientist*, pp. 447–454, 20 November.

STOBAUGH, R., & YERGIN, D., eds., 1979: *Energy Future: Report of the Energy Project at the Harvard Business School*, Random House/Ballantine, NY.

STOCKHOLM INTERNATIONAL PEACE RESEARCH INSTITUTE: see SIPRI.

STOCKMAN, D.A. 1977: "Conservative Economics and Free Market Philosophy Say 'No' to the Clinch River Breeder Project," 17 September letter to USHR colleagues, and accompanying memorandum "The Market Case Against the Clinch River Breeder Project."

STODDARD, F.S. 1981: application for DOE AT Small Grant, Stoddard Consulting, PO Box 311, Amherst MA 01004.

STOVER, J.G. *et al.* 1978: "Incorporating Uncertainty in Energy Supply Models," EA-703, February report by The Futures Group to Electric Power Research Institute, Palo Alto CA.

STRAITS TIMES 1980: "Power strike threatens Queensland with blackout," UPI story datelined Brisbane, p. 5, 28 March.

STUDY OF MAN'S IMPACT ON CLIMATE 1971: *Inadvertent Climate Modification*, Wilson, C.L. & Matthews, W.H., eds., MIT Press, Cambridge MA 02139.

SUBCOMMITTEE ON ENERGY & POWER 1977: "The New York City Blackout of July 13, 1977," 13 October hearing, USHR Committee on Interstate & Foreign Commerce, 95th Congr., 1st Sess., Serial #95-88, USGPO (1978).

—1978: "Energy Impacts of the Coal Strike," 16 February hearings, USHR Committee on Interstate & Foreign Commerce, 95th Congr., 2nd Sess., Serial #95-132, USGPO.

—1978a: "New York Blackout of July 13, 1977; Costs and Preventive Action," 10 July hearings, USHR Committee on Interstate & Foreign Commerce, 95th Congr., 2nd Sess., Serial #95-148, USGPO.

SUBCOMMITTEE ON ENERGY & THE ENVIRONMENT 1977: "Nuclear Reactor Security Against Sabotage," 5 May hearing, USHR Committee on Interior & Insular Affairs, 95th Congr., 1st Sess., Serial #95-13, USGPO.

—1977a: "Allegations Concerning Lax Security in the Domestic Nuclear Industry," 29 July hearing, USHR Committee on Interior & Insular Affairs, 95th Congr., 1st Sess., Serial #95-23, USGPO.

—1979: "Security in the Domestic Nuclear Industry," 11 June hearing, USHR Committee on Interior & Insular Affairs, 96th Congr., 1st Sess., Serial #96-8, USGPO.

SUBCOMMITTEE ON ENERGY CONSERVATION & POWER 1981: "National Security Implications of Centralized Energy Sources," 17 February briefing, USHR Committee on Energy & Commerce, 97th Congr., 1st Sess., Serial #97-7, USGPO.

SUN*UP 1981: "So You Want to Sell Back Power to Your Utility Co.", pp. 4ff, March; 56020 Santa Fe Trail, Suite O, Yucca Valley CA 92284.

SUNWORLD 1980: "Energy for Industry," 4(4):134 (Pergamon).

SUPERINSULATED BUILDING: monthly technical

newsletter starting May 1981, $25 per year, 5006 V St NW, Suite 207, Washington DC 20007.

SUTHERLAND, J.P. 1974: "Multiple Stable Points in Natural Communities," *American Naturalist* **108**:859–873.

SYSTEMS CONTROL, Inc. 1980: *Decentralized Energy Technology Integration Assessment Study: Second Principal Report,* summary & report vols., SCI Project 5278, December, for USDOE Office of Policy & Evaluation, from SCI, 1801 Page Mill Rd., Palo Alto CA 94304.

—1980a: *The Effect of Distributed Power Systems on Customer Service Reliability,* June, SCI.

—1980b: *Study of Dispersed Small Wind Systems Interconnected with a Utility Distribution System: Interim Report: Preliminary Hardware Assessment,* March, for Rockwell International Corp., from SCI.

TALBOT, S., & DANN, J. 1981: "Broken Arrows, Broken Sleep," *Los Angeles Times,* p. II:7, 18 March.

TALBOT, D., & MORGAN, R.E. 1981: *Power and Light: Political Strategies for the Solar Transition,* Pilgrim Press, New York.

TANDEM COMPUTERS, INC. 1981: "The Non-Stop® Network," advertising brochure, 19333 Vallco Pkwy, Cuptertino CA 95104.

TANNER, H. 1978: "Terrorist Bombs Badly Damage Rome Power Plant," *New York Times,* pp. A3 & A8, 15 June.

TATOM, J.W., COLCORD, A.R., KNIGHT, J.A., & ELSON, L.W. 1976: "Clean Fuels from Agricultural and Forestry Wastes," EPA-600/2-76-090, April report to Office of R&D, U.S. Environmental Protection Agency, Washington DC 20460, from Engineering Experiment Station, Georgia Inst. of Technology, Atlanta 30332; data updated by J.W. Tatom, personal communications, 1978.

TAYLOR, T.B. 1973: "Diversion by Non-Governmental Organizations," pp. 176–198 in Willrich, M., ed., *International Safeguards and Nuclear Industry,* American Society of International Law / John Hopkins U. Press, Baltimore MD.

TAYLOR, M.D. 1976: *Precarious Security,* Norton, New York, quoted in Bucknell 1979.

TAYLOR, V. 1980: "The End of the Oil Age," *The Ecologist* [UK] **10**(8/9):303ff, October/November.

—1980a: "Electric Utilities: The Transition from Oil," 9 December testimony to Subcommittee on Oversight & Investigations, Committee on Interstate & Foreign Commerce; available from Union of Concerned Scientists, 1384 Massachusetts Ave, Cambridge MA 02238.

TAYLOR, T.B. 1981: written statement of 23 October to Subcommittee on Oversight & Investigations, Committee on Interior & Insular Affairs, USHR.

TAYLOR, R.P. 1981a: *Rural Energy Development in China,* Resources for the Future, Washington DC / Johns Hopkins U. Press, Baltimore MD.

TAYLOR, T.B., & TAYLOR, C. 1981: newsletters of community energy project, from 10325 Bethesda Church Road, Damascus MD 20750.

TELSON, M.L. 1975: "The economics of alternative levels of reliability for electric power generation systems," *Bell Journal of Economics* **6**(2):679–694.

TERA 1982: "Flat-Plate Solar Collection System for Commercial/Residential Development," February report, TERA Advanced Services Corporation, Berkeley CA.

TERRY, S. 1981: "Solar energy gets a new 'lease' in Oceanside, Calif.," *Christian Science Monitor,* 30 December.

THOM, R. 1975: *Structural Stability and Morphogenesis,* Addison-Wesley, Reading, Massachusetts.

THOMAS, W. DUB., & SCHWENDTNER, A.H. 1972: "LNG Carriers: The Current State of the Art," Paper 13, LNG/LPG Conference, London, 21–22 March 1972, *Shipbuilding & Shipping Record;* also in *Transactions of the Society of Naval Architects and Marine Engineers* **79**:440ff (1971).

THOMPSON, T.J., & BECKERLEY, J.G., eds. 1964–70: *The Technology of Nuclear Reactor Safety,* 2 vols., MIT Press, Cambridge MA 02139.

TIMES 1974: "Suspicion falls on Nepal as uranium gang's HQ," p. 8, 2 May, London.

—1974a: "Thefts of metal at nuclear dockyard," p. 1, 16 July.

—1975: "Radioactive waste drums concealed cannabis," 25 November.

—1975a: "Warning to tankers of hijack plan," p. 6, 6 May.

—1978: "Basque bomb protest against nuclear plant," p. 6, 2 March.

—1981: "Tanker hits jetty," p. 3, col. 2, 26 January.

TINKERMAN, R.M. 1981: 27 April testimony to Subcommittee on Energy Conservation & Power, Committee on Energy & Commerce, USHR, for Transition Energy Projects Institute, 2995 Van Ness Ave, San Francisco CA 94109.

TOMASI, T. *et al.* 1981: *Local Energy Initiatives: A Second Look,* California Office of Appropriate Technology, Sacramento.

TOTH, R.C. 1981: "Terrorists: Threat of A-Weapons," *Los Angeles Times,* p. I:1, 25 May.

TREBLE, F.C. 1980: "Photovoltaic Pilot Projects in the European Community," *Sun at Work in Britain* 11:47–51, UK Section of the International Solar Energy Society (Pergamon).

TRW 1979: "Appendix—Data Base on Automobile Energy Conservation Technology," 25 September, Energy Systems Planning Division, TRW, Inc., McLean VA.

TSONGAS, P. 1980: "The Massachusetts Plan: Through Survival to Stability," from Senator Tsongas, 2003-F, JFK Building, Government Center, Boston MA 02203.

TSUCHIYA, H. 1981: "Efficient Energy Use and Renewable Energy in Japan," paper to Second International Conference on Soft Energy Paths, Rome, January, excerpted in *Soft Energy Notes* 4(1) 8–9, February/March, from IPSEP, 1045 Sansome St, San Francisco CA 94111.

TURNER, S.E., MCCULLOUGH, C.R., & LYERLY, R.L. 1970: "Industrial Sabotage in Nuclear Power Plants," *Nuclear Safety* 11(2) 107–114.

TURNER, W. 1977: "Alaska Oil Flow Reaches Valdez After Delays and Pipeline Mishaps," *New York Times,* pp. 1 & 5, 30 July.

UNITED STATES: See U.S.

UNIVERSITY OF SASKATCHEWAN 1979: *Low Energy Passive Solar Housing Handbook,* Division of Extension & Community Relations, U. Sask., Saskatoon; updated October 1980 as *Energy Efficient Housing: A Prairie Approach,* Alberta Energy & Natural Resources, Energy Conservation Branch (Edmonton) and Saskatchewan Mineral Resources, Office of Energy Conservation (Regina).

UNIVERSITY OF ARIZONA 1981: "Arizona's Energy Future: Making the Transition to a New Mix," Frank, H., ed., October report to Arizona Academy, Phoenix.

URBAN SOLAR ENERGY ASSOCIATION 1981: *USEA Newsletter,* Somerville MA.

UREY, H. 1945: *New Republic,* p. 885, 31 December.

URSU, I., & VAMANU, D. 1979: "Motivations and Attitudes in the Long-Term Planning of Alternative Energy Systems," paper to 26 November–7 December UNITAR Conference on Long-Term Energy Resources (Montréal).

U.S. GENERAL ACCOUNTING OFFICE 1979, Letter to Secretary of Energy on National Energy Planning II (EMD-80-43), 28 December.

USGPO: U. S. Government Printing Office. See under author or title.

USHR: United States House of Representatives. See under committee name.

VACCA, R. 1974: *The Coming Dark Age—What Will Happen When Modern Technology Breaks Down?,* Anchor, New York.

VICKER, R. 1981: "Civil Defense Wins More Corporate Converts, But Industry Is Still Vulnerable to Nuclear Attack," *Wall Street Journal,* p. 48, 17 June.

VINE, E. 1981: *Solarizing America: The Davis Experience,* Conference on Alternative State and Local Policies (*q.v.*).

VOLKSWAGEN OF AMERICA, INC. 1980: "VW Develops 60 MPG Experimental Safety Car," undated press packet, VWA, Englewood Cliffs NJ.

VOLLENWEIDER, R.A. 1970: *Scientific Fundamentals of the Eutrophication of Lakes and Flowing Waters,* OECD, Paris.

VON HIPPEL, F. 1981: "Forty Miles a Gallon by 1995 at the Very Least: Why the US Needs a New Automotive Efficiency Goal," Part III in Yergin, D., ed., *The Dependence Dilemma: Gasoline Consumption and America's Security,* in press, Harvard University; preprinted in 1980 as PU/CEES-104, Center for Energy & Environmental Studies, Princeton University, Princeton NJ 08540.

VON NEUMANN, J. 1956: "Probabilistic logic and the synthesis of reliable organisms from unreliable components," at 43-98 in Shannon, C.E., & Moore, E.F., eds., *Automata Studies,* Annals of Mathematics Studies #34,

Princeton University Press, Princeton NJ 08540.

—1966: *Theory of Self-Reproducing Automata,* U. of Illinois Press, Urbana.

WAGNER, N.R. 1977: *A Survey of Threat Studies Related to the Nuclear Power Industry,* SAND 77-8254, August, Sandia Laboratories, Albuquerque.

WALKER, P.F. 1981: "Precision-guided Weapons," *Scientific American* **245**(2):36–45, August.

WALKER, D.N., ADAMS, S.L., & PLACEK, R.J. 1981: "Torsional Vibration and Fatigue of Turbine-Generator Shafts," *IEEE Transactions on Power Apparatus & Systems* **PAS-100**:4373–4380.

WALL, I.B. 1974: "Probabilistic Assessment of Aircraft Risk for Nuclear Power Plants," *Nuclear Safety* **15**(3):276–284, May-June.

WALL STREET JOURNAL 1977: "Puerto Rican Utility Is Struck in Dispute Over Wage Increase," p. 21, 28 December.

—1979: "Philadelphia Electric Nuclear Plant Worker Is Fired for Tampering," p. 2, 1 October.

—1980: "Tosco Says Refinery Was Hit by Sabotage, Dampening Earnings," p. 6, 4 April.

—1980a: "Oil Facilities in Iran Are Further Damaged by Fires, Explosions," p. 7, 7 April.

—1980b: "Angolan Saboteurs . . .," P. 30, 13 August.

—1981: "Business Bulletin: Energy Audits . . .," p. 1, 30 July.

WALLS, W.L. 1963: "LP-Gas Tank Truck Accident and Fire," *Fire International* **3**:12.

WALSH, J. 1981: "Genetic Vulnerability Down on the Farm," *Science* **214**:161ff.

WANG, D.I.C., BIOCIK, E., FANG, H.F., & WANG, S.D. 1979: "Direct microbiological conversion of cellulosic biomass to ethanol," *Proceedings of the Third Annual Biomass Energy Systems Conference,* at 61ff.

WASHINGTON POST 1975: "Explosion Precedes B-52 Crash," p. A4, 4 September.

—1979: "Half Million Lose Electricity After Storm in Northwest," p. A10, 25 December.

1981: "Report on Collapse of Oil Rig Assails Design, Safety Training," p. A19, 4 April, Reuters report.

—1981a: "New England Energy Costs," p. A4, 4 April.

WATTS, R.L., SMITH, S.A., & MAZZUCCHI, R.P. 1981: *Photovoltaic Product Directory and Buyers Guide,* Battelle Pacific Northwest Laboratory, available from National Technical Information Service, Springfield VA 22161.

WAYS AND MEANS: bimonthly newsletter of Conference on Alternative State and Local Policies (*q.v.*).

WEEKLY ENERGY REPORT 1975: "FEA Push for Smaller, More Reliable Power Plants Is Likely," **3**(3):10, 10 March.

WEGLEY, H.L., ORGILL, M.M., & DRAKE, R.L. 1978: *A Siting Handbook for Small Wind Energy Conversion Systems,* PNL-2521, May, Battelle Pacific Northwest Laboratories, Richland WA 99352.

WEINBERG, A.M. 1973: "Can Man Live With Fission—A Prospectus," Project on Sustainable Growth, Woodrow Wilson International Center for Scholars, Washington DC, 18 June.

WEINBERG, G.M. 1975: *An Introduction to General Systems Thinking,* Wiley/Interscience, New York.

WEINGART, J.M. 1977: "Systems Aspects of Large-Scale Solar Energy Conversion," RM-77_23, International Institute for Applied Systems Analysis, Laxenburg, Austria.

WEINTZ, M. 1981: "Florida Begins to Put More Sunshine Into Its Lagging House-Building Industry," *Los Angeles Times,* p. I-B:14, 19 November.

WELCH, H. 1965: *Taoism: The Parting of the Way,* Beacon Press, Boston.

WENTZEL, A.K. 1979: "The Vulnerable Society," Swedish Government report to December seminar at Ljubljana (Yugoslavia) of Senior Advisors to ECE Governments on Environmental Problems, "Alternative Patterns of Development and Lifetyles," U.N. Economic Commission for Europe, Geneva, ENV/SEM.11/R.15, 25 October.

WEST, R. 1976: "Tanker Blows Up in L.A. Harbor," *Los Angeles Times,* pp. I:1 & :26, 18 December.

WHEELER, J., GRAUBARD, M., & ACTON, J.P. 1975: "How Business in Los Angeles Cut Energy Use by 20 Percent," P-5417, report to Office of Conservation & Environment, Federal Energy Administration; USGPO #041-108-00042.

WIEGNER, E. 1977: "Tax incentives and utility

cash flow," *Proceedings of the Atomic Industrial Forum Conference on Nuclear Financial Considerations, 24–27 July, Seattle, Washington*, AIF, Washington DC.

WILBURN, G. 1981: "Terrorism, Sabotage Are Growing Worries for Petroleum Industry's Security Chiefs," *The Oil Daily*, pp. 1 & 2, 28 December.

WILLIAMS, LT. CMDR. H.D. 1971: *Proceedings of the Marine Safety Safety Council* (U.S. Coast Guard) **28**(9):162ff.

—1972: *id.* **29**(10):203ff.

WILLIAMS, R.H. 1978: "Industrial Cogeneration," *Annual Review of Energy* **3**:313–356.

WILLIAMSON, B.R., & MANN, L.R.B. 1981: "Thermal Hazards from Propane (LPG) Fireballs," *Combustion Science & Technology* **25**:141–145.

WILSON, W.L. 1976: *Energy World* **26**:2, Institute of Fuel (succeeded by Institute of Energy), London.

WILSON, T.W. JR. 1980: "National Security and the Politics of the Present Predicament," 15 November lecture to Naval Postgraduate School, Monterey CA.

WILSON, T. 1981: *Home Remedies*, Mid-Atlantic Solar Energy Association, Philadelphia.

WISCONSIN PUBLIC SERVICE COMMISSION 1977: *Environmental Review and Consumer Analysis*, Division of System Planning, Madison.

WITTENBERG, L.J., & HARRIS, M.J. 1980: "City of Miamisburg heats pool with solar gradient pond," *Solar Engineering*, pp. 26–28, April.

WOODCOCK, A., & DAVIS, D. 1978: *Catastrophe Theory*, E.P. Dutton, New York.

WOOLSON, A., & KLEINMAN, R. 1981: *County Energy Production Planning Handbook*, National Association of Counties, Washington DC.

WORCESTER [MASSACHUSETTS] POLYTECHNIC INSTITUTE 1978: *Proceedings of the First New England Site-Built Solar Collector Conference*, Dept. of Mechanical Engineering, May.

WOYCHIK, E. 1981: "Double Envelope Conquers Arctic Cold," *Soft Energy Notes* **4**(2):50–51, April/May.

YANDA, B., & FISHER, R. 1980: *The Food and Heat Producing Solar Greenhouse*, John Muir Publications, PO Box 613, Santa Fe NM 87501.

YORKE, V. 1980: *The Gulf in the 1980's*, Chatham House Paper 6, Royal Institute of International Affairs, London.

Index

About the Authors

Amory B. Lovins is a consultant physicist active in energy policy in over fifteen countries. He was born in Washington, D.C. in 1947. After two years each at Harvard College and at Magdalen College, Oxford, he became a Junior Research Fellow of Merton College, Oxford in 1969. He resigned in 1971 to work full-time from a London base for Friends of the Earth, a U.S. non-profit conservation group. He became Vice-President of Friends of the Earth Foundation in 1979 and returned to the United States in 1981.

Mr. Lovins received an Oxford M.A. degree by Special Resolution in 1971 and honorary D.Sc. degrees from Bates College (1979) and Williams College (1981). Twice Regents' Lecturer in the University of California (Berkeley, energy policy, spring 1978, and Riverside, economics, spring 1980), he was Grauer Lecturer in the University of British Columbia (autumn 1979) and Distinguished Visiting Professor in the University of Colorado (summer 1982).

His experimental physics consultancy (1965–) shifted to energy and resource strategy in the early 1970s. His clients have included several United Nations agencies, the Organization for Economic Cooperation and Development (OECD), the International Federation of Institutes for Advanced Studies (IFIAS), the Science Council of Canada, Petro-Canada, the U.S. Department of Energy, the U.S. Congress's Office of Technology Assessment, the U.S. Solar Energy Research Institute, Resources for the Future, and various state and foreign governments and financial institutions. He has published eleven previous books and numerous technical papers. During 1980–81 he served on the Energy Research Advisory Board of the U.S. Department of Energy.

In 1979 Mr. Lovins married L. Hunter Sheldon, Esq. They work as a team on energy policy, and are joint Policy Advisors to Friends of the Earth and members of the Committee for National Security.

L. Hunter Lovins is a lawyer, political scientist, sociologist, and forester. Born in Vermont in 1950, she received a B.A. degree from Pitzer College in political studies and sociology. Her J.D. degree from Loyola University School of Law (Los Angeles) was accompanied by the Alumni Award for Outstanding Service. Since 1975

485

she has been a member of the California Bar and a partner of Hirschtick & Sheldon, Los Angeles.

From 1974 to 1979 Ms. Lovins served as Assistant Director of the California Conservation Project ("Tree People"), which she helped to establish in Los Angeles. She designed and implemented the Project's energy and environmental education projects, coordinated community participation in urban forestry, and served as photographer, firefighter, and emergency logistics and disaster relief coordinator. She has lectured and consulted widely on energy and environmental education, community organizing, urban forestry, and biomass energy, and has co-instructed energy workshops for the University of Oklahoma, the American Association for the Advancement of Science, and others. In 1979 she served on the City of Los Angeles Energy Management Advisory Board.

Ms. Lovins has co-authored and edited other recent publications, including the Summer 1980 *Foreign Affairs* article "Nuclear Power and Nuclear Bombs" and its expansion *Energy/War: Breaking the Nuclear Link.* She was co-investigator under contract to the German Federal Environment Agency in a study published as *Least-Cost Energy: Solving the CO_2 Problem,* and to the U.S. Defense Civil Preparedness Agency in the technical study which preceded this book.

In 1982 the Lovinses were Luce Visiting Professors of Environmental Studies at Dartmouth College, and received a Mitchell Prize for their analysis of how electric utilities can regain financial health. Their work is the subject of the 16mm film "Lovins on the Soft Path."

Alec Jenkins, who supplied much of the material in Chapter Seventeen, holds a degree in electrical engineering from Johns Hopkins University and has done graduate work in business management at the University of California, Los Angeles. In 1974, in a Los Angeles hard hit by the Arab oil embargo, he chaired the Task Force on Energy Alternatives for Mayor Tom Bradley's Citizens' Energy Policy Committee. He then became the first member of the California Energy Commission's engineering staff, managed the Commission's Solar Office during 1975–77, and has since been the state's program specialist for solar energy. He represented California in the formation of Western SUN, nurtured the Municipal Solar Utility concept in its early years, and organized the state's 1981–82 photovoltaic demonstration program. In 1979 he created ON THE RISE, an annual program on policy issues sponsored by the American Section of the International Solar Energy Society (AS/ISES), whose Socio-Economic Division and Divisions Committee he chairs. He has edited two volumes of ON THE RISE Proceedings and authored "Community Energy Mobilization," published in *The Energy Consumer* in January/February 1981. In his private capacity (in which he participated in preparing this book) he writes and lectures on community programs to improve energy resilience.